The Crescent
and the Couch

BOOKS BY SALMAN AKHTAR

Psychiatry and Psychoanalysis

Broken Structures (1992)
Quest for Answers (1995)
Inner Torment (1999)
Immigration and Identity (1999)
New Clinical Realms (2003)
Regarding Others (2007)
Turning Points in Dynamic Psychotherapy (in press)
The Alphabet of Psychoanalysis (in press)
Passions or Poisons (in press)
The Trauma of Dislocation (in press)

Popular/Nonfiction

Objects of Our Desire (2005)

Urdu Poetry

Ku-ba-ku (1976)
Doosra Ghar (1986)
Nadi Ke Pas (2004)

English Poetry

The Hidden Knot (1985)
Conditions (1993)
Turned to Light (1998)

Edited

New Psychiatric Syndromes (1983)
The Trauma of Transgression (1991)
Beyond the Symbiotic Orbit (1991)
When the Body Speaks (1992)
Mahler and Kohut (1994)
The Birth of Hatred (1995)
The Internal Mother (1995)
Intimacy and Infidelity (1996)
The Seasons of Life (1997)
The Seed of Madness (1997)
The Colors of Childhood (1998)
Brothers and Sisters (1999)
Thicker than Blood (2000)
Does God Help? (2001)
Three Faces of Mourning (2001)
Real and Imaginary Fathers (2004)

Cultural Zoo (2005)
Mental Zoo (2005)
The Language of Emotions (2005)
Freud Along the Ganges (2005)
Interpersonal Boundaries (2006)
Listening to Others (2007)
Severe Personality Disorders (2007)
Geography of Meanings (2007)
On Freud's "The Future of an Illusion"
  (in press)
The Orient and the Unconscious (in press)
The Unbroken Soul (in press)
Culture and Psychoanalysis (in press)
On Freud's "Beyond the Pleasure Principle"
  (in press)

The Crescent and the Couch

Cross-Currents between
Islam and Psychoanalysis

Edited by
Salman Akhtar

JASON ARONSON
Lanham • Boulder • New York • Toronto • Plymouth, UK

Chapter 13, "Hindi-Muslim Relations: India" previously appeared in *Freud Along the Ganges: Psychoanalytic Reflections upon the People and Culture of India*, ed. S. Akhtar, pp. 91–137. New York: Other Press. Reprinted with permission of the publisher.

Published in the United States of America
by Jason Aronson
An imprint of Rowman & Littlefield Publishers, Inc.

A wholly owned subsidary of
The Rowman & Littlefield Publishing Group, Inc.
4501 Forbes Boulevard, Suite 200, Lanham, Maryland 20706
www.rowmanlittlefield.com

Estover Road
Plymouth PL6 7PY
United Kingdom

Copyright © 2008 by Jason Aronson

British Library Cataloguing in Publication Information Available

Library of Congress Cataloging-in-Publication Data

The crescent and the couch : cross-currents between Islam and psychoanalysis / edited by Salman Akhtar.
    p. cm.
 Includes bibliographical references and index.
 ISBN-13: 978-0-7657-0574-7 (cloth : alk. paper)
 ISBN-10: 0-7657-0574-5 (cloth : alk. paper)
 1. Psychoanalysis and religion. 2. Psychotherapy—Religious aspects—Islam. 3. Islam—Psychology. I. Akhtar, Salman, 1946 July 31–
    BF175.4.R44C74 2008
    297.2'61—dc22   2007036298

Printed in the United States of America

♾^{TM} The paper used in this publication meets the minimum requirements of American National Standard for Information Sciences—Permanence of Paper for Printed Library Materials, ANSI/NISO Z39.48-1992.

To
the memory of my maternal grandfather

CHOWDHRY SIRAJ-UL-HAQ

a devout Muslim and a good man

Contents

Acknowledgments   xi

Introduction   xiii

Part I: Prologue

1   Basic History and Tenets of Islam: A Brief Introduction   3
Hamada Hamid

2   The Prophet Muhammad: Man, Fountainhead, and Leader   21
George Awad

Part II: Characters

3   Rapture and Poetry: Rumi   43
M. Hossein Etezady

4   Vision and Modernization: Atatürk   63
Vamik D. Volkan and Norman Itzkowitz

5   Destiny and Nationalism: Mohammad Ali Jinnah   79
Salman Akhtar and Manasi Kumar

6 Ideology and Aggression: Osama bin Laden   103
      Peter A. Olsson

Part III: Culture

7 Islam and Family Structure   123
      Samar A. Jasser

8 Islam, Sex, and Women   141
      Shahrzad Siassi and Guilan Siassi

9 Sufi Perspective on Human Suffering and Its Relief   161
      Mohammad Shafii

10 Religious Identity Formation in the Children of Immigrant
      Muslim Parents   181
      Mali A. Mann

Part IV: Confluence

11 Christian-Muslim Relations: The Axis of Balkans and the West 199
      M. Sagman Kayatekin

12 Jewish-Muslim Relations: Middle East   217
      Joseph V. Montville

13 Hindu-Muslim Relations: India   231
      Salman Akhtar

Part V: Creativity

14 Some Reflections on Arab Cinema   267
      Iman Roushdy-Hammady

15 Oedipus in Egypt: A Twentieth-Century Rendition of
      Majnun Layla   283
      Ruqayya Yasmine Khan

16 Cultural Nationalism in Indo-Muslim Art 295
Manail Anis Ahmed

Part VI: Epilogue

17 Muslims in the Psychoanalytic World 315
Salman Akhtar

18 Whose Side Are You On? Muslim Psychoanalysts Treating
Non-Muslim Patients 335
Aisha Abbasi

Notes 351

References 371

Index 393

About the Editor and Contributors 413

Acknowledgments

I wish to thank the distinguished colleagues whose contributions appear in this volume. I am also thankful to Michael Vergare, M.D., who, as the chairman of the Department of Psychiatry and Human Behavior at Jefferson Medical College, Philadelphia, gave unwavering support to my work. My wife, Dr. Monisha Nayar, helped clarify my thinking at crucial junctures. Many psychoanalytic colleagues, especially Drs. Jennifer Bonovitz, Ira Brenner, Jaswant Guzder, Saida Koita, and Frank Maleson, gave me useful advice during the preparation of this book. My personal friends, A. Abdullah, Shantanu Maitra, and Farida Mazhar also helped in subtle and explicit ways. My uncle and aunt, Mr. Abu Salim and Mrs. Hamida Salim, who are distinguished academics in their own right, gave me meaningful feedback on the chapters I have written for this book. Dr. Vinay Bharadwaj of Delhi University kindly provided much-needed historical information for one of the chapters. Ms. Melia Awad, Ms. Kakul Hai, Ms. Farrah Qidwai, and Drs. Zhabiz Kazminezhad, Rajnish Mago, Mallika Patri, and J. Anderson Thomson, Jr. located useful references and offered suggestions that helped improve the book. My secretary, Melissa Nevin, offered devoted help with tasks that went beyond manuscript preparation. To all these individuals, I offer my sincere thanks.

Introduction

Roll down the screen and begin the PowerPoint™ presentation on Islam. Here is what you see:

- Click: Muslim hijackers ramming a plane full of passengers into the World Trade Center towers in New York.
- Click: Muslim young men, who would later blow up a commuter train, captured by video surveillance at a suburban tube station in London.
- Click: Muslim mobs setting fire to the Danish Embassy in Lebanon to register protest against newspaper cartoons ridiculing Prophet Mohammed.
- Click: Stills and movies footage of anti-Western and anti-Israeli diatribes by the likes of Moammar Khaddafi, Ayatollah Khomeini, Saddam Hussein, Osama bin Laden, and the current Iranian president, Mahmoud Ahmadinejad.

Fill your mind with these pictures. Now commit words like *al-Qaeda*, *Mujahadeen*, *Taliban*, *Hamas*, and *Hizbollah* to your memory. Add the images of veiled Middle-Eastern women, poverty-ridden Afghani old men, stone-throwing Palestinian kids, people dying in stampede during the Muslim pilgrimage to Mecca, and Kalishnakov-waving "terrorists" and "insurgents" of this or that Islamic stripe. Having accomplished this, you may join the ranks of other non-Muslim citizens of the Western hemisphere who carry similar visions of Islam in their minds.

Islam, for them, is a creed of ignorance, intolerance, and violence. It is a religion of rigid principles, austere lifestyle, strict demands, and harsh retributions. Followers of Islam seem narrow-minded, averse to modernization, and hateful toward those of other faiths. They devalue women, beat children, and their arrogance precludes participation in the democratic forms of government and administration. All in all, Islam is a religion of darkness and evil.

This is what most people in the West, especially the United States, think of Islam. And, with a few exceptions, popular media support and perpetuate this vision. To be sure, there are elements of truth in such a negative portrayal, but then a similar caricature can be drawn of the current Western culture as well. Imagine, for instance, a description of the United States that solely relies upon its genocide of American Indians, dark record of slavery and racial discrimination, bombing of Hiroshima and Nagasaki, pillage of Vietnam and Cambodia, fabricated reasons for invading Iraq, highest infant mortality rate in the Western world, widespread belief in creationism, child molesters and serial killers, staggering divorce rate, hopelessly mangled healthcare system, and prohibitively expensive educational institutions. Despite containing elements of truth, such a portrait would be factually unrealistic, morally unfair, and socio-politically unhelpful. The United States deserves a kinder, deeper, and more nuanced description in the cultural and historical annals of our world.

Likewise, Islam needs to be viewed in a broader light. This book is intended to provide such illumination. It offers information that could help contextualize the negative, bring in the neutral, and put forward the positive in the realm of Islam. To begin with facts, it notes that Islam is not an esoteric whimsy of a few, but the religion of nearly 1.5 billion people of this world. Its followers live all over the globe; indeed, 57 out of 191 countries holding membership of the United Nations are predominantly Muslim in their census. Contrary to the popular assumption, not all Muslims are Arabs and not all Arabs are Muslims. Actually, Arabs constitute only 20 percent of the world's Muslims. The remaining 80 percent have diverse national origins including Indonesia, India, Pakistan, Bangladesh, Turkey, Iran, Philippines, Thailand, and various regions of the former Soviet Union, as well as many African countries and China. There is a sizable population of Muslims in Europe as well (e.g., in Bosnia, Kosovo, and Albania) who are not immigrants from other countries. Indonesia is the country with the largest Muslim population, with Pakistan, India, and Bangladesh closely following, in that order. The geophysical landscape of the world's Muslims is hardly uniform. It ranges from the bustling markets of Cairo to the snow-peaked mountains of Kashmir, from the harsh ravines of Afganistan to the shimmering skyscrapers of Dubai, from the civilized housing societies of Karachi to the old coffeehouses of Ankara, and from the *diwaniyas* of Kuwait City to the rug stores of Dearborn, Michigan. The linguistic, vestmentary, culinary, and cultural preferences and practices of Muslims are also not monolithic. While retaining certain core principles, their religion is divided into many sects and is subject to textural variations in accordance with the geographical peculiarities and historical traditions of the land where it has taken root.

This book underscores these facts. It also brings to attention the truly majestic nature of the artistic, literary, and philosophical traditions of Islam. It highlights the seminal contributions in these realms by philosophers like Ibn Rushd (known in the West as Averroes), Imam Abu Hanifa, Imam Ibn Taimiya, Imam Ghazali, Ibn Khaldun, and Abu Raihan al Bairuni, physicians like Ibn Sina (better known as Avicenna), mathematicians like Al-Khwarizmi (the eighth-century founder of algebra), and Nasir-uddin Al-Tusi, explorers like Ibn Batuta, and Sulaiman al Mahiri, poets like Mosleh-al-din Saadi, Shams-uddin Hafiz, Jalal-uddin Rumi, and Omar Khayyam (Persian), Nizar Qabbani (Arabic), Nazim Hikmat (Turkish), Mir Taqi Mir, Mirza Asad-ullah Khan Ghalib, Mohammad Iqbal, and Faiz Ahmad Faiz (Urdu), novelists like Salman Rushdie, Naghib Mahfouz, and Orhan Pamuk (English), and Vaikom Mohammad Bashir (Malyalam), musicians like Mian Tansen, Amir Khusrau, Umm Kulsum, and Ustad Allah-uddin Khan, artists like Abdul Rahman Chughtai, Sadeqain, Maqbool Fida Hussain, and Raza, political leaders like Mustafa Kemal Ataturk, Gamal Abdel Nasser, Mohammad Ali Jinnah, Yasser Arafat, Sheikh Mujib-ur Rahman, and Anwar Saadat.

Matters do not end here. Just note the awe-inspiring mosques of Istanbul and Marrakesh, the breathtaking monuments of Alhambra and Delhi, the entrancing museums of Alexandria and Cairo, and the imposing libraries of Cordoba and Damascus. The panorama of Islamic architecture, bibliophilia, miniature painting, carpet weaving, and calligraphy is truly something to behold. And, the history of such great achievements goes far and deep in the ever-pulsating heart of time. A return to our PowerPoint™ presentation readily confirms.

- Click: Major libraries of sacred texts were established as early as A.D. 634 at the al-Aqsa Mosque in Jerusalem and in A.D. 721 at the Umyyad Mosque in Damascus. While focusing on Islamic culture, scholars at these and other similar institutions studied important literary texts from far away lands as well. A most striking cross-cultural accomplishment of this era was the translation of the great Indian collection of fables, the *Panchtantra*, into Arabic around A.D. 750. The Hindu discovery of the number zero was transmitted to the Western mathematical world only after its assimilation in the Arabic numerals. The greatest think-tank ever seen by the medieval world was established by Caliph al-Mamun in A.D. 1004 in Baghdad, the capital of the Abbasid Empire. It was called *Bayt al-Hikmah* (the House of Wisdom). Without the translations and research that went on there, much of the Greek, Latin, and Egyptian knowledge would have been lost to the world. By the middle

of the thirteenth century, Baghdad alone had thirty-six libraries, and
similar enthusiasm about scholarship was evident in Cairo, Aleppo, and
the major cities of Iran and Central Asia.

- Click: The Muslim world is replete with complex and elaborate fiction,
  rich parables, and heart-melting poetry of epic proportions. Perhaps the
  most outstanding among this literature is the *Shah-nama* ("The Book of
  Kings") that was written in Persian circa A.D. 1010 by Abdul Qasim
  Mansur Firdausi. It was a poem of sixty thousand verses (seven times the
  length of Homer's *Iliad*), detailing the history of the Persian kings from
  their legendary beginnings to Khusrau II in the seventh century A.D. It has
  remained the great national poem of Iran and is a preeminent literary work
  of the Muslim world. The great Arabic tale of *Alf Layla wa-Layla*, the old
  Urdu tract of *Tilism-e-Hoshruba*, the medieval romantic stories of *Majnun-
  Layla* (Arabic) and *Shirin-Farhad* (Persian), as well as the moving nine-
  teenth-century love saga of *Heer-Ranjha* (Punjabi), are among some other
  immortal contributions of Muslims to the world literature.
- Click: While the canvas of Islamic art is broad and its palette quite diverse, calligraphy, glazed ceramics, miniature paintings depicting historical narrative scenes, illustrated manuscripts, intricately weaved prayer
  rugs, and ornately inscribed Holy Qurans are among its prime illustrations. Collections of such items from as far back as the ninth century A.D.
  exist in The British Museum, the Museum of Modern Art in New York,
  The Brooklyn Museum, and the Freer and Sackler Galleries of the
  Smithsonian Institution in Washington, D.C. An encounter with these
  stunning antiquities leaves one speechless.
- Click: It was a Muslim Emperor of India, namely, Khurram Shahab-
  uddin Mohammad Shah Jahan, who built Taj Mahal (A.D. 1631), which
  is arguably one of the most beautiful architectural achievements of human civilization.

Lest this appear water under the bridge, harping on "chosen glories," and
lacking pertinence to a useful contemporary understanding of Islam, let us
take a look at some recent developments.

- Click: Five Muslims have recently received the Nobel Prize for Peace:
  Anwar Sadaat (1978), Yasser Arafat (1994), Shirin Ebadi (2003), Mohammad El Baradei (2006), and Mohammed Yunus (2007).
- An additional two Muslims have been awarded the Nobel Prize for Literature: Naghib Mahfouz (1988) and Orhan Pamuk (2007).
- Click: Literary works produced by Muslim authors have been far from
  state-controlled, timid hagiographies. Qazi Abdul Ghaffar and Ismat

Chughtai (Urdu) have given voice to the Muslim feminist cause as early as in the 1930s and 1940s. Saadat Hasan Manto (Urdu) and Iraj Mirza (Persian) have exposed the sexual hypocrisies of Muslim societies. Iftikhar Nasim (Urdu) and Irshad Manji (English) have authored daring books on the vicissitudes of homoerotic praxis in Muslim societies. Salman Rushdie (English) and Taslima Nasreen (Bengali) have flirted with blasphemy in challenging the mythic and structural features central to Islam. Orhan Pamuk (English) has questioned dearly held views of some problematic aspects of Turkish history. These are but a few examples of the defiant creativity of Muslim authors. Add the deliciously labyrinthine and socially aware novels of Naghib Mahfouz to this list, and you get the lay of the Muslim literary land.

- Click: Five Muslim women have held the highest elected office of their nation: Benazir Bhutto (Prime Minister of Pakistan, 1988–1990, and 1993–1996), Tansu Ciller (Prime Minister of Turkey, 1993–1996), Sheikh Hasina Wajid (Prime Minister of Bangladesh, 1996–2000), Begum Khalida Zia (Prime Minister of Banglades, 1991–1996, and 2001–present), and Meghawati Sukarnoputri (President of Indonesia, 2001–2004).
- Click: The noted American journalist, Thomas Freidman, observes that India and Bangladesh, two countries with extremely large Muslim populations, show no evidence of anti-American or anti-Semitic sentiment.

But what does all this have to do with psychoanalysis? The answer is manifold. *First and foremost*, psychoanalysis, both as a field of study and professional discipline, is anchored in reality. Its handling of intrapsychic conflicts takes place within the context of the individual's external environment. It recognizes that the integrity of psychic structure is dependent upon stimulus nutriment from outer reality, and ego's compromise formations take environmental vectors into account. Islam is part of external reality. For large parts of the world, this was always the case. For the West, it has become insistently so ever since the events of September 11, 2001. Insofar as this is true, feelings and fantasies about Islam often find their way in the analytic chambers. Muslims and their faith can thus become the containers of all sorts of projections, the interpretive deconstruction of which will require some factual knowledge about Islam and Muslim societies. It will also necessitate the overcoming of shared ethnic scotomas when neither of the two parties in the clinical situation is Muslim.

A *second* matter is the direct encounter of clinical psychoanalysis with Muslims. With the rapidly changing demography of the West and the influx of immigrants from Islamic countries, the number of Muslims seeking analytic treatment seems to be increasing. The hitherto negligible proportion of Muslims in the ranks of analytic candidates and practicing psychoanalysts is also changing. Cultural sensitivity toward the former and the possible theoretical and technical innovations by the latter have the potential of enriching psychoanalysis. Nuances of idiom and culturally determined iridescence of transference and countertransference phenomena, when one or both partners in the clinical dyad are Muslims, can also help refine the dynamic and developmental hypotheses of psychoanalysis.

With such sociocultural rejuvenation of psychoanalysis in the offing, a *third* interface between it and Islam appears on the horizon. This pertains to the application of psychoanalytic ideas to interethnic conflict resolution. Knowledge about Islam and its historical traditions and politico-economic concerns thus comes to acquire a great importance in the contemporary development of applied psychoanalysis. How can one understand the minds of Muslim fundamentalists and the so-called terrorists that one is trying to "tame" unless one tries to learn something about their thinking and what that thinking is based upon?

Finally, Islamic perspectives on the dilemmas of human separateness, the usefulness of self-knowledge, the role of courage and stoicism in the conduct of daily life, and the healing powers of silence and humility have the potential of enriching certain notions of psychoanalysis, especially those enunciated by its independent British tradition. The Sufi offshoot of Islam is especially pertinent in this context. Its emphasis upon the need for interaction with a selfless *pir* (an elder or a guide), in order to free oneself from conceit and conflict, has parallels in the increasing recognition of development-facilitating role of the psychoanalyst. Sufi and psychoanalytic views on the ego-refueling prowess of music have considerable overlap with each other. The respect given by the Sufi tradition to the emotional dimension of transcendent experience seems akin to the current views of psychoanalysis that value nonverbal interactions and interventions in clinical work. Both Sufism and the "romantic" vision of psychoanalysis encourage authenticity and both remain aware of the existentially misguiding nature of narcissism.

Clearly, the time has come for a hearty dialogue between psychoanalysis and Islam. However, it should not be overlooked that such crosscurrents can also become turbulent. This risk is heightened if one mental set attempts to colonize or cannibalize the other. Reflexively pathologizing one or the other form of thought is also unhelpful. To avoid such hermeneutic conundrums, one needs scholarly rigor, genuine respect for intracultural viewpoints, and interdisciplinary input. Prejudice on the part of both parties has to be set aside. The capacity for perceptual surprise and heuristic innovation must be in place.

It is with such caveats and with enthusiasm for the potential enhancement of knowledge that I offer *The Crescent and the Couch* to the reader. In closing, I wish to bring an additional matter to the reader's attention. This involves the great variability in the spellings of the name of Prophet Mohammed and Islam's holy book, the Quran. Instead of homogenizing these spellings throughout the book, I have allowed each contributor's version to stand as is.

The book's main purpose is to bring the awesome history and rich cultural traditions of Islam to enter into a dialectical exchange with the multilayered conceptualizations of psychoanalysis. Its message is directed toward both the Muslim and psychoanalytic communities. It contains contributions from distinguished Muslim and non-Muslim authors from many parts of the world. These authors represent the fields of psychoanalysis, psychiatry, political science, diplomacy, anthropology, literary studies, art history, and comparative religion. Their works help us delve into the psychological aspects of the religious, historical, political, literary, and artistic traditions of Islam. Together, their voices create an intelligent symphony of insight where Islamic history and thought meet psychoanalysis. Listening to this symphony is not only a profound instruction for the mind, but a great pleasure for the senses as well.

1

PROLOGUE

1

Basic History and Tenets of Islam

A Brief Introduction

Hamada Hamid

> For him who seeks the truth, there is nothing of higher value that truth it-
> self; it never cheapens or abases him who reaches for it, but ennobles and
> honors him.
>
> —al-Kindi, in *Nasr* 1964, 37

The question of how one understands "the Muslim mind" assumes that Muslims are monolithic, a simple, predictable body of people. Muslims constitute
at least 1.5 billion people; they inhabit every continent in the world and come
from multiple, diverse cultural backgrounds. Narrowing an approach to "the
Muslim mind" is as dubious an enterprise as isolating "the" approach to the
black, white, Jewish, or Christian mind. Each individual has distinct personal,
developmental, and biological dispositions and needs, and the social labels
we apply to them (and the extent to which they identify with those categories
themselves) may or may not help us provide optimal mental healthcare. This
cursory introduction of a tradition that evolved over fourteen centuries and includes people from thousands of different societies serves only to highlight
the cultural and historical factors[1] that may play a role in a Muslim's psychological profile and life experience.

My emphasis on the fact that religion is culturally constructed and that
Muslims come from all walks of life is not meant to suggest that it is a demographic incidental that therapists should simply ignore. Islam is a major
world tradition and Muslims share common histories, intellectual genealo-
gies, religious canons, and sets of pedagogical and ritual practices. The failure to take Islam seriously as a major dimension in the lives of many Muslims would be as problematic as assuming that there is one monolithic

3

approach to "the Muslim psyche" or that Islam operates as an ahistorical, programmatic social force in the lives of all Muslims. For many Muslims, their religion plays a critical role in the ways they view themselves and informs their value systems and their behavior. Rituals, religious narratives, and legal injunctions influence life decisions and may be invoked to resolve or defend against, either adaptively or maladaptively, mundane personal conflicts. Muslims transfer their own object-relations paradigms, defensive structures, and personality traits into the Islamic tradition, continuously reconstructing their relationship with Islam. For instance, an obsessive-compulsive personality may focus on the highly nuanced writings of Islamic jurisprudence and, therefore, may experience Islam as a religion that micromanages a person's daily affairs. Meanwhile, a neurotic (in the healthy, psychoanalytic sense) Muslim may reconcile a traumatic life event as being "God's will" and resolve a potential interpsychic conflict without negative sequelae. An individual's personality style has as much to do with how she experiences Islam as the formal dictates of the tradition itself. In this chapter, I provide a brief overview of the central tenets of Islam and the cultural contexts and historical narratives that may figure prominently in the minds of Muslim patients.

DEFINING ISLAM THROUGH SACRED TEXT

The word Islam is derived from the Arabic verb *salama*, which means "to submit." A Muslim, by definition, is the active participant who submits to the will of God. The very name of the religion is distinct from others in that it is not based on its founder or followers, but by its central tenant, which is to obey God. A central theological concept in Islam is that humankind owes a cosmic debt to their Creator.[2] Muslims view Islam as a primordial religion of the omnipotent and omniscient God who created the universe and willed mankind to be tested, judged, and rewarded or punished in the afterlife. The message of Islam was first presented to Adam and Eve, who were cast from the heavens as a consequence of disregarding God's command. In contrast to the Old Testament account, however, God forgave Adam and Eve of their heedlessness because they repented.[3] Satan was also expelled from the heavens because he arrogantly rejected God's command to prostrate to Adam, and his condemnation to hell is the consequence of not seeking God's forgiveness. Satan's disobedience to God is considered the first act of evil. Satan personifies evil; he is referred to as the archenemy of humans, using deception and temptation to morally mislead mankind. However, Muslims do not simply externalize the source of their immoral behavior as the machinations of Satan because humans also posses a level of agency that makes each individual accountable for her actions. Importantly, evil is defined and determined as acts of disobedience to God. Human beings, by their nature, are inclined to forget their cosmic debt to God. In fact, the word humankind in Arabic, "*insan*," a term used throughout the *Quran* (the holy book of Islam), shares an etymological root to the word "*nasa*," which means to forget. Consequently, the primary purpose of religious rituals, such as the five daily prayers, is to train Muslims to be mindful of their mundane actions and conscientious of their moral responsibilities.

In the moral history of the *Quran*, prophets were appointed to each society to call their people to submit to God's will. Therefore, in the Muslim tradition, all prophets delivered the same divine message, obeyed God's law, and were by definition "Muslim" (a person who submits to God's law). Likewise, the followers of God's prophets, for instance, the Israelites who obeyed Moses are considered believers. Muslims believe that the distortions and innovations introduced into prophetic teaching led to the construction of different religions. Each prophet came to correct the deviations of the previous prophet's followers. So, for instance, Jesus came as a divine corrective to the Jews of Israel. Mohammed ibn Abdullah of seventh-century Arabia came as the "seal of prophets," or the final prophet, and Muslims believe that Islam will be God's final message until Judgment Day. The two sources of sacred knowledge in Islam are the Prophet's teachings called the *Sunna*, which includes his normative behavior as well as his recorded and explicit instructions, and the *Quran*, the word of God revealed to Prophet Muhammad.

The *Quran*: Revealed Word of God

Muhammad received Quranic revelations in the form of high Arabic poetry, a genre that appealed to the Arabs who cherished poetry in general, calling humankind to the worship of the one God. Quranic verses were revealed gradually over the course of Muhammad's life, many times as a response to specific events. Each verse of the *Quran* is universally instructive but also particular and socially situated. The primary message of Muhammad was that there is one God who is the Creator of the Universe and should be worshipped. The central theme of early Quranic revelation was the nature of God, (in Arabic, *Allah*).[4] The term Allah was not new to the pagan, Christian, and Jewish Arabs who used the term to describe the Supreme Lord.

From the outset, the *Quran* and the *Sunna* regulated human behavior and directed believers to worship and reflection. Fazlur Rahman (1994) describes three key terms repeated throughout the *Quran* related to security.[5] The first term *iman* means "faith," but comes from the root word *amana*, which means "to be at peace," implying that faith leads to feeling at peace. The term *Islam* shares etymological origins to the term *salam*, which also means peace,[6] suggesting that if one surrenders to the law of God, both inner peace in this world and everlasting peace in the afterlife will be achieved. The third term, *taqwa*, originates from the root *wa ka ya*, which means to avoid, prevent, or protect. *Taqwa* denotes the active avoidance of peril for the sake of piety. Rahman suggests that having *taqwa* prevents Muslims from encountering danger. *Taqwa* is the mindfulness of one's actions and the remembrance of God's omniscience that drives a Muslim to regulate her behavior and to cultivate an affective relationship to God. Collectively, these terms suggest that security, morality, and good judgment are dependent on God's will. An individual's judgment is always blurred by personal desires, worldly distractions, and the immediacy of selfish (and, ultimately, self-destructive) interests; however, *taqwa* heightens the believer's perception of the cosmic reality and his desire to live a righteous and successful life. The sense of *taqwa*, or the motivation to please God, also inspires believers to reevaluate their intentions and actions.[7] Introspection and critical analysis of one's environment is encouraged throughout the *Quran* and Muslim writings.

A central tenet in Islam is that God alone determines the fate of individuals; therefore, people should rely on God (a concept termed *tawakkul*) and refrain from the impulse to behave immorally.[8] *Tawakkul* is invoked as a coping strategy to endure hardships, premised by the idea that God provides relief after hardships.[9] Hardships are understood either as divine tests or as worldly punishments (which are preferable to punishments in the afterlife).[10] Therefore, a Muslim should embody *tawakkul* by demonstrating patience and perseverance in the face of hardships. Conversely, the term tawakkul is sometimes used by Muslims to justify inaction. For instance, refusing medication may be rationalized as resigning to God's will.

The Prophet: Model Life and Model Community

The *Quran* and the Prophet's teachings are the two main sources of sacred knowledge. The Quranic verses are immutable but cannot be understood in the absence of the historical context in which they were revealed to the Prophet. Muslims accept the Prophet as the most balanced and perfect human being. Therefore, the way he worshiped, related to others, interacted with his family, resolved conflicts, mourned loss, and led the community remains a model of optimal human behavior in the Muslim view. This is why early Muslim scholars went to such great lengths to record with exactitude the Prophet's behavior and teachings in a canon of literature known as hadith.

Pre-Islamic Arabia during Muhammad's time consisted mostly of pagan cults, although there was a viable Christian and Jewish presence. People transmitted their values and legends through oral narratives and poetry. Mecca, a southwest Arabian city, boasted one of the major shrines for worship. The Kaa'ba was the central sacred refuge in Mecca, believed by Arab tradition to have been built by Abraham and his son Ishmael many centuries earlier. By the sixth century, it was a sacred sanctuary for many of Arabia's animist religions, and many tribes throughout the Arabian peninsula made spiritual pilgrimages to honor it. Trade routes toward Mecca and other cities were formed as a result of religious pilgrimage and the Meccans greatly benefited from the spiritual pilgrims both politically and economically. Festivals were held and poetry, their dominant form of entertainment and media, was recited to pay homage to the idols of Mecca and to transmit the social values of the time.

Muhammad was born in the arid climate of Mecca to the most powerful Arabian clan, the Qurish. He was orphaned at an early age and raised by a poor wet-nurse. He was eventually taken under the guardianship of his uncle, who was the head of his clan. Muhammad, during his adult years, became a trader in Mecca and developed a reputation as a quiet, even-tempered, and trustworthy gentleman. At the age of twenty-five, he married a wealthy widow and independent businesswoman named Khadija, who was approximately fifteen years his senior. His relationship with her is described as a warm and reverent romance and he relied on her for emotional support. Most of his early career was spent managing Khadija's businesses. During his leisure time, Muhammad secluded himself into the mountains of Mecca, contemplating life's mysteries. On one of these occasions, at the age of forty, he received revelation in the form of the vision of the archangel Gabriel urging him to recite lyrical prose that would later be recorded as the first verses of the *Quran*.[11]

The message of Islam challenged Arabian pagan beliefs and directly criticized many social norms in Meccan society. Allah had no partners, no intermediaries, and no demigods. The pagan Arabs were urged to become Muslims by rejecting and abandoning their idols and objects of worship, and submitting only to Allah as prescribed by the teachings of Muhammad. The *Quran* condemned Meccan practices such as worshipping idols,[12] burying unwanted infant daughters alive, and the maltreatment of orphans and the poor. The *Quran* decreed women the rights to inheritance and placed them as spiritual equals in the eyes of God, a radical concept in seventh-century Arabia.[13] Furthermore, the Quranic message undermined tribal authority and commanded the Meccans to submit to God and the true religion, Islam. Muhammad began gaining followers, mostly freed slaves, family members, and occasionally noble members of the community. Just as Muhammad's following was gaining momentum, his beloved Khadija died. The Prophet was deeply saddened. Not long after Khadija's death, Muhammad's guardian uncle, whose tribal status provided protection for Muhammad and his followers from political and social persecution in Mecca, also died. These two emotionally devastating events marked this year of his life as *A'mr Husn*, or the Year of Sadness.

Without the political support of the prophet's uncles, the persecution of the Muslim community in Mecca intensified. The followers of the new religion were subject to economic sanctions, social humiliation, and even bodily torture by the tribal elites. Quranic verses reassured the bourgeoning Muslim community that their suffering was a rite of passage and recounted the persecution of the earlier prophetic nations, such as the followers of Moses and Noah. Throughout history, Muslims have drawn on this oppressive period of the Prophet's life and the perseverance of his community as an instructive example of maintaining a resilient faith and steadfastness in the most dire of conditions.

By the thirteenth year after his initial revelation, Muhammad and his several thousand followers fled from the oppression of the Meccans and migrated to a northern city called Medina. This emigration marks a key turning point in the Prophetic biography. To underscore the importance of this moment in Islamic history, the Islamic lunar calendar begins with the date of migration to Medina and the establishment of the Islamic community. Muhammad made a pact with the people of Medina, establishing himself as both religious leader and statesman. Dislocated from their homes, many Muslims were separated from their families and relied on the hospitality and generosity of their hosts. The Quranic verses revealed in Medina maintained an overall emphasis on devotion to God, the afterlife, and the Day of Judgment, but they also integrated issues relevant to civil life such as marriage and divorce law, rights of inheritance, fair trade, and circulation of wealth to the poor. This pivotal moment in Islamic history marked the transformation of the Muslim community from an oppressed marginalized cult to a growing religious community and influential political entity. The collective Muslim community was called *ummah*. Dissolving tribal and ethnic differences and establishing all Muslims as brothers and sisters within a universal spiritual community became central to Muhammad's mission. The community in Medina would serve as the idealized model of an Islamic polity and spiritual community for centuries to come.

Displaced from their homes, property, and businesses, the new Muslim community took hold of trade routes and claimed the bounties of incoming caravans enroot to Mecca. The Quraish of Mecca responded militarily, and several major battles ensued. After a truce and establishing diplomatic ties with other tribes, Mohammad and his army entered Mecca in a bloodless coup. Mohammad spared the lives of his former persecutors and appointed many of the tribal leaders to positions of power within the new Islamic state, thereby easing the humiliation of the defeated Quraish and strengthening Meccan public opinion and diplomatic support. The remaining years of Mohammad's life were spent building the Muslim polity and unifying all the Arab tribes under the banner of Islam. By his death, in approximately 632 C.E., much of Arabia had converted to Islam through his missionary work and exceptional diplomacy.

This early history of Muhammad's life became the cornerstone of Muslims' religious imagination. Narratives of Muhammad's life and teachings were immortalized through the minutely detailed accounts of his companions and devoted followers. The stories of individual personalities and the triumph over the initial persecution would be related over generations by Muslim poets, scholars, and mystics. The detailed descriptions of Muhammad's personal struggles with the responsibility of carrying his divine message, his profound grief as his loved ones passed, the families torn apart by the migration to Medina, the inspiring loyalties of the Prophet's inner circle, the painful betrayal by his fellow tribesmen, and the epic battles that threatened the survival of Islam permeated throughout Arab traditions and spread, as Islam expanded into neighboring regions. The details of these stories have been elaborated and continue to carry a mythic quality, relaying moral lessons and providing a shared legacy across Muslim cultures.

EARLY EXPANSION, INTELLECTUAL DEVELOPMENT, AND CULTURAL EXCHANGE

Whereas the first two decades after the Prophet's death witnessed rapid expansion of the Islamic state through conquests, there were important political and ideological conflicts that resulted in the creation of sects, the development of diverse schools of thought, and, in some cases, the emergence of rigid and brutal rulers. Academics have amply documented that the notion that Islam was "spread by the sword" is embellished historical fiction. The first seven centuries of Islamic history are marked by the rapid spread of the Arabic language, followed by the *gradual* conversion to Islam, as well as by major cultural and intellectual contributions by non-Arab Muslims. As newly-found wealth poured into the new Islamic state, Muslim leaders built a standing military and invested in intellectual projects and institutions.

Early Crisis and Political Authority and Rapid Expansion

After Muhammad's death, the question of who should lead the Muslim community was quickly resolved when Muhammad's closest companions and several tribal leaders appointed Abu Bakr, the Prophet's father-in-law, closest friend, and one of his first converts, as the first Caliph (which literally means "successor"). Shortly, thereafter, several tribes challenged Abu Bakr's political authority, and several leaders even claimed to be new prophets. Abu Bakr mobilized the Muslims and engaged what is now known as the Apostasy War. Abu Bakr's victory not only unified all of Arabia for the first time under the banner of Islam, it also placed Arabia in position to face both the Byzantine and Sasanian armies. Over the next two decades and two caliphs later, Muslim conquests included lands that began to flow into the newly centralized Islamic state, and Arabs began to enjoy material wealth like never before. Wealth was redistributed through a tax system first articulated by the Prophet and later modified by the second and third caliphs; a standing army was provided a salary for the first time, and garrisons throughout the newly ruled lands were under the command of the Caliph. Armies were still being led by many of the close companions of the Prophet, and many of these Muslims were committed to establishing the righteous order of Islam, including the just distribution of resources.

Approximately a decade after the Prophet's death, there was a second crisis in political authority. In the context of an increasingly wealthy and rapidly expanding Islamic state, the third Caliph, Uthman ibn Affan, had appointed many family members of questionable qualifications to important government positions. Increasingly, tensions among tribal leaders culminated in the assassination of Uthman. The cousin of the Prophet, Ali ibn Abi-Taleb, succeeded Uthman as Caliph. Insistent on avenging Uthman's death, many of members of Uthman's tribe subverted Ali's authority. This resulted in a series of battles and assassinations, which included the death of Ali, his two sons, and many important leaders of the early Islamic community. This period marked a critical junction in Islamic history. It is termed *Fitna al-Kubra* (the "Great Calamity") and is labeled by some historians as the first civil war of the Islamic state. The Shiite sect emerged against this backdrop, initially supporting Ali against Uthman's tribe, and later asserting that Ali should have been Muhammad's immediate successor and that he had been wrongfully passed over in favor of the pervious three Caliphs. Some historians report that the term Shiite emerged from the group named "Shiite Ali," which translates as The Party of Ali.

Shiites over the next few centuries developed their own expressions of piety, legal interpretations, and political structures. Although Shiites, who currently constitute around 10 percent to 15 percent of the world's Muslim population, maintain the core tenets of Islam, including the belief in the divine message of the *Quran*, the centrality and finality of Muhammad's prophesy, the religious obligations of five daily prayers, fasting during the

Islamic month of Ramadan, and performing the pilgrimage to Mecca, and so on, they differ in the construction of religious and political authority. The Imam, or leader of the Muslim community, according to Shiites, could only be a descendent of the Prophet. In contrast, Sunnis believe anyone, depending on the level of piety and religious knowledge could be a potential leader. Some Shiites believe that Imams inherit a secret knowledge required for religious leadership.[14] After the violent killings of Ali and his sons, the tribe of the third Caliph, Uthman, called the Ummayads (661–7501 C.E.), led a Sunni Islamic absolutist monarchy. This important shift in the political establishment was the beginning of a period characterized by authoritarian Caliphs, who were often brutal rulers. In order to sustain their legitimacy in the public eye as Commanders of the Faithful, these rulers maintained an Islamic identity and supported Muslim institutions. The Ummayads, cautious not to lose their wealth and power, swiftly and violently destroyed their critics—both Sunni and Shiite. Many Sunni tribes, especially non-Arab Muslims, united with oppressed Shiite communities to overthrow the Ummayads, leading to the Abbassid dynasty. Political divisions over the course of these two dynasties (and the other constellations of power in the peripheral areas of the Muslim world) tended to revolve around tribal loyalties. Despite these political rifts, a shared Islamic identity preserved a level of social cohesion across different regions and over many centuries, facilitating intellectual exchange across different cultures.

Development of Islamic Law: The Shariah

With the exception of the Fatimid dynasty,[15] which controlled most of North Africa during much of the eighth century, Sunni Islam dominated state law and scholarly legal discourse. Sunni Islam always constituted the majority of the Muslim population, and is often inappropriately named "Orthodox Islam" by Westerners. Currently, over 85 percent of the world's Muslims are Sunni.

The first two centuries after the death of prophet is often conceptualized as the formative period in Islamic legal history. During this time, a great deal of intellectual energy was spent preserving the traditions of the prophet as *hadith*, developing exegeses of the *Quran*, and systematizing Islamic law. During the formative period, many legal schools of thought emerged with different approaches to interpreting sacred text and formulating Islamic law, known as *shariah*.

In Sunni Islam, four legal schools prevailed, each named after its founder: *Hanafi* (Imam Abu Hanifa), *Maliki* (Imam Anas ibn Malik), *Shafai* (Imam Mohammad Idris Al-Shafa'i), and *Hanbali* (Imam Ahmed ibn Hanbal). These schools gained popularity throughout different areas of the Muslim world mostly because of the work and dedication of the disciples of the original founders. While each school has a distinct approach to drawing on the traditions of the Prophet, considering local cultural practices, and determining the role of independent reason independent of sacred text, each school is perceived as being equally valid. Legal discourse among and between schools occurs mostly at the academic and juristic level, and, in the modern period, only a minority of Muslims feel bound to a particular school. Most lay Muslims do not appreciate the seemingly minute differences between the schools. With that said, each school has developed a highly systematized approach to jurisprudence in which social welfare, justice, local customs, sacred text, and case precedents are considered when establishing a legal opinion. A legal opinion is called a *fatwa* and is a nonbinding position of an Islamic jurist that may or may not be incorporated into state law.[16]

Shariah, in both Sunni and Shiite Islam, regulates a broad range of Muslim behavior, such as ritual washing to prepare for prayer, valid forms of worship, rights and obligations of spouses, inheritance law, trade, and criminal law. Some of these rules were regulated to the realm of individual observance, whereas others were to be administered by the state. Although there was never a "separation between church and state" as we understand it in the West, historically, there has been an important distinction between Islamic scholars and political statesmen.

Intellectual and Scientific Exchanges

Shariah and legal discourse evolved slowly over the first few centuries after the Prophet's death and was influenced by the cultural exchange within conquered lands. The influence of non-Arab Muslim thinkers was critical for the intellectual growth of Muslim civilization. Arabic, the official language of the Islamic state, was adapted quickly, whereas conversion to Islam occurred more gradually over the course of many centuries. Persian, Byzantine, and Greek philosophy and literature were translated into Arabic in the late Ummayad period. However, it was during the early Abbasid period that the state invested enormous resources into translating classical works. As all academic researchers know, government funding and institutional support is critical for the development of science and technology. Handsome endowments and grants drew scientists from distant lands to Baghdad, the capital of the Islamic state in that period. These scholars, mostly from Persia and Central Asia, translated classical Greek and Indian texts into Arabic and added brilliant commentaries.

As networks of intellectual exchanges emerged throughout the caliphate during this period, institutions of higher learning thrived, and Cordoba, Fez,

Cairo, Damascus, and Ifsahan became emergent academic centers where science and new technology flourished. From a Muslim perspective, religion and science are not seen as oppositions, inherently in conflict. Rather, science is viewed as evidence of God's precise and perfectly calculated creation of the universe.[17] The exploration of the patterns and laws of the physical world only affirms the perfection of God's design. In the classical period of Islamic history, much of applied science was used for religious purposes. For instance, knowledge of astronomy was used to calculate the times of prayer, the month of Ramadan, and the direction of Mecca in order to perform the five ritual prayers.

The specific interest in the celestial led to great advances across the fields of mathematics and applied sciences. Ptolemaic astronomy was translated in the eighth and ninth century. Mathematics from India was synthesized with ancient Greek trigonometry and used to correct and advance Ptolemy's original calculations and theories. The interest in the physical laws of geology and astronomy crossed over into the development of theoretical mathematics and led to the restructuring of these disciplines. Most notably, Al-Khwarizimi, a ninth-century Persian philosopher, wrote *Kitab al-Jabr wa-l-Muqabala* (literally, "the book of compulsion and comparison"), now known as the *Book of Alegbra*. This work was not an isolated contribution; during the next several centuries, thousands of manuscripts were produced furthering mathematical tools from operations of polynomials, extraction of irrational roots, and measurement of spherical shapes, and helped develop the field of optics by the geometric study of vision. Through his research on mirrors and lenses, the eleventh-century scholar Ibn al Haythem (known as Alhazan in the West) developed the fundamental principles of dioptrics and the index of refraction. By the ninth century, Galenic humoral medicine has been integrated and synthesized by Muslim doctors. In the tenth century, Al-Razi (Averroes) and Ibn Sina (Avicenna) (author of *The Canon of Medicine*, perhaps the most important medieval medical treatise) championed the shift from theoretical to clinical medicine.

Mental illness was approached as a medical condition early in medieval Islamic scholarship. In Al-Razi's medical encyclopedia, "Continens" or Kitab al-Hawi, a chapter was devoted to melancholia. He listed symptoms, such as sorrow, sadness, fear, irritation, seclusion, and difficulty sleeping, as markers for the disease and, consistent with the Galenic influence, prescribed medications targeted to remove the patient's black bile. Al-Razi was both a philosopher and physician. He directed a major hospital in Baghdad during the Abbasid period, and his treaties on repelling vices, such as envy, conceit, grief, greed, drunkenness, sexual passion, and so on, were as philosophical as they were medical. Al-Razi coined the Arabic term al-Ilaj annafsani, literally translating to the "treatment of the self."[18] He argued that if the physician encouraged the patient to care for her soul, the body would follow. Ibn Sina extensively wrote about illnesses related to mental health, with his most important contribution related to the correlation of fever and delirium, which he attributed to the boiling of yellow bile. These physician-philosophers contested the idea that delirium and seizures were caused by spirit possessions and advocated the use of medications, herbs, perfumes, and music to treat these ailments. The famous Caliph Harun Rashid established the first Muslim hospital in Baghdad in the tenth century. Unlike medieval European hospitals, which were born out of the Church, these hospitals were state-established institutions supported by endowments and administered by physician-philosophers.

In addition to science and technology, the translations of Greek philosophy profoundly impacted Islamic theology, law, and moral discourse. Beginning with Al-Kindi in the ninth century, the study of philosophy was used to reconcile principles of Islamic faith, including the proofs of the existence of God, prophetic revelations, creation of the universe, and the resurrection of the body after death. Much of the discourse was driven by exchanges with Christian theologians to contest anthropomorphism. By the late ninth century, some Islamic philosophers claimed that rational philosophy itself purified the soul and morality could be known outside of revelation. Heavily influenced by Plato, Al-Rhazi held the position that revelation is superfluous to reason, and there are objective moral truths that may be known by intelligent, independent inquiry. This was one among many positions taken up by the Mutazilite rationalist theological school. Later philosophers, such as Al-Farabi and Ibn Sina, drew on both Platonic and Aristotelian concepts of individual happiness and utopian societies to develop a new Muslim political philosophy.

The major thinker attributed to having undermined the hegemony of the Mutazilite rational school of thought is the legal scholar and master Sufi theologian Imam Hamed Al-Ghazali, with his seminal work, *Incoherence of the Philosophers*. One consequence of the Mutazilite rational movement's demise was the overall acceptance of the traditionalist's doctrine of the source of moral reason. In contradistinction to the Mutazalites, who felt that objective moral truths were universal across cultures and peoples, traditionalists argued that mankind's limited perception, experience, and cognitive capacity restricted reason to the subjective product of mankind's selfish desires. This "theoretical subjectivism" was accepted by traditionalists, including theologians and legal jurists, as well as the majority of Sufi scholars.

Sufism and Spirituality

The spiritual dimension of Islam, while a formal focus of the Sufis, is central to many Muslims' lives. This stems from the central doctrine that all of creation is dependent on God. Therefore, every condition and circumstance is by God's will. Many Muslims hold that a sincere believer endures a hardship as a test or an unforeseen benefit and ideally will pronounce "*Alhamdulliah*," meaning "All praises are due to God" in the face of personal tragedy. Religious sentiment is so pervasive in Muslim cultures that to this day, secular humanists and atheists still reflexively respond to "How are you?" with "*Alhamdullilah*."

As early as the second century of Islamic history, Sufism emerged from circles of more spiritually-minded Muslim thinkers. In part, this spiritualist tradition was a reaction to the growing opulence of Muslim society and the corresponding focus on material gain as Islamdom expanded, as well as a corrective to the overwhelming dominance of the legal, philosophical, and theological inquiries of Muslim intellectuals. Sufism provided an avenue to develop the "inner self" and the spiritual relationship with God, an area that both Islamic jurists and theologians paid less attention to. Sufi scholars developed systematic approaches to controlling one's desires through prayer and formal chants from the *Quran* and the prophet called "dihkr," which translates to "remembrance." They organized themselves into new social orders, each called a "tariqa," which literally means path. The tariqa system reshaped social organization throughout the thirteenth to eighteenth centuries and often became important centers for political change as well. Despite the shifting constellations of political dynasties and foreign occupations, Sufi orders served as a stable and constant communal movement. During the colonial era when European imperial forces began to infiltrate Muslim lands, Sufi orders were a major buffer against Western political and cultural dominance. Many Muslims were more impressed by the access to divine wisdom their Sufi sheiks provided than the worldly knowledge of material science and technology that Westerners offered.

THE MODERN ERA

The Colonial Legacy

The impact of the colonial era still affects the Muslim world economically, politically, and psychologically. The legacy of colonialism effectively led to the division of the Ottoman Empire into separate nation-states. Many of these states were constructed for geopolitical purposes, such Afghanistan, which was created to politically buffer Russia from India. Economically, the British carved out oil-rich coastal countries from the Arabian Peninsula into smaller, easier to maintain gulf states, such as Kuwait, United Arab Emirates, and Qatar. Lebanon, colonized by the French, was separated from Syria to promote a dominantly Christian Arab state.

The colonial powers differed in the styles of management; however, they shared the policy of building infrastructures and institutions to maximize the funneling of resources from their colonies into the economies of the empire. Educational institutions were established throughout the Muslim world for the education of the elites of society. In the nineteenth century, significant cultural shifts in the Muslim world equated high social status with the level of Western education achieved and one's familiarity with European languages and cultures. Development and modernization became coterminous with Westernization. Wearing Western clothes, listening to Western music, and being well read in Western literature identified one as "modern."

Many reform movements during the nineteenth and twentieth centuries elaborated reactionary, Islamic visions for social and political relations and reinforced the collective Muslim identity. Across the Muslim world, these reform movements served as viable and culturally authentic alternatives to colonization and Westernization, and, in some regions, they became the dominant political force ousting the colonial rulers. Many of these reformers, such as Mawlana Mawdudi in India or Sayyed Qutb in Egypt, rejected Western secularism and called for a return to Islamic ideals. They invoked the historical legacy and past success of the Islamic civilization and attributed deterioration of the Muslim world to moral deviances.

As Muslims throughout the world grapple with the complexities of modernity and the perceived demise of their civilization, they continue to project their political and social frustrations onto the West. Many Muslims tend to split themselves and the West into categories that do not necessarily follow, idealizing one and vindicating the other. For instance, for some Muslims, modernity and development is considered a Western phenomenon. Capitalism, secular humanism, and Western-style democracy is idealized; meanwhile, tradition, religion, and eastern culture are branded as backward and crippling. Conversely, some Muslims reject Western values as secular, hedonistic, materialistic, and fundamentally opposed to the Islamic tradition, and with it they reject Western philosophy and culture.

Islam in America

Muslim "immigration" to the United States began with forced migration of African slaves; approximately 10 percent of them were Muslims (Austin, 1997). The conditions of American slavery, however, made it impossible for the slaves to sustain their religious identity or pass it on to their children. The first voluntary immigrants to the United States are the economic sojourners from the declining Ottoman Empire in the nineteenth century.[19] They were typically uneducated, middle-class Arabs from modern-day Syria and

Lebanon. This wave of immigrants tended to settle in large urban centers, such as Detroit and Chicago, working as peddlers or in industrial factories. A smaller group of South Asian immigrants, mostly from British India, began to enter the United States around 1900. The demographics and patterns of immigration were dependent on both international politics, as well as American domestic policy. For instance, Asian immigration to the United States was halted after World War I with the Barred Zone Act of 1917 and the National Origins Quota Act of 1924, which favored European immigrants over Asians. The early immigrants who did reach the United States were often from minority communities and marginalized groups. Consequently, the demographies of immigrant Arabs and South Asians in the early twentieth century is often inversely related to the composition of the Muslim world such that there is a significantly large proportion of Christian Arabs, Shiia', and heterodox Muslim sects in the United States. With the civil rights movement of the 1950s and 1960s, immigration policy shifted again, resulting in a dramatic increase of Sunni Arab and South-Asian Muslims' immigration. Wealthier, highly educated immigrants began immigrating to the United States mostly in search of economic opportunities. This new wave of immigrants began investing resources into building mosques and Islamic schools and more recently cultural centers and politically based institutions.

African-American Muslims, who constitute the largest ethnic group of Muslims in the United States, have a distinct history and culture compared to their immigrant coreligionists. During the end of the nineteenth century, many black nationalist and Afrocentric movements emerged to combat white supremacy and reframe black identity (McCoud 1993). Turning to their African ancestry, many movements looked to reappropriate symbols of Islam as a charged political and religious move against white supremacy. The first such movement, The Moorish Science Temple, was founded by Noble Drew Ali in 1913, followed by numerous others, including the popular Nation of Islam. These movements focused on Quranic concepts like the purposeful creation of God, justice, freedom of will, refraining from alcohol and drugs, and organized religious community. Many of their religious claims, however, are alien to the global tradition of Islam. For example, Elijah Muhammad, the leader of the Nation of Islam (NOI) taught that "the white man" was Satan, that God was black. Elijah Muhammad claimed that he was God's messenger; his teachings inspired and empowered a group of disenfranchised people in the height of racial segregation, public lynching, and blatant discrimination, with little to no access to the global tradition of Islam. With the influx of immigrants from the Muslim world in the 1960s and onward, and with the direction of important black Muslim leaders like Malcolm X and Elijah Muhammad's son, Warith Deen Muhammad, black

Muslims embraced Sunni Islam, which is now the dominant expression of Islam in the African-American community.[20]

For many first- and second-generation Muslims in America, whether immigrant or African American, navigating their belief system and dominant cultural norms can be both challenging and stressful. As minorities, issues of acculturation, displacement (physical or social), and the creation of cultural spaces for the authentic expressions of their values in a socially and politically hostile environment remain central issues for Muslim Americans. Muslim Americans often experience internal conflict as they explore what it means to live as a Muslim in the United States. For instance, the challenge of observing the Islamic prohibition on physical intimacy outside of marriage may be overwhelming in the context of high school dances, college parties, and the culture of casual dating, given people's desires for social acceptance and sexual intimacy. Furthermore, Muslim Americans often feel distressed over the ways Islam is construed as backward, radical, and sometimes as even a terrorist religion by other Americans. For many Muslim Americans, there is also the perceived and sometimes real threat of discrimination, especially after the September 11 tragedy.

CONCLUDING THOUGHTS

This brief sketch is intended as an overview of the tenets of Islam and the historical narratives that may figure prominently in the minds of Muslim patients. However, this cursory history is also intended a cautionary note. Just as 1,400 years of the rich history of a civilization that spanned from Spain to China (and now includes millions in the United States) cannot be done justice in a short chapter, the psychological dispositions of billions of people cannot be reduced to a simplistic construct of "the Muslim mind." Local cultures, customs, and turns of events have shaped Muslim histories throughout the world, and individual Muslim's personalities and life experiences frame their engagements with their religious tradition. While the Islamic tradition inevitably influences Muslim patients worldwide, understanding a specific individual's worldview requires a sensitive and systematic clinical approach.[21] Consequently, to discuss the "Muslim mind" or the "Muslim family structure" as unqualified abstractions obscures numerous psychosocial factors, such as culture, socioeconomic status, personality styles, and biological predispositions. Furthermore, psychoanalytic histories pose methodological problems because historical figures are being analyzed outside of therapy and across temporal and social gaps and differences, which may be invisible to the analyst. Placing Muslim personalities, societies, and interpersonal dynamics under the psychoanalytic lens may be both an interesting intellectual exercise and potentially useful; however, I hope that the richness of the Islamic tradition and the histories and the complexities of this people sketched out in this chapter humbles our scholarly enterprise. We must be careful not to allow our own cultural histories and intellectual paradigms to propagate a racist discourse that measures the Muslim "other" against dominant Western norms, or arrogantly constructs the Muslim world as fluid waves crashing on the unmoving, static shore of Western psychoanalysis. Rather, our subtitle "Crosscurrents between Islam and Psychoanalysis" invokes the image of two bodies of water meeting, a meeting characterized by unfixable boundaries and perpetual movement. My suggestion is that the meeting of these two traditions could be analytically productive, teeming with lively possibilities, but also that the metaphor of fluidity leaves open the possibility that our assumptions and intellectual certainties might also be transformed and remade in the crosscurrents.

2

The Prophet Muhammad

Man, Fountainhead, and Leader

George Awad

And when Jesus, the son of Mary said, "O Children of Israel, I am God's messenger to you, bringing affirmation of the Torah before me and giving the good news of prophet who will come after me and who shall be called the Praised One."

—*Qur'an* 61:6

In a book that ranks the most influential persons in history, Hart (1996) lists the Prophet Muhammad[1] as number one (of note, Jesus was number three and Freud was number sixty-nine). Although there may be disagreement about the order of any such list, I agree with listing Muhammad as number one. I will discuss his life and achievements, and I hope that I will be able to demonstrate this in this chapter.

SOME CAVEATS

Unfortunately, we know little about Muhammad. The books written about him are of two types. Some were written by Muslims, whose goals were to defend the Prophet and Islam and to counterattack their opponents (Gibbs 1970). Their approach to the subject of Muhammad is philological, repeating two biographies of the Prophet that were written more than a century after his death. They are not allowed or cannot allow themselves to critically evaluate the old texts for fear of being accused of apostasy; instead the writers uncritically regurgitate what was written centuries before. The second group of authors are Orientalists,[2] whose views were "colored by the belief that Islam is an inferior religion" (Gibbs 1970, vi).[3] Lockman (2004) captured this attitude during the Middle Ages: "Nothing was so outrageous or completely unsupported by evidence that it could not be said about Muhammad" (p. 35). It is important to approach the subject of the Prophet with an empathic, sympathetic, and respectful attitude, but subject it to critical thinking. Furthermore, any discussion of Muhammad has to be approached with the current political and intellectual milieu, and we must realize that our transferences and countertransferences, as well as conscious and unconscious prejudices and fears, shape how we write about Muhammad. This is the approach that I will take.

It may be interesting to some readers that the author of this chapter is not a Muslim. I wanted to write this chapter because of the personal relationship I feel that I have had with Muhammad since my adolescence. I was born and lived my first six years in Acre, Palestine, and the next twenty years in Beirut, Lebanon. Both were coastal cities with mixed Eastern Christian and Muslim populations, and both were in contact with Europe. As a nominal Christian, I grew up within a Muslim majority. I enjoyed being part of this mixed Arab culture and being surrounded by Islam. Consequently, I became interested in Muhammad in an attempt to understand the religion of the people that I befriended and loved. Furthermore, I grew up in a secular Arab atmosphere that made me experience Muslims as self-objects, who were both parts of my self, as it were, as well as distinctly others. Muhammad was often referred to as "the Arab Prophet." He is an Arab, and so am I, and thus, he was part of my personal Arab heritage.

Undoubtedly, language plays an important role in the aforementioned relationship. There is something magical about the language of the *Qur'an* that every Arab, Christian, or Muslim enjoys. Some are even mesmerized by it. The magic increased when I realized that when I am listening to the *Qur'an*, I am listening to the same words that Muhammad himself had used. No translations and minimal changes are required as I listen; and I understand almost every word the Prophet uttered. There is something distancing in reading the *Bible* in a third language. Jesus spoke Aramaic, the *Bible* was written in Greek, and then translated into the vernacular. There is no sense that I am listening to Jesus' words as said by him. Another reason for my interest is political. Muhammad united the Arab tribes into a community before Islam became universal. Thus, I relate to and appreciate whatever unites the Arabs.

An important question is: Is there anything new that can be discovered about Muhammad? I believe so. However, a devout and practicing Muslim may not be able do so. According to Islam, the *Qur'an* is the *words of God* and the Prophet was *his messenger*. Consequently, reading the *Qur'an* will thus not teach us anything new about Muhammad, as the words are from God and not from the Prophet. However, what if the text of the *Qur'an* was read

developmentally and chronologically and as if it is what Muhammad said?
Thus, if he said this, then what can the text tell us about the Prophet? I hope
that even the religious Muslims can accept this approach, because the qualities that are in the *Qur'an* must be the qualities of the Prophet. God must have
chosen him because he must have had these qualities.

Currently, there are a number of biographies about the Prophet, each presented to serve a particular purpose: For example, the socioeconomic milieu
of his time, the religious ideas, the laws expounded by Muhammad, and so
forth.[4] However, there are little psychoanalytically-oriented studies about
Muhammad. I could only find one 1921 article in the *International Journal
of Psychoanalysis* (Berkeley-Hill 1921). Following the lead of Karl Abraham's analysis of the Egyptian Pharaoh Amenhotep IV, and within a few sentences and without any data, Berkeley-Hill starts with asserting the Muhammad suffered from an intense "father-complex." Muhammad also suffered
from a "daughter-complex" and "sister-complex" (p. 43), whatever those
terms mean. Furthermore Muhammad's chastity during his marriage to his
first wife was due to "the repression of every impulse towards sexual experience was due to the immensity of certain incestuous fixations" (p. 44). Whatever happened to the repression of the Prophet's libido during the Madinah
period, when he had several wives? Reflecting the racist attitudes of that period, not only the British Raj, but also the editors of the *International Journal
of Psychoanalysis*, we are told that the secret for the tremendous success of
Islam is because, "Islam stirs up the deeply buried and unconscious complex
against the father, which is an attribute that pervades the minds of all men."
To add insult to injury, this is followed by: "From hardly any other sources
could there spring those wild torrents of emotion that enable men, 'utterly lost
to every call of honour, or patriotism, or family affection, whose only occupation is eating, and whose only reaction is woman, to thrill with excitement
at the summons of faith, and meet death with a contempt the Red Indian could
only envy.'" While I am not judging a previous era with our current ideas
about racism, I think that Berkeley-Hill's article does not add much to our attempts to understand Muhammad.

On other hand, I found one book that uses a psychoanalytic frame to study
Muhammad (Indamdar 2001). I found it intriguing that Indamdar starts by referring to his hometown of Mumbasa, in Kenya, as the place where Africa
collided with the seafaring Indian, Arab, and European worlds. This is similar to my background, which motivated me, a non-Muslim, to rise to the defense of Islam, because of the unfair, inaccurate, and demeaning way in which
it is depicted in the West. I do not know whether Indamar is a Muslim; however, I see his efforts, like mine, as attempts to put the life of Muhammad, and
subsequently of Islam, in a universal, psychoanalytic, and, human frame. The

focus of the book, as the title indicates (*Muhammad and the Rise of Islam: The Creation of Group Identity*), covers similar territory as this chapter. However, there are some differences in focus and interpretations, but it is beyond the focus of a short chapter to get into.

Taking a different approach, this presentation is a short, psychoanalytically oriented biography of Muhammad. I want to describe Muhammad *the individual,* the man, the human being who suffered many losses, and *the group leader* who united warring tribes into a community.

THE LIFE OF MUHAMMAD[5]

Birth and Childhood

Toward the end of the sixth and the beginning of the seventh century A.D., the Arabian Peninsula was outside the influence or control of the major civilizations of that period, namely the Byzantine, Persian, Abyssinian, and the distant Indian cultures. Makkah was the most important city in Hejaz (west-central Arabia) and the religious center of the area. It was a city-state with a thriving business: the transportation center between India and both the Byzantine and Persian empires. The Arabs of this city were the middlemen. In addition, Makkah was a center for polytheistic deities, where pilgrimages were held regularly. The story is that the *Ka'bah* was built in Makkah by Abraham for the worship of *Allah,* (God), but it contained several "daughters of God" who interceded with God. Makkah's ruling group was the Qureish tribe, consisting of several clans, one them being Hashim.

Muhammad ibn Abdullah was born around A.D. 570 in Makkah. His father was Abdullah, from the Hashim clan and his mother Amina, was from Madinah, a city two hundred miles north of Makkah. Abdullah died just before Muhammad was born, and thus Muhammad was left fatherless and an only child. His eighty-year-old grandfather, Abd al-Muttalib, took him and his mother to live with the family. Two years later, his grandfather died, and his uncle, Abu Talib became his guardian. Furthermore, and following custom, he was sent away to be nursed by a woman from a nomadic clan. At the age of six years, Muhammad's mother took him back to his uncle's family, however, she died either during the trip back or soon after. This is what we know about the first six years of Muhammad's life.

It would be fair to say that losses (father,[6] grandfather, and mother), and separations (mother, uncle, and foster mother) dominated the first six years of Muhammad's life. I was unable to find the exact ages of the separation from his mother, the length of said separation, and no direct evidence about the quality of his early object relationships or his reactions to them. This lack of information was filled in more than a century later, when biographies of Muhammad were written in a most idealized way. Thus, any formulations about the impact of these separations and losses must be speculative. However, as previously mentioned, if we look at the *Qur'an* as being about Muhammad, then what is revealed is a sensitive man, who cared deeply about the underprivileged and the ostracized. For example, orphans are mentioned twenty-one times in the *Qur'an*, and always in a supportive and sympathetic manner.[7] The first mention of orphans occurs in the second Surah (*The cow*): "And (remember) when We made a covenant with the children of Israel, (saying): worship none save Allah (only), and be good to parents and to kindered and to orphans and the needy, and speak kindly to mankind: and to establish worship and pay the poor-due." (Pickthal 2002, 2:83).[8] This verse is quintessential Muhammad: caring for the underprivileged, especially the poor and the orphans, in the midst of the central teaching of Islam, worshiping the one and only Allah. Thus, one could conclude that the effects of losses and separations made Muhammad sensitive and caring, not bitter, angry, and hateful as some who had sustained such aforementioned difficulties. This may add support to the later claims that his family's care was good enough,[9] yet it must be noted that a sense of sadness permeates Muhammad's early life, which is understandable from such a history.

Adolescence

Even less is known about Muhammad during this period. We know that he grew up as an orphan in his uncle's house, that he worked on caravans that went to Syria, and earned a reputation for being honest and hardworking, and was given the nickname *al-Amin*, which means the "trustworthy." There is a notable story about Muhammad going on a caravan with his uncle Abu Talib to Syria. In a city called Bostra, a monk recognized him as a prophet, and told his uncle to go back home and protect him.

Adulthood

We learn more about Muhammad after the age of twenty-five. The major event in his life for the next fifteen years began with his marriage to a forty-year-old woman named Khadijah, a successful businesswoman who ran caravans. Muhammad himself ran some of her caravans, and she was so impressed by him that she proposed marriage and he accepted. The evidence from most narratives is that this was a successful and happy marriage. Undoubtedly, the maternal element in the love of this supportive wife compensated for what he lost early in his childhood. He was no longer the poor orphan, but a successful businessman, with a loving wife with whom he had four daughters. The one thing that she could not give him was a son, as two were born, but both died in infancy (more losses). It may be hard for a Westerner to understand the sense of loss and shame that an Arab, from Muhammad's age and even today, will inevitably feel if they are not able to produce a son. There is no question that both the society and the individual himself attribute that failure to the man. There is even a name for such men in Arabic, *abtar,* which means, incomplete. This must have undoubtedly affected Muhammad, most probably shame, because the *Qur'an* accuses the Prophets' enemies of being *abtars.* Some men denied their role, blamed their wives, and remarried until a son is born. Muhammad remained monogamous throughout their twenty-three-year-long marriage that ended with Khadijah's death.

Old Age and Death

During his marriage, he became the messenger of God, and Khadijah is considered to be the first convert to Islam. Soon after her death and due to increased persecution of the Muslim community in Makkah in A.D. 622, Muhammad and the Muslims immigrated to Madinah, a city two hundred miles north of Makkah. There, he built a Muslim community, married a number of women, was able to conquer Makkah, and became the ruler of all of Arabia by the time of his death, A.D. 632.

THE BEGINNINGS OF ISLAM AND THE MAKKAN PERIOD

In A.D. 610, Muhammad was approaching forty and, externally, things were going well for him. However, he was struggling internally. It was the custom of some Arabs in Makkah to withdraw to the surrounding hills for a period of time to be alone, to reflect, and to pray to their Gods and seek wisdom. On a yearly basis, and with little provisions, Muhammad traveled to a cave on a hill outside Makkah, and spent time in reflection and prayer. Who did he pray for? The answers are only speculative.

When Muhammad turned forty, he withdrew again and did so back and forth for some time. Watt (1974, 14) refers to two dreams or "visions" that Muhammad had while at the cave, but only one is clearly reported in the *Qur'an* (Pickthal 2002, 53:6–11):

> One vigorous; and he grew clear to view
>> When he was on the uppermost horizon.
>> Then he drew nigh and came down

Till he was (distant) two bows' length or even nearer,
And he revealed unto His slave that which he revealed.
That heart lied not (in seeing) what it saw.

The second reference only says that "surely he beheld him on the clear horizon" (Pickthal 2002, 81:23).[10]

Muhammad then became afraid that the *Jinns* (unseen spirits) were affecting him. He shared that with his wife, who reassured him. One day as he was sleeping in the cave, an angel appeared to him holding a paper, and the angel said, "Read." Muhammad was taken back and answered, "What shall I read?" He felt as if the angel was choking him and the angel said, "Read." Muhammad replied, "What shall I read?" He again felt as if the angel was choking him and he repeated, "What shall I read?" The angel answered (Pickthal 2002; 96:1–5):

Read: In the Name of thy Lord who creates,
    Creates man from a clot.
    Read: And thy Lord is the Most Bounteous,
    Who teaches by the pen,
    Teaches man that which he knew not.
    This is considered to be the first revelation.

Muhammad woke up in terror and ran out of the cave. While he was in the middle of the hill, he heard a voice calling him. In terror, he raised his head and looked at the sky and saw an angel in the figure of a man. He was so terrified that, for a while, he did not move. Finally, he rushed home and shared what had happened with his wife, who reassured him of the meaning of what had happened. He was so exhausted that he fell asleep, and when he awoke he began his new life as the messenger of God. Clearly Khadijah was both a self-object in Kohut's term and a supportive object who "affirmed" him (Killingmo 1995).[11] Wolf (1988), a Kohutian, defined the term self-object as "an intrapsychic events and is subjectively experiences. Furthermore, when is functioning appropriately, it evokes and maintains the self and its concomitant sense of selfhood" (p. 54). On the other hand, Killingmo defined an affirmative intervention as a communication that removes doubt about the experience of reality and thereby reestablishes a feeling of identity. Clinically, affirmation may function both as a silent background and as a delimited intervention in the foreground.

What is one to make of these experiences? This is the believers' explanation: that the angel was Gabriel, teaching Muhammad God's words. For those of us who are not Muslims, we have to offer another explanation, one of which is a psychological one. However, and unfortunately, some Orientalists abused the psychological explanations. They used the material described above to claim that Muhammad was hallucinating, and thus he must either be psychotic or epileptic. However, the experiences described by Muhammad do not fit the clinical descriptions of either epilepsy or psychosis. Specifically, the hallucinations of a psychotic or an epileptic are not expressed in such cohesive sentences as those that came from Muhammad's mouth. The words that came from Muhammad during a trance and from similar states over the next twenty years compromise a book of over five hundred pages that serves as a belief system of over one billion human beings all over the world.

Another accusation leveled by some Orientalists who claimed that Muhammad was a charlatan and was lying and manipulating, cited that some verses were influenced and even determined by the personal situation of the Prophet or his community. Needless to say, I do not agree with these explanations. I believe that Muhammad's experiences were real and honest. So then, how do we explain these phenomena? More than a hundred years ago, William James addressed these phenomena in his classic, *The Varieties of Religious Experience* (2002). He stated that religious leaders have been subject to abnormal "psychical visitations" and "frequently they have fallen into trances, heard voices, seen visions, and presented all sorts of peculiarities which are ordinarily classed as pathological"(p. 9). The whole of the first lecture of his book is to disprove that such phenomena were pathological, but that they were religious experiences. Subsequently, James defines this state: "There is a state of mind, known to religious men, but to no others, in which the will to assert ourselves and hold our own has been displaced by a willingness to close our mouths and be as nothing in the floods and waterspouts of God" (p. 54). Even though the book was about the experience of Westerners, James mentioned Muhammad as someone who indeed had these types of experiences, which James later attributed to the "subconscious" (p. 524). To continue, this type of religious experience is about an external force taking over Muhammad's body and mind, and not the oceanic sense of fusion. Here, there was no sense of fusion between Muhammad and God, but a sense of self-object differentiation was clear. On many occasions, God chides, supports, and commends Muhammad.

While accepting that these were religious and not pathological experiences, how then do we explain them? An incomplete explanation is that Muhammad's experiences at the cave and his mental state when he recites the verses that became the *Qur'an*, were manifestations of unconscious beliefs, attitudes, and wishes. However, I can accept that it was Muhammad's "psychic reality" that Gabriel was talking to him and that God was talking through him. The support for the unconscious source of Muhammad's revelation is supported by the way they were manifested. Firstly, these phenomena were manifested in dreams and subsequently in trances. Every psychoanalyst would accept the unconscious sources of both phenomena. However, we have to accept that these trances and coherent verses were unusual manifestations of the unconscious and may only occur in religious individuals. Furthermore, our attitude toward these explanations is vital.

I consider myself a "Freudian" with regards to religion (Freud 1930). I think that some people simply have faith, and others, like myself, simply do not and cannot have faith, no matter how hard we try. However, I do not agree with Freud that the "scientific" attitude is superior to the "religious" attitude. Meissner's erudite chapter (2001) on faith discusses the relationship between faith and regression, which permits a relaxation in the organization of psychic functioning that permits greater cognitive flexibility (p. 92). Furthermore, he discusses the instinctual base of faith, it relationship to narcissism, and to basic trust and fidelity. One cannot leave this chapter thinking that faith is simply primitive, unscientific, and in existential areas, inferior to reason. Thus, both reason and faith are narratives and neither is superior nor inferior; they are just different.

After the aforementioned experiences, Muhammad began to preach and a small group of believers gathered around him. This early period is fascinating because the few revelations of this period teach us about both the "origins" of Islam and about Muhammad's personality. So what were the earliest revelations? Unfortunately, the *Qur'an* is not chronological, but attempts were made to assert what these early revelations were, namely before Muhammad posed danger to the established order in Makkah and his group became the object of persecution. Watt (1974) summarized these early messages as indicating: (1) God's goodness and power (and surely your Lord will give unto you so that you will be *content*) (Pickthal 2002, 93:5), (2) the return to God for judgment, (3) man's response—gratitude and worship, (4) Man's response to God—generosity, and (5) Muhammad's own vocation (italics added).

These verses reminded me of the psychoanalytic concepts of health, particularly those of Melanie Klein (1975). Muhammad's inner world was populated by good and giving objects, giving him a sense of contentment, and he reciprocated with gratitude to the good objects. According to Watt (1974), the early meaning of the word *kafir* (unbeliever) could have the meaning of "ungrateful" (p. 29). Those with such experiences can be, and are, generous to others. Yet, there are superegos and ego-ideals to regulate us and help us live good and moral lives (judgment day in the afterlife).

Soon after Muhammad began preaching, many powerful groups in Makkah opposed him for a variety of reasons. One was that he was a monotheist at a time when polytheism prevailed. If he was successful, then his "Allah" will triumph over their gods. The second reason was economic. Makkah was a place where each group had its own stone god in the Ka'bah and each group made pilgrimage to the shrine. Such visits were a source of income for Makkans, and thus, they feared that the elimination of polytheism would affect their economy. The opposition became violent and the Muslims were persecuted. A number of revelations occurred during this period, and the *Surahs* (chapters) that were revealed during that period are referred to as the Makkan Surahs. Most of the revelations addressed the daily life of the small and beleaguered community, and thus, it is proper to suggest that the *Qur'an* is biographical (Inamdar 2001). One example of how the revelations related to the life of the community is illustrated by the following example. When persecution became more violent, Muhammad advised a group of supporters to emigrate to Ethiopia, whose Christian king was reputed to be just. Before they left, he recited the Surah of Mary (No. 19), which shows the similarities between Christianity and Islam. When the Makkans went to Ethiopia to extradite the Muslims, the Muslims recited the Mary Surah and the king would not send them back. The brilliance of Muhammad was to provide the immigrants with useful information, whose timing was perfect. Such timing was repeated in the future.

Muhammad experienced two other losses three years before the immigration to Madinah. In A.D. 619, his beloved Khadijah, undoubtedly his mother-figure, and his protector and father-figure, Abu Talib, died within a few days of each other. Then, in A.D. 621, during the annual pilgrimage to the Ka'bah, a group from the city of Yathrib, later renamed Madinah, approached Muhammad to move there and lead their city. Subsequently, in 622, a group from Madinah entered into a formal agreement with Muhammad that included a pledge to fight to protect him. Thus, Muhammad and his small group of believers escaped to Madinah. Of note, this waiting of one year, despite the persecution that the Muslims were being subjected to, is characteristic of the Prophet's planning. Realizing that the Makkans were going to fight him, he gave the people of Madinah one year to think of the fighting that would ensue after Muhammad moved there.

THE HIJRAH AND THE MADINAH PERIOD

The year A.D. 622 is known as the year of the *Hijrah* (immigration, exile), and marks the beginning of the Lunar Muslim calendar. This period was fundamentally different from the Makkan period, when Muhammad was the leader of a small group who lived under threats. During this period, A.D. 622–632, he showed his charisma and brilliance as a political leader through his ability to form an *umma* (community)[12] from tribal groups who had constantly fought and raided each other, and had no sense of unity or belonging. However, two issues continue to be brought up by both the old and current Orientalists, particularly the American Christian fundamentalists, who viciously attack the Prophet, calling him a terrorist and a pedophile.[13] Such accusations refer to the fact that Muhammad led the Mulims in battle and that he married several women, the most controversial of whom were Aisha (who was a child when he married her) and Zaynab bint Jahsh who was his "adoptive" son's wife.[14]

Let me begin with the Prophet's role as a group leader who forged a community that spread all over the world. In Madinah, the Muslims achieved Freud's definition of a group: "*A primary group of this kind is a number of individuals who have put one and the same object in the place of their ego ideal and have consequently identified themselves with one another in their ego*" (Freud 1921, 116; italics in the original). I think that the Prophet did what needed to be done, *at that time and in that place,* to build such a community. His acts ranged from preaching, punishment, gratification, expulsion, massacres, and forgiveness, and each act was brilliantly calculated and well timed to unite and strengthen his community.

When the Prophet arrived in Madinah, there were four groups living there: the new converts from Madinah, the Jews, the pagans, and the Muslim immigrants from Makkah. An agreement was written stating that, "the believers *and* Muslims of Quraysh and Yathrib [Madinah] and those who follow them and are attached to them and fight alongside them . . . form a single community [*umma*] distinct from other men" (Rodinson 1976, 152; italics added). It is clear that the Jews, namely the believers, were considered to be part of the community. Of note, Muhammad was also willing to coexist with the pagans. The community was not made up of individuals, but of groups. Eleven clans, eight Arab and three Jewish, were mentioned in that agreement. Furthermore, the Muslims were bound by a number of obligations. Muhammad was Allah's intermediary in settling disputes and quarrels between members of the community. It took Muhammad's wisdom and abilities and the help of his counselors to turn what was simply his moral authority into an effective practical power.

Muhammad was aware that if he succeeded in solidifying his power in Madinah, the Makkans would attack him. Furthermore, Makkah was the religious and commercial center of the Hejaz and he had to conquer it eventually. He started attacking the Makkan caravans, on their way to or from Syria, which achieved two goals: weakening the Makkans and the looting was a source of income for the immigrants. The Makkans then realized that they had to attack the Muslims. The first big battle between the Makkans and the

Muslims occurred in A.D. 624, at an oasis called Badr.[15] The Muslims were victorious despite having a smaller number of fighters. This gave the Muslims a certain authority and influence among the local tribes.

Three important events followed this victory that aimed to consolidate Muhammad's power. The first was the assassination of certain poets whose poems attacked the Prophet. No verbal opposition was tolerated. The second event was the use of a fight between a group of Jews and Muslims in the market, supposedly when a Jewish goldsmith pinned down the dress of a Muslim woman while she was sitting so that when she stood up, her dress was torn and she was exposed. A Muslim killed the goldsmith, and then a Jew killed the Muslim. The Jews retired to their fort, and the Muslims laid siege. After fifteen days, the Jews surrendered and they were allowed to leave, but they had to leave their property behind to be distributed among the immigrants.[16] This event achieved two goals: the removal of a potential enemy and financial rewards for the immigrants. Perhaps more important was the psychological impact. The immigrants suffered with the Prophet, and now they were compensated through his leadership. Such a process of deprivation and satisfaction, both due to one individual, increased their attachment to him and to his teachings. In more dynamic terms, these events helped internalize Muhammad and his teachings into their superegos and ego-ideals as what binds them as a community.

The post-Badr period was also the beginning of the establishment of a proto- and theocratic state. One important issue was how to regulate the spoils of war. The *Anfal* (Surah 8) came within a month after the Badr battle: "They ask you (O Muhammad) of the spoils of war. Say: the spoils of war belong to Allah and the Messenger, so keep your duty to Allah, and adjust the matter of your difference, and obey God and Messenger, if you are (true) believers" (Pickthal 2002, 8:1). Was this a revolutionary decision? It depends. Allowing the spoils to be kept was the only rational thing Muhammad could do to keep the loyalty of tribal groups. However, he invoked God and the messenger as the state to receive the spoils. Thus, Muhammad became the state. The spoils were divided among the fighters, and some were kept for the Prophet. However, it is known beyond any doubt that the Prophet did not benefit personally from the spoils. He continued to live a simple and public life until his death. What was left for the Prophet was put toward the first "state budget" to be used for the purpose of keeping the cohesion of the community. Thus, looting was regulated but not banned.

The second battle occurred in A.D. 625. An army of three thousand warriors from Makkah came to destroy Madinah. The two groups battled at place called Uhud, and the Muslims were defeated and Muhammad was wounded. However, he was able to quickly reorganize his warriors, and when the Makkahans discovered that the Prophet was not killed, they withdrew back to Makkah. Thus, total defeat was avoided by the stamina and leadership of Muhammad. Some historians consider this battle to have been a draw, despite the major loss of Muslim men. However, this defeat lowered the prestige of the Muslims among the Arab tribes and the Jews of Madinah. The Women Surah (No. 4) came several months after this battle, where many women were widowed and children were orphaned. This Surah regulated marriage and inheritance, and compared to what prevailed, these rules were ahead of their time. Of note, certain well-known rules, such as the right to have four wives and the rule that daughters inherit half of what sons inherit, are not acceptable today and go against the Universal Declaration of Human Rights (OHCOR 1948).

After Uhud, Muhammad was weakened, and yet he had to deal with potential enemies. He focused on one of the two Jewish tribes left in Madinah, the Bani Nadir, whom he felt were conspiring against him. He besieged their quarters, and when they surrendered, he exiled them to Khybar, a city seventy miles north of Madinah. Their land and property were then distributed among the immigrants, and again in one strike he achieved two goals: eliminating a rival tribe, and satisfying his followers. The second Surah, the *Al-Baquara*, came during this period and lists most of the Jewish prophets and Jesus, clearly showing that Muhammad saw himself as a continuation of said prophets. The anti-Jewish sentiment expressed in this Surah has to be understood within that time and these events.

The third major battle occurred in A.D. 627. This time, the Makkans were well prepared. They had their tribal allies to join them and thus sent ten thousand warriors to attack Madinah. However, Muhammad's unusual strategy was to build a trench around Madinah and defend it from inside. Usually, Arab warriors met in the open. The war was inconclusive and the Makkans withdrew, and this weakened them and strengthened the Muslims. At this time, news came that the Jewish tribe, the Bani Qurayzah, had defected to the enemy. Muhammad, thus, laid siege to their quarter until they surrendered. Here, their fate was different from the two previously-mentioned Jewish tribes. The Bani Qurayzah asked to be judged by a member of an Arab tribe to which they were affiliated. The judgment given was the execution of the men and enslavement of the women and children. It is possible that the man who made the judgment was the receptor of what we would now call 'projective identification.' If this, in fact, represented Muhammad's wishes, they are understandable in the context of the time. If this group reached Khybar, where the Bani Nadir was already in exile, the city would have been strengthened, making it a second front in addition to the Makkan danger.

The next important incident occurred in A.D. 628, and was of a personal nature. During the Muslim's return from a campaign against an opposing tribe,

A'isha, the Prophet's young wife was left behind by mistake. A young Muslim found her and brought her to the Muslim camp, causing hints of infidelity. This dispute was settled by a revelation from God in Aisha's favor. Of note, the said incident has been used by "Orientalists" as an example of Muhammad's charlatanism. Of course, the previous interpretation accepted in this chapter is that such revelations represent Muhammad's wishes and beliefs, delivered in the unique way of a trance.

SOME CONTROVERSIAL ASPECTS OF THE PROPHET'S LIFE

The Satanic Verses

An incident from the early Makkan period was that of the "Satanic Verses." Those were two or three verses (Watt 1974, 26) that permitted the intercession of other deities besides "Allah" at some shrines outside of Makkah. Such verses accepted other gods in addition to "Allah," and thus, were polytheistic and contradictory to the central teachings of Islam, which is monotheistic. Muhammad later withdrew those verses and attributed them to Satan cheating him. The psychological explanation for Muhammad's recitation of these verses is that he wished for compromise with those who opposed him. Thus, in his trance he uttered these wish-fulfilling and probably unconscious wishes. When he either realized that these verses were contradictory, or that this compromise would not change the attitudes of his opponents, he recanted these verses.

This, in a hyperbolic form, became the nidus of a chapter in Salman Rushdie's (1988) novel, *The Satanic Verses*, which created a furor all over the Islamic world. Nothing infuriates Muslims more than insulting or ridiculing the Prophet. At times, there is conflict between our Western ideas about freedom of expression and the need to respect the sensitivities of others. I think that the Salman Rushdie affair was typical of the Western attitude.[17] What was the Salman Rushdie affair? Let me start by condemning the *fatwa* against Rushdie's life. However, my opinion may not be acceptable in the West. Rushdie ridiculed, insulted, and humiliated the Prophet, by offering, in a sarcastic way, the Orientalist explanations of some aspects of Muhammad's life. Rushdie knew what he was doing, but his grandiosity let him believe that he would get away with it. I believe that controversial events about the Prophet's life can be brought up and discussed with respect and without assaulting him.[18] I do not think that my freedom of expression is limited by my not ridiculing or insulting the Prophet, and infuriating about a billion human beings. Unfortunately, this digression distracted attention from the main focus of the book, *The Satanic Verses*, which, in my mind, was a brilliant narrative of migration.

Muhammad and the Jews

It is difficult (impossible?) to discuss this issue without it being colored by the current Middle Eastern conflict. However, to ascribe modern implication to this relationship is ludicrous. The issue here is that Muhammad was trying to consolidate his community. He wanted to be seen as part of the Abrahamic religions, a prophet following Moses and Jesus. Yet, it was clear that there were contradictions between what was revealed to Muhammad and the Old Testament. Thus, the Jews did not accept him and raised doubts about his message. Furthermore, there were alliances between one important Arab faction, referred to in the *Qur'an* as "Hypocrites," and certain Jewish tribes that threatened Muhammad's goals. Muhammad realized that he could possibly win over the Hypocrites, but that the Jews, with an already coherent belief system, were out of reach. Thus, for this place and time, the only ways to get rid of such danger, were expulsion or death. Muhammad did both.

Muhammad's Marriages

The third series of events, not all occurring after Badr, were aimed at consolidating his power through his relationships with the leaders around him through marriages. First, his cousin and fourth Caliph, Ali, married Muhammad's daughter Fatima. Then, Uthman, the third Caliph, who was married to one of the Prophet's daughters, married a second daughter when the first daughter died. Muhammad married the daughter of Umar, the second Caliph. In A.D. 623, he had married Aisha, referred to as the beloved of Muhammad, who was the daughter of Abu Bakr, the first Caliph. Thus, there is consensus (Ahmed 1992; Rodinson 1976; Watt 1974), that marriages were often politically based. There were other marriages, however, where passion was as important as politics. Islam stresses that Muhammad was human, and as such, he had sexual desires. In his time, polygamy was the norm and he lived it.[19] To view it with today's social prism is a historical fallacy.

Two of Muhammad's marriages continue to cause criticism until today. One was his marriage to Aisha, whom he married when she was nine and he was fifty-three years old. Of note, it was the custom not to have a sexual relationship until after menstruation. From reports, it was clear that he loved Aisha and that the age difference did not have had the same significance that it has today. The second was his marriage to Zaynab, his "adopted" son Zayd's ex-wife. I put the word "adopted" in quotation marks because the translation of the actual word used in the *Qur'an* is not the current Arabic word for adoption. Zayd was a slave whom his first wife Khadijah bought and freed, and that she and Muhammad brought up as if he were their son. The story is that Muhammad went to see Zayd at his home, but he was not there. He accidentally saw Zaynab, who was not fully clothed. Zayd then felt that Muhammad was attracted to his wife and offered to divorce her, but Muhammad forbade him. Nonetheless, Zayd divorced Zaynab, and consequently, Muhammad married her. This event must have aroused questioning, because the *Qur'an* addressed them. These verses have a defensive tone, deny the equality of "adopted" children, and allowed the Prophet to marry Zaynab: "and when you said unto him on whom Allah has conferred favor and you have conferred favor: Keep your wife to yourself, and fear Allah. And you did hide in your mind that which Allah was to bring to light, and you did fear mankind whereas Allah had a better right that you should fear him. So when Zayd had performed the necessary formality (of divorce) from her, "We gave her unto you in marriage, so that (henceforth) there may be no sin for believers in respect of their "adopted" sons, when the latter have performed the necessary formality (of release) from them. The commandments of Allah must be fulfilled." (Pickthal 2002; 33:37; quotation marks added).

While three translations of the *Qur'an* that I consulted use the term "adopted," the Arabic word used in the above verse is not the current Arabic word for adoption. The word used in the verse was *Ad'eya'um.* The current Arabic word for adoption is *Tabani,* which clearly has no connection with *Ad'eya'um. Ad'eya'um* is a complex word: *'um* means "them," while *Ad'ey'a* refers to those who *d'eya' (verb),* namely to claim. In the verse mentioned above, Ade'ya'um refers to those who claim that you are their father, while in reality you are not. This could very well be Muhammad's experience. He was orphaned, but he knew who his father and his mother were. I found this particular verse to be harsh. I read it as the psychological father's response is to remind the child that he is not the "real" father. In many situations that we face today, we do not know who the biological father is. The Islamic attitude is: "I am not your father and, thus, do not attach to me as if I am your father." It represents the triumph of biology over psychology, of dogma over empiricism. We know that children can attach to foster or adoptive parents, "as if" they were their "real" fathers. Such subtlety is missed in this verse.

Pickthal, the English convert to Islam, and whose translation I have used, said the following in his introduction to the Clan Surah (No. 33), "the prophet was commanded to marry her in order, by his example, to disown the superstitious custom of the pagan Arabs of treating their adopted son as their real sons" (Pickthal 2004, 397). It is clear today that, "the superstitious custom of the pagan Arabs" were psychologically ahead of the Muslims. Tragically, until today, Islam does not recognize adoption and such children are institutionalized or ambivalently held by families who believe that they are not allowed to treat them "as if" they were their own children. We know that both alternatives are harmful.

Any explanation of this marriage is marred by the lack of details of this incident. The explanations that this marriage was due to lust, political expediency, or to ensure Zaynab's future, who was about thirty-eight years old and probably too old to marry again, are based on wishful thinking and political agendas. Whatever the reasons were, this incident has had some harmful results on some aspects of Islamic family law. Such verses make some aspects of *Shari'a* incompatible with our knowledge about attachment and psychological ties, especially in regards to children's needs for a sense of belonging (Fonagy 2001; Goldstein, Freud, and Solnit, 1973).[20]

BACK TO MAKKAH

During the same year, the Prophet had another vision (a dream?): "Allah has fulfilled the vision for his messenger in very truth. You shall indeed enter the Sacred Mosque, if Allah will, secure, (having your hair) shaven and cut, not fearing. But that which you know not, and has given you a near victory beforehand" (Pickthal 2002, 48:27). So Muhamad gathered 1,500 men, all dressed as pilgrims, and set out to Makkah. As he approached the city, the Makkans put on their warrior clothes and set out to meet him. He ordered his men to go to *Hudaybiyah,* a range of mountain gorges and sought to open negotiations. The agreement they reached, called the 'Truce of Hudaybiyah' enshrined the cessation of hostilities between Makkah and the Muslims for ten years. It also included a controversial stipulation that Muhamad would return any Makkan who had moved to Madinah to join the Prophet, while if his followers joined the Makkans, they would not be returned. However, probably the most important aspect to the agreement was that the Makkans would evacuate the city for three days next year for the Muslims to perform their pilgrimage.

Two major events occurred in A.D. 629: Muhammad was becoming the ruler of Arabia and dealt with one of his opponents. He attacked Khybar, where the Jews gathered and turned them into tenants of the Muslims. Then, according to the truce of Hudaybah, the Muslims made the pilgrimage to Makkah, while the non-Muslims evacuated the city for three days. In the eighth year, the Makkans broke the truce and attacked a tribe allied with the Prophet. Muhammad marched to Makkah with a large army and conquered it, with the Makkans offering little resistance. Despite being from Makkah, the commercial and transportation center of central Arabia, Muhammad chose to return to Madinah. During the next year, tribes from all over Arabia came to Madinah to swear allegiance to the Prophet and to learn the *Qur'an.*

Ten years after his escape to Medina, the Prophet made his last pilgrimage to Makkah and gave what would later become known as the Farewell Pilgrimage. One of his main points was the following: "All mankind is from Adam and Eve, an Arab has no superiority over a non-Arab nor a non-Arab has any superiority over an Arab; also a white has no superiority over a black nor a black has any superiority over a white—except by piety and good action. Learn that every Muslim is a brother to every Muslim and that the Muslims constitute one brotherhood. Nothing shall be legitimate to a Muslim which belongs to a fellow Muslim unless it was given freely and willingly. Do not therefore do injustice to yourselves. Remember one day you will meet Allah and answer your deeds. So beware: do not stray from the path of righteousness after I am gone." While his focus had been on Arabia and the Arabs, he now pointed to the future universality of Islam.

CONCLUDING REMARKS

Muhammad was both a great man and a unique Prophet. Those of us who are Jewish or Christian have mental representations of prophets as old, asexual men preaching, threatening, and cajoling the sinners to repent. Muhammad was a different type of prophet. First and foremost, he was a man like you and me, but he was also more. He was a man of his time and yet beyond his time. He was a deeply religious man, a preacher, an only child, an orphan, a husband, a sexual being, a father, a grandfather, a businessman, a religious leader of a small and beleaguered community, a temporal and political leader of a growing community, and a military leader. His message arose in a place where social organization was fragmented and primitive. He could not leave to Caesar what was to Caesar because there was no Caesar. He had to be both Caesar and representative of God.

With the exception of changing attitudes about adoption, all of Muhammad's changes improved the social cohesion of his forming group and gave more protection and rights to women and children than had ever been available. However, the idea that if some psychological or social solutions were adaptive at a certain time and in one place, then they shall be adaptive forever and in all places is alien to psychoanalysis. The most adaptive solutions have to continue to change and be elaborated. In fact, one definition of pathology is that it is a rigid and unchanging adaptive solution to particular problems at a particular time. Thus, one can continue to admire Muhammad and learn from his life, yet one has to questions the timelessness and universality of *any* teachings and behaviors that developed in one time and for one place. It is the tension between respectful admiration and healthy and courageous curiosity that leads to human growth.

I would like to conclude by stating that these issues discussed in this chapter are not the illusions of a Westernized Christian psychoanalyst, but they express the struggle of dedicated and thoughtful groups of secularists, Muslims, and Islamists, as illustrated in a book dedicated to these issues (Abu-Rabi' 2004).

II

CHARACTERS

3

Rapture and Poetry

Rumi

M. Hossein Etezady

When nothing was, then God was there; had nothing been, God would have been. My being has defeated me. Had I not been, what would have been?

— Mirza Asad Ullah Ghalib, 1856, cited in Russell, 2003, p. 18

Jalal-uddin Mohammad Rumi, the great Sufi poet, was born in the vicinity of Balkh (currently in the region of Afghanistan that borders on Iran) on September 30, 1207, to a prominent Muslim family of mystics and scholars. Seeking safety from the menacing invasion of the Mongols, the family traveled extensively westward through the Muslim world and finally settled in Konia, then a part of Iran under the Seljuk Empire. Rumi believed in the Islamic principle of unity and singularity of God. He dedicated his life to the worshipful pursuit of spiritual purity and was energized by the consuming passion that fueled his devotion to truth. As much as any other aspect of Rumi's personal attributes, the element of faith as a determining factor in his life and creative work is deserving of special attention.

As a driving force in the life of people, faith has been the subject of much deliberation in philosophy, literature, religion, and sciences. From a psychoanalytic perspective, we can consider faith as a state of relatedness to an object whose dimensions exceed the reach of experiential and cognitive grasp. Viewed in the context of relatedness, faith rests on the intersubjective matrix of interactional reciprocity. Faith is based on the belief in the willful interventions of an omnipotent object, even though the effect or the manifestations of such interventions might lie beyond the operative expanse of perceptual experience. Through a sense of connectedness to the omnipotent creator, faith serves to maintain a background of safety (Sandler 1960)

43

and to provide self-object functions that underpin regulation of homeostasis and emotional stability.

Faith in the benevolence of the object is rooted in early experience of the child when the mother's libidinal availability and the child's omnipotent illusion of symbiotic dual unity provide a background of safety. The quality of the experience with the maternal object in early childhood determines the state of future object relations and the fate of future attachments. When early object relations are disrupted, disorganized, or dismissive, narcissistic fixation and self-pathology may ensue. In such instances, the development of self-reflection, self, and object constancy (Mahler et al. 1975) and the capacity for affect modulation will be impeded. Signal affects are not available. Magical thinking and narcissistic defenses of a primitive nature will dominate. Self-concept and self-regulation will be unstable and unduly vulnerable to precarious vicissitudes of external events or the perceived views of others (Blum 1996). The quality of relatedness to the object will continue to be based on states of need and deficit, creating great instability and a sense of loss of control and helplessness. Primitive idealization (Kernberg 1976) inflates objects into hollow phantasms of perfection and grandiosity, and disillusionment creates frightful monsters of persecutory intent or degraded refuse of no worth and value. Relatedness is experienced in coercive and sadomasochistic terms. This prevents the development of the capacity to empathize and reciprocate and being able to understand and appreciate others realistically, in their own right as intentional and feeling individuals. When the development of object relationships has been optimal, secure attachment and object consistency become possible. Understanding of one's own mind and the capacity to empathize with others can grow (Fonagy and Target 1997). Mutuality becomes possible. Judgmental decisions, based on intuitively accurate appreciation of the internal state of self and others, become more realistic and reliable. "Blind faith" or baseless optimism regarding others will not prevail any more than paranoia and bitter disillusionment. A person who does not know his own needs and internal states cannot know or appreciate the state of the mind of others. It has been said if you know yourself, you know God. When we encounter arrested development in the course of early object relationships, the pathological manifestations of this arrest can be observed in the individual's quality of faith and his attitudinal disposition toward the deity.

Although we know little about the specifics of Rumi's early life, we might assume that he enjoyed the benefits of an "average expectable environment" (Hartmann 1939) in an intact family headed by an enlightened and prominent figure of high moral, social, and scholarly standards. Rumi was endowed with exceptional intelligence and intuitive resonance that enabled him to reach deep into the mysteries of hearts and minds and to gain penetrating access to transcendental insights conceivable only by the exceptional genius of the rare few who are destined to leave their indelible mark on the course of human history and the basic tenets of civilization.

Rumi, we may safely assume, knew his own mind and the mind of others, and he knew God as the omnipotent object of his worship, whose dimensions he understood to reach beyond the limited confines of cognitive and emotional grasp. His faith was transcendental, rooted in the basic trust of his early upbringing, fostered by the spiritual orientation of his cultural and educational milieu, and honed by his own pursuit of the surpassing truth and absolute beauty that he found pervading every manifestation of existence.

RUMI'S WORLDVIEW AND LANGUAGE

Some seven centuries ago, Rumi was one of the best known and most popular of the classical Persian poets. Today, he is ranked among the top six great luminaries of the world of classical poetry for which the Persian culture and literature claims right of pride and unequaled magnificence. It is owing to the penetrating power of genius and the creativity encapsulated in the world of great Persian poets that today's Persian language has maintained its native fluency, immediacy, and communicative instrumentality. Through centuries of change and turmoil, the Persian language and national identity have withstood the test of tumult, conflict, calamity, defeat, and victory. In the face of powerful and often coercive influences from competing powers of the neighboring cultures, rulers, enemies, and friends, the Persian culture and literature have endured and bonded people together from land to land and generation to generation.

Rumi's language of seven centuries ago is as current in form, presentation, and sophistication today, as it was when first spoken. Were it not for the language of the Persian great classical poets, such as Firdausi, Hafez, Saadi, and Rumi, the Persian language may not have survived the onslaught of intrusion, coercion, and official animosity from competing influences beyond the oscillating boundaries of the country. Without the life-enhancing influence of its poetry, today's Persian language might not be as rich and as great a source of inspiration to as many thinkers, men of knowledge, and masters of art, letters, and lexicon for centuries, spanning the Asian continent from China to North Africa and the Mediterranean. Foreign dominance and influence included extended periods of government by Islamic conquerors and their caliphs under whose rule the Arabic language dominated science, commerce, politics, and the international climate of the day over great expanses of time and geography. Equally pervasive was the invasion and domination of the Mongols, including Genghis Khan, Taimur. and Halakoo, conquerors who completely dominated life over hundreds of years, while the past glory of Persian native culture and the majestic power of Persian kings had to yield to the disruptive intrusion of these alien invaders. With the passage of time, the native Persian culture absorbed these external elements, and metabolized and transformed them into internal components of the surviving culture, language, art, poetry, and literature. The language and the native culture were thus enriched as they assimilated many beneficial elements from a multiplicity of origins and divergent sources.

I leave the detailed discussion of Rumi's life, poetry, and philosophical perspective to the scholarship of those who have studied his life and the enormous body of his work in great depth (e.g., Nicholson 1926; Turkman 1962; Barks 1995; Gamard 2004). Here, I only aim to provide some explanation from a psychoanalytic perspective for Rumi's universal appeal, observations on his worldview, his creativity, and his sense of rapture that he lived, described, and exuded in his creative work.

Rumi was revered in his own lifetime, as he is now in the Persian-speaking world, as well as in other cultures. During his lifetime, he was among the most sought-after teachers and figures of moral prominence. He was well versed in all branches of knowledge and spoke many languages. During the period of time that he lived in the area now known as Turkey, he quickly achieved the same prominence and reverence among the Turkish-speaking populace of his time as he maintains today. During a period of history when kings, monarchs, and potentates dictated conduct and one could be beheaded for uttering the wrong word or displaying the wrong gesture, Rumi was able to speak frankly, emphatically, clearly, and without any restraints. He spoke directly to man, woman, child, old, poor, powerful, the mighty, the wise, and the simple-minded. His words and poetry were equally acclaimed and devoured by people from all ranks, intellectual levels, and social strata. He possessed a universal appeal that combined soothing, solace, consolation, inspiration, hope, direction, enticement, enlightenment, reason, and resolution. It expressed a bittersweet longing that fills the heart of humanity from cradle to grave. Rumi speaks of love, timeless, infinite, ever present, forever nurturing the soul, and enriching the spirit. He depicts this everlasting love as a source of excitation that energizes the soul, kindles life, and sets hearts on fire—a fire without which there might as well be no life.

He sees love as the activator of life and the fire that enlightens the soul. He finds love accessible, attainable, to be pursued with all-consuming fervor, sacrificing all one possesses on the way to its attainment. In Rumi's view, our birth into the physical world was an act of separation from the original source of life and creation. Our soul leads our life in a course of seeking and reaching, longing for re-fusion. Death is the final return of the eternal soul to its origin.

Man, once an angel, can recover his lost place in paradise by actively seeking proximity to the creator and by acknowledging the oneness of existence where the boundaries between the self and other signify unity as much as they designate distinction. There is an intelligent design in a universe of predetermined order where all elements and entities are in eternal harmony, conducting time and the living physical world from here into the infinite future, in accordance to an order that supercedes the confines of place or time. There are other dimensions beyond our perceptual capacity and other worlds beyond the scope of cognition or imagination. Our awareness of existence is woefully limited as is that of a worm living inside an apple. While all animals are granted the gift of life, man alone is bestowed with "human life," blessed and burdened by the ability to discriminate, and by his need, as well as the ability, to reflect upon events and to arrive at judgment pertaining to his own behavior and his choices. Man alone possesses the governing sense of agency and awareness of how he can plan, prepare, proceed, and conclude a sequence using available means and various choices, to actualize dreams and to bring about desired results, and to satisfy wishes and to influence the future. Man alone can reflect on his own feelings, thoughts, decisions, and behavior in the light of obligation, respect, and responsibility to others as dictated by arbitrations of his conscience.

THREE TYPES OF KNOWLEDGE

In Rumi's view, knowledge exists in three varieties: intuitive knowledge, experimental knowledge, and imitational knowledge. Intuitive knowledge is independent of the senses. It is uncommon and exceptional, involuntary, and a product of a daydream-like activity. Rumi believes purifying the spirit and polishing the soul, like a mirror, can reflect the face of reality more vividly. "Remove the swab of doubt from your ear so you can hear the roar of the universe. The ear of your heart is where you hear the voice of truth. What is the voice of truth if not a sense from within." He believes direct access to the source of inspiration and creativity is available to anyone, in proportion to the extent of one's effort, the purity of spirit, and the taming of instinctual urges. Experimental knowledge is physically organized and it is based on perception, sensory organs, and neurological structure. Here, information is hierarchically organized, based on past acquisitions and deletions. Imitational knowledge is acquired by adopting information imparted to us by others or from other existing sources, such as books.

Rumi regards the Holy Spirit as the original fountainhead of inspiration and intuitive consciousness. Access to this sort of knowledge is the means to reaching the genuine article, bypassing reason and logic on the road to the final destination. The leg of the rationalist is wooden, and a wooden leg is woefully inadequate for this journey. This level of consciousness that Rumi describes exists in the domain of faith, certitude, and the "confident expectation" (Benedek 1938) that is reached, not in sequential steps or in the collective accumulation of individual scientific achievements, but in a single and complete flight unhindered by limits of reason or restrictions of the perceived objective reality. Just as light emanates from the sun, but it is not the sun, intuitive consciousness guiding inspiration comes from the Holy Spirit but is not the Holy Spirit itself.

It is noteworthy that our more recent discoveries and observations, derived from quantum mechanics and chaos theory for instance, are compatible with much of what Rumi's worldview takes for granted. One such example is lack of certainty and unpredictability of likely events, juxtaposed with the notion that anything that is possible can happen at any given time. In Rumi's vision, miracles can happen. Miracles indeed are at the heart of the magical mystery of life and the mind-boggling mathematics of existence itself, rather than being the uncommon exceptions of a dubious claim. Positives do not rule out the negative, and paradox weaves the essential fabric of the mundane reality. Albert Einstein, reflecting on the reductionistic nature of our scientific assertions that attribute the miraculous emergence of life to accidental permutations of random chance, mused: "God does not play dice."

In Rumi's cosmic consciousness, there is order in the apparent chaos as the willful elaborations of an exquisitely intelligent design unfolds in the universal dimensions of space and the eternity of time. The capacity to comprehend the unitary logic of such an infallible order exceeds all limits of mentation and scientific understanding. The mind is incapable of conceiving the extent of the complexity of a design so infinitely grand, much as the worm in the apple is incapable of considering the age of the apple tree or the history of the orchard in which the apple tree is located. We can never conceive all there is to know and will never master infinity. We can only know and speak of some aspects of what has preceded and the fragments of our present. What the future and its predestined course will bring cannot be known.

> Living inside the apple, you're no diff'rent than the worm.
> What news might you bring 'bout the tree, the orchard or its form?

THE SEVEN STATIONS OF DEVOTION

In his pursuit of true knowledge, justice, and grace, it is the aim of the Sufi seeker to free his mind of the corrupting influences of physical dictates and to rein the wild horse of corporal passion, rage, and conceitful grandiosity by applying vigilant restraint. Enslaving commitment to the material and worldly concerns weakens spirituality. Denial of or restraining temptations of the flesh brings one closer to fulfillment of the goals of spiritual uplifting. It is through inhibition, restraint, and denial of desires and the temptations of the physical world that ultimate freedom and liberation of the soul can be accomplished. Rumi as a Sufi is dedicated to the purification of the soul as he devoutly seeks an encounter with the vision of the countenance of his creator. The seeker can achieve this vision, reflected in the mirror of his soul. When the mirror is polished, clear, untainted, and carefully positioned, it reflects the countenance of the beloved. The magnificence of this awesome vision of eternal beauty exceeds all boundaries of imagination, powers of attribution, and all means of description.

Upon this pursuit, the Sufi in training dedicates his resources and future to the devoted obedience of an older master who guides his way through the seven arduous stations of devotion.

1. *Longing and pursuit*: This involves a concentrated search for the mysteries beyond the confines of physical limitations and boundaries. Without a willing commitment, one can not put foot on the road of spiritual refinement. The seeker shall find. Persistence and sacrifice are needed for reaching the goal.

2. *Love and abandon*: Spiritual awakening depends upon a passionate and consuming love that fuels such search. This love sustains the traveler on this treacherous journey that is overtaxing beyond human tolerance and requires endurance past all physical possibility. As with the moth encircling the candle with abandon, drawn ever closer to the fiery center of the source of light, wings can burn, lives may be sacrificed, and the self annihilated at the worshipful altar of the beloved. The heart is so attached to the beloved that separation creates an insatiable desire to grope for the moment of reunion, fearless of the fire and heedless of doubt, certainty, good, or evil, and regardless of any consequences.

3. *Awareness of divinity*: This involves an encounter with supreme wisdom. While there is a cosmic dimension to the experience, each traveler has his own endowment of knowledge that gives shape to it. Accordingly, each has chosen his own path of servitude, be it the temple or the idol, each grasping to the extent of their own capacity. On the road to this goal, countless thousands are lost before any find the key to unlocking the secrets of existence. The value of each individual is at the level of his relationship to divinity.

4. *Needlessness*: The wise and compassionate individual on the way to his goal needs nothing from the physical world or the people in it. In his

eye, the universe is no more real than a picture on a plate. There is no picture once the plate breaks.

5. *Oneness*: Reaching this station, the traveler sees oneness in all diversity and finds God in all there is. God is the creator of all existence and nothing would exist without his will. All else is, therefore, immaterial and may be dismissed. Here, the separation between self and other disappears.

6. *Wonderment*: At this station, the traveler realizes how little he knows, is completely lost, and discovers the depths of his own ignorance. He loses his identity. He knows nothing and knows nothing about the extent of his ignorance.

7. *Selflessness*: This involves the loss of self, desires, and passions and pride of conceit. In losing himself, he has fused with the universe of unity, like an instrument accompanying others in creating a glorious melody in a concert of irreducible totality of the creation. In letting go of his own existence, he reaches the truth and joins infinity.

DEATH AS A RETURN TO GOD

Rumi's cosmic continuity supports and maintains physical life, as well as the eternal life of the soul. In the Persian language, there exists a word with no English equivalent. It is a very important and common word with biological, psychological, philosophical, and colloquial significance. *Jaan* (pronounced as the American "John") is the nonphysical element that is granted by the creator in order to bring the physical vessel into life, movement, and awareness. *Jaan* is surrendered or taken back at the time of death. Without the physical vessel (i.e., before birth and after death), there is no *jaan*, but there is the soul that is reunited with eternity after death. The soul or the spirit of man, bestowed upon him by the creator distinguishes him as the most exalted of all creatures. Rumi sees man's existence as the evolutionary waystation preceded by plant life and inanimate material. From the inanimate material came the plant world, from the plants came animals. The next level of honor and exaltation was to become a human being. This is an intriguing insight that is in substantial accord with our current theories of evolution. The only higher station would be the otherworldly angelic state of no time and no space, no physical vessel to confine and pose limits or to create carnal temptation and physical burdens. Rumi sees death as the end of one process and the beginning of the next, elevating the soul toward a higher plane of spiritual purity and increased proximity to the supreme creator. Since death at every level sets the stage for entering a higher plane of existence, we can only gain in dying, which Rumi celebrates enthusiastically and anticipates with hope and faith that the best is yet to come.

MEANING AND *ERFAN*

In Persian tradition and philosophy, *erfan* (gnosis) refers to a state of "knowing" or level of consciousness greater than mere possession of facts and objective information in any specific field or about a given subject. In *erfan*, access to truth is not achieved by means that are exclusive to the domain of scientific inquiry or objective verification. While rationality, intelligence, discrimination, and logic are essential in establishing a scientific discourse, they, in fact, might hinder access to the unifying truth that governs disparate facts and irreconcilable events. Since our intelligence, powers of discrimination, and the grasp of our logic are finite, our cognitive tools are limited in their reach and are, therefore, capable of addressing not all, but merely a circumscribed face of reality, under particular conditions, from specific points of view. In this sense, our perceptions, thoughts, calculations, and scientific elaborations can lead us at best to assumptions and understandings that are limited in scope. Confinement to the objective certitude of scientific endeavor blocks access to the totality of reality, which cannot be defined or appreciated by our limited cognitive resources and our finite capacity for understanding. Reaching true knowledge and the ultimate truth requires reaching beyond the limits of logic and the boundaries of comprehension. It calls for entering into the boundless realm of intuitive inspiration that reaches beyond the limits of our intellectual confinement. In the perspective gained from *erfan*, the pervasive light of eternal truth shines in the heart, enlightens the soul, and elevates the mind into the overwhelming ecstasy of transcendence, boundless compassion, exquisite humility, joyful surrender, encompassing peace, expanded consciousness, and liberating wisdom (Neher 1980).

Grounded in *erfan*, Rumi's lofty view of nothingness versus the unitary totality of oneness derives from the belief that first there was nothing and then, in a single instant, all of creation came into being. This Islamic perspective regards the entirety of existence as a singular presence of a unitary entity— one with infinite variations, countless permutations extended in innumerable dimensions, seemingly separate, distinct, dissimilar, incompatible, contradictory, and yet combined and contained in the eternal singularity of a holistic unitary presence of one.

Rumi sees man's existence and the universe of his perceived experience as a manifestation of this eternal unity. In this vision, the totality of all creation exists, evolves, functions, and proceeds in a single direction, governed by a unitary rule of law and under the supreme intelligent intent and willful command of the omnipotent creator. Life and the entirety of all creation is driven by a single unitary force assuming infinite dimensions; eternal in its permanence, yet constantly in transformation; immutably singular, yet infinite in variation; continually generating, yet forever inexhaustible; and preordained and predestined, yet utterly unpredictable—multitudes of forms and states merely signifying the incomprehensible singularity of the ultimate source of power, intelligence, light, truth, and creativity; constancy preserved through inevitable and endless change; life generated from nothingness and light from primordial darkness; destruction intertwined with creative construction; opposites indispensably interdependent and the positive invariably complemented by the negative; and paradox binding the irreconcilable extremes of incompatibility as chaos constitutes the elemental order of predetermined destiny. The only thing certain is uncertainty, and nothing is constant but change itself. The ultimate in wisdom and the overarching principle is the recognition that what is known, knowable, and within our intellectual reach is an infinitely small fragment of the ultimate truth, much like a drop of dew in size and significance, compared to the oceans.

Recognizing man's meager resources, his uncertain yet predetermined destiny, his hopelessly narrow view of reality, and his incurable vulnerability, Rumi advocates one remedy. He resorts to total submission to the ultimate and solitary source of power, intelligence, enlightenment, creativity, and absolute beauty. He advises yielding to the supreme will that governs the entirety of all that now exists, ever has, or ever will. Submitting to this will and surrendering to the empowering servitude of this power is the only viable course to salvation and the sole straight path to the destination of fulfillment, enlightenment, transcendent consciousness, and sustaining peace. As if blissfully nestled in the warm, comforting containment of a nurturing benevolent bosom, he drinks from the intoxicating fountain head of love, eternal life, absolute beauty, and inexhaustible strength to which unconditional access is granted for the mere intent to seek and the determination to sustain the search in confident expectation.

RAPTURE, LIBERATION, INTUITION, AND CREATIVITY

Rapture is a positively charged state of vitality and energetic exuberance that reaches or surpasses the outer limits of emotional registry and affective range in the vast repertoire of our subjective experience. More than a simple state of well-being and compelling joy, rapture connotes a state of ecstatic exuberance associated with a sense of buoyancy, boundless freedom, and liberating fulfillment (Neher 1980). It emanates from a sense of complete contentment wherein coveted wishes have been entirely gratified and all obstacles have been surmounted. It is experienced as an expansive sense of being at one with the boundless infinitude of the universe. In this state of imperturbable oceanic bliss, the remote and the alien become close, familiar, and comprehensible. Disparate elements of isolated experience are collectively linked and meaningfully interconnected; the novel turns familiar, and the absurd gains depth and validity; meaning is securely anchored internally, is profoundly pervasive, and hence thoroughly self-affirming; self-other boundaries fade and the internal universe interpenetrates and comingles with the external; boundaries of the ego are expanded and its strength and resources multiplied; optimism, hope, compassion, and confidence abound; wisdom, insight, and creativity are in ample supply; acceptance, surrender, gratitude, and peace are at hand; past, present, and future unite to exceed the confining boundaries of birth and demise. There is a subjective sense of fusion and continuity with all that exists, as the self and other merge into one. Senses are stronger, reach deeper, span more broadly, and receive impression from higher orbits of influence. Perception is similarly more direct, clear, better integrated, and more stimulating. Thinking is better grounded in greater quantities of factual references, both objective and intuitive. Cognition is unimpeded. Inner urges, needs, and drives are more syntonic and free of contradiction, conflict, remorse, guilt, or shame. Self-awareness and realistic assessment of self and others, along with reality processing, are enhanced in the absence of defensive grandiosity and regressive narcissistic idealization. The mundane and the tedious acquire their own rightful significance, assume higher levels of meaning, and can be a source of insight, inspiration, and fascination. Empathy, intuition, and objective engagement are facilitated. Truth is perceived to be self-evident, more compelling, easily accessed, and readily accommodated. Ambiguity, errors, and shortcomings of self and others are embraced with tolerance. Events and actions are perceived in a transcendental context rather than in the isolative restriction of self-centeredness.

In the psychoanalytic view, creativity begins as a developmental capacity, embedded in the initial emergence of the transitional phenomena (Winnicott 1953). This originally begins when an object is imbued by the infant with a personal meaning that is different from what it might otherwise stand for, outside the realm of the child's subjective experience. To the child, a security blanket simultaneously represents the satisfying mother, the currently gratified self, and past self-object experiences of a restorative nature. It represents an illusion of safety and control, at a time when any absence of the maternal object threatens to undermine the child's sense of connectedness and symbiotic, magical control of the object. Transitional objects become operational toward the end of the first year of life when self and object differentiation has begun and the boundaries between the self and the object are being clearly delineated. This developmental progression is heralded by the appearance of stranger reaction, which is known as Spitz's "second organizer" (1965) of the psyche and which ushers in Stern's (1985) intersubjective realm of self-experience. The monadic pattern of psychological functioning of early infancy, operative until now, enters the dyadic mode of operation. Transitional objects and phenomena emerging at this point can serve self-regulation, independence, and autonomy from the maternal object, who by now is becoming a target of primitive ambivalence and normative oral and anal-sadistic conflicts. Until and beyond the end of the third year, when object constancy and the triadic mode of experience begin to emerge, transitional objects and phenomena, as the child's first product of creativity, become a means of self-soothing, undoing separation and building the illusion of control and safety. This primary creativity in time develops in innumerable directions to enrich the experiential universe, connect individuals, groups, and communities on a subliminal level and produce art, literature, music, and miracles of science and technology.

Choosing and combining of familiar and available elements to produce new formations, which represent freshly emerging meanings and bring forth novel solutions, are indispensable elements among the constituents of the process of creativity. An important condition of creativity is the ability to access acquisitions and experiences of the past and to combine with the intuitive sense of what may be added from the possibilities or necessities of the present, in order to contend with the contingencies that may lie ahead in the uncertainties of the future.

Creating something new is always gratifying and often generates a sense of mastery, self-affirmation, liberation, and elated emotions. Participating in the enjoyment of someone else's product of creativity can be a source of similar gratification and excitement. It creates an emotional bond that brings people together in a deeply compelling manner. It appeals to a universal component of our humanity that is dormantly expectant, as if waiting to be recognized, awakened, and satisfied. It is a consoling reminder that we are embedded in a communal universality shared by all humanity and that in our subjective sense of individual isolation, anxieties, aspirations, and fantasies, we are not alone after all.

While creativity may serve an invaluable adaptive function in everyday life on many levels, it can also be used successfully in psychologically defensive terms, as well as in instances of regression and pathological formations (Beres 1951; Modell 1970; Hamilton 1969). There are innumerable examples of artistic and innovative creativity that have contributed to transformation of individual lives or have brought about revolutionary alterations affecting nations, generations, and the course of history (Rose 1964; Niederland 1976). The history of art and sciences is replete with dramatic instances of such monumental examples of creativity.

The newborn creates the world by opening his eyes. Creating the world representionally is the mind's unique function. Representational thought and symbols bring the physical reality of objects into the internal sphere of subjective experience and intersubjective cocreation (Eigen 1983; Mitchell 1988). To contend with fear of loss, separation, abandonment, bodily injury, and death, the mind is shielded at first in the delusion of symbiotic dual unity (Mahler et al. 1975). Later, the emerging intersubjective mode of relatedness provides the context in which meaning is cocreated. In this mode, the delusion of symbiotic dual unity may be replaced by a defensive illusion of safety, such as may be represented by transitional objects and phenomena. The intentional evocation of creativity or the capacity to seek and engage in a creative experience or in the sharing of its products, rests upon the individual's ability to induce and submit to a state of mind in which the formation and utilization of illusions are permitted. Illusions similar to dreams, jokes, and problem solving, combine the past and the present with the future, fantasy, with reality, the internal with the external wish with reality, and primary process thinking with secondary. For this reason, an important component of creativity is the element of surprise, since there is always something new and unexpected that is introduced de novo.

Akhtar (2000) has described a sequence of events leading from the impingement of initial impression to the final formation of a creative product. This sequence begins with an initial recoiling followed by a period of incubation. This is then followed by the activation of internal resources in a flurry of integrative coalescence of disparate ingredients. A period of intense engagement, technical refinement, and energetic productivity may then ensue, resulting in the formation of the final creative product. When the course is run to its completion, there is a self-affirming sense of accomplishment, relief, and euphoric buoyancy. When the initial trigger is traumatic or a source of emotional pain, the creative process can serve as a healing agent that serves to objectify, externalize, and process the initial disturbance. This diminishes the traumatic impact of the event, which is integrated from a more tolerable distance and at a higher level, thereby contributing to a newly gained internal strength. Sharing the final product with receptive others provides further self-affirmation, objectivity, a comforting sense of communion and restorative sharing.

Creative thinking inevitably draws on intuition. However, in our scientific bias, we tend to be suspicious of intuition and whatever impressions that might be grounded in the subjective realm of experience, since they are characteristically idiosyncratic and so personal as to not be available to direct experience by another person. Intuition primarily relies on unconscious emotional indicators not always in agreement with or under the control of objective rationality. Intuitive understanding may therefore be unverifiable and not subject to scientific validation. Indeed, we often hold the rational as the polar opposite of the emotional and the intuitive. Emotions have their own kind of logic that tend to vary, depending on their intensity or context. They convey with them the context of previous events and their physical/organic counterparts, accommodations, and procedural memories. When we know something intuitively, we say we know it in our bones, heart, pit of the stomach, and so forth. Intuition is grounded on unconscious memory traces of ontogenetic, as well as phylogenetic heritage that reach deep into our nature and precede establishment of cortical centers needed for the use of language, abstract thinking, and cognitive maturity needed for self-reflection. To understand Rumi's intuitive approach and his sense of rapture and boundless creativity, it is important to remember the essentials of his spiritual and cultural background.

A DIGRESSION INTO PERSIAN POETRY AT LARGE

Persians produce and consume a great deal of poetry. They take their poetry seriously, hold it in high regard, and are proud of their national literary heritage. In Iran, you are taught poetry as a child, memorize it in school, and delve into its depth more eagerly in the later stages of life. One is literally surrounded by poetry. Buildings, buses, taxicabs, tombstones, storefronts, and monuments are all adorned with verses of famous or not-so-famous poetic statements: to console, alert, advise, humor, warn, amuse, or inform. One is likely to hear poetry recited by almost anyone, as a shorthand retort, philosophical pondering, subtle disapproval, romantic persuasion, or praise. It may come from an imminent authority, a farmer or an isolated shepherd, or a grandmother lamenting days gone by or putting a child to bed. Poetry has long been a vehicle for verbal transmission of intergenerational narratives. The effiacy and practicality of this mode of transmission across generations is enhanced by the unique features of a poem, not the least of which are rhyme, rhythm, and meter, along with the irresistible appeal of the form and structure of the poem.

In much of classical Persian poetry, *erfan* is a guiding light that illuminates the path of the faithful, as faith is the ever-present connection that maintains a permanent tie with the creator. Persian poetry has been intimately connected with *erfan* and cosmic consciousness. There is a tradition of extensive use of allegories and metaphors that serve to connect the explicit surface to the implicit core, the concrete to the abstract, and the immediate senses to the intangible sentiments. Metaphors and allegories serve to disguise the unspoken intentions contained in the narrative that is presented in apparent simplicity, as incontrovertible statements not likely to invoke the wrath of an intolerant dictator or a religious authority. If the message appears intolerable in its profundity and evocation of deep resonance, it may be instead taken at its literal and concrete facade. If the surface encounter smacks of excess, deviation, or banality, it can instead be interpreted at its transcendental intent, thereby rescuing the poem and perhaps the poet from impending denunciation or demise.

Translation of any work of linguistic art or literature from one to another language suffers the fate similar to dismantling an artifact in order to pack it into a new container intended for an item of a different shape and function. It "loses in translation" and it can lose its message, its nuance, color, character, emphasis, aesthetic value, or expressive quality. In translating Persian poetry, this difficulty is greatly exaggerated since allegories and metaphors are deeply rooted in the native history and culture, and often bear no equivalent in English or in Western culture. A sample of common words with dual references both in lay as well as *erfan* lexicon might include flower, nightingale, fire, flame, moth, eye, ear, water, garden, wheel, bread, wine, bird, love, slave, friend, thorn, gazelle, king, pauper, and so on. While these expressions contain great intrinsic beauty and poetic delicacy, in an English text they often sound strange and out of place or annoyingly pedestrian. The reader of such a poem in English is often disoriented, as if trapped in an esthetic void searching for familiar grounding.

There are other words without equivalents in English, such as *Jaan* and *yaar*. More will be said about *Jaan* later. *Yaar*, a very important word, is referred to a benevolent object of affection and attachment, longed for and constantly searched for. Reaching the *yaar*, sharing with and being with the *yaar* is the ultimate in all yearning and is a source of motivation, as well as existential anxiety. *Yaar* can be a friend, a partner, a teammate, a lover, a beloved, or a sympathetic supporter. He can be faithful to the promise of loyalty and reliability or, on the other hand, may fall short of the ideal purity of faithfulness, reciprocity, or the faithful promise of fulfillment. Without a *yaar*, life is barren and empty. Nights are long and unbearable; days are dark and hope is dim. In classical Persian poetry, references to reaching or reunion with the *yaar* as the ultimate in gratification, solace, and cohesion, are innumerable. In today's psychological jargon, searching and longing for the *yaar* would include striving for ultimate fulfillment, secure attachment, satisfying object hunger, undoing separation, and securing self-object functions. In classical poetry of *erfan*, *yaar* stands for the beckoning illusion that creates devotion, direction, and intent. It is the central core of what supplies dedicated persistence on the road to the final destination in one's emotional and spiritual journey.

As seen in Rumi's creative work, faith and religious practices flourish in the spiritual values of the cultural environment. Spiritual objectives reach for lasting values that are not confined to the boundaries of time and individual lifespan. A spiritual perspective contrasts the transience and even the "futility" of material or earthly and physical existence to the reality and permanence of the "eternal life" in the "hereafter," for which our brief worldly existence is regarded as mere preparation. For the believer, faith delivers eternal life, promise of salvation, access to relief, solace, and contentment, through attaining peace by surrendering to the will of a supreme source of intelligence and omnipotence. For some, faith is the most important element in their lives. For others, it is a very important source of strength, and for still others, it is an important element even if it is pushed asides at times, in part or completely. Each person's relationship to the object of their faith is unique and highly personal, depending on the specific elements of the initial relationships with their early objects of attachment. From this perspective, we can see faith as a state of relatedness to an object whose dimensions reach beyond the limits of cognitive or emotional grasp. While beliefs and opinions are supported and substantiated by objective evidence, faith needs no objective validation, but gathers and forms evidence that is based on preexisting conviction. While objective knowledge accrues in small steps and an orderly process of serial sequencing of logic, faith, by contrast, may defy objectivity, logic, and reason, as it brings deep conviction and enduring belief in a single giant leap unimpeded by requirements of objectivity or reason.

Even when there is no faith, one may see parallels to early object relationships where the individual might go to extremes in order to avoid interaction or reliance on another. In such cases, one might find the need to deny the significance or presence of the other and to keep a watchful distance guarding against annihilation, rejection, disappointment, or disillusionment. There may also be an unconscious wish, as well as a corresponding fear, of being devoured or engulfed by the narcissistically archaic object. Such a wish may threaten the tenuously maintained self boundaries or the integrity of a fragile sense of self that may still be in a vulnerable state of equilibrium. Defiant rejection of divinity can be encountered in individuals who grew up needing to rely on their own resources because of actual or perceived abandonment by troubled caregivers. These individuals might become resolutely independent minded investigators who can only trust the certainty of their own incontrovertible findings or scientific discoveries. Others may turn to self-reliant solitary adventures, seeking to repeatedly confirm their ability to survive without needing to turn to anyone else as vulnerable recipients of help.

The sense that one is forever in the presence of an omniscient other, who witnesses and judges thoughts, actions, and predicaments, can be immensely reassuring or intensely unsettling. If the early object relationships have been burdensome, conflictual, or severely ambivalent, the quality of subsequent relationships and dispositional attitude toward others will be reflective of those early difficulties. As transference in the course of analysis allows for the externalization and projection of early introjects, so in the case of faith, God may be experienced as punitive, vengeful, or alternately benevolent, or loving.

In absence of "basic trust" (Erikson 1950), when strategies for maintaining attachment are disorganized and confused, the outcome may be a narcissistic or schizoid retreat rather than submission to a coercive and sadomasochistic engagement. In such a case, submission may be tantamount to disintegration and the loss of the self in a state of overwhelming need and vulnerability. Another scenario might be the sense of being dominated, negated, mistreated, and controlled by the will and whim of an arrogant and persecutory sadistic other. The ongoing drama of life is confronting and coping with loss, disillusionment, and fear. Fixation at or regression to a "schizoid position" (Fairbairn 1952) in the face of a challenge may be one solution, while the alternative would be to move on by letting go and, through constructive mourning, being able to attain internal resources that foster reorganization, growth, and change. In such a "depressive position," living in the present allows us to prepare for the contingencies of the future and the inevitable loss and disillusionment, which is the unavoidable lot of imperfect human beings populating an imperfect world. Schizoid position is self-focused, in the service of adhering to the narcissistic grandiosity and omnipotence of the pleasure ego. The depressive position accepts the loss and contends with the pain. The disturbance that ensues can lead to adaptive structure formation and progressive reorganization. The depressive position allows for the ability to relinquish omnipotent control of the object, and moving beyond rage and destruction by tolerating the inevitable pain of loss and generating new solutions through reorganizing and creating new internal resources that are needed for successful adaptation and developmental progress.

Rumi's poetic and compassionate lamentation of separation, loss, and passionate longing is rooted in such a depressive position and leads us in the direction of subjective introspection, expanding self-knowledge and transcendental consciousness. It is not whether life contains loss, separation, anguish, regret, and despondency, but how one endures adversity, accommodates the pain and gains from each loss, in order to sustain cohesion, integrity, and resilience in the face of the unrelenting demands of reality. Rumi's rendering lamentations of the "nay"[1] reverberates with existential void of every heart as it provides solace, consolation, and hope. His engaging tone throbs to the universal beat of the timeless rhythm that moves human beings together, in respect, compassion, love, and empathic resonance.

Akhtar (2000) has likened the therapeutic benefits of poetry, music, and creative art to that of the remedial effects of salve when applied to a wound. We find Rumi's transcendental perspective and his depressive position, based on *erfan* and relatedness to the creator, more than palliative and soothing. It introduces a compelling opening into the universe of benevolent and restorative self-object experience with unlimited supplies of spiritual fulfillment and emotional sustenance. This is a resource well capable of neutralization of disabling pain and devastating frustrations inherent in life and its inevitable deficits, unavoidable disruptions, incurable afflictions, or the ominous vicissitudes of unfavorable fate.

CONCLUDING REMARKS

Rumi's worldview, rooted in ancient Persian values of righteousness and integrity, is supplemented by his Islamic faith. It models ideals that are in accord with the exemplary life of the prophet Mohammad and the teachings of the Holy *Quran*. Persian *erfan* (gnosis) is the guiding light that illuminates Rumi's intellectual and emotional universe, as he pursues proximity and subservience to the absolute objective truth that governs life. This guiding influence can be seen in the transcendental perspective manifested in the exuberance of his unsurpassed creativity and the cosmic consciousness of his rapturous poetry. *Erfan* is also a fundamental element in his attitudinal orientation as the founder of a Sufi sect with ardent followers, some still practicing their beliefs in parts of Iran, as well as in other parts of the Middle East and elsewhere.

While the psychoanalytic tradition of scientific objectivity might seem at odds with Rumi's primacy of the subjective realm, divine inspiration, and intuitive knowledge, the pursuit of meaning in the context of the uniquely personal experience of the individual is the main focus for both disciplines. Also, in both these viewpoints, we find that it is through the taming of the instinctual drives and the reigning mastery of the biological imperatives that emotional maturity and psychological equilibrium can be achieved.

While self-actualization through conflict resolution may be considered to be the ultimate objective in psychoanalysis, Rumi's faith-based mystical and transcendental journey reaches beyond the corporal confines of the physical and spiritual self, as it advocates seeking and surrendering to the consuming passion that soars beyond the physical and spiritual self, toward the ultimate destination of dissolution of boundaries and loss of personal identity, through immersion in a spiritual state of oneness and boundless fusion with the deity, as an object of relatedness.

Rumi's creative work and worldview contain elements of ancient Persian culture and moral codes, the teachings of Islam, and the tradition modeled after the exemplary life and virtues of the prophet Mohammad. I have presented Persian *erfan* as a guiding light that illuminates the path of the seeker of the ultimate truth, provides access to transcendental knowledge emanating from cosmic consciousness, and elevates the soul to the lofty heights of proximity and the fusion with the singular unity that is the source and the essence of all existence.

I have commented on creativity and rapture generally, as well as particularly in reference to Rumi and in psychoanalytic theory. I have stressed the pursuit of meaning and the primacy of the subjective experience in Rumi's work and worldview, as an essential element of basic commonality with the psychoanalytic perspective. The precursors of creativity begin with the dawn of awareness, the emergence of meaning, the intersubjective context of meaning, and the appearance of transitional phenomena (Winnicott, 1953) before the end of the first year of life. We think of transitional objects as the child's first and earliest creation, invented to guard against separation anxiety, representing an illusion of safety and control at a time when the internal representation of the mother begins to be a target of the child's ambivalence and is threatened by primitive aggression. As the child's first invention, the transitional object and phenomena combine representations of the gratified self, the satisfying mother, and the restorative interactions of the past. They integrate divergent elements of past and present, wish and reality, internal and external, passive and active, and self versus the other. Later on, they bring together primary and secondary process thinking, as well as primary and secondary narcissism (Etezady 1995). We may call this "primary creativity."

Mature creativity calls for the ability to intentionally evoke a state of mind that allows illusion and seeks novelty and surprise. Sharing and narrative formation, each ranking among important developmental capabilities, are indispensable constituents of creativity and the intrinsic value of a creative product. We need narratives and are fascinated by stories, as they help us organize, elucidate, integrate, and communicate our subjective experiences in order to reach others and to be reached, understood, appreciated, and affirmed by others. We need a sense of belonging and affiliation if we are individuals unique in our personal sense of identity and isolated subjectivity.

Subjectivity courses through an initial monadic mode, followed by a dyadic intersubjective and finally the triadic, narrative organization of the

Oedipal period. The transition from the dyadic to the triadic mode of relatedness hinges upon the optimal resolution of rapprochement conflict (Mahler et al. 1975) in the latter half of the second year. Such an optimal resolution requires the libidinal availability of the caregiver and her ability to survive the child's primitive aggression, protect his primary narcissism, and tolerate his normative oral and anal-sadistic conflicts. Most importantly, she needs to be able to stay attuned and to empathically contain the toddler's conflicted push-and-pull of separation versus engulfment, as well as individuation versus de-differentiation.

When rapprochement resolution fails, primitive aggression can not be neutralized, affect modulation and internal regulation are impeded, and splitting and primitive defense persist. The signal function of affects and repression as a higher level of defensive operation cannot develop. Self and object constancy will not consolidate. Infantile omnipotence can not be relinquished and the schizoid position prevails while the depressive position is not established. The triadic mode of relatedness will not emerge. Ego and superego development suffer, as triangulation and infantile neurosis and its Oedipal resolution will not be possible. Progression from primary process thinking to secondary and from primary narcissism to secondary narcissism will fail. Reflective function, narrative formation, abstraction and symbolic thinking, empathy, and realistic assessment of one's own inner states, as well as those of others will be impaired. Boundary negotiations, essential for developmental progression and interpersonal tolerance, create disorganization and chaos. Secure attachment can not be achieved and resiliency has no chance. Pathological narcissism and failure of self and interactive regulation will be a matter of course. Primary creativity of the pre-Oedipal period remains arrested in its initial primitive and primary narcissistic nature.

Rumi's boundless creativity and transcendental consciousness, guided by his consuming faith, challenges us to define faith and its unconscious, intuitive, inspirational, and developmental attributes. I have suggested that if we view faith as a state of relatedness to an object whose dimensions exceed the limits of emotional or cognitive mentation, we can utilize an object relations model of the mind, separation-individuation theory, and the intersubjective view of the dyadic experience to define and elucidate faith as an individual experience, as well as an organizing agent of communal and sociological impact and enduring significance.

4

Vision and Modernization

Atatürk

Vamik D. Volkan and Norman Itzkowitz

> Civilization is built by the artists, by the literary exponent, by the ability
> to generate beauty and music and the new methods of expression. Civi-
> lization advances when there is a premium, not a fatwa, on originality of
> thought.
>
> —Khaled Abou El Fadl, cited in Manji 2003, p. 188

Mustafa Kemal Atatürk, the founder and first president of modern Turkey,
died in 1938. Most of the cultural/religious revolutions he led took place after the establishment of the Republic of Turkey in 1923. Since he lived and
worked so long ago, why is it important to include a chapter on him in a book
that primarily focuses on the current relationships between Islam and the
Western world?

Foremost among the reasons for telling Atatürk's story in this context is to
counteract the creation of an illusion in post–September 11, 2001 America,
and to a lesser degree in Europe, that puts all Muslims of the world together
as the unwanted and dangerous "other." Many, of course, will object to such
a characterization of the American/Western world attitude. There are countless open-mined, well-educated, worldly Americans and Europeans who
know that Muslims, just like Christians, Jews, and those from other religions,
have their own ethnic or national variations and subgroups in their own countries. Muslims are not monolithic. They are composed of different sects, such
as Sunnis and Shi'a; the Shi'a are themselves divided into different groups,
such as Seveners and Twelvers, depending upon which of the earliest Imams,
the seventh or the twelfth, they follow. Just as Christians and others do, Muslims establish alliances and/or fight among themselves. Some Muslims col-
laborate politically and work with (or fight against) other countries that are

populated mostly by non-Muslims. The idea of a clash between civilizations and religions gets support from the continuing mental images of past history, such as the Crusades, and, at the present time, the more we go along with such an idea, the more we provide fuel for it. Atatürk's story is an antidote for the clash of civilizations idea. It tells how he came from a Muslim culture, fought against some great Western powers in World War I, and, in its aftermath, dedicated the rest of his life to the task of integrating modern Turkey—99 percent of whose population is Muslim—into the Western world.

A second reason is associated with the Western world's "search" for an Islamic leader, an authority figure, to speak for all or most of the world's Muslims—as the Pope speaks for most of the Catholics. Such a leader hopefully would condemn al-Queda supporters who sponsor terrorism and divide the world into "believers" and "nonbelievers." This contemporary search has gotten nowhere, whereas Atatürk's story tells of the abolition of the caliphate on March 3, 1924, and the departure of the Caliph, Adulmecid Efendi, from Turkey the following day. Despite the fact that the law governing the expulsion of the Caliph and the other members of the House of Osman gave him ten days to leave the country, he left for Switzerland on March 4.

Even prior to the abolition of the caliphate in 1924, European powers that controlled those Arab lands from Libya to Iraq, which were previously Ottoman lands mostly as mandate powers, watched as the authorities in some of those Muslim countries tried to reestablish the caliphate and appoint a new Caliph. King Husayn of the Hijaz accepted the title from neighboring Arab lands. But, within a year, a Wahhabi force took both his kinship and his caliphate. In Libya, the name of King Victor Emmanuel III was inserted into the khutba (the Friday sermon) in place of that of the Ottoman Caliph, but it did not last long. Those Western manipulations left a bad taste with the Arabs. An examination of the consequences of the abolition of the caliphate by Atatürk and its reflection on the post–September 11 world, we think, would be an interesting and important topic. In this chapter, we will examine some of Atatürk's personal motivations for the abolition of the caliphate and the creation of modern Turkey as a secular republic.

The third reason is the Americans' and the Europeans' quest for "models" for modernization in many countries with Muslim populations. There is not much reference to the "model" posed by Atatürk in the available scholarship. Sometimes, when there is a reference to it, that reference is made in an inappropriate and simplistic fashion. When President George Bush visited Turkey in 2004, he told the Turkish president, Ahmet Sezer, to use Turkey as a mode for other Islamic governments. The Turkish president, as we understand it, was upset with this request. President Bush overlooked the fact that Turkey is a secular republic and was treating Turkey as though it were an Islamic one.

President Bush's approach also angered Turkish intellectuals. But, we think that President Bush has a reason to speak as he did. Whereas the Turkish president is a staunch secularist, the prime minister of Turkey, Ragib Erdoğan, presents himself as a devout Muslim and champions Islamic cultural norms. This may have given President Bush a reason to suggest that Turkey become a "model" for Islamic countries. But, Erdoğan himself is in favor of the separation of religion and state.

There are other serious considerations why Atatürk and "his" Turkey cannot be a "model" for "Islamic countries." The history of Atatürk's time and his own personality-organization dovetailed in the creation of modern Turkey. It is as impossible to transfer actual historical events of the past to the present as it is to "clone" Atatürk's personality-organization in modern leaders of the current world. Having said this, we should also take into account the fact that Atatürk indeed inspired some Muslim leaders, whereas some other Muslim leaders considered him a "nonbeliever." For example, the late Egyptian president, Anwar Sadat (El-Sadat 1979), refers in his memoirs to his having received inspiration from Atatürk. Indeed, he grew up with a picture of Atatürk hanging on a wall in his house. We are not aware of any direct remarks by Ibn bin Laden about Atatürk. On one of his taped interviews, however, he speaks of Turks (meaning the type of Turks who followed Atatürk's revolutions) as not being true Muslims.

With the above thoughts in mind, in this chapter, we will tell Atatürk's story and examine some of his motivations for creating Turkey as a secular republic. The authors of this chapter first met in 1973, at a meeting at Princeton University at a conference devoted to psychology and Middle Eastern Studies (Brown and Itzkowitz 1977). Surprisingly, both authors had come to this conference with papers entitled, "Atatürk and his Women." This led to a seven-year collaboration between the authors and resulted in a coauthored book, *The Immortal Atatürk: A Psychobiography* (Volkan and Itzkowitz 1984). Since this work is available and we are under space restrictions, we will only focus on the following:

1. A brief history of Atatürk's life—This will be presented in a style similar to what it usually presented as a background for a psychoanalytic case study. In other words, instead of focusing on his activities as a great military mind and as a "teacher" of new ideas to his followers, we will provide some details from his childhood and refer to certain behavior patterns that he repeated.
2. Aspects of his creativity—We will not provide a full psychobiographical understanding of Atatürk's internal world, the nature of his object relations, his separation-individuation issues, his Oedipal concerns, his

personality-organization, and related phenomena. Instead, we will deal with him as a creative person—his creative product being modern Turkey—and report one key source that gave direction to his creativity and another source on how he achieved his creative aim.

3. A brief discussion of some reflections of Atatürk's achievements on present-day Turkey and Turkey's relationships with the Western world.

ATATÜRK'S PERSONAL HISTORY

The child of a minor customs official, whose wife was twenty years his junior, Mustafa (who later was known as Atatürk) was born, most likely in 1881, in Salonika (today's Thessalonica in Greece). At that time, Salonika, a city of some eighty thousand people, was populated by Jews (about 50 percent), Turks (about 25 percent), Greeks, Slavs, and Albanians—in that order of percentage of the population (Darques 2000, 21–61). Atatürk's parents has recently come there from the then Ottoman post, consisting of several buildings, at the Ottoman Empire-Greece border near Mount Olympus, a harsh environment that was home also to Greek bandits. At this border post, Atatürk's mother and father had three other children, two boys and a girl, and they lost all three of them, one after the other in their childhood (one lived to be seven years old).

Mustafa's birth coincided with an all-too-brief period of family prosperity. The move to Salonika was facilitated by a wealthy lumber merchant who had made Mustafa's father a partner in the lumber business. While in Salonika, Mustafa's mother bore two more children, both girls. Mustafa and his sisters were the only children to survive into adulthood. Furthermore, when Mustafa was seven years old, his father died, leaving his mother widowed at the age of twenty-seven. It can be said that Mustafa was born into "a house of death." His mother, in mourning, turned to God for solace. Later, she would be called a "molla," a person seeking mystical union with God. She was also known for being headstrong and unconventional.

Prior to his death, Mustafa's father had directed that his son be educated in a modern elementary school instead of in a religious school, which was preferred by the child's mother. At that time, Turkish parents living in large cities of the Ottoman Empire, including Salonika, could elect either kind of training for their children. Atatürk's earliest memory was the disagreement between his parents over his schooling. He recalled how skillfully his father worked out a solution. First, the child entered a religious school with the traditional ceremony. "Thus, my mother's heart was made good," Atatürk recalled. But, a few days later, he left the religious school and was registered by his father in a modern school. "Soon after this my father died" (Emin 1922).

This pattern of "compromise" would be used by Atatürk later on; he would pay "homage" to his religious mother/her substitutes first and then turn to the West and modernization.

After the father's death, his widow and children had to seek support from a relative who lived on a farm outside of Salonika. Mustafa eventually returned to Salonika to live with an aunt while he went to another school, a secular secondary one. One of his teachers in that school appears to have been rather sadistic and known for his prereligion views. One day, he beat Mustafa harshly. Atatürk recalled that, "All my body was covered in blood" (Emin 1922).

Mustafa's interest in the military arose in his prepuberty years when he felt jealous of the military school uniform worn by a neighborhood boy (Emin 1922). Without consulting his mother, Mustafa took and passed the entrance examination for a military secondary school. Around this time his mother remarried, angering Mustafa greatly (Aydemir, personal communication, November 20 and December 13, 1974). He left home and enrolled in a military boarding school, where he quickly excelled in mathematics. He mathematics teacher gave him the nickname of "Kemal," meaning perfect, and thus he became Mustafa Kemal.

Continuing his military education, Mustafa Kemal went to the War College and later to the Staff College, both in Istanbul, the capital of the Ottoman Empire since the mid-fifteenth century. While Mustafa Kemal was a military student, the Ottoman Empire was already collapsing. At the War College and later at the Staff College, Mustafa Kemal began to declare himself to be a special being. He gathered friends about him who shared his self-ascribed mission to save the empire. He was introduced to the world of Turkish and French literature and developed his powers of oratory. Mustafa Kemal was interested in the work of the nationalist poet Namik Kemal. One of Namik Kemal's best known verses tells how:

The enemy put his knife at the throat of the country—
There is no one save mother (meaning the country)
From her black fate.

Mustafa Kemal would paraphrase this, substituting for the second line: "There is someone to save the mother from her black fate."

One catches in that poem an echo of a little boy who wanted to save his mother from distress in a house of death. As a young man, he wanted to save the country that was collapsing.

Charged with what the government deemed to be inappropriate political activity, the Ottoman Sultan's functionaries sent Mustafa Kemal into "exile" by assigning him to duties away from Istanbul. For example, Mustafa Kemal was sent to Syria for two years, and later he was the Military Attache to Bulgaria. While in Sofia, he was able to see what "westernization" had done for Bulgaria, a former part of the Ottoman Empire. He also fell in love with a Bulgarian woman whose family would not allow a marriage between the dashingly handsome, and Muslim, Mustafa Kemal and their daughter.

When World War I came, Mustafa Kemal, as a young military commander, became a hero at Gallipoli against Britain and her allies, especially the Australians and the New Zealanders. In a battle in Gallipoli, he was struck over the heart by a bit of shrapnel as he recklessly stood in the line of fire. The shrapnel, however, shattered the watch in his breast pocket without seriously injuring him. In our psychobiographical study of his life, we concluded that this event had deep psychological effects on him, crystallizing his belief that he indeed was a special person who could take risks and who was destined to do special deeds.

Subsequently, in World War I Mustafa Kemal was promoted to general, a rank that carried with it the title of Pasha. He was now known as Mustafa Kemal Pasha. He was one of the Turkish commanders who did not lose a battle during the war. But, the defeat of the Ottoman Empire resulted in the Allied fleet entering the harbor of Istanbul. The Ottoman parliament was dissolved and the British, French, and Italians prepared to partition the Ottoman Empire. In addition, when the Paris Peace conference was slow in recognizing Greece's claims to parts of western Anatolia, the Greeks would land troops at Izmir (Symrna).

After the defeat of the Ottoman Empire, Mustafa Kemal joined his mother, who had come to Istanbul without her second husband to live with her daughter in the occupied Ottoman capital. One evening, he had dinner with his mother in the old traditional Muslim style, in other words, symbolically paying "homage" to her. The next morning, Mustafa Kemal and his entourage left Istanbul by boat for Anatolia from where he would lead the Turkish War of Independence. The Sultan would later order his capture and death. Against great odds and relying heavily on his charismatic personality, he raised an army loyal to the Sultan, the Allied forces, as well as the Greek forces that pressed on into Anatolia from Izmir; Mustafa Kemal defeated all the forces arrayed against him, winning the War of Turkish Independence. Even before the war was officially over, he married a highly westernized woman from Izmir, Latife, daughter of Ushakizade Muammer Bey, a wealthy businessman, on January 29, 1923. That marriage, entered into shortly after the death of Mustafa Kemal's mother, did not last long, being dissolved on August 5, 1925, by which time Mustafa Kemal was the first president of the Republic of Turkey, proclaimed on October 29, 1923.

With the proclamation of the Republic of Turkey, Atatürk embarked upon his cultural revolution often referred to as "westernization" or "modernization." The sultanate and then the caliphate were abolished, the latter on March 3, 1924. The following day of the Caliph, Abdulmecid, left for exile in Switzerland where his arrival with his two wives did not sit too well with the Swiss. Mustafa Kemal refused the title of either Sultan or Caliph.

In Mustafa Kemal's activities concerned with his cultural revolution, he often repeated the pattern that could be seen in his first memory of life: to please mother first before following his father, as well as his first teacher, Shemsi Efendi, in the secular school, in the directions of westernization. We will have more to say about Shemsi Efendi later in this chapter. For example, he developed a ritual: each day after waking up—he would enter his mother's quarters, she now lived in the presidential compound in Ankara, and kiss her hand in the accepted fashion before going to work. She died in 1923. In 1934, four years before his own death at fifty-seven, when a new law required that Turkish citizens use surnames, Mustafa Kemal was given the surname of Atatürk, meaning Father Turk, by a special law.

Religion had colored almost every aspect of daily life in the Ottoman Empire, including law, customs, and medicine. There had been earlier attempts in the Ottoman Empire at westernization/modernization, starting with the successful adoption of gunpowder in the fifteenth century. The process continued in the military sphere, especially in the reign of Selim (1789–1807). Over time, modernization and westernization became practically synonymous in the Ottoman Empire. Western nations who had been the traditional enemies of the empire, such as the Austro-Hungarian Empire, began to offer greater resistance to the territorial advance of the Ottoman Empire and even started to liberate former territories from Ottoman control. Russia, which had begun to westernize seriously under Peter the Great (1689–1725), had become a newly formidable foe. The Russo-Ottoman War that ended in 1774 by the Treaty of Kücük-Kaynarca (Itzkowitz and Mote 1970) made military reform along modern/western lines an absolute necessity. Selim III tried unsuccessfully to rid himself of the by then ineffective Jannisary Corps. That process was successfully undertaken by Sultan Mahmud II in 1826. For the next half century, the main advisers to and props of the Ottoman Empire were the British. They were then followed by the Germans. As a young army officer, Mustafa Kemal had translated German military field manuals into Turkish.

What has distinguished early Ottoman reform attempts from the cultural revolution of Atatürk was that the earlier reforms has not touched religious issues and icons, Atatürk initiated a thorough-going process of modernization/westernization that began with some of the most sacred elements of

Ottoman society, the sultanate and the caliphate. That process can be conceptualized as an attempted "purificantion" (Volkan 2004) that would remove those aspects of religious or semi-religious influences he saw as "bad" from Turkey, and that he associated with the religious side of his mother's preoccupations.

In addition, Atatürk proscribed education based on the sacred values and symbols of the Koran. He also modernized the legal systems that had been based on the Shariah, replacing them with the Swiss Civil Code, the Italian Penal Code, and German business law. He introduced western dress for men, banishing the fez in favor of the fedora, and discouraged veils for women. He began purging Turkish of its Arabic and Persian influences, creating new words in the process. Latin characters replaced the old Arabic ones. Experts advised that it would take five years to change the alphabet, but he granted only three months for the task and took to the countryside with blackboard and chalk to instruct his people in the new script and acted as a teacher.

Atatürk had become so revered that when he died in 1938, the Turks could not bring themselves to bury him in the ground. His body was preserved for fifteen years (an act against Muslim tradition), awaiting the construction of his mausoleum that now stands on a hill in Ankara that was once his favorite place to ride on horseback.

ATATÜRK'S CREATIVITY

We will only look at two aspects of Atatürk's creativity: (1) the role of being born in a house of death in giving direction to his creativity, and (2) the role of his "transitional activities" (Volkan and Itzkowitz 1984) at his dining table, after he became the president of Turkey, in enabling him to carry out his creative urges.

Being Born in a House of Death

To be raised by a mother in chronic mourning does not necessarily make the living child a creative person when he or she becomes an adult. In Atatürk's case, we are interested in examining how having such a childhood environment led him to develop an unconscious fantasy of being a "savior." His unconscious fantasy was to make his mother in mourning "happy" in order for him to have better mothering. This gave a direction to his creativity.

In 1930, Atatürk wrote some essays that are available in his handwriting today. His essay entitled "Freedom," we believe, refers to "freedom" he was searching for as a child from his mother in mourning and transferring this type of wish and activity to the historical arena in his search for "freedom" for his new country. This essay opens with a discussion of the relationship between man and nature: man does not decide whether or not to be born. At the moment of his birth, he is at the mercy of nature and a host of creatures other than himself. He needs to be protected, to be fed, to be looked after, to be helped to grow (Atatürk 1930, 77–78). He goes on to speak about "primitive people" who live in fear of thunder, the darkness of the night, floods, wild animals, and even one another.

Atatürk's essay on "freedom" makes more sense by our adding new information about his childhood. It should be recalled that three of his older siblings had died before Mustafa was born, when the family lived in an isolated border post. Apparently, one of his brothers was buried near the shore. The night following his burial, the rising sea flooded the grave. This resulted in the exposure of the boy's corpse, which was torn apart by animals. That story was told and retold in the family. We think that it became a symbol of this particular "house of death" and a focal point of lurking dangers in the dark in little Mustafa's mind. One wonders if his mother expected losing her fourth child, too. In the essay, Atatürk as child (we think that "primitive people" stands for his child-self) seeks protection from adults, basically representing from his mother. But, he is not sure if his mother, because of her chronic mournings, can respond to his need for protection. This worry appears in another one of his essays written earlier, in 1927: "Since my childhood, in my home, I have not liked being together with my mother or sister, or a friend. I have always preferred to be alone and independent, and I have lived this way always" (Aydemir 1969, vol. 1, 484).

His essay indicates that he had to turn to his own internal strength in order to protect himself against the fate of his siblings who had died and against having a mother in chronic mourning. He experienced what Arnold Modell (1976) calls a "premature maturation," that is the seed of increased narcissism and its crystallization as a core of a personality with excessive self-reliance.

In 1927, he also wrote that if someone gives him advice, the expected thing is either to accept it or reject it. He added: "I have the peculiarity of being unable to tolerate being given advice by my mother, sister, or any close friend according to their mentality and conception of the world" (Aydermir 1969, vol. 1, 484).

His turning to his own self and establishing his exaggerated self-reliance can be seen in one of his earlier essays. This one was written in 1918, when he was ill and had gone to Karlsbad for treatment. His illness and being away from his country might have him regress and reminded him of his childhood helplessness and being at the mercy of others. Thus, he wrote to shore up his won power (his increased narcissism, his increased self-reliance was a defense

against his childhood helplessness in dealing with a mother in chronic mourning and not having good enough mothering). In this essay he says: "If I obtain
great authority and power [it should be recalled that he believed in having it
when, in military school he would tell other students how he would be a leader
and that he would assign them different tasks under his leadership], I think I
will bring about a coup—suddenly in one moment—the desired revolution in
our social life. Because, unlike others, I do not believe that this deed can be
achieved by raising the intelligence of others slowly to the level of my own.
My soul rebels against such a course. Why, after my years of education, after
studying civilization and the socializing processes, after spending my life and
my time to gain pleasure through freedom, should I descend to the level of
common people? I will make them rise to my level. Let me not resemble
them; they should resemble me" (Aydemir 1969, vol. 3, 482).

What was his mother's "mentality and conception of the world" that Atatürk
could not accept? As we stated earlier, his mother, in chronic mourning, had
tried to find solace in religion. Perhaps through religion and a belief in heaven,
she might wish to find a connection with her dead children. Benefiting from
our clinical work with mothers who had lost multiple children, we assumed
that Atatürk's mother had two opposing perceptions of her living son: (1) This
child is also destined to die, therefore I should not be too close to him, and
(2) This child will live, replace all the dead ones, become the sunshine of my
life and save me from my unending mourning. This child is special.

We think that Mustafa sensed both aspects of his mother's perception of
him. In a sense, he had "two mothers." He wanted to be the special child of
the "second mother," but he was afraid that the "first mother's" expectation
could materialize. One way to deal with it was a wish to be immortal, which
would also save his mother from her chronic mourning. Both "mothers'" relationships to him fed into his increasing self-reliance. As an adult, he wanted
the Turkish nation to become "civilized," saying that religious beliefs and
practices [of his childhood mother] "numb the mind" instead of letting in the
vigor of civilization and science. He especially wanted to get rid of the religious emphasis on attempting contact with the dead [his dead siblings]. "To
seek help from the dead is a blot on any civilization," he declared (Atatürk
1925, vol. 2, 214–15).

We are only focusing on Atatürk's difficulties in dealing with his early
mother with two opposing perceptions on her living son and the reflection of
this difficulty on adult Atatürk's concerns with "bad" habits of religion. But,
the reader should be aware that in addition to his early motivation to deal with
"bad" religious influences on society, he had other motivations coming from
the more advanced age of his childhood, such as having been beaten by a
religious-mind teacher.

His first memory of life, reported earlier, refers to his finding a "model," provided by his father just before the older man's death, for "repairing" his mother first, and then freeing himself from her influence and separating from her opposing images, both of which were most burdensome for him. But, when he found a "model" to separate from his mother, he could not truly be free from her and thus continued to spend his main energy in the historical arena from repairing her substitute, the new Turkey (it was said that after the Balkan Wars and World War I, when walking in the streets of Istanbul, one literally could hear families grieving over their lost sons.) Grieving Turkey represented his mother in chronic mourning and he tried—curing all his adult life—to make his country happy and remove the religious influences from it. It was clear that he would get rid of not only the Sultan, but also the Caliph as well.

His teacher, Shemsi Efendi, became his father figure after his father's death. Religious zealots on occasion would raid Shemsi Efendi's school and destroy it. Shemsi Efendi was "stubborn," he would repair his school and continue teaching. Atatürk's identification with his father and Shemsi Efendi became a model for him in his revolutionary activities as the president of modern Turkey. It is fascinating that recently, through contacts among Istanbul Turks whose origins stem from the Dönme community of Salonkia, we have learned that Shemsi Efendi was a Dönme. The Dönmes were that group of Jews in the Ottoman Empire who followed the teachings of Shabbatai Zvi, born in Izmir in August 1626. In May 1665, while in Palestine, he proclaimed himself the messiah, and then eventually moved on to Istanbul. The Grand Vezir, concerned with the general public unrest due to the arrival of the messiah, ordered his arrest. On April 19, 1666, he was imprisoned in Gallipoli. Later, from there he was removed to Adrianople, arriving on September 15 and, the following day, he appeared before Sultan Mehmed IV in the divan (council). After the Sultan's mother interceded on his behalf, the Sultan made him an offer—either he converted to Islam or he would be killed. He converted, as would many of his followers (Scholem 1973). The Turkish noun "dönmek" means to turn, and they became known as the "Dönmeler" (pl.), those who had "turned" or converted to Islam.

Shemsi Efendi apparently was one of the Turks of Greece who were returned in the population exchange arranged for in the Treaty of Lausanne. He went to Istanbul and died in 1927 or 1928 and was buried in the Dönme Cemetary, Bülbül Deresi Cemetary, in Uskudar on the Asian side of Istanbul.

Atatürk's "Transitional Activities"

As the first president of Turkey, Atatürk had guests each night for dinner until, in his last few months, such gatherings were forbidden by his physicians.

Statesmen, politicians, literary celebrities, scholars, artists, singers, and even children were invited to such gatherings. But, his cronies, most of them friends from his childhood or military school days, could come without invitation. Records were kept of who attended each night.

We see a ritualistic aspect of these dinner gatherings. It repeated a pattern that we have already mentioned: Atatürk would regress and meet his mother (her symbolic image), pay his "homage" to her, and then he would identify with the image of his father/Shemsi Efendi and repair the grieving mother/country. He would become the "Father Turk" (Atatürk).

Drinking and dining began early in the evening and continued well into the early morning. Atatürk drank for hours before addressing his need for food. The food served to him was that which he had preferred as a child, for example, beans and rice pilaf. He might order an omelet "like my mother used to make," and we know that on one occasion he sent the omelet back three times because it fell below his mother's standards. As the evening wore on, he was apt to call for songs of his childhood. In summary, he would "regress" and be with his mother's image before he would "progress" the next day again and repair her religious image in mourning.

After a long night of drinking and eating, before sunrise, he might go hunting with his friend Nuri Conker, in the hills where he is now buried (Tesal, personal communication, May 13, 1975). He usually went to bed in the morning hours and rose shortly after noon and became "Father Turk."

Our informants provided data which suggest that he was like a child at play during each night. At his table, exhibitionistic behavior was common, along with boasts. Sometimes, there were scuffles among the guests, and soldiers assigned to the presidential palace gave exhibitions of wrestling (the national sport), in which Atatürk himself might join. With his guests, he was also involved in serious discussions of this revolutionary ideas. A blackboard at hand made the dining room a kind of lecture hall (Afetinan 1971; Tesal 1975) and a place for developing theories about the Turkish past. Regression and reorganization at the dinning room table was under Atatürk's complete control. We are reminded of Donald W. Winnicott's (1971) statement that "in playing, and perhaps only in playing, the child or adult is free to be creative" (p. 53).

In our psychobiography on Atatürk, we named Atatürk's nightly activities as "transitional activities," recalling Winnicott's (1953) remarks that connect creativity with transitional objects and transitional phenomena. Atatürk's dining room activities were repetitive and he was "addicted" to them like a child becomes "addicted" to his or her transitional objects or phenomena.

Of special interest is his creation of new words representing a child's learning how to speak. He was redoing his childhood and "purifying" what he considered to be "bad" in the mother/child relationship and was creating a "happy" Turkey. He would spend hours to find a new word that would be "pure Turkish." During Ottoman times, especially in official circles, the spoken or written Turkish was heavily contaminated by the Arabic and Persian languages. In Atatürk's mind, the Arabic and Persian languages were associated with the Muslim religion that his mother had turned to in her grief. In his play with words, Atatürk was trying to remove sadness/mourning from his mother. After writing a newly created word in a sentence on the blackboard, Ataürk often summoned a youngster (representing young Mustafa) to the dining room and asked the child to read it aloud so that he could listen to the way it sounded (Tesal, personal communication, May 13, 1975). His creative use of language can be considered parallel to a child's creation of neologisms, the developmental aspects of which are examined by Weich (1978) from the viewpoint of the transitional phenomenon. The next day, or sometimes later, as "Father Turk," Atatürk would make the new word official in the Turkish language, thus accomplishing a change from his childhood, a new "Turkishman" without the burden of "Arabicman" or "Persianman," which were associated with Islam.

ATATÜRK'S STORY IN TODAY'S WORLD

When we examined aspects of Atatürk's life (again, in this brief chapter, we left out many other important elements of his life) from a psychoanalytic angle, we saw his internal motivations for removing the "bad" influences of religion on modern Turkey, separating religion from politics, abolishing the caliphate, and insisting on the creation of a secular republic. Knowing this, of course, does not diminish the effects of many other reasons for his cultural revolution. We are not examining them in this chapter. To say that Atatürk modernized Turkey just because he wanted to change his mother in mourning would be simplistic and reductionistic. Over a foundation of unconscious motivations related to childhood traumas and defenses and adaptations that deal with these traumas, other psychological factors add bricks and stones to build a higher structure, in Atatürk's case, the new secular Turkey. One important issue is whether the leader sublimated the internal urges that may find an echo in the historical arena. One year before his death, on March 17, 1937, Atatürk said the following: "Man, as an individual, is condemned to death. To work, not for oneself but for those who will come after, is the first connection of happiness that any individual can reach in life. Each person has his own preferences. Some people like gardening and growing flowers. Others prefer to train men. Does the man who grows flowers expect anything from them? He who trains men ought to work like the man who grows flowers" (Volkan and Itzkowitz, 1984).

Atatürk as a revolutionary leader worked as the man who grows flowers. In the above statement, we can catch an echo of an unconscious wish that if his dead siblings came out of their graves and were like roses (reincarnated), he would have a mother who would not be in chronic mourning and who would have given little Mustafa better mothering. But in the real world, what counted were Atatürk's actual accomplishments, like a man who in reality creates a rose garden.

Turks, in general, could not allow a charismatic leader like Atatürk to die. They made him "The Immortal Atatürk," which is the title of our psychobiographical study of him. It was during his presidency of Turkey that Turgut Ozal (1927–1933) openly reminded the citizens of Turkey that, after all, Atatürk was just a man. The Turks, as the heirs of the Ottoman Empire, would not mourn losing their empire, their old glories, or their status as having been at one time one of the most powerful empires in world history, as long as their "gain" against those losses would be keeping alive the image of their charismatic leader Atatürk as an immortal human being. Turgut Ozal, on the one hand, inflicted a deep wound on the psyche of the Turks, but on the other, he began the process through which the Turks would become able to view Atatürk not as immortal, but as a man, albeit a great, great man. Shared mental images of lost shared glories (as well as traumas), however, do not disappear (Volkan 1997; 2004), but rather continue to influence societal/political processes for years or centuries to come. Decades after Atatürk's death, the Turks, we believe, began mourning things from Ottoman times that were now gone, including aspects of the Muslim religion. Ozal, who was an effective leader and modernized Turkey's economy and its relations with the West, also allowed the opening of religious schools.

Today, Turkey is run by leaders who are openly "religious." For example, the wives of the prime minister and foreign minister wear religious head scarves, but they are products of well-known fashion designers. These two leaders and their entourage do not drink alcoholic beverages, at least in public. The lost "past" customs related symbolically to the Muslim religion have come back for "review." Such reviews are the core activity of the work of mourning and are, in the case of today's Turkey, a work of group mourning that gets reflected in societal processes. Meanwhile, there are Turkish intellectuals, including the present Turkish president who believes that Atatürk would have been extremely upset if he knew that some present-day Turkish wives wear religious head coverings. The wives of the prime minister and the foreign minister are not invited to official ceremonies at the Turkish president's residence simply because they do not appear "modern" and they do not follow what Atatürk wishes for Turkish women.

The group mourning is not a total reactivation of the past for a review, but it also includes clashing of new investments with old ones and sometimes integrating them. What does all this mean? Does it mean that there is a danger that Turkey may become like Iran? All indications are that this will not happen. The present "religious" government's main preoccupation is to become a member of the European Union and to follow strict rules of that Union, including "freedom" of religion.

Turkey presently is struggling with a process of integration of what has returned from the past (as part of delayed large group mourning; Volkan, 1988) with what had been gained through Atatürk's revolution. How much this integration will take place and create a new type of Turkish citizen is something that we have to wait and see. But what Atatürk's revolution created in Turkey still remains after many decades as the major core of present Turkey's orientation toward freedom and democracy. It appears that what has been reactivated from the past will be absorbed by this core adaptively.

Turkey's membership in the European Union (EU) will guarantee the continuation of this adaptive absorption. Meanwhile, it appears that the idea of having Turkey as a member of the EU has reactivated Christian Europeans' images of the Muslim Ottomans and these images, to some extent, are being projected on present Turkey. This needs to be studied carefully in order to make good and realistic political decisions and not let religion (Christian or Muslim) distort the Turkey-Europe relationships. This is, of course, another long topic for consideration above and beyond this chapter.

5

Destiny and Nationalism

Mohammad Ali Jinnah

Salman Akhtar and Manasi Kumar

I once had a brother in Iraq. I would go to him when times were bad and say, "Give me some of your money." He would throw me his purse for me to take what I wanted. Then one day I came to him and said, "I need something." He asked, "How much do you want?" And so the sweetness of brotherhood left my heart.

—al-Ghazali, cited in Fadman and Frager, 1997, 222

The epigraph for this chapter captures the subjectivity of the great Muslim leader, Mohammad Ali Jinnah (1876–1948), who, along with Mohandas Karamchand Gandhi (1869–1948), dominated the Indian political scene during the first half of the twentieth century that culminated in the country's independence from British rule and its partition into India and Pakistan. In a few elegant words, al-Ghazali's parable portrays the psychodynamics of the loss of "sweetness" that comes with a change of heart and, thus, puts an unblinking spotlight upon how this forceful lawyer-turned-politician got transformed from a highly secular freedom fighter into a militant activist of narrow ethnic nationalism. This is by no means to deny that Jinnah was—and remains—a political leader of great significance. Indeed, in the words of his preeminent biographer Stanley Wolpert, "Few individuals significantly alter the course of history. Fewer still modify the map of the world. Hardly anyone can be credited with creating a nation-state. Mohammad Ali Jinnah did all three. Hailed a 'Great Leader' (*Quaid-e-Azam*) of Pakistan and its first governor-general, Jinnah virtually conjured that country into statehood by the force of his indomitable will" (1984, i).

Whether this statement contains any element of hyperbole and oversimplification born out of literary cleverness and emotional idealization that characterize most biographies should become clear as we proceed with our treatment of the subject. Clearly, our psychoanalytic orientation compels us to view all interpersonal events, even the grand and truly historical ones, as multiply determined (Waelder 1936). It is our contention that, besides sociopolitical and interpersonal variables, major events in the course of human history are also governed by the personality style, emotional hues, conscious and unconscious fantasies, and the formative childhood experiences of the leader(s) involved. Therefore, we hold that the pivotal turn that changed Jinnah's conceptual path from that of pluralism to divisiveness originated from not only the traumatizing experiences he faced at the hands of his political rivals, but also from a long-held turmoil about the motifs of unity and separateness at the deepest core of his psyche.

In order to highlight and explicate this proposition, we offer a brief biographical sketch of Jinnah, alongside an account of his political career. We do this in the hope of elucidating the complex interplay of intrapsychic and reality factors in the dramatic turn that his trajectory ultimately took. Being mindful of the traps and pitfalls in an undertaking of this sort, we wish to enter some caveats at the outset.

SOME CAVEATS

First and foremost, we acknowledge that we are not historians, and the topic we are addressing here requires a deep familiarity with the nineteenth and twentieth century history of India. Besides being prohibitive in its amount and scope, the pertinent literature emanates from too many vantage points. Dichotomies that pervade these tracts exist along the lines of the religious-secular, Hindu-Muslim, intracultural-extracultural, and Indian-Pakistani schisms. To complicate matters, Jinnah is hardly an uncontroversial figure. As a result, the tendency toward sycophantism, as well as demonization, is rampant in writings about him. The resulting difficulty in separating the wheat from chaff, combined with our overall lack of historical expertise, carries the potential of rendering our arguments a bit tentative.

Second, in focusing upon the political shifts and turns of Jinnah's life, we may end up giving short shrift to the intrapsychic lives of other significant players in the India's freedom struggle, even though their subjectivities must have entered into a dialectical relationship with what unfolded in our protagonist's mind. Prominent among such dramatis personae, besides Gandhi, are Jawaharlal Nehru (1889–1964), Sardar Vallabhai Patel (1875–1950), and Maulana Abul-Kalam Azad (1888–1958), to name a few.

Third, a "psychobiography" of an individual who is long deceased and who left no personal diary and few intimate letters and correspondence behind is a risky enterprise. Avenues of direct information are meager and dwindling; reliance upon secondary sources has its limitations.

Fourth, a certain amount of personal bias becomes unavoidable in this sort of undertaking. This is true of both its writers and the readers. We are immigrant Indians (one Muslim, the other Hindu) of a politically liberal and religiously secular stripe. While we strive to maintain conceptual vulnerability, our stance that the partition of India and creation of Pakistan was a national tragedy is bound to color our portrayal of history and biography in this chapter. Biases might also come from the side of its readers. Feeling validated or invalidated in their own ethnopolitical convictions, they are vulnerable to emotionality and partisanship. Therefore, both positive and negative verdicts on our contribution need to be taken with a grain of salt.

Finally, the lock-stock-and-barrel transport of psychoanalytic theory across cultures has its own pitfalls.[1] Roland's (1996) questioning whether the "psychoanalytic self," as conceptualized in the West, exists universally in that very form is a point to keep in mind here. Societies in which collective and communal identities supercede individual autonomy might require a wider lens of determinism in order to avoid psychoanalytic reductionism. Yet, it is also true that present day conflicts can hardly be comprehended "without first understanding how historical hurts and grievances survive from generation to generation" (Volkan 2004, 51). The fact that such grievances emanate from both group trauma and personal history goes without saying.

FROM THE PROVINCIAL "MOHAMMAD ALI JINNAHBHAI POONJA" TO THE ANGLICIZED "M. A. JINNAH"

Mohammad Ali Jinnah was born on December 25, 1876, in a tenement house named Wazir Mansion in Karachi (at that time in India, now in Pakistan) to a family that originally came from the Kathiawar peninsula of the Gujarat State in India. This "official" date of birth, however, seems fictitious since the register preserved at the Sindh Madarsa-ul-Islam, Karachi, the first school Jinnah attended, notes October 20, 1875, as his birth date (Harvani 1996, 48; see also Ahmed 1997). While the discrepancy can be attributed to the lackadaisical attitude about recording birthdates prevalent among lower- and middle-class Indians of that era, there might be something of greater significance here. Why has, for instance, the government of Pakistan, which celebrates its founder's birthday on Christmas day, failed to look into its calendar veracity?

More importantly, is it possible that in claiming that he was born on the same day as Jesus Christ, Jinnah was deftly creating a grand self-image for both his and others' subliminal consumption? The fact that, decades later, a crucifixion-resurrection sequence, too, awaited him is, however, ironical. But let us not get ahead of our story and return to Jinnah's origin.

His father, Jinnahbhai Poonja (1857–1901), had moved from Gujarat to Sindh at the turn of the century. Jinnah was the eldest of the eight children, having four younger sisters and three younger brothers. Jinnahbhai Poonja belonged to the *Khoja* (a spoiled form of the Persian word *Khwaja*, meaning a nobleman) community, a splinter Muslim group of the Ismaili sect that regarded Agha Khan I (1800–1881) as its spiritual head. Most Muslims regarded Khojas, business-oriented and temperamentally akin to Hindu *banias*, to be apostates. The fact is that Khojas felt closer to the fire-worshipping Zoroastrains (*Parsis*) and settled in India, since both groups had fled persecution in Persia. This further marginalized them in the eyes of Muslims at large. The "Muslim" foundations of Jinnah's identity were thus weak to begin with.

Further intrigue is added by the fact that no less than *five* different versions exist about his ancestral roots. The first version traces his family's origin to Iran and attributes the apparently Hindu names of his paternal uncles (Valji and Nathoo) and aunt (Manbai), somewhat incredulously, to their immigrant Muslim ancestors (Ahmed 1997). The second version proclaims that one of Jinnah's male ancestors was a Rajput from Punjab who had married into Ismaili Khojas and settled in Kathiawar, Gujarat, where Jinnah's father was later born (Beg 1977). A related third version notes that Jinnah's paternal grandfather was Hindu and had "for some obscure reason converted to Islam" (Collins and Lapierre 1985, 26), and had this not occurred, "the two political foes (Gandhi and Jinnah) would have been born into the same caste" (p. 27). A fourth story suggests that Jinnah's paternal grandfather was a Parsi who had lost all three of his children during their infancy, and had prayed while looking at *Zuljinnah*[2] in a Moharram procession that if he had a son who lived, he would name him after the divine creature. The child he subsequently received was named Poonja Jinnah. This inspired the originally Parsi family to convert to Islam. Subsequently, Poonja Jinnah gave an unmistakably Muslim name to his son: Mohammad Ali Jinnahbhai Poonja. Finally, there is the version of Jinnah's origins that states that Jinnah's non-Muslim (Parsi? Hindu?) mother used to visit a Muslim saint's *dargah* (a grave-cum-shrine) in Kutch, Gujarat, while pregnant with him and had vowed to give a Muslim name to her child; it is even believed that this saint's name was Mohammad Ali, and Jinnah was named after him.

Regardless of which of these narratives one chooses to believe, one fact does come across loud and clear. Mohammad Ali Jinnah did not come from a long lineage of Muslims. His ancestors were non-Muslims, most likely Hindu, and their conversion to Islam could hardly be devoid of emotional consequences. What were the subtle and gross avenues by which the sentiments associated with this religious conversion got transgenerationally transmitted to the young Jinnah, we do not know. What we do know is that such "deposited representations" (Volkan 1981) do affect the "basic core" (Weil 1970) of identity which, in turn, dictates the career path one selects for oneself.

Let us back up a little and note that as an infant, Jinnah was weak and underweight. His parents constantly worried about his health, even though the family physician assured them that there was nothing wrong with him. Nonetheless, he appeared to be a weak and tiny boy with slim hands. Young Jinnah got his early education at home by private tutors and, curiously, was not sent to a formal school till the age of eleven. To what extent this delay of schooling was related to his physical frailty remains unclear. When he did go, he enrolled at the Sindh Madarassa-ul-Islam but, a few months later, transferred to the Christian Missionary Society High School in Karachi (Ahmed 1997; Moore 1983).[3] It was there that he perhaps first came to realize the mythic significance of December 25 (Wolpert 1984, 7), which he was to later "adopt" as his birth date!

As a schoolboy, Jinnah was indifferent to studies. His "tolerance for formal education was never high . . . and he cut classes regularly" (Wolpert 1984, 6). However, he soon came in contact with Sir Frederick Leigh Croft, who came to Karachi as the general manager of Douglas, Graham, and Company, a firm that had extensive dealings with Jinnah's father's import-export business. Sir Frederick liked the teenaged Jinnah and recommended him for an apprenticeship at his firm's home office in London in 1892. "That single letter to London lifted young Jinnah from provincial obscurity into the orbit of British imperial prominence, accessible at that time to fewer than one in a million Indians" (Wolpert 1984, 7).

Jinnah left for London in January 1893, at the age of seventeen. His mother vehemently opposed his departure and gave her consent on the condition that he would get married before he left. Jinnah protested at first but, seeing such surrender as the only way to receive her permission, consented. Soon he was married to a fourteen-year-old distant relative named Emibai, and only days after their wedding sailed for England. Emibai died shortly afterward. A few months later, Jinnah lost his mother as well. The latter loss devastated him. Many authors (Bolitho 1954; Collins and Lapierre 1985) note that from this time onward, Jinnah developed a certain emotional reserve with which he took personal decisions in his life. He also began to appear more intellectualized and, at times, rather coldly candid. It is as if the sentimental part of his heart died with the concurrence of these multiple traumas (loss of country, loss of wife, and loss of mother). At seventeen/eighteen years old, Jinnah was on his own.

He now took two important decisions. First, he decided to quit the business firm, where he had been clerking on the recommendation of Sir Frederick, and pursue studies in law. Second, he dropped *bhai* from his surname (Jinnahbhai); the deleted portion, "*bhai*,"[4] literally meant "brother" and, in general, stood for a sense of fraternal bonding. His original name, Mohammad Ali Jinnahbhai Poonja (he had stopped using the last word upon his entry in the Christian Missionary School in Karachi), was thus transformed into the crisp and suave M. A. Jinnah. Pressures of postmigration acculturation most likely played a role in this decision. At the same time, the implicit severing of the primary ties created an ominous periphery of loneliness and distance from others that marked his being for the rest of his life. Perhaps, the name change was an attempt to carve out a new identity for himself in a new land and bidding goodbye to the past. Paradoxically, by "anglicizing" his name, Jinnah was also showing a need to belong with his British peers. This particular tension, namely between isolation and attachment, would appear again and again in his personal and political life, as it unfolded over the subsequent six decades.

At that time, though, "M. A. Jinnah" felt quite welcomed at the gates of Lincoln Inn, which he joined on June 5, 1893. The legal institution's lobby bore pictures of Prophet Mohammad in flowing green robes; the picture resounded with the young man's inner values and ideals of honesty and justice. He was energized, and later, at the age of twenty, became the youngest Indian citizen ever to get a law degree from England. His years of study led to him becoming increasingly self-assured. He traded in his traditional Sindhi long coat for smartly tailored Saville Row suits and heavily-starched detachable collar shirts. His shoes always shone with polish and he took great pride in never wearing a silk tie twice. "Jinnah was to remain a model of sartorial elegance for the rest of his life, carefully selecting the finest clothes for the 200-odd hand-tailored suits in his wardrobe closet by the end of his life" (Wolpert 1984, 9). The time he spent in England had not only armed him with a law degree and sharpened his intellect, it also led him to become "anglicized" in dress, manner, culinary preferences, and his overall lifestyle.[5]

Jinnah left England for Bombay in 1897 to set up a law practice there. He was instantly successful. As a prominent member of the Bombay intelligentsia, Jinnah also started to keep on eye on national politics and began associating with the senior members of the Indian National Congress, such as the Ismaili Muslim Badar-uddin Tyabji (1844–1906), the Parsi Sir Phirozeshah Mehta (1845–1915), and the highly revered Hindu Gopal Krishna Gokhale (1866–1915). This was a partly social necessity and partly a matter of actual growing interest in politics. The death of Jinnah's father around this time perhaps also contributed, though subterraneanly, to the development of these ties.

Jinnah's anglicized get-up, sharp intellect, and impressive oratory made him a star barrister at the Bombay bar, earning a whopping sum of forty thousand rupees a month.[6] Impeccably dressed and often wearing a monocle (in an identification with one of his British heroes, Joseph Chamberlain), Jinnah showed special fondness for oysters, champagne, whiskey, and pork (all of which, except oysters, are prohibited by Islam). He "sounded like Ronald Coleman, dressed like Anthony Eden, and was adored by most women at first sight, and admired or envied by most men" (Harvani 1996, 59). All in all, he cut a rather formidable figure, though a covert tenderness remained visible to the discerning eye. Sarojini Naidu (1879–1949), the great Indian poet and parliamentarian, described Jinnah with unparalleled eloquence:

> Tall and stately, but thin to the point of emaciation, languid and luxurious of habit, Mohammad Ali Jinnah's attenuated form is a deceptive sheath of a spirit of exceptional vitality and endurance. Somewhat formal and fastidious, and a little imperious of manner, the calm hauteur of his accustomed reserve but masks—for those who know him—a naïve and eager humanity, an intuition quick and tender as a woman's, a humor gay and whining as a child's. Nonetheless, he is preeminently rational and practical, discreet and dispassionate in his estimation and acceptance of life. The obvious sanity and serenity of his worldly wisdom effectually disguises a shy and splendid idealism, which is of the very essence of the man. (Naidu, quoted in Harvani, 1996, 46–47)

On April 19, 1918, Jinnah entered his second marriage. He was forty-two years old and Ruttenbai Petit (born February 20, 1900), the woman he married, had just turned eighteen. The courtship had actually begun a year earlier, but, ever mindful of legalities, Jinnah decided to formalize the bond only after she had reached the proper age of consent; this was especially needed since her wealthy and influential father, Sir Dinshaw Petit, was strongly opposed to this union (Collins and Lapierre 1985). The young woman he married was Parsi, but three days before the wedding, converted to Islam and took on the name Mariam (a vernacular form of Mary). The marriage was tumultuous as the two partners turned out to have great temperamental differences. Jinnah was formal, meticulous, and emotionally restricted. His wife was mercurial, moody, wore headbands, smoked cigarettes, and dressed in a provocative manner. She addressed Jinnah as "Jay," a practice to which the latter somehow never objected. The birth of a daughter, named Dina, did little to save this flamboyant, colorful, but essentially doomed marriage.

To take a step back, however, it should be noted that not too long after setting up a law practice in Bombay, Jinnah became formally involved in national politics. A heady era of secular, anti-British activism followed. During this time, Jinnah and his wife often appeared publicly, to much fawning and admiration. Then, feeling narcissistically injured and outshined by Gandhi's popularity with the Indian masses, he withdrew from the political stage and returned to full time practice of law.

"The death of his nationalist career in politics coincided with changes in his relationship to Ruttie. Their lives were less glamorous now, less exciting. Jinnah was no longer the rising political hero . . . he (had) aged. . . . The rakish beau of forty-two was transformed—overnight, it seemed—into an elder statesman, a careful barrister of forty-five, who had precious little time for the whims and fancies of a young wife and infant daughter" (Wolpert 1987, 73).

Jinnah's wife now turned to pets and the spiritual world for company, spending time in séances with mediums and joining the theosophical movement. While Jinnah soon returned to active politics, Ruttie never joined him with gusto again. Indeed, in September 1922, she left for London with her daughter. This was the beginning of the end of their marriage.

Ruttie Jinnah returned to Bombay a year or so later, but soon developed a relationship with a Parsi[7] lawyer from Bombay, named Kanji Dwarkadas. This relationship grew from written correspondence and solace-seeking to nearly daily meetings and, most likely, a romantic and sexual affair.[8] Ruttie nonetheless regressed, became melancholic, and developed a morphine addiction (Collins and Lapierre 1985; Wolpert 1984). She became increasingly estranged from her husband and died on February 18, 1929, two days short of her twenty-ninth birthday.

> The funeral was held at Bombay's Muslim cemetery on February 22. Kanji met Jinnah's train at Grant Road Station and drove him there, trying to convince him "that Ruttie would have liked to be cremated" but "she was buried under Muslim rites." It was a painfully slow ritual. Jinnah sat silent through all of its five hours. "Then, as Ruttie's body was being lowered into the grave, Jinnah, as the nearest relative, was the first to throw the earth on the grave and he broke down suddenly and sobbed and wept like a child for minutes together." M. C. Chagla was also there, and he, too, recalled "there were actually tears in his eyes," adding, "That was the only time when I found Jinnah betraying some shadow of human weakness." (Wolpert 1984, 105)

Burying the grief beneath his industrious self, Jinnah soon resumed his political life, which kept him exceedingly busy and in great national prominence for the next few years. Once again, however, he was frustrated and lost faith in both his Muslim and Hindu colleagues. He was fed up and decided to transfer his practice entirely to appeals before London's Privy Council, the highest court in the British Empire. Ever guarded and secretive, he told practically no one about this move.

Jinnah lived in London from 1931 to 1934. His unmarried sister, Fatima, lived with him. His eleven-year-old daughter, Dina, was enrolled in a nearby boarding school. While Jinnah participated in the Indian national affairs in London, these were "the quietest, least political years of his adult life" (Wolpert 1984, 129). He worked hard, but did not succeed in his practice in the Privy Council to the extent he had expected. By now, fifty-nine years old, Jinnah had "paced off every inch of Hampstead Heath and probably eaten in every decent restaurant in London. Even if theater continued to lure him to the West End and old friends to Oxford or Cambridge, there was really nothing to tax his talents, no challenge left to his life, no summits to win, no opponents worthy of his genius to vanquish. At fifty-five, he appeared to have achieved a routine resembling the perfect tranquility of the grave" (Wolpert 1984, 130).

He decided to return to India in 1934. On the surface, he was persuaded by Sir Mohammad Iqbal (1877–1938), the great Urdu poet and German-educated barrister, who had become increasingly vocal on behalf of the right-wing Muslims of India. Deep down though, his ambitious nature was perhaps looking for renewed challenges.

Three years after arriving in India, Jinnah explicitly joined the rank of Muslim separatists. The 1937 Muslim League session in Lucknow was the end point of a long journey. The city where, twenty-four years ago, he had forged a pact of unity between Congress and Muslim League now became the starting point of a vendetta. Having faced many harsh confrontations with his Hindu political colleagues and many crushing disappointments to his ambition, Jinnah had now gone over to the other side completely.

During the 1940s, Jinnah lived at a frenetic pace, traveling, speaking, arguing, discussing, preparing drafts, and conducting negotiations at all hours of the day and night. His health began to deteriorate. Extreme stress of work and frequent bronchitis (which turned out to be rather severe tuberculosis) took a heavy toll upon his weak constitution. He was now frequently thinking of his death and leaned heavily on Fatima for emotional and intellectual support. Appearing more gaunt each day, Jinnah handed over the charge of the daily grind of the political movement to his trusted lieutenant, Liaquat Ali Khan (1896–1951). He kept addressing the issues of a separate political identity and statehood for Muslims, while carefully deflecting any allusion to his deteriorating health in public. In the words of his personal physician, Dr. Jal Patel (curiously, a Hindu), Jinnah lived the last three years of his life on "willpower, whiskey, and cigarettes" (quoted in Collins and Lapierre 1985, 129).

The idea of a separate homeland for Muslims, long voiced before, took a concrete form in 1940, but was not administratively formalized until June 3, 1947. Two-and-a-half months later, on August 14, 1947, a dominion of Pakistan was created, with Jinnah as its first Governor General. He was overjoyed. Soon, however, the pyrrhic political victory, coupled with failing physical health, brought him to the threshold of despair. His lung disease worsened by his smoking (nearly fifty cigarettes a day!), a habit that paradoxically became more tenacious with its deleterious impact. Always thin and emaciated looking, he began to rapidly lose weight; toward the last few days of his life, he barely weighed seventy pounds. Spitting blood, thrown upward by his tuberculosis-infested lungs, Jinnah died on September 11, 1948, at the age of seventy-one, in an ambulance that had broken down on its way from Ziarat to Quetta (Bolitho 1954). This account, corroborated by the depiction in Christopher Lee's 1998 movie *Jinnah*, is questioned by Wolpert (1984). He mostly agrees with Bolitho's (1954) version, but insists that Jinnah died in a government bungalow, where he had been transported following the ambulance breakdown, two days later. The exact location of Jinnah's death is thus also shrouded with a bit of mystery, just the way his ancestry and date of birth had been.

Fatima was the only family member around when Jinnah died, although his daughter, Dina, from whom he had become estranged,[9] did come to attend his funeral a few days later. He was buried in Karachi. Life had sent him away on a fibrillating sojourn of turmoil and transformation. Death brought him back, full circle, to the city of his birth.

FROM "THE AMBASSADOR OF HINDU-MUSLIM UNITY" TO "QUAID-E-AZAM" OF PAKISTAN

The long and complex saga of Jinnah's political career has been the subject of many books (Bolitho, 1954; Ahmed, 1997; Wolpert, 1984; Wells, 2005) and what we offer here is but a brief summary of it. Our goal is to link the personal and the social in this intriguing man's life, so that we can highlight how external events affect a leader's intrapsychic life and how that, in turn, shapes his political ideology (Volkan et al, 1998). In keeping with the spirit of our agenda, we wish to begin this section by pointing out four important facts about Jinnah's sociopolitical life.

1. Jinnah was not a practicing Muslim. He came from a marginal Islamic group and his Muslim ancestry was questionable. He hardly ever visited a mosque or prayed to Allah; it is doubtful that he had ever read the

Quran. He drank alcohol and ate pork regularly. Indeed, his lifestyle was closer to that of British gentry than to the North Indian Muslims he claimed to represent toward the last part of his political career.

2. Jinnah was not the founder of Indian Muslim League. This political party was founded in December 1906, when a group of Muslims seeking proportionate representation of their community of all government jobs met in Dhaka under the leadership of Sultan Mohammad Shah (Aga Khan III); the name "All India Muslim League" was the brainchild of Sir Mian Mohammad Shafi. Mohammad Ali Jinnah, an active member of the secular Indian National Congress, was much later asked to also join the Muslim League by Congress; it was hoped that he would create bridges between the two groups.

3. Jinnah did not come up with the idea of Pakistan. The notion of a separate and independent Muslim nation-state carved out of India was the brainchild of Indian Muslim immigrants in London, who were spurred on by the activities of Muslim League "back home" in India. It was especially given shape by Sir Mohammad Iqbal (1877–1938), and the name of Pakistan itself was coined by the Muslim League leader, Choudhary Rahmat Ali (1897–1951) in 1933.

4. Jinnah did not welcome the idea of Pakistan when it was first presented to him. He found it unacceptable to think that Indian Muslims should part ways from their Hindu brethren. He scoffed at the notion of a separate Muslim nation carved of India and dismissed Chowdhry Rahmat Ali and others who had suggested the idea to him with considerable scorn (Collins and Lapierre, 1985).

With these facts in mind, let us return to the beginnings of Jinnah's political career. As we have already noted, he completed his education in London and returned to India in 1896. This highly anglicized man, who, in the words of Sarojini Naidu, was "Hindu by race and Muslim by religion" (1918, 3–4), symbolized the composite culture of the Indian society at that time. Becoming a Reader to the Advocate-General of Bombay launched him into social prominence and laid the groundwork for a successful legal career. In London, Jinnah had already come in contact with the stalwart of Indian National Congress, Dadabhai Nairoji (1825–1917); this had sowed the seed of political leanings in his mind. In Bombay, Jinnah began associating with prominent Congress leaders (e.g., Tyabji, Mehta, and Gokhale) and soon formally joined the secular Indian National Congress Party. By 1908, he was a highly-sought-out lawyer and a well-recognized sociopolitical figure. Then, the Minto-Morley reforms in 1909 introduced a separate electorate for Muslims. This opened a new avenue for Jinnah. He was nominated to the Imperial

Legislative Council by the Muslims of Bombay Presidency. He thus came to represent the Muslim community within the Hindu-dominated, even though secular, Congress Party. As a true nationalist, he was gaining prominence. His main strength was his keen grasp of law and a strong advocacy of progressive legislation. As one of the first Muslim members elected to the Viceroy's Central Legislative Council in 1910, Jinnah emerged as a formidable advocate of the principle of merit through qualification.

The next few years saw him forging, strengthening, and championing Hindu-Muslim alliances within the Congress party. He saw the two communities firmly united in a common front against the British and he chose to operate within the system to consolidate this. The unity articulated by Jinnah embodied a liberal, democratic, and enlightened worldview. His vision accommodated the heterodox units of a diverse and complex social order. Secular nationalism was the political space to which Jinnah committed himself, along with the centrist and moderate leadership of Congress, and from where he launched himself into the stratosphere of Indian freedom struggle. In an apt, if a bit grandiloquent, appreciation of this, Sarojini Naidu (1918) conferred upon him the title of "The Ambassador of Hindu-Muslim Unity."

Along with Gandhi and other major congress leaders (e.g., Motilal Nehru, Jawaharlal Nehru, Sardar Vallabhai Patel, and Maulana Abul-Kalam Azad, to name a few), Jinnah spearheaded the combined Hindu-Muslim struggle against the British Imperial power, with the goal of establishing a free India within the British Commonwealth. Underlying Jinnah's vision was a deep faith in the dignity and equality guaranteed by the British law to all citizens (Wolpert, 1984). Thus for him, the constitutional means were the only legitimate way to achieve this goal.[10]

The year 1913 presented a major political opportunity for Jinnah. As a high-ranking member of Congress, he was invited to address the meeting of the All India Muslim League, held in the city of Lucknow. There, he pronounced

> the goal of attainment under the aegis of British crown of a system of self-government suitable to India through constitutional means, *by promoting national unity*, by fostering public spirit among the people of India, and by cooperating with the communities for the said purpose. (quoted in Naidu 1918, 6, italics added)

Jinnah thus spelled out his future strategy in explicit detail and thinned down the distinction between Congress and the Muslim League to its narrowest limit. Not surprisingly, the next couple of years saw him as the chief human link between the aims and strategies of the two political parties.

The first crack came with the British seeking to recruit Indians in their army during World War I. Gandhi supported this, arguing that cooperation with the British would lead to the latter granting greater freedoms to Indians.

Jinnah vehemently opposed such cooperation. He demanded greater civil rights and a citizenship status for Indians that was equal to the British themselves as a condition for extending cooperation to the allied powers led by the British. Why should Indians act as mere pawns? If they have to take up arms, he argued, they should do so as citizens and not subjects. Few can deny that he showed greater shrewdness and rationality than Gandhi in bargaining with the British in their hour of crisis.[11]

Yet, Gandhi was emerging as the undisputed leader of India's struggle for freedom from the British. His rise was, at least in part, based upon his having adopted a predominately Hindu idiom in both the daily conduct of his life and his political message. Words like *satyagraha* (insistence upon truth), *ahimsa* (nonviolence), and *swadeshi raj* (self-rule) were the daily staple of his addresses to the Indian masses. Gandhi's attire (a simple *dhoti,* loincloth), language (ordinary Hindi sprinkled with catchy Sanskrit-derived phrases), dietary habits (eschewing meat and alcohol), and easy mobility through the hearths and hearts of the Indian people stood in sharp contrast to Jinnah's formal, even if suave, Western persona and intricate legal arguments. Gandhi's frequent resorting to "hunger strikes" through fasting also differed dramatically from Jinnah's frontally assertive methodology that relied upon logic and reason.

Jinnah's privileged position within the Congress rank-and-file was seriously threatened by the ushering in of mass politics with Hindu religious nuances. Gandhi's vernacular juggernaut transformed Congress overnight from a private club of elite upper-class professionals, notable academicians, and affluent lawyers, into a mass organization thronged by starved and semi-starved peasants, poorly paid workers, and unemployed faceless crowds. "Gandhi's Congress" was far from "Jinnah's Congress"; broadly speaking, the former represented an idiom of heart and the latter an idiom of mind. Jinnah grew increasingly disenchanted, as a result, and resigned from Congress in 1920.

He was also affected by the death, around this time, of Dadabhai Nairoji and Sir Phirozeshah Mehta, who had been the voices of moderation in the Congress Party and his long-term senior friends. The changing colors of Congress now made Jinnah increasingly aware of the difference between majority and minority politics. He was also distressed by another development—the poisoning of sociopolitical atmosphere by the increasingly strident voice of Rashtriya Sevak Sangh (RSS). The RSS was an explicitly pro-Hindu political faction founded in 1925 by Vinayak Damodar Savarkar (1883–1966), an ardent admirer of Mussolini and Hitler (Jafferlot 1996).[12] Its followers detested Muslims and aspired to restrict their civil rights if and when India gained independence and became a sovereign nation. Jinnah began to fear political isolation, experience religious discrimination, and sense that the chances of his rise to administrative power in a postindependence India were becoming dim.

Jinnah also despised the ways by which Gandhi achieved success. He doubted that Gandhi's call for "civil disobedience" was an appropriate way of gaining independence from the British; he felt that legislative reform was a better method to achieve the goal. He was convinced that Gandhi's program was taking the country in a wrong direction. He felt that if Gandhi opposed schools based upon the British system, he must build nationally oriented schools in their place. Jinnah would accept Gandhi's boycott of British consumer goods only if Indians built their own mills and competed with the West-like men. In other words, he dared to drag Gandhi's dream to reality. In addition to resonating with Gandhi's pain at India's emasculation by the British, Jinnah felt the impotence of Indian Muslims under Gandhi's ascetic totalitarianism.[13]

The high point of bitterness between the two came in the wake of Government of India Act of 1935. This act provided greater provincial autonomy and buttressed the dyarchical substrate of regional legislative councils laid down earlier by the Montague-Chelmsford Reforms of 1919. Jinnah's dream of holding power through elected office (and enjoying the patronage that came along with it) now got strengthened. This, in turn, became a source of friction between him and Nehru, the handpicked heir apparent of Gandhi.

Nehru insisted that Congress was capable of representing the interests of both the majority Hindus and the minority Muslims, since it was a secular party. Jinnah, increasingly wary of the Gandhian "Hinduization" of national politics, opposed this. The seeds of the parting of their ways were sown by the refusal of the Congress high command to accord proper representation, after its 1937 electoral victory, to the Congress-League Coalition. As a result, in Hindu majority provinces, ministries were formed with only the members of Congress, entirely excluding those of the Muslim League. This enraged Jinnah. Bitter arguments, angry mistrust, and vituperative mudslinging now became the order of the day. The dream of Hindu-Muslim unity was shattered. According to Wolpert, "The separate electorate formula (which) was initially rejected by Jinnah on grounds of national principle (now) served to raise his personal consciousness of Muslim identity" (1984, 29). The "*Quaid-e-Azam*" ("Great Leader") of Pakistan was thus born.

Two other events, which took place around this time, paved the way for the creation of Pakistan. The first was the arrival on Jinnah's desk of a letter by Sir Mohammad Iqbal, which grimly declared that "an organization which gives no promise of improving the lot of average Muslims can not attract our masses" (Iqbal, March 8, 1938, quoted in Bolitho, 1954, 117); the fact that Iqbal was referring to the Congress Party goes without saying. Such an emphatic statement from the revered and influential poet-cum-politician had a great impact upon Jinnah. His suspicions were "confirmed" and his quest for leadership and popularity with multitudes—through becoming the head of a newly created nation—was fueled. The second event was the increasing popularity of the Muslim League among the religiously leaning Muslim youth in high schools, colleges, and universities throughout the country. They were clamoring for a political platform of equality with Hindus or to severe ties with them altogether. Jinnah now became convinced a Western parliamentary democracy, based upon an ethnically homogenous nation, was not applicable to the pluralistic society of India; more than a third of its non-Hindu inhabitants were, in his view, at the risk of being excluded from national administration.

Around this time (circa 1940), a commission led by Sir Stafford Cripps (1889–1952) arrived from England. After studying the political situation in India, this commission proposed a dominion status for a "Union of India." Though it did not accept the idea of Pakistan *per se*, the mission did accord various Indian provinces the right to secede from the "Union" on the basis of a plebiscite. Jinnah and the Muslim League, with which he had become synonymous by now, saw this as a tacit approval of their demand for Pakistan. Congress objected to such interpretation of the Cripps Commission Report, but Jinnah found legal loopholes in its objections. He began to insist that England needed to frame a new constitution dividing India into two sovereign states of India and Pakistan (Moore 1983, 553). Gandhi tried to dissuade Jinnah. They met many times but their talks failed. Jinnah's resolve was unbeatable.

A new impetus to ending the British rule over India came with the end of the World War II, in 1945. With the unconditional surrender by the Japanese, the fear of the invading India[14] subsided (Bolitho 1954). This diminished the "necessity" of Indo-British coalition on the military level and loosened the imperial grip on India's destiny. The next year saw general elections in India. The Muslim League won by overwhelming majority in the United Provinces and in the Central Assembly. Emboldened by this victory, it sanctioned a "Direct Action Day" on August 16, 1946, to force the creation of Pakistan. Drowning the secular and "pro-Indian" voices within their own community, right-wing Muslims filled the streets with loud processions. Jinnah had them mesmerized.

Sensing the fast approaching demise of the imperial reign, the British Empire, led by King George VI, dispatched Earl Louis Mountbatten (1900–1979) as the last Viceroy of India in early 1947. Jinnah and Mountbatten held six intense meetings in the first two weeks of April 1947. However, the Viceroy was unable to persuade Jinnah to give up his demand for Pakistan. For Jinnah, India's partition was now the natural course, and he insisted that the state of Punjab and Bengal, despite their substantial Hindu populations, should go to Pakistan. Mountbatten found this demand unagreeable. Jinnah was the absolute dictator of the Muslim League by this time and warned that, if partition was not agreed upon, India would descend into chaos, if not a civil war. Mountbatten relented. Right-wing Hindu nationalists, who had their own ethnocentric agendas and wanted Muslims to get out of India, rejoiced. Gandhi wept, but to no avail. Nehru and Patel, worn out by years of political struggle, were themselves now eager to acquire positions of prestige and power. Instead of letting Jinnah lead a coalition government of undivided India, they seemed to "prefer" ruling a partitioned India. All arrows now pointed in the same direction.

In June 1947, Sir Cyril Radcliffe (1899–1977) was invited to India by Mountbatten to give reality to the country's partition. Arriving from England and soon confining himself to a government bungalow near Patna in the Eastern province of Bihar, this architect and draftsman, who had never stepped on Indian soil before, drew bloody lines on the country's map. In a period of about eight weeks, he vivisected India "much like a surgeon using scalpel to sever the bone and muscle of a limb in an amputation" (Collins and Lapierre 1985, 128). On August 7, 1947, Jinnah flew from New Delhi to Karachi to become the Government General of Pakistan, a week later when India was divided and Pakistan came into existence. The fact that he had inflicted a catastrophic wound upon India's soul was far from his mind. He was beaming with joy and seemed to have played his inning well.[15]

FROM A DIVIDED SELF TO A DIVIDED COUNTRY

In order to establish links between the personal and political elements of Jinnah's life, we turn to the psychoanalytic perspective. The first thing we become aware of is that Jinnah's story is that of a series of transformations. On multiple fronts—nominal, vestimentary, residential, and ideological—Jinnah repeatedly emerged afresh and, at times, unrecognizably changed. He seemed to be involved in a process of constant self-invention. From the clumsy-sounding mouthful of "Mohammad Ali Jinnahbhai Poonja," he became the sleek and easy to pronounce "M. A. Jinnah." From the provincial Sindhi attire, he went to a stylish Western wardrobe, only to give it up in favor of traditional Muslim clothes when that appeared suitable for his political image. From Karachi he moved to London, from London to Bombay, from Bombay to London, then back again to Bombay, from there to New Delhi, and finally he came full circle back to Karachi. This peripatetic course was largely dictated by external contingencies, but it was also an outward manifestation of his emotional turmoil.

The alterations of name, attire, and residence, however, pale in comparison with the ideological transformation that characterized Jinnah's life. From a successful anglicized barrister, he became an anti-British politician and, in the latter realm, had a stunning change of heart. Celebrated as "the Ambassador of Hindu-Muslim Unity," he became a hateful divider of the two communities. Admired by both Hindus and Muslims at first, Jinnah became the darling of right-wing Muslims and the nemesis of Hindus. In Pakistan, the country he founded, he is revered. In India, his name is taken with contempt and hatred. What led to this Janus-faced outcome? What factors contributed to his transformation from a secular nationalist to a political opportunist who exploited the "Muslim cause" for his own narcissistic purposes?

Our search for answers to these questions leads us not only to the adult life frustrations he faced (and also unwittingly engineered), but also to the traumas of his childhood as well. Consequently, our reconstruction of what actually happened includes not only what he consciously registered, but also what he might not have been consciously aware of; we see his political transformation as a combined result of adulthood and childhood frustrations, conscious and unconscious motivation, and real as well as fantasized scenarios.

Consideration of his childhood brings attention to four important facts. The first pertains to a Hindu-Muslim split at the most fundamental core of Jinnah's psyche. Since Jinnah's parents or grandparents had undergone a religious conversion, there is a strong likelihood that as a child he received mixed, even if quite subtle, messages about his religious identity. Such spoken and unspoken "family myths, conflictual and nonconflictual wishes on the part of parents, and intergenerational transmission of traumatic events play an important role in child's identity formation" (Akhtar 1999, 50). In Jinnah's case, this could translate into a divided core of the self, with his Hindu ancestors depositing their incompletely renounced religious allegiances deep inside the child's overtly Muslim identity.[16] The emotional cues emanating from Jinnah's interpersonal and inanimate surrounding, therefore, might have been contradictory. The culinary and vestmental preferences of his family, for instance, might have been more "Hindu" and the religious inclinations more "Muslim." Were there allusions to Hindu mythology in the lullabies his grandmother and mother sung to him? Did the mention of those ancestors who had not converted to Islam ever appear in family reminiscences? If so, what sort of sentiments accompanied such recollections and what was the impact of these on the young Jinnah? We do not know the answers to such questions, but they are certainly important to raise since thinking along these lines helps us imaginatively map out Jinnah's inner "representational world" (Sandler and Rosenblatt 1962).

A closely related second issue is that the origins of his name are shrouded in mystery. Did a Parsi or Hindu mother name her son after a Muslim saint? Was the name derived from a revered but grievously injured animal (*Zuljin-nah*)? What possible psychological impact could either of these derivations have upon the identity of someone named in this fashion? Abraham's (1911) early paper on the determining power of names addresses this point, noting how the name a child receives often ends up contributing significantly to his identity and course of life.

A third psychologically significant fact about Jinnah's childhood is his apparent physical weakness and emaciated appearance. Since the family's physician ruled out any actual ailment, one is forced to wonder about the psychic determinants of this Shakespearean "lean and hungry look." Was Jinnah, as an infant and later as a child and adolescent, not eating properly? Why? Was there some anger underlying such refusal of nourishment? Was the hauntingly gaunt look (which persisted throughout his life) a psychosomatic signal, a silent but forceful appeal to be fed and taken care of? Did his so-called weakness cause him shame? And, if his not being sent to school until age eleven was due to his "weakness," did that cause him further narcissistic injury?

This brings up the fourth interesting feature of his childhood. Jinnah's mother gave birth to eight children altogether. Jinnah was the first and "her favorite" (Wolpert 1984, 7). This laid down the ground for his great emotional strength and resilience. Freud's (1917) correlation of "confidence in success" with being mother's "undisputed darling" (p. 156) and Abraham's (1924) linking "imperturbable optimism" (p. 399) with a profoundly gratifying infancy readily come to mind in this context. At the same time, inevitable breaches in the relationship with his mother, resulting from seven subsequent pregnancies could have stirred up hurt, yearning for mother, fear of losing her, and resentment of siblings who took her attention away from him again and again. A split self-representation would develop under such circumstances: confident and optimistic on the one hand, vulnerable and jealous on the other.

Now, if one puts these four elements of Jinnah's formative years (namely, the non-Muslim deposits in a Muslim psyche, the physical weakness caused probably by eating inhibitions, the curious origins of his name, and the favored child status with a mother who produced seven other children), we begin to sense that his core self was a peculiarly contradictory amalgam of Hindu and Muslim traditions, resilience and vulnerability, strength and weakness, and longing for attachment and defensive aloofness. Things simply did not fit well.

For a person with such psychic structure, the challenges of young adulthood can prove to be difficult. In Jinnah's case, this step got further complicated by immigration; he lived from the age of seventeen to twenty in London, which was culturally quite different from his native Karachi. He faced the challenging task of postmigration acculturation and identity transformation (Akhtar 1999; Grinberg and Grinberg 1989). Shortening his name and changing his wardrobe were the outward manifestations of this inner identity alteration. The increased aloofness he developed soon after his mother's death[17] was most likely a further "deployment" (Moses-Hrushowski 1994) of the narcissistic self-sufficiency he had earlier evolved to deal with his mother's repeated pregnancies.

Another psychologically significant aspect of Jinnah's adult life pertains to his sexuality. His first marriage was most likely unconsummated, and his second marriage took place when he was forty-two years old. There is little evidence of any romantic relationship that he had until then. Was he actually celibate until the age of forty-two? Or, did he have some fleeting sexual encounters that have gone unrecorded? The latter possibility is less likely in light of his immensely public life. If true, what does his prolonged celibacy tell us? Was it "organic" in etiology, a continuation of his childhood "weakness?" Or, did it betray a narcissistic dread of vulnerability that invariably accompanies attachment to others. Was he incapable of falling in love? In commenting upon such an emotional handicap elsewhere, one of us had drawn a portrait that resembles that of Jinnah.

> Individuals suffering from this malady have pronounced deficits in their capacities for concern, empathy, and basic trust. They can not develop closeness with others. They lack spontaneity and manage their interpersonal lives on a factual basis. They also lack the capacity for "sexual overvaluation" (Freud 1921) and idealization (Bergmann 1980; Kernberg 1974), which is a mandatory initial ingredient of falling in love. They are too "realistic" in their estimation of others and cannot allow themselves the perceptual compromise needed for idealization of another individual. (Akhtar 1999b, 79)

Impaired in his capacities for intimacy, relaxation, and love, Jinnah must have felt emotionally alone on a chronic basis. The inner splits resulting from his childhood (Hindu-Muslim, favorite-rejected, confident-jealous) were now getting condensed with conflictual schisms of adult life (Indian-British; poor student as a child-great scholar and orator as an adult; normal sexual yearning-sexual celibacy). The emotional turmoil of living a life like this can be great.

Jinnah found three solutions in succession to his inner chaos. The first was to fervently devote himself to work; this "manic defense" (Klein 1935) became an integral part of his character armor. His desire to be accepted and loved manifested in his "counterphobic assimilation" (Teja and Akhtar 1981) with the British culture. His impeccable attire, his monocle, and drinking alcohol and eating pork were all garnish to this defensive acculturation. By being British (i.e., Christian), he could erase the ill-fitting Hindu-Muslim substrate of his identity. This line of thinking gains support from his having adopted Christ's birth date and having given Ruttie, his already quite Westernized second wife, the name Mariam (Mary) after her conversion to Islam. From our psychoanalytic perspective, we can not but wonder if he was at all aware that by naming her after Jesus' mother, he (who claimed to be born on the same day as Jesus) was enacting a powerful Oedipal wish to erotically possess his mother? Could the gap of nearly a generation between their ages (twenty-eight years) have been a reversed manifestation of the same Oedipal wish? And, could these seemingly Oedipal enactments have hidden a deeper, pre-Oedipal hunger for mother's love and acceptance? We will never know. What we do know is that Jinnah's "Christian solution" to his inner division did work to a considerable extent and remained in place even when newer salves for the psychic wound (remember *Zuljinnah?*) had to be found.

The next phase in Jinnah's self-healing was his anti-British activism. This was largely determined by the politics of the day, but it seems to have also been an unconscious way of getting rid of his anglicized "false self" (Winnicott 1960). If the British would leave India, Hindus and Muslims could live in harmony. The rational and admirable political dream fitted nicely with Jinnah's "self-righting" (Lichtenberg 1989) need to heal his own inner ethnic split. In other words, the external solution actualized the desire for the internal "mending" of his ill-fitting Hindu and Muslim self-representations. No wonder Jinnah worked for Hindu-Muslim cooperation with remarkable intensity and soon became the "Ambassador" of their unity. Great optimism flooded his ego.

Around this time, Jinnah experienced many narcissistic injuries, some of them being quite severe. The most prominent among these was Gandhi's overtaking him in popularity with the Indian masses. Gandhi's ready-made access to the Hindu idiom of majority India and a lifestyle that resembled that of the country's poor made him an immediate hero. Jinnah, with his Western attire, manner, and intellect failed to endear himself to ordinary folks. This injury to his self-esteem mobilized a great amount of "narcissistic rage" (Kohut 1972) and led to him beginning to hate all things Hindu (which stood for his chief rival, Gandhi). The fact that Gandhi favored Nehru over him added insult to injury. The poison of jealousy began to flow through his veins.

Among other blows to his self-esteem were the failure of his marriage to Ruttie and her involvement with Kanji Dwarkadas. He also felt that his Congress League liaison building efforts were not duly rewarded. This also hurt and angered him. Gandhi, Nehru, and Kanji seemed to rob him of all glow.[18] There was no coherence to his life. He was anglicized but not British. He was secular but regarded a Muslim. He was industrious but passed over for rewards. As if this was not enough, his health also began to deteriorate. One narcissistic blow after another left him reeling. He was looking for a way out.

The third and, to use a notorious phrase from Hitler's (1925) lexicon, "final solution" was now presented to him. Organizationally cornered and narcissistically bruised, Jinnah decided to pull the two warring factions of his psyche—and their externalized representations—as far apart as he could. The "Ambassador of Hindu-Muslim Unity" drove an intractable wedge between his two selves and between the two groups that represented them in outer reality. This perhaps also accounts for the fact that a highly logical and calculating person like Jinnah could not see that a country with two parts (West Pakistan and East Pakistan), separated by a distance of over one thousand miles, was a geographical absurdity.[19] To be sure, the states of Punjab in the east and Bengal in the west did have considerable Muslim populations, but the hope to forge a unified nation out of two regions with such cultural disparity and topographical distance seems to have been emotionally driven, to say the least. It is as if by "joining" two very different and far apart areas of land, he would accomplish a harmonious union of his own ill-fitting self-representations.

Disregarding geocultural considerations and putting a premium on his ambition and drive, Jinnah coopted the idea of Pakistan (which he had earlier ridiculed) and reinvented himself as a great Muslim. To symbolize this dramatic shift: "Jinnah changed his attire, shedding the Saville Row suit in which he had arrived for a black Punjabi sherwani long coat, donned for the first time in public on the morning of October 15, 1937. He had spent the night at Mahmudabad House, and after breakfasting with the Raja, was about to leave for the packed meeting outside when his eye was attracted to a black Persian lamb cap worn by Nawab Mohammad Ismail Khan, one of the greatest provincial League leaders. He asked his friend if he might try on that compact cap, which would soon be known throughout the world as a "Jinnah cap." When he saw how handsome it looked over the white of his sideburns in the mirror, he knew that it was just the headgear needed to give his Muslim costume its crowning touch" (Harvani 1996, 87).

Far more ominous was Jinnah's exploitation of the Muslim separatist cause. Mocking his fellow Muslims who were true Indian nationalists,[20] he grabbed the role of the Muslim community's savior. Lacking any Muslim credentials of faith and religious practice whatsoever, Jinnah's latched on the Pakistan bandwagon in a transparently opportunistic move. Like Gloucester in the opening soliloquy to Shakespeare's *Richard III*, Jinnah declared:

> And therefore, since learn not prove a lover,
> To entertain these fair well-spoken days,
> I am determined to prove a villain,
> And hate the idle pleasures of these days
>
> —Shakespeare, 1593, p. 210

In discussing the deeper psychological meaning of this statement, Freud (1916) has offered a succinct paraphrasing of it: "Nature has done me a grievous wrong in denying me the beauty of form which wins human love. Life owes me reparation for this, and I will see that I get it. I have a right to be an exception, to disregard the scruples by which others let themselves be held back. I may do wrong myself, since wrong has be done to me" (p. 314–15).

Failed as a pseudo-Christian and as a Hindu-Muslim unifier, Jinnah felt wronged by all others around him. The dormant traumas of his childhood were revived. Feeling excluded and enraged, he decided to become a traitor to his own cause of communal unification. Genuine sublimation gave way to selfish and corrupt ambition.

In becoming a "destructive pied piper" (Blum 1995, 18) who led many million Indian Muslims to create a separate nation, Jinnah disregarded that an even greater number of them did not want India's partition. He seemed to care little about the fact that he was jeopardizing the fate of Muslims left behind in India since they would, as a result of his self-aggrandizing antics, be forever viewed with a bit of suspicion by their fellow Hindu citizens. Drunk with dreams of power and reincarnated as the glorious *Quaid-e-Azam*, he cared little for the fact that nearly ten million (seven million Hindus and three million Muslims) people got displaced from their homes and nearly 300,000 of them were brutally massacred in the course of India's partition. The man who once had noble aspirations was now content with self-glorification.

CODA

In an attempted synthesis of the personal and political in Mohammad Ali Jinnah's life, we have underscored the essential complimentary of intrapsychic and reality determinants. Behind each step in his majestic but troubled (and troubling) sojourn, a complex dialectic of characterological issues and social events is evident. Jinnah's enigmatic ancestry and traumatic childhood delineated his destiny as much as his fierce struggles with his political rivals did. For the Hindu-Muslim split that lay at the deepest core of his psyche, he found three successive solutions: (1) avoidance of conflict via manic anglicization, (2) attempted synthesis via enthusiastic secularism, and (3) violent compartmentalization by identification with one self-view (Muslim) and repudiation of the other (Hindu). Since none of these solutions were based upon valid ancestry, authentic belief systems, and healthy identifications, Jinnah's life ended up having a chameleon-like and caricatured quality. He kept changing names, residences, attires, and ideologies. Lacking love, which is the "glue of a unified self-representation" (Settlage 1992, 6), Jinnah had to rely on the fuel of hatred. Unfortunately, however, hatred does not bind. It splits things apart and destroys links. In the near-demonic quest of power and glory, Jinnah became a human scalpel that cut his motherland apart. Sweetness, which defined his early secular inclinations and to which this chapter's epigraph by al-Ghazali referred to so eloquently, had certainly left his heart.

6

Ideology and Aggression

Osama bin Laden

Peter A. Olsson

Do you know what sappeth the foundation of Islam, and ruineth it? The errors of the learned destroy it, and the disputants of the hypocrite, and the orders of kings who have lost the road.

—Prophet Mohammad, cited in Abdullah
and Al-Suhrawardy, 1990, p. 93

What is in the mind of Osama bin Laden? What can we surmise about his unconscious motivations? Why does he want to kill or hurt Americans? Some of the psychodynamic parallels between destructive and apocalyptic cult leaders and Osama bin Laden are striking. Osama's cyberspace fundraising, his charismatic, religion-flavored recruitment techniques, and his rebellion against his Saudi homeland community and America are all similar to psychodynamic and group dynamic features of destructive cults and their leaders. Osama bin Laden seems to harbor unconscious childhood resentments, stemming from his childhood disappointments and losses. Do these inner psychological issues drive him to relentlessly seek symbolic father and brother figures to compensate for his losses, and then heal and sustain his inner coherence of self? Do his childhood narcissistic wounds live on in the current moment? Does he seek inner spurious symbolic restitution and revenge for these narcissistic wounds by acting out his narcissistic rage via terrorism? Osama simultaneously has also become the great leader-parent figure for disaffected Muslim and Arab youth. Indeed, Osama has become a heroic Robin Hood figure for many disaffected Arab and Muslim adults around the world. They perceive him as selflessly using his wealth to fight big and powerful invaders and oppressors, such as Russia, America, and Israel. However, Osama can also be viewed as the ultimate terror cult leader or malignant pied piper.

Osama clearly takes a paranoid stance toward Americans and Israelis. Paul Berman, writing in the *New York Times*, describes the Al Qaeda terror cult in these terms: "Al Qaeda upholds a paranoid and apocalyptic worldview, according to which 'crusaders and Zionists' have been conspiring for centuries to destroy Islam. And this worldview turns out to be widely accepted in many places . . . a worldview that allowed many millions of people to regard the 9/11 attacks as an Israeli conspiracy, or perhaps a C.I.A. conspiracy, to undo Islam" (2003, 4).

Biographical details about Osama bin Laden's childhood and early family history reveal similar patterns to the psychological dynamics and character patterns that occur in destructive cult leaders (Olsson 2005). The psychobiographical information about Osama bin Laden is incomplete, but there is enough data to form psychoanalytic hunches and some solid conclusions about bin Laden's personality and psychodynamics.

There is an uncanny social-psychological fit between the religiously flavored charismatic leadership of a man like Osama and the group psychology of communities where he and his colleagues and mentors recruit devoted terrorists. It is a serious mistake to glibly label and dismiss bin Laden as simply a mass murderer or only a criminal. As ancient martial arts and warrior codes say: (1) Hasty declaration of war inflates the status and grandiosity of the enemy, (2) Contempt fuels the enemy's outrage, and (3) Incorrect and dangerous assumptions are easily made about an unknown enemy for whom one only holds contempt. "If you know the enemy and know yourself, you need not fear the result of a hundred battles. If you know yourself, but not the enemy, for every victory gained, you will also suffer a defeat" (Sun Tzu, 500 B.C.).

This chapter is an effort to know our enemy, Osama bin Laden, from psychobiographical, psychodynamic, and psychosocial perspectives. First, we will look into some psychobiographical details about Osama bin Laden and some of the readily apparent psychodynamic patterns that we can discern.

PSYCHOBIOGRAPHY OF OSAMA BIN LADEN

Osama's father, Mohammad, was born in about 1930 and immigrated as a laborer from a poor Yemeni family to Saudi Arabia in the late 1950s. Osama was born in Saudi Arabia on March 10, 1957, in Riyadh. Osama means "young lion" in Arabic. Mohammad bin Laden became a skilled engineer and started a construction company. He gained the respect and favor of both King Saud and his successor, King Faisal. Mohammad was a valued confidante of King Saud. King Faisal awarded Mohammad bin Laden the contract to structurally look after the Islamic holy sites at Mecca and Medina in 1973.

Mohammad bin Laden had eleven wives and Osama has more than fifty siblings. Osama's mother, Hamida, is Syrian. Osama is the only son of her marriage to Mohammad bin Laden. Hamida refused to accept the traditionally passive female role in her marriage. Sharp conflicts arose in the marriage and Mohammad banished Hamida to another town (Tabuk). Osama, already lowly ranked as the seventeenth son, lost his mother because she lived in a separate household. How unfortunate that Osama could not have had more influence from an independent-minded woman of apparent dignity such as Hamida. His stepmother, Al Khalifa, another woman with a strong personality, raised Osama. Supposedly, Osama eventually, on a day-to-day basis, held respect and affection for Khalifa, despite the loss of his real mother. (Robinson 2001, 39–40).

Mohammad bin Laden spent his time making hundreds of millions of dollars for his Bin Laden Corporation. Osama spent some time with his father during an annual week-long, "male bonding" winter hunting vacation in the wild desert regions of the Saudi Kingdom. Osama shone brightly during these brief trips with his father and his royal friends. Mohammad was impressed with Osama's prowess on these trips and probably recalled his own boyhood adventures in the Yemeni desert. Osama also excelled in Islamic studies, which drew positive attention and praise from his father. Sadly, those father-son times were far too brief. Robinson's implication that it left a profound father-hunger in Osama's heart is very likely true.

Father's Death as Psychological Wound and Narcissistic Injury

Mohammad bin Laden, though a multimillionaire, was poverty stricken when it came to paying the piper of parenthood. It was impossible for him to spend quality time with each of fifty children, particularly his bright and perceptive son of the "lesser" Syrian wife. Mohammad espoused religious piety. Miliora (2004, 127,137) indicates that Mohammad bin Laden was a devout Wahhabi fundamentalist, and that Osama was undoubtedly exposed to anti-United States sentiments during his upbringing and development as a Wahhabi. So at an unconscious level, Osama must have felt torn between his father's strict Wahhabism and the fact that his father worshipped money and its accumulation.

Osama was ten when his father died. Mohammad bin Laden's helicopter crashed in the desert while he was traveling home. Ten thousand men gathered for his funeral. Of Osama, Robinson says: "His grief was deeper than simply the loss of a loved one. Beneath the surface, he had long repressed a deep gouge in his psyche caused by the partial loss of his mother (via divorce) and a relationship with his father shared with so many siblings, a handful of wives, and the pressure of a vast business empire" (2001, 54–55). Robinson continues: "Before his [father's] tragic death, his [Osama's] interest in Islam had drawn him closer to his father. It was a paternal relationship he [Osama] craved; yet Mohammad's sudden death had robbed the youngster of a chance to enjoy anything other than fleeting moments of satisfaction. Family members recall him reeling emotionally."

Osama withdrew into himself for months. His grief was actually no different from that of any other young man with unresolved ambivalence toward his father. Note in the connection, Freud's (1900) description to his own father's death: "It was, I found, a portion of my own self-analysis, my reaction to my father's death—that is to say, to the most important event, the most poignant loss, of a man's life. Having discovered that this was so, I felt unable to obliterate the traces of the experience" (Freud 1900). Osama bin Laden's loss of his father was poignant, but also seemed filled with profound ambivalence. The powerful echoes of that ambivalence follow Osama down the path of his life.

Shame and Humiliation as the "Son of the Slave"

Another narcissistic wound in Osama's childhood is found in the way he was treated by his half-siblings in the household. Osama`s banished birth mother, Hamida, was spitefully referred to as *Al Abeda* (the slave). Osama was cruelly labeled *Iban al Abeda* (son of the slave). The teasing and devaluation of Osama by his half-siblings hurt and deeply festered in his heart (Robinson 2001, 39).

Osama was sent to Tabuk after his father's death. He thus joined his mother in their exile from the rest of the family. He tried to get reacquainted with her, but Robinson says: "Some of the [bin Laden] family today explain that Osama came to resent both his father for removing him from his mother, and his mother for not attempting to bridge the gap with his father for his sake. The wounds healed, but the scars remained" (2001, 40).

Early Loss of a Best Friend

Osama had one true best childhood friend. This friendship with Abdul Aziz Fahd began during the annual father-son desert camping trips they took with their fathers. Because their fathers were close, they enjoyed frequent visits and they spoke on the phone frequently. When Mohammad bin Laden died when Osama was ten, the two families' relationship changed; closeness between them ceased.

Once, after Osama returned to Jeddah from Tabuk, he was delighted to learn that Prince Fahd was soon coming to Jeddah for a visit. His best friend, Abdul Aziz, would be with the Prince. Osama tried dozens of times to contact his friend by phone during that visit, but was rebuffed. Osama was even turned away from the door of the house where Abdul was staying. Osama has never heard from or seen his friend again. This clearly added another element to the basis for Osama's acted-out hatred toward the "Father-brother-land" (Robinson 2001, 60) of Saudi Arabia.

Mohammad bin Laden let money be his major payment to the piper of parenthood. He did pay for good schools for his children. Osama went to high school in Jeddah, then studied management and economics at King Abdul Aziz University, in Jeddah also. Osama's personal adolescent searches reflected some of the turmoil of the Arab Middle East in the late 1970s. Robinson (2001), Bodansky (1999), and Dennis (2002) describe Osama as going through typical adolescent rebellion. They report that he was a playboy, drinker, and womanizer in Beirut. However, Peter Bergen, in his book *Holy War, Inc.* (2001, 55), insists that Osama was always serious, devout, and well behaved.

Relentless Search for Father Figures

Bergen (2001) observes that Osama idealized his father; Osama told a Pakistani journalist: "My father is very keen that one of his sons should fight against the enemies of Islam. So I am the one son who is acting according to the wishes of his father" (p. 55). Bergen says, "Having lost his deeply religious, [*but also very materialistic*] father, while he was still a child, bin Laden would, throughout his life, be influenced by religiously radical older men" (p. 55; italicized words are author's own). Psychoanalysts can find this observation to be important and compatible with a psychodynamic hypothesis about Osama's lifelong ambivalent and hungry search for father figures. Let's now meet several of these key men in Osama's young adult life.

Osama began to show intense interest in Islamic studies during his college years. He was greatly influenced by several mentors. The first, Sheik Yussuf Abdallah Azzam, was born in a village near Jenin, Palestine, in 1941. Azzam was sixteen years older than Osama. He graduated with a degree in theology from Damascus University in 1966. Assam hated Israel, which he blamed for taking Palestinian land. In the 1967 War, Azzam fought against Israel. Azzam received a master's degree and doctorate in Islamic jurisprudence at al-Azhar University in Cairo by 1973. The eloquent and charismatic Azzam established the worldwide network of jihad that won the Afghan War against the Russian communists. Azzam, and subsequently Osama, believed fanatically in the need for *Khalifa*, the dream that Muslims around the world could be united under one devout Islamist ruler (Miliora 2004).

Azzam was a friend of the famous jihad ideologue Sayyid Qtub and the Egyptian Sheik Omar Abdel Rahman (who inspired the 1993 bombing of the World Trade Center towers). These three heroes and mentors of Osama were leaders in the formation of an Internet network of holy warriors in the 1980s.

Muhammad Qtub was another of Osama's influential mentors and the brother of Sayyid Qtub (1906–1966), the philosopher and hero of all the groups that eventually joined the Al Qaeda network. Even though Sayyid Qtub was executed in 1966, his writings in prison have led him to be called the Karl Marx of Islamist global jihad. Qtub wrote *Milestones*, as well as his masterwork, *In the Shade of the Quran*. Qtub's writings have inspired Al Qaeda, Egyptian Islamic jihad, the Islamic Group (Egypt), and the Muslim Brotherhood (Egypt's Islamic fundamentalist movement in the 1950s and 1960s).

Qtub's work makes fifteen thick volumes in English. His ideas are articulate, sophisticated, and powerful. Qtub had a traditional Muslim education and had memorized the Koran by age ten. He went to college in Cairo and did further studies in literature. He wrote novels, poems, and a book that is still well regarded, called *Literary Criticism: Its Principles and Methodology*. Qtub traveled to the United States in the 1940s and got a master's degree in education from the Colorado State College of Education.

Qtub's radical Muslim youth-inspiring prose comes not from a university campus, but from an Egyptian prison, where anti-Western hatreds found their spiritual headwaters. Paul Berman (2003) summarizes the partially prescient core of Qtub's sophisticated theology of hatred toward the West:

> Qtub wrote that, all over the world, humans had reached a moment of unbearable crisis. The human race had lost touch with human nature. Man's inspiration, intelligence, and morality were degenerating. Sexual relations were deteriorating "to a level lower than the beasts." Man was miserable, anxious, and skeptical, sinking into insanity and crime. People were turning, in their unhappiness, to drugs, alcohol, and existentialism. Qtub admired economic productivity and scientific knowledge. But, he did not think that wealth and science were rescuing the human race. He figured that, on the contrary, the richest countries were the unhappiest of all. And what was the cause of this unhappiness?— This wretched split between man's truest nature and modern life! (p. 4)

This depth of thought and idealism appeals to youth in all societies because of its eerie iconoclastic truth. (One can see a nostalgia here for an earlier, simpler time that resonates in Western philosophy from Rousseau to Thoreau and many twentieth-century poets, songwriters, and others who reject the materialism of modern life and yearn for a preindustrial Eden of some kind.) But Qtub's writing grew angrier, and has been used to encourage martyrdom and violence. It is similar to the way that Abbie Hoffman indirectly inspired violence against the "Establishment" in the 1960s or, more recently, the way anti-abortion preachers have encouraged schizoid idealistic loners to assassinate physicians at abortion clinics or other terrorist acts in the United States (Stern 2004).

OSAMA'S LIFE JOURNEY

His deranged nephew, Prince Faisal ibn Musaid, assassinated Saudi Arabia's King Faisal in 1975. Osama's radical professors/father figures said the assassin had been driven insane by exposure to Western ways. Osama's Islamist Saudi teachers taught that the terrible pain of the Lebanese in their 1975 war was a punishment from God for their sinful acceptance of modern Western materialism and excess. The fatherless Osama was deeply impressed by his conservative Islamist professors who taught that only return to strict Islamism could liberate Muslims from the sins and materialism of the "Satanic West" (Bodansky 1999, 3).

Another Muslim and father figure to bin Laden is Hassan Abdullah al-Turabi. Turabi was born in 1932, in Kassala, eastern Sudan. Turabi received a secular Sudanese education in British schools. He got a law degree at Gordon University in Khartoum in 1955. Turabi was a clandestine member of the Egyptian Muslim brotherhood, even as he earned a degree in law on scholarship to the University of London in 1957. He got his doctorate at the Sorbonne in 1964. Turabi became the spiritual leader of the National Islamic Front (NIF). He became Sudan's spiritual leader after General Omar al-Bashin's coup in June 1989. Turabi's radical Islamist influence is probably present in the violence and genocide in Sudan today.

Bin Laden returned to Saudi Arabia in 1989, after serving as a hero of great renown in the successful jihad and defeat of the Soviet Union in Afghanistan. On August 2, 1990, Iraq invaded Kuwait. Osama presented his detailed but grandiose plan for self-defense of the Saudi kingdom. He felt confident in and bolstered by battle-hardened Saudis who had fought in Afghanistan. Bin Laden offered to heavily recruit the "Afghans." He promised that his family construction company could quickly build fortifications. Osama angrily warned that inviting or permitting infidel Western forces into the sacred lands of the kingdom would be against the teachings of Islam and offend the sensibilities of all Muslims.

Osama was not alone in these concerns among the Saudi leadership, but his offer was ignored. Osama's narcissistic rage was further stirred by the Saudi rulers' turning to the United States for help and protection. Miliora (2004) astutely observes that not only did Osama "lose all trust that the House of Saud was a reliable interpreter of Islam but, in permitting the United States to increase its foothold in the Middle East, he saw his nation as having made a deal with the devil and having become a protectorate of the greatest enemy of Islam" (p. 129).

Osama's disappointment and rage took the form of intense, aggressive criticism of the Saudi rulers. Osama continued to grow so critical and threatening that the Saudi leadership threatened his extended family. Osama began to fear reprisals for his outspoken anti-American and anti-Saudi pronouncements. In 1991, Osama bitterly left for exile in the more friendly land of his father figure Hassan Turabi.

Osama seems to have been perpetually (unconsciously) caught between his fervent Islamist beliefs and the dazzling financial success from his dead father's affiliation with the materialistic Saudi leaders and their American "friends." Osama seems to seek both the destruction of the father figures of the Saudi regime that disowned him and the casting out or destruction of the Saudis's American "friends." On a conscious level, he idealized his father, but on an unconscious level, he even held tremendous ambivalence toward his admired mentor Azzam.

A psychoanalytic theory is that unresolved grief, disappointment, and shame over his dead father's Western materialism have focused and magnified Osama's identity as a self-appointed anti-Western, radical Muslim warrior chieftain. Osama's relentless grief-laden search led him to find other radical, admired, and admiring father figures. Osama's relationships with Azzam of Afghanistan and Turabi of Sudan became bolstering inner introjected fortresses. In his book, *Bin Laden: The Man Who Declared War On America*, Bodansky (1999) documents in great depth and detail the mutual admiration reverberating between Osama and these figures of Osama's identification and identity formation.

SYMBOLIC BROTHER FIGURES

Ayman al Zawahiri, the Egyptian physician turned radical Islamist, and Mullah Huhammad Omar, leader of Afghanistan's Taliban, became Osama's brothers in rebellion and rage. They served as a replacement for Osama's Saudi half-brothers, who eventually disowned him over his terrorist commitments.

Dr. Ayman al-Zawahiri was born in Egypt in 1951, six years before Osama bin Laden. He comes from an aristocratic, affluent Egyptian family. Ayman was educated as a pediatrician. As a medical student in 1973, he joined an electrical engineer and an army officer in forming the Egyptian Islamic Group, which dedicated itself to the violent overthrow of the Egyptian state. Al-Zawahiri served as a medical officer in Afghanistan, where he was regarded as a hero, along with bin Laden, in the jihad against the Soviet Union's occupying army. Alzawahiri was very close to Egyptian Sheik Omar Abdel Rahman, the so-called blind sheik behind the 1993 bombing of the World Trade Center towers and the assassination of Egyptian President Anwar Sadat in 1981.

Zawahiri has grown very close to Osama (an older brother/father figure) over the years of their alliance in building what Bergen calls "Holy War, Inc." Some experts think that al-Zawahiri is the man who influenced Osama to morph from a donor of money to a warrior of violent jihad. He has been a constant companion and mentor of bin Laden. In a psychodynamic sense, Zawahiri has psychologically replaced and compensated for Osama's painful loss of his best friend, Abdul Aziz Fahd, in his childhood (Robinson 2001; Bergen 2002).

Osama was a heroic, fearless military leader in Afghanistan's successful war against the Soviet Union. The Afghanistan War was, for Osama, a profoundly spiritual experience. He became both an admired warrior son of radical terrorist state leaders and a legendary hero/older brother/mentor for millions of angry young Muslims. Money has never been able to compensate for Osama's grief over and ambivalence about a father who was not around when the adolescent Osama needed his guidance the most. Fathers of adolescent sons often feel superfluous or devalued by their sons. However, beneath this surface of rebellion in the service of fledgling independence and identity searching, is a desperate need for a father with moral strength and dignity. All destructive cult leaders seem to have unconscious ambivalent longing for, but also hatred of, the father who did not stand up to them and for them. This leads them to be the ultimate father/themselves, unto themselves. Osama is, in this sense, an ultimate terror cult leader whose acted-out hatred and rage captures the imagination of many young Arab men.

Gunaratna (2002) gives good examples of Osama's severely ambivalent conflicts with even his mentor/father figure Azzam. Azzam asserted that noncombatant women and children should not be killed in the jihad. In his strict Wahhabi fundamentalism, Osama felt that all infidels should die—even women and children. Gunaratna raises the serious question of whether Osama held symbolic patricidal urges, as he may have participated in Azzam's assassination.

OSAMA'S POETRY

The *New York Times* published a poem on April 7, 2002, called, "The Travail of a Child Who Has Left the Land of the Holy Shrines." It was coauthored by

Osama bin Laden and the poet Dr. Abd-ar-Rahman al-Ashrawi. Half of the forty-two verses were written by Osama bin Laden. Eighteen of Osama's verses mention father, son, brother, child, or family. One line mentions mother. A few annotated verses are presented here because of their reflection of bin Laden's psychological search for his father/himself.

> Father, where is the way out?
> When are we to have a settled home?
> Oh, Father, do you not
> See encircling danger?
> Long have you made me travel, father,
> Through deserts and through settled lands.
> Long have you made me travel, father,
> In many a sloping valley,
> So I forget my kinsfolk,
> My cousins, and all men.
> Why has my mother not returned? [*Early childhood separation?*]
> How strange! Has she taken a taste for travel?

And later:

> Why, father, have they sent?
> these missiles thick as rain, [*Because of your 9/11-type attacks!*]
> Showing mercy neither to a child
> Nor to a man shattered by old age?
> Father, what has happened
> so we are pursued by perils? [*Actually a tragic tit-for-tat?*]
> It is a world of criminality, my son
> Where children are, like cattle, slaughtered.
> Zion is murdering my brothers,
> And the Arabs hold a congress! (italicized words are author's own)

Bin Laden's poem lines can be seen as free associations, similar to those a psychoanalyst hears from the couch. In the following lines of this poignant poem, bin Laden reveals his search for a home and a father figure in Sudan and Afghanistan:

> A decade has passed, whose years were spent
> In homelessness and wanderings.
> I have migrated westward
> To a land where flows the Nile. [*Clear reference to father surrogate Turabi of Sudan*]
> Of Khartoum I love the character,
> But I was not permitted to reside.

So then I traveled eastward
Where there are men of radiant brows.
Kabul holds its head up high [*idealized Afghan fighter fathers and brothers*]
Despite the hardship and the danger.
Kabul, with a shining face,
Offers all-comers shelter and help. (italicized words are author's own)

When captured by the poetic muse, the poet often reveals his or her inner feelings about the core of self. Poetry of this sort provides access to the more unconscious levels of the poet's psyche. Osama's vulnerability peeks at us in and between these lines of his poetry.

Osama seems to have both found and become his own lost father, brother, mother, and family in the far-off terror training camps of Afghanistan. Osama's painful losses and unconscious disappointment in his parents led to a fixation in the form of his search for his grandiose omnipotent father/himself. His ambivalence and narcissistic rage has relentlessly been acted out via terrorist acts. His personal psychodynamics have an uncanny resonance with thousands of father-hungry young Muslims around the world. Osama seems in denial of his own grief, loss, and fear of being alone or dying (Becker 1973). This denial dynamic becomes part of the appealing illusions that he offers his young terror cult followers. Osama cloaks these illusions in the radical Koranic misinterpretations offered by his mentors. (Might it be just as likely that a suicide bomber will be greeted in Eternity by God's frown as by his smile?)

Many Muslim clerics who are sympathetic to bin Laden's radical Islamist theology of hatred, teach in Madrassahs all over the Muslim world. They act as lieutenants to recruit and indoctrinate followers for Al Qaeda and its warrior prophet bin Laden. Al Qaeda has even successfully appealed to American youths John Walker Lindh and Jose Padilla. Osama bin Laden's pied piper music goes on, and on, and on.

THE ANTIHERO AS A TERROR CULT LEADER

Osama bin Laden's life trajectory shows evidence of what I have called elsewhere "dark epiphanies" (Olsson 2005, 18) in destructive cult leaders. Such later life experiences reify and magnify their earlier molding experiences of disappointment, neglect, shame, and humiliation influenced by parents and other childhood role models. Adolescents or young adults often chose antiheroes to counteract disappointment or humiliation/shame experiences they have had with parental figures.

Osama bin Laden's appeal has a unique "fit" for normal adolescent rebelliousness. Anna Freud said of adolescents, "On the one hand, they throw themselves enthusiastically into the life of the community, and on the other, they have an overpowering longing for solitude. They oscillate between blind submission to some self-chosen leader and defiant rebellion against any and every authority. They are selfish and materially minded and at the same time full of lofty idealism" (1936, 137–38).

What would be normal adolescent rebellion and protest for young people become terrorist actions under the influence of charismatic fundamentalist leaders, whether they are Al Qaeda leaders or American "Save the Babies" antiabortionist fundamentalists. The volatile contemporary American political and economic circumstances and the Arab world's seeming endless turmoil find many young adults who are in the phase of what psychoanalysts call "prolonged adolescence." Siegfried Bernfeld described a specific kind of male adolescent development called "the protracted type." "It extends far beyond the usual time frame of adolescent characteristics and is conspicuous by "tendencies toward productivity, whether artistic, literary, or scientific, and by a strong bend toward idealistic aims and spiritual values and activities." (1923, p. 64).

There are similarities in "follower psychology" between Al Qaeda recruits and recruits in many destructive cults and social movements. Stern (2004, 85–106), traces the history and the striking, chilling similarities between Jewish extremists, American fundamentalist extremists who murder abortion doctors, and Al Qaeda franchises. The followers are not exclusively poor or uneducated young people. Bin Laden's lieutenants and Al Qaeda leader colleagues are predominantly educated and dedicated to his ideal of jihad. Radical Islamofascists like bin Laden recruit by using personal charisma and manipulating the Koran to form attractive mixtures of theology turned into a radical political action ideology.

In Arabic, Al-Qaeda means "the base." In addition to well-educated youth, radical Islamists also recruit poor and less-educated Muslim "foot soldiers." They do this via religious Madrassah schools and young-adult mosque programs and activities. Osama's jihad appeals particularly to disaffected Arab and Muslim youth. These adolescents and young adults have suffered while witnessing their parents being humiliated, oppressed, and impoverished in countries ruled by wealthy dictators who are perceived as puppets of America. Madrassah-type "schools" offer economic advantages and spiritual inspiration to families and Muslim communities that have few alternatives.

The recruiting techniques of Al Qaeda and its franchises are savvy, creative, and diverse in their applied theology distortions

Grandiose Personality Extensions of the Dark Epiphany

The early childhood disappointments, shame, and empathic parental failures of future destructive cult leaders are further magnified and compounded by "dark epiphany" experiences in late adolescence or young adulthood (Olsson 2005, 38–39). This is true for Osama bin Laden. Let's backtrack a little to focus on one of Osama's dark epiphanies.

Osama returned to Saudi Arabia in 1989, as a hero of the war against the Soviet Union in Afghanistan. Osama was even admired by some Americans when he was killing Soviet soldiers. However, events of the next two years left him feeling rejected and threatened by the Saudi leadership, who ignored his offers to help defend the country when Iraq invaded Kuwait. This rejection slowly smoldered into molten rage and vengeance toward the betraying Saudi father figures and their American "infidel friends." Miliora (2004) concludes: "Because of his grossly inflated grandiosity about having won the 'holy' war against the Soviets and his seeing himself as an instrument of divine will, his reactive narcissistic rage was similarly inflated, and it may have reached a psychotic level. He focused his violent fantasies against Saudi Arabia, as well the United States, both for revenge and to show that he, representing true Islam and the will of Allah, was the more potent force" (p. 132).

Miliora (2004) and others make a strong case that Osama has intense grandiose fantasies of identification (probably introjection/merger) with Muhammad the warrior-prophet who will restore Islam as the most powerful force in the world. Osama wears a long trimmed beard, dresses in simple white robes dating back to the prophet Muhammad and recites poetry in front of caves—bathed in sunlight like the prophet was alleged to have done.

In Afghanistan after the Soviets left, America and our Saudi "friends" did not pay the piper. The United States (and the "free" world) abandoned a crumbled Afghanistan. A Robin Hood-like Osama bin Laden emerged. Today, there are many future bin Ladens born daily around the world. American foreign policy does have life or death consequences for us. America can no longer give billions to repressive dictators in Arab countries to protect only our own interests with no benefits to ordinary people.

Radical Islamist groups make extensive social and educational offerings to everyday needy people in the Muslim world. They gain people power and good will through these social, economic, and educational programs. They inspire communities' spirits, not just give them financial aid. Volkan (2004) observes that the very name of the Taliban movement means "students" and that in the post-Soviet power vacuum, the *Haggania madrassah* taught hatred of "infidels," jihadist ideology, and hero worship of Osama bin Laden (p. 156).

Volkan resonates with and extends the theme of Osama's narcissistically tinged search for a father figure saying: "It seems to me that in Afghanistan, there was a particularly 'good fit' between a hurt and victimized country and a man whose extreme hate may be a reflection of personal pain and sense of victimization. Bin Laden first became interested in Afghanistan through his spiritual mentor, Azzam—who, impressed by the devotion and heroism of the *mujahidin,* had moved his family to Pakistan just one year after the Soviet invasion. Already a father figure to bin Laden, Azzam founded the Mujahidin Services House in Peshawar, Pakistan, and supplied help to the Afghan opposition cause, including volunteers to fight. And Osama's millions of dollars in contributions helped the cause" (156–57).

Volkan has traced the powerful connections between a hurt and victimized country and the spiritual-warrior leader who feels personally victimized. A large group or country thus claims a leader to focus its collective hate, revenge, and hoped for triumph. Volkan also asks a fascinating and important question: "But how does a pathologically vengeful individual such as Osama bin Laden persuade other individuals to die intentionally for his politicoreligious cause?" (p. 157). In essence, Volkan's answer is that through charismatically applied, religiously saturated indoctrination, education, and social approval, a person's large-group identity/group-self is made to supercede his individual identity. Volkan concludes: "Thus, future suicide bombers feel normal and often experience an enhanced self-esteem. They become, in a sense, a spokesperson for the traumatized community and assume that they, at least temporarily, can reverse the shared sense of victimization and helplessness by expressing the community's rage" (2004, 159).

The Uncanny Impact of the Popular Media

Cults and terrorism as tactics of spiritual rebellion and political/social control have existed since antiquity. In a confounding paradoxical way, modern worldwide instantaneous media coverage provides a perfect psychodrama stage for the terrorist's ghastly reality drama. If Al-Qaeda had to purchase television time to cover their events, they would have to pay millions of dollars for what they now get for free. The media provides both publicity for the terror event and grandiose narcissistic affirmation of the terror cult and its leader. Osama's hubristic videotape performances give evidence of this point. Osama becomes an exciting, flamboyant, and darkly charismatic television celebrity. Osama had issued threats and warnings shortly before his terror cult's actions. This gave a magical, grandiose, "prophecy come true" quality to the media covered 9/11 events.

Many people who saw the World Trade Center towers hit by airliners said, "It was surreal!" or "It looked like a Hollywood movie." Good moviemakers or horror fiction writers exploit the same experience of "the uncanny" that terrorists do (Freud 1919). By intuition and/or conscious calculation, the terrorist act impacts on the tendency of people to regress to magical, black-and-white, superstitious, or primitive thinking under severe stress or shock. Minds in shock become more fragile and vulnerable.

A Resemblance to Hitler's Apocalyptic Delusions

In addition to Osama's grandiose narcissistic states and paranoia, Miliora (2004) makes the chilling observation that Osama's Manichean view of reality strikingly resembles that of Hitler. (Manichaen involves stark perceptions of good and evil, black and white, and "us" versus "them.") Miliora's cogent argument begins with Osama's murderous hatred of Israel and the United States, its parallel with Hitler's anti-Semitism, and proceeds as follows: "Much like Hitler, with regard to his claim about the loss of Germanic soil after the First World War, bin Laden stakes a moral claim that his people have suffered injuries perpetrated by the West and avows that it is the sacred duty of Muslims to restore Islamic lands to rightful control. And also like Hitler, bin Laden promotes his rigid, totalitarian ideology with utter self-righteousness. Moreover, both bin Laden and Hitler imagine that their atrocious mass murders are consistent with the will of God and imbue their sociopathic behavior with religious significance" (2004, 134).

Hitler's messianic and apocalyptic visions are well-known. Miliora (2004) quotes bin Laden's apocalyptic visions (from a 2001 home video of bin Laden and friends) for America (and by implications, Islam): "I tell you, freedom and human rights in America are doomed. The United States government will lead the American people and the West in general into an unbearable hell and a choking life."

There are other views beyond bin Laden's fundamentalist mentality. Kohut (1975) made the following poignant and prescient statement:

What moves society towards health is that of creative individuals in religion, philosophy, art, and in the sciences concerned with man (sociology, political science, history, psychology). These "leaders" are in empathic contact with the illness of the group-self and, through their work and thought, mobilize the unfulfilled narcissistic needs and point the way toward vital internal change. It follows that during crisis and periods of regressive identification of the group-self with pathological leaders, there is an absence of creativity in religion, philosophy, art, and the sciences of man. The absence of experimental art during such periods is a striking phenomenon. Creativity in all fields is choked off. There is no one in empathic touch with the diseased group-self. This points toward the increasingly worsening condition of the group-self (corresponding to the disintegration threat of incipient psychosis in individual psychology) and leads to pathological ad hoc solutions. (p. 247–48)

There is strong evidence for diseased group-selves in the Middle East (Israel and Palestinians), in Bin Laden's Al Qaeda's jihad, and the American notion of preemptive war. The work of psychoanalysts, such as Vamik Volkan, adds "unofficial diplomacy" (i.e., psychoanalytically informed dialogue between national representatives) to the "leaders" Kohut mentions above. There is hope, but as Volkan (2004) describes, the road is not easy.

CONCLUDING REMARKS

Osama bin Laden will never knock on a psychoanalyst's door. It is worthwhile, however, to apply psychoanalytically informed approaches to understanding, as well as possible, how he thinks, feels, and behaves. We have looked at evidence that Osama bin Laden manifests intense "archaic narcissistic states" as Miliora accurately describes and illustrates them (2004, 121). Osama's unconscious and conscious narcissistic fantasies stem from profound childhood losses (father and best friend), separations (from his mother via parental separation before the death of his father when Osama was ten years old), and profound ambivalence and disappointment (admiration/identification with his father's devout Wahhabism, but unconscious rage and disappointment in his father's devotion to money and "Western materialism"). These narcissistic wounds have led Osama on a lifelong quest to find, befriend, and incorporate the ideas and philosophy of older father and brother figures (Azzam, Turabi, Qtub, al-Zawahiri, Mullah Omar, and others).

Osama also experienced dark epiphanies (Olsson 2005, 38–39, 148). When Osama returned from Afghanistan a conquering hero, his offer to lead forces to protect Saudi Arabia from Iraq was ignored in favor of protection from American forces whose presence he despised. His rage at Saudi leaders and their counteranger at him, led to Osama losing his Saudi citizenship and fleeing to exile in Sudan and later Afghanistan.

It also is fruitful to undertake the applied self-psychological study of how Osama and other terror cult leaders influence disaffected Arab, Muslim, and even a few American/Western youths? These adolescents and young adults have often suffered while watching their parents being humiliated, oppressed, and impoverished in countries ruled by wealthy dictators who are perceived as puppets of America. They idolize Osama and resonate with the suffering of his life journey and his heroism during the defeat of the Soviets in Afghanistan. Osama's personal rebellious identity and jihad of acting out, has led to a peculiar celebrity status as an anti-American, anti-Western, anti-Israeli pied piper and Robin Hood-like mythic hero. An understanding of Osama's mind and those of his followers can help with American diplomacy, foreign aid, and education policy formation.

III

CULTURE

7

Islam and Family Structure

Samar A. Jasser

In Islam, life in general—and the family life in particular in all its
aspects—is an indivisible unity in which the spiritual is not separate from
the mundane.

—Nasr 1991, 207

Literally meaning "submission to the will of God," Islam reaches deeply into
all aspects of human existence. Two of its five basic obligations, namely *Za-kat* (giving alms to the poor) and *Hajj* (pilgrimage to Mecca), assume human
linkages to society and the world at large. No wonder, then, the messages of
the *Koran* and the teachings of Prophet Muhammad frequently refer to man's
duty toward others, especially his family. Actually, the family unit is considered the single most nonreducible unit of the Islamic faith, underscored only
by the individual and her personal spiritual-religious path. Thus, the family
can be considered the natural evolution of an individual's religious observance, the foundation upon which any communal, national, or world Islamic
view must rest. The family unit, in its unique relationship to God, has been
described as the link uniting the closely-knit individual relations within the
family on one hand and the relationships between families within the community at large on the other hand (Nasr 1991). As such, the development of a
family structure and progression to this next natural step of religious development beyond the individual self is considered to be a duty incumbent upon
any Muslim who is genuinely "able" to do so (Nasr 1991; Farah 2003; Esposito 2005).

Herein lies a point of contention, however. In common practice, this question of "ability" to successfully engage in family settlement is interpreted primarily as a measure of financial and/or physical capacity to fulfill the task of family development. However, a less common, but arguably equally exigent consideration, is the ability of an individual, at a given point in her psychosocial development, to engage in this pursuit in a mentally healthy way. Assessment of this psychological realm is not as straightforward as those of reproductive or financial means. Yet, it is at this interface between religion-in-practice and underlying psychological realities where there is great need for discussion. This discussion will rouse reappraisal of popular assumptions about accepted variations of accepted Islamic practice that are consonant with mental health, and what might be considered universally unsound from a psychological standpoint. One may find that what are often accepted at face value as practices reflecting religious tradition are instead normalizations of behaviors that are advantageous to the pathological potential of all human beings. To attempt to make this distinction is to find the balance between respecting the inherently "nonrational" nature of religious practice and challenging believers of all faiths to confront the ways in which their most basic drives might be masked by their declared beliefs.

One means of assessing the integrity of a given practice or belief is to analyze its internal and external consistency within the greater context of believers-at-large. In addressing this prodigious task, I will not attempt to cover each and every area of family structure and family dynamics within Islam. Instead, I will focus upon marriage and parent-child relationships, while also attempting to elucidate the contextual variations of these in different Islamic societies.

SOME CAVEATS

First, I must emphasize that making any generalization in the realm under consideration is extremely difficult and problematic. At the same time, it is necessary to do so in order to achieve some didactic coherence. Therefore, I need to remind the reader that wherever generalizations are made, they are made in an effort to characterize and distinguish the Islamic faith, as it is laid out in the *Koran* and the teachings of the Prophet Muhammad, from the manifold interpretive practices in which it manifests across the globe. The day-to-day manifestations of Christianity, Judaism, Hinduism, Buddhism, and other major world religions in practice vary incredibly from one region to the next, as well as in the level of orthodoxy practiced within a given region; Islam is no exception to this variability. Thus, generalizations are made a priori, in the effort to convey unified, core principles of the Islamic faith, but not without recognition of their inherent limitations.

Second, the regional variations in interpretation of the core Islamic principles across cultural traditions are still important to recognize insofar as any discussion of family structure in Islam hinges upon these reality-based contexts. To make such distinctions about Islamic family structure on a culture-by-culture, region-by-region basis is beyond the scope of this chapter and could be the subject of an entire text unto itself. However, in the final section of the chapter, I will draw on examples from a few distinct cultural regions within the Islamic world in order to demonstrate this phenotypic variability.

Third, much of what is known about the Islamic religious and cultural practices across the globe is based upon phenomenological observation and large-scale trends rather than raw data of family therapy. There are very few, if any, carefully controlled epidemiologic studies that shed light upon the prevailing beliefs about Islamic family structure in a given region. As a result, the nature references drawn upon here have a tremendous variability. However, I have mostly tried to cite authors who demonstrate cultural and historical awareness, as well as a scholarly understanding of Islam.

THE CRUX: TENETS OF THE FAITH

Perhaps the foremost tenet of the Islamic faith is a belief in the oneness and ultimate nature of God. This is a very literal and serious edict of the religion, stated a countless number of times throughout the *Koran*. The practical translation of this belief is that followers of the Islamic faith worship God as one unified entity, who, though he may have distinctly enumerated traits and facets of divinity, is to be considered as one, nonpartnered creator of life as we know it. He is also distinctly described as a nonformed being, not able to be conceptualized in the way that humans consider form, body, and physical features (Farah 2003). Similarly, in Islam, the rules, boundaries, expectations, logic, feeling, and directionality that constitute human existence cannot be transmuted into a concept of God. It is this nondeducible quality of the Islam, side-by-side with its strict aversion to any present-day human proxy of divine will, which magnifies the importance of the *Koran* as an enduring source of understanding and guidance for practitioners of the religion.

Deriving from this primary belief are the other four core tenets of the faith, including: a belief in the angels of God, a belief in *all* of the prophets of God throughout time (the last recognized being Muhammad), a belief in the scriptures revealed through these prophets (the *Koran* being the final revelation), and a belief in the day of judgment (Farah 2003), where it is held that each and every human being will be held accountable to God for the way in which he or she has conducted himself or herself throughout existence.

Beyond these specific core tenets of Islam, several of the essential teachings of the faith overlap significantly with those of the other major religions across the globe. These commonly include: "(1) Acknowledging there is no god whatsoever but God, (2) Honoring and respecting parents, (3) Respecting the rights of others, (4) Being generous but not a squanderer, (5) Avoiding killing except for justifiable cause, (6) Not committing adultery, (7) Safeguarding the possessions of orphans, (8) Dealing justly and equitably, (9) Being pure of heart and mind, and (10) Being humble and unpretentious" (Farah 2003, 113–14).

Each of these facets, as can be readily seen, impacts upon the daily conduct of life, both on a personal and societal level. Together, these facets come into a dialectical play with the cultural traditions and interpretive applications of the *Koran* and give shape to Islamic practice across the globe today.

MARRIAGE IN ISLAM

Marriage is considered to be the ultimate and ordained resolution to the conflict between the drives of the human flesh and the unconscious pressure toward psychospiritual development (Nasr 1991). It is referred to in several places (Galwash 1963; Farah 2003) as comprising "half" of an individual's religious practice and "an abode of peace and serenity, a link of mutual love and compassions—all being God's sign for those who reflect" (*The Holy Koran* 30:21). The foundation of a family, as well as every element of its ensuing structure, is dependent first and foremost upon the selection of a mate in marriage. Contrary to contemporary portrayals of this process in the Islamic world as an arranged, precontracted process, the *Koran* explicitly acknowledges the right of a woman to contract her marriage to a chosen husband (Esposito 2005). It is strictly a matter of mutual consent between the man and woman (Galwash 1963). Circumstances in which this is not the case reflect particular cultural norms rather than religious prescription. Furthermore, the ceremonial instatement of the contract for marriage is not, per se, a religiously prescribed procedure. Rather, it is witnessed according to the cultural and legal practices of the society in which it is created (Farah 2003).

Magnification of the hallowed nature of sexuality within the construct of marriage, to the exclusion of either partner having sexual relations outside of their marriage, has led to the extreme range of "modesty" observed women's clothing in self-declared Islamic cities and countries across the globe. All the variations of belief about religiously ordained dress code stem from the Koranic instruction that *both* men and women dress modestly (*The Holy Koran*, 24:30–31). Furthermore, as Esposito (2005) writes, "the Quran does not stipulate veiling or seclusion. On the contrary, it tends to emphasize the partici-pation and religious responsibility of both men and women in society." (Esposito 2005).

While many texts (Haddad and Lummis 1987; Abdul-Rauf 1989) refer to the act of marriage primarily as a protection against sinful pursuit of sexual relations outside the bonds of a sacred commitment and higher religious in-tent, most of them also recognize the more subtle, spiritual facets of marriage. The couple's capacity to experience each other as a joyful respite from the de-mands of daily living is underscored by Islamic scholars (Abdul-Rauf 1989). One author effectively summarizes this multidimensional role of marriage: "It is said that it is wise to divide one's time over three types of activities: wor-shiping the Lord, self-examination, and entertainment of the heart" (Abdul-Rauf 1989), for according to religious and spiritual practices in Islam, mar-riage may play a pivotal role in all three of these activities. Unfortunately, the same authors often speak of the pleasure-satiating role of marriage solely from the perspective of the male partner, leading many to conclude that the Islamic view of erotic pleasure as one-sided and sexist. This overlooks the limitations of translating Arabic into English, especially with regard to the inherently gender-specific pronouns and grammatical structure. No doubt, in order for a couple to support each other in all three of the aforementioned facets of mar-riage simultaneously, there is a minimal level of compatibility and mutual par-ticipation that must be present, far beyond what can be forced arbitrarily upon any couple asked to unite for the sake of marriage itself.

Mate Selection

Significantly, the *Koran* is much more specific in enumerating who is *not* ac-ceptable as a partner in marriage than it is in delineating who is: "Prohibited to you (for marriage) are: Your mothers, daughters, sisters; father's sisters, mother's sisters; brother's daughters, sister's daughters; foster-mothers (who [breastfed you]), foster-sisters; your wives' mothers; your step-daughters un-der your guardianship, born of your wives [with] whom ye have [had inter-course]—no prohibition if ye have not [had intercourse]—; (Those who have been) wives of your sons proceeding from your loins; and two sisters in wed-lock at one and the same time, except for what is past" (*The Holy Koran* 4:23).

We further notice that the *Koran* declares that it is acceptable for a man to marry a non-Muslim woman of monotheistic faith (i.e., a Jew or Christian) (*The Holy Koran*, 5:5–6), but says nothing about the correctness of a Muslim woman marrying a non-Muslim man. A result of this omission is the preva-lent belief that a Muslim woman is discouraged and forbidden from marrying a non-Muslim man. Scholars have gone on to speculate rationale to justify this interpretation (Abd al Ati 1977), but many of these rationalizations are easily arguable in the context of several modern-day cultures, especially those that are "westernized." For both men and women, Islam forbids marriage to a person who is statedly polytheistic "until they believe" (*The Holy Koran*, 2:221). The idea behind this is that harmonious union within a family and the sharing of core values would be nearly impossible in a situation with such a pervasive disconnect in belief between partners.

The lack of specific religious restrictions in marriage is often rigidly translated in "scholarly" circles in the most literal and dry manner, with the implication that one is "better safe than sorry." Alternatively, the literality of these translations, while seeming cold and overly factual, has essentially left it to the individual and her culture to contribute superimposed aesthetics, expectations, and modes of religious observance within marriage as they please. For example, what is not said in Islam about the quality of the love between a married couple could be interpreted as disregard of the aesthetics of marital love and eroticism. The *Koran* addresses the nature of this closeness between mates, particularly husband and wife, in a way that is certainly open to literary and allegorical interpretation. It is perhaps most directly addressed in the story of Adam and Eve, where it is described that mankind is created from "a single soul" beginning with Adam, and then with Eve (*The Holy Koran*, 39:6). Thus, the *Koran* has laid a very tangible foundation for a belief in soul mates—the idea that two souls were once united, separated, and then found each other again to unite in this lifetime. This conceptualization is certainly one that is founded in a union based upon a bond that is deeper than a simple contractual agreement between two people to coordinate their reproductive, financial, and religious responsibilities. Still, Abd al Ati (1977) argues that "love and marriage are two modes of experience that are by no means identified with each other or with normality. Mate selection has been governed by rules and considerations that may or may not include the priority of love" (p. 85). One may add fuel to the fire of such rhetoric by stating that the necessity of love as a basis for marriage is a romanticized Western ideal that is not a valid universal expectation from the institution of marriage. Thus, the conflict surrounding a patient's idea of love or lack thereof in the context of their marital relationship hinges strongly upon the cultural context of both their upbringing and present beliefs. Is love something that must be present prior to commitment in marriage, or is it something that can develop between any two people who openly commit themselves to each other and spend a lifetime together? It is difficult to argue that our response to this question is not culturally bound.

The *Koran* itself does comment on the intention of a loving and compassionate relationship between spouses and the necessity of these qualities for a relationship between a married couple to last, though it does not necessarily imply the *sequence* of development in love and marriage (*The Holy Koran*, 30:21). Thus, the patient's entire belief system surrounding love and relationships becomes an important realm to explore before any "diagnostic" or "ameliorating" interventions directed at that system can be employed.

Polygamy

The issue of polygamy is another misunderstood aspect of the Islamic faith. There are several culturally based practices in the Arab world that predate the revelation of the *Koran* and were subsequently incorporated, in modified form, into the manifest teachings of the Prophet as he revealed the *Koran* to the people of the time (Galwash 1963; Farah 2003). Bearing multiple wives most certainly falls under this category of practices. In Islam, monogamy is the rule, with "permission" granted to man by God to take on additional wives in marriage, *if necessary*, and *only* under the condition that he is able financially, physically, *and* psychologically to treat each wife in an equal manner (Galwash 1963).[1] One could easily argue from a psychological standpoint that this essentially prohibits the act. After all, it is hard to imagine a human psyche that would not come to prefer one spouse over another at some point in time and express this preference in conscious or unconscious ways. Furthermore, the conditions surrounding such "necessity" were rooted in a time, social setting, and political climate very different from where we find ourselves today. The practice was carried over at a time of repeated wars of conquest and in the context of an attempt to survive the revelations of the new Islamic religion. This is a far cry from the setting of most modern civilizations, and even within those areas of current political upheaval, is still distinct in its implications. Even so, a more compelling argument against the idea that the permissibility of polygamy in under any circumstance is a statement against women's rights in Islam lies in the fact that Islamic law allows for the prenuptial stipulation by any woman that she will pursue dissolution of the marriage should her husband choose to pursue another wife without her consent. Thus, the groundwork is laid for the couple to discuss and share their ideologies before marriage in order to avoid the unexpected overstepping of either person's rights by divergences in their beliefs.

As esoteric as this mention of polygamy may initially seem, it raises a highly relevant, more general clinical point, namely the discussion of psychological capacity within the context of obligations in Islamic marriage and family structure. It is emphasized that the act of polygamy is only sanctioned according to a specific ideal of impartiality on the husband's part, anything short of which is forbidden. Such recognition of human limitations next to what is allowed or prohibited by the *Koran* is not isolated to discussions of polygamy. Yet, it is easy to extract from the concretized, black-and-white appearing translations of the *Koran* available today absolute statements that, when taken out of context, fail to convey this underlying appreciation for the human struggle that underlies all aspirations toward religious idealism. On the contrary, in practice and throughout the *Koran*, it is repeatedly emphasized that the practice of Islam is not to be undertaken primarily as a hardship—as a compulsive act of rigidity isolated from spiritual growth and development. Rather, it is to be understood in a way that is at once harmonious with the soul and instructional: "God will help you follow the easiest path. He makes laws that are easy for the souls to accept and the mind to understand" (*The Holy Koran*, 87:8). There are many secular cultural norms with implicit ethical expectations that, when extracted and enumerated as doctrines of practice in a particular context, would sound potentially unforgiving and harsh if received in another time and place. For example, descriptions of the expected behaviors of a man engaged in the courtship of a woman in high society, Victorian America could sound strikingly similar to the scriptural descriptions of a husband's obligation of dowry to his courted wife. Similarly, practices that are translated concretely out of the context of cultural norms in the Arab world at the time of the Prophet Muhammad may appear to be pure objectifications of the wife at the hand of the husband. To fixate on these at the expense of the underlying principles is to be in danger of disregarding the more essential teachings of Islam that serve to guide each couple in their union and building of new family foundations.

Divorce

Like many other religions, Islam regards divorce as permissible. It is permitted as a kind of necessary evil in situations in which a couple find themselves absolutely unable to work through their difficulties toward mutual peace and harmony (Galwash 1963). When faced with unbearable internal and/or external turmoil within a marriage, which plagues each spouse's ability to maintain equanimity and pious observance in other realms of their mental life, divorce is regarded as the lesser of two evils. The acceptable extent of efforts to restore harmony to the marriage prior to pursuit of divorce is not specifically outlined, however. Herein lies another area of clinical interest. For it is during these times of extreme discontent, unworkability, and turmoil that Muslims might seek psychiatric help, whether in the form of couples counseling or individual psychotherapy. For this reason, it is important for psychotherapists to be aware of this weighted flexibility within the religion.

The Islamic conditions that constitute a permissible pursuit of divorce by a court of law (in a case where the effort may not be mutual between husband

and wife) are quite general and include things such as "habitual ill-treatment, nonfulfillment of the terms of the marriage contract, insanity, and incurable incompetence" (Galwash 1963). It's hard to imagine a situation of matrimonial discord that would not fall under the umbrella of this description. Furthermore, it is written in the *Koran*: "And if husband and wife do separate, God shall provide for each of them out of His abundance: for God is indeed infinite, wise" (*The Holy Koran* 7:19). Thus, the decision of "incurable incompetence" and "insanity" is arguably primarily a clinical rather than religious one, and there is significant potential for psychotherapy to assist a couple, together or individually, in gaining greater insight into their motivations and etiology of their difficulties. Perhaps only with this knowledge is it possible for each to know, in good conscience, by knowing themselves, that they are making choices based on real deficiencies rather than projected realities.

THE ROLE OF MOTHER AND FATHER

The *Koran* says more about the role of children in respecting their parents, especially the mother (Abd al Ati, 1977; *The Holy Koran* 19:32), than it does about the specific duties of the mother and father in the family structure. Children are advised throughout the *Koran* to help their parents as much as possible (*The Holy Koran* 2:215), including financially (*The Holy Koran* 2:180). The admonishment to "be good" to one's parents is found repeatedly throughout the *Koran* (*The Holy Koran* 4:36, 2:83, 6:151). This is stated in mostly general terms, with the exception of one explicit verse that addresses a child's verbal containment of any discontent with his parents (*The Holy Koran* 17:23).

In contrast to such emphasis upon respecting parents, the *Koran* says little about the roles of mother and father with respect to the children. Scholars (e.g., Abd al Ati 1977) have speculated about the reason for this lack of Koranic guidance regarding parental responsibilities, suggesting that parental care for offspring is such an intrinsic biological drive that to describe it as an obligation beyond what can be naturally intuited by any ethically conscious human being is unnecessary. As previously discussed, wherever a lack of specific guidance exists in any religious framework, the cultural norms of observance in a given region will often dictate or at least heavily influence the interpretations that are taught from one generation to the next. Moreover, from a purely religious standpoint, it is written in the *Koran* that even the Prophet Muhammad was warned against forbidding acts that are not explicitly forbidden in the *Koran* and thus permitted by God (*The Holy Koran* 66:1). Thus, it remains important to distinguish religious teachings from cultural norms, for patients with pathology related to interpretation of religious expectations will often fuel the continued existence of ego-dystonic beliefs because of the perceived gravity of these religious "obligations." Considering how little is specifically written in the *Koran* with regard to the expected roles of each parent, there is much room for a Muslim couple to come to an agreement about parental roles, whether they choose to abide by the gender-specific traditions of their regional culture or not. This is an important awareness to have clinically, for the pathological feelings of guilt, betrayal, and inadequacy that might plague a parent are thus much more likely to be founded in cultural family expectations than in the heaven-or-hell level of religious profundity that fuels their guilt.

One of the most consistently cited roles of parental duties is the generational bequeathing of Islamic values and teachings. Abd al Ati argues that this is the reason for the asymmetry in recognizing interfaith marriage for Muslim men but not Muslim women. In other words, it is the father whose firmness and traditionally stricter disposition toward the child is best suited toward the teaching of religious observance, and, thus, it is most likely his faith that will be passed on to the children (Abd al Ati 1977). This is strictly hypothesis, however, and not a reflection of the specific teachings of the *Koran*. Regardless of any parental duty toward religious teaching and upbringing, however, it is explicitly stated in the *Koran* that in the end, on the day of judgment, each human being is to stand before God and answer for his or her life as an individual, where the roles of parent, child, and otherwise will no longer have any bearing: "O mankind! Do your duty to your Lord, and fear (the coming of) a Day when no father can avail [anything] for his son, nor a son avail [anything] for his father. Verily, the promise of Allah is true: let not then this present life deceive you, nor let the chief Deceiver deceive you about Allah" (*The Holy Koran* 31:33).

Fascinatingly, this rather Western value of autonomy is arguably a core principle of the Islamic faith (Zepp 1992). There is "no compulsion in Islam" and the free will behind a person's choices to worship God and live a pious life is essential to the value of their observance: "If it had been thy Lord's will, they would all have believed, all who are on earth! Wilt thou then compel mankind, against their will, to believe!" (*The Holy Koran* 10:99). While no child could possibly be expected to challenge what he is taught or exert a will toward or away from the environmental influences he receives throughout his development, this responsibility to explore, contemplate, and choose how and even whether to worship God is laid upon him in his adulthood.

Thus, much weight is essentially removed from the parents with regard to the outcome of their efforts to guide their children religiously. In fact, the *Koran* admonishes against enmeshment, that it might threaten the parent's capacity to carry out her own worship: "Let not your riches or your children divert you from the remembrance of God" (*The Holy Koran* 63:9). The *Koran* emphasizes the separate religiospiritual responsibilities of the children from the parents by going so far as to warn parents that their children may come to occupy oppositional stations in life, becoming a lure *away* from worship should the parents become obsessed with maintaining family "harmony" over their own transcendental responsibilities: "O ye who believe! Truly, among your wives and your children are (some that are) enemies to yourselves: so beware of them! But if ye forgive and overlook, and cover up (their faults), verily Allah is Oft-Forgiving, Most Merciful" (*The Holy Koran* 64:14).

It is even suggested in the *Koran* that the power of the emotions invoked in the parent's love for his child, such as passion, aggression, protectiveness, and desire, are a test for the believer—a challenge to maintain equanimity in his devotion to God above all other drives (*The Holy Koran* 64:5). The parent is warned against demoralization by the perceived failures of his child in fulfilling his expectations, as well as against the vanity of pride in the material successes of his child (*The Holy Koran* 9:85). Thus, the greater challenge for the Muslim parent is framed in terms of maintaining her own religion in the face of the demands of her children, rather than successfully effecting a generational translation of her beliefs in those of her children's. Mahler's delineation of separation-individuation (Mahler et al. 1975) can thus be seen as consistent with the Islamic teachings of "normal" parent-child relations. That individuation is both inevitable and necessary for fulfilling religious responsibility is reflected in the aforementioned verses.

CULTURAL VARIATIONS

One Islam or Many?

Nearly 70 percent of the world's Muslims live in the continent of Asia, and less than 1 percent in North America. Less than 15 percent of Muslims are Arab. In order of frequency, the non-Arab Muslims live in Indonesia, Pakistan, Bangladesh, India, Iran, Turkey, Egypt, and Nigeria, to name a few (*Encyclopedia Britannia Yearbook* 1997). This vast dispersion of Muslims across the world lays the groundwork for cultural variation in religious practice. This leads to much confusion in third-party observations of what reflects the Islamic religion rather than cultural practice descended by tradition through time. Matters are further complicated by the overlay of different schools of Islamic thought (e.g., Sunni, Shiite, Sufi, etc.) across various cultures. While a distinguishing feature of Islam is considered by Muslims to be its unity of belief, there are nonetheless distinct modes of practice found across the world. The historical elements of these divisions can be explored elsewhere (Armstrong 2000; Zepp 1992; Nasr 2003), but we will address their clinically relevant fundamental divergences here.

Sunni Muslims comprise about 85 to 90 percent of the world Muslim population today (Zepp 1992). Their practices represent the tradition and teachings of the Prophet Muhammad. Subsequent religious leaders are not emphasized in this sect as much as in the Shiite tradition. There are two main schools of philosophical thought within the Sunni tradition, the *Mutazilites* and the *Asharites*. Their differences in practice are relevant clinical distinctions that influence how patients will confront any conflict they face in the practice of their religion. The Mutazilite school emphasizes reason as an arbitrator in the face of any conflict involving matters of faith; it places a high premium upon human freedom and responsibility. *Mutazilites* emphasize an allegorical rather than literal interpretation of the *Koran*. They believe that the *Koran* is timeless, but that many of its specific messages were revealed to address the Arab societal conditions of the seventh century. The *Asharites*, on the other hand, place emphasis on the Koranic revelation as the final authority and the way Islam was practiced at the time of the prophet. They believe predestination to be central to Islam (Zepp 1992). Thus, the family structure and values instated by a *Mutazilite* in her family are likely to be much more workable clinically in the face of conflict than the circumstances surrounding dysfunction that might arise in an *Asharite* family dynamic. Addressing these fundamental beliefs and models of family values in our patients becomes an important task up front, so that when various realms of dysfunction reveal themselves in therapy, they may be considered within the framework of the patient's religious presuppositions.

Even within the Sunni tradition, there are four major schools of law: (1) the *Hanafi*, located primarily in Turkey, India, Pakistan, and Afghanistan, (2) the *Maliki*, located primarily in West Africa and North Africa, (3) the *Shafi*, located in Indonesia, Egypt, the Phillipines, Malaysia, and Sri Lanka, and (4) the *Hanbali*, located primarily in Saudi Arabia (Zepp 1992). The components of these laws as they apply to marriage and other family-related rituals vary from each other, even though they retain a core of austere conservativeness typical of Islam.

In contrast, Sufism, which is the mystical strand of the Islamic faith, offers less strict interpretation of scripture. Instead, it focuses upon meditative practices for knowing one's self, with the greater goal of becoming free from the constraints of narcissism and materialism. The family structure laid out in the Sufi tradition has much less of an expectation for specific duties, member obligations, and predetermined roles. It is rather an idealized way of relating for harmony and union among family members. The love within a family becomes an ecstatic projection of the individual souls' realization of a familial-type connection to God's love. Thus, from a clinical perspective, the presence of a Sufi predisposition in a Muslim patient is likely a positive prognostic indicator, signaling the potential for psychotherapy to be a productive adjuvant to the person's spiritual practice in her effort toward equanimity and mental health. It adds the richness of expressiveness, emotion, and inner life to the bare-bones fulfillment of diligent adherence to obligations of Islamic worship of God, making it perhaps even more conducive to the work of psychotherapy than many other religious traditions.

Variations in Marriage Ceremonies

A specific marriage ceremony of one or the other kind is neither outlined in nor required by the *Koran*. Various rituals that have arisen and become commonplace are expressions specific to the culture of the bride and groom (Galwash 1963). Marriage in Islam is defined primarily by the drafting and instatement of a marriage contract, which is considered to be a sacred covenant between the bride and groom (*The Holy Quran* 4:21). The primary components of the ceremony in which the contract is instated are: (1) the mutual, written agreement for marriage of the bride and groom, which can contain the intentions and provisions of their choosing and is perhaps analogous to the Western "vows" of marriage, (2) two adult witnesses, (3) a state-appointed Muslim official carrying out the marriage ceremony, and (4) the marriage gift from the husband to the wife (Hussaini 1996). This contractual ceremony is often referred to as the *Kitab*. The marriage banquet, referred to as the *Nikah*, is recommended as a social seal to the marriage whereby the community bears witness to the bride and groom's union. It is completely unscripted by the *Koran* and analogous to the wedding reception celebrations in the West. Thus, the marriage banquet, which can occur as completely separate from or in continuity with the marriage contract ceremony, is inextricable from cultural tradition and transpires according to the cultural preferences of the bride and groom's community. I will explore a few instances its variety here.

For example, in the Asian Indian Muslim tradition, the wedding ceremonies traditionally transpire over three days of specifically sequenced celebration. *Mehndi* celebrations are held at the home of the bride on the night or couple days before the planned wedding date, involving the application of *mehndi* to the bride's hands and feet, traditional song, and dance. Then, by traditional custom, the bride is not to step outside her house until her marriage. At the wedding, a band announces the arrival of the groom; he shares a drink of *sherbet* with the bride's brothers, and the bride's sisters chidingly pat guests with batons made of flowers. The Nikah ceremony is carried out in either one of the homes or some other venue. The Maulavi, or priest, conducts the actual marriage ceremony in the presence of the closest family members and relatives, and this portion of the ceremony is completed following the groom's proposal and bride's acceptance of the terms of marriage. In this culture, the elders of the family meet on the day of the marriage and mutually decide on the amount of the dowry to be offered by the groom to the bride. It is only after the lavish dinner following the ceremony that the bride and groom sit together for the first time, though their heads are covered while reading prayers under the Maulavi's direction. During this piece, the *Koran* is placed between the couple, and they are only allowed to see each other through mirrors. After the ceremony and banquet, the bride is sent off by her family and departs to the husband's home, where she is first welcomed by the groom's mother in another lavish reception, the *Valimah*. On the fourth day after the wedding, the bride visits her parent's home in a celebratory return.[2]

In Egyptian tradition, most of the friends and family of the bride and groom attend the engagement party, which occurs on a day determined at the time of the preparation of the marriage contract. At this party, which typically occurs in a banquet hall, the bride wears a nonwhite engagement dress, and the ring is placed on her finger by the groom. The dowry is given at this time as well, and there is a large celebratory feast with ornate decorations. The date of the wedding is determined by the date of completion/preparation of a new home for the bride and groom. The night before the wedding day, the women gather for song, dance, and celebration at the bride's house, and the men at the groom's house. On the wedding day, the wedding contract is signed in the presence of a religious official, in a mosque or the bride's home, with friends and family present. The wedding party begins after sunset, and the white wedding dress and black suit are worn by bride and groom. Unlike the Indian tradition described above, the bride and groom enter the hall and greet their guests together upon entering, before taking seats next to each other. The party begins with a drink called *Sharbat*, a rose-water juice, followed by singing, dancing, and the feast. Afterward, the new couple is taken (traditionally on horse- or camel-back accompanied by a musical band) to their new home.

In Syrian custom, there is significant variability in the significance and financial embellishment of the marriage ceremony. The bride and groom will have met either by family-sanctioned introduction or independently in their places of work, school, or other social setting. They will express an initial mutual interest to each other, which will then be socially sanctioned by the visiting of the groom's family to the home of the prospective bride. Family status, including intellectually, economically, and socially, is given high value with regard to the acceptability of any couple's union. If both families are in agreement with the couple's expressed desire for each other, the groom will offer the bride an engagement ring as a sentiment of committed intention, religiously sanctifying the time they might subsequently spend getting to know each other. The initiation of the marriage contract, referred to as *al-kitab*, is conducted either in combination with the wedding reception ceremony (which allows for consummation of the marriage) or on a separate, earlier occasion. The *kitab* will often take place in the home of the bride or groom, with the official of the ceremony being led by a legal representative rather than a religious leader. The wedding reception often occurs in a hotel or other public banquet space. Often, the cost of the wedding contract ceremony is borne by the family of the bride, and the financial responsibility of the wedding reception is carried by the family of the groom.

Thus, a common theme in Muslim marriages across cultures is that the marriage contract is considered the key element of the actual wedding of any couple—that any separation subsequent to this ceremony is considered a divorce. The public celebrations involved in the wedding banquet or reception, on the other hand, are a distinct cultural phenomenon and bear witness to the marriage in a way that religiously sanctifies it as socially witnessed and allows for consummation of the marriage. The proximity of these two events—the marriage contract and the marriage celebration—is highly variable across cultures, sometimes determining the length and role of the engagement accordingly in cases where the marriage contract is initiated at engagement. In orthodox Muslim communities across cultures, the marriage celebrations are carried out with men and women attendants seated in separate areas, in order to maintain the sacredness of modesty and chastity that is so frequently magnified in orthodoxy. Yet another universal underpinning of an Islamic marriage is that the mutual consent of both the bride and groom is crucial to the religious validity of the marriage. In this way, the common uniting theme of the Islamic teachings is free-willed human submission to the will of God, without compulsion or the overstepping of free agency, and this penetrates every aspect of Muslim life.

Some Rituals Pertaining to Childhood

Passage through developmental epochs of childhood and adolescence often requires external markers. The rituals of baptism and confirmation among Christians and bar or bat mitzvah among Jews are prominent examples of this. Among Muslims, too, there are social events of this sort. The degree to which they are directly connected with Islam as against being derived from local customs and traditions is however unclear. While these rituals are too numerous to mention, two outstanding ones among them are those surrounding a child's arrival in this world and, in the case of a male child, the act of circumcision.[3]

Traditionally in Islam, a goat or ram is sacrificed on behalf of a newborn child, on the seventh day after his or her birth. The Arabic word for this ritual is *aqiqa*. According to Prophet Mohammad: "On the seventh day, a name should be prescribed for the child. Its hair and all filth should be removed and sacrifice should be performed on his behalf" (cited in Al-Bukhari, cited in Khan, 1995). Interpreted differently in different regions of the Muslim world, the *aqiqa* celebration involves shaving of the child's head in India and occurs at the time of circumcision of the male child in Pakistan. The connection between the *aqiqa* and circumcision draws upon the conventional wisdom that the foreskin of the penis is not conducive to cleanliness of this area of the body and should thus be removed as part of the "removal of filth" in the *aqiqa* ritual. Still, in other cultural traditions, particularly those with a more Western influence, the *aqiqa* is more simply a nonspecific celebration of the baby's birth.

One of the most important aspects of variation in the religious practice of circumcision in male children is the age in which the act is performed. For example, in the Jewish traditions, circumcision occurs on the eighth day after birth. As a result, it does not cause any alteration of body image and plays no role in the later phenomenon of castration anxiety. In Islamic tradition, however, the age at which circumcision is performed varies greatly. In Syria, Jordan, and the United States, Muslims have their sons circumcised soon after birth. In India, Pakistan, and Bangladesh, the tradition is to perform circumcision when the boy is between three to five years of age. This has an impact on body image and also on the Oedipal conflicts of the boy; depending upon fantasy elaborations, circumcision at this age can certainly intensify castration anxiety. Besides the difference in the age when circumcision is performed, who actually does the act also varies from region to region. Among the Muslims residing in more advanced countries, for instance, circumcision is performed by physicians. In other parts of the world, it is usually the family barber who does the deed, often without the use of any local anesthesia. Although little data is available in this regard, it seems safe to assume that such variations of age, personnel, and the actual procedure, can have different fantasy elaborations and behavioral consequences.

CONCLUDING REMARKS

By elucidating the principles of Islamic teachings about family structure, including marriage and the relationship between parents and children, juxtaposed with the diverging philosophical schools of Islamic observance, I have attempted to inspire awareness as to the profound complexity of the interaction between religion and human practice. The perspective of this complexity is a lens that can be analogously applied to the appreciation of any religion and its culturally variable traditions. It can serve to humble us as clinicians to remain aware of our unconscious associations to the categorized beliefs of our patients and open to the unique way in which any belief structure will play out in our patients' lives. Psychopathology and, thus, the psychotherapeutic goal with any patient cannot be properly addressed without this kind of diligence in challenging our own fundamental assumptions about individuals and their families.

8

Islam, Sex, and Women

Shahrzad Siassi and Guilan Siassi

> He who spends his fortune to educate two daughters or sisters, paradise
> will be due to him by the grace of God.
>
> — Prophet Mohammad, cited in al-Amily 2005, 192

When thinking about Islam, it is not unlikely that the train of one's free associations should take an etymological turn, coming to rest on the word's literal meaning of submission. Moreover, as psychoanalysts with a legitimate
interest in the impact that religion has on the psyche of its followers, we cannot but notice the gendered valences of this term when considered alongside
the religion's most conspicuous symbol: the Muslim woman's veil. At one
level, Islam refers to the submission that goes hand-in-hand with faith in God,
his will, and his law. Taken in this sense, the meaning of Islam has much in
common with the doctrinal and spiritual tenets of the other two religions of
The Book, and most explicitly with Judaism (consider for instance, the centrality ascribed in both faiths to the story of Abraham's sacrifice). But on a
day-to-day basis, religious practice also entails obedience to regulatory and
prohibitory codes of social conduct, which, as Freud so perceptively noted,
both form the basis of civilization and inaugurate our psychic malaise. From
this perspective, Islam's meaning of submission also intimates the unconditional surrender of one's instinctual life to the law of God.

Insofar as it addresses this general need to subdue id impulses for the sake
of civilized social existence, Islam differs very little from other world religions. However, what is distinctive are the practices and attitudes to which
the religion has given rise in responding to this age-old problem and the new
forms taken by that historical response in the modern world, which are most

visible in the past several decades. In contrast to the moral codes of Christianity, for instance, Islamic law does not demand a renunciation or repression of the sexual and aggressive instincts, but rather prescribes their social regulation. Indeed, Islam's attitude toward sexuality would seem relatively open and accepting when compared to the largely antagonistic relationship to sexuality that for so many years characterized Christianity—one whose dynamics have not only been documented by psychoanalysts since the inception of our field, but have also become familiar in common parlance, for instance, as the phenomenon of "Catholic guilt." As opposed to Christianity's control of sexuality via guilt (for instance, through a preoccupation with original sin) and fear, spread through both official channels and popular culture (e.g., "fire and brimstone" sermons, the common myth that masturbation causes blindness, etc.), Islam does not forbid, but instead codifies, the expression of human sexual needs and desires.

Of course, it goes without saying that we do not intend to isolate Islam as a codified religion preoccupied only with the instinctual conduct of its followers. We draw this parallel not to essentialize the nature of religiosity but simply to highlight the relationship of Islam, in its social function, to the psychic domain of drives and desires. Seen in this light, Islam's frank dealing with sexuality could even be seen to carry relative advantages for psychic health, warding off a number of neurotic afflictions caused by the repression of sexual feelings.[1]

To the extent that Islamic law offers general guidelines for integrating the instincts into social and political life, or at least stipulates certain "legitimate" outlets for them, it is no more "radical" than Orthodox Judaism, which also imposes similar legal codes and disciplinary regimes, including veiling, on its followers. However, given the Jews' status as an oft-persecuted minority group living in exile for many centuries, it is not surprising that orthodox observance within the diaspora would weaken or that Jewish communities in Western Europe, in keeping with the region's increasing secularization from the enlightenment onward, would adhere less strictly to the letter of religious law. By contrast, the forms of Islam that are most commonly or at least most visibly practiced today continue to embrace such laws as veiling, fasting, daily prayer, and so on, just as they insist on codifying, thoroughly and systematically, the expressions of erotic desire.[2]

Insofar as Islamic law continues to be applied to various aspects of public and private life in this way, it intervenes far more actively in the psychic life of its average practitioner. Moreover, we find a rather excessive preoccupation with the laws governing sexuality and gender relations within various schools of Islamic jurisprudence today: groups whose zealotry no doubt serves the interests of autocratic state sponsors and supporters. While we do not deny the political motivations of such complicity, we are concerned here, first and foremost, with the psychological underpinnings of the attitudes that these fundamentalist forms of Islam have in common: namely, the fear of female sexuality and the hostility toward women in general who, because of their power to arouse sexual desire in men, are viewed suspiciously as a disruptive force—a potential threat to the social order that must be, often violently, controlled and subdued.

When the social regulatory function of any religion is manipulated to serve as a mechanism of mass control, not only is its ability to serve individual spiritual needs diminished, but this perversion of religiosity for political ends also has serious consequences for individual psychic life. In the case of Islam today, the privileging of sociopolitical aims of the religion at the expense of personal spirituality can have a significant impact on male-female sexual dynamics in general, and on Muslim men's attitudes toward women in particular.

SUBMISSION

In this chapter, the subject matter is Islam as observed through a psychoanalytic lens and, in particular, the Islamic practices either enshrined in or traditionally justified by the *Shari'a*,[3] which generate an exaggerated unevenness of gender relations and an unjustified hostility toward women in general. A caveat is in order: as the root causes of current practices are beyond the scope of this chapter, the reader is referred to secondary sources for information in this regard beyond the brief speculations or passing comments made here. We are concerned first and foremost with the psychological dimensions of religious belief and practice: namely, the psychological ramifications of Islam's institutional regulation of sexual life and the implications of religious discourse in shaping the self-image, mental representations, and object relations of male and female Muslims.

Although all three religions reflect and endorse a strongly patriarchal social order, Islam's emphasis on submission seems to translate more readily into expectations of female subordination. Sabbah (1984) makes this connection explicit in noting that "the ideal of female beauty in Islam is obedience, silence, and immobility. . . . In fact, these three attributes of female beauty are the three qualities of the believer vis-à-vis God. . . . The female condition and the male condition are not different in the end to which they are directed, but in the pole around which they orbit" (p. 118). Islamic discourse and the extreme interpretations of female submission to which it lends itself thus has unique consequences for the instinctual life of Muslim men and women. However, insofar as instinctual urges are mediated through religious law, the call for submission that lies at the heart of Islam must be understood as an imperative grounded in something more than the guilt feelings that give rise to superego demands. Rather, "submission" in this sense must be understood as a libidinal structure that implicates and determines an entire system of social relations.

Our contention is that a literal and rigid interpretation of submission within Islam, along with the *Shari'a's* extensive codification and regulation of the sexual instinct, have given rise to a great antagonism within the instinctual lives of Muslim men, shaping their sexual relations on the basis of mistrust and inducing an unconscious fear of women as instigators of their illicit desires, which consequently render the latter as objects of fear and subjects of control. Interestingly, this denunciation within doctrinal practice of the potentially "toxic" effects of female sexuality has been reversed among non-orthodox Islamic poets, who instead associate feminine beauty with the "intoxicating" power of divine love. That is, erotic desire for the beloved is seen to be not only consistent with, but even exemplary of, the sublime desire for union with God; accordingly, the power of this figure to unhinge a man from his corporal equilibrium and ordinary state of consciousness is not shunned, but rather embraced.

There is, then, a stark contrast between Islamic practices emanating from the premise that "heterosexual love is dangerous to Allah's order" (Mernissi 1987, 19) and culminating in an unconscious fear of women (a fear camouflaged by a misogynistic religious discourse and a fastidious concern with sexually oriented doctrinal minutiae), and the Sufi poetic mindset, which introduces a refreshingly friendly attitude toward sexuality and a romantic adulation of women as sources of inspiration and healthy desire. It is the two sides of this ambivalent relationship to women, reflecting two extremes of Koranic exegesis, which this chapter will explore.

MULLAHS AND MYSTICS

There is no denying that as Islam rose and spread through Arabia and the Near East from the seventh century onward, it affiliated itself with and was shaped by the existing androcentric customs and traditions of other ethnic and religious groups in the region.[4] Likewise, from the earliest years of its institutionalization, Islamic discourse was subject to variant interpretations, some emphasizing the ethical and spiritual dimensions of Mohammad's teachings and the egalitarian social principles he promoted, and others insisting on the utilitarian function of the religion as a principle of social organization and control. As Leila Ahmed (1992) explains, these two competing perspectives correspond to "two competing understandings of gender, one expressed in the pragmatic regulations for society . . . the other in the articulation of an ethical vision" (pp. 65–66). However, these divergent modes of interpreting the scriptural writings on gender specificity and difference also reflect very different strategic views on how to integrate the libido into social life. A brief historical overview of these exegetical tendencies and the tension between their respective approaches to this problem will help us to better understand how Islamic discourse gives rise to such a great ambivalence toward female sexuality in general.

Ahmed (1992) holds that the women of pre-Islamic Arabia participated more actively in social life and enjoyed a greater degree of sexual autonomy and self-determination than they did under Islam, particularly when it came to matters of marriage and personal wealth. With Islam, there arose a different relationship between the sexes modeled on that of neighboring urban city-states whose hierarchical class system gave rise to an institutionalized, codified, and state-supported patriarchal order that aimed to "guarantee the paternity of property heirs [by] vesting in men the control of female sexuality" (p. 12). Thus, as the normative practices of the pre-Islamic, or *jahaliya* period—when the woman and her tribe had a legitimate claim to her sexuality and offspring—were replaced by a new socioreligious order that viewed marriage as "a proprietary male right" (Ahmed 1992, 62), relations between the sexes also became inscribed in a new cultural paradigm: men now had the right and, indeed, the religious sanction to control women by way of various strategies, but most importantly, as Mernissi (1987) has astutely observed, through the delimitation and regulation of sexual space, of which veiling and harem seclusion are the most obvious examples.

Mernissi (1987) rightly points out that the source of sexual inequality in Islamic societies is not to be found in some notion of female inferiority propagated by the religion, but rather in its affirmation of the "potential equality of the sexes" and in a prevailing social assumption that "women are powerful and dangerous beings" (p. 42). From this perspective, both the universal Islamic sexual institutions Mernissi describes (such as polygamy, segregation, repudiation), as well as region-specific practices implemented, justified, and upheld in the name of Islam (such as female circumcision in Egypt and the Sudan, honor killings in Jordan, and temporary marriage in Iran), can be understood as strategies for the containment of female power.

One would be hard-pressed to find any religion whose general ethical guidelines and spiritual ideals could be readily translated into socially viable (let alone appealing) doctrinal or legal forms. An orthodoxy fashioned not on

a strict adherence to the letter of the holy text, but rather on a selective interpretation aligned with existing hegemonic structures, has historically proven
to be far more politically expedient. However, as long as there have existed
governmental bodies, from the medieval caliphates to modern nation-states,
claiming to rule according to the spirit of Islam, there have also been dis-
senting voices challenging their "orthodox" interpretations. One place where
these voices of opposition have found a home is in Sufi poetry.

The history of the rise of mystic poetry in Islamic lands would itself be a
worthwhile sociopsychological study. Most fully developed as a religiocultural phenomenon in Iran and finding its fullest elaboration in lyric poetry
written in the Persian language, Sufism (Islamic mysticism) was tied to a
mixture of popular but hardly orthodox religious practices, some elements of
which were appropriated and selectively adapted to what would become
Shi'ism (Babayan 1994), the branch of Islam that is now the official religion
of Iran. Despite its origins in a blend of local myth, legend, and folk religious
activity, Shi'ism eventually, of political necessity, became an orthodoxy in
its own right, with all the inflexibility, impersonality, and doctrinal rigidity
of any such system of belief. Sufism, however, always remained marginal to
the ordained religion, embracing a symbolic rather than a literal reading of
the *Koran*, which often entailed a critique of orthodox religious practices that
was expressed through the double meaning of poetic language. The Sufis,
then, were and continue to be nonconformists and free-thinkers who reject
the distance that the institutional religion creates between the Creator and the
human individual.

Islamic mysticism, then, can be seen as the spiritual arm of doctrinaire religious practice, which not surprisingly softens the religiosity of its adherents
and sympathizers. Sufi poetry, in accordance with this more humanized approach to spirituality and religious observance, aims above all to illuminate
the path to truth rather than to just enumerate the mandates to live by. This
poetry, replete with sensual images of women contrasts sharply to the adversarial relationship with instinctual life embedded in the orthodox excesses
characterized by gender splitting, gender hegemony, and rigid gender identities on the basis of seclusion and exclusion. Recontextualizing the instinctual
life in a loving relationship to a sort of feminine incarnation of God on earth,
the Sufis recast the doctrinaire discourse on raw sexuality as a relation of desire and longing for union with the beloved. Through an idealization of feminine beauty, as well as an exaltation of the beloved's power to bring out the
most sublime emotions in man, the Sufis provide a humanistic twist to the orthodox discourse and present a less prohibitory, disciplinarian conception of
God: a God for whom the realms of sensuality and spirituality are not mutually exclusive, but rather intertwined.

THE NEGATIVE SIDE OF AMBIVALENCE

The literal understanding of submission among Islamic fundamentalists has been used not only to justify female subordination and segregation within the patriarchal hierarchy, but also has given rise to an antagonism toward sexuality in general. Such religious attitudes have been conducive to a view of sexuality and libidinal pleasure as raw instinct,[5] excluded from the social sphere and viewed in isolation from any context of intersubjective relationality. The famous eleventh-century theologian al-Ghazali, whose influential writings shaped and legitimated in the name of "orthodoxy" what would become the normative views and practices of sexuality in many Islamic societies, presents sexual union as a purely biological, even mechanical process. His horticultural metaphor for copulation (whereby the man implants his seed in the woman for cultivation) suggests an encounter devoid of intimacy or emotional investment and entered into with minimal discrimination in the choice of partners: any woman's "field," it would seem, is as good as another's. In fact, al-Ghazali even denounces those men who would be so "mad" as to fall in love and to desire one woman only: "It is to ignore completely why copulation was created. It is to sink to the level of beasts as far as domination and mastery of oneself go. Because a man passionately in love does not look for the mere desire to copulate, which is already the ugliest of all desires and of which one should be ashamed, but he goes as far as to believe that this appetite cannot be satisfied except with a specific object (quoted in Mernissi 1987, 110).

The key words in the above quote are "domination" and "mastery of oneself." Ghazali's description of sexuality as a purely biological function defends against man's susceptibility to female seduction. Falling prey to a woman by falling in love with her is to voluntarily assume the status of a beast in relation to man. The ironic subtext of this analogy, however, is that before beasts were brutally tamed and domesticated, they did indeed have powers that far exceeded man's. When we extend this analogy to women, it becomes clear that the place from which their hidden, suppressed, "bestial" powers arise is, in fact, their sexuality. Indeed, al-Ghazali attributes to women an almost phallic power of sexuality in his description of fertilization as dependant on both the male and the female "sperm" and in his discussions of the harmfulness of withdrawing from a woman before she has attained her "ejaculation" (Mernissi 1987, 37–38). Moreover, he depicts a sexually frustrated woman as one of the gravest threats to the social order, an uncontrollable and disruptive force that must be defended against at all costs.

Exploring how such attitudes find expression in cultural discourse, Fatna Sabbah (1984) has conducted some interesting research on Arabic erotic literature, drawing attention to its representation of woman (who has all but been reduced to her sexual organ) as a creature devoid of consciousness who can never be sexually satiated (p. 24). In these tales,[6] we are constantly made aware of the inadequacy of the man's penis for the woman's vagina. For instance, in a popular fifteenth-century text that is still widely available and sold cheaply in Arabic cities, we find the following assertion: "Certain wise men hold that the sperm of the ass always outnumber those of man. In the case of a woman who has copulated with a hundred men and one ass, it is the ass which prevails" (quoted in Sabbah 1984, 30). A number of comical, even farcical tales in this corpus depict how the voracious woman, never satisfied with an ordinary-sized phallus, resorts to bestiality as a final recourse to sexual satisfaction. Each time, there emerges a triangular situation where a subhuman creature with superhuman sexual capacities "seduces" or is pursued by a women while the ordinary man is left in the lurch. As Sabbah aptly puts it, "Every time that man is placed in competition with an ass, he loses out" (p. 30).

The preoccupation with such themes in these fictional tales suggests a certain anxiety of men vis-à-vis the carnal appetites of women which can be seen in popular legends going as far back as the *The Thousand and One Nights* (Haddawy 1990).[7] It would seem from these tales that a mere display of virility is not enough to spare a man from a woman's rejection; in order to please her, he must possess a superhuman capacity to satisfy the nymphomaniac's omnisexual, devouring appetite. We could speculate that such stories, with their low-brow humor, serve a similar function as jokes in externalizing elements of the unconscious. Not only do they allow their authors to project and vicariously enact their paranoid fantasies on the page, but they also strike chords in the psyche of readers who have consumed this erotic literature over the centuries. Similar and shared plot elements point to at least one unconscious source for these fantastic tales of sex-crazed harpies: a deep-seated fear of humiliation and narcissistic injury at the hands of an uncontrollable woman who chooses an indisputably inferior rival to be the object of her attentions.

It is in light of the unconscious meanings embedded in such stories that we can understand the exaggerated contention, often voiced by Muslim men, that the unveiling of women, or any other transgression of the orthodox sexual order, would give rise to *fitna*, a dissolution of the entire social fabric:[8] that is, the explicitly voiced fear of anarchy masks an implicit fear of symbolic castration and Oedipal defeat.[9] As Deutsch (1933) has argued, sexual inhibition, in men and women alike, takes its origins in the castration complex. When the sexual instinct is directed at a woman who cannot be possessed, the fear of castration and emasculation is amplified, just as the force with which one's sexuality is suppressed increases.

Consequently, sexuality becomes subject to copious restrictions and shame-evoking attitudes. Caught in a seemingly no-win situation, man tries to avoid emasculation by suppressing the very same instinct that in the collective imaginary is equated with manhood and power. This perpetual danger of losing one's potency and having to compensate by inhibiting one's sexuality would seem to put the Muslim man between the devil and the deep blue sea. However, all theses dangers are lifted once the fear of the sexual instinct and the responsibility for its control are displaced onto women. In this way, men are spared from the potential fate of self-castration triggered by extreme sexual inhibition and loss of control and are simultaneously protected against rejection and engulfment by the insatiable woman.

In addition, Islamic law sanctions means by which the relationship of man to his sexuality does not have to be one of constant deprivation. The analization of Muslim men's sexuality as a curse in the public sphere is thus checked by the possibility for its gratuitous, uninhibited expression in the domestic sphere (harems, polygamy, temporary marriage, etc.). Consequently, while the presence of sexuality as a force to be reckoned with is forcibly suppressed and disavowed in the public sphere, in the private sphere, there are practically no bounds and no inhibitions restricting the expression of the sexual instincts.

However, it is hard to see how such provisions would not exacerbate the man's already ambivalent relationship to the sexual instinct as they encourage a jerky shifting between bipolar extremes: Anna Freud's (1936) juxtaposition of the asceticism of religious fanatics to that of adolescents offers some insight into how an individual negotiates, psychologically, between these contradictory attitudes. She maintains that because a continuous, indiscriminate state of instinctual deprivation would eventually result in a complete paralysis of vital activities; recovery through such excessive indulgences become necessary. Thus, alternation between ascetic deprivation on one hand and indulgent excesses on the other tempers the antagonism of the ego toward the instincts so as to relieve pressure and restore a precarious psychic balance.

The inhibition of romantic intimacy and the segregation of gender roles further destabilizes this uneasy equilibrium as it strips sexuality of any relational quality, a sine qua non for the humanization of sexuality as desire. In some ways, the literal treatment of instinctual life appears to be conducive to a paranoid schizoid position fraught with regressive distortions that affect the self and other representations. Accordingly, this mindset precludes any sort of benevolence vis-à-vis the sexual impulses and replaces it with a fear of the raw sexual instinct as a dangerous enemy, a fear projected onto woman as a potential seductresses who must be desexualized by being rendered invisible in the public sphere.

The locus of control is thus shifted from the self, the Muslim man, to the other, the Muslim woman, who, for the sake of an expedient adaptation (Ghent 1990), in turn, accepts this projection of fear and begins to perceive her own femininity as something dangerous that needs to be hidden behind the veil. Through this projection of the Muslim man's fear onto women and the woman's identification with it, the control and the taming of male sexuality is no longer his responsibility but becomes a challenge for both men and women. Thus, personal responsibility in terms of ownership of one's instinctual life, as well as acknowledgment of the centrality of emotions and affects in one's interpersonal life, are denied and any quest to free the "emotional self" (Symington 2004) is blocked.

Onto the figure of woman is projected not only the man's fear of his instincts, but also his shame vis-à-vis sexual hunger. This situation forces her to perform a mental acrobatics of sorts, by which she is perpetually trying to disprove that she is the instigator of the lust projected onto her. The outcome, as the following quote from the sociologist Nilufer Gole (2001) demonstrates, is that she is the one who has to justify a certain image of herself in the society and most importantly in relationship to herself: "The veiling is not only just covering the head; it indicates a way of behavior, which is called to be more modest, more pure—Puritan maybe—which means you limit your presence in public life. For instance, the way you look at people. You have to cast down the eyes. The way your body occupies the space in public. That means you shouldn't be too loud—laughing, for instance. So, it means a way of behaving, more modest behavior. It comes from *hija* [*hiya*], meaning being more cautious, being more modest."

In the above quote, we see how the Islamic expectation of women to communicate through a shy demeanor requires a self-imposed exclusion from the world of sexuality, a disavowal of their existence as desiring individuals and of the power of their banned sexuality. Dimen's (1991) observation of the difference, and not essence, at the core of gender (that is, how one is gendered through absorption of the contrast between male and female) is well illustrated by this delineation of gender role differences in Islam. Gender is covertly constructed (Scott 1988) on the basis of mutually exclusive role expectations that give rise not only to a cultural split between the genders, but also to a psychological rift within oneself. The ensuing cultural, interpersonal, and intrapsychic ramifications of this mode of conceptualization are far-reaching.

Since in reality, the woman is no longer an asexual child, she has to endure the psychological gymnastics of perpetually denying her physical and psychological experience of desire and desirability: because, in her self-representations, she is a time-bomb of sexuality that has to be monitored through invisibility and untouchability, it is she who feels herself responsible and culpable for triggering the shameful impulses of men, and it is she who bears the onus of reassuring them. Her ever-present sexuality becomes a danger to morality and the social order unless she suppresses and eventually represses any acknowledgment of it.

IMPACT ON WOMEN

The potential repercussions of this mindset are worth some speculation. It is not farfetched to hypothesize that a compromised relationship with one's body/self will result in all kinds of phobic avoidances, that the prohibition of any normal enjoyment of one's body, and the aversion toward any form of eroticism can take on pathological forms, such as unwillingness to touch one's body even for hygienic purposes (Mernissi 1987). Within this orthodox perspective and its puritanical regime that leaves no room for woman's sexuality as a reality to be reckoned with, frigidity would seem preferable to *fitna* (chaos), the perceived inevitable consequence of expressing desires publicly or admitting intimacy into sexual relations.

We can also imagine the extent to which such erotic impoverishment would compromise maternal aptitude (Deutsch 1933), feeding into the vicious circle of man's fear of women—that is, sons of mothers lacking the "soothing erotic touch" (Eleanor Galenson, personal communication, April 2003) would be more inclined to perpetuate the cycle of generational gender hostility. And yet, as Mernissi (1987) has pointed out, the mother-son relationship in Muslim societies is as highly valorized as the conjugal bond is deemphasized: a man is expected to be unfailingly loyal to his mother, who is "the only woman [he] is allowed to love at all" (p. 121). This expectation of gratitude is internalized by the man as a duty not only to open his house to his widowed or deserted mother when he gets married, but also to bestow on her absolute control over that household. The resulting competition and antagonism between the young wife and her mother-in-law consequently becomes one of the greatest obstacles to conjugal intimacy.

Stereotypes depicting the despised mother-in-law as a harsh, vicious, and abusive character abound in popular culture. We find a striking cinematic representation of this tyrannical figure in the film *Inch' Allah Dimanche* (2001, directed by Y. Benguigui), the story of a young wife who leaves Algeria with her three children and mother-in-law to rejoin her husband in France, where he had been recruited to work ten years earlier. The grandmother's power over the domestic sphere, which she guards jealously, is symbolized by her possession of the kitchen cabinet keys. Throughout the film, we observe her great hostility toward the daughter-in-law, at whom she does not cease hurling malicious insults for alleged domestic inadequacies. Moreover, the elderly figure acts as a sort of externalized socioreligious conscience, conveying, in a grating, accusatory tone of voice, all the shame-inducing taboos placed on the young woman's sexuality. For instance, in one scene in which the wife gets into a physical scuffle with her xenophobic next-door neighbor in the front yard, the mother-in-law does not rebuke her for having attacked the other woman, but for having exposed her hair and legs during the fight!

We find a similarly phallic image of the aging Muslim women in the semi-autobiographical novel *Fantasia: An Algerian Cavalcade*, by the well-known Algerian writer Assia Djebar (1985), who describes the terrifying presence of a senile old woman who lived with the family of her best friend: "Sometimes the youngest sister and I venture as far as the doorway, petrified by the sound of her cracked voice, now moaning, now uttering vague accusations. . . . The presence of this ancient, with one foot already in the grave, ensures that the other women of the household never miss one of their daily prayers" (pp. 9–10). Such representations both suggest the long-term impact of sexual repression and demonstrate the way that the negative attitudes toward female sexuality are transmitted among women themselves. Whether depicted as a rancorous shrew or a demented hag, the postmenopausal Muslim woman embodies the cumulative detrimental effects of disavowed sexuality. Having renounced the last vestiges of her femininity, she becomes an ominous presence haunting the lives of younger women. The elderly woman, who has internalized the Islamic/patriarchal laws regarding female sexual decorum by provoking fear and shame among women who are in their sexual prime, reinforces those prohibitions and thus ensures their transgenerational perpetuation.

Negative cultural and religious attitudes toward female sexuality also have a significant impact on the psychic lives of Muslim men, as can be seen in their often violent response to the sexual transgressions of women. Nowhere is the regressed aspect of Muslim man's struggle with his masculinity better demonstrated than in the culturally condoned practice of honor killing in certain Arab countries, like Jordan. This form of revenge is unique from the honor killings that take place among other ethnic groups (e.g., Albanians, Sicilians) because it is directed at the object of desire, the woman, rather than the rival. On a social level, the cultural endorsement is such that even a rumor, justified or not, provides the license to kill as the only way to wash the family's disgrace. As Faqir (2005) points out, attaching such great significance to the sexual reputation of women is one method of keeping them subordinate and policing them. On a psychological level, we could see this mode of control to operate like a childhood solution applied to an adult adaptational difficulty: one which can only result in the aggravation of a man's fear and rage when he finds that his attempts at control have failed. Consequently, instead of a psychological solution, the culture provides a concrete, social remedy—the act of violence, with its power to magically erase shame—for the failure of these regressive repetitions. Nevertheless, this external "solution" applied to an intrapsychic problem ultimately fails to allow the Muslim man to master the narcissistic dimension of his Oedipal conflict.

Moreover, inasmuch as the culture does not expect the man to face the actual Oedipal triangle by confronting the rival, it reinforces his position within a dyadic merger with the feared object. In this regressed narcissistic drama with its phobia of triangulation, the villain to be eliminated is always the feared woman whose control is lost. The call for her elimination stands irrespective of whether she is guilty of willful adultery or whether she is the victim of a rape. This latter irrelevancy of the woman's guilt to the final punishment exposes a mindset that defines honor and pride outside the Oedipal triangle and on the basis of a dyadic omnipotent control. Regardless of her actual actions, the woman is felt to have betrayed the man, simply because she has failed in her assigned/implanted psychological function of safeguarding his self-worth. This leads us to wonder whether honor killing is about upholding virtuous values in the society or about perpetuating a regressed social order in which Muslim men can address the narcissistic dimension of a disavowed Oedipal conflict outside of triangulation. In any case, the practice seems to reinforce the man in his position of dogged watchfulness and exacerbate his paranoid mistrust of women.

In summary, we find that in this archaic mode of perceiving and relating to woman, whose religiously sanctioned social role is defined by a literal translation of submission, acquires central importance in the psychic functioning of the man. First, she is empowered as the keeper of his sexual impulses and as the party responsible for obviating the triangulation of desire and containing his shame. Her subordination as possessed object in the dyadic merger becomes a crucial strategy to quell the man's anxiety over defeat at the hands of an omnipotent, hypervirile rival. A relationship of mistrust and suspicion subsequently takes shape as the man both depends on the woman to protect and validate his self-esteem, and yet fears her potential failure to fulfill those functions.

THE POSITIVE SIDE OF AMBIVALENCE

In contrast to the orthodox practitioners and champions of Islam, Islamic mystics and pantheistic thinkers bring the emotional dimension of human relationality and erotic life to the fore of the religion. These nonorthodox Muslims pay little heed to the concrete directives and codified mandates for behavior that are given so much attention in the official Islamic discourses. Unlike the traditional disciplinarian attitudes, their religious perspective is one that reduces the antagonism between body (instinctual drives emanating from the id) and mind (ego/superego, or self-consciousness/social conscience). A closer look at the poetry of one such free-thinking Muslim, the famous fourteenth-century Persian poet, Hafez (1320–1389), will reveal how another interpretation of Islam as spiritual surrender can indeed embrace sensuality as a precondition for the experience of closeness with God. His lyric poems, which draw heavily on religious symbolism and engage many of the spiritual tenets of Sufism, articulate the idea that an affective investment in earthly relations opens one up to the ecstatic experience of divine love. This more broad-minded Islamic perspective thus conveys a radically different sense of relationship to God in which the feminine or feminized other becomes the key to spiritual fulfillment.[10]

The moderate Islamic viewpoint expressed in Hafez's poetry shifts the interpretive emphasis of Islam from an attitude of submission to an ideal of surrender. While both terms encompass an idea of self-renunciation, submission tends to translate into a practice of sacrificing of one's wishes in order to appease the other and often results in a certain resignation and stagnation of the self, whereas surrender has as its goal a joyful *liberation* of oneself through union and dissolution of the ego. While orthodox Islamic discourse presents us with a remote, distant God whose mercy must be sought through strict piousness and submission, Hafez's poetry conveys the fundamental Sufi principle that God lies within oneself. In the words of Grotstein (2004), "God is no longer an object but a subject with whom one attempts to be not in identification but in a transient dissolution of self" (p. 86). And, like many Muslim mystics, Hafez believes that one can tap into the divine love within and thus attain this authentic experience of self in union with God only by entering into a platonic relationship of love with a human other: the beloved.

While the beloved's gender often remains ambiguous in Sufi poetry, and particularly in the Persian Sufi poetry that will be discussed here (all Persian nouns are gender-neutral and the language has only one third-person pronoun that could mean either "he" or "she" in any given context), the effeminate features of this figure cannot be denied. While we do not disregard ongoing debates about whether this character should be interpreted as an actual human love interest (the object of hetero or homoerotic longing) or as an allegorical symbol of a purely platonic love (one which, by definition could never be consummated), in this chapter, we will refer to the beloved as a "she." In doing so, we seek only to underscore the prevalence of feminine attributes ascribed to this Sufi ideal and to contrast this view of the feminine with the orthodox one: namely, whereas the latter discourse presents the female body as a dehumanized receptacle of the male seed, the Sufi paradigm feminizes the body of the beloved so as to inscribe it with sublime potentiality, presenting it as the aim of an erotic desire that gives meaning to life and connects the human realm with the divine.

Hence, austere reverence toward God is replaced by a kind of friendship with God, who is transformed from a distant figure demanding obedience and servitude (the projected harsh superego) into the awe-inspiring beauty and alluring presence of the beloved. The following verses, engraved on Hafez's tomb, capture his burning desire for this effeminate and interweave references to both earthly and divine union:

Where are the tidings of union with you? That I may arise from the inner depths
   of my soul,
Aloft in the heavens, I rise from the snares of the world.
Should you call me slave in your domain,
I would renounce my position as master of this earthly realm.
O God, send down rain from the cloud of guidance,
Before I disappear like dust from here.
Sit at the foot of my grave with wine and music
So that your scent should bring me out dancing from my coffin.
Rise up and show yourself oh you sweet-moving idol
So I should rise up with upraised arms from this world and earthly life.
Though I be old, pull me tightly into your nightly embrace,
So that when dawn comes I should awaken, young again, by your side

—Hafez 1345, 33[11]

These verses are as much about celebrating the rejuvenating power of the other's embrace as it is about the yearning for spiritual union. The life-exuding, youth-promoting embrace of the beloved harkens back to the maternal presence, which is passionately longed for as the revitalizing source of absolute connectedness with one's world. Indeed, from a psychological perspective, the gnostic longing for union with God could be seen as a yearning to return to the crucible of that mother-infant relationship. From a more materialistic and plebian standpoint, one could read this longing for oneness, as well as its corresponding notion of surrender, in terms of the quite literal, physical union of lovers that reproduces a momentary loss of self in the other at the moment of orgasm.

In any case, one seeks a dissolution of the ego that would result in the kind of "oceanic feeling" of oneness with the world that Freud (1930) so astutely deconstructed in his *Civilization and its Discontents*. Such a religious attitude, as opposed to the puritanical socioreligious views, contextualizes the instincts and bodily drives in the domain of affects and emotions and humanizes sexuality/sensuality as an experience of interpersonal desire. The primordial model of sexual union as a purely biological need is elevated to a paradigm of transcendent desire. It is as though the poet intimates how the sexual drives can lend themselves to sublimation, how the power of sensuality can be channeled into creative outlets that bring one closer to the ultimate creator himself.

In the following poem, one observes the poet's progression from a celebration of the beloved's irresistible sensuality to a denouncement of the asceticism and acts of penitence falsely practiced in the name of God:

> Hair disheveled, cheeks flushed, she bore a smile on her lips and was drunk;
> Her shirt torn, chanting a lyric, a carafe in her hand.
> With a frenzied look in her eyes, and the power of enthrallment on her lips
> She came late last night to my bedside and sat.
> She brought her head close to my ear, and with a sad voice
> Complained, oh my long-time lover, how could you be sleeping?
> The lover to whom is given such an intoxicating night cap,
> Would be a blasphemer of love indeed if he did not worship that wine.
> Go away you righteous ones, and don't admonish the wine-makers,
> Because from the first day of creation, we were given nothing but this gift.
> Whatever He poured into our goblets we drank,
> Whether it came from the winery of heaven or from the inebriating cup.
> The laughter of the wine-cup and the tangled locks of that Beauty,
> All this makes repentance seem pointless, as it breaks Hafez away from his
>   penance."

—Hafez 1345, 1–2

The bold and overpowering eroticism of these verses is astonishing. Hafez' symbolic use of wine and his unabashed adulation of the beloved here is in direct opposition opposed to the prohibition of alcohol in the Shari'a and to the orthodox abhorrence of feminine power. These seemingly profane comments, coming from the pen of a poet who earned his title of Hafez, "The Keeper," for his ability to recite the entire *Koran* by heart, cannot be attributed to any ignorance of Islamic doctrine. Rather, they reflect the poet's informed decision to emphasize religious principles that cannot be accessed through a blind adherence to the law and his focus on pursuing the path of truth and revelation (*tarighat*), rather than on following the mandates of the Shari'a.

While some commentators argue that all imagery of forbidden pleasures in Hafez's poetry (wine, dancing, unveiling, loving) should be read allegorically for their religious meaning rather than literally a sign of earthly "debauchery," one could hardly deny the unmistakable allusion to sensual love in this provocative scene. We find here a poet who is enticed by the worldly beauty and carefree playfulness of the beloved, who does not hesitate to seduce the poet and demand love by awakening him in the middle of the night. There is an easy flow of role responsiveness between the two lovers, an absence of puritanical gender differentiation or active/passive role assignment in the expressed sensuality. This dramatic tableau of unguarded sensuality between two lovers is presented in counterpoint to the abstinence of the "righteous one" who preaches virtue and refrains from seeking and surrendering himself to such love. In this way, ascetiscism is explicitly renounced and denounced, while feminine beauty is exalted. And indeed, this beauty is meant to be provocatively exposed and *not* veiled.

Hafez thus advocates and rejoices in an uncensored, unveiled expression of love and feminine beauty—even if this beauty is such as to make a slave of man. In light of this reversal of traditional gender roles and hierarchies, it is not surprising that the more literal readings of Hafez's poetry have been suppressed and the critics have passionately denied all but a purely allegorical (i.e., religious) meaning of such verses: indeed, for a man to willingly accept such treatment from a woman and to let her exert her power over him would be anathema to orthodox believers and upholders of tradition. Nonetheless, in keeping with the Sufi tradition, Hafez "shamelessly" depicts the beloved as occupying a position of superiority over the lover—a position of power from which she shuns his every attempt to get close to her, as we see in the following famous poem:

> If that Turk from Shiraz, should ever take my heart in hand,
> For her Hindu mole, I would renounce the wealth of Bukhara and Samarqand.
> Oh cup-bearer, pour us that leftover wine, since even in paradise one could not find
> The banks of the Roknabad and the rose gardens of Mosalla.
> Alas! These sweetly jesting and playful city-ravaging gypsies
> Like Turks plundering the spoils of war, have stolen patience from the heart.
> I have heard of Joseph's daily-increasing beauty,
> The love of which brought Zuleikhah out from behind her veil of chastity.
> The beauty of the Friend has no need for our imperfect love.
> What need has the beautiful face of adorning colors and painted lines?
> You spoke harsh words to me. I don't mind, you spoke well.
> A bitter answer suits those sugar-crunching ruby lips.
> Listen to these words of advice, my soul: happy are those youths
> who hold the councils of the sage above concerns for their soul.

Tell of minstrels and wine and seek less the secrets of the two worlds;
No one has and no one shall unravel that enigma through worldly wisdom.
You've recited a ghazal and threaded pearls, so sing it well, Hafez!
Because your verse is such that it will scatter the chain of the Pleiades.

—Hafez 1345, 203

The poet's humble surrender of his ego to the cruel Turkish beauty ultimately empowers him to string the pearls of his experience of love into a form that rivals the harmonious order of the cosmos. In other words, surrender to the beloved brings man closer to God because it inspires him and permits the sublimation of libidinal energies into the poetical production of meaning and other creative forms of cultural activity.

By presenting sensuality as God's gift and not his curse, Hafez's poetry suggests that the erotic drives should not be relegated to the private confines of one's home in an emotionally detached context of satisfying raw physiological needs, but rather, should be publicly celebrated in song. A positive, embracing attitude toward such sensual delights in an interpersonal context translates into the possibility for a transcendental spiritual experience of surrender. It is not human sexuality and female desirability that is sinful, but rather the antagonistic attitude of orthodox believers toward those God-given gifts and their harsh religious injunctions directed against them, which only deprive us of an essential means to attaining an authentic experience of love. The creative and philosophical writings of moderate Muslims, like Hafez, thus critique the reactionary stance upheld by those who insist on traditionalist readings of the *Koran*. These enlightened Muslims advocate instead an appreciation of earthly beauty and an openness to sensual rapture, which will not only foster an erotic relationship to the world and to human others within it, but will also allow one to attain the ultimate goal of mystical transcendence.

CONCLUDING REMARKS

At the heart of this discussion about the Islamic ambivalence toward women, represented by conservative religious practices on one hand and the sensual allusions made in poetry on the other, we have distinguished two modes of relating to God: submission and surrender. The nuanced distinction between these two modes defines not only man's relationship to God, but also his relationship to himself and to his sexual/aggressive instincts. Grotstein's (2004) distinction between institutionalized religion and private spirituality is relevant here. Like all organized religions, which inevitably operate on a more primitive level because their functioning is driven by political motives, Islam, as a patriarchal institution with its own political interests, demands a categorical submission on behalf of its followers. And yet, its strict codification of sexual life, with the strong division of what is acceptable in the public versus the private sphere, ultimately advances a regressed or, at best, artificial relationship with oneself and others. The institutional preoccupation with sexuality as a raw instinct gives rise to an "on-again/off-again" mode of extreme disavowal and excessive gratification and as such, thwarts the integration of instincts into the affective current and, thus, inhibits this hallmark of mature love relationships. Insofar as the orthodox discourse fails to promote sexual practices grounded in healthy human relationships of desire, the call for submission translates into a call to suppress not only sexuality, but also one's identity and self-awareness as an embodied subject.

If the road to submission, from an orthodox perspective, is paved with suppression of the instincts, the path of spiritual surrender embraced by the Muslim mystics and poets depends on an acceptance of those erotic drives. Such a loving orientation toward the sensual body offers a remedy to the joyless denial and atrophy of self that so often results from too strict an interpretation of Islam. However, we must admit that even the "positive" Islamic attitudes toward female sexuality articulated in the nonorthodox poetic tradition do not necessarily resolve the underlying problem of ambivalence toward the power of the feminine, and are hardly conducive to the development of a practical model for relating to women in everyday life. Neither perspective, insofar as it lacks a fluid notion of gender identity, promotes a balanced adaptation of the man to the female other, since both compromise agency by shifting the locus of control from the self (man) to the other (woman). However, the poetic ideal of the feminized beloved has a greater potential to mitigate this tendency, in that it emphasizes reciprocality rather than hierarchy by presenting the love relationship as the ultimate source of spiritual knowledge and human empowerment. In any case, both extremes of fear-induced misogyny versus idealistic adulation expressed by the two currents of Islamic exegesis reveal the ever-present centrality of woman as an object of desire and as a source of maternal comfort.

With this in mind and by way of conclusion, it would not be out of place to add a third axis to our dialectical conceptualization of Islam in terms of submission/surrender. This refer to the key attributes of beneficence, compassion, and mercy (invoked with the name of God at the beginning of the *Koran* and at the head of every chapter, as well as at the opening of every prayer) are *bismallah-e-al-rahman-al-rahim*, or "begin with the name of Allah, the Beneficent and the Merciful." Strikingly, the Arabic words (*al-rahman, al-rahim*) designating these qualities derive from the same root as the word for "womb" (*al-rahm*). Murata (1992) rightly points out that these essential names of God are, if not equal, then second only to the all-inclusive name of *Allah*. This more feminized or "matriarchal" description of divine power suggests a gentleness and receptivity of God that act as yin to the yang of his activity, which is emphasized in the "patriarchal" view (Murata 1992, 208). Aligning these observations with those we have set out in this chapter, it would appear that Islamic beliefs and practices in the modern world acquire their distinctive form and color by privileging one or the other of such key terms as submission, surrender, mercy—or indeed, by striking a delicate balance between them. But, it still remains to be seen how believers will fare as they struggle toward the goal of overcoming conflict and living a virtuous (but not necessarily balanced) life and how successfully Islam can forge their path to that proverbial Rome.

9

Sufi Perspective on Human Suffering and Its Relief

Mohammad Shafii

Do not take a step on the path of love without a guide, I tried it one hundred times failed.

—Hafiz, 1389, cited in Ghazvini and Ghani, 1941, p. 71

The West is gradually recognizing that the East has used effective psychotherapeutic techniques in dealing with human suffering for thousands of years. Comparative study of Western psychotherapeutic techniques with Eastern "psychomystical" practices can further our knowledge of human development, health, and integration. In this chapter, the Sufis' concept of emotional and spiritual suffering and their methods of all alleviating these sufferings and achieving human integration will be discussed and compared with the concepts of psychopathology and treatment methods in psychoanalysis and dynamic psychotherapy.

SEPARATION: SICKNESS OF THE MIND

According to the Sufis, human beings are separated from their origin in nature and from reality, truth, and God (*haqq*). They believe that emotional suffering originates from this separation (*firaq*). Jalal-uddin Rumi (1207–1273), the great Sufi poet, repeatedly voiced the human dilemma of separation from nature in his poetry and fables.

The intensity of the sickness of separation, including a possible remedy for it, is especially exemplified in Rumi's first story of the *Mathnawi*:

A King fell in love with a slave maiden. He bought the maiden, but before enjoying her company, she became sick, lost weight, looked pale, and each day

161

became weaker. The King consulted many physicians, and numerous remedies were prescribed to no avail. As time passed, the slave maiden came close to death. The King was in agony and despair. In the depths of hopelessness during a dream, the King heard a voice saying that a spiritual physician would arrive the next day to relieve the girl's misery.

The next day, a Sufi *pir* appeared in the court. The King knew at once that he was the physician revealed in the dream. The physician examined the maiden carefully and realized that he sickness was "of the heart and the mind," a sickness of separation and love.

The maiden would not reveal to the physician whom she loved. The physician through an ingenious method tried to uncover the identity of her beloved. While taking her pulse, he mentioned the names of all the provinces. The name of one of the provinces caused "her pulse to jump." Then he mentioned Samarqand and the maiden's pulse jumped again. Then he asked for someone who was quite familiar with the city of Samarqand and the people living there. After mentioning quarters, streets, and finally a particular household, it was discovered that the maiden was deeply in love with a certain goldsmith.

The physician felt the remedy for the girl's sickness was temporary reunion with her lover. They brought the goldsmith and the two enjoyed each other's union. Gradually the goldsmith was given "a poisonous draught." He became weak, lost his strength, charm, and finally the favor of the maiden. Later, the maiden and the King were reunited (Rumi 1925, vol. 1, 3–17).

In this story, the king symbolically represents the self of the seeker who is in search of a spiritual physician to uncover the reason for anxieties and sorrows and for guidance on the path of security and integration. Recognition of separation and fragmentation as the origins of all sickness of the mind and heart, and overcoming this separation through the fire of love and the intense relationship with the spiritual physician, are the first steps on the way to recovery, communion, and integration.

The maiden and the goldsmith symbolize the male and female aspects of nature that are hidden in all of us, and also reflect manifest phenomena of life, such as physical appearance and animal desires. The goldsmith symbolizes the temporal self and the animal *nafs*. Temporal love—which originates from animal desires—can be transformed through loss of self by the help of a spiritual physician into the permanent love of existential communion.

The king also represents the searching soul who is seeking relief and comfort from the anxieties of separation. The king, with all his power and gold, was not able to find comfort. Reunion and integration occurred with the help of a Sufi guide. Rumi himself insightfully concluded the story by saying that, in actuality, the king, the maiden, and the goldsmith are metaphors for various parts of the self at odds with each other. The integration of all these fragmented parts can occur through love and with the help of a *pir*. Sufis feel that God's life-giving breath bestows on human beings the potential for existential communion, the oneness of all with All. In human beings, maturity, and freedom may be achieved by completing the circle of evolution and returning to the origin, which is universal reality (God, *haqq*).

FORGETFULNESS AND IGNORANCE

Sufis feel that human beings have a tendency to forget their origin in nature in order to avoid the sadness and anxieties of separation. This forgetfulness (*ghaflat*) expresses itself in the form of forgetting, neglecting, heedlessness, and ignorance.

However, forgetfulness does not alleviate the anxieties of separation, but actually intensifies them. In the state of forgetfulness, the individual behaves like a wounded beast imprisoned in a cage. The beast does not know the source of its pain, the remedy for it, or the way to freedom. The beast hits itself against the cage, attacks the doctor and jailer alike, and eventually exhausts itself.

Forgetfulness results in *hijab*, meaning veiling, concealing, a partition, a curtain, and, specifically, ignorance. In Sufism, ignorance refers to the individual's psychospiritual blindness, lack of insight, preoccupation with pride, and self-conceit. Hujwiri, more than nine hundred years ago, pointedly entitled his book on Sufism, "The Uncovering of the Veils" (*Kashf Al-Mahjub*). He explored and described the ways of overcoming forgetfulness and ignorance on the Sufi Path. According to him, the only way one can overcome forgetfulness and ignorance is through awareness and knowledge of reality: "Knowledge is the life of the heart, which delivers it from the death of ignorance" (1967, 16–17). Abu Yazid of Bistam said: "I strove in the spiritual combat for thirty years, and I found nothing harder to me than knowledge and its pursuit" (1967, 18). Hujwiri, in discussing ignorance, wrote: "Man, enamoured of his gross environment, remains sunk in ignorance and apathy, making no attempt to cast off the veil that has fallen upon him. Blind to the beauty of oneness, he turns away from God to seek the vanities of this world and allows his appetites to domineer over his reason, notwithstanding that the animal soul . . . is the greatest of all veils between God and man" (1967, 9).

Indulgence in animal desires (*nafs*) and enslavement in habits are the core of ignorance and veiling. Al-Amuli, a Sufi *pir*, said: "Acquiescence in natural habits prevents a man from attaining to the exalted degrees of spirituality" (cited in Hujwiri 1967, 149).

SEPARATION SICKNESS IN SUFISM AND
SEPARATION ANXIETY IN PSYCHOANALYSIS

In classical psychoanalysis, emotional suffering and neurotic disorders were conceptualized as symptomatic expressions of repressed intrapsychic traumas and conflicts between id impulses and superego prohibitions. Fear of parental punishment and societal prohibitions, in the form of castration anxiety in the phallic-Oedipal stage psychosexual development, were the roots of emotional suffering and psychopathology. This theoretical position has been modified extensively during the last few decades with the advancements in ego psychology, child developmental studies, and attachment theory.

At the present time, attachment behaviors are perceived as essential for the survival. Bowlby (1958), inspired by the works of ethologists, suggested that attachment behaviors in human beings (sucking, clinging, following, crying, and smiling) are instinctual. In the infant six to twelve months of age, these behaviors are integrated in the form of an innate instinctual attachment toward mother beyond the need for satiation or sexual and aggressive drives of the id (Shafii and Shafii 1982, 15).

Disturbances in human attachment, disorders of mothering, and the experience of a loss of a loved one in early childhood contribute significantly to the development of chronic anxiety, depression, and, in severe cases, to narcissistic disturbances of personality, antisocial behavior, addiction, or even psychotic disturbances.

It appears that the Sufis, more than one thousand years ago, became aware of the anxieties of separation and their possible pathological influence on the self, not only within the context of the mother-child relationship, but also separation sickness from the animal, vegetative, and mineral parts of the self, other human beings, and, above all, universal reality.

Even within psychoanalysis, Fromm (1956) lucidly discussed man's separation from nature as the origin of anxieties: "[Man] . . . has emerged from the animal kingdom from instinctive adaptation . . . he has transcended nature— although he never leaves it; he is a part of it—and yet once torn away from nature, he cannot return to it; once thrown out of paradise—the state of original oneness with nature . . . . Man can only go forward by developing his reason, by finding a new harmony, a human one, instead of the prehuman harmony which is irretrievably lost" (p. 6).

According to Fromm, the development of reason brings with it a sense of awareness—awareness of the moment, the past, the future, the self and others. Awareness contributes to seeing the self as a separate entity. Separateness brings with it the possibility of choice and freedom. But at the same time, separateness makes one aware of being alone. Fromm's formulation concerning human beings' separateness from nature is similar to the Sufis' ideas of separation.

FORGETFULNESS AND IGNORANCE IN SUFISM VERSUS REPRESSION AND DENIAL IN PSYCHOANALYSIS

The concept of "forgetfulness" in Sufism is similar to the defense mechanisms of repression and denial in psychoanalysis. Repression is a psychological defense mechanism that consists of the expelling from conscious awareness of an idea or feeling that is painful and related to anxiety or guilt. Although some repression is necessary for daily adaptation, extensive repression contributes to the development of inhibition, neurotic tendencies, lack of curiosity, and ignorance.

One of the major goals of exploratory psychotherapy and psychoanalysis is helping the individual modify the defensive posture of repression through free associations in order to become aware of the origin of earlier traumatic experiences and anxieties that have been repressed and forgotten. In effect, both Sufis and psychoanalysts feel that extensive forgetfulness or repression may contribute to feelings of fragmentation, psychic suffering, and arrest in development.

Forgetfulness in Sufism has similarities to the defense mechanism of denial (i.e., the ego's avoidance of acknowledging painful aspects of reality). Extensive use of denial may contribute to the development of severe psychopathology and, even in limited amounts, the defense can lead to ignorance, dishonesty, and psychological insensitivity.

Ignorance and veiling in Sufism also have similarities to the concept of psychological blind spots in psychoanalysis, which refer to the individual's psychological unawareness of tendencies and shortcomings. In Sufism, being unaware of oneself is worse than being veiled from reality. Lings (1971) quoted a Sufi *pir* of the twentieth century, Shaykh Al-'Alawi: "The veiled are ranged in hierarchy: the veiled from his Lord, and the veiled from himself. And the veiled from himself is more heavily veiled than the veiled from his Lord" (p. 205).

The Sufis' concept of ignorance goes beyond the present concepts of repression, denial, and psychological blind spots in psychoanalysis. For instance, Nasafi, in the thirteenth century, regarding forgetfulness and ignorance, wrote: "[Most people] fall to the animal level of existence and never reach the human level because they are preoccupied in this world with the passions of consuming, sexual desires, and preoccupation with their offspring. From the beginning of life to the end of life all of their efforts are for these. They do not know anything else but these three things. . . . A few when they are freed from these fetishes become enslaved by three bigger fetishes. They pass these three veils, but become entangled by three larger veils. The three larger veils are preoccupation with physical appearance, possessions, and position" (1962, 228–29).

According to Nasafi, there are seven veils on the path of reality: worship of the self, passion of consumption, indulgence in sexual desires, preoccupation with offspring, preoccupation with appearance, preoccupation with possession, and love of position. These seven veils consume a person's life and contribute to the continuation of ignorance and forgetfulness (p. 230).

OVERCOMING THE SICKNESS WITH THE HELP OF *ISHQ*

Internal conflicts, such as the struggle between moral values and impulsive wishes, intellect and emotion, certainty and insecurity, and the conscious and unconscious, which are manifestations of the sickness of separation, can only be overcome through union of all internal and external forces.

Sufis believe that union is achieved by the intensive emotional involvement of the seeker with the Sufi *pir*, or "spiritual physician." The seeker totally devotes and surrenders the self to the *pir*. Intense love, *ishq*, is the essence of this relationship and its integrative energy.

"*Ishq*" is an Arabic word meaning intense and passionate attachment to a love object and dying for love. It does not have an English equivalent. The closest meaning of *ishq* in English would be intense love and devotion. The word "love," however, does not represent the totality, intensity, dynamism, and irrationally of *ishq*.

The word "*ishq*" originates from "*ashiqa.*" *Ashiqa* is the name of a type of vine that attaches itself to a tree. This vine grows on the tree, taking nourishment and sustenance from it. Eventually, the tree dies and loses itself to the vine (Valiuddin 1972, 1). The loss of self in the beloved through intense love (*ishq*) is the essential core of Sufism.

Sufis feel that intense love is dormant in all beings. When it is activated in human beings through psychological reawakening, it starts to grow. The fertile ground of intense love is the unconscious. Gradually, animal instincts, such as anger and passion, are transformed through the alchemy of intense love to an integrative energy for existential communion.

The Sufi's experience of *ishq* cannot be fully understood unless one becomes familiar with the concepts of *mihr* and *mahabbar*. "*Mihr*" is a Persian word encompassing a broad spectrum of related meanings—sun, light, matter, mother, love, and death. "*Mohabbat*" is an Arabic word meaning affection, and originates from the word "*hubb*," meaning seed. The Sufis believe that the rays of the sun of reality (God, *haqq*) manifests in the world of existence in the forms of love and light (*mihr*) and find concrete representation in human beings in the form of affection (*mohabbat*). Affection that exists in all of us is the dormant seed of *ishq* (intense love).

In Sufi thinking, the seed welcomes the pain and suffering of cold winter and the torment of spring. Finally, the seed loses its identity (dies) and becomes a new plant that flowers and bears seeds. By loss of the temporal self, the seed continues its permanent existence. Sufis call this process *mahabbat*. They feel strongly that the seed of growth and integration is dormant in each person in the form of intense love. Through psychological reawakening, and by the help and affection of a Sufi *pir*, the dormant seed of intense love germinates and unleashes the energy for final integration and existential communion. An individual, then, loses temporal individuality and becomes one with the existential cycle of life—transcending the self to become truly human.

ATTRIBUTES OF THE *PIR*

Pir is a Persian word meaning aged, old, or elder. In Sufism, *pir* means spiritual guide or physician of the soul.[1] The *pir* plays a significant role in the psychospiritual development of the disciple, seeker, or *myrid*. The attributes of a *pir* includes the following:

- *Pukhta* (maturity)—A Persian phrase beautifully describes the concept of *pir*. The *pir* is called *mard-i-pukhta-va-johan-didah-mard*, meaning man; *pukhta*, meaning cooked, ripe, mature; and *johan-didah*, meaning seeing or having seen the world and knowing mankind. A *pir*, then, is a seasoned and mature human being, who has traveled extensively both in the world and on the path of reality.
- *Sabr* (patience)—A *pir* spends years as a seeker while progressing through the various stages of human development on the Sufi path. Ibn 'Arabi, the Sufi saint of Andalusia, described an interaction with his Sufi *pir*: "One day, while we were walking together by the sea, he [my *pir*] asked me a question concerning God's saying, "I require no provision from them, nor do I need then to feed Me" [*Koran*, Sura 101:57]. I did not answer him, but left him. Four years later, I met him and told him that I had the answer to his question. He said, 'Let me have your answer, for after four years the time is ripe for it.' I then gave him my answer and marveled that he had remembered the verse" (1971, 119).

The question asked by the Sufi *pir* transcended the intellectual mean-ing of the Koranic verse. Although Ibn Arabi from a very young age had a reputation for understanding and interpreting verses from the *Koran*, he perceived his *pir*'s question on a deeper experiential and spiritual level. Ibn 'Arabi realized that he was not ready to comprehend or appreciate the meaning of the verse with his whole being. He knew that an imme-diate or impulsive response would be merely an intellectual exercise. He left his *pir* without saying a word, and patiently meditated upon the verse for four years. Through patience and continuous internal experience of the verse, Ibn 'Arabi became enlightened.

- *Total awareness of the disciple*—It is essential for the *pir* to be emptied of self-preoccupation in order to be in tune with the disciple's physical, psychological, and spiritual states. The *pir* becomes a mirror, not only for reflecting the beloved reality and the beauty of nature, but also for intu-itively perceiving the disciple's inward state and outward condition. Through psychospiritual communion beyond words, thoughts, time, space, and temporal reality, the *pir* helps the disciple become aware of the unconscious and universal reality.

They are in tune with each other verbally and nonverbally. Frequently, communication and revelations occur in both of them simultaneously, while they are meditating or during dreams. Instead of using words to communicate, the *pir* and the seeker are in psychological communion be-yond the limitations of time and space. Moreover, one does not become a *pir*—it is, itself, a sign of self-aggrandizement and a veil on the Path of Reality. A true Sufi *pir* does not claim to be a *pir*.

- *Freedom from illusions*—Attributes of the *pir* have been exalted in Sufi poetry. Depending upon the era, the cultural situation, and the seeker's own needs, metaphysical powers (such as mental telepathy, clairvoy-ance, and even miracles) have been ascribed to the *pirs*. But, in most Sufi writing, emphasis is on the *pir* as an integrated or universal human be-ing, rather than as a person with magical or omnipotent powers.

- *Fana* (Freedom from the self)—Although not every *pir* can reach free-dom from the self (*fana*), it is essential that every *pir* constantly work on freeing the self from self-conceit, selfishness, greed, thirst for power, and prejudice. The *pir* is ready to give up and sacrifice everything for hu-manity. He or she lives by serving others willingly, enthusiastically, and humbly.

- *Being of the world*—A Sufi *pir* is of the world, at the same time, free from the world. A Sufi is expected to have a job and be useful in the com-munity. He or she is encouraged to be married. Marriage and the respon-sibility of parenthood are helpful in dealing with daily reality and are essential for the development of maturity. The biographies of the Sufi *pirs* reveal that most of them excelled in a profession or a skill.

* *Freedom from the world*—The *pir* treated rulers and beggars alike. Frequently, the *pir* directly questioned and confronted the worldly preoccupation of the ruler. The following story is an example of such an encounter between Ebrahim Ibn Adham, the King of Balkh, and a Sufi *pir*.

> Suddenly a man with an awful mien entered the chamber, so terrible to look upon that none of the royal retinue, and servants dared asked him his name; the tongues of all clove to their throats. He advanced solemnly till he stood before the throne.
>
> "What do you want?" demanded Ebrahim.
>
> "I have just alighted at the caravanserai," referring to the king's palace as a motel, said the man.
>
> "This is not a caravanserai: this is my palace. You are mad," shouted Ebrahim.
>
> "Who owned this palace before you?" asked the man.
>
> "My father," Ebrahim replied.
>
> "And before him?"
>
> "My grandfather."
>
> "And before him?"
>
> "So-and-so."
>
> "And before him?"
>
> "The father of So-and-so."
>
> "Where have they all departed?" asked the man.
>
> "They have gone. They are dead," Ebrahim replied.
>
> "Then is this not a caravanserai which one man enters and another leaves?" With these words the stranger vanished (Attar 1966, 63–64).

This encounter, among others, blazed the flame of reawakening and repentance in Ebrahim. Soon after, he renounced the Kingdom of Balkh and pursued abstinence and renunciation on the Sufi path of reality.

THE NEED FOR A *PIR*

The Sufis believe that maturity cannot be achieved alone. They feel that there is a great need for guidance and discipline. The path is unknown, the night is dark and the road is full of danger. Danger of preoccupation with selfishness, false vision, misinterpretation of mystical states, arrest in development, fixation in a particular state, appeal to various drugs to create false mystical experiences, and, not infrequently, overwhelming anxiety and insanity.

Transcending the temporal self cannot be accomplished by the self alone. However, emotional readiness is necessary to benefit from the psychological and spiritual guidance of the *pir*. The metaphor of making wine is frequently used to describe this readiness. The grapes are picked when ripe. Then they are crushed by the wine maker and allowed to sit for some time to ferment. The final quality of the wine depends more on the grape than on the ability of the wine maker. In this metaphor, the grape is the seeker, the wine maker is the *pir*, the crushing is the process of freeing the self, and the quiescence is meditation.

After a seeker becomes aware of the need for further integration, the search for a *pir* begins. The search may take a short time or many years. A true search is not a whim of the moment. It is a serious endeavor originating from the seeker's heartfelt need. If the search is undertaken out of self-conceit, pride, or material or societal gain, it becomes an obstacle on the path and will further fragment the seeker's soul. The more sincere and devoted the seeker is in this search, the closer the goal.

Such need and search for a guide is not unique to Sufism. The guru in yoga, the Zen master in Zen Buddhism, and the spiritual director in Christianity are all guides on the path. Also, the need for a spiritual teacher is mentioned in the Cabala, the Jewish mystical tradition. According to the Cabala, to understand the Book Yestsirah, even God's chosen Prophet, Abraham, needed a teacher: "He [Abraham] sat alone and mediated (me'ayyen) on it, but could understand nothing until a heavenly voice went forth and said to him: "Are you trying to set yourself up as my equal? I am One and have created the Book Yetsirah and studied it: but you by yourself cannot understand it. Therefore take a companion, and mediate on it together, and you will understand it." Thereupon Abraham went to his teacher Shem, son of Noah, and sat with him for three years and they meditated on it until they knew how to create a world. And to this day there is no one who can understand it alone" (Scholem 1965, 176).

PIR–SEEKER RELATIONSHIP

Initially the *pir* interviews the seeker privately. The nature and the content of the interview are not disclosed and are considered "secrets of love." Often, the *pir* asks the seeker about motivation, internal pain and suffering, visions, dreams, past experience, and misdeeds. The seeker at this time experiences feelings of excitement, turbulence, and ecstasy. With humbleness and honesty, the seeker gives mind and heart to the *pir*.

Generally, the *pir* does not accept a seeker immediately. He or she advises patience, self-observation, repentance, and purification. The seeker is put through many tests to assess sincerity of commitment, intensity of devotion, and strength of personality for tolerating the trials and tribulations of the path. Obedience and total trust in the *pir* are important steps for the novice (Nurbakhsh 1978; Royster 1979).

However, the "physician" has to be worthy of this trust. Throughout the ages, there have been many excellent *pirs*, but also some corrupt ones. These few corrupt *pirs* exploited the trust of their disciples for personal, political, and financial gains. The downfall of Sufi orders in Turkey, Persia, and other Islamic countries may be attributed to corrupt practices of some the Sufi *pirs*. This is similar to unethical physicians today who exploit their patients and commit egregious boundary violations (Celenza 2007; Gabbard and Lester 1997). However, the abuse or exploitation by a few physicians does not mean that the field of medicine should be abandoned.

Hazrat Inayat Khan (1964), the founder of the Sufi Order of the West, wrote:

> Then there arises the question of how to fine the real guru. Very often, people are in doubt, they do not know whether the guru they see is true or a false guru. Frequently, a person comes into contact with a false guru in this world where there is so much falsehood. But at the same time a real seeker, one who is not false to himself, will always meet with the truth, with the real, because it is his own real faith, his own sincerity in earnest seeking that will become his torch. The real teacher is within, the lover of reality is one's own sincere self, and if one is really seeking truth, sooner or later one will certainly find a true teacher. And supposing one came into contact with a false teacher, what then? Then the real One will turn the false teacher also into a real teacher, because reality is greater than falsehood. (p. 65)

Initiation

Initiation to the Sufi Path frequently occurs through symbolic and highly emotional ceremonies. At this time, the *pir* instructs the seeker with *zikr*, one of the names of God. The disciple learns to inhale and exhale *zikr* silently. This is referred to as "secret *zikr*." The practice of *zikr* is similar to the practice of mantra in Yoga. It is the first step of the meditative experience. The seeker may at times feel elated and at other times sorrowful. Feelings pour out from within. Tears may flow quietly and profusely.

As a seeker, one knows that the *pir* is aware of one's internal states at all times. So one feels there is no need to communicate one's feelings verbally except when the *pir* asks. At this phase, emphasis is upon the internalization of the *pir* and his attributes. At times this internal process is so intensive that the seeker does not think about anything but the *pir*.

The seeker is expected to come regularly, usually twice a week, to the place of Sufi gathering (*khaneqah*). In the gathering, the seeker serves his brothers and sisters in any capacity, such as cleaning, serving tea, and helping the needy. Serving others helps to decrease selfishness and "I-ness." The Sufis read mystical poetry and are involved in group *zikr*. They chant one of the names of God or a poem together until an intensive emotional experience occurs. Many cry in joy and ecstasy. Some will be blessed by a "vision."

The seeker is expected to keep silence and reveals visions or dreams only to the *pir*. The *pir* at this stage is essential in helping the seeker develop further on the path of integration. It is not uncommon for a seeker to express psychomystical experiences in symbolic poetry, but often silence is advised. Silence is considered a sign of growth and maturity. The *pir* listens attentively to the seeker. He may ask a few questions and make occasional suggestions, clarification, or interpretations. This process helps the seeker become aware of animal *nafs* and the tendencies for avoiding and resisting. The *pir* constantly helps the seeker chip away at self-conceit, illusions, and false expectations.

Halat (Mystical States)

The seeker's intensive emotional experiences on the Sufi Path are called "*halat*." *Halat* is the plural of the word "*hal*," which means condition, state, and feeling. Hujwiri (1967) stated: "*Hal* . . . is something that descends from God into a man's heart, without his being able to repel it when it comes or to attract it when it goes" (p. 181). In this statement, the involuntary and spontaneous aspects of *hal* are emphasized. Jonaid of Baghdad wrote that mystical states (*halat*) "are like flashes of lightning: their permanence is merely a suggestion of the lower soul (*nafs*)" (Hujwiri 1967, 128).

Sarraj (1914) described ten mystical states in detail: observation, nearness, love, fear, hope, longing, intimacy, tranquility, vision, and certainty. These states are progressive. The Sufis in each stage of personality development reexperience these mystical states spontaneously. Affective and emotional experiences are like intense fires that melt away impurities and help in polishing the mirror of the heart. Tears, sensory vibration, hair-raising goose bumps, and changes in respiration are experienced during such mystical states. There is a temporary suspension of thought processes, as the individual becomes totally filled with visceral or vegetative sensations.[2] These mystical experiences help the Sufi further along the path of truth toward a deeper experience of reality.

Origins of Suffering

Sufis and psychotherapists differ on the origin of suffering and anxieties. Classical psychoanalysts emphasize neurotic conflicts originating from the phallic-

Oedipal phase of psychosexual development as being the origin of patients' anxieties and suffering. In the last few decades, with the contributions of child analysis and developmental psychology, we have become aware that attachment behavior and the mother-child relationship throughout pregnancy and the first two to three years of life play an important role in the formation of personality and in the development of psychopathology. Attachment behavior and its manifestations in the form of separation anxiety now seem to have much more impact on the development of the self than the Oedipal conflict. The Sufis, too, perceive "separation" as the basis of anxieties and disorders of the mind. However, they not only include separation of the child from the mother, but also separation of human beings from each other, from nature, and from universal reality. Sufis feel that the greater the separation, the more intense are the feelings of fragmentation and distress.

In recent years, psychoanalysts, such as Kohut (1971; 1977) and Kernberg (1975), have recognized that frequent separations of the child from the mother or uneven mothering have significant impact on the development of a variety of psychopathologies that come under the heading of narcissistic and borderline personality disorders and center upon defects in the self coherence rather than intrapsychic conflicts. These disorders differ from neurotic disturbances.

The Sufis too have been aware of the human tendency toward self-gratification, self-conceit, and overestimation and underestimation of the self. They do not use the terms neurosis or narcissistic personality disorder, but at the core of their conception of the disorders of the mind is the individual's relationship with the self, others, nature, and God. Sufis feel that separation from nature and God and dualistic thinking are the roots of selfishness, self-conceit, and fragmentation. Constant attacking and chipping away at narcissistic tendencies is the essence of the therapeutic methods in Sufism.

Assessment

The Sufi *pir* interviews the seeker and observes not only verbal expressions, but also actions and attitudes. In the interview, there is less emphasis on early childhood development, although past experiences and frightening and hurtful behavior toward others are explored. The Sufi *pir* is particularly interested in assessing the seeker's tendencies toward pride and self-conceit, insincerity, lack of commitment, and emotional instability. The process of assessment may take a short time or years.

The Sufi *pir* looks for two major things. The first is the extent and nature of the seeker's psychic suffering. Is the seeker looking for a quick relief to avoid pain? Or is the person seeking knowledge and reality? If the seeker is looking for a quick relief from pain, Sufism is not the answer. On the other

hand, if seekers are sincerely seeking truth and are unhappy with their present condition, then they are welcomed to the path. The assessment of the intensity of suffering is primarily nonverbal, observational, and intuitive.
Pointed, and at times apparently irrational, illogical, or even rude comments
are made by the *pir* in the initial interview to put the seeker off guard or jolt
him or her. In this manner, the *pir* assesses the individual's response to the unfamiliar, paradoxical, or irrational. Flexibility, receptiveness, and thirst for
knowledge are important qualities for a seeker. Argumentativeness, rigidity,
and particularly rationalistic tendencies are signs of potential limitations.

Treatment

In psychotherapy, the premise is that by gaining insight through self-
examination of past traumatic experiences, and their re-creations in transference, improvement will occur. The Sufis, in contrast, feel the psychic suffering and pain are essential throughout life. The goals of the Sufis are the
vision of reality, union with the beloved, and integration of personality. This
requires pain, suffering, and sacrifice. Alleviation of symptoms and the development of health and well-being are not the goals but the side effects.

Let us say, for instance, that a seeker suffers from sleeplessness. If the
sleeplessness is to be related to psychological or spiritual causes, the *pir* may
say, "This sleeplessness is a sign of your psychic suffering. Use the hours of
wakefulness to meditate and read Sufi poetry, and if you feel like crying, let
the tears flow. This turmoil will help you become like steel in the fires of
agony and despair." The Sufis do not avoid grief, depression, temporary irrationality, or the experience of intense feelings. They see all of these experiences as ingredients for purification. However, if a seeker becomes too anxious, distraught, or fragmented, the sensitive and experienced *pir* will advise
decreasing the intensity and frequency of meditation, and prescribe concrete
and specific tasks in the form of serving others in order to modify the intensity of what we now would refer to as "regression."

There is a limitation in the therapeutic effects of psychotherapy or psychoanalysis. A number of studies show that it does not matter what type of therapy one applies, be it psychoanalysis, exploratory psychotherapy, behavior
therapy, or faith-healing, the outcome is about the same. Approximately
two-thirds of the patients experience relief and alleviation of symptoms. In
psychoanalysis, there is now less emphasis on "treatment" and more emphasis on acquiring knowledge and insight about the self and one's relationship with others.

Here again, Sufism and psychotherapy meet. The only difference is that the
Sufis' purpose from the beginning is not "treatment." The Sufis feel that

knowledge of the self is only the first stage of experiencing true knowledge or universal reality.

Intense Love in Sufism and Transference in Psychotherapy

Intense love (*ishq*) is the integrative energy in Sufism. Imam Ja'far as-Sadiq, one of the greatest teachers of Sufism, stated that intense love is "a divine fire that devours man completely" (cited in Schimmel 1975, 41). Sufis from that time on searched for this "divine fire," which they felt was the source of light.

The intense relationship between the seeker and the *pir* rekindles the divine fire and unleashes extensive and, at times, overwhelming emotional experiences in the seeker. The relationship between the *pir* and the seeker can be compared to the relationship between parent and child, beloved and lover, candle and moth, rose and nightingale, and physician of the soul and the patient. Such relationship has similarities with the transference relationship in psychoanalysis and psychotherapy, but at the same time transcends it.

The most important and significant person in the seeker's life is the *pir*. The seeker projects and displaces inner thoughts, ideas, feelings, wishes, and hopes onto the *pir*. The *pir* is frequently idealized as a benevolent father or mother who is, at all times, aware of the physical, emotional, and spiritual state of the disciple. Occasionally, magical thoughts and omnipotent fantasies are projected onto the *pir*. Generally, negative, angry, and hostile feelings toward the *pir* are not directly expressed, as is encouraged in psychotherapy. However, in many situations, such hostile feelings may find a way of expression through dreams and visual or auditory experiences in meditation. The seeker shared dreams, visions, and thoughts openly with the *pir*. The *pir* then makes comments to help the seeker modify anxiety, guilt, and sexual or aggressive impulses of the animal *nafs*. The major emphasis is on confronting and modifying the narcissistic aspects of the self. In Sufism, "working through" varieties of narcissistic postures and tendencies frequently occurs by the process of displacement. Sufi stories, metaphors, symbolic poetry, anecdotes, and brief sayings of past *pirs* are used extensively for clarification, confrontation, and interpretation (Deikman 1977).

In Sufism, the seeker, through intense love and total trust, is expected to give up will and desires and totally follow the will of the *pir*. This is called *iradah*. The *iradah* literally means "will," but in Sufism it refers specifically to enthusiastically, willingly, and unconditionally giving up one's will to the will of the *pir* and the will of God. This complete giving up of one's will without doubt or ambivalence helps the seeker on the path of liberation and freedom from the self. The Sufis feel strongly that one cannot be freed from the conditioned self and animal *nafs* until one freely gives up one's will and totally trusts the *pir* as a guide on the path of reality. *Iradah* transcends the concept of transference in psychotherapy. Transference is based on infantile wishes and desires of the id, and *iradah* is based upon the highest level of human love for psychospiritual integration and existential communion (Nurbakhsh 1978).

Avoidance in Sufism and Resistance in Psychotherapy

Sufi *pirs* are aware of the seeker's tendency for avoiding regular meditative practices, for giving in to impulses, and for avoiding pain and frustration on the path. Total trust or "surrender" to the *pir* helps the seeker in overcoming these avoidances. Rumi, in Book 1 of *Mathnawi*, portrays the seeker's tendency toward avoidance: "It was the custom of the men of Qazwin to have various devices tattooed upon their bodies. A certain coward went to the artist to have such a device tattooed on his back and desired that it might be the figure of a lion. But when he felt the pricks of the needles he roared with pain, and said to the artist, 'What part of lion are you now painting?' The artist replied, 'I am doing the tail.' The patient cried, 'Never mind the tail; go on with another part.' The artist accordingly began in another part, but the patient again cried out and told him to try somewhere else. Wherever the artist applied his needles, the patient raised similar objections, till at last the artist dashed all his needles and pigments on the ground, and refuse to proceed any further" (Rumi, cited in Whinfield 1973, 44–45).

The artist said, "Who has ever seen a lion without a head, tail, stomach, or back?" Here, Rumi emphasized the physical and emotional pain that a seeker needs to go through to become a fully integrated being. Sufis do not use the term "resistance" to express the seeker's conscious and unconscious hesitations for further development. They generally use the terms "avoidance," "fear," or "cowardice" to describe what we call "resistance."

In the initial phase of the meditative experience, fantasies, and visions occur frequently. At the time, the Sufi *pir* is helpful in assisting the seeker to overcome preoccupations with self-satisfying and self-deluding visions. These visual experiences may become a source of avoidance and resistance on the path, as demonstrated in the following story.

A disciple formed the notion that he had attained a degree of perfection.

"It is better for me to be alone," he thought.

So he withdrew into a corner and sat there for a space. It so fell out that every night he was brought a camel and told, "We will convey you to Paradise." He would sit on the camel and ride until he arrived at a pleasant and cheerful spot,

thronged with handsome folk and abounding in choice dishes and running water. There he would remain till dawn; then he would fall asleep, and awake to
find himself in his cell. He now became proud and very conceited.

"Every night I am taken to Paradise," he would boast.

His words came to Jonaid's ears. He at once arose and proceeded to his cell,
where he found him putting on the greatest airs. He asked him what had happened, and he told the whole story to the sheikh.

"Tonight when you are taken there," Jonaid told him, "say thrice 'There is no
strength nor power save with God, the Sublime, the Almighty.'"

That night the disciple was transported as usual. He disbelieved in his heart
what the sheikh had told him; nevertheless, when he reached that place he uttered as an experiment, "There is no strength nor power." The company all
screamed and fled, and he found himself on a dunghill with bones lying before
him. Realizing his error, he repented and repaired to Jonaid's circle. He had
learned that for a disciple to dwell alone is mortal poison (Attar, 1966, 208–9).

The story clearly illustrates that the seeker, when withdrawn to the self in quiescence and meditation, may experience illusions and hallucinations. The disciple was preoccupied with narcissistic delusions and self-gratifying hallucinations. He perceived these illusions as true mystical experiences. He avoided
the rigors of meditation, discipline, and sleeplessness for the pleasures of
sleep and illusionary experiences. Also, he became more conceited and felt no
need to contact his *pir*. He had the illusion that he had attained the highest
level of spiritual development.

Jonaid was acutely aware of the regressive power of meditation and isolation. In this situation, Jonaid recognized that because these visions were so
gratifying (ego syntonic) it would be of no use to confront the seeker directly.
He decided to redirect the seeker's emotional investment from these illusions.

The verse from the *Koran*, "There is not strength nor power save with
God," is commonly uttered by the Sufis when they want to determine whether
they are experiencing something real or illusionary. It is believed that by repeating this verse three times and relying totally on the power of God, illusionary experiences will disappear. Jonaid tactfully, on a nonverbal level,
communicated to the seeker the illusionary nature of his experiences by suggesting the utterance of the Koranic verse three times. By this process, Jonaid reawakened the observing part of the seeker's ego without increasing his
narcissistic defensive postures and thereby helped him overcome these illusionary experiences.

The seeker "repented" and gave up his delusions. From a psychoanalytic
point of view, the seeker was acting out transference resistances and, with
Jonaid's help, was able to "work through" these resistances by the process of
repentance. As we shall see, repentance, or reawakening, although it is the

first stage of human development in Sufism, is at the same time a dynamic process that continues throughout the Sufi's life.

The Self in Sufism and Psychic Trauma in Psychotherapy

Interpretation, whether dynamic or genetic, plays an important role in psychoanalytic therapies. The essence of interpretation is connecting the patient's present behaviors, feelings, and associations in the psychotherapeutic situation with unconscious residues of traumatic childhood experiences.

Sufi *pirs* do less interpretation. When they do interpret, it is related to the narcissistic self of the seeker. From a psychoanalytic point of view, the Sufi *pir* focuses more directly on the self and the primary and secondary narcissistic tendencies of the seeker. The *pir* does not permit the seeker to indulge in self-pity because of "earlier traumatic experiences." Interpretation in Sufism frequently transcends the dynamic and genetic interpretation of psychoanalysis and psychotherapy. It is existential interpretation, facilitating constant examination of the seeker's relationship with the self, others, nature, the cosmos, and universal reality.

THERAPEUTIC METHODS IN SUFISM

The Sufis' methods for helping a seeker on the path toward integration are numerous. Some of them include:

1. Silent meditation—Performed at least daily (usually before dawn), and preferably two to three times a day following prayers.
2. Regular attendance—Regular attendance at Sufi gatherings is essential.
3. Regular interviews—Interviews with the Sufi *pir*, which are referred to as "experiencing the presence" (*huzur*) of the *pir*. This presence can be for either a short or long time—as short as a glance, or as long as a day or two. Generally, it is fifteen minutes to an hour long, and occurs at least twice weekly in the place of Sufi gathering. Meeting with the *pir* may be more frequent, at times daily, depending upon the *pir's* assessment of the seeker's psychospiritual state.
4. Group meditation—Regular contact with other Sufis at least twice weekly is essential. The Sufis sit in a circle on the floor, cross-legged, with knees lightly touching, forming a "chain." They meditate silently for a period of time, usually thirty to ninety minutes.
5. Chanting—This is also called *zikr-i-jali*, which means glorious outward meditation. Here, under the guidance of the *pir*, the Sufis rhythmically chant a *zikr*, which is often a short verse from the *Koran* in praise of

God. This group chanting can be a very powerful experience. At times, the whole group functions as one entity, like "a ship in a tumultuous sea of unity." Some of the Sufis temporarily lose consciousness and, for many, silent tears flow. After reaching a crescendo under the direction of the *pir*, the rhythm becomes slower and finally quiescence prevails. Most of the Sufis experience spiritual uplifting, profound joy, and elation after these sessions.

6. Use of poetry—Reading mystical poetry or expressing one's psycho-mystical experiences in the metaphor of poetry is a common phenomenon. Sublimation of urges also finds an expression through Sufi poetry. Frequently, the Sufi poems are sung in melodic tones. This helps the Sufi experience beyond words the feelings and spiritual states of other Sufis.

7. Use of music and dance—Although the use of music in the orthodox Islamic religion is forbidden, the Sufis have discovered that it may help significantly in meditative practices. To them, music transcends words and logic. Music goes to the heart of nature, connecting the seeker to the invisible rhythms of existence. Rumi, the founder of the whirling dervishes, used music extensively in Sufi group meditative practices, *Sema*. Sufis are aware of the powerful and significant effects on the rhythmical movement of music and dance on catharsis of emotion, creation of a feeling of well-being, and the enhancement of internal peace and tranquility.

8. Seclusion—The Sufi *pir* advises some of the seekers, particularly those who have passed the initial phase and still have overwhelming narcissistic tendencies, to isolate themselves from others for a period of forty days (*chilla*). Also, periods of seclusion may help a Sufi or Sufi *pir* to refocus all energies and attention on reality.

CONCLUDING REMARKS

The goal of psychoanalysis and psychotherapy is helping the individual become more independent, to have freedom of choice, and to adapt more effectively with the environment, resulting in strengthening of the ego and the self. The Sufis' goal is freeing the self from the self. Emphasis is on interdependence rather than independence. It is becoming one with all; experiencing existential communion. In existential communion, one gives up individuality, but gains the essence and spirit of all beings.

10

Religious Identity Formation in the Children of Immigrant Muslim Parents

Mali A. Mann

Some simplify their existing name or adopt a diminutive, especially for the first name (Bill for Bilal, Jim for Jamil, Alan for Ali, and so on), some move a letter in the name, alter the pronunciation or the placing of an accent. Among the South Asian Muslims I met, only one "Khan" had changed his name to "Kahn."

—Aminah Mohammad-Arif 2002

The struggle for assimilation, integration, and self-identity formation among immigrant parents and their children in a new host country becomes even more complex when the parents are Muslims. For a variety of reasons, the September 11, 2001 terrorist attacks on the United States and the label imposed on them, "Islamic terrorism," has increased hostility toward Muslims among some in Western nations. In turn, "Western" ideas and culture have come to be seen by some Muslims as destructive of Islamic values. Scattered groups within Islam and Christianity today view each other as "the enemy," which is similar to what occurred during the Crusades (A.D. 1100–1400).

Researchers, theorists, and statesmen have written about the conflict between religious and philosophical-based systems since the end of the cold war. For Huntington (1993), the current divisions among nations and people involve a clash of culture, including fundamental differences over religion. Iran's former President Mohammad Khatami agrees, joining calls for a "dialogue of civilizations" at the United Nations to lessen conflict (1998).

Others have studied these clashes on a family and individual level. Freud (1927) writes that religion is an illusory attempt to console, the best illusion that man has yet been able to invent for the indoctrination of children. Marks (2004) notes the importance of religious interactions, rituals, and practices in

Christian, Jewish, Mormon, and Muslim families. Rehman and Dziegielewski (2003) report significant challenges involving family life for Muslims living in the West, including issues involving dress and attire, learning and practicing the basic tenets of the faith, and, for women, avoiding physical contact with men who are not related by a blood or marital bond. Adams (1984) and Carolan et al. (2000) note the importance of loyalty to family, to home country, and to religion that is part of the Middle Eastern cultures, and Shavit and Pierce (1991) observe, additionally, the importance of patrilineage (*hamula*). Ambali (1987) admonishes parents to teach their children acceptable moral behavior based on Islam in order to strengthen the positives and weaken the negatives in adolescent behavior.

Another group of researchers focus on the importance of religion in the formation of identity. Royle et al. (1999) note that religion was a salient aspect of Egyptian children and reports evidence that some of them engaged in intergroup comparison, in-group favoritism, and out-group denigration based on religious identity. Ian (2000) writes that children do not invent their religions and do not design the symbolic order in which they seek to play a meaningful role; rather, they inherit them from their parents and use them to configure Oedipal constellations.

In a study of Hindu and Muslim male and female children, Hassan (1987) observes that the highest degree of religious prejudice was shown by children with prejudiced parents, raised under restrictive and authoritarian discipline. Bocock (1993) writes that violence by children against others of different ethnic and religious groups often has roots in their own childhood experiences. Foley (2003) reports the difficulties that legal systems face in custody disputes due to the difficulty reconciling interpretations of Islamic Shari'a law and the best interests of the child. These studies help underscore the difficulty that Muslim parents in the West face in the raising of their children, aspiring toward integration, yet trying to maintain their religious beliefs and practices.

Islam is the third and youngest of three great monotheistic faiths, built on earlier foundations of Christianity and Judaism. The teaching of the *Koran*, Islam's holy book, is primarily concerned with the transmission of God's spiritual message to humankind as a corrective measure. Islam is essentially a simple faith. Five basic duties are required of the believer, five pillars of the house of Islam: profession of faith, prayer five times a day, the obligation to share, fasting one month a year, and the pilgrimage, as well as a set of ethical and moral teaching. Islam has many points in common with Judaism and Christianity. All three are monotheistic religions, having the fundamental belief in one God.

Psychoanalytic understanding of the genesis of pervasive cultural, religious attitudes of parents during their children's early childhood offers enlightenment about the effect and importance of parental religious identity on their children's religious identities. Parental expectations about transmitting their religious faith to their children can present an undue pressure on the children who are living in Western culture. The pressures children feel have increased even more, in lieu of more recent increase in racism and religious hatred toward Moslem families. In addition to their normal developmental tasks, these children have to witness parental mourning of their lost motherland. They are expected to learn religious principles, as well as practicing them on a daily basis.

The following two cases may show us how some of the parental religious conflicts color the healthy identification with the parent of same sex and the love of the parent of the opposite sex. Unresolved pre-Oedipal and Oedipal conflicts also color the relationships with other children in school.

THE CASE OF HASAN

Hasan was a first-grader, a handsome boy of six from India who entered in treatment because of ritualistic behavior of hand-washing for fear of getting them dirty. His parents observed this symptom for one-and-a-half years before they sought my help.

He was apprehensive about participating in play activities with other children in his school for fear of being treated badly since his skin color was darker. He worried about being criticized for his imperfection by his teachers. He struggled to be successful. He also showed unwillingness to work at tasks in the classroom, especially after school. He reported to his parents that he had "bad thoughts" when he started in analysis with me and kept repeating: "Oh, never mind," "I don't remember my bad thought to tell you today!" or "I don't want to say what I think out loud."

Hasan's underlying low self-esteem became obvious to his parents. Parental expectations of him to have scholastic success left more pressure on him to perform accordingly. He had mistrust in his ability to make friends and his classmates. He was unsure if they would appreciate him as a friend if he just offered himself, with all he knew and with all his charm. He wished he would be accepted into the popular cliques and he could share the way he practiced Moslem religion in his family environment. He wanted them to learn his ethnocultural values, too.

His mother infantilized him and treated him deferentially, like a little prince. She would also expect his two older sisters to do the same, despite their expressed feelings of envy. His sisters resented the restricted freedom they had in the way they dressed and not being allowed to talk to any boys in their schools.

His relationship with his father contained many positive elements, but during his phallic and Oedipal phases, his father showed concern about his obsessive-compulsive symptoms, since he himself recalled being the same way as a young boy and even during his later life as an adult. He did not spend much time with Hasan at home because of his "busy schedule" at work. Hasan would spend a lot of time with his mother, who adored him without setting any boundaries.

His father decided that Hasan had to go to a special private Islamic school. His father was very proud that he was able to find the school where his friends and acquaintances would send their children. He wanted to make sure Hasan would learn important concepts from the Koran: charity, good deeds, hospitality, moderation of desire, the faithful keeping of promises, love of one's neighborhood, respect for one's parents, and returning good for evil.

The first of summer of his treatment with me, his parents took a trip to Saudi Arabia with him, going to Mecca. This was an important pilgrimage since his father wanted to pass his religious legacy to Hasan, just like his father did by taking him to Mecca. When he returned, he told me all about his trip and he also told his friends in public school. His friends told him, "You are not supposed to talk about all of these weird things." He was hurt and did not know why they weren't interested in his story. This was one of the many factors that motivated his father to find a private Muslim school. In his new school, he was welcomed since they were all Muslims, mostly Sunnis and some Shiites. His family was Shi'ite. His father, who worked for a high tech company, did not socialize with people who were not Muslims. Hasan had only Muslim friends. His teachers were also Moslem and were supportive of him. He had to go to classes in Islamic Studies, learn the Arabic language, and memorize the Koran.

He tried to make an extra effort to learn Arabic by taking private lessons. He often times talked in frustration that he was ready to give up all attempts at mastery of Arabic language. He questioned how he would be able to use it elsewhere, except in the mosque or in his school. He was afraid that when he would grow older, other children would make fun of him in middle and high school. There was no private Islamic school as far as he could tell. He was extremely ambivalent about mastering the Arabic language since it was a big challenge for him. His father insisted that he should read it every night and get a good grade. Hasan did not do well in one of his exams and disappointed his parents.

His science teacher was a German-born woman who was married to a Moslem-Indian man. He found his teacher's conversion to Islam very interesting and curious. If his teacher willingly accepted a new religion, then it may not be too odd for him to declare his Islamic faith to the outside world without fear of being ridiculed by non-Moslem students in his neighborhood. He also showed his curiosity about my hyphenated name (Persian-German) and its implication was similar to what he was feeling about his science teacher. He wanted to make sure I could at least recognize a few words.

He found it interesting that I could say a few Arabic words when he brought in his language workbook one day. Hasan was happy with the friends he had, since they all had immigrant parents and they were Muslims. When he got pressured to do well in his school, his hand-washing and dirt phobia would worsen, and he would throw temper tantrums at home. His mother would give in to his wishes, and he would feel triumphant, which followed by feelings of guilt over his power.

His father would condemn him when he could not do well in his religious study class. His father would display his harsh condemnation only in this one area. He was disappointed that Hasan was going to embarrass him for not knowing his Arabic well. He also had extreme sense of shame and sense of defeat for not having been able to pass on the importance of adhering to his religious practice and belief to his son.

During his early latency, the stressful experience again brought up a developmental conflict in the form of a threatening superego introject. Hasan's latency conflicts were exacerbated by the fact that he experienced father's disapproval of his poor grades. I tried to help his parents help him modify his inner turmoil and improve his adjustment to the school environment. They were able to see how Hasan regressed from his latency instinctually and structurally. His use of externalization brought about ego regression, as well as drive regression and a regression in his object relationships. He became clingier to his mother and actively sought out his father's approval.

His regressions were primarily defensive in nature. He developed stool retention and would not go to the bathroom in his school. He was afraid other children's urine would accidentally soil him. This was even more shameful since according to Islam he had to be very clean. He was fearful to be seen as "*najis*," meaning "unclean," according to his religion, which added even more anxiety lead to avoidance of going to the bathroom. His father started therapy as well, per my recommendation. During the course of our ongoing work (with his parents' participation on weekly parent consultation), he gradually was able to overcome his problems and developed a better sense of reality and autonomy. I also helped him to define his own sense of body boundary and self-organization over the course of our work.

The forever-permanent loss of motherland with no hope to return created a complex mix of intense anger, helplessness, or a sense of shame attached to being ineffectual as a parent was a common theme for his parents, especially his father. This would propel groups of parents similar to Hasan's to enforce

their ideals with irrational aggressive force, and their anger remains unresolved, fueled more with outside experience of racial prejudice. These parents anxiously cling to the hope that they would be the ones who could create a perfect home in fantasy, which is permanent and indestructible. The one
they would never leave and remain permanent. The "all-good-place," wishes
to pray with freedom in religious practice with a sense of pride, stays as an
unconscious fantasy.

Anger after a loss may be turned to guilt. The idealization of the lost land
or a place to worship God is another part of the grief process among these
Moslem parents. This is why building a mosque is an important event in a foreign land. It is an attempt to recreate the landscape of the motherland. This
coincides with the acceptance of the lost person or landscape, which was left
behind. Bowlby (1969) refers to this stage in mourning as a process in which
the mourner's identification with the lost person or place is overshadowed by
depression and despair. Through this, the bereaved may come to terms with
the reality of the loss and begin a new life. Unfortunately, the latter process
fails to happen in these groups of immigrants who are Moslem.

Hasan's father told me Muslims, whatever their nationalities, do not count
as foreigners in the eyes of other Muslims; therefore, I was not a foreigner in
his eyes. This was one important reason that Hasan's father decided to get
help from me since he found out my maiden name was Amirsoleimani, and
his insurance providers list my last name as Amirsoleimani-Mann. Then he
learned that I was Persian in origin. He also assumed that I must have been a
Shi'ite Muslim and could understand their religious background. (In fact, I
was born in a liberal Muslim family, but my father was more Zoroastrian in
his ethno-cultural and religious ideals. This stems from the fact that he felt Islamic forces invaded Persia, and the Moslem religion was imposed upon the
Persian people. He had been ambivalent about being Moslem. He did not enforce it on his children. I learned how to recite the Koran as a child and had
to study Shariyat in elementary school.)

Hasan often would bring up questions like, "We are fasting because it is
Ramadan; are you not fasting?" "Do you not know we do not celebrate
Christmas?" To his questions I responded that I thought they might have
wanted to observe both holidays. He said affirmatively, "No, only ours!"
Hasan continued his studies during Christmas break, and Halloween did not
mean anything to his family. They did not have any trick-or-treaters coming
to their house. That was not so puzzling since the neighbors learned their
house should be skipped from their previous years of contacts. When I asked
how it was possible for him not to have any feelings about not being part of
it, he responded matter-of-factly, "We do not decorate and leave the lights out
for any trick-or-treaters. They look strange; I do not like candies any way!!"

Hasan was feeling very ambivalent. Seeing the whole world around him changing the color and form was unavoidable.

How could he not think about his outer world and its seasonal changes? In one of our sessions, Hasan saw a young girl leave my office in her costume. She was dressed since she was on her way to go trick-or-treating in her neighborhood. He looked at her and walked into my office without saying a word about what he saw that day. His association went back to what attire Islam allows in his school. "In Islam, you are supposed to cover yourself when you are a girl, but I wear a blue top and pants uniform." Another day, he saw the same girl leaving my office carrying a cup of hot chocolate. He asked, "Did you make that for her?" I responded, "Yes. Remember I offered you once, but you decided not to have it since you promised your parents not to drink hot chocolate with a marshmallow in it." This was because marshmallows was made of pig fat, according to the parents. The family would purchase their meat from a special store in order to have *Halal* (Kosher) meat.

During the month of Ramadan, he would go through fasting along with his parents. He was able to complete the two days of fasting, but gave up because it was a hardship for him. He was curious as to whether I was observing Moslem religious duties, such as fasting. He learned I was not practicing his religion, which made him silent for a while during that session. He said at that point that he knew I was able to say few words in Arabic and read some lines from Koran. This reminder meant *we* were still from the same faith, and he did not have to feel uncomfortable.

There were many themes with respect as to how I was living my life with family and within that community that occupied his mind in his transference manifestation toward me. The theme about his competency in comparison to others, including his father, came up.

I kept his parents involved in his treatment and made myself available to answer their questions.

THE CASE OF MEHRAN

Mehran is a ten-year-old, attractive, well-developed Iranian youngster, born in the United States, the older of two children. He came to see me because his father thought he was very unhappy, and he did not know why. During his first visit, he told me that he did not want me to see him wearing his glasses. He was not sure if I would like him with his glasses since his classmates teased him, and it added more to his problem of being "different."

Both parents came to the United States as emigrant exiles from Iran because of the political turmoil and their opposition to the hard-liners. Mehran's mother left him as a young infant to pursue her political ambition in Iraq as the extension of her resistance in Iran by joining Mojahedin to overthrow Khomeini's followers. Mehran's father was dismayed with his wife's decision, but had no choice but to raise his son as a single father until Mehran turned five, at which time he married a new Iranian wife. The couple waited until Mehran was seven years old before they had a baby girl. Mehran's sister was fourteen months old when he started seeing me in treatment.

Mehran's grades plummeted from As to C+s. He left a note saying he wished he were not alive, so the parents' first contact was initiated on an emergency basis. When another mental health professional made the referral to me, his father was pleased that I was an "Iranian child psychiatrist who was ethno-culturally informed about Iranian and their immigration problems." He was happy to know that I was in the United States before the revolution and had no political interest or ties in the present regime. He was afraid that once I learned about of his political orientation, I would become critical of him while he was in Iran during Khomeini's regime since he had hoped Khomeini would bring justice to underprivileged Iranians. He was disenchanted and had to leave the country.

Although Mehran's father at first saw me as an immediate ally, he appeared ambivalent about his son needing help in the first place. Although he was referred to me about a year earlier, he had waited to consult with me until after Mehran expressed a wish for not wanting to be alive to his teacher.

He worried that I would also possibly become critical of him and his wife, Mehran's mother, who was a religious activist in Iran. He was torn with feelings of guilt and accused himself for having not provided the right kind of parenting or fathering for his son. He expressed doubts about his own lack of cultural integration in the United States and its immediate effect on Mehran. His father was not concerned about Mehran's religious identity since he adopted a liberal attitude toward Islam. The initial evaluation consisted of an effort to disentangle Mehran's symptoms as a troubled, unhappy youngster from any significant cultural and religious determinants. His father's hopes that Mehran would be seen only a limited number of times ended in disappointment at first. He thought Mehran was going through something of a transitional phase and did not require intensive treatment. I emphasized the importance of frequency and he finally agreed to bring him in regularly and as frequent as he was able to. He was resistance to more in-depth treatment and saw my more frequent visits per week recommendation as more of a sign of his parental incompetency. He also felt I was being assertive and firm, unlike what he was used to in women of his family of origin. The father was also afraid that I would hold both him and his wife in contempt for their perceived failure as parents.

He was trying to decide whether to pay for Mehran's psychiatric treatment or to send his son to a private school. His reason for the latter was that he would be protected from "bullies." He also felt justified in pushing him for higher achievement at school. Mehran had complained to his father that children would tease him and would pick on him because he was Iranian, and Iran was seen as "the axis of evil" in which terrorists breed!

He would cry and defend his ethno-national connection to Iran, his parents' motherland. The feeling of shame was carried through his father, who came as an exile, and now they had to feel even more shame for being labeled as coming from a terrorist country. In one of his sessions with me, Mehran said, "I have been in their school for three years, and my classmates know me too much, and they tease me, but in a new school, I won't get teased because they won't know much about my parent's birth country." When I asked how he would feel about hiding his identity in the new school, he did not know what to say. Then, I empathized with him for feeling shame and needing to keep it from his fellow students. I said it must have been a great burden to feel what he was feeling.

He did not know the new wave of racism about Iranian was post-9/11 phenomenon. He wanted to know if I was subjected to children's ridicule when I was his age. I said he would feel more understood by me if I had a similar experience as he did. He said children in his class think he must have gone to schools where they train terrorists. He felt singled out, ashamed, and confused. He did not know whom to turn to. His father went to talk to his teacher to seek support for him.

Meanwhile, I got the school reports that Mehran was friendless; he would stare into space, spend his time alone walking in the schoolyard, and would not return his classroom assignments on time. He just did not know what he could have done to deserve such rejection from his classmates. He was very sensitive to the voice of his teacher, Mrs. R., who would call his name "Mehran!" as a warning signal. He also needed to get away from his class because "they could not understand my feeling." He was dropped from the principal's honor roll, which was puzzling to him and a few of his classmates, who liked him for his intelligence; he had been on the honor roll for more than two years.

The main motivating factor that prompted his father to seek consultation was Mehran's academic decline, rather than his lack of friends or his unhappiness. His father's disappointment was also related to the experience of his son running into difficulties and needing psychiatric help as a sign of parental failure in setting a secure and stable home in the United States. He wondered, after all, what else did Mehran need? They provided him with a computer, a CD player, and access to TV programs when he was through with his homework.

Mehran reported that he was bored most of the time and could not finish his homework. Although he was a very good student, he failed to complete his assignments. He admitted that he stared into space and "daydreamed." His biggest punishment was that his computer would be taken away from him. He was a voracious reader; he had subscriptions to four different children's magazines and would read constantly. He even sneaked and read in the dark after he would go to bed when the lights were out, pretending that he was asleep. Once his father found out about it, he took his computer privilege away. He was very unhappy about that and threw a temper tantrum. He felt people were being unfair at home, as well as at school. He thought that he was being treated at home like a five-year-old; after all, he knew that he had to wash his hands before dinnertime and he had to take a shower before he went to bed, and he did not understand why his mother would remind him, "like a five-year-old." He felt that as a ten-year-old, he knew what he should be doing and, therefore, he did not need to be reminded of it.

When it came to describing his feelings of unhappiness, he related that he was kind of "bored" and kind of unhappy and friendless. He also did not enjoy being left with his fourteen-month-old sister because he had more important things to do than watch his sister for an hour or so when his mother went to the supermarket.

In one of his sessions, when I announced the end of our meeting, he pulled out several meters of elastic that he had stuffed in his pocket (rubber bands that he had tied together and made into a very long rope). He dazzled me by the length of his rubber-band rope, and when I thought all of it must have come out of his pocket, he had even with a big smile on his face. He looked excited at the sight of the lengthy rope that he had made himself, and he definitely wanted to show it off to me. This was after a sad account of how he was badly treated in his class when he was questioned about his family background.

The early deprivation and maternal neglect Mehran experienced with his mother was revived and intensified by the birth of his sister. He was both excited by her birth and at the same time felt neglected. All his pre-Oedipal and Oedipal conflicts were interwoven, and Oedipal problems seemed particularly significant in his masochistic need to feel badly and to be "the unimportant person in the household."

His feeling of abandonment by his mother who left him at the age of eighteen months in the hands of his father intensified even more by him feeling rejected and ridiculed at school. His new host country was also a rejecting mother like his birth mother. He felt overwhelmed with intense affects of rage, shame, and helplessness. He often felt being "so different" from other children in his school that he wanted just to disappear and never come back. Friendship with the boys in his class was so important to him that he was willing to work his hardest to win their favor without much luck. He also felt his teacher did not seem to be supportive of him and his fear. His teacher, who could have been like a mother substitute for him, seemed to be indifferent and not empathic when there was a class discussion about current events. His father reported that despite of his explanation to his teacher about them being "Persian" and not being "Arab," the teacher did not believe him. He explained to the principal that where he came from, there were no schools for terrorist training, in the hope she would support Mehran. He would not get invited to the birthday parties and it added more psychological pain for him.

I decided to go to the school conference to help Mehran's situation. I explained how important friendship is for latency-age children and especially for Mehran. To my surprise, there were a lot of preconceived ideas about Iranian and Moslem religion. His peer group and his teacher slowly received Mehran with cautious reservation. I continued my work with his parents to help him to feel better about himself and his parental identity. Obviously, our work needed to continue for a long time.

DISCUSSION

There have been relatively few articles in this area of working with immigrant parents dealing with their latency-age children. The struggle of assimilation, integration in new host country, and self-identity formation among immigrant parents and their children becomes even more complex when the parents are Muslims. Hatred against people of different ethnic and religious groups tend to be seen by many people in the affluent Western countries as being rooted in historical, national, or ethnic conflicts between adults who involve children in their warfare. Psychoanalysts named the beginning school years the "latency period." As we know, Freud referred to this chronological time as the quiet phase between the conflict prone pre-Oedipal and Oedipal periods, and the stormy period of adolescence. Latency was after "the dissolution of the Oedipal conflict and creation or consolidation of the superego and creation of ethical and aesthetic barriers in the ego" (1926, 114).

The latency child needs to establish friendly peer relations outside of home, as well as needing secure parental objects to permit the child to have a life of his own in the broader outside world. Turning away from the primary object for latency child is a developmental step forward. The immigrant parents who have endured losses of their country of origin may be engaged in the mourning process and be preoccupied with their own grief. Therefore, they inevitably are not able to provide their children with a smoother transition into the outside world of friends. The children turning away more from them is going to be perceived as an act of disloyalty. The parents may have inherited in their fantasy compensation or antidote in creative self-expression, which becomes a defense in dealing with an incomplete mourning. They may try to master their trauma in their own terms. Bowlby (1986) compares the unresolved grief of such a child with recurrent physical illness, and the same analogy may be true of the survivor immigrant parent who had left his own motherland for political reasons.

Psychological responses to survival, as to all forms of loss, vary greatly from person to person. They depend not only on the duration and intensity of the trauma and the conditions for mourning, but also on the individual's make-up, particularly his early developmental and family history, which makes the person, react in a certain pattern under the stressful situation. The immigrant parents' main defense against survivor guilt is a numbing feeling, which enables them to function in the new land. At the same time, they are unable to tap into the sources of joy, growth, and happiness. During the period of yearning and searching for the attributes of their customs and religious practice, the immigrant parents may find it is possible to revive the same degree and intensity of vested emotions attached to their religious beliefs from their past into the new host land. Children who are respondent to parental wishes and guilt feel obligated to comply with parental dictum. During the period of yearning and searching for the dead (Bowlby 1980), the searcher still believes that "the lost" can be found and resurrected. The parental irrational hope for "the lost" brings about a surge of anxiety, which can impact the children's psychic structures. The impact of such parental demand and expectation on their children causes undue stress. If they do comply with parental wishes, they may save themselves trouble with them, but they also have to reconcile their differences and conflicts in the outside world. These children comply out of loyalty to parental wishes and expectations and feel tormented following their wish to turn away from their parental dictum.

There is a potential disorganization and regression in the face of parental grief process. As parents are engaged in the yearning and searching process, they assimilate emotions derived from the lost place where the family used to go to pray or the people they would do the prayer with. The wish will appear in the form of nostalgia and an attempt to seek an outlet when the mourning process is not yet complete. When the disbelief and denial of the loss is mixed with some level of acceptance, denial take a form of "holding on" to the lost motherland with its entire religious and other cultural attributes (Aberbach 1989). The insistence of keeping things alive and passing their beliefs and customs to the children becomes highly invested with libidnized emotions. Their parents are in search of perfecting the customs and religious beliefs; their disguised bereavement is in the center stage of this highly fueled state and ready to go through a process of the discovery of lost ideals. Any outside threat, insult, or disrespect to the way they practice their religion may lead to more disorganization or a rigid defensive insistence and adherence to being more of a Moslem in their own eyes or others. If the immigrant parent is an exiled one, whose migration is permanent without any hope for a return, their expressions of grief and mourning process can become even more complicated. There is a difference between the immigrant parents who are forced to leave their motherland for political reasons and those who chose to immigrate to a new host country. The grief process has a much more complex and intense momentum in the former group. The exiled immigrant parents have a much more fierce denial of the loss of their motherland, needing to assert their religious identity.

I have described two cases of latency-age children who show how their parental religious affiliations, rituals, and practice influence their identity formation. Religion is an important aspect of the children's identity and under normal circumstances of a stable environment, we see a more robust integration and solidification with other kinds of identities, ensuring a more secure self-identity formation. When parental religious identity is under the threat of diffusion and disorganization because of the threat of racism in wider society or religious conflicts with the host country, they influence their children's sense of stability and security.

Parents who do not feel free to practice their religion or feel ambivalent about teaching their children their faith will feel a sense of shame and loss. The parent's anxiety of being misunderstood or unsupported by Western society for their cultural differences and attributes intensifies. They feel that Western society attributes all of their being "different" to be derived from Islam.

My focus on this topic comes from experience as a child psychiatrist and analyst with immigrant parents' difficulty in negotiating their religious ideals with their children, especially latency-age children. These children who live in America experience the contrast between their own parental inherited and adopted religious ideals and the external world in which they live. They are unfamiliar about what is expected of them from inside of their family home and from the outside world of neighborhood and schools. When they face parental ambivalence in adopting new values in the host county, in return, they become confused as to how to negotiate parental expectations, as well as bicultural ideals.

My role in working with immigrant parents, nonimmigrant parents, and their children has shown me that the ways children grow and change are extremely complex. I try to assist parents to help their children adjust to the new school environment and the world outside. I try to show them what role they play in facilitating or complicating their children's development. By learning about the immigrant parent's expectations, I try to support parent's psychological "agency" (Pine 2006) in their effort at creating a greater flexibility to regulate and organize their own strength, and consequently on a larger scale over their children. They will learn how they can help their children to adjust and transition from the home environment to their schools and the outside world.

The immigrant parental issues vary, and among many of these are the following: mourning of their lost motherland, fear of loss of their own religious and cultural identity, fear of not being able to transmit their religious beliefs to their children, separation issues, immigration as "a third individuation" (Akhtar 1999), and dealing with their children's peer relationships in the greater circle of school and outer world. The "latency" period, along with its critical developmental issues, does not simply rest with the intrapsychic processes of sexualized prelatency years; rather, the school-age years are characterized by an extremely active exchange between the child's inner world and the world around him. For our purpose, I did not focus on a psychoanalytic view of the latency period by reviewing biological, ego-psychological, temperamental, cognitive, or cultural influences. My focus was only on the religious identity of immigrant parents and their school-age children, omitting other attributes of cultural identity.

My own psychoanalytic interest in the normal development of latency-age children brought up the following questions: How do latency-age children of a Moslem background negotiate their problems around parental religious beliefs while living in an environment surrounded with other religious affiliations that are not only unfriendly but actually hostile? How do they comprehend these differences; what do they do when their parents are preoccupied with their own sets of unresolved issues?

We have been witnessing in recent years how immigrant families create more constraints and demands on their children defensively on the one hand, and how the community or society of the new host country reacts fearfully with hostility toward immigrant Moslem families. Since September 11, I have observed another layer of stressor and hardships added to the already stressed immigrant parents' mental apparatus. They have to deal with many parental tasks, going through their own mourning process of their lost motherlands and dealing with the overt and covert hostile reception of the Western host country. I tried to point out various factors that play in the complex dynamic of these groups of parents and their children.

CONCLUDING REMARKS

There is a reciprocal interaction between parent and children, which is not a static process, but a constantly evolving dynamic. Likewise, society also changes over time and is in reciprocal interaction with immigrant families, as well as nonimmigrant families. The two clinical cases I described might show some of the struggles these children face when the different religions are added to their already overwhelmed psychic structures. How do they view other children, and how do they view their peers who are already well-grounded in Western culture? These kinds of questions require knowledge about the adaptive functions and problem-solving capacity of parents and their latency-age children, parental attachment patterns to their children, temperamental traits, and cognitive and emotional capacities. Hasan's mother sought out professional help by seeing a Western therapist of her own choice. She accepted her own traditional role and place in the family. She knew she had to deal with domestic tasks and care for her children. She would also wear a traditional costume that covered all of her body except her head. She would bring Hasan to his sessions and would wait until I would invite her in sometimes for a parent's conference. On Islamic holidays, she would appear in attire appropriate to the occasion with somber colors or cheery ones if it were Eid. Hasan's father was educated in the United States, caught in limbo dealing with both cultures in intimate ways. He wanted his son to carry on his legacy by following strictly the moral codes of Islam as expressed in the Koran. Mehran's father, an exiled immigrant, felt he should be his son's teacher and guide in the absence of proper religious education in the new country. He was intent in teaching his son Farsi and respecting Islam. He was conscious of his shortcomings and feared he would not be a perfect father and would fail in transmitting his family legacy. He would blame the government of the present regime and was prone to self-blame for having been naïve and idealistic in his political view.

My work involving parents in the treatment of these children and understanding how well or poorly they function as immigrant parents in the new host country suggests many new ideas for treatment. The most important among these is to recognize that if the parents have not adequately mourned their immigration trauma, they are vulnerable to bring their psychic disequilibria to their children.

IV

CONFLUENCE

11

Christian-Muslim Relations

The Axis of Balkans and the West

M. Sagman Kayatekin

> The figure of Jesus is the one common denominator of Christianity and Islam, and consequently, any talk or discussion of the relationship between the two religions, can, failing all else, start with him. . . . But this also creates a gulf between the two religions in that the precise nature, role, and significance of Jesus in each are quite different.
>
> —Muntasir Mir, 2005, p. 116

The stunning terrorist attacks of 9/11 sent tremors around the globe, evoking a broad array of reactions. The Islamic fundamentalists whose brethren killed thousands of innocent civilians in the name of Allah were viewing themselves as holy warriors of Jihad in the land of the infidels. In some Muslim countries, men and women were dancing in the streets celebrating the horrendous attacks. Pictures were published of a little boy holding a photograph of the Sears Tower, implying that when he grew up, he would be the one to bring it down; his parents were in the background with approving and proud smiles. The United States: the country under assault. Initial disbelief was followed by revulsion, sadness, and fury. In one instance, ordinary citizens attacked people wearing turbans, assuming them to be Muslims, and killed one. They actually were Sikhs. Some stated that all Muslims should take a lie detector test and be executed if they could not pass. There were a few, otherwise respectable, academicians who openly recommended that the United States should "nuke 'em." The "Crusades" became a familiar theme. The Islamic fundamentalists thought they had attacked "evil," whereas the Americans thought that they were attacked by "evil." Despite the overwhelming condemnation, some between the lines of "I told you so" and "now it's is your turn" responses were coming from Middle Eastern countries that had been struggling with Islamic fundamentalism for many decades.

Christianity and Islam had a peaceful stretch during the twentieth century. As a solution to the "Eastern problem," the Christian West had utilized political Islam at the beginning of the twentieth century in the dismantling of the "Sick Man of Europe" and the collapse of the "Sick Man of the West," the Soviet Empire. With this collaboration, memories of the perennial conflict between Islam and Christianity faded away. Toward the end of the twentieth century, the old conflict had started to simmer (Roy 2004), but when 9/11 shook the whole world, the overwhelming majority in the Christian West had only hazy images of primitive, heroic Muslims who had defeated Ottomans (as were depicted in the films of Lawrence of Arabia) or the brave Muslims freedom fighters who brought down the evil empire of the Soviets (as portrayed in *Rambo*). September 11 severed the century-old partnership between political Islam and Western Christianity and awakened the ghosts that were lying dormant. These were archaic, distorted, stereotypical images held by each side about one another. A chronicler of the First Crusade documented the ancient birth of these disfigured images of the "other." The year is 1097 and the stage is Anatolia (present-day Turkey).

> With the advances of our knights, Turks, Arabs, Saracens, Angulans, and all other barbarians ran away to the passages of mountains and plains. Excluding the Arabs, whose numbers only God would know, our enemies Turks, Persians, Saracens, Pavlicians, Angulans, and other idolators were a total of 360,000 people. . . . We killed them all day long, amassing gold, silver, donkeys, camels, sheep, cows and numerous other things that we had no idea about . . . two of our knights died with honor. . . . Is there anyone who is knowledgeable or wise enough to describe the military prowess, tact, and patience of Turks? Turks thought they would overwhelm the Franks with the threat of their arrows—as they did Arabs, Armenians, Saracens, Assyrians, and Greeks. But with the help of God, they will never defeat people as great as us. Turks state they are from the same race as Francs and claim that only they and Francs can be called "knights." Let me say something that no one would contest: if they had an unfathomable belief in Jesus, Holy Christianity, Holy Trinity, and Resurrection, then there would be no one stronger, more valiant, and capable than Turks. (Gurel 1985)

Compared to the distortions that would be created in the following centuries, the ambivalence against the adversary is acknowledged in an admirably open and sincere way. In addition, the narrator has a propensity to lump the ethnicities together. In the Western mind, it took many centuries to distinguish between the diverse ethnicities of the Near/Middle East. This differentiation is still a ephemeral one; even in highly educated circles, there is an amalgamated image of the geography and various ethnicities of that region. Unlike Africans or Asians whose physical attributes make them easily discernable, peoples of the Near East, like Armenians, were vague figures in the minds of Western Christians, and thus easy targets for projection. On the other side of the coin, there was a stereotypical "Europe," "West," or "Christian" in the minds of Muslims. This vague, hazy "other" was a precondition for disowning, projecting, and creating simplistic, stereotypical, shared representations of the "other." This chapter is about the history of such distorted representations of "self" and "other."

A BRIEF HISTORY

Islam and Christianity shaped and created one another within a very old neighboring relationship around the Mediterranean Basin. The two key points of contact in this tumultuous relationship were the Iberian Peninsula and Anatolian Peninsula/Balkans. The first major actors on the historical stage were the Arabs. Beginning with a "Medieval Blitzkrieg" in the seventh century, in a matter of decades, Arabs took control of the southern and eastern coasts of the Mediterranean, laid siege to Constantinople, and carried out an European invasion through present-day Spain. Abbasid and then Umayyad, the two Arab empires that came out of this expansion, were the dominant civilizations of the region until the end of the first millennium.

After the Arabs, nomads from Central Asia, "Muslim Turks," appeared as a new force in Anatolia and became the main medium for contact between Christianity and Islam. For several centuries, they continued a westward expansion, invading/infiltrating the lands inhabited by Christian people and gradually establishing political dominance, first as Seljuks, then as Ottomans. Alongside their conquest of Anatolia and the Middle East, Ottomans started invading the Balkans around the mid-fourteenth century, and in 1453, captured Constantinople, severing the European connection to East, which was a major impetus behind the great expeditions that eventually led to European discovery of the Americas. Around the mid-seventeenth century, the continued Ottoman expansion into Christian territory reached its zenith at the gates of Vienna. By then, the Balkans, Middle East, Northern Africa, Black Sea, and Eastern Mediterranean were under Ottoman control. It was an impressive civilization with overwhelming military prowess.

Meanwhile, European lands had been undergoing dramatic economical/cultural changes for several centuries, and by the seventeenth century, Europe was a powerful continent, capable of containing the Ottoman expansion. The centuries that followed saw the consolidation of the European supremacy and continual dissolution for Ottomans. In the nineteenth century, all European territories and North Africa were lost, and by the beginning of the twentieth century, so was the whole Middle East. Ottomans were barely capable of securing what today is known as Turkey.

OTTOMANS AND THE WEST

One of the nodal, psychologically transforming points in the history of these two faiths was the 1453 conquest of Constantinople. This majestic city had survived many sieges, and the only time she had surrendered was the result of an assault from the "inside" in 1201, when the Latin Crusaders sacked the city on their way to Promised Lands (Kilicbay 1985). When Constantinople was lost to the Ottomans, the repercussions were felt all through Europe. The sentiment was one of defeat, hopelessness, and fury. New Rome, New Jerusalem, the city of the first Christian Emperor Constantine, had fallen into the hands of the "infidel." There was disbelief, failed attempts to start a new crusade, and self-blame. A widespread interpretation was that this was God's punishment for their sins (Turkic nomads received this projective image quite regularly; about a thousand years back, Attila the Hun was portrayed similarly as the "whip of God"). The Ottoman Sultan was named "Satan, Beast of The Apocalypse." The image of Turks as cruel, lustful, bestial perverts was spreading rapidly through Europe.

As Ottomans entered the city and turned Hagia Sophia to a mosque, Ducas said the following:

> He (Mehmet II, the Ottoman Sultan) summoned one of his vile priests who ascended the pulpit to call out his foul prayer. The son of iniquity, the forerunner of Antichrist, ascending the holy alter, offered the prayer. Alas the calamity! Alack the horrendous deed. Woe is me. What has befallen us? Oh! Oh! What have we witnessed? An infidel Turk standing on the holy Altar, in whose foundation the relics of Apostles and Martyrs have been deposited. Shudder O sun! Where is the Lamb of God, and where is the son, and Logos of Father Who is sacrificed thereon and eaten and never consumed? Truly we have been reckoned as frauds! Our worship has been reckoned as nothing by the nations. Because of our sins the temple, which was rebuilt in the name of the wisdom of Logos of God and is called the Temple of the Holy Trinity and Great Church and New Scion, today has become the Altar of barbarians, and has been named and has become the House of Muhammad. Just is Thy judgment, O Lord. (Wheatcroft 2004, 194–95)

It was a moment of tremendous pride for Ottomans. They had conquered the New Jerusalem and cleared the entire East of Christian domination. The conquest of Istanbul was the only victory Ottomans celebrated. Even in current-day Turkey, it is still a nationally recognized day. In Greece on the other hand, Tuesday, the day of capture, is viewed as an unpropitious day (Volkan and Itzkowitz 1994, 35–46). The Satan of the West was the hero of Ottomans, and his epithet "Faith"—"Conqueror"—is a common name given to boys in current-day Turkey. The glory of Ottomans and trauma of Byzantium was etched into the shared representations of both sides.

Ottomans were traumatized, too, and they were aware of the magnificence of what Eastern Rome had accomplished, but, despite that, the first-hand witnessing of the glorious edifices of Constantinople was a clear narcissistic injury (the first sight of the magnificent American skyscrapers probably has the same effect). From this point on, Ottoman architecture would be deeply influenced by the grand architecture of Byzantium, and it would try to emulate and surpass it.

A century later, during the reign of the great-great grandson of Mehmet the Conqueror, Suleiman the First, Ottomans reached the limit of their intrusion into Europe and the grandiose self-image of the empire crystallized in the self-description of Suleiman:

> I am Suleiman, Sultan of Sultans, sovereign of sovereigns, distributor of crowns to the lords of the surface of the globe. I am Suleiman, the Shadow of God on earth, and Commander of the Faithful, Servant, and Protector of the Holy Places. I am Suleiman, ruler of the two lands and the two seas, Sultan and Padishah of the White Sea and of the Black, of Rumelia, of Anatolia, of Karamania, and of the land of Rum [Rome]. I am Caesar of Rum. I am lord of Damascus, of Aleppo, lord of Cairo, lord of Mecca, of Medina, of Jerusalem, of all Arabia, of Yemen and of many other lands which my noble forefathers and illustrious ancestors (may God brighten their tombs) conquered by the force of their arms and which my majesty has subdued with my flaming sword and my victorious blade. I am Sultan Suleiman Han, son of Sultan Selim Han, son of Sultan Bayezid Han. I am Suleiman. To the east, I am the Lawgiver. To the west, I am the Magnificent. (Smith 1996)

In contrast to this content with its grandiose self-image, Europe was inundated with publications, paintings, rumors, and stories creating an image of a brutal, bloodthirsty Ottoman who was a pederast, sodomite, and devotee of impalement of the Westerners. As often happens, there was envy, ambivalence, and "identification with the aggressor": Suleiman was given the title of "magnificent," an interesting contrast to the pervasive negative image (it probably was related to an Ottoman involvement in European politics and their helping of the French). Also, a symbol of the dominant power of the times, "turbans" became fashionable in Christian Europe (Timur 1993). It is very similar to how a prominent symbol of America, the baseball hat, had spread through the whole world. In current-day Turkey for example, one can talk with a young man who is expressing very strong anti-American sentiments while he is wearing a New York Yankees cap. Ottomans didn't project to Christian Europe with the same degree of passion. It was a simple world; they were the best, most dominate, and "good" ones.

This period was the pinnacle of Ottoman architecture. Under the brilliant creativity of their chief architect, Sinan, the Ottomans finally felt that they had managed to surpass the splendor of Byzantine architecture with the Selimye mosque, the jewel of this era. The point of pride about this magnificent mosque was the fact that Sinan finally had built a dome that was larger than St. Sophia's! This was the end of the Ottomans' mourning over the narcissistic injury implemented a century before when they witnessed the grandeur of Eastern Rome, symbolized by the great church, Hagia Sophia (Volkan and Itzkowitz 1994, 47–52).

Akin to Narcissus losing himself and dying in the pursuit of the love of his self-image, Ottoman grandiosity and self-content brought the beginning of decline (Inalcik 2004). In 1571, several years after the death of Suleiman, the battle of Lepanto proved to be the first significant defeat of the Ottoman Navy. A navy composed of many European nations in the old Crusaders' spirit, crushed the Ottoman Navy, destroyed the whole fleet, and killed its admiral. Lepanto was a counterpoint to the loss of Constantinople, and there was a unification of the whole of Christian Europe around this victory. From Spain to England to Rome, all of Western Europe held ecstatic celebrations. There were plays, poems, and songs written about the event. Even in France where, for political reasons, the most Christian King preserved good relations with the Ottomans, there were processions and church services in the smallest of towns and villages. In Protestant England, there were days of exuberant celebration in London. German towns went wild with delight. Perhaps for the last time, the sense of universal participation in a holy war transcended the chasm between Catholic and Protestant. A year later, the Pope decreed that the feast of the Rosary should be celebrated on the anniversary of Lepanto (Wheatcroft 2004, 3–35). The theme of Lepanto recurred in the image of the West for many centuries.

The famous comments of the Ottoman Grand Vizier Sokullu to the Venetian Emissary Barbaro summarized the Ottoman efforts to avoid mourning and repair their devastated narcissism: "In taking Cyprus from you, we deprived you of an arm. By defeating our fleet, you have only shaved our beard. A cut off arm can never come back, but a shaven beard will grow back stronger" (*Turk Tarihi* 2005).

After the seventeenth century, the asymmetry[1] between Europe and the Ottomans shifted toward the dominance of Europe. Once a feared foe, Ottomans never regained their political/military supremacy. As their capacity to be a threat to the West vanished, the images of the Ottomans in the West altered: the negative, vilified image of the Muslim Turk subsided and was replaced by a widespread fascination of Ottomans as objects of interest, and they began to be depicted as somewhat inferior, primitive, and different, something to be curious about. "When the first Ottoman embassies came to France in 1720s, turbans heavy silks, furs, and flying robes suddenly became immensely desirable. The fashion for being painted in oriental dress: 'a la Turque' spread throughout Europe's aristocracies. For the west, flowers, silk, and flowing robes suggested an indolent life, rather than the rigors of the field of battle. . . . Where once the limitless and boundless energy of the sultan and his pashas had evoked blood and gore, now images of them suggested ravening lust, raw sex, and brutal passions in the harem" (Wheatcroft 2004, 266–67).

Ottomans, yet again, didn't counter the curiosity of the Europeans. Partly related to the belated entry of printing to their lands, Ottoman masses and even the elite were largely oblivious to the outer world (Quataet 2003, 74–88). There were some "soul searching" going on, but it was restricted to a small minority; the mass awakening of the Ottoman elite would not occur until early in the nineteenth century. "Prior to this time (the Greek rebellion in 1820), Ottoman ruling elite knew very little about Europe and were not noticeably interested in learning more. When they thought about Europe at all, it was with a vague comforting idea that Europe was inferior to their own world" (Itzkowitz 1972, 104–7).

This peculiar, harmless, lustful image of the Ottomans held by Christian Europe and the Ottoman ignorance of the "other," ended around the beginning of the nineteenth century. It was the age of Imperialism; the Americas, Africa, and Asia were being divided between the mighty powers of Europe, and Ottomans became the recipient of intense projective distortions. Perhaps the most poignant representative of these projections can be found in the writings of the renowned British politician of the nineteenth century, the "Grand Old Man of Liberalism," William Ewart Gladstone, who was publishing pamphlets on the conflict in the Balkans. In these widely-read essays, he was painting a gruesome, distorted, almost sadomasochistic image of the process of Balkanization, with descriptions like "the only refinement of which Turkey boasts!—The utter disregard of sex and age—the abominable and bestial lust—and the utter and violent lawlessness . . . murdering, burning, impaling, roasting men women and children indiscriminately, with the extreme refinements of cruelty . . . scenes at which hell itself might almost blush . . . Satanic orgies . . . unbounded savagery . . . unbridled and bestial lust . . . ferocious passions . . . horrible outrages" (Loewenberg 1995). There is no doubt that Gladstone's savagery of the "other" was accentuated by his secret, intense, conflicted interest in pornography, prostitutes, and sado-masochistic perversions.

The era spanning the nineteenth century through the beginning of the twentieth is known as the "longest century of Ottomans." During this epoch, the world as they knew it collapsed. "Their" lands in Europe were being taken away, forcing mass migrations of Muslims back to Anatolia. The cataclysmic dissolution of the Balkans crushed the Ottoman self-image of "good/superior," evoked a clear awareness of we/them, and started a deep search for an identity. The question of "who am I?" found several answers: Ottomanism, Pan-Islam, Pan-Turkism, and Westernization. During this "longest century," some old, important elements of the hazily defined Ottoman self-image transformed and became central ingredients in a well-delineated self-image. As an example, for many centuries, the term "Ottoman" was used to refer to the ruling class. Now it became a defining element of a core identity. In a similar vein, when Ottoman society was integrating various ethnicities and religions into its fabric, "Turk" was a somewhat insignificant member of the wider society. In contrast, during the nineteenth century "Turk" emerged with a very strong emphasis, as a defining element in contrast to the new national identities of the Balkans:[2] Greeks, Bulgarians, Serbians, and Romanians (Ortayli 2003, 23–33).

Another solution to this search was to identify with the West. All through the nineteenth century, during the time of "Ottoman Modernization," sweeping reforms were made to accomplish this ambitious transformation (Ortayli 1985, 3–13). The main structure of the society—government, education, and military—were reformed to meet the standards of what was seen as Western norms. Even the daily attire was forced to change. The centuries-old turban, "sarik" was discarded and fez (originally a Greek hat) was accepted as the symbol of the image of modern Ottoman. A century later, after the collapse of the empire, when modern Turkey was being established, the second wave of modernization would discard the fez and the Panama hat would be introduced. The most remarkable of these attempts of Westernization was the abandonment of Arabic scripture in favor of the Latin alphabet in the 1920s. These zealous identifications with the West were countered by a vilifying of the West in the Islamist circles in which the West was seen as an aging monster that was on the verge of collapse.

It is an unexamined fact of history that the identities of "Pan Ottoman," "Pan Turk," and "Pan Islam" were not "internal" creations of the Ottoman society, but, in actuality, they originated in the eyes of the West. Once initiated in the West and projected, Ottomans identified or counteridentified with images, a similar process to what is defined in analytic literature as projective identification (Klein 1946; Shapiro and Carr 1991). The story of Pan Islam provides a good illustration for this fascinating phenomenon.

> All the western writers point to the absence of one such organization prior to the era of Abdulhamid the Second (1876–1909). On the other hand Europe, who was struggling with the "Pan" movements within herself (Pan Germanism, Pan Slavism) interpreted the events in her colonies (the Punjab revolt in 1820s, Algerian resistance against France in 1830) through the same lens. By the end of the 1860s, Europe has come to the conclusion that there was a threat of Pan Islam in the East. Whereas there was no mention of any such term in the East, a European author who lived in Istanbul during 1820–1870, states he saw no evidence of people riding horses with their swords and fighting like another Mohammed trying to convert others to Islam—the image of Panislamist is nonexistent. (Kologlu 1990)

Once the "other" (Ottomans) identified with the images projected by the "self" (European powers) and with the internalization of the projections, Islam became a central, politically motivating element of Ottoman identity.

> For twenty-five years before the Great War, the German government with its diplomats and military officers worked to cultivate the Ottoman Empire. All this time, they were clearly preparing for a world war in which Turkey was to play a decisive role. Undoubtedly, Turkey's policy fitted with the German plans. In Istanbul, German ambassador Wangenheim purchased one of the largest Turkish newspapers, Ikdam, which immediately began to praise Germany and abuse Entente. The Osmanischer Lloyd, published in French and German, was already the official organ of the German embassy. Baron Max von Oppenheim, who was supposedly an archaeologist, but known to the British as "the Kaiser's spy," traveled all over Turkey manufacturing public opinion against England and France, opening offices everywhere for this propaganda facility. Kaiser Wilhelm suddenly became "Haci Wilheim" ("Haci" is a person who has completed a ritual pilgrimage to Muslim Holy sites on the Arabian Peninsula), the great protector of Islam (during the earlier part of the Second World War when Turkey was close to Germany the same rumors would spread about Hitler).
> The Turkish populace was informed that Moslems of India and Egypt were about to revolt and overthrow their English tyrants. In his illuminating article, Hamed reported that Baron Oppenheim "was also known to lose no opportunity of reminding the Egyptian nationalist press of the syllogism that Islam was threatened with extinction by Europe, that Britain and France were at the head

of the anti-Islamic movement, that the Sultan was the last hope of the faithful, and that Germany was the friend of the Sultan and, therefore, the only Muslim-minded European power . . . . The plan behind Germany's deliberate policy to support pan-Islamism was to stir Muslims up against the English and the Russians in order to force them to make peace. The Holy War was a means for destroying the English and French influence in the territories where Germany had economic interests." (Deren 2002)

There were also high stakes for Britain. An ally of Ottomans during the Russian wars in the mid-nineteenth century, now Britain was developing a negative image of the Ottomans, as Ottomans and Germans were becoming allies:

> Kitchener, like most Britons who lived in the East, believed that in the Moslem world religion counts for everything . . . the field marshal and his colleagues mistakenly seemed to believe that Mohammedanism was a centralized authoritarian structure. They regarded Islam as a single entity, as an "It," as an organization. They believed that it obeyed its leaders. In much the same spirit, Kitchener and his colleagues believed that Islam could be bought, manipulated, or captured by buying, manipulating, or capturing its religious leadership. . . . Central to Kitchener's analysis was the contention that Caliph had fallen into the hands of Jews and Germans. The Director of Information, John Buchanan dramatized these fears in his 1916 novel titled *Greenmantle*, in which Germany makes use of a Moslem prophet in a plot to destroy Britain's empire. The prophet appears in Turkey. . . . Kitchener's proposal was that after the war, Britain should arrange for her own nominee to become the Caliph. Mohammed has been an Arabian. Kitchener proposed to encourage the view that Mohammed's successors as Caliph should be Arabian, too . . . an obvious candidate to be that Arabian Caliph was the ruler of Mecca. (Fromkin 2001)

By 1918, at the end of the Great War, the Ottoman Empire was dismantled, and the millennia-old Christian/Moslem conflict receded. Shadows of their once-mighty selves, the Ottomans were encapsulated in their original nucleus in Anatolia, trying to recover from the calamitous blows of the previous hundred years. With the subordination of Ottomans, another shift occurred in the eyes of the West: there was a change from malevolent to inferior/naïve/primitive. A good example of this is the Greek perception of Ottomans at the end of World War I when, in an attempt to reconquer a land that was lost to Turks one thousand years before, the Greek army landed in Izmir on 1919, and started an eastward move into Anatolia:

> The landing was the high point of Prime Minister Elefterios Venizelos' relentless pursuit of the Megali Idea, "The Great Idea" of a resurrected Greek empire with Constantinople as its capital, uniting all Greeks under the flag of Hellas. Linking twentieth-century Greece with its illustrious imperial past, Venizelos

based his claim to substantial parts of western Asia Minor, not on the mere existence of a sizeable Greek Minority there, but also on (alleged) Greek cultural
superiority, which made the Greeks far more "suitable" than Turks to rule these
areas. The Greeks, he argued, represented "an old and advanced civilization,"
whereas the Turks were good workers, honest in their relations, and good people as subjects. But as rulers, they were insupportable and a disgrace to civilization. (Karsh and Karsh 1999)

As Volkan and Itzkowitz demonstrate in this book in their chapter on Atatürk
(chapter 4), Turks counteridentified with this image.

TURKEY AND THE WEST

Now, we will expand our tour further west; the history of Turkish/American
relations will shed further light on the central themes of this chapter. One of
the first American chroniclers of Ottomans was Mark Twain. In his travels
during the mid-nineteenth century, with his usual self-effacing wit, Twain
made humorous comments about Ottoman lands, more in the line of observing some harmless, peculiar, primitive people (Twain 1966). This uninformed
and fantasy image of Ottomans changed with increased American political interest in the Middle East. During World War I and afterward, as the Turkish
War of Independence (1920–1923) unfolded, a negative image of Turkey
gradually developed in the American public. But this image did not live long
and saw a positive change by the end of the 1920s. Probably due to an increased American awareness of the fact that the Soviet Union had withstood
the first Western assault and needed to be taken into consideration, American
policy shifted toward befriending Turkey, who was positioned geographically
in the underbelly of this new power, almost as Cuba is in relation to the
United States. This brought intense efforts on both sides to clear the public
image of the Turk in the United States (Yilmaz 2003).

   After World War II, as the cold war was warming up, a very significant gesture was made: in 1946, the battleship USS *Missouri* visited Turkey. The *Missouri* was an American icon, imprinted in the world's memoirs with the scene
of the surrender of Japan to the West, symbolized in the proud persona of
General MacArthur. The ship was bringing the remains of the Turkish Ambassador, who had died in 1944, to the United States. The fact that the remains of the Turkish ambassador were brought back on the *Missouri* (instead
of being flown on a plane) was a remarkable statement to Turkey and her
neighbor the Soviet Union.

   In return, Turkey sent troops to Korea in 1950. The bravery of Turkish soldiers was highly praised by Americans. Turkey was a staunch ally against

Communism and was praised as a vital constituent of the West. With these events in the background, in 1952, Turkey applied to NATO and was immediately accepted as a member. Turkey was a secular country, and being the only NATO member with a predominately Muslim population elated the Turks.

It was fashionable to use American and Western names in Turkey: In "Missouri Café" you could play pool, backgammon, cards, or drink tea, and smoke your water pipe. "NATO Drycleaners" was a neighborhood shop. Or you could have an elegant dinner at the "Washington Restaurant." The Turkish government that had recently joined NATO was euphoric, and there was talk about becoming the "Little America." The Turkish President Celal Bayar made a month-long trip to the United States in 1954, where he was received with fanfare (Bali 2004). Following this bizarrely long visit, on his homecoming to Istanbul, the president had a ticker-tape parade on Istiklal Avenue (Grand Rue de Pera, apparently the Turkish equivalent of Broadway) (Barkay 2003), a style of celebration that was never used before or since. The process of becoming "Little America" had begun, with an intriguing level of idealization of/identification with America and gave a clear boost to the depleted narcissism of the Turks.

References were made to how Istanbul, Ankara, and Izmir were similar to New York, Washington, and San Francisco respectively (Alkan 2003). Turkey had her share of the global anti-American sentiment of the 1960s and 1970s, but on the whole, in the latter half of the twentieth century, there was a widespread positive public image of America in the minds of Turkish masses/elite. In 2003, the second war in Iraq caused a major rupture. Turkey's decision to not be involved was a serious setback for American plans. With the souring of relations, some very disturbing images of the "other" appeared on both sides. On the American side, in a primetime series, the American president was portrayed as heroically interfering to save the life of a Turkish woman who was going to be executed by beheading for the crime of adultery (Turkey does not have a death penalty, and France is the only European country where beheadings are utilized). Victims, threatening, belittling remarks about Turkey poured out of prominent newspapers. Re-runs of *Lawrence of Arabia* (where Arabs revolted against Ottomans during World War I) appeared on television. One TV series told the story of a dormant Turkish terrorist cell in the United States.

The shift on the Turkish side reached massive proportions; it engulfed the bulk of the nation, from cab drivers to academics to generals. Turkey was going through the most pervasive, vicious anti-American, anti-Christian upheaval of the last hundred years. A Turkish bestseller of 2005 was a novel about the United States invading Turkey. As the United States was bombing, destroying the whole country, Turks, in return, were exploding nuclear bombs in the United States. Another novel was written stating that now Turks were invading the United States. As the new occupiers of the White House, Turks changed the name to "Red and White House" (after the colors of the Turkish flag) and naturally, the new American president was a Turk!

TURKEY–EUROPEAN UNION NEGOTIATIONS

Regressions in the images of self/other also occur during periods of massive large-group movements, such as in mass immigrations. A contemporaneous example of these phenomena is the history of the negotiations between Turkey and the European Union (EU). Turkey has been interested in becoming a member of the EU since 1963. There were deep ambivalences on both sides (Uyar 2004). The Turkish side finally overcame the decades-long reluctance, applied for full membership, and on December of 2004, was given a date when she would begin negotiations with the members of the EU. The final years of this process created substantial splits in Turkey on whether they should join the EU. The intensity of the debate was enormous, each side accusing the other of treason. There were similar splits in Europe.

The political cartoons of 2000–2002 offered a good window into the archaic self/other images that were awakened:

Due to the fact the political cartoons lack political correctness, they reveal the deepest and most spontaneous feelings and images about their objects almost without any mental filtration. . . . Cartoons exhibit the unveiled portrait of societies. . . . On the European side, there is a tendency to understand Turkey as a stereotypical homogenous, politically undeveloped entity. In the cartoons where they depict a well-known Western figure (say American President Bush or British Prime Minister Blair), the Western character is discernible (it may be mocked—for example, Bush may be portrayed as a chimpanzee), but the Turkish figure is anonymous, stereotypical, usually wearing a fez or turban. Usually the character has excess bodily hair—moustache, hairy hands, and bushy eyebrows. There are some instances where a Turk is drawn as a childlike, immature figure, sometimes deformed and even animal like. Also the greedy, fat image with a devilish, foxy smile is another stereotype. Belly dancing, Taliban-like figures are also utilized. . . . On the Turkish side, there is duality of the images as is well expected. These images of the other are between an "Imperial West" and a "Civilized West." There are remarks on Europe being a train that Turks need to catch, a castle that they need to conquer. There is a condensation of the West—Europe is joined with the United States, and the differences within Europe are ignored. (Erensu and Adanali 2004)

The distortion seen in the cartoons was all around; as the day of negotiations approached, primitive images of the other were leaking from high-level talks. Behind closed doors, comparisons were made between the Turkish government and carpet sellers, bazaar traders, and vegetable sellers. On the Turkish side, there were cutting remarks referring to the bureaucrats of Brussels as rich, arrogant fat cats who lead decadent immoral lives (Deutsche Welle 2004).

This irrationality climaxed on December 17, 2004, when Turkey was finally given a date for the beginning of negotiations for membership. Here are some samples from the Turkish conservative and liberal sides:

- The civilization of exploitation is intent on leveling the world to slavery, blood, and tears. The only way of rising against EU, United States, Israel, and England is "The National Attitude." This is an attitude of peace, justice, equality, dialogue, freedom against exploitation and slavery. They are pretending as if they don't want Turkey in EU—they will try to trap us in the jail of EU. The Western powers are trying to take away our independence (*Milli Gazete,* December 18, 2004—conservative).
- December 17, 2004—It is the great day of our history. Being able to live this day in Brussels must be one of this highest privileges granted by history to an individual. And I was one of those individuals. There was a dramatic "diplomatic warfare" over the course of some hours: Turkey on one side and a twenty-five-member body on the other side. A political body that has rigid rule, important difference within itself despite a basic sense of unity. . . . And our Prime Minister won this "war of diplomacy and nerves." This was a glorious victory—the most important in the last forty years according to some, and 200 years according to others. . . . It went back and forth. We were saved from being strung up . . . and history was written. . . . Really, history was written. . . . We are not saying this—our European "partners" are. We can all them "partners" now. Because now, Turkey is on the "Interstate EU." This interstate is not without bumps. There are bumps, potholes, dangerous turns, and it is a long journey for Turkey. But Turkey is not any more on a dirt road, a side street, or a street. She is on the "EU Interstate," moving toward the tollbooths. Once we pass them, we will be in (Candar 2004, liberal).
- "Turkish Republic entered the most important part of its history. These are some of our happiest days. We are on the verge of actualizing Atatürk's will. Turkey set sail for contemporary civilization. . . . Today is a turning point in modern history of Turkey. . . . Today is the beginning of the end of the identity problem of Turkey. . . . We are told we may play in the major leagues now. . . . The wheels of an enormous project of change have started turning—a project that will not only change Turkey,

but the whole of Europe. From this point on, let's use our power to the end. We started like Germans, let's finish like British. Let's not give up in the middle of this road" (Birand 2004, liberal).

The interpretations are quite dramatic: Turkey was on the verge of being "hanged" if she was not given a date. When she got the date, it was the most important event in the last two hundred years. These are images of dirt road, side streets versus interstate highways. Clearly, there was an amazing degree of envy/admiration on the Turkish side and the battered, proud heirs of Ottomans were hungry for praise and acceptance.

As the French and Dutch referendums of 2005 (where the majority of the population said "no" to the proposed EU Constitution) demonstrate, Turkey's getting a date for negotiations and the possibility of joining EU created regressive swings and substantial splits in Europe (BBC News 2005). The perfect summary of the negative European reactions to the prospect of an inflated Muslim population appeared on the cover page of a prominent weekly magazine in which an icon of the West, the *Mona Lisa*—the famous painting by Leonardo Da Vinci—was portrayed as wearing a turban!

CONCLUDING REMARKS

Large groups create distorted, stereotypical shared representations of self and others that are unstable, susceptible to regressive shifts in response to boundary transformations (Volkan 2004, 23–55). These representations that are encoded in diametrically opposite concepts of good/bad, superior/inferior, beautiful/ugly, simplify the complexities of the world and create, synoptic, ideological, "fast-food" interpretation of history available for the quick consumption of the masses. Once created, these images gain autonomy and become one of the determinants of history; they initiate projective identificatory processes and have a remarkable potential to mobilize/guide the masses as an ideological/political roadmap.

History becomes much more complicated if we are not exclusively motivated to create an ideological narrative that serves the pragmatic needs of a political agenda. As an example, we can propose diverse interpretations to the topics that we outlined above.

The process that culminated in the formation of Ottoman Empire was one in which the nomads of Central Asia, in their relentless push westward, were in a very complicated relationship with the autochthonous cultures they were conquering. Somewhat similar to the "barbarian conquest of Rome," when the conquerors melted into the conquered civilization, the great Arabic, Persian,

Byzantine civilizations were incorporated into the rich fabric of Ottoman civilization. They were not aiming at creating a Moslem-Turk supremacy (Inalcik 1987, 137–84). The rulers of this new formation deeply identified with the conquered culture and didn't view themselves as centrally Muslim or Turk until the late nineteenth century (Ortayli 2003, 23–33). The clearest example of this is seen in the aforementioned self-description of the grandest of Ottomans, Suleiman the First. He described himself as the "Han," "Sultan," "Padishah," and the "Caesar of Rome." These are, in that order, Turkish, Arabic, Persian, and Eastern Roman titles.

The conquest/fall of Istanbul can be interpreted as a victory of Islam over Christianity, but in reality was much more complicated. A brother of Mehmet the Conqueror, Orhan, was fighting on the side of Byzantium and was killed on the walls of Constantinople while defending the city (Inalcik 2004, 30–39). The Conqueror made every effort to protect the status of the Orthodox Patriarch as the Ecumenical Center of Eastern Christianity; the current-day flag of the Archpatriate in Istanbul was given by the Conqueror. He was probably Greek on his maternal side and had a deep interest in Greek/Latin culture. There were some personal sides to him that would be very hard to reconcile with the current-day interpretation of Islam: he would drink wine (so did Suleiman) and had his portrait painted, both of which are considered idolatrous. It is most likely that he considered himself the new Emperor of Eastern Rome rather than anything else.

On the other side of the coin, the history of "West" and "Christian" are also infinitely complicated, as an average reader of this chapter would very well know. What is depicted as West/Christian has a long and bloody history of religious and ethnic/national schisms that would easily defy proposing these terms as unifying, defining concepts of "self" or "other." West and Christian are clearly ideological representations that serve political agendas and are not fair representations of historical complexity.

This overview of the ideological, distorted self/other images of Islam and Christianity has an important implication for our times. Today, the United States and Europe, the two dominating economical/cultural foci of the world, are undergoing challenging boundary transformations. Europe, through migration and Turkey's potential EU membership, is facing a massive increase in her Muslim population. The United States, on the other hand, is struggling with a rapid acceleration in the growth of its Latino population, mainly through migration from Mexico. These large-group movements, which are happening on a scale that has never been seen before, have stirred up an "identity confusion" in the United States and Europe, and opened a heated debate of "who are we?" (Strath 2001). When there was an outside "other"— Communism, the Evil Empire of the Soviets—the United States and Europe were content with a vague self-image of "goodness." But with the threat coming from the inside, similar to the struggle of Ottomans a century ago, there is a push for self-definitions that are different from the simple "goodness." In Europe and the United States, a narcissistically cathected, harshly demarcated image of "white/Protestant (United States), white/Christian (Europe)" self in contrast to the "Latino, Muslim" other are being proposed. In the way it is defined, this "self" is seen as superior to the "other," claiming ownership of a geographic territory and expecting the other to dissolve in self, if it wants to live in that territory. This internal turmoil is also projected to the outer world.

Samuel Huntington is probably the most prominent expositor of this new ideology. Huntington, who coined the inauspicious term of "clash of civilizations," is also the author of an influential article on "Hispanic Challenge," in which he interprets the massive Hispanic migration to the United States as an internal clash. Somewhat analogous to Gladstone, who was viewing the outer world through the lens of his own personal, troubled internal world, Huntington, on a different level, is seeing the world through the lens of the troubled internal affairs of the United States. His political agenda and ideological interpretations, which are finding wide acceptance as theories both in the United States and in the outer world, are offering an ominous prognosis for the young century (Huntington 1993; 2004).

These are challenging times for the world, times where the way in which we conceptualize the world and base our political strategies will be of enormous significance. We have the option of either seeing "evil," "inevitable clashes," thus creating global witch hunts, and evoking regressions in large groups—or, we have the option of perceiving "conflicts," and facilitating "conflict resolution" through peaceful processes. The great wars of the twentieth century in which millions perished are examples of the former option. The great negotiations of the latter half of the twentieth century—between the United States and Mexico, between Europe and Turkey—are examples of the latter.

A luminous son of Ottomans, Mustafa Kemal (Atatürk) was the victorious general of one of the fiercest battles of the Great War—Gallipoli. It was a deadly skirmish between Allies and Ottomans in 1915, where both sides lost tens of thousands of their sons. In 1933, Mustafa Kemal, who proved to be a brilliant, vicious, fearless general in these wars and who ordered many thousands on his side to die and took the lives of thousands on the other side, was delivering this eulogy to his once-enemies, ANZACS, now buried in Turkish soil: "These heroes that shed their blood and lost their lives. . . . You are now lying in the soil of a friendly country. Therefore, rest in peace. There is no difference between the Johnnies and the Mehmets to us, where they lie side by side here in this country of ours. . . . You, the mothers, who sent their sons from far away countries, wipe away your tears; your sons are now lying in our bosom and are in peace. After having lost their lives on this land, they have become our sons as well" (ANZAC monument in Gelibolu, Turkey). A year later, Turkey turned the glorious Hagia Sophia, which had been converted to a mosque by the Conqueror, into a museum. Mustafa Kemal wanted this magnificent edifice to be a symbol of the joining of West and East, of Christianity and Islam. He was offering to see the "self" in the "other." In 1933, Sigmund Freud, the brilliant leader of battles with the demons of the human psyche, was making a similar proposition: "*Wo Es war, soll Ich werden*" (Freud 1933). Mustafa Kemal and Freud were in essence offering us the hopeful concept that if we chose to see the "self" in the "other," or ponder the possibility of seeing "self" in "it," then we will not have to be trapped in a defeatist determinism in which we prophesize the inevitable clash of civilizations or the unrivaled dominance of the "it."

In the same year, 1933, a choice with atrocious consequences to follow was being made in the middle of Christian Europe. A choice where "it" was severed from "self," where "other" was seen as "not self": the gates of the first official German concentration camp—Dachau—had opened.

12

Jewish-Muslim Relations

Middle East

Joseph V. Montville

We have sent revelation to you as we did to Noah and the prophets after him, To Abraham, Ishmael, Isaac, Jacob, and the Tribes, to Jesus, Job, Jonah, Aaron, and Solomon, and to David we gave the Psalms.

—Qur'an 4:163

On August 18, 1988, the Islamic Resistance Movement in Palestine, better known as Hamas, published its covenant. It contains a statement of special interest for a psychodynamic assessment of Jewish-Muslim relations: "The injustice of next-of-kin is harder to bear than the smite of the Indian sword" (Avalon Project 1988, 5). The Internet provides a drawing of a weapon said to be an Indian sword—short, but wide at the hilt, tapering to a sharp point. Its reputation for murderous efficiency would appear to be great in Muslim memory. But the phrase that is most significant in the Hamas statement is "the injustice of next-of-kin," in the context of bitter condemnation of Israel. This chapter attempts to explain why this might be so.

There is an intimate historical relationship between Jews and Muslims starting with the experience of the Prophet Muhammad in Mecca and Medina in the late sixth and early seventh centuries C.E., extending to the Islamic conquest of Mesopotamia and the encounter with the Exilarch (Resh Galutha) or head of the Jewish community in the Sassanian (Persian) Empire based in Babylonia. The relationship reached its creative peak in Muslim Spain from the incursion by Tariq ibn Ziyad in 711 C.E. through the tenth-century Caliphate of Abd al-Rahman III in Cordoba, and even through the political collapse of the Caliphate and the rise in the eleventh century of competing city-states in Al-Andalus, as Muslim Spain was called in Arabic.

Nissim Rejwan, the Baghdad-born Israeli historian, has written that in the era of Muslim Spain, the majority of the Jewish people lived under Arab rule in the broad Mediterranean region. "It was at this point that began the long and brilliant period which can be said to have been the most flourishing in Jewish history, and whose significance for the Jews and for Judaism to this day cannot be exaggerated" (1997, 1). The Umayyad Caliphate in Cordoba became a political and cultural center of legendary beauty and great achievement. The city had some 700 mosques, over 3,000 public baths, street lamps, and many libraries. It is said that the caliph's library had 400,000 manuscripts.

According to historian Erna Paris, "public literacy was a government priority. Successive caliphs built libraries that were open to all; in fact, one tenth-century ruler, Hakam II, was so obsessed with books that he sent emissaries to Baghdad with orders to buy every manuscript that had ever been produced . . . . The Jewish poets of Andalusia were profoundly influenced by their Muslim compatriots, and from the tenth to the twelfth century, during the justly named Golden age of the Spanish Jews, they, too, wrote remarkably beautiful verse" (1995, 42).

This special period in Muslim-Jewish relations in Al-Andalus came to an abrupt and brutal end, with the completion of the Spanish Reconquista by the Catholic King and Queen of Castile and Aragon, Ferdinand and Isabella, and the surrender of the last Muslim city-state of Granada, on January 2, 1492. The edict expelling the Jews and Muslims from now completely Christian-dominated Spain was signed on March 31, 1492. But, there was to be relief for most of these Jews rejected by the Christian kings.

The Ottoman Empire had been providing a refuge for Jews from Spain and Portugal in Istanbul, the Balkan provinces, and the city of Salonika, which became a major center of Jewish life until its population was sent to the death camps in World War II. Sultan Bayezid II (1481–1512 C.E.) also welcomed Iberian Jews to the newly conquered Arab provinces of Egypt, Syria, and Palestine. Norman Stillman reported, "Bayezid and his courtiers are said to have considered Ferdinand of Spain a fool for impoverishing his own kingdom while enriching theirs. Some of the Sefardic (sic) immigrants were skilled in the art of manufacturing weapons and helped the Turks produce some of their cannon and powder" (1979, 87). Indeed, many of the Jewish refugees were skilled agriculturalists, artisans, merchants, physicians, artists, and linguists. Some historians believe that it took centuries for the newly Christian Spanish economy to recover from the sudden loss of its Jewish population.

During the fifteenth, sixteenth, and part of the seventeenth centuries under Ottoman rule, Jews, some of whom were immigrants from Christian Europe, played complementary roles to the Turks in society and the economy. They often conducted diplomatic missions for the Ottoman government in Europe. They were sources of investment capital for the empire through extended networks of entrepreneurs. The Turks, for their part, preferred to use Jews in these special roles rather that members of the Christian minority. The latter was made up of Greeks, Armenians, Italians, and Arabic-speaking Christians from the Levant. Because of the steady encroachment of Christian European powers on the lands of the Ottoman Empire, Jews were more trusted than Christian subjects, who could be expected to intrigue with their coreligionists who continuously threatened the Sultanate.

Inevitably, as Ottoman Turkey became more known as the "sick man of Europe" and with Latin and Protestant Christian powers pushing from the west and Orthodox Christian Russia pushing down from the north, Ottoman Christian subjects became bolder in promoting themselves and pushing the Jews aside in economic and social competition. Immigration of Ashkenazi Jews from Europe to the Ottoman Empire started to dry up in the seventeenth century and, thus, the contacts Ottoman Jews had had with Europe dried up also. As Ottoman Christians increased their ties to Europe, sending their sons to local Christian or European schools for educations, they came to replace Jews in privileged positions of service to the government. For example, in the age-old honored profession of physicians to the Ottoman nobility, Jews gave ground to better-educated Greek physicians.

As Bernard Lewis (1984) put it, by the eighteenth century,

[T]he Jews . . . had to endure the consequences of the rising power of Christendom. The [Ottoman] Christians had many friends in Europe; the Jews had few. The Christians had ships; the Jews had none. And above all, the Christians could count on the support, the Jews on the ill will, of European traders, and, by this time, it was the preferences of European Christians, rather of Muslim Turks, that counted. (1984, 144)

Nissim Rejwan wrote in a 1980 essay that there were three great civilizations with which the Jews had significant contact: Greek, Arab-Muslim, and Roman-Germanic. He cites the late Princeton historian Shlomo Dov Goitein as saying that the closest symbiosis was with the civilization of Arabic Islam. For over a thousand years, from the seventh to the seventeenth centuries, Jews were part of this civilization. Goitein wrote that the civilization of the ancient Greeks was for Jews like modern Western civilization, essentially unconnected with the religious culture of the Jews. He explained that, "Islam is of the very flesh and bone of Judaism."

Rejwan cites another respected authority, Professor Erwin Rosenthal of Cambridge University, saying: "There was never more similarity between a tolerated Judaism and its adherents and a civilized, masterful overlord until the post-emancipation period. . . . The Jews adopted the Arabic language of their conquerors and, with it, many a norm and quite a few ideas. And yet, despite all assimilation to the Muslim mode of life and to Muslim ways of thought, the Jews under Islam maintained, even enriched, their distinctive character as Jews with a vigor and determination hitherto unknown" (1980, 4).

Of course, a parallel drama was moving toward its denouement for the Jews of Christian Europe. The pathological anti-Semitism rooted in the dogma of the church never abated, even with the French revolutionary emancipation of all subject citizens regardless of race or creed. Under the Rights of Man, every person enjoyed equality, but as an individual, not as a member of a specific group. Thus Jews, as Jews, were not recognized as a distinct people in the new secular era. Yet, they were increasingly subject to discrimination as a distinct people in Western and Eastern Europe and especially in Russia, where the Czarist inspired or approved pogroms of the nineteenth century against Jewish villages and communities became more frequent and brutal.

It would come as no surprise, at least in retrospect, that amidst the surge of ethnic nationalisms in the era of declining empires, a Jewish national movement would arise out of despair that European Christendom would ever accept Jews as free and equal. Zionism became a force that would eventually loom large in the history of the twentieth and twenty-first centuries. The quest for a Jewish state that would make all Jews safe was forged in the crucible of enduring and apparently incurable Christian hatred of Jews collectively and for all time for their alleged responsibility in the crucifixion of Christ. The result was the establishment of Israel in 1948, an event that would profoundly affect the tradition of close, nonpathological, Jewish-Muslim relations going back to the time of the Prophet Muhammad some 1,300 years earlier. Unlike Christendom, in Islam, the Jews were never a problem to be solved. They were, in the bitterly ironic perspective of today's headlines, indeed theologically next-of-kin to the Muslims. To comprehend the psychodynamic importance of this fact, it is essential to take at least a broad brushed history of the Muslim-Jewish relationship from its origin.

It is particularly important to get this early history right because of its false but widespread belief in pubic opinion that Islam has been an implacable enemy from the very beginning.

THE PROPHET AND THE JEWS

Historians believe that Muhammad's first contacts with Christians and Jews occurred during his years in Mecca where he was born around 571 C.E.[1] Jewish communities in cities in Southern Arabia went back to biblical times as evidenced by the story of Solomon and the Queen of Sheba. In the northern oases of the peninsula, Jews probably settled in the era of the Second Temple, and after the Romans destroyed the Temple in 70 C.E., refugees from Judea moved south for safety. The Jews of the region were thought to be a mix of some who fled Palestine, but were mostly local Arab converts to Judaism.

The trade route from Mecca to Damascus passed through the Wadi al-Qura, The Valley of the Villages, which had a sizable population of Jews. Muslim historians believe that Muhammad made two or three caravan trips to Damascus, and he must have met Jews—and Christians—en route.

Because the *Qur'an* has so many references to the Hebrew *Bible* and the Christian *New Testament*, some historians have speculated that Muhammad must have read these books. Traditional Muslim historians contend that Muhammad was illiterate and therefore incapable of reading the sacred texts. Any such references the *Qur'an* has to these texts or material in them, therefore, came directly from God through revelations to Muhammad.[2] Other researchers believe that, given the cosmopolitan nature of Mecca as a major trade and pilgrimage center and that Muhammad helped his wife, Khadija, with her trading business, he must have had functional literacy. Almost all historians seem to agree that he did not read the *Bible*, either *Old* or *New Testament*, but that monotheism was in the air, and he is very likely to have heard missionaries talk about the revealed word of God, dominant polytheism notwithstanding.

The serious engagement of the Prophet with Jews began after his *Hijra* or flight from his enemies in Mecca to Medina—then called Yathrib—in 622 C.E. There were twenty Jewish clans, the three largest of which were the Qunayqa, the Nadir, and the Qurayza. Eight clans were composed of Arab polytheists or pagans who settled the oasis when the Jews were predominant, but had since asserted their authority. The Jews made protective alliances with Arab clans, the most powerful of which were the Aws and the Khazraj, who were bitter rivals. Because of intermarriage between Jews and Arabs, it was difficult to distinguish among them, although the clans in general lived in each their own neighborhood. The Jews identified themselves not as one religious community but by their clan identity.

Muhammad had been sought out in Mecca by representatives of the Aws and Khazraj, who were constantly feuding because of the declining resource base of Medina. They wanted a respected and neutral Hakam or arbiter to help them settle their disputes with the minimum amount of costly violence. The Jewish clans did not take part in this invitation to Muhammad.

Muhammad started out in a relatively weak position in Medina. He had a sense of mission to create an Ummah—a community of Muslims—who would rise above the combative tribal ways of the nomadic tradition and live an orderly, law-abiding life as settled urban societies. He also had strong beliefs about social justice and responsibility for widows, orphans, the poor, and otherwise needy members of society. His values were almost identical to those of Jesus in Palestine some six hundred years earlier. Indeed, Jesus is one of the most respected of the prophets mentioned numerous times in the *Qur'an.*

In Muhammad's view, the people of Mecca were not only misguided polytheists, but also self-centered individuals whose major goal was to enrich themselves through their control of a major trade entrepôt and the income derived from pilgrims coming to visit their false gods. One of the surahs in the *Qur'an* was focused on the dominant tribe of Mecca, the Quraysh: "Woe to every slanderer and backbiter, Who amasses wealth, hoarding it to himself. Does he really think his wealth will make him immortal? By no means! He will be cast into the fire kindled by God" (*Qur'an* 104:4–6).

Through the traditional practice of raiding caravans without shedding blood, Muhammad and his followers generated a needed income stream, but also kept also the attention of the Meccans who remained hostile to the Prophet and the Muslims, determined to crush their very troubling challenge to the Meccan way of life and business. The antagonism resulted in several historic battles between Muhammad's forces from Medina and attacking Meccan forces allied ad hoc with neighboring Bedouin tribes. These battles not only established the political, military, and moral power of the Muslims, but also had important consequences for Muhammad's relationships with the three principal Jewish clans in Medina.

In 624, Muhammad heard of a very large caravan headed to Mecca from Palestine. He gathered three hundred men for a raid. But on arrival at the city of Badr, the party was greeted by a Qurayshi body of a thousand warriors ready to chase off and finally defeat the tiresome upstarts from Medina. Some persons who knew of Muhammad's plan had passed it on to the Quraysh. There were spies in the midst of the Muslims. In what commentators characterize as a miracle, the outnumbered Muslims routed the Quraysh, losing only twelve of their own fighters. In this victory, Muhammad established himself a winner in the only way that mattered with other men and tribes. Large numbers of clan members moved to Medina to ally themselves with the Prophet.

As for the spies who alerted the Quraysh on the planned caravan raid, Muhammad suspected the Jewish Qaynuqa clan. This was the wealthiest clan because of its very profitable trade in dates, wine, and arms with Mecca and also because of its previous control of the local market in Medina, which was ended when Muhammad banned the Qaynuqa's monopoly regime of taxes and fees. In effect, the Muslims' conflict with Mecca was bad for business and the very important relationship with the Quraysh. As Reza Aslan writes,

"Despite the victory at Badr, there was still no reason to believe Muhammad could actually conquer the Quraysh. Eventually the Meccans would regroup and return to defeat the Prophet. And when that happened, it would be imperative for the Jewish clans to make their loyalties to the Quraysh absolutely clear" (2005, 89).

Almost immediately after the Battle of Badr, the Prophet drew up the so-called Constitution of Medina that laid out the responsibility of all inhabitants of the city to aid in its defense. For the Jewish clans, the document guaranteed religious and social freedoms. It said, "to the Jews their religion and to the Muslims their religion." Violation of the constitution by any individual or clan would be considered treason and, under tribal law, punishable by death to the men, slavery to the women and children, and distribution of property among the troops. However, the Prophet decided against tribal law and allowed the Qaynuqa to go into exile, taking the bulk of their property with them.

One year later, in a return match with the Quraysh and their allies at Uhud near Medina, the Muslims were beaten badly when overzealous soldiers that were told to guard the flank foolishly left their position after an enemy retreat to gather booty from the battlefield. The Quraysh regrouped and destroyed the Muslim force, almost killing the Prophet, who had his jaw broken and teeth smashed. He was rescued by one of his fighters and carried to safety in a cave.

Muhammad learned after the battle that the shaykh of the Jewish Nadir clan had met with the commander of the Meccan forces and the shaykh tried to assassinate Muhammad. Once again, as with the Qaynuqa, a Muslim force, this one somewhat ragged, laid siege to the Nadir stronghold. The latter appealed to the only remaining large Jewish clan for aid, but the Qurayza declined. To the reported disgust of the Muslim troops who had suffered terrible losses at Uhud, the Prophet again agreed to allow the Nadir, clearly guilty of treason under the Constitution of Medina, to go move to the oasis of Khaybar, with their property.

The final and definitive battle with the Meccans came at the Battle of the Trench in 627 C.E. Muhammad had reportedly learned from a Persian veteran the technique of defending a city by surrounding it with a deep trench. After a month-long siege, the Meccans and their allies could not advance on Medina, and weary and out of supplies, they gave up and returned home. For some reason, the last of the large Jewish clans, the Qurayza, openly supported the Meccan forces during the siege, providing them with weapons and supplies. They may have still believed that Muhammad would eventually be defeated, and as they had no religious loyalty to him because he allowed them to keep their faith, they wanted to hedge their bets and preserve their Meccan ties.

They may also have believed that even if the Muslims won, the worst that could happen to them was exile with their property, as had happened to the Qaynuqa and Nadir. If this is so, they could not have been more mistaken.

Muhammad drew the line with the Qurayza. He asked a neutral Hakam or arbiter to decide the fate of the clan. The Hakam, the Shaykh of the Arab Aws clan, with which the Qurayza actually had a client relationship, decided to invoke tribal justice. Thus, several hundred men were executed, the women and children enslaved, and the property divided among the Muslims. Some commentators have said that the killing of the Qurayza men was cruel. Francesco Gabrieli, a noted scholar of Islam wrote that the execution, reaffirms "our consciousness as Christian and civilized men, that this God, or at least this aspect of Him, is not ours" (Aslan 2005, 92). Others of the more polemical school of historians have held that the execution was an early example the historic hostility of Islam to the Jewish people. However, Norman Stillman, an observant Jew, has written that the killing of the Qurayza was consistent with the tribal justice of the time.

Yet, even sympathetic historians have said that the conflict with the Jewish clans in Medina was a sign of profound theological difference between the Muslims and the Jews. There is an undocumented tradition among some historians that the Prophet and the Jews debated the accuracy of the *Bible* and the *Qur'an*, which at the time was not yet written down. Certainly there are passages in the *Qur'an* that show serious impatience and frustration with the Jews, but most scholars do not believe this was over theology. The Prophet criticized Jews for failing to live up to their religion, as did the Biblical prophets and Jesus in the *New Testament*. Apparently in response to political exigencies of the time, later Muslim chroniclers put anti-Jewish words into the mouth of the Prophet that are completely inconsistent with his belief that the Jews, Christian, and Muslims were all part of a monotheistic family who worshiped God and who, if they led moral lives and believed in the last day, would reap their reward in heaven.

THE PEOPLE OF THE BOOK

The critical concept in the *Qur'an* that undergirds the idea of family of believers is that God's revelation to Muhammad is a confirmation of the books revealed to the Jews and the Christians. There are several references in the *Qur'an* to the "*Umm al-Kitab*," "Mother of the Book," the original source of God's guidance that God keeps and from which the *Torah* and the Gospels of Jesus and the *Qur'an* were drawn. Reza Aslan writes, "Muhammad may have understood the *Umm al-Kitab* to mean not only that the Jews, Christians, and

Muslims shared a single divine scripture, but also that they constituted a single divine *Ummah* (community of believers). As far as Muhammad was concerned, the Jews and the Christians were 'People of the Book' . . . spiritual cousins who, as opposed to the pagans and polytheists of Arabia, worshipped the same God, read the same scriptures, and shared the same moral values as his Muslim community. Although each faith comprised its own distinct religious community (its own individual Ummah), together they formed one united Ummah" (2005, 11).

Indeed, Muhammad asked his followers to fast on Yom Kippur and to pay special homage to Jerusalem. He also followed most of the Jewish dietary and marriage laws. In quite a surprise to this author, according to Nabia Abbott, Muslims studied the *Torah* alongside the *Qur'an* for the first two centuries after the Prophet's death.[3] Moses has the largest number of references in the *Qur'an*, at 140. It is true that Muslim scriptural and legal scholars in later centuries rejected the Prophet's idea that Jews and Christians were part of the Ummah, and instead designated them unbelievers. They asserted that the *Qur'an* superceded the *Bible* and *New Testament* rather than supplemented it. This was the ideology of political religion speaking, with Muslims wanting to distinguish themselves from their monotheistic competitors. This phenomenon has been noted by *New Testament* scholars who assert that the authors of the Gospel of John put unbelievable words in the mouth of Jesus, an observant and loving Jew, condemning "the Jews" as the children of Satan at a difficult time—seventy to one hundred years after Jesus' death—when Christians were trying to set themselves apart from traditional Jews.

Further evidence of the respected place of Judaism in early Islam is the story of the Muslim conquest of Babylonia, the chief center of Jewish life for two centuries before the rise of Islam. The Muslim military leaders singled out the Resh Galutha (or Exilarch)—head of the Jewish community in the Sasanian Empire—for a special honor. Norman Stillman writes that the Exilarch, Boustanay ibn Haninay, "was considered to be a descendent of King David, whom they [the Muslims] revered as a prophet. According to Jewish tradition, Bustanay was given the captive daughter of the last Sasanian shah for a wife. The gesture was clearly to emphasize his own noble lineage and the esteem he held in the eyes of the Muslims. After all, Caliph Ali (ruled 656–661) gave another Persian princess to his own son Husayn, who was a grandson of the Prophet Muhammad" (1979, 30).

To sum up the Muslim-Jewish relationship through the high Middle Ages, one may refer to Bernard Lewis writing that there was, "in earlier, though not later, Islamic times, a kind of symbiosis between Jews and their neighbors that had no parallel in the Western world between the Hellenistic and modern ages. Jews and Muslims had extensive and intimate contacts that involved social, as well as intellectual association—cooperation, commingling, even personal friendship . . . there was no inclination on the Muslim side to concede equality; but there was nevertheless an attitude of live and let live, and even a certain respect for the possessors and transmitters of older cultures and revelations" (1984, 88).

JEWS AND MUSLIMS TODAY: CHRISTENDOM'S DEBT

What happened to get Muslims to consider Jews as embodied in Israel as the essence of evil? What caused the late King Faysal of Saudi Arabia to tell an Egyptian publication in 1972: "Israel has had malicious intentions since ancient times. Its objective is the destruction of all other religions. It is proven from history that they are the ones who ignited the Crusades at the time of Saladin the Ayyubid so that the war would lead to the weakening of both Muslims and Christians . . . and on the subject of vengeance—they have a certain day on which they mix the blood of non-Jews into their bread and eat it. . . . This shows you what is the extent of their hatred and malice toward non-Jewish people?" (Lewis 1984, 187).

What made Hamas state in its 1988 charter, "They were behind World War I, when they were able to destroy the Islamic Caliphate, making financial gains and controlling resources. They obtained the Balfour Declaration, formed the League of Nations through which they could rule the world. They were behind World War II, through which they made huge financial gains by trading in armaments, and paved the way for the establishment of their state. It was they who instigated the replacement of the League of Nations with the United Nations and the Security Council to enable them to rule the world through them. There is no war going on anywhere, without having their finger in it?" (Avalon Project 1988, 15). These are paranoid fantasies about the mystical powers of Jews in collaboration with their Christian backers who have humiliated Arabs and Muslims in modern times. But the true story is much more bizarre.

In the examination of the Jewish-Muslim relationship, the barely acknowledged moral debt of Christendom to the Jews of Europe is the proverbial elephant in the room. There is a direct link between the condemnatory language of the Gospel of John laying responsibility for the killing of Christ on "the Jews" and the decision of European Jews in the nineteenth century to follow the lead of Theodore Herzl to seek creation of a Jewish state. As James Carroll says in his monumental *Constantine's Sword*, "The Jews have become not just the historical enemy [of the small Jesus movement] but the ontological enemy—the negative against which every positive aspect of Christianity is defined. The Manichean demonizing of the Jews by the first-century followers of Jesus—themselves mostly Jews—and the sanctioning of that demonizing in the canonizing of the Scriptures are what made this story murderous down through the centuries" (2001, 93).

In 388 C.E., the Archbishop of Antioch, St. John Chrysostom, revered by the Eastern Orthodox Church today, said: "A place where a whore stands on display is a whorehouse. What is more, the synagogue is not only a whorehouse and a theater, it is also a den of thieves and a haunt of wild animals. . . . No better disposed than pigs or goats, [the Jews] live by the rule of debauchery and inordinate gluttony. . . . When animals are unfit for work, they are marked for slaughter, and this is the thing which the Jews have experienced. By making themselves unfit for work, they have become ready for the slaughter" (Ruether 1974, 179). In 404 C.E., the first recorded pogrom—or slaughter—took place in Alexandria when the ancient and highly respected Jewish community was destroyed.

As Pope Urban II stirred up Christians in France and Germany in 1096 C.E. to launch the First Crusade to free Jerusalem from the Saracens, the murderous passions of the recruits were first directed toward Rhineland Jews. Up to 10,000 men, women, and children were killed in Speyer and Worms. In Mainz, the Christians told the cowering Jews, hoping in vain for the archbishop's protection, "You are the children of those who killed our object of veneration, hanging him from a tree; and he himself had said: 'There will yet come a day when my children will come and avenge my blood.' We are his children and it is therefore obligatory for us to avenge him since you are the ones who rebel and disbelieve him" (Eidelberg 1977, 32). Of course, there is no credible evidence that Jesus ever spoke of vengeance. In fact, the very idea would be totally inconsistent with his ministry. But the mob felt otherwise. About 1,000 Jewish men, women, and children faced a force of 12,000 Christians. The choice was to convert or die. They chose to die—adults first killed their children with knives and then each other until no one was left standing.

The history of the Jews in Christian Europe is one of episodic expulsions, pogroms, mass murders, and existential misery. This is a history that ultimately produced Zionism—the nationalist movement based on the European Jews' instinct to survive. This is a history that has nothing to do with the life of Jews under Muslim rule, who were nonetheless mobilized to join and defend the new Jewish state. It is also a history that Arabs and Muslims must learn if they are to get a conceptual grip on the struggle between Israel and the Palestinians and other Arabs in the twenty-first century. Christendom is the father of Zionism, and Christendom owes an enormous moral debt to Ashkenazi and Sephardi Jews and the Palestinian people and, for many more reasons, to the Arab and Muslim world.

Reconciliation is possible between Jews and Muslims, but there is a prodigious amount of work to be done to bring it about. The psychological tasks of healing requires parallel processes of engagement between Jews and Christendom embodied in the Church of Rome, where the founding dogmas were set creating the misery for the Jews who lived under Christian rule. The Vatican II Council of 1962–1965, in its declaration *Nostra Aetate* (In Our Day), made a significant start in acknowledging that the wrongdoing of some Jews during the Passion of Christ should not be attributed to all Jews for all time. The Church instructed its bishops and priests to remove from the Good Friday liturgy the condemnation of the "perfidious Jews" for the killing of Christ. The document also recognized the legitimacy of God's covenant with the Jewish people. But the Council did not apologize to the Jews of Europe for the Church's sins over the centuries. Indeed, even the late John Paul II, who was the most outspoken in acknowledging and asking forgiveness for Christian debts to the Jews, would not concede that the Church as an institution could sin. The Holocaust was not a freak Nazi phenomenon. It was the logical consequence of almost two millennia of the hounding, persecution, degradation, and killing of the Jews of Europe by Christians—revenge for the alleged Jews' killing of Jesus. This truth must become part of the conventional wisdom of the dominant Christian West, including Russia and the Orthodox traditions.

The Christian-Jewish engagement in coming to terms with history must resume with greater commitment and in public view, with participation of Muslims at least as observer/learners. (James Carroll has proposed a Vatican III.) There should be a simultaneous process in which the founders and descendents of Zionism and the State of Israel engage with the Palestinian people to acknowledge the latter's losses as the state was built. Indeed, it is Israeli Jewish historians who have undermined the founding myth that the Palestinian refugees left their homes in 1948 at the urging of Arab leaders. It was an Israeli Jewish psychiatrist in this author's presence who pleaded with Arabs in a 1980 workshop to understand that the Jews came to Palestine to build a state because people in Europe were trying to wipe them out. The Jews were a "people in distress." And because the Jewish state was established, the Palestinians became "a people in distress," and Israel had to acknowledge this fact and the moral responsibility it carried. This acknowledgement of moral debt by an Israeli to the Arabs present had a profound positive effect on the discourse in the meeting.

This author has written elsewhere on the psychodynamics of ethnic and sectarian conflict analysis and reconciliation strategies.[4] Key to the process is honest conversations about the past, in particular, the losses remembered most painfully by each side in the conflict. Almost as important is the re-humanization of the relationship through the exploration of shared values and positive memories.

This chapter has focused on what could be called Jewish-Muslim family values that are rooted in basic religious history of the two peoples. In so many ways that could only be hinted at in these pages, Jews and particularly Arab Muslims are "next-of-kin." Returning to Nissim Rejwan's Jerusalem Post essay cited above, Professor Rosenthal of Cambridge University is quoted, in 1960, as saying, "The strength or otherwise of the Muslim consciousness will largely determine whether or not long-term self-interest will bring the Arab states nearer to Israel. On the Jewish side, more than a return to the ancient homeland, more than a physical return to the cradle of the religious Semitic civilization is needed. One of the preconditions for a positive solution of the present conflict is, at any rate, the conscious realization on both sides that to a large measure, they share a good deal of common ground in the religious ordering of their lives in the past, and that much of their cultural achievement springs from the same spiritual roots . . . To become aware of one's roots is the first step for believer and agnostic alike, on both sides, toward forging a new link for the future on a basis more solid and stable than political expediency and material aspirations."

Forty-five years later, in 2005, there is a glimmer of hope in the direction proposed by Professor Rosenthal. After hosting Muslim-Christian dialogues in 2003 and 2004 in Doha, Qatar, Shaykh Hamad bin Khalifa al-Thani proposed that it might be "useful to widen the dialogue in next year's seminar to [include] the participation of representatives of the Jewish religion which concurs with Islam and Christianity in the belief in the oneness of God." Mark R. Cohen, a rabbi and a professor of Near Eastern studies at Princeton, who has written extensively on the difference between the Jewish experience under Christian and Muslim rule,[5] participated in the Doha conference in July 2005.

Cohen reported that there was a remarkable frankness in the meeting with some Muslim scholars criticizing others for excess in their attacks on Christians and Jews and for failure to acknowledge the excesses and conflicts within the Muslim world. There was a strong call by Muslim speakers for Muslim critical self-analysis. This was all the more remarkable in a country where, at least nominally, the extremely conservative Wahhabi school of Islamic thought is dominant. Cohen recalled the contrast of the experience of being Jewish under Christian rule as opposed to being Jewish under Muslim rule. "Jews living in Muslim lands, even where in recent centuries they were downtrodden and sometimes oppressed, felt embedded in the society around them, and friendships with Muslims often outweighed enmity." He concluded his speech by calling for much more Islamic-Jewish dialogue within the Muslim world, saying, "We need it desperately, lest the hatred of the present, existing on both sides, completely snuff out the memory of the age-old commonalities of the Judeo-Islamic tradition, which could form the foundation of a meaningful and peaceful discussion of what has bound us together in the past and can, with good will, bring us together in the present and the future" (2005, 2).

The good news for the readers of this chapter is that the Muslim-Jewish dialogue project, based on shared religious values, is going forward in Qatar and in other parts of the Arab world, and an Israeli rabbi participated in the Doha conference in 2007.

13

Hindu-Muslim Relations

India

Salman Akhtar

O Hindus and Muslims! Do you belong to a country other than India? Don't you live on this soil and are you not buried under it or cremated on its *ghats*? If you live and die on this land, then, bear in mind, that "Hindu" and "Muslim" is but a religious word; all the Hindus, Muslims and Christians who live in this country are one nation.

—Sir Syed Ahamd Khan, January 27, 1884

Hindus and Muslims have lived together in India for over 1,200 years. The saga of their coexistence is, however, far from smooth. It is characterized by the contradictory hues of strife and synchrony, hatred and harmony, and conflict and cooperation. Whereas different eras might have witnessed one or the other extreme of such polarities, both ends of this emotional spectrum have usually been evident throughout the mutual history of these groups. Moreover, when it comes to the love-hate economy within their relationship, neither of these groups has acted entirely one way or the other. Neither can claim to be merely a victim and neither can be labeled simply a perpetrator. Both have loved each other and both have hated each other. In the end, their story is one of a close but ambivalent sibling bond.

As a result, which facet of their history gets highlighted, under what circumstances, by whom, for what purpose, and with what consequences become important questions to consider. It is in this spirit, that I offer the following exploration of the recent crisis in Hindu-Muslim relations in India. The threat posed by this crisis to India's secular, multicultural, and democratic fabric has drawn urgent attention from the worldwide community of social scientists (Gopal 1991; Hasan 1991; Mukherjee 1991; Rudolph and Rudolph 1993; van der Veer 1994; Jafferlot 1996; Kakar 1996; Ludden 1996;

231

Manuel 1996; Varshney 2002). This chapter constitutes a modest attempt at integrating and extending their valuable contributions.

SOME CAVEATS

First, the subject lies beyond the clinical realm that is the area of my expertise as a psychoanalyst. Well-versed in depth-psychology of individuals, I find myself ill-equipped to explain matters involving large groups of people. Though my tenure on the Group for Advancement of Psychiatry's Committee on International Relations (1996–2001), my work in the area of immigration and cross-cultural psychotherapy (Akhtar 1995a; 1999; 1999d; Akhtar and Choi 2003; Huang and Akhtar, 2005), my reading of the post-Freudian psychoanalytic literature on large-group psychology (especially Volkan 1988; 1997; 2004), and my participation in the International Psychoanalytic Association's Working Group on Terror and Terrorism (2002–2005), as well as my own work toward understanding terrorism (Akhtar 1999a; 2003), have given me some insights in the realm of social turmoil, the field still remains somewhat unfamiliar to me.

Second, in addressing the specifics of the Hindu-Muslim conflict, one faces the risk of overlooking the fact that such conflicts and the prejudices that fuel them are universal. It is, therefore, important to remind oneself that the roots of ethnic, racial, and religious prejudice (at least in its ubiquitous, mild, and dormant forms) are to be found in the ordinary and inevitable experiences of human childhood: "stranger anxiety" of infancy, later disappointment with maternal care, anger at the father for being the "invader" of the mother's body, resentment of younger siblings as unwelcome intruders, repudiation of pregenital sexuality, and the need for an "other" for the purposes of self-identity consolidation (Akhtar 2003; Freud 1900, quoted in Gay 1988, 55; Bird 1956; Parens 1999; Spitz 1965; Sterba 1947; Thomson et al. 1993). Together, these factors give rise to a universal vulnerability to prejudice. However, more than such ordinary childhood frustrations is needed to turn this "seed of prejudice" into a cactus of actual hatred of others. Factors pertaining to the real world (e.g., economic hardship) and to group psychology (e.g., intensification of emotions and lowering of critical judgment, as noted by Freud in his 1921 paper) are required to transform this hatred into ethnic violence. All in all, while the factors giving color to a specific ethnic conflict might vary from situation to situation, the factors preparing a human being for possessing such a potential are universal. Study of a particular situation, therefore, teaches us about both that situation, as well as about the human condition in general.

Third, any consideration of the topic of the Hindu-Muslim conflict warrants a serious reading of the history of these two groups in India, and this brings its own hurdles. The material is too voluminous to cover and emanates from too many vantage points. Dichotomies that pervade this literature exist along the religious—secular, Muslim—Hindu, left—right, intracultural—extracultural, and Indian—non-Indian schisms. Historical tracts written by liberal Hindus and Muslims accord well with each other, whereas those authored by conservative Hindus and Muslims differ sharply in their accounts. British, North American, and European scholars bring their own perspectives. Different historians offer varying interpretations of the same historical fact, and even the facts they report often do not coincide with each other. One views a Muslim emperor's effort to bring Islam and Hinduism together as heretic and the other views as admirably secular. One emphasizes the early Muslim invaders' atrocities while the other highlights the later Muslims' contributions in the realm of architecture, music, and films. One says that Muslims caused the partition of India while the other reminds that a large number of Muslims were strongly against it. One underscores the differences between the Hindu-Muslim communities while the other brings out their similarities and overlaps, and, so on.

Fourth, writing on matters of interfaith strife stirs up anxiety and conflict. On the one hand, there is the risk of offending those Hindus and Muslims whose viewpoints are different from mine. On the other hand, it would be shameful to skirt honesty for the purpose of appeasing others. It is not easy to find out a way of this conundrum.

Fifth, in focusing upon the conflictual aspects of Hindu-Muslim relations, one runs the risk of overlooking the fact that the majority of individuals from both these groups are friendly and affectionate toward each other. The current rift between the two communities is largely engineered by the Hindu nationalists of the right, who receive ample justification from the outrageous political stands taken by the narrow-minded Muslim religious leaders[1] of the country.

Sixth, a certain amount of personal bias becomes impossible to avoid in this sort of undertaking. No matter how hard one tries for it not to be the case, the picture one paints ends up receiving color not only from one's professional discipline, but also from the deepest core of one's personal identity. I am no exception in this regard. It is therefore best that I put my cards on the table and let the reader know that I am, politically, a democrat; religiously, a nonpracticing individual; and professionally, a psychoanalyst. I was born in a highly creative, politically active, nationalist Muslim family of North India and have deep and abiding love for my motherland.

Finally, reading essays such as this is not done in a state of psychic equanimity and neutrality. Feeling validated or invalidated in his own ethnopolitical convictions and thus narcissistically exalted or injured, the reader is himself vulnerable to regressive simplification, emotionality, and partisanship. Therefore, both positive and negative verdicts on this essay need to be taken with a grain of salt.

It is with such caveats in mind that my contribution should be approached. In this chapter, I will present my understanding of the nature of the current increase in the Hindu-Muslim strife in India. I will also outline some psychoanalytically informed social interventions to minimize this problem. I will, however, begin with my reading of the history of the Hindu-Muslim coexistence in India. A background of this sort should be helpful since "[P]resent-day conflicts cannot be fully understood without first understanding how historical hurts and grievances survive from generation to generation as 'chosen traumas.' These psychological 'genes' exist within many large groups and can be manipulated by leaders in subsequent generations to mobilize the group" (Volkan 2004, 51).

HISTORICAL BACKGROUND

Hindus had lived in India for many centuries before scattered settlements of Muslim traders began to appear along the Southern coastal areas of the country. This development, also evident in parts of Sindh and Gujrat, occurred around the early eighth century. Invaders representing various Middle Eastern regimes also appeared on the scene around this time. One of them, namely Mohmmad-bin-Qasim, an emissary of Hajjaj bin Yusuf, the Umayyad governor of Baghdad, went as far as to establish his control over Sindh and parts of Punjab by A.D. 713. However, his administration soon faltered and a sustained dynasty formation did not follow. Muslim life in India returned to its relatively quiet status.

As the years passed, a modicum of cultural exchange between Hindus and Muslims occurred. Musical instruments of the two began to acquire hybrid forms. Patterns of attire were subtly affected, and the necessity to learn each other's language was felt. Even folklore began to be shared. The most striking cross-cultural accomplishment of this era is the translation of the great Indian collection of fables, the *Panchtantra*, into Arabic around A.D. 750 (Mani 1975). All in all, life seemed relatively peaceful.

This changed with the massive and invasive influx of Muslims into India, beginning around the mid-eleventh century A.D. Indeed, their history from then onward reveals a complex and contradictory pattern of plunder and patronage, bloodshed and beautification, coercion and cooperation, and repression and reform. The Turkish, Afghan, and Mongol invaders of the northwestern provinces of India were indeed plunderers. They showed little respect for the culture of the local masses and had no hesitation in denuding respected Hindu palaces and sacred temples of their valuable objects. The pain caused by their desecration of Hindu icons and shrines continues to throb in the Indian psyche, even though nearly a thousand years have since passed.

The most significant and permanent military movement of Muslims into North India occurred in the late twelfth century A.D., and was carried out by a Turkish dynasty that arose from the ruins of the Abbasid Caliphate. The road to their conquest was, however, prepared by Sultan Mahmud of Ghazna (Ghazni in today's Afghanistan), who conducted more than twenty raids into North-West India between A.D. 1001 and A.D. 1027 and established a large but short-lived empire in Punjab. Mahmud Ghaznavi (the name by which he was widely recognized) only gave the impression of wanting to conquer and rule. Actually, he was more interested in robbing the local treasuries and Hindu temples that stored gold and precious jewels for religious purposes. His goal was to use this wealth to finance his campaigns in Central Asia where he *did* want to build an empire. Little did he know that one of his raids (A.D. 1026), at the magnificent Hindu temple of *Somnath* in the Junagadh district of Gujrat, would be evoked as a "chosen trauma" (Volkan 1997) by the Hindu consciousness many centuries later.[2]

At the risk of straying from the chronological progression of events, let me clarify the reasons behind Somnath temple's demolition becoming a persistent and ever aching emblem of Muslim atrocities toward Hindus. First and foremost, the sheer grandeur of the shrine made its demolition hard to fathom and mourn. Second, its demolition was not a one-time occurrence; the temple was reconstructed again and again by Hindus, only to destroyed each time by one or the other Muslim invader or ruler (at least six such attacks, i.e., those in A.D. 1026, A.D. 1297, A.D. 1394, A.D. 1413, A.D. 1459, and A.D. 1669, are well documented) As a result, the site became a chronic reminder of large-group humiliation for Hindus. Finally, the fact that the two Muslims considered most nefarious by Hindus were *both* responsible, at different times, for the temple's demolition, also fixated the trauma in an emotionally powerful way.

Whereas this deep wound will reappear in a later part of our discourse, for the time being, allow me to rejoin the advancing march of time after Mahmud Ghaznavi's invasions. As I do so, I note that the next wave of Muslims who arrived in India included other plunderers like Mohammed Ghauri, as well as imperial expansionists of the Middle East, with aims to establish their rule over parts of India. The latter group did *not* view themselves as the keepers of Turkish, Afghan, or Iranian outposts; they were truly Indian rulers. Qutubuddin Aybak established the first Muslim headquarters in Delhi, the heart of India, in A.D. 1193. He and the subsequent Muslim rulers were well-grounded in the local idiom, took pride in their new nation, and sought ways for its improvement. This trend continued and, with the passage of time, the Indian-born progeny of these Muslim rulers began to ascend to power. They built major highways (e.g., Sher Shah Suri constructed the road known as the Grand Trunk Road today), created *sarais* for travelers, and even founded new cities (e.g., Ahmed Shah, Sikander Lodhi, Adil Shah, and Quli Qutub Shah founded Ahmedabad, Agra, Bijapur, and Hyderabad respectively). They invested funds in building canals, stepwells, and underground water channels. They also constructed buildings of great splendor, many of which (e.g., Fatehpur Sikri, Red Fort of Delhi, and Taj Mahal) continue to be the source of national pride today. Muslim rulers also established *Karkhanas* in Khurja for pottery, Moradabad for brassware, Mirzapur for carpets, Firozabad for glassware, Farrukhabad for printing, Saharanpur and Nagina for woodcarving, Lucknow for *chikan* and *zardozi* work, and Srinagar for papier-mâché.

To be sure, the ancestral religion of these rulers was Central Asian, but even that began to have pliability and admixture. A near-pagan taint had already seeped in Islam via the Sufi movements of Persia and Afghanistan that utilized devotional singing, dancing, and trance-like states; their dialogue seemed to be with a God who was friendlier and more "human" than the strict and foreboding God of the *Quran*. This trend received further color from the pantheistic culture of India that placed idol worship as a stepping stone for spiritual self-realization and union with God.[3]

There were considerable differences in the way various Muslim regimes responded to this encounter between their ascetic monotheism and the more relaxed and colorful spiritual life in the land they were governing. Some emperors, like Ghyas-uddin Balban (A.D. 1200–1287) and Alamgir Aurangzeb (A.D. 1618–1707), recoiled, asserted their religious ancestry, suppressed local customs, levied extra taxes upon Hindus, demolished Hindu temples, and forced Hindus to convert to Islam. Others reacted with ambivalence. Ala-uddin Khalji (A.D. 1255–1316), for instance, plundered Hindu kingdoms in South India and yet married a Hindu princess and opened the gates to prominent Hindus and Jains to participate in his administration. Still others went much farther in adapting to India. Firoz Shah Tuglaq, who reigned from A.D. 1351 to A.D. 1388, conducted discourses with Hindu saints, commissioned Persian translation of important Sanskrit texts, and erected a pillar to commemorate the life of the great Hindu King Ashoka (who reigned from 273–232 B.C.) at a prominent place in his palace. Without openly violating the *Shari'ah* (the Islamic law), Firoz Shah Tughlaq, and many Muslim emperors after him, made sure that the policy of the state was based increasingly upon the opinion of court advisors and not on religious considerations. They supplemented *Shari'ah* by framing *Zawabit* (their own state laws) that, in cases of conflict, overrode the universal Muslim law.

Jalaluddin Mohammad Akbar (A.D. 1542–1605) married a Hindu princess, Jodha Bai, and later their son, Jahangir, ascended to the throne of India. Akbar appointed three Hindus (Raja Mansingh, Raja Todar Mal, and Raja Birbal) to the nine-member advisory council (*nav-ratna*) to their court.[4] He incorporated Hindu etiquette in his personal behavior (e.g., he often wore a *tilak* on his forehead) and banned certain practices (e.g., marriage between cousins) commonly associated with Islam. Akbar even sought to create a hybrid religion (*Din-e-Ilahi*), which had attributes of Islam and Hinduism. His grandson, Shah Jahan (the builder of Taj Mahal), was deeply interested in the Hindu culture, and his great-grandson, Dara Shikoh (the elder brother of Aurangzeb, to wit), translated *Upanishads* into Persian. Dara Shikoh himself authored a book called *The Meeting of the Two Oceans of Sufism and Vedantism* that elucidated the intellectual confluence of these traditions (Radhakrishnan 1975).

Despite such rapprochement, tensions frequently flared up between Hindus and Muslims. However, not all such friction was religion-based. Most of it resulted from territorial battles that cut across the lines of religious faith. For instance, the Mughal emperor Akbar's general was Raja Mansingh, a Hindu Rajput. Aurangzeb fought his three brothers (Dara Shikoh, Shujaa, and Murad) for the throne with the help of Hindu allies, and each of his brothers had Hindu allies themselves. The Muslim rulers of Deccan and Gujrat had similar alliances, and when the Marathas fought the Mughals, Shivaji's campaign had many Muslim lieutenants. In sum, Hindus and Muslims stood with each other on the basis of their political alliances more often than they did on account of their religious faith. Sher Shah Suri's appointment of Hemu Bhargava as his chief of intelligence and Sultan Mohammad Adil's later appointment of him as his Prime Minister are striking examples of such strategic pluralism of the times.

The Muslim-Hindu blending of culture, however, went beyond the mixture of blood, politics, and religion. It also became evident in architecture, music, and language. Muslim kings frequently employed Hindu artisans, and the resulting confluence of aesthetics gave a uniquely charming texture to their buildings. Mosques built by Muslim rulers in India, for instance, began to have four minarets, in contrast to their Middle Eastern counterparts, which had only one. The single minaret mosques were efforts to replicate the *Ka'bba* (the "first mosque") in Mecca. The four minaret mosques reproduced the Hindu motif of symmetry in design and architecture.

Music was another realm in which Muslim-Hindu cooperation led to impressively productive results. Indeed, Manuel (1996), who has written extensively on this topic, declares that music might be the only sphere in which the followers of these two religions have led a completely harmonious existence over the last one thousand years. The talent of Hindu musicians was regularly nourished by their regional Muslim rulers.[5] Some among the latter made innovative additions to the Indian classical singing; the most outstanding example of this is Sultan Hussain Shariqi of Jaunpur, who introduced *Khayal* in Indian *gayiki* (circa A.D. 1430). Amir Khusrau (A.D. 1253–1325) evolved *sitar* by conflating the features of the South Indian *rudraveena* with various Persian and Afghani drone instruments, and Mian Sarang, an eminent musician in the dying Mughal court of Mohammad Shah Rangeelay, invented a remarkable string instrument that was named *sarangi* after him. Currently the preeminent exponents of *Dhurpad*, a deeply devotional Hindu raga, are Muslim singers, especially the Daggar brothers.

Muslim intermingling with the Hindu mainstream of North India also resulted in the birth of a new language, Urdu (circa A.D. 1500). Derived from lexical betrothal of Persian, Turkish, and Arabic nouns and adjectives to the verbs and adverbs of the local *Braj-bhasha* and *Awadhi* dialects, Urdu (itself a Turkish word meaning "contonement") became the language of the "commoners," while Persian was retained for judicial and administrative transactions of the court. This led the littérateurs to shun Urdu at first. Gradually, however, a distinguished cadre of Urdu writers and poets emerged that ranged from the pioneering Wali Gujrati through the great Mir Taqi Mir and playful Nazir Akbarabadi to the immortal Mirza Ghalib. Even Bahadur Shah Zafar (A.D. 1775–1862), the last Mughal king of India, before the country came under British domination, wrote poetry in Urdu.

The language, with its lyrical cadence, became a deeply loved medium of expression for vast segments of the North Indian population regardless of their religious affiliation. Many Hindus came to be recognized as great contributors to Urdu literature. This vast list extends from Har Gopal Tafta (a favorite disciple of Ghalib), Daya Shankar Nasim, and Ratan Nath Sarshar through Munshi Premchand and Braj Narain Chakbast to Anand Narain Mulla, Raghupati Sahai ("Firaq Gorakhpuri"), Krishna Chandra, Mahindra Nath, Tilok Chand Mehroom, Upendra Nath Ashk, Kanhayya Lal Kapur, and Jagan Nath Azad. The most authoritative source on Ghalib's work in contemporary India, Malik Ram, was a Hindu and so is the eminent Urdu scholar, Gopi Chand Narang, who currently heads the national Sahitya Academy. Besides directly contributing to it, Hindus also took a lead in publishing Urdu literature, a tradition that has ranged from Munshi Nawal Kishore, the original publisher of the great *Diwan-e-Ghalib*, through *Biswin Sadi's* pseudonymous "Khushtar Garaami," to Amar Nath Varma, the founder of the current Star Publications in New Delhi.

With British rule over India (1858–1947) came subtle divisions among Hindus and Muslims, largely at the behest of their colonizer's "divide and rule" policy. The most virulent aspect of this tactic was the establishment of separate, religion-based electorates for the two communities. However, as van der Veer (1994) reminds us: "This is not to say that there was no division of Hindu and Muslim communities in the precolonial period. There was: the division was not a colonial invention. But to count these communities and to have leaders represent them was a colonial novelty, and it was fundamental to the emergence of religious nationalism" (pp. 19–20).

Nonetheless, Muslims continued to feel deep loyalty to India and the early uprisings against the British rule had prominent Muslim participation. The legendary Tipu Sultan of Mysore,[6] Begum Hazrat Mahal of Oudh, and Nawab Ali Bahadur of Banda (who fought the British alongside Maharani Lakshmibai of Jhansi in the 1858 battle of Kalpi) readily come to mind in this connection, though an actual list of such freedom fighters is certainly much longer. Countless is the number of Muslim soldiers who fought shoulder to shoulder with their Hindu counterparts against the British on the battlefronts of Lucknow, Patna, and Meerut.

All in all, Hindus and Muslims led a peaceful coexistence during the nineteenth and early twentieth centuries. In the Gangetic plain state of United Provinces (later named Uttar Pradesh) especially, a hybrid culture of sublime elegance prevailed; the *Ganga-Jamani tehzib* of Lucknow was the epitome of such confluence (Sharar 1920; Mohan 1997; Oldenburg 2001). Hindu nobility kept *taazias* (an Indianized replica of Prophet Mohammed's grandson Hussain's tomb) during *Moharram* (the month in the Islamic calendar in which Hussain was killed in a battle in Karbala, Iraq). Raja Tikait Rai and Raja Bilas Rai went as far as building their own *imambaras* (Shia religious shrines) in Lucknow to house *alams* (scepters) representing the A.D. 680 battle of Karbala. The Hindu Lambadi community in Andhra Pradesh had (in fact, continues to have to this day) their own genre of *Moharram* lamentation songs in Telgu. Much more curious was the emergence of the small *Hussaini Brahamin* sect in the rural Punjab (Sikand 2004). They practiced an intriguing blend of Muslim and Hindu traditions and based their name on the claim that their Hindu ancestors had traveled to Karbala and fought in the army of Hussain. They believed that the sacred Hindu text, *Bhagavad Gita*, had foretold the event of Hussain's death at Karbala. They also held Hussain's father, Ali, in great respect and referred to him as *Om Murti*.[7] While they are very extreme in their hybrid beliefs, *Hussaini Brahmins* were by no means the only Hindu community that straddled the frontier between Hinduism and Islam.

Muslims, on their part, took delight in participating in the *Diwali* and *Dusshera* festivals. They joyously played *Holi* (the Hindu festival of colors) all across North India. Wajid Ali Shah (A.D. 1827–1887), the famous Nawab of Oudh, learned the *Kathak* dance from Hindu teachers of Banaras. He would sometimes dress up as Krishna and at other times as a *Gopi* to celebrate the love of Krishna and Radha in his palace. Abdul Rahim Khankhanan (A.D. 1556–1627) and Malik Mohammad Jaisi (circa A.D. 1500) wrote outstanding devotional poetry about this paradigmatic romantic couple of Hinduism. In Southern parts of the country, too, Muslims intermingled peacefully with Hindus, and their regional culture was a shared one. Muslims of Andhra Pradesh, Tamil Nadu, Karnataka, and Kerala spoke Telgu, Tamil, Kannada, and Malyalam, respectively, and not Urdu. In Bengal, Islam especially assimilated many values and practices that were not in conformity with the precepts of the *Quran*.[8] All in all, throughout India, regional commonality determined linguistic, sartorial, and culinary preferences to a greater extent than did religion. Interethnic strife was infrequent.

In such placid centerstage notwithstanding, trouble was brewing in the wings. This was constituted by the foundation of the Muslim League in 1906 and Rashtriya Sevak Sangh (RSS) in 1925. The Muslim League was pro-Muslim and anti-Hindu. RSS was pro-Hindu and anti-Muslim. Both promulgated discrimination and prejudice. And, despite their narrow "nationalisms" ("Muslim nationalism" of the League and "Hindu nationalism" of the RSS), both were opposed to India's independence struggle with the British. Another similarity between them was that they both received inspiration from events outside India. The Muslim League gained strength from the *Khilafat* movement (the adversarial relationship between the Turkish Caliph and the British government of that time), and RSS drew fervor from its ideological links with the European fascists; Veer Savarkar "wrote approvingly of the occupation of Sudetenland by Germany on the grounds that its inhabitants shared common blood and language with the Germans. In the late 1930s, both *Hindu Outlook* and *Maharatta* praised Franco, Mussolini, and Hitler" (Jafferlot 1996, 51). All in all, both Muslim League and RSS sowed the seeds of organized hatred between the outer fringes of the Hindu and Muslim communities. This was later exploited by the British.

Then, the freedom movement of the mid-twentieth century came. Initially united with their Hindu brethren in opposing the British rule, Indian Muslims found themselves suddenly caught up in an immensely painful dilemma. Feeling unfairly treated in the distribution of political power, a segment of them sought not only independence from the British, but also secession from the country in order to form their own nation. The Muslim intelligentsia was divided with prominent activists on both sides of the dreaded choice. Mohammad Ali Jinnah, who had been dubbed "the ambassador of Hindu-Muslim unity" in 1916 by Sarojini Naidu (The Encyclopedia of Asian History and Asia Society 1988) and who had harshly rejected the idea of Muslim secession from India proposed to him by immigrant Muslims in London a few years ago (Collins and Lapierre 1975), now became the chief spokesman of a virulent ethnic megalomania. Liaqat Ali and Sikander Mirza also took the side of carving out a separate nation for Muslims, arguing that Hindus and Muslims were fundamentally different[9] and that Muslims could not expect fair treatment in a post-British independent India. Maulana Abul Kalam Azad, Khan Abdul Ghaffar Khan ("Frontier Gandhi"), Rafi Ahmad Kidwai, the Ansari brothers, Hakim Ajmal Khan, Mohammad Yunus, and Ansar Harvani were among the outstanding nationalist Muslims fiercely opposed to the country's partition. The first group felt that they were Muslims first, and Indians later. The second group felt the opposite. Muslim masses were torn.[10]

The radical Muslims, hell-bent upon seeking a separate country, were unwittingly aided by the right-wing Hindu ideologues, such as Veer Savarkar and Madhav Sadashiv Golwalkar, who also subscribed to the idea that Hindus and Muslims of India were two entirely irreconcilable nations. They wanted the Muslims "traitors" to be kept away from grabbing power in a government that would be formed once the British left. Lord Mountbatten, the last Imperial Viceroy of British India, was also in a haste to hand over an empire that had lost its *raison d'etre* with the post-World War II economic crisis. He facilitated the tragic partition of India. The country's body and soul were mutilated in 1947, and what was India ended up becoming India and Pakistan in a dark moment of the subcontinent's history. "Never before in South Asian history, did so few decide the fate of so many. And never before did so few ignore the wishes and sentiments of so many in the subcontinent" (Hasan 1991, 108). Gandhi protested to no avail and wept.[11]

This macabre territorial surgery was accompanied by a major population exchange whereby a large number of Hindus from Punjab, Sindh, and Bengal moved into "India," and a multitude of Muslims migrated from United and Central Provinces (Uttar and Madhya Pradesh, respectively), Bihar, Bengal, and a few other areas to the newly formed Pakistan. Looting, chaos, and communal violence accompanied this exodus. The degree to which both Hindus and Muslims sank in this bloody orgy of dehumanization and sadism is beyond description. Trains would arrive from what is now Pakistan filled with corpses of Hindus killed by Muslims. Entire families of Hindus were frequently murdered by Muslims, who also tortured Hindu children and pregnant women. Not ones to be left behind, Hindus killed numerous Muslims, raped Muslim women escaping India, castrated Muslim men and threw bucketsful of circumcised penises in mosques to taunt the Muslim community. A diabolical nightmare of religious persecution was unleashed on both sides and humanity was degraded in the name of *Allah* and *Ram*. All in all, ten million Hindus and seven million Muslims moved across the newly created boundaries, and nearly three hundred thousand individuals were killed in the process.

While the Muslims who moved to Pakistan were traumatized by the sudden dislocation, the suffering of Hindus who came to the vivisected India was greater. The former were pursuing a dream, the latter were pushed into a nightmare. The former, even in the midst of suffering, were buoyed with "nationalistic" optimism, whereas the latter had little reason for hope. Most among the former had opted to emigrate, while the majority among the latter were forced out of their ancestral lands. The trauma of exile was great in the latter and its mourning blocked by necessities of adapting to new circumstances.[12] It would take another fifty years before the psychosocial working through of this massive trauma would resume. Until then, the pain would remain subject to transgenerational transmission. Let me not rush though, and return to the immediate post-independence period.

After the partition, both sides sought to deal with the refugees that had freshly arrived in their respective countries. Independence from the British was a heady affair, nation building a priority. Gradually, the dust settled. India glowed with national pride and chose an insistently secular fabric for its constitution. Here, credit is owed to the enlightened vision of those Hindus (including Jawahar Lal Nehru, Rajindra Prasad, Sarvapalli Radhakrishnan, and C. Rajgopalacharya) who opted for making the territorially amputated India a secular rather than a Hindu religious state. The basically liberal and forgiving majority among the Indian Hindus accepted this secular constitution and embraced those Muslims who had chosen to stay in India with relative equanimity.

This group of Muslims received a treatment in the postpartition India that was roughly equal to that offered to the majority Hindus. India's secular constitution offered them safety and, by in large, protected their cultural and educational institutions. If there were poor, illiterate, and hungry among them, they differed little from the Hindus in the same boat. If there were occasional outbreaks of violence against them, these were regularly followed by communal contrition and reparative gestures. Outside of such situations, most Muslims muddled along in a fashion similar to their Hindu brethren, and some truly prospered and acquired great fame and success. The contributions of these Muslims to the contemporary Indian culture over the last fifty years are indeed remarkable.

Let me name the most influential among these: *presidents of India*: Zakir Hussain, Fakhruddin Ali Ahmed, and A. P. J. Abul Kalam; *parliamentarians* like Maulana Abul Kalam Azad, Rafi Ahmad Kidwai, M.C. Chagla, Ansar Harvani, Humayun Kabir, and Najma Heptullah; *jurists* like Chief Justice Hidayatullah, who also served as the acting President of India for a brief period of time; *diplomats* like Abid Hussain, India's Ambassador to United States from 1990 to 1992; *film actors* like Yusuf Khan ("Dilip Kumar"),[13] Yaqub, Zakaria Khan ("Jayant"), Rahman, Sheikh Mukhtar, Hamid Ali Khan ("Ajit"), Badruddin Ahmed ("Johnny Walker"), Mehmood, Firoze Khan, Abbas Khan ("Sanjay"), Amjad Khan, Naseeruddin Shah, Shahrukh Khan, Salman Khan,

Aamir Khan, and Saif Ali Khan; *film actresses* like Naseem, Fatima Bai ("Nargis"), Begum Paara, Surraiya, Mumtaz Jahan ("Madhubala"), Mahjabeen Ara ("Meena Kumari"), Shakila, Waheeda Rehman, Saira Banu, Mumtaz, Zeenat Aman, and Shabana Azmi; *movie directors* like Mehboob Khan, M. Sadiq, Kamal Amrohi, Nasir Hussain, and Farhan Akhtar; *Bollywood music makers* like Mohmmed Rafi, Talat Mehmood, Naushad, Shamshad Begum, and A. R. Rahman; *Urdu poets*[14] *and film lyricists* like Sahir Ludhianvi, Shakeel Badayuni, Jan-Nisar Akhtar, Majaz, Ali Sardar Jafri, Makhdoom Mohiuddin, Kaifi Azmi, Majrooh Sultanpuri, Rahi Masoom Raza,[15] Shaharyar, Nida Fazli, and Javed Akhtar,[16] *journalists* like K. A. Abbas, Hamid Dalwai, and M. J. Akbar; *physician-educators* like Mahdi Hasan; *ornithologists* like Salim Ali; *sportsmen* like Nisar Ahmad, Mushtaq Ali, Abbas Ali Beg, Mansoor Ali Khan ("Nawab of Pataudi"), and Azharuddin; *artists* like M.F. Hussain; *theater personalities* like Habib Tanvir, Shaukat Azmi, and Firoz Khan; *fiction writers* like Ismat Chughtai, Qurrat-ul-Ain Haider, Razia Sajjad Zaheer, and Wajida Tabassum; *literateurs* like Sajjad Zaheer, Aal Ahmad Suroor, Ehtisham Hussain, Mohammad Hasan, Safia Akhtar, Baqar Mehdi, Zoe Ansari, and Shams-ur-Rehman Farooqui; *academicians* like Irfan Habib, Asghar Ali Engineer, Mushirul Hasan, and Zoya Hasan; *art and antique collectors* like Salaar Jung of Hyderabad; *exponents of vocal and instrumental classical music of India* like Bade Ghulam Ali Khan, Allaudin Khan (the teacher and former father-in-law of the world-renowned Ravi Shankar), Allah Rakkha, Bismillah Khan, Ali Akbar Khan, Begum Akhtar, the Dagar Brothers, Amjad Ali Khan, and Zakir Hussain; and, finally, *Muslims of the Indian diaspora*, like the novelist Salman Rushdie, the artist Raza, the filmmaker Ismail Merchant, the academic Aqeel Bilgirami, the community workers like A. Abdullah and A. R. Nakdar, and the journalist Fareed Zakaria.

The contributions of these individuals to the Indian society can only be denied by the truly irrational. Yet, a culturally subversive effort to do precisely this is evident in today's India. Before describing this sinister scenario, however, I would like to conclude my historical survey[17] and move on to an overall picture of the Hindu-Muslim tension in India and the complex forces that fuel such prejudice from within both these communities.

MUSLIM CONTRIBUTIONS TO THE HINDU-MUSLIM TENSION

The current rise of anti-Muslim prejudice in India might make it seem out of place to mention, but the fact is that Muslim community has also contributed to the difficulties it faces in India. The ways in which they have, wittingly or unwittingly, contributed to the Hindu-Muslim strife can be grouped under five categories: (1) some of their inherent characteristics, (2) their ongoing "love affair" with a nostalgically idealized past, (3) prejudicial attitudes held by some members of their community, (4) the absence of secular and progressive leadership in the Muslim community, and (5) certain constitutional exceptions and privileges enjoyed by them. Together, these five factors have a synergistic effect of alienating Hindus.

Inherent Characteristics

The religious faith of Indian Muslims originated in Saudi Arabia (i.e., a place that is outside India). Their chief holy cities include Mecca and Medina, Jerusalem, and Karbala and Najaf, which happen to be in Saudi Arabia, Israel, and Iraq, respectively. In offering *namaaz* (daily prayers), all Muslims of the world turn to face Mecca; Indian Muslims are no exceptions in this regard. Such commitments and practices have the potential of making them appear "not fully Indian" to Hindu eyes. There is little, however, an Indian Muslim can do about this except to point out that extraterritorial religious loyalties are not to be equated with extraterritorial political loyalties. He or she can also remind his critics in this regard that such extraterritorial religious loyalties are the credo of vast segments of the world's population, including the Hindus living outside India. However logical such rejoinder might be, it might still fail to correct the emotionally charged perception of Muslims having "foreign" ties. The situation is not helped by the fact that Indian Muslims have retained names that have Persian, Turkish, and Arabic origins, even though this is not in any way different from migrant groups in other parts of the world.

Pathological Nostalgia

More problematic is the Muslim attitude of covert self-aggrandizement. In a self-deceptive act of ethnic elitism, they establish a mental link between themselves and the grand Islamic empire that once spanned from South Eastern Europe and Africa through the Middle East to India. By fabricating a kinship with the Turkish sultans of centuries ago, an Indian Muslim can put a bandage of illustrious ancestry over the wounds of his daily hardship. This defensive maneuver, however, creates a dreamy quality to existence and cleaves the imaginative potential from the sunlight of effort.

A more severe problem is that the average Muslim has not fully accepted the fact that his coreligionists are no longer the rulers of the land. A mentality of *pidram sultan bood* ("my father was a king") prevails at a preconscious level and creates abhorrence of actual praxis and toil. It is as if the individual is saying, "Look, we have already made the Taj Mahal, so we do not need to study hard for college or medical school entrance examinations." Such exaggerated "nostalgia" perpetuates complacency and a cryptic air of unearned superiority.

Prejudicial Attitudes

A third aspect of Muslim psychosocial life hurtful to Hindus is that some Muslims, especially those whose relatives moved across the borders during the country's partition, continue to have emotional ties with Pakistan. Mostly dormant, this proclivity can become overt during an Indo-Pakistan cricket match or during a border skirmish between the two nations. Fortunately, with each passing day, partition is receding back in time and memory; the numbers of those with pro-Pakistan feelings seems to be diminishing in tandem. It must also be emphasized that such individuals did not and do not represent the sentiments of the majority among Indian Muslims.

A bigger problem is that many Muslims hold secret prejudices against Hindus. They regard Hindus as having plebian minds, low valor, and gaudy aesthetics (for the last mentioned point especially, see Kakar 1996, 182). They hold scornful attitudes about Hindu animistic mythology and reified gods. In this, they are "empowered" by their religion, which declares all "idol worshippers" as *Kuffar* (plural of *Kafir*, meaning "the blasphemer"), and by the socially irresponsible rhetoric of their religious leaders.

Absence of Progressive and Secular Leadership

Indian Muslims also suffer from the fact that they have never had a progressive, liberal, and secular leadership. It is not that their community has not produced such individuals. It has. However, in a trend set with the Muslim League-Congress schism of the early twentieth century, most of the post-independence secular Muslims stayed within the folds of the Congress party. Some joined the Communist Party of India. In either case, secular Indian Muslims never developed an *en bloc*, separate political voice of their own. An unfortunate consequence of this was that religious Muslim leaders became the community's political spokesmen also. A recipe for social disaster was set. Bound to orthodox beliefs and literal interpretations of the *Quranic* law, the Muslim clerics took every opportunity to steer the Muslim masses toward thinking that their faith was continually endangered in India. Using the age-old device of encouraging a sense of victimhood, they strengthened their grips on Muslim masses and, thus, became a political lobby of considerable importance with the central government. This frequently resulted in administrative decisions being made that were not only deeply annoying to Hindus, but, in the long run, were harmful to Muslims as well.

Take the example of the October 15, 1988 banning of Salman Rushdie's (1988) controversial novel, *The Satanic Verses*, in India. The ban attacked the right to freedom of expression that lies at the foundation of a democratic society. It strengthened the hand of right-wing Muslims in India, for instance, Imam Bukhari of Delhi, who had engineered anti-Rushdie riots in Bombay. And, it perpetuated the image of Muslims in the Hindu eyes as an overindulged minority. All in all, the decision made by Rajiv Gandhi (the Congress Party's leader and the Prime Minister of India at the time) was a shameful capitulation to the Muslim religious "leadership"; it was a terrible decision that might have done more harm than good in the long run.

Constitutional Privileges

Indian constitution allows Muslims to have a separate family law governing matters of marriage, divorce, and inheritance. The renowned *Shah Bano* case, involving a divorced Muslim woman who had sued her former husband in order to get alimony, had brought this dilemma out in open. While the ever just Supreme Court of the country ruled in her favor in 1985, the then Prime Minister, Rajiv Gandhi (representing the Congress Party) overruled the verdict, largely as an appeasement of the right-wing Muslim politicians and religious leaders. This was truly unfortunate, as an opportunity for initiating an important paradigm shift was lost. To perpetuate separate laws for Hindus and Muslims is to create an imbalance. And, for Muslims to "enjoy" and feel entitled to such privilege is shortsighted, to say the least. It certainly does not help their cause for social justice and equity.

All in all, the "foreign" religious loyalties of Muslims, their covert nostalgic attitude of superiority, their ethnic prejudices, the lack of secular leadership in their community, and their reveling in having separate constitutional privileges, all tend to create serious difficulties in the Hindus forming harmonious relations with them. To complicate matters, the Hindus bring their own negative attitudes toward Muslims to the table.

HINDU CONTRIBUTIONS TO THE HINDU–MUSLIM TENSION

In the light of the historical and social accounts provided previously in this chapter, it is not surprising that Hindus experience a certain ambivalence toward their fellow Muslim citizens. The vicissitudes of this tenuously balanced love-hate economy are such that a tilt toward intensified hate is an ever-present possibility. A flare-up of unrest in the predominantly Muslim state of Kashmir, a border skirmish with Pakistan, an India-Pakistan cricket match, news regarding anti-Hindu activities in the neighboring nation of Bangladesh, an economic policy of the government that threatens the majority interests, and a civic dispute regarding arrangements about the way one community's religious festival affects the other's existence for a mere day or two—are all potent triggers to tip the scales of the Hindu ambivalence toward heightened mistrust and dislike of Muslims.

Even in the absence of such intensified aggression, subterranean negative images of Muslims lurk in the minds of many Hindus. A population survey conducted by Varma et al. (1973) revealed that such anti-Muslim prejudice is more marked in lower middle-class Hindus than in those who are truly poor. Frenkel-Brunswick and associates' (1954) early observation that socioeconomic marginality and not socioeconomic class is a crucial factor in the origin of ethnic prejudice was thus supported by Varma and associates' study. Another finding of this investigation was the close association of anti-Muslim sentiment with ethnocentrism, politicoeconomic conservatism, and antidemocratic attitudes. Those who were prejudiced believed that Muslims are given to "escapist activists like poetry, music, and dance" (p. 158), beside being clannish, smelly, unkempt, and dirty.

There also exists a myth that Muslims might one day outnumber Hindus since they are polygamous and produce many more children than Hindus. The reality is that according to 1992 Census of India, there were 2.5 million *less* females than males among the Indian Muslims. So where are the alleged four wives for each Muslim man going to come from? To wit, the incidence of polygamy was 15 percent among the tribals, 8 percent among Buddhists, 7 percent among Jains, 6 percent among Hindus, and 5 percent among Muslims; these findings have also been reported in a recent book by Jagruthi (2003). And, in the same census figures, the Muslim birth rate was only marginally higher (.01 percent) than that of Hindus. Given these facts, how is it possible that they will outnumber Hindus? And yet, the myth persists.

Were it only for such malevolent notions, matters might not be so bad after all. However, the situation has become worse over the last two decades. India's proud metropolitan centers have lost their spirit of ethnic camaraderie. Violence threatens to erupt readily through a thin veneer of tolerance. "Narcissism of minor differences" (Freud 1918, 199) has become sadism of manufactured animosities. This unfortunate turn of events seems to have resulted from the confluence of the following five unconscious factors operating in certain sections of the Hindu majority.

Post-Muslim Domination Trauma

The history of Muslims in India is a complex and contradictory tapestry of larceny and largesse, blood and blossoms, and domination and devotion. They came from foreign lands, plundered and established their empire that extended quite widely over the country's terrain. Although over the course of time, they became increasingly assimilated into the Indian culture and enriched it by their profoundly significant contributions, the fact that a minority had been the ruler of a majority left its indelible mark on the latter's collective psyche. This wound continues to affect the national recall of this historical fact. According to Kakar (1996),

> [T]here are two overarching histories of Hindu-Muslim relations—with many local variations—which have been used by varying political interests and ideologies and have been jostling for position for many centuries. In times of heighten conflict between the two communities, the Hindu nationalist history that supports the version of conflict between the two assumes preeminence and organizes cultural memory in one particular direction. In times of relative peace, the focus shifts back to the history emphasizing commonalties and shared pieces of the past. (p. 24)

I, however, believe that the traffic between the predominant historical paradigm and ethnic conflict goes in both directions. Kakar suggests that in conflictual times, people "prefer" a Hindu nationalist version, and in peaceful times, people "prefer" a secularist version of history. I agree with him, but add that the opposite might also be true. In other words, when a Hindu nationalist version of history is "preferred," then conflict between the two communities ensues, and when a secularist version is "preferred," then peace between them results. Further complexity is added to the situation by the retrospective embellishment of Muslim atrocities by one group and of Muslim contributions by the other. Fact and fiction get mixed up, as they often do in the creation of history (Loewenberg 1995). The ground gets well prepared for a harvest of hatred and gleefully welcomes the poisonous seed of further divisiveness.

Postpartition Unresolved Mourning

The refugees from those areas of pre-1947 India that became Pakistan were not able to fully mourn their trauma. Regardless of whether their losses were of lives or property or only of psychosocial continuity, their pain was great and a deep mourning of it was not possible. Deprived of the "protective rites of farewell" (Grinberg and Grinberg 1989), physically overwhelmed, emotionally shattered, and lacking the possibility of "emotional refueling"

(Mahler et al. 1975) from their lost motherland, they suppressed their anguish. The need to reestablish their lives in a new land also shifted the tension away from inner sadness. Surviving occupied them more than reminiscing.

However, their unresolved grief and its associated emotions of hurt, shame, rage, and sadness became susceptible to transgenerational transmission. A tear shed at the mention of an old neighborhood, a sigh heaved at the sight of a sewing machine (the like of which was lost to looting during the riots), an absent-minded caress of a scar, and an unexplained silence in response to a seemingly innocent question, all became encoded signals to carry this grief into the souls of the next generation. Also passed was the unspoken (and not entirely unreasonable) fear and dislike of Muslims. It took the second or third generation of these refugees to open up the wounds of partition for understanding and resolution. Movies and plays regarding partition of India and its bloody aftermath have only recently begun to be made. Otherwise, silence had prevailed, and under the cloak of wordlessness, pain and hate were being passed on to the next generation.

Postcolonial Villain Hunger

A certain amount of ethnic xenophobia is perhaps ubiquitous. It results from the universal tendency to externalize aggression. This helps human beings demarcate their own group boundaries and protects them from feeling weak and helpless vis-à-vis life's hardships. Having someone to blame keeps sadness and mourning in abeyance. Anger makes one feel strong. Paranoia becomes a psychic vitamin for threatened identity and a powerful anodyne against the pain that results from genuine self-reflection. This is the essential dynamics of what I call a "villain hunger." And, this hunger gets readily activated when a large group's identity is threatened from external or internal sources. Most such threats are constituted by economic upheaval, but sometimes the sudden disappearance of a well-known "enemy" can also destabilize the group. The fall of the U.S.S.R., for instance, created a vacuum in the American large-group dynamics and, in part, led to the finding of a new enemy in the form of Islamic fundamentalism (not that these Muslims did not "invite" such an occurrence).

Within the Indian context, independence from the British had a similar effect.[18] After nearly two decades of patriotic exaltation, the masses gradually realized that the mere departure of the British hardly made their problems vanish. *Swaraj* (self-governance) gave them pride, but did not take away poverty, epidemics, overpopulation, regional conflicts, and so on. Needing someone to "blame" for their continuing hardships, people unconsciously sought a new villain and Muslims appeared "suitable reservoirs for externalization" (Volkan

1997). After all, they had ancestors who had come from foreign countries, caused bloodshed, and became rulers of the land (disregard the fact that this was hundreds of years ago). And, the fact that their religion originated outside of India "confirmed" that they were basically "not Indians."

The rampant national hunger for an enemy was exploited by the right-wing Hindu leaders who publicly emphasized the negative aspects of Muslim history. The *Jana Sangh* stalwart Balraj Madhok, who had earlier (1970) proposed a program for the "Indianization" of Muslims, now declared that they "have no legal or moral claim or right on this country" (1983). His call, along with similar rhetoric from other right-wing Hindu leaders, turned Muslims into the hated "other." However, like events in individual mind, matters of large-group psychology are also "multidetermined" (Waelder 1936). The departure of the British seems to be one among many factors leading to the intensified anti-Muslim sentiment in India over the last two or three decades. Another factor was an intramural economic threat.

Post-Mandal Commission Economic Threat

In August 1990, the Government of India, led by the secular and socialist-leaning *Janata Dal*, implemented the final report from an Advisory Commission that had been set up earlier to study ways to improve economic lives of the country's lower socioeconomic class. This commission, led by Justice A. K. Mandal, recommended that 27 percent of all federal level jobs be reserved for the "backwards classes." Coupled with an already existing quota of 15 percent for the "untouchables" and 7 percent for the tribals, this meant that 49 percent[19] of government jobs were now out of the reach for the majority of Hindus. This resulted in a jolt of economic threat to the Hindu middle and lower classes. In their vulnerability, the right-wing Hindu leaders found an opportunity to mine political capital. They began to exploit the group frustration and to stir up a sense of victimization in the group. They fueled its rage and "offered" Muslims as the scapegoats for its aggression. BJP leadership had clearly sensed an opportunity to snatch power from the secular forces at the national level.[20]

Postmigration Hypernationalism and Its Boomerang Effect upon India

The smoldering passions stirred up by the right-wing Hindus in India received further impetus from the immigrant Indians (commonly known as "nonresident Indians," or NRIs) in the United States. This group was largely comprised of physicians, academics, and technocrats. Their encounter with the North American culture of consumerism, competitiveness, sexual freedom, broken families, and multiculturalism produced interesting results. On the one hand, these Indians rose rapidly in the ranks of economic hierarchy. Indeed, by the mid-1990s, immigrant Indians had become the most affluent ethnic group (*including* the white Anglo-Saxons) in the United States. Armed with first-class educational credentials, unburdened with student loans that plagued their American counterparts, and given to disciplined hard work, these immigrant Indians acquired great material success; the self-mocking quip by an Indian colleague that "no Indian shall die without a Mercedes" paints a fitting, if facile, verbal portrait of this group. It also hints at the gnawing uncertainty about the inner self that propels the "need" to own palatial houses and status-brandishing cars. There was evidence of pain here.

The Hindu community among the Indian immigrants was especially shaken up by finding itself to be a small minority in a nation largely made up of Christians and Jews. Even Muslims, with their multiple nationalities (Indian, Pakistani, Bangladeshi, Iranian, Saudi Arabian, Iraqi, Palestinian, Syrian, Egyptian, and so on) seemed to outnumber them in the United States. Not used to being a minority or being a target of prejudicial attitudes, this community was quite traumatized. Judging from their "modal" reactions, the members of the NRI Hindu community seem to belong to three groups. The first group was constituted by those who were able to adjust to this "ethnic downgrading" with wry humor, pride in efficacy, and a bicultural transformation of identity. They did have occasional bouts of nostalgia, but these tended to diminish with the passage of time (Akhtar 1999; 1999d). Their turning to religion had a "soft" and private quality, and their inner definition of India remained pluralistic and secular. Their self-esteem was sustained by their professional and familial achievements, as well as by the fact that they helped India by investing funds, pro bono teaching and consultancy, and the construction of schools and clinics, especially in rural areas in the country. In contrast, the second group was constituted by individuals who became overidentified with the West in a massive "counterphobic assimilation" (Teja and Akhtar 1981). They renounced all sense of belonging to the Indian community and its rich traditions.

The third group of NRI Hindus resorted to defensive hypernationalism and ethnic grandiloquence. This helped in easing the pain of temporal discontinuity and made it possible for them to withstand ethnic caricature by the American community. They valiantly attempted to rectify the frequently biased and negative portrayal of India in the North American press. Unfortunately, their hypernationalism also had some problematic aspects, including: (1) the mistaken equation of Indian culture with Hinduism, (2) a conviction that the mankind's wisdom sprung only from Hindu religious thought, (3) an insistence that while Hindu culture provided concepts and imaginative potential to both the West and Far East, nothing significant from those regions contributed to the Hindu culture, (4) an exaggerated and paranoid sense of cultural victimization by the West, and (5) a doomsday scenario, suggesting that Christian evangelists proselytizing in India would gradually convert so many people to their faith that the demographic dominance of Hindus would be threatened. Not surprisingly, a close liaison developed between the North American NRI's holding such sentiments and the VHP-BJP politburo in India.[21] This ethnocentric twinship "benefited" both parties. Celebrations of Indian heritage in American cities became increasingly the solipsistic serenade of Hinduism, with VHP and BJP leadership often appearing at them. In turn, the Hindu nationalist NRIs of the United States began funneling huge amounts of money to support the anti-secular agenda of these political parties in India.

RECENT FIASCOS

The five factors mentioned above (namely, the lasting impact of Muslim rule over India, the unresolved grief over partition, the villain hunger subsequent to the departure of the British, the impact of the Mandal Commission report, and the dark fraternity between the diaspora Indians' hypernationalism and the BJP-VHP political juggernaut back in India) combined, in various permutations and at different levels of abstraction and consciousness, to make Hindu masses immensely susceptible to manipulation by the right-wing leaders of their community. Muslim religious leaders' outrageous proclamations provided further fuel to this fire. Hindu nationalist parties benefited greatly from all this and rose to power, and ultimately formed the national government.

There now began a virulent drum beat that sought to evoke religious fervor in the Hindu masses. Right-wing leaders of the *Sangh Parivar* (BJP, VHP, RSS, Bajrang Dal, etc.) evoked "chosen traumas" (Volkan 1997) (i.e., old injuries to the group's pride) and with their fiery rhetoric, created a sense of "time collapse." As a result, centuries-old wounds acquired the emotional intensity of yesterday's laceration and the fundamentally kind, multivocal, and pluralistic Hindu religion was hijacked by these "destructive pied pipers" (Blum 1995, 18) of the right. In North India, at least, the vast and deeply evocative pantheon of Hinduism was reduced to a monolithic exaltation of one particular deity, namely *Rama*. This was done in order to stir up the emotional delirium needed to destroy an A.D. 1528 mosque (*Babri Masjid*) that was presumably built by a Muslim ruler, Mohiuddin

Babar (reigned A.D. 1530–1540 and A.D. 1555–1556), on the site of Rama's birth place (*Ramjananbhoomi*).

The fever spread widely. In the United States, Hindu nationalist NRIs took out ads in ethnic newspapers of the Indian community soliciting money for the construction of *Ramjananbhoomi* and implicitly endorsing the destruction of *Babri Masjid*. The very people who felt so proud of India thus openly mocked the country's secular constitution. No one seemed to notice this contradiction. There was madness in the air.

Back in India, L. K. Advani, a prominent BJP leader undertook a 10,000-kilometer *Rathyatra* (travel by chariot) that took him across many North Indian states to the site of this mosque in Uttar Pradesh. "The Toyota van in which the BJP leader traveled was decorated to make it resemble the chariot of the legendary hero Arjuna, as shown in the immensely popular television serial of the *Mahabharata*. Advani's chariot aroused intense fervor among the Hindus. Crowds thronged the roads to catch a glimpse of the *rath*, showered flower petals on the cavalcade, as it passed through their villages and towns, and the vehicle itself became a new object of worship, as women offered ritual prayer with coconut, burning incense, and sandlewood paste at each of its stops" (Kakar 1996, 49).

All along the way, Advani called for the destruction of this Muslim place of worship[22] and "there were incidents of violence between Hindus and Muslims in the wake of the *rathyatra*" (Kakar 1996, 49). In a clever political ploy that added a dream-like quality to all this, Advani chose *Somnath* as the starting point of his sojourn. The message was loud and clear. By destroying *Babri Masjid*, the Hindus would be avenging Mahmud Ghaznavi's A.D. 1020 attack on *Somnath* temple. That the two events would occur in different cultural contexts, under different political systems of government, for different purposes, and would be separated by nearly one thousand years, did not seem to matter. Such is the power of large-group regression (Freud 1921) and the activation of its unmourned traumas (Volkan 1997, 2004). Under the sway of emotions, people lost their critical abilities and submitted to their mesmerizing leader. Personal morality was sacrificed on the altar of resurgent large-group identity.

On December 6, 1992, the *Babri Masjid* was destroyed by a frenzied Hindu mob "with prominent members of BJP, VHP, Bajrang Dal, etc., aiding and abetting the destruction. No police/Center Forces were used by the State government to stop the destruction" (Prasad et al. 1993, 113). The entire nation watched this horrible event in utter disbelief on television. The Muslim citizens of India were humiliated to the bone. The liberal Hindus of the country felt remorseful and outraged at what the right-wing zealots had done. To the country's credit and to the credit of the liberal Hindus, a nongovernmental

Citizens Tribunal headed by three Hindu judges, namely Justice O. Chinappa Reddy, Justice D. A. Desai, and Justice D. S. Tewatia, conducted a thorough investigation and, on the basis of "voluminous body of evidence, eye-witness accounts, and submissions, the honourable judges concluded: '[T]here is a moral certainty that there was a well-laid conspiracy to demolish the Babri Masjid,' and indicted the top leaders of the BJP, VHP, RSS, Bajrang Dal, and Shiv Sena for hatching the conspiracy. They also held the Government of India 'guilty of culpable negligence and a willful refusal to discharge its obligation as a Constitutional Government' and observed that its 'inaction was deliberate and with full knowledge of the likely outcome'" (Prasad et al. 1993, x).

Existing parallel to such shiningly secular jurisprudence was the persistent knife of anti-Muslim hatred, still bloodthirsty and in search of victims. "In Bombay in early January, a month after the destruction of the Babri Masjid, the militantly Hindu, Muslim-hating Shiv Sena acted out the fiery images and language of its campaign videos by torching Muslim homes and shops. The Bombay elite's sense of being in charge and safe in India's most cosmopolitan city was shattered, when roving bands searched for Muslim names in elegant apartments along hitherto sacrosanct Marine Drive, Club Road, and Malabar Hill" (Rudolph and Rudolph 1993, 29).

Never having suffered such national level humiliation, the Muslim community of India was stunned. Indian Muslims living abroad became queasy about visiting their own motherland, and those who lived in India felt robbed of civic dignity. As time passed, three unfortunate reactions to this onslaught became crystallized in the Indian Muslim community: (1) many became fearful and silent, (2) others turned to regressive, pan-Islamic fanaticism, with individuals like Imam Bukhari of New Delhi's *Jama Masjid* counting himself among the "brothers" of Osama bin Laden, and (3) a few Muslims resorted to destructive acts against Hindus and their properties which, in turn, evoked greater violence toward the Muslim community.

In 2002, some members of this last mentioned group set fire to a train passing by the town of Godhra in the state of Gujrat and, in the process, killed about sixty Hindus, including women and children. This cruel and deplorable act was followed by the massacre of over two thousand Muslims in Gujrat, especially in the city of Ahmedabad. Hindu mobs killed Muslims, raped their women, destroyed their properties, and burned their shrines. They cut the water and electric supplies to Muslim areas, creating pogroms of terror and despair. They even leveled the grave of the great (and arguably the first) Urdu poet, Wali Gujrati, in a callous attack on language and metaphor, which are the hallmarks of human civilization. Most disturbing about all this was the undeniable element of state complicity with the right-wing Hindu government of

Gujrat, headed by Narendra Modi, not only standing away from the site of the carnage, but actually facilitating in this attempted genocide of Muslims.

The BJP government, by now firmly ensconced in New Delhi, did not dissolve the state government, nor did it remove Narendra Modi from his post, both of which it could have readily done. It was busy in implementing its agenda of "Hinduttva," an important element of which was rewriting the early history of India "often with a bizarre content" (Sainath 2004). School curricula were changed "without consulting the educational bodies that had earlier routinely consulted, such as, the Central Advisory Board of Education" (Thapar 2004, 10). Such revisionism was intended to: (1) blur the boundaries between mythology, literature, and history, (2) demonize the British,[23] (3) "deny the contributions the Muslims have made to India" (*Economist*, May 22, 2004, 10), and (4) replace the well-established early Aryan invasion of India by the assertion that no such thing took place and these progenitors of North Indian Hindus had lived in India from the times immemorial. Essentially the Hindu nationalist version

> divides Indian history into a Hindu period (1000 B.C. to A.D. 1200) and a Muslim period (A.D. 1200–1800) on the basis of the religion of some of the ruling dynasties. It brackets together Arabs, Turks, and Persians under the term "Muslims," even though that term is rarely used in contemporary sources before the thirteenth century. It uses the term "Hindu" as if it described a unified religious community, despite the fact that the term is not found in pre-Islamic sources. (It was first used by Arabs and later by others to refer to the inhabitants of the area near the river Sind or the Indus.) Basically, it is an ahistorical view of the past in its denial of discontinuity and its assertion of essentialized categories. (van der Veer 1994, 152)

The Hindu nationalist portrayal of Indian history is actually a jump backward to the assumptions of the nineteenth century colonial history, according to the preeminent scholar Romila Thapar. In her view:

> The colonial interpretation was carefully developed through the nineteenth century. By 1823, the *History of British India*, written by James Mill, was available and widely read. This was the hegemonic text in which Mill periodized Indian history into three periods: Hindu civilization, Muslim civilization, and the British period. . . . Mill argued that the Hindu civilization was stagnant and backward, the Muslim only marginally better and the British colonial power an agency of progress because it could legislate for improvement in India. In the Hinduttva version, this periodization remains, only the colors have changed: the Hindu period is the golden age, the Muslim period, the black, dark age of tyranny and oppression, and the colonial period is a gray age of almost of marginal importance compared to the earlier two. (Lecture in February 2003 cited in Gatade 2003, 4)

Thapar (2004) emphasized that there was nothing new in the Hindu nationalist version of history except its aim to "bring about a new bonding by privileging the identity and origins of the majority community" (p. 27). The political capital gained out of denying the Aryan invasion was especially great. This so-called "modern viewpoint" facilitated the denial of Aryan suppression of the darker skinned original inhabitants (*Dravids*) of the region. Moreover, it led to the obvious conclusion that the only Indians who had "foreign" roots were Muslims. They could, therefore, be declared to be not really Indians. The growth of Muslim labor migration to the Middle East further "confirmed" their foreignness.

On commenting upon some of these developments under the BJP government, British journalist Gwynne Dyer says: "The most spectacular recent manifestation of its Hindu-first, anti-minority policy was the massacre of Muslims in Gujrat in 2002, which had the tacit support of the BJP state government. More insidious for the long run was the deliberate attack on the education system. School textbooks have been systematically rewritten to represent a victimized and downtrodden majority, and to portray Muslims and Christians as somehow foreign and disloyal to the real, Hindu India" (2004, A-19).

Veteran Indian journalist Kuldip Nayar, who happens to be Hindu, wistfully acknowledges that "A preponderant number of Hindus have felt small even over the manner in which the BJP and other members of the *Sangh Parivar* have disfigured Hinduism, from its image of tolerance to fanaticism" (2004, 6).

Clearly, both Hindus and Muslims of India have been harmed by the rightwing, religious nationalism of Hindus. The ultimate conflict therefore seems to be not between Hindus and Muslims, but between those who are fundamentalists and those are secular. Awareness of this creates the potential for fresh thinking in this realm. It sustains hope.

The Proverbial Silver Lining to the Cloud

One good outcome of the troika of Muslim narcissistic mortification (the *Babri Masjid* destruction, the politically driven rewriting of history, and the Gujrat riot) was that educated and liberal Muslims have begun to organize themselves into a political voice of robust secularism. They are seeking to delink Muslim societal concerns from religious orthodoxy and to mobilize the Muslim voting block by appealing to their politicoeconomic concerns rather than to their religious doctrines.

More importantly, there is evidence that the callous noose of Hindu fundamentalism has failed to strangulate the secular and democratic spirit of India.

Its people, though poor and superstitious in Western eyes, are highly sophisticated when it comes to the power of their electoral vote. This democratic process, which removed Congress Party's leader Indira Gandhi from national office after she had arrogantly assumed near dictatorial powers, has once again shown its strength. In a stunning reversal of fortune, the Indian electorate delivered a resounding defeat to the Hindu nationalist BJP government in May 2004, replacing it with a coalition government led by the secular Congress Party. And, *within the first week* of coming in power, the education ministry of this government, headed by Arjun Singh, announced that it would take immediate steps to recall the school textbooks distorted by the Hindu nationalist agenda.

Though immensely reassuring, this is only a first step. The path to resolve the Hindu-Muslim conflict and reduce anti-Muslim prejudices is a long one. It needs many types of interventions by both governmental and grassroots level organizations.

SUGGESTED REMEDIES

I will outline seven psychoanalytically informed social strategies aimed at ameliorating the Hindu-Muslim conflict in India. These measures pertain to the (1) educational, (2) cultural, (3) experiential, (4) economic, (5) political, (6) judicial, and (7) constitutional realms. I make these suggestions with humility and wish to enter two caveats at the outset. First, since the foundations of prejudice rest upon ubiquitous childhood experiences, it is not possible to eliminate all such feelings; one can only hope to lessen their intensity. Second, while illustrations will be given here from the specific Hindu-Muslim context, some of these guidelines could possibly be applicable to other ethnic conflicts as well.

Educational Measures

While prejudice emanates from deep emotional roots going back to childhood, knowledge deficit and misinformation also play a role in its perpetuation and intensification. To combat this aspect of prejudice, educational measures must be set into motion. A multipronged approach is needed. Government agencies and NGOs, including those set up by progressive and secular Hindus and Muslims, should take it upon themselves to spread positive information about the minorities. Billboards, with simple messages to such effect, can go a long way in this regard. Imagine billboards, in the predominantly Hindu areas of New Delhi, Bombay, and other similar parts of

India, declaring that "many Muslims were against the partition of India," "Muslims fought hard for the independence of India," and "Muslims have greatly enriched Indian culture." And, now imagine billboards in the high-density Muslim cities of Aligarh, Srinagar, and Hyderabad declaring that "Hindus have safeguarded the beauty of Taj Mahal," "Hindus have a hand in India's having had three Muslim Presidents" and "Hindus played an important role in post-partition India being a secular nation." While certainly untested, it is my hypothesis that such billboards can have a powerful impact upon the consciousness of the masses.[24] Radio and television, especially in India where the central government has considerable say in the media's programming, can similarly broadcast antiprejudice messages.

A scrutiny of what is being taught to schoolchildren might also be needed. Clearly, their textbooks need to incorporate both Hindu and Muslim figures who have contributed to the evolving history of the nation. Instruction along these lines during formative years of childhood could have a major impact upon the view that Hindu and Muslim children will have of their counterparts as both of them grow up to become adult citizens of a secular country.

More importantly than this, the possibility of teaching children and adolescents about the nature of human prejudice should be considered. India might take the lead in the free world by introducing required courses in elementary and higher secondary education about the emotional forces that create and sustain man's hatred for his fellow beings. Such early sensitization would hopefully "inoculate" them against future vulnerability to be exploited by religious politics, regardless of whether it is of Hindu or Muslim stripe. However, in contrast to what the BJP administration did, none of these changes should be made by government fiat and without detailed, critical, and thorough review by various academic bodies representing multiple disciplines and interests. It should be remembered that "authoritarianism of the left" is not the corrective to the "authoritarianism of the right."

Cultural Measures

Another avenue to approach this matter is through Hindi movies. India is the largest producer of movies in the world, and its people are avid watchers of these mostly caricatured and maudlin, song-laden family dramas. One particular genre among such movies goes by the curious title of "Muslim socials." They depict a colorful and seemingly positive, but nonetheless highly caricatured, view of Indian Muslims. The era depicted is always that of princely states, never the contemporary one. The hero is invariably inclined to poetry and the heroine is a *purdah*-clad stunning beauty. There is also the required courtesan-cum-prostitute. These movies (e.g., *Chaudvin Ka Chand, Mere*

Mehboob, Palki, Bahu Begum, Pakeezah, and *Mehboob Ki Mehndi*), usually produced on a lavish scale, are quite popular among the masses, the majority of whom happen to be Hindus. Perhaps, the idealization of Muslims by these movies is enjoyed on a conscious level as a defense against the doubt and suspicion toward them in the unconscious. Actually, these movies are harmful since they perpetuate a stereotypic view of Muslims as merely given to matters of heart and leisure. Indeed, they also fuel the Muslims' retrospectively embellished nostalgia for their past days of royal glory; such idealization helps them deny their legacy of early atrocities toward Hindus. Either way, these movies perpetuate stereotyping of Muslims and thus potentially fuel prejudice toward them. Their production needs to be discouraged.[25]

Fascinatingly, even outside of this specific genre, when a Muslim character is shown in a Hindi movie, he is bearded, interested in *qawwali* (a Sufi-derived form of Muslim devotional singing), and attired in a caricatured "Muslim" way. All this needs correction. Just the way political action is being taken in the United States to check the depiction of gratuitous violence in movies and on television, the Indian social activists should also launch a campaign to have Muslims shown in movies as regular, working-class people like everybody else. Movies that have incidental, even minor, Muslim characters who behave and dress like ordinary people on the street should be given tax benefits by the government. Such depictions will subtly help erode the stereotyping mentioned above.

Another cultural avenue to reduce Hindu-Muslim friction is to encourage the production of plays and movies depicting friendly relations between them. These could be drawn from either their early history (imagine a movie or stage play on the life of Shah Jahan's son Dara Shikoh who translated *Upanashids* into Persian) or from some exceptional moments during recent times (for instance, Hindu and Muslims sheltering each other's relatives during the bloodshed associated with the partition of India). Witnessing such material, especially the setting of a theater, can have powerful kindling effects and recharge submerged memories of good relations between the two groups.[26]

Experiential Measures

Closely parallel to the educational and cultural measures outlined above are methods of interventions that are "experiential" in nature. Two such measures readily come to mind. One pertains to creating opportunities for children, adolescents, and young adults of the two faiths to actually live with a family of the opposite faith. The Bombay-based liberal journalist, Hamid Dalwai, did succeed during the late 1960s to create such an "exchange program."

Those Muslim and Hindu kids who participated in it, and their host families, found the interaction immensely beneficial. This goes to show that there is no substitute to the knowledge of the other gained by the mutuality of actually living together on a day-to-day basis. The Kids for Peace sports camp in rural Connecticut hosting Israeli and Palestinian youngsters also confirms the value of such one-to-one human experience. Such programs need to be supported and popularized throughout India.[27]

Yet another study in this realm was conducted in an Israel school. In a class exclusively made up of Jewish children, half were given an Arab identity for a period of a few days and then the situation was reversed so that the remaining half got to be "Arab" also. The results of this study (Rena Moses-Hrushovski 1999, personal communication) demonstrated a heightened sensitivity toward the feelings of minority as a result of putting oneself in another's shoes. Perhaps, it is time that some Indian schools attempt to undertake such experiential exercises?

Economic Measures

Frequently, it is a real or imagined threat to economic safety that leads a group to start scapegoating a religious or ethnic minority. The threat is exaggerated by the majority's leaders who point fingers to the minority as lazy and unentitled devourers of scarce resources. Such threats to economic safety must be combated by legislative reforms, whereby the "need" for viewing others with suspicion of thievery or parasitism would not arise or, at least, stay within containable limits. Moreover, when and if extra provisions for a minority are democratically put into place, the government should make concerted efforts to educate the majority about the nature, reasons, and limits of such provisions. This would be akin to good parents' ensuring that an older sibling does not feel totally displaced by the arrival of a new baby. In the United States, a chronic source of irritation for white racists is the government's policy of "affirmative action" toward the African-American population. However, few white people know the actual details of the policy. And, few white people truly appreciate the duration and extent of subjugation and abuse of blacks that has necessitated such reparation.

In the context of India, the mid-1990s outbreak of anti-Muslim violence all over the nation followed the release of the Mandal Commission Report (1990), which proposed that a proportion of federal jobs be reserved for ethnic minorities; curiously, the "minority" being offered the greatest protection was the lower caste Hindus! However, feeling suddenly threatened in their search for employment, the upwardly mobile, lower-middle-class Hindu youth was rendered vulnerable to find scapegoats for its frustration. This vulnerability was exploited by right-wing Hindu leaders in order to fuel communal hatred. In light of all this, it is my sense that the economic reform needed to diminish ethnic prejudice should involve: (1) actual improvements in the monetary status of the entire group and (2) careful education to combat the view of protected minorities as pampered and overindulged.

Political Measures

From psychodynamic studies of leadership patterns (Volkan et al. 1998; Steinberg 1996; Post 1983, 1991; Post and Robins 1993; Robins 1986), it can be safely assumed that some character attributes in an individual headed toward a leadership position should be a cause for alarm. While "healthy narcissism" (Kernberg 1976) is a needed attribute in a leader, pathological degrees of self-absorption, especially when combined with paranoid tendencies, can impair the leader's decision making and render him prone to marked devaluation of others. The dreaded resurgence of inferiority feelings from within is then handled by attributing "badness" to others and creating ethnic targets of the consequent hatred. "At these moments, the leader loses the adaptive elements. The means no longer serve the initial goals/ends. The pathologically paranoid leader projects hostility onto an enemy, likening this enemy to a cancer, or a disease. The leader selects a nation, group, a cultural entity, and/or a religious entity that has to be destroyed. The leader is forever obsessed with hatred and fear towards these entities" (Volkan et al. 1998, 155).

By instituting a system of checks and balances, such individuals could be prevented from ascending to positions of power. What exactly would constitute such a psychosocial filter and how effective—without acquiring fascist overtones itself—it would be, remains to be explored. Indeed, some might question whether this approach is practical at all. Yet, psychoanalytically informed social interventions (e.g., consultations with political parties, disseminating pertinent information to significant nongovernmental organizations or NGOs, public lectures) might help create enough concern about potentially dangerous individuals to prevent them from acquiring much power. The sharp rejection of Richard Haider, the pro-Nazi leader, in 2000, by the Austrian public and government alike is a case in point here. If psychoanalytically informed social activism could achieve even this much, it would be a great service.

Judicial Measures

While the actual deterrent value of retributive justice still needs study, democratic societies can hardly afford to look the other way when calculated efforts are made to hurt a minority group. Indeed, crimes emanating from racial or religious bigotry—*hate crimes*—need swift and condign punishment. Regardless of their social stature, individuals deemed responsible for inciting communal hatred and violence should be brought to justice. This might or might not deter others with similar plans, but it will certainly make the victimized group feel vindicated.[28] The latter's sense of full citizenship and the inalienable rights that it bestows will be restored. And, the secular conscience of the nation will be upheld, thus enhancing its esteem and democratic efficacy.

Within India's context, the indictment of Shiv Sena leader Bala Saheb Thackeray by the Bombay High Court was a shining example of this sort. By declaring the powerful head of the preeminent Hindu militant organization accountable for his role in the anti-Muslim carnage in Bombay, the Indian justice system injected a dose of confidence in the nation's commitment to secularism. Also, when Thackeray was accused in 1995 by for soliciting votes in the name of religion in contravention of existing lanes, the Bombay High Court barred him from voting for six years as a punishment. In tragic contrast is the miscarriage (or should we say abortion?) of justice in the recent Gujrat situation. Clearly, one hopes that courts in India will act in a fair, swift, and strict manner when dealing with anti-Muslim or anti-Hindu hate crimes.

Constitutional Measures

While the secular nature of India's constitution is to be applauded, its provision of a separate family law for Muslims is something that needs reconsideration. On the one hand, it lets them conduct the transactions of marriage, divorce, and inheritance in accordance with their religious dictates and, therefore, makes them feel secure about their identity. On the other hand, it separates them from the Hindu majority who feel that Muslims are being "pampered." This leads to friction between the two groups. Therefore, it might be worthwhile to reconsider such provisions. The disadvantage of Muslims' feeling deprived of erstwhile privileges and trampled upon in their religious freedom needs to be weighed against the societal damage done by the country's having two civil laws. To be sure, the entire issue needs to be revisited, debated, and researched in its constitutional, human rights, civic benefit, and legal aspects. It should be remembered that the country's criminal law for Hindus and Muslims is the same. And, it should be registered that other secular democracies of the world (e.g., the United States) do not allow religious minorities to have separate family laws. Of course, lacking the historical complexity and cultural diversity of India, the Western democracies might have found such legal homogenization easier. This rationalization should, however, not be allowed to deter India's constitutional experts from courageously facing the possibility of changing course in regard to the civil laws of the nation. And, Muslims of India should learn that to be truly equal with Hindus, they require two separate measures. On the one hand, they must be offered comparable socioeconomic opportunities. On the other hand, they must renounce the constitutional privileges not available to Hindus. Social dignity can be bestowed to only a certain extent. Mostly, it is an earned commodity.

CONCLUSION

After entering some caveats, I have highlighted the nodal points in the thirteen-hundred-year (A.D. 700–A.D. 2000) history of the Hindu–Muslim coexistence in India. After this, I have discussed the anti-Hindu feelings of Muslims and the anti-Muslim feelings of Hindus, highlighting their actual, as well as retrospectively embellished, roots in history. I have also addressed the origins of the increased strife between the two communities in the contemporary politicoeconomic scenario of India. I have then suggested seven psychoanalytically informed social strategies to combat such ethnic tension. I have spread my net wide, spoke in a spirit of informed altruism, and maintained a secular and psychoanalytic perspective throughout this chapter. However, it is not lost upon me that no matter what I say and what some others, like me, might express, the fundamentalist Hindu and Muslim forces against a kinder, more tolerant, interethnic stance are indeed powerful. Much governmental and nongovernmental intervention, concerted interdisciplinary research, and social activism on the part of both liberal Hindus and Muslims are needed to combat such forces. For my own humble contribution, a fitting conclusion comes from a couplet of the late Jigar Muradabadi (1896–1982), a renowned Urdu poet of India: "*Unka jo kaam hai, voh ehl-e-siaysat jaanen; Mera paigham mohabbat hai, jahan tak pohnchey.*"[29]

ACKNOWLEDGMENTS

I am thankful to many individuals who read earlier versions of this chapter and provided valuable input. Prominent among these are Javed Akhtar, Anju Bhargava, Subhash Bhatia, Ira Brenner, Naresh Julka, Saida Koita, Shantanu Maitra, Harish Malhotra, Tarnjit Saini, Abu Salim, Hamida Salim, J. Anderson Thomson Jr, and Vamik Volkan. I have incorporated many of their suggestions and the chapter is certainly enriched as a result.

V

CREATIVITY

14

Some Reflections on Arab Cinema

Iman Roushdy-Hammady

Into the mirror of my cup, the reflection of your glorious face fell
And from the gentle laughter of love, into a drunken state of longing I fell
Struck with wonder by the beauty of the picture that within my cup I beheld
The picture of this world of illusion from the reflection of my mind fell.

—Hafiz, A.D. 1370, cited in Ghavzini and Jhani 1941, p. 133

Films are recording mirrors. They record societal history through the representation of an image, which can be true or deceptive. In light of this, the historical portrayal of the Arab in local and global cinematic discourses deserves attention. The focus here is on the different genres of Arabic cinema, which have counterparts in Hollywood for purposes of analysis. American cinema has global hegemony over the presentation of the image, which reflects a complex infrastructure of a cultural political economy. On the other hand, the selection of Arabic film is largely Egyptian. Egypt has the early lead in the art of cinema on the regional level and represents its biggest industry.

The birth of a cinematic genre and its corresponding representations carries an agenda with it. The nature and aims of this agenda, disguised under the innocuous form of entertainment, can be an amalgamation of public opinion manipulation, education, reinforcement of the status quo, or resistance, to mention a few. In this light, the image of the Arab engages in the dramatization of multiple issues including gender, class, colonialism, religion—especially Islam, exoticism, orientalism, and local and global political economies. This engagement translates the historical and political circumstances, which, in turn, have shaped the presentation of the image in question.

In film, the presented image becomes so alive and personified, thus lending the screen the charisma of leadership and justifying its presentation. The power of the image is the outcome of an interplay of factors; some of them are tangible, like the filmmaker and consumer/viewer, whereas others are more abstract and uncontrollable, such as history, culture, and stereotypes.

THE IMAGINARY AND THE EXOTIC

The screen preaches. The image becomes a religion. With its inherent charisma the screen "preaches" about this created religion "the truth of the presented image." The audience grows up socialized to follow this charismatic entity. This charisma has the power to create and even change history.

The first genre of American movies about the Middle East started when the region was entirely under European colonial control, early in the twentieth century. One of the striking geographic differences distinctive to the Middle East is the vast and varying desert, which was mentioned in the memoirs and writings of a number of colonial officers, such as *Bonaparte and the Earl of Cromer* (1908) in the case of Egypt. These descriptions were positive at times and negative at others, but they generally allude to the mysterious quality of this geography with all the challenge, exotics, and the romance it entails. This perspective was reflected in the movie *Son of the Sheik* (1926).

This genre, however, was by far outlived by another, which appeared with the exotic, magical, and supernatural elements of *One Thousand and One Arabian Nights*. These include movies like *The Thief of Baghdad* (1924), the series of Sindbad movies, and *The Wonders of Aladdin* (1961). Here, women are represented as sex objects, as the target of sexual drive, as part of the state of nature, to borrow a Lévi-Straussian conception of women. This is manifested in scenes portraying harems and baths, where women are shown in excessively revealing clothes. The main female character plays the role of a beautiful woman, who is waiting to be saved from (marrying) the evil character in the movie. The woman is the trophy for the charming man, who survives adventurous dangers. In these exotic lands, the abundance of women and sex goes hand-in-hand with the excessive wealth, strange creatures, and magic. The victory of the camera in visually overcoming the "inaccessible" mirrors the colonialist victory and predominance over the colonized, a process during which the images of women's bodies were particularly exploited, being seen at times as mere erotic sex objects.

The genre of a magical Arab world has its Egyptian counterpart, which developed around the same time as in America. This started in the 1930s with the Thousand and One Night stories, like *Ali Baba wa al-Arba'in Harami* (Ali Baba and the Forty Thieves) (1936) and *Nur al-Din wa al-Bahhararah al-thalahtah* (Nur al-Din and the Three Sailors) (1938). Although there are no nude presentations, women are dressed in the harem-like outfits, which resemble those shown in the famous American T.V. show *I Dream of Jeannie*. Women are still the prizes won by the good guys. Yet, the good guy is often depicted as hardworking, industrious, and charming, unlike the lazy depiction of his American counterpart as shown in *The Thief of Baghdad* (1924). However, Egypt soon domesticated this genre and made it of cultural relevance. This resulted in a genre of movies, emphasizing images of resistance, which originally developed in the 1940s and 1950s in Egypt. In these movies, the time frame is purposefully unidentified, but the entire setting—with palaces, markets, wealth, costumes, harem-like-dressed-women—looks like a mixture of One Thousand and One Nights in Baghdad and Egypt under Memluk rule (A.D. 1250–1517). Examples of this genre are *Al-Saqr* (The Eagle, 1950), *Amir al-Intiqam* (The Prince of Revenge, adapted from Don Quixote, 1950), and *Dananir* (1940), in which the main female character was Umm Kulthum (1900–1975), the most famous singer on the local and regional levels. Umm Kulthum avoided portraying her image in the garb of orientalism, and yet she was not absorbed in the Western *chic* either. She completely rejected any projection of sexuality. Her image and songs came to embody hopes for a bright future for the Arab world, while keeping her appeal as a woman rooted in the tradition of the countryside. She represented a symbolic mother figure for the people in the region (Graham-Brown 1988).

The main theme is usually a battle between powerful good and bad men to rule a particular land, very much like Memluk princes. The woman in this genre is the trophy, as she also symbolizes the land. She is the beautiful *garia* (slave girl or courtesan), whom princes bought from the slave market for entertainment. However, the main female character is not passive. She falls in love with the good guy and, in arrangement with her lover, is sold to the opponent on whom she would spy. She can play tricks using her charm and beauty, and is able to alert her lover, who is loyal to the land, to all possible dangers and traps prepared for him. Eventually, the lover wins the battle. The prince usually highlights the vital role, which his *garia* played, and then marries her!

Though the stories and the plots seem simple, these movies implicate autocratic, unjust ruling, either directly or indirectly. The distinction is made between a helpless, nominal king, and the actual subrulers, some of whom are loyal and the others are traitors. At the time when these movies were made, this scenario seems to have implicated local politics. For example, in the 1950s, when Egypt was still under monarchy, the king's authorities were becoming more and more nominal toward the end of the British rule in Egypt. Among the subrulers, there were those in favor of the status quo, and those who opposed it and sought freedom. Within an evasive time frame with fancy palaces and fashion, this movie genre seems to have provided a safe way to express resistance and opposition to the existing sociopolitical regime.

This genre of movies was presented frequently on Arabic television during the time when the Arab League, which was supposed to represent all Arab countries in defending Iraq as perceived by many Arabs, had failed in its efforts to stop the American war against Iraq. In April 2003, Arabs residing all over the world shunned the Arab League and blamed its failure on the dependency that every country represented in it had on the United States (Roushdy-Hammady 2006).

The exotic and the mysterious thoughts about the Middle East continued to manifest in movies like *Casablanca* (1942) and later in *Naked Lunch* (1991). The first movie clearly depicts Morocco as a place in which it explores socio-historical facets of human experience in the context of the World War II period. In the second example, however, the plot is set in an exotic country that is not explicitly defined. Yet, the call for Muslim prayer, the Arabic dialect heard in the hallucination scenes of the protagonist (especially where a sex creature develops from an Arabic typewriter), the clothing of cast, and the accompanying Arabic dialect in the background streets, all indicate that this place must be either Morocco or an imaginary place like Morocco. It is a place of hallucinations, unusual sex experiences, and adventure.

REGIONAL POLITICS

In Egyptian cinema, there is a genre of movies that has become timeless in representing the Arab struggle—movies that are played intensively on different Arab television stations at different times of political unrest, including the period during the invasion of Iraq on March 19–20 2003. It is a genre of movies that had actually developed under Nasser's regimes in Egypt, yet is set in pre-1952 revolution in Egypt. Some of these movies highlight the vital role of the "Free Officers" in ending Egypt's colonial rule and monarchy, such as *Ghurub wa Shuruq* (Sunset and Sunrise, 1970), whereas others glorify martyrdom for the Palestinian cause, such as *Fi Baytina Rajul* (A Man in Our House).

After the 1967 Arab defeat at the hands of Israel, Nasser was lamenting with the Arab people, sharing their agonies, and trying to restore their self-esteem. The songs and movies that appeared in that period, such as *Fida'i* (Martyr) and feature films like *'Awdat al-Ibn al-Dal* (Return of the Prodigal Son, 1970), respectively, expressed the pain of the loss as part of the experience and served as an impetus to keep struggling and look toward a brighter future (Roushdy-Hammady 2006).

The Arab/Israeli conflict, since 1948, along with (neo-) colonialism, formed a locus, around which societal topics in Arabic cinema were explored. Throughout the 1970s, Egyptian cinema presented a whole series of films about the 1973 war with Israel, usually referred to as a victory in Arabic discourses, and how it affected people's lives. These films usually portray the lives and reactions of the average, middle, and lower middle classes. This genre includes films like *Al-rosasah l tazal fi gaybi* (The Bullet is Still in My Pocket, 1974) and *Budur* (1974). The plots dramatically depict how a young man has to leave his people, dependents, and the woman he loves to go and fight. The war conditions change everybody, and people rethink their personal problems and get them solved by the time the war ends. The female character usually tries to survive her problems, taking up a job to support dependents, fighting a bad guy who tries to rape her, pursue her education, or take a nursing course to treat war patients.

Women in this genre represent peaceful Egypt and a refuge for men. After going through the war, the man comes back—and he may be wounded—but he comes back to Egypt and his lover, alive. Since the word "Egypt" is referred to in the feminine case in Arabic, this metaphor is easier to depict by viewers on the regional level. Within the context of this historical framework, the enemy is usually recreated within a male figure in Egyptian movies. The male representation of the enemy seems to have a linguistic base—as the word "enemy" is in the masculine case in the Arabic language. Thus, the 1967 war, in light of this film genre, could be seen as a sexualized assault by the "male enemy" on "female" Egypt, while the 1973 war, the victory, is metaphorically referred to as the act of "washing off the shame (of defeat)" and "restoring the honor and dignity (of the Arab Nation and/or Egypt)."

The Middle East conflict was accompanied by three major events: (1) the Peace Treaty between Egypt and Israel in 1977, and the accompanying efforts to "normalize" the relationships between Israel and its Arab neighbors, (2) the Khomeini Revolution in Iran, and the accompanying Islamic movements throughout the region, and (3) the change of politicoeconomic ideology in Egypt. In 1974, three years into the rule of President Anwar al-Sadat (1918–1981), Egypt adopted an open economy approach, referred to as the Open-Door-Economic-Policy (ODEP). Accordingly, Egypt opened its doors to foreign (including Arab Gulf) investment, exported labor to oil countries for workers' remittances, and imported Western and Arabian cultures, embedded in consumer goods and services. This policy has had far-reaching effects on the social aspect of life in Egypt, some of which are negative, such as the spread of consumerism, single-parent families, an unfavorable change in the structure of economic activity, especially in the countryside (Richard 1991).

Along with the war movies, a different genre developed in the middle of the 1970s with the introduction of the ODEP, reviving the culture of belly dancers. This seems to reflect the huge investment in casinos and nightclubs in Egypt, which have been popular attractions for Arab tourists. The first category of this film genre takes up biographies of female artists—dancers and singers—back in the nineteenth century, and early and middle of the twentieth century. *Badi'ah Masabni* (1975) and *Bambah Kashar* (1974) provide typical examples. The female artist, at one point of her life, would fall in love with a man of an aristocratic background. They do not get married due to class difference, but she gets pregnant, and the rich family of her lover takes the baby. The "victimized" woman ends up being an entertainer, especially for men, which the society, in general, does not see as a respectful career. This genre presents belly dancers and singers at these times as victims of the prevailing class structure of the society. They seem to create the illusion that class difference, discrimination, and corruption are an act of the past colonial and monarchical rule, while providing a great deal of belly dancing and musical entertainment.

Another more contemporary variation of this genre portrays the challenges of being a college student while maintaining a family profession as a third-class belly dancer in the movie *Khalli Balak min Zuzu* (Watch Out for Zuzu, 1972). The film depicts differences between social classes in the Egyptian society. The dancer proves to have better morals than her rich respectful counterpart, and wins the man she wants. Having the man as the trophy is an interesting change, and yet justifies certain powers of the dancer over the respectful woman, and the threat that the former, despite her low social status, poses on the latter. Elevating the morals of a lower socioeconomic class woman over those of her upper class counterpart is a trend in Egyptian cinema, which has its roots in the early 1950s with the beginning of the Nasserist revolution in 1952 Egypt. It is the cinema's way to express the idea of removing class barriers, which was one of the revolution's main slogans.

The idea of presenting the belly dancer as the victim of society extends to present her as the victim of colonialism in a different genre of film. This genre developed after the 1952 revolution, showing the drawbacks and scandals of Egypt under the monarchy and British colonialism from the point of view of the revolution. Examples of this genre are *Al-Qahirah 30* (Cairo in 1930, 1966) and *Zuqaq al-Midaqq* (Al-Midaqq Alley, 1963). Everything is reversed compared to the Western movies and to stereotypes about the Westerner and the Egyptian (the Middle Easterner): the British are the bad guys, some of the old Egyptian aristocracy are "kind," and the middle and lower local classes are the good guys. This genre seems to represent resistance to the British, who did not think highly of the local population. The belly dancers and prostitutes who fill the bars and the casinos to entertain the British soldiers, symbolize the humiliation and control exercised by the colonizers. In other treatments, peasant women who were victims of sexual abuse by British soldiers and rich landlords threatened the honor of peasant men. Nevertheless, the urban poor women are typically picked and seduced by a local man who introduces them to the profitable "career," thus showing the double exploitation of the Egyptian woman. The exposure of the Egyptian woman's body to the aristocracy and the colonizers symbolizes utmost corruption and humiliation. Raping an Egyptian by a British sometimes is explicitly paralleled with "raping Egypt."

The prevailing genre in Egypt from the 1980s to the present is one that reveals the ills of the ODEP on the society, among others. In the sweeping materialism, there is almost no distinction between the role of men and women in these movies. The government is usually the target of sharp critique, burdened by a society suffering an ever-widening gap between the social classes. *Awdat Muwatin* (The Return of a Citizen, 1990), for example, portrays how a man with a typical middle-class background decides to come back and live with his four siblings in Egypt, after having spent fifteen years in a Gulf country to make money, only to find that the society he left is not the same anymore. His sister starts a bakery and caters for a casino, the manager of which likes her. He arranges an apartment for her. While unmarried people, especially women, usually stay in their parents' house, the older sister decides to complete her independence by living on her own. The other sister, who has a college degree, works in a bar. One of the brothers does not find work years after he graduates from college and becomes addicted to drugs. The last one joins a political group clandestinely working against the government.

Each one of these characters represents a paradigm that developed in the context of the ODEP and the surrounding global economy. This genre of film is a very good reflection of Egypt (and some Arab) thought. Whereas ills in the society were attributed to the preindependence era, the belief in economic and cultural colonialism as a continuum of political colonialism is seen as a cause of contemporary problems. This latter form of colonialism specifically refers to the ODEP. A number of imbalances and contradictory developments in Egyptian and other Arab societies are seen as the outcome of this politicoeconomic policy: a new form of Islamic movement with its new dress code (most significantly affecting women), Westernism with both its positive and negative implications, change in cultural values, consumerism, and the increasing gaps between socioeconomic classes (Richard 1991). The film excellently depicts the reasons behind these developments in society and how they have managed to weaken the values, traditions, and ties of one of the historically strongest institution in the Middle East, the family. The screen

conveys hopelessness, emphasizing the difficulty of going against the hegemonic politicoeconomic power, when the protagonist changes his mind about
staying in Egypt with his family and goes back to the Gulf.

THE MUMMY

Another stereotype of the Arab in American cinema includes the element of
danger, whether in the magical or the political sense. The magical genre includes films like *The Mummy* (1932). The plot usually depicts a female and a
male archeologist, who are threatened by the mummy itself or its physical
reincarnated soul. If the mummy represents a male character, it pursues the
Western woman and threatens the male archaeologist, and the opposite is true
if the mummy belongs to a female soul. In the latter case, the Egyptian
woman, represented by the powerful, magical soul released from the
mummy—through the curiosity of the scientist—symbolizes the threat.
Though she might temporarily capture the heart of the white archaeologist
through her mysterious, exotic attractiveness, he decides that her love could
be destructive, as this mummy has the evil power to destroy. Therefore, he ultimately chooses the Western woman, who embodies the familiar. Solving the
mysteries associated with Pharaonic curse, and the archaeologist legitimately
destroys the evil Egyptian spirit, and captures her back in the mummy. The
mummy embodies the old civilizations and their power, which have decayed
with time to be replaced by Western civilization. The finale legitimizes Western superiority and modernity. The "primitive" mummy and the "modern"
scientist also legitimize the logical aspects of the human mind, and the victory of the latter in such movies underscores the western infatuation with rationality over intuition.

Turning to Egyptian cinema, the mummy becomes an icon of an entirely
different sort. It is a complex amalgamation of pride in their glorious civilization and a celebration of ancestral heritage, treasures, and blessing. In
times of war, these amalgamations play a more intricate role in manifesting
historical and cultural values, and bringing up questions of identity. One of
the movies evoking these images is *Al-Mumya* (The Mummy, 1969, but pre-
miering in 1978). This movie concentrates on the problem of smuggling ancient Egyptian antiques, using the local people in a village, to complete Westerners' collections. The film controversially examines the virtue of modern
science and its efficacy in elevating societies. A member of a village, which
survives on antique smuggling in the turn of the century, decides to inform
the Egyptian archaeologist about their treasure. The archaeologist comes with
his superior, who is French, and transports the contents of a major burial site

to the museum. Nevertheless, this moral act was never rewarded. Preserving the past, modern science left the present without offering an alternative. The villager gained nothing and lost his community support on whom he turned his back. The community itself is left without an alternative income. On the one hand, the film questions the ethical dimensions of modern science, especially the different shape of exploitation in the name of Western technology. The political implications of this depiction to the relationship between the core and the periphery are rather critical. On the other hand, the film takes concepts of exploitation and loss and extends them to the deeper level of identity on both the individual and the communal levels. The perplexing identity crisis and questioned raison d'être implicated in the loss of past and future, incarnates itself in a profound dimension if we consider the production date of the movie. The film was produced in 1969, two years after the 1967 Arab/Israeli war, and directly parallels emotive senses that reflect loss of land and identity, as well as defeat.

MORE DANGER

Under the genre of "danger" classification in American cinema are movies associated with terrorism, which developed in the late 1970s and throughout the 1980s. The development of this genre is contemporary to the Iranian Islamic revolution and the rise of Ayatollah Khomeini (1900–1989) in the late 1970s, as a challenging power to the West, especially after the 1979 capture of American hostages in Iran.

A variation of the mysterious, the "in-between" stage of the visible and the invisible, is the dialectical problem between the absolutely seen, between the veiling and the nude, especially with reference to women in the Middle East. This time, however, the seen and the unseen is taken to a different level, reflecting the value system of the West on judging the Arab woman and comparing her to her Western counterpart in various historical times. When the ideal image of the Western woman was that of modesty and reserved sexuality in the late nineteenth and early twentieth century, the image of the Arab woman, even though veiled, was that of wild openness and eroticism. Now that the image of the almost nude, white female body is publicly displayed in advertisement, photography, and film, the Arab woman is portrayed as veiled, submissive, and oppressed in the context of the West's perception of the contemporary Islamic movement. These prevailing stereotypes about the Arab in the West have been directly or indirectly supported by Western social science. Lévi-Strauss's description of the woman as nature, which brings to mind the idea of unmanageable sexuality, and men as culture, are cases in point (Strauss 1967).

FEMINISM AND FILM

The spirit of feminism on the Egyptian scene is well captured in Nobel Prize winner Naghib Mahfuz's trilogy *Bayn al-Qasrayn, Qasr al-Shawq*, and *al-Sukkariyah*, which were translated and turned into three movies under the titles of *Between the Two Palaces* (1958), *The Palace of Desire* (1964), and *Sugar Street* (1973), respectively. The trilogy navigates us through some of the most volatile political decades in Egyptian history through a traditional family, starting from World War I until the Nasser revolution in 1952. The most famous character turned out to be the dominant male family head, who is married to an obedient housewife, and who imposes his children's respect to him through fear. Nevertheless, the film juxtaposes the viewer to the development of women's status and the accompanying change in societal values. We encounter the obedient housewife, the concubine, the belly dancer, then the student, the protesting veiled woman, the traditional, and the modern woman. Meanwhile, we get a vivid feeling of the different political developments and a social history of the different political movements, including feminism.

Efforts of feminists in the periphery have been largely concerned with local problems. In the Middle East, especially Egypt, nationalism gave legitimacy to the rise of women's movements. This started by partaking in the resistance against the colonial occupation. In the early 1920s, long before the feminist activism of Simone de Bolivar's (1908–1986) and Betty Friedan's (1921–2006) call for women's rights, the Egyptian Feminist Union was formed, and a women's committee was simultaneously started as part of the Wafd Party, a major opposition party until today. Aside from practicing political independence, women's groups have been largely occupied with women's issues on the local level: education, the right to work, social reforms regarding family life, and the personal status law, an issue which concerns Egyptian feminists. Before 1910, nine women's journals had appeared in Egypt (Graham-Brown 1988).

Fighting for political rights in Egypt is another major task, which occupied feminists since the 1920s, until women finally obtained their right to vote in 1956—thirty years before their counterparts in Switzerland. Feminists in Egypt had to fight in different frontiers, including religion. Durriyah Shafiq (1908–1975) a born feminist, so to speak, studied at the Sorbonne in France with support from Huda Sha'rawi (1879–1947), the leading feminist at the time. In 1945, Shafiq completed her doctoral dissertation on *La femme Egyptienne et l'Islam*, and returned to Egypt where she founded a number of feminist magazines, most important of which was *Magallat Bint al-Nil* (the Daughter of the Nile Magazine), which soon included a section called "Political Daughter of the Nile." Focusing on female literacy and the political rights of women, she founded *The Daughter of the Nile Union* in 1948, a broadly middle-class feminist association with branches in a number of cities (Badran and Cooke 1990; Graham-Brown 1988). Shafiq provides an excellent example of an Arab feminist who engaged Western ideas about women's liberation through education in local traditions and religion in order to reform views about women and their rights. On May 14, *Al-Misri* (The Egyptian), a liberal Wafdist paper, published Shafiq's article, "Whom should we follow—The present *Mufti* [Chief of Muslim Clergy] or the previous *Mufti*?" She attacked the views of the *Mufti*, backing her argument up with the views of the preceding *Mufti*, in addition to a number of secular and religious statements on the issue of women's voting rights:

When Shaykh Alam Nasser was *Mufti* of Egypt he said, "Islam looks at women as it looks at men with respect to humanity, rights, and personality. Islam does not distinguish between the sexes with respect to humanity. . . . Women and men in the judgment of Islam are equal (Shafiq, cited in Badran and Cooke 1990, 354–55).

In the twentieth century, with the development of nationalism, women were politically active. Images of Arab women marching in demonstrations and attending international conferences were not only shown in local media, but also presented in Western press. During revolutions, the image of women in their traditional clothes, protesting, and shouting, while actively engaging the public into the protest, largely shocked the British officials. Women's political activism then became a familiar scene in Egypt, especially after the formation of the different women's groups. In some parts of the Middle East, such as Algeria, the female dress became part of the national symbol and, hence, of defense against colonialist rule. In the 1950s, the veil became the weapon of the oppressed in Algeria: "[H]iding a face is also disguising a secret," as Fanon (1986, 42) argues.

Egyptian cinema captured these critical developments not only through the art of acting, but also through documentaries. In feature movies like those based on the trilogy of Naghib Mahfuz, for example, documentary excerpts of Egyptian women demonstrating against the British, students' riots, and the different nationalist revolutions were inserted into the weave of film to make vivid the events and draw attention to their significance. In that respect, the trilogy and movies of the same genre serve as dramatized archives of national sociohistory.

OLD TABOOS CONFRONTED

A genre of film that was taboo for a long time surfaced to address issues related to sexuality, sex education, "informal marriage," virginity, rape/marriage, hymen-reconstructive surgery, and the image of a moral woman. In the movie *Asrar al-Banat* (The Girls' Secrets, 2001), these issues become vivid and challenge Arab audiences to engage in a dialogue about questions so sensitive they were only hinted at metaphorically on the screen for many decades. The plot is in a traditional middle class neighborhood in Cairo, where a pious Muslim married couple live with their thirteen-year-old daughter. The movie pays attention to the modest dress code of this family, compared to the mother's sister who adopts a less conservative life style and approach in raising their daughter. Other problems represented were the inadequate sex education in some public schools and the associated discomfort that still prevails in the classroom. This leads to the male teacher's theorizing and using less concrete imagery, which leaves the female teenagers with no clear understanding of their reproductive system. From here stems the problem of the movie: when the thirteen-year-old is seduced with fear and resistance into sexual intimacy with the son of the neighbor's, which leaves her pregnant; this comes as a surprise to her since she was not actually penetrated. The audience navigates with these young teens the streets of Cairo on the screen to clandestine abortion clinics and shares the disappointment at the skyrocketing prices, far beyond the reach of the desperate girl. The events develop when finally the girl gives birth in the bathroom, after she had managed to hide her growing belly for many months. At the emergency unit, accompanied by her family and immediate relatives, the girl falls victim to a radical gynecologist, who—examining her newly torn hymen as a result of delivery—takes the responsibility upon himself to discipline the girl by circumcising her, without telling the family. The traumatized family, however, was busy taking care of informing the boy's family about the incident, and arranging for their marriage, so the girl's reputation would not be compromised.

The movie addresses the issues in a way that sympathizes with the victimized girl, while highlighting the factors that lead these circumstances. It also problematizes societal fear of shame on multiple levels: hiding the truth of events from the society, which paradoxically perpetuates problematic patterns, and abstaining from using one's right to take legal action toward a noncompliant doctor. The screen succeeds in portraying societal fears as agents empowering others, who do not have the right to control our bodies and lives. Furthermore, it challenges the viewer's notions of religion, its role in society, and the consequences of seeking a religious façade in the context of societal fear.

Whereas dramatic treatment of virginity loss is not new to Egyptian cinema, having been depicted in movies such as *Zuqaq al-Midaqq* (Al-Midaqq Alley 1963) and *Du'a' al-Karawan* (The Nightingale's Prayer 1959), *Asrar al-Banat* encapsulates the interrelated complexities of contemporary Egypt and exposes audiences to reconsider definitions of religiosity and proper behavior in an open, nonaccusative format. The definition of a virgin female body according to many Muslim communities hinges on the presence of a nontorn hymen. Losing this indicator of virginity puts women's reputation and social value at risk. The societal pressures and cultural definitions of the female body lead to an emergent need for hymen-reconstruction surgeries. Women who learn about their broken hymen immediately resort to this surgery before their wedding night to save themselves and their families from grave societal shame and resentment. There is common belief that a hymen is expected to be intact until first sexual intercourse; otherwise, a woman is accused to have engaged in premarital sex. It is observed that the demand for hymen-reconstruction surgeries has risen tremendously in many Arab countries, as well as immigration concentration in Europe. This type of surgery is considered illegal in the Arab world and, hence, it has a relative high cost.

This movie appears in the context of a current lively discourse on women issues in Egypt, which includes feminists, religious, and legal figures. The Mufti Ali Gom'ah answers the audience's questions on Arabic television about the stand of Islamic views vis-à-vis definitions of virginity. His well-informed views highlight the coinciding of the Islamic interpretation with the medical interpretation of virginity, which states that no matter the status of her hymen, a woman is virgin until she has sexual intercourse with a man. Yet, he resents hymen reconstructive surgeries, as they provide a fictitious solution built on a lie, fear, and lack of trust. On the other hand, in other areas of women's issues, alternative solutions are being sought to replace long established ones that no longer seem to fit the society's value system. For example, traditionally, if a woman is raped, and the rapist is "compatible," then marriage was seen as a natural solution. This scenario seems to confuse rape with seduction, and desire with unwanted sex. On Arabic Radio and Television (ART), which presents Arabic-speaking audiences with Arabic satellite channels globally, sociologist Samia Al-Sa'ati ardently explains to legal and religious authorities the psychological and societal damage that can result from a marriage built on a rape experience. She also draws attention to the traumatic experience of unwanted sex for a woman and suggests a reconsideration of addressing legal settlements.

CINEMATIC DEVELOPMENTS AFTER SEPTEMBER 11, 2001

Awareness of global hegemony in Egyptian cinema found its way to its American counterpart. The image of the Arab in American cinema made a clear shift with the screening of *Syriana* (2005) and *Munich* (2005), in which militant activities associated with Arabs were for the first time contextual-ized within a framework of intertwined local and global politicodynamic structures. This approach has long characterized similar treatments in Arabic cinema and is slowly finding its way on the American screen. The American viewer finds it daring and controversial, while the Arab saw it compatible with familiar local discourses. The movie *Syriana* reveals the complex global relationships and politicoeconomic interests between the American CIA, factions of the government, and Arab leaders on the one hand, and the resulting economic effect on labor migration in the Gulf, poverty, and class and Islamic militancy on the other. The movie starts its events with the mov-ing scene of lined up Pakistani workers after the merge of two major oil companies, waiting to hear, in translation, that they have to submit their passports and go home, while celebrations of the big events are taking place in the United States. The constant juxtaposition of the viewer to simultane-ous events in the core and the periphery, and the links between them, urges one to question concepts of cause and effect, the meaning of peace and war, and global hegemony and power legitimacy.

The movie premiered at a time when more and more people in America and globally are questioning the legitimacy of the American elections, the real im-petus of the war against Iraq, and skepticism surrounding the authority's ini-tiatives to prevent the human losses associated with the hurricane disasters in 2005. As for the Arab audience, the screened experience leads to a reiterated, communal embodiment of suffering. This phenomenology of suffering under concentric hegemonies is both local and global, based on histories of uncer-tainties and sequential oppression (Roushdy-Hammady 2006).

Munich (2005) on the other hand, presents the image of the Arab directly through the Arab/Israeli conflict. Through showing a terrorist attack on Israeli athletes in the Munich Olympics in association with the Arab as the point of departure, *Munich* attempts to create a dialogue that recognizes Palestinian humanity and suffering, as well as highlighting the victimization and manip-ulation of the Palestinian and the Israeli humans alike by Israeli politics in a complex network of global political terrorism in the 1970s. Giving the Pales-tinian viewpoint space on the screen, presenting their right to exist and their suffering at the hand of Israeli regimes, the movie weaves in this space in a complex quandary of Israeli identity and self-realization. Israelis face an ex-istential question, being morally torn between acknowledging the invasion of Palestinian lands, and its caused dislocation and suffering, and their Israeli nationalism and belief in a Zionist and/or religious cause that answers their call for freedom in the context of the Holocaust. This results in a rather com-pound and paradoxical phenomenology, in which one agent is the embodi-ment of suffering in one sociohistorical context, yet an inflictor of it in another. Furthermore, suffering is embodied in one geographical area, but extends to groups of people associated with it, across national and international borders. The resulting controversial phenomenology of suffering is reflected in the audiences and critics evaluation of the movie: some Zionist American Jews thought of it as a pro-Arab movie that denied Jewish suffering and right to exist, while some Arabs in America felt that the movie was only a feeble attempt to recognize the Palestinian perspective and right to the land, and was rather a justification of Israeli coercive policies, as the spectator is constantly bombarded with flashy bloody scenes showing Palestinians as terrorists attacking innocent Israeli athletes. Yet, there is no doubt that the average audience found a message between these two extremes that urged him/her to ponder the Palestinian question and recognize coercive measures of Israeli politicians in new light.

Turning to Egyptian cinema, an interesting landmark from the 1960s titled *Al-Naser Salah al-Din* (The Victor Saladdin, 1963) deserves a closer consideration in light of the political events since September 11. The movie depicts the Arab victory under the leadership of Salah al-Din al-Ayyubi (A.D. 1137–1193) over the Crusaders' attacks in the battle of Hittin in A.D. 1187. One of its main messages is its emphasis on the importance of Arab unity and nationalism, overriding any religious differences. As such, it depicts Issa ibn-al-'Awwam, an Arab Christian who was a main figure in Salah al-Din's army, resenting the wars of the Crusaders, even though they were fought under the sign of the cross. It is common in Arabic discourses to accuse the Crusaders of being colonizers hiding behind the façade of religion to achieve their political ends. Bush's attacking threat to launch a "Crusaders' fight against [Islam]" after September 11, and also, prior to the war against Iraq, when he identified Americans (and Europeans) with Christians, thus reiterated long-established ideas in Islamic and Arabic perceptions of the West, and framed American politics as another extension of neocolonialism.

More recent films addressing global hegemonies focused on resulting controversial elements in the Arab society. The feature film *Muwatin wa-Mukhbir wa-Harami* (A Citizen, a Detective, and a Thief, Abd al-Sayyid 2001) is a case in point. The film is richly symbolic on multiple levels. It philosophically examines the human condition under different circumstances and in response to power pressure. Doing so, it talks about class structure and its change in Egyptian society as a result of the corresponding political regimes and the open-door economic policy. On a different level, each class symbolically represents a nation and, among those nations, the film shows which one will have ultimate hegemony and be able to manipulate others to follow suit, either by force or by "treaty politics" (Roushdy-Hammady 2006).

CONCLUDING REMARKS

Dealing with the presentation of the Arab image in film urges us to ask the following question: Who watches these movies? The American film is watched in the West and the Middle East. The Egyptian film is seen on the regional level, and some are shown in European festivals. The mode of distribution empowers a certain image of the Middle East created by Hollywood. So, what are the implications of this for Western and local discourses? How is this powerful presentation of the image confronted, if at all? Is the presentation of the image created in local cinema more accurate? Is there such a thing as imaging a reality?

The myriad of genre presented here aimed at pronouncing the relationship between the film industry, the sociopolitical and historical context that surrounded the production of a film, and the image of the Arab on the screen. These relationships are not to be taken lightly, as they reflect and shape the cultural and political attitudes toward that Arab. If we consider American cinema and its presentation of the Arab, we find that for the longest time, it emphasized difference. The Arab is different because he/she is exotic, coming from foreign lands of different moral values, from a geographical region of political conflict and instability, with a different package of religion and culture, and, therefore, is associated with violence and danger. Even when recognizing the old glorious civilizations that existed in Arab lands, the audience is assured that these civilizations are extinct, decadent, and are no longer a threat or a match to the advanced, modern, and superior Western hegemony.

The events of September 11 and the following host of questionable local and international politics that shaped the face of America urged a reexamination of the image of the Arab, with a focus on its human existential responses to global hegemonies of unequal power weights. This rather slowly developing approach on the screen might provoke an interpretive understanding of a people's behavior in the context of political, economic, and cultural environments, rather than the easy and shallow blame on "cultural and religious differences."

On the other hand, the Egyptian cinema grew in different directions simultaneously to address the myriad of issues that erupted on the societal scene. Ranging from *problematiques* related to colonialism, post, and neocolonialism, this industry placed the sociocultural changes of the local people in contexts that challenged societal, traditional, and religious values. The myriad treatment of images in Egyptian cinema further extends to elucidate local views and explication of causal chains on the regional and global levels. It is the critical examination of these treatments by global political hegemonies that may lead to a true appreciation of Arab cultures.

15

Oedipus in Egypt

A Twentieth-Century Rendition of *Majnun Layla*

Ruqayya Yasmine Khan

I asked a Bedouin Arab about passionate love (*'ishq*) and he said, "It is too sublime to be seen and it is hidden from the eyes of mortals, for it is concealed in the breast like the latent fire in a flint, which when struck, produces fire, this fire remaining hidden as long as it is left alone.

—al-Asma'i, ninth century

Although romantic love in its emotional immediacy defies all attempts at reductionism, the fact is that shadows of childhood urges and fantasies are ever present in adult love choices (Freud 1910; 1912; 1914). However, to extend these psychoanalytic notions to religiocultural settings and temporal eras vastly apart from those associated with the discovery and evolution of psychoanalytic theories is an exercise beset with conceptual difficulties (Roland 1988, 1996; Akhtar 1999b; Kakar 1985; Homans 1984). Nonetheless, there is merit to applying psychoanalytic perspectives to the examination of such religiocultural settings, including their literary products. First, this application lends support to the universality of the intrapsychic relational configurations delineated by Freud and his followers. Second, both psychoanalysis and cross-cultural studies benefit from such an application and integration of Freudian and, especially, post-Freudian psychodynamic concepts. For example, the insights gained from such an application bolster those gained from clinical observation and hence, culture and psychoanalysis, literature and psychoanalysis become heuristic allies in the genesis, refinement, and growth of developmental and conceptual hypotheses in psychoanalysis. Cross-cultural studies involving the Islamic world (including, for example, the contiguous subfields of Islamic studies, Arabic literary criticism, and Middle East studies) benefit insofar as the application addresses

existing lacunae as regards to the study of the human unconscious and its
representations in the material and phenomena with which these subfields
deal. Far more attention needs to be paid to the presence of unconscious
processes in these subfields' data (textual or otherwise)—whether it is
through using psychoanalytic theory as a tool for deciphering symbolic material, analyzing modes of self and other, and/or understanding representations of childhood experiences and family dynamics. For reasons that are
somewhat complicated, while the integration of psychoanalytic concepts
and methods has occurred and continues to occur with the research and
study of Christianity, Judaism, Hinduism, and Buddhism—it has scarcely
happened in the scholarship on Islam and Middle East studies.[1]

It is with this aim in mind that I offer a reading of the contemporary Egyptian playright Salah Abd as-Sabur's (1970) play, *Layla Wal-Majnun* (*Layla
Majnun*), which, as I shall show in this chapter, has further "Oedipalized" the
tenth-century classical Arabic love story from which the play stems. I initially
offer some brief introductory remarks on the content and history of the classical love story by way of informing a primarily Western audience.

THE CLASSICAL *MAJNUN*

Majnun (meaning "one who is possessed or mad") is the name of the "most
famous of the famous" lovers in the Islamic world. Majnun is both a poet and
a character in the Arabic romance associated with his name (i.e., the love
story of *Majnun* and *Layla*)—a romance that is equally renowned in the Islamic world.[2] The Arabic title of the romance means Majnun of Layla, or the
"madman" of Layla. This love story blossomed in the Arabo-Islamic world
during roughly the tenth century. It belongs to a rich orally transmitted, as
well as written, corpus of stories known as the "Udhri romances"—a corpus
that is most fully recorded in the tenth-century multivolume work *Kitab al-
Aghani* (Book of Songs), produced by a Baghdadi courtier named Abu al-
Faraj al-Isfahani. In this classical story, the two—who are cousins—meet as
children and fall in love in a pastoral setting. Majnun expresses this in the following verses:

> I fell in love with Layla when she was just a child with ringlets
> and no sign of her budding breasts had yet appeared to playmates.
> Two children tending the lambs,
> would that we never had grown up, nor had
> the lambs grown old.
>
> —al-Isfahani 1992, 11[3]

Majnun grows into a handsome youth with a flair for poetry who frequently visits and serenades his beautiful beloved Layla in his verses. But some of these verses turn out to be rather risqué and impugn the chastity of his beloved. In so doing, he transgresses the social norms of early Arabo-Islamic society and culture. Consequently, Layla's father (who is also his paternal uncle) is so offended and enraged that he bans him from seeing or visiting her. He also flatly refuses Majnun's rather desperate proposal of marriage. Thus rejected, Majnun becomes somewhat deranged and emotionally instable, in spite of numerous attempts by his kin to help him. He begins to madly wander about and live with the beasts in the desert, where he continues to compose beautiful verses about his love for Layla that gain further renown as they circulate in the region. Even after Layla is married to a rich man from another tribe, Majnun continues nostalgically to recall his beloved through his poetry.

> O beauty of this world, beauty which I am unable to attain,
> the parting from whom cannot be fathomed by my heart . . .
> The soul does not refrain from remembrance of you for even a moment
> Even if I at times chastise it much."
>
> —al-Isfahani, 1992, 84

According to some passages, Majnun and Layla continue to have trysts even after she is married (when her husband is away), and it is also related that her husband and Majnun engage in verbal jousts with each other over the issue of Majnun's continued public declamation of poetry about her. Majnun, however, remains in the desert wilderness, and in the end, dies a lonely death amid the desert rocks, and yet, his poetry becomes even more famous after his death. Appropriately, Majnun is found dead by a fan of his verses, who had travelled to Majnun's clan to hear and collect his poems. Moreover, a slip is found in his garb containing a bitter couplet in which he curses Layla's father and invokes upon him the same misery and wretchedness that he had to face in his life due to the loss of his beloved. He also assails her father not only for the breakdown of the love affair, but also for the madness that afflicts him after the reversal in the affair.

> O Shaykh, one who was not pleased with us,
> May you be wretched and not enjoy life's comfort and ease;
> May you be miserable just as you made me miserable and left me to roam with
> the perishing and not taste sleep."
>
> —al-Isfahani 1992, 92

The burial lament for Majnun is attended by people from Layla's clan, including her father who repents his earlier harshness to the youth.

Rather like a traveling folktale (and as Northrop Frye has pointed out, the genre of romance descends from the folktale), the love story of *Majnun Layla* has crossed many chronological and cultural boundaries, and has spread throughout the whole Islamic world. It has been composed and recomposed in Persian, Arabic, Turkish, and Urdu literatures in the form of poetry, romance, drama, and even has been set to film.[4] Two great premodern Persian poets and writers who composed narratives celebrating these two lovers are Nizami (1141–1203) and Jami (1414–1492). Often known in non-Arabic literatures through the inverted title of *Layli Majnun* or the Layla of Majnun, this literary history of the love story has played a role in the development of Islamic mystical literatures, as well as of early Persian and Urdu love poetry, not to mention, according to some scholars, medieval European romance. Because elements of tragedy are to be found in the classical Arabic love story of *Majnun Layla*, it has lent itself to dramatic treatment during the modern period.

OEDIPAL THEMES AND THE MODERN *MAJNUN*

In the Arab world, since the mid-1800s, this love story has been adapted to drama, and some of these plays have been staged during the twentieth century.[5] Indeed, an eminent critic of the Majnun love legend, As'ad Khairallah, remarks that the story has been amenable to both theater and cinema in the modern period: "Since the middle of the last [nineteenth] century, tens of plays and some motion pictures and operas have been adding original variations on the old theme through the medium of the dramatic arts. In Arabic, the last hundred years have witnessed at least ten plays on the theme, many of which were produced on stage or in the cinema. This vogue is the same in most Islamic languages: in Urdu, for instance, the Majnun story was adapted for stage as early as the middle of the last century" (Khairallah 1995, 162).

Two modern Egyptian dramatic versions are dated 1933 and 1970, respectively. The 1933 version (also entitled *Majnun Layla*) is composed by the famous neoclassical Egyptian poet Ahmad Shawqi[6] (1933), and has been adapted to film containing some popular Arabic lyrics by the singer Muhammad Abdelwahhab.[7] The 1970 play is by the renowned modernist Egyptian poet Salah 'Abd as-Sabur, and it bears the title *Layla wal-Majnun* (*Layla and the Madman*). Whereas Shawqi clearly draws from and models his drama after the classical tenth-century *Majnun Layla,* his play, in turn, functions as the intertextual model for 'Abd as-Sabur's late twentieth-century drama (Khairallah 1995, 164–65).

The setting, imagery, and story line in Shawqi's 1933 play goes back to the classical tenth-century Arabic rendition.[8] Khairallah points out, "It follows all previous versions in retaining [the early Bedouin] setting" (Khairallah 1995, 169). This is not surprising, given that, as just remarked, Shawqi was a neo-classist. Admittedly, he was influenced by French playwrights (it was while he was in France that his interest in theater was born, influenced especially by Corneille and Racine),[9] and yet, as Badawi has observed, "He may have borrowed the external form of Western literature, but for his language and for his inspiration, he was an Arab revivalist, turning back to the past poetic achievements" (Badawi 1975, 31). Shawqi's reliance on classical Arabic poetic conventions, diction, and imagery had a valuable cultural function, given the fact that at the time he composed and wrote his works, "Arabs felt that their cultural identity, among other things, was being threatened by powerful alien forces" (Badawi 1975, 34). Hence, Shawqi's act of composing the play can be viewed as part of a nationalist project to rediscover the classical Arabic heritage during the time of the Nahdah (or Renaissance in modern Arabic literature), a Renaissance accompanied by a reassertion of national identity.[10]

Issues of nationalism and colonialism are especially salient to the post-World War II context in which 'Abd as-Sabur's play was written (in the late 1960s, of the Jamal 'Abd al-Nasser era).[11] It falls within the period of a recoil from romanticism in modern Arabic literature, when, instead, the idea or ideal of political commitment in literature gained popularity (Allen 2000). In Arab states, such as Egypt, conditions were ripe for revolutionary change: privileged feudal elites were under attack and with the migration of masses of rural people to overcrowded urban cities, such as Cairo, a widening of the gap between the rich and poor occurred. The revolution of 1952 in Egypt overthrew the monarchy and broke the great landowners' power. The literary critic M. Badawi has asserted this revolution was a landmark in the history of modern Egyptian and Arabic drama as a whole (1992; 1987): "A remarkable revival of the Egyptian theater occurred during the late fifties and the sixties, following the mood of euphoria and optimism that swept over the country in the wake of the revolution" (Jayyusi 1995, 6).

Consistent with 'Abd as-Sabur's modernism, his 1970 drama is a radical departure from all previous versions: not only is its setting and time altered (as we shall see), the character is also framed differently. What really sets apart 'Abd as-Sabur's innovative drama from the all previous versions, including the classical rendition of *Majnun Layla* (to which Shawqi's play is a throwback), is that it directly deals with the interior or psychological states of its characters, particularly Majnun. This does not mean that the classical Arabic rendition of *Majnun Layla* does not address issues of the subjectivity and interiority, indeed it does, but in rather disguised and elliptical ways—relying more on figurative language (metaphor, allusion, symbol) to accomplish this task. But the modern version by 'Abd as-Sabur is more explicit about the treatment of character, and it does so through techniques utilizing memory, fantasy, projection, splitting, and so forth. Remarkably, 'Abd as-Sabur deftly inserts an Oedipal subtext in his play such that it is the occurrence of intra-psychic conflicts within the protagonist, rather than his social transgressions, that is the fundamental reason for the break-up of the love relation. As'ad Khairallah draws our attention to this subtext when he remarks that "what 'Abdassabur seems to add is a Freudian dimension that emphasizes the scars deeply carved in Sai'd's psyche by social conditions," but he does not explore this dimension[12] (Khairallah 1995, 172). Before I offer a reading of Abd as-Sabur's play *Layla Wal-Majnun* that teases out and treats this Oedipal subtext, I present the following summary of the play:[13]

Abd as-Sabur's drama, divided into three acts, presents a group of revolution-ary journalists in modern Cairo. In the beginning of the first act, these young revolutionaries and their newspaper director are shown discussing the fate of their fledgling paper with its tiny circulation. Amid references to and evoca-tions of patriotic matters, such as love for motherland, love of the people for freedom, love of mothers for sons that have been imprisoned, mention is made of the most famous of famous Arabic love stories (i.e., that of Shawqi's *Maj-nun Layla*). The director then proposes that the group of writers and revolu-tionaries act out the play. "In the distribution of the roles, the role of Majnun falls on Sa'id, an idealist and a poet, while the role of Layla falls on a fellow journalist, who goes by the name Layla in real life. Following two months of rehearsal, the two major protagonists discover that this play-within-a-play be-comes a reality for them." With the boundaries between fiction and reality dis-solving, with reality mimicking art, the two fall in love with each other in the enactment of the love story. But the protagonist is unable to consummate his love, unable to make love to his Layla, not because of dictates of social honor and propriety, but because of a deep intrapsychic conflict stemming from his childhood experiences and fantasies. Layla, a vibrant and warm young woman, desires Sa'id and articulates this desire to him, but Sa'id expresses an aversion to sex. He recounts to her some traumatic childhood scenes in which he has witnessed his mother submitting to sex with his father, and then later, his step-father, but being repulsed afterward. "Layla, sympathetic, but despairing over his rejection, yields herself to another member of this young group of revolu-tionaries named Husam (meaning the sword). Just at about this time, the others in the group discover that this same Husam is a traitor who is collaborating as an agent and denouncing them." The climax of the drama occurs in Act Two. Upon discovering the true identity of Husam, the others hurry to his apartment, and there, a fight erupts between Sa'id and Husam. But Husam gets away. However, Sa'id finds Layla there, half-clothed, in Husam's bedroom. She con-cedes that he had just made love to her, whereupon Sa'id loses consciousness, muttering: *Layla Layla ummi* (Layla, Layla my mother). "Suddenly Husam reappears and tries to kick Sa'id out, but the latter comes to consciousness, grabs a statue, and batters Husam almost to death. Husam escapes and reports Saʿid to the authorities, who then ends up in jail."

Through this device of a play-in-a-play, a device that is exercised only after an explicit reference to Shawqi's *Majnun Layla*, ʿAbd as-Sabur deliberately and consciously rereads and critiques the entire literary tradition associated with the classical *Majnun Layla* romance, including, by implication, Shawqi's text. ʿAbd as-Sabur radically alters the setting (modern urban Cairo), time (post-1952 revolution), characters (young journalists and revolutionaries), to mention some of the more obvious transformations. Having already remarked that what is unique about ʿAbd as-Sabur's play is the insertion of an Oedipal angle, it would not be incorrect to now say that what ʿAbd as-Sabur does is to take an Oedipal subtext already present in the classical rendition and bring it to the foreground, that is, render it prominent in his version.

Indeed, psychoanalytic dimensions are not absent from the classical Arabic corpus of ʿUdhri romances (the word "Udhri" means virginal; i.e., the concern with sexuality is reflected in the very name), including the love story of *Majnun Layla*.[14] The Oedipal subtext in the classical romance is discerned in the following cluster of elements: the recurrent motif of the hostility between the youthful protagonist and his paternal uncle (i.e., the beloved's father who functions as a kind of surrogate father figure for Majnun); the near absence of any role of the mothers—indeed the maternal role is supplanted by that of Layla, the idealized beloved; the motif of the unavailability of this female beloved—she always belongs to another man (first her father and then her husband) and in some subsequent versions (including those by Nizami and Shawqi), this motif of unavailability is intensified: the beloved remains chaste even after marriage; the proliferation of triangulated relations in the romance, which often comprise two males and one female (with the female always being Layla, the adored and elusive beloved, and one of the males always being Majnun).[15]

In ʿAbd as-Sabur's play, this underlying Oedipal subtext emerges: the protagonist, Saʿid, cannot consummate his relation with Layla, not because of prohibitive social conventions or class differences, but because of an emotional trauma and intrapsychic conflict with which he is emotionally burdened. As mentioned earlier, there are, to be sure, important ideological and political angles in the play. This is to be expected considering that ʿAbd as-Sabur wrote his play in an age of social realism characterizing modern Arabic literature, especially the literature by Egyptian writers. The drama was written after the revolution of 1952 in Egypt—a revolution that eradicated the monarchy and destroyed the power landowners' holdings. In the play, the very backdrop against which the relations between Saʿid and Layla unfold is one in which a group of young men and women journalists are working together to put an end to the extreme political social inequities in Egypt prior to the 1952 Revolution. A sustained sociopolitical matrix informs the play: for example, associations exist between the symbolism of the independent, vibrant beloved Layla and a vision of the "New Egypt," and as critic Ali al-Rai'i points out: "Both Layla and Egypt are victims of indecision and lack of purpose on the part of their lovers and supporters" (1992, 363). There also exist symbolic links between the impoverished and mistreated mother of Sa'id and the former, colonized motherland of Egypt.[16] Moreover, 'Abd as-Sabur's modernism regarding gender issues is discernible in how, for instance, he transforms the character of Layla: she is not a beloved set upon a pedestal, not a mere abstract ideal, as often is the case in the premodern versions of the love story. Rather, she has a concrete personality; she articulates her feelings, she is a working professional and active participant in the prevailing ideological, revolutionary struggles, and she chooses the man she wants to be with and love. As Khairallah has observed, "the [very] title of the play mentions Layla first and on equal footing with Majnun" (1995, 170).

Still, I would argue that a dimension that is very powerfully brought to the fore in the drama (as powerfully as the sociopolitical dimensions) is the psychological one (i.e., the intrapsychic state of the protagonist and its impact upon his relations with others). The play provides much detail regarding childhood experiences, and the way childhood trauma is integrated with the drama suggests that privileging merely the sociopolitical factors does not allow for an optimal interpretation of the text. The Oedipal content relating to this psychological state most fully emerges in scene I, act II of the drama: this scene presents a divided stage containing two scenes, one illuminated and the other in darkness. In the illuminated scene, Layla is shown visiting Sa'id, the journalist and poet upon whom the role of Majnun has fallen; the scene takes place in Sa'id's apartment. The conversation between them revolves around the issues of marriage, love, and mothers. Layla gently tries to get Sa'id to talk about the possibility of love and marriage between them. But Sa'id—who first induces Layla to talk about her mother—then begins to "open the chamber of his own dark memories" (in his words) and turns to the subject of his own mother. His initial comments recall memories of his mother vomiting after having had sex with his father. Midstream in his dialogue (while he is discussing his father's death that occurred when he was ten years old), the other side of the divided stage is illuminated while the first one is darkened. This other side reveals a room exhibiting extreme poverty in which the boy, Sa'id, and his mother are sleeping. The entire first scene of Act II alternates between these two sides of the stage: the present (i.e., Sa'id and Layla conversing in the apartment) and the past (successive bleak scenes of childhood, nearly all of them characterized by interactions between mother and son). In the childhood scenes, the mother is shown increasingly sinking into deep poverty and the young boy Sa'id is often shown suffering from hunger. Eventually, the mother is compelled to marry a man who already has another wife. The following is a translation of the penultimate segment of scene I, act II (1970, 75–77):[17]

> The light dims a little in the left half so that we see a man of towering height wearing an overcoat. His height, rough boots, and twirled mustache make him stand out. He strides in and plants himself between the woman and the child.
>
> *The Man*: "The night has been inauspicious from the beginning! And this foolish child doesn't want to budge. Dirty woman's child, make some space for me to spread out!"
>
> *The Mother*: (as she grips the shoe of the man) "Patience until the child goes to sleep and the time is right."
>
> *The Man*: "I don't have time to enjoy your coquetry. The child won't protect you. You're a woman in trouble. I sent you food today. Did your belly fill up?" (He feels her belly with his shoe.)
> "Did your belly fill up, dirty woman's son? You're voracious, like a tapeworm—and uncouth also when you ogle us." (He prods the child's stomach with his shoe.)
>
> *The Mother*: "Please, leave him be. You're a good man. Don't pick on a poor lad."
>
> *The Man*: "Ha, Ha! Do I now take lessons from a filthy woman?! How can I be—as she said—a man. . . . But I'll show her—I am a man and more [than a man]!!"
> He tries to lift her off, but she keeps her ground. Then, the man falls on top of her and the stage becomes completely dark. After a moment, we hear the woman moaning in pain.
>
> The Child: (crying loudly . . .) "Mother, my mother."

Character is stripped to base identities (through the bare and simple labels of "the Man" [*al-Rajul*], "the Mother" [*al-Umm*], and "the Child" [*al-Tifl*]), which permits 'Abd as-Sabur to enhance the drama of the triangulated Oedipal conflict. The towering, contemptuous, and rough "Man" or stepfather "plants himself between the woman and the child," and he mocks his wife's insistence upon "waiting until the child goes to sleep" before they engage in coitus. Both her insistence upon this and his preceding command of "Make some space for me to spread out!" indicate that all three, parents and the child, share one bedroom. Interestingly, 'Abd as-Sabur employs the Arabic word *basbasa*, which means "to ogle," to convey something of the excitement and curiosity (in addition to fear) in the child's gaze—a gaze that the stepfather is aware of and with which he is somewhat perturbed. Nonetheless, at the end of the scene, he rapes his wife in the presence of the child, Sa'id. Through this childhood flashback and others, 'Abd as-Sabur presents the young boy's repeated witnessing of the coercive bedroom scenes as an important source for the adult Sa'id's emotional problems. No doubt the violence and the degradation inherent in the symbolism of the rape lends itself to feminist and/or postcolonial readings (i.e., the intruding, powerful, and exploitative second husband represents the colonizers who are raping the motherland of Egypt). Among the most distinctive traits of the stepfather, or "the Man," are his shoes or boots with which he roughly prods both the mother and boy—imagery evocative of the stereotype of the enemy soldier kicking or otherwise maltreating his colonial subjects. Without belittling these readings, it should be pointed out that the rape symbolism may have other psychodynamic dimensions as well: according to psychoanalytic data from patient fantasies, children often imagine that their mother is being forced to have sex by the father so that they can free themselves of the guilt stemming from desiring the mother (read: "I should get her because he is mistreating her").

'Abd as-Sabur showcases the psychological trauma of the child's recurrent witnessing of the primal scene (i.e., the sexual act between the parents) as one of the causes of Sa'id's neurosis as an adult. This is consistent with Freudian psychoanalysis that identifies the child's being overstimulated from the repeated witnessing of the primal scene as a contributing factor in the formation of an Oedipal complex. Sudhir Kakar (1985) has observed that in Indian and other non-Western cultures, the opportunities for the child to witness parental coitus are common because often parents and children sleep and, in fact, live in one room (precisely what is depicted in 'Abd as-Sabur's play). But, to quote him, "The sexual excitement caused by these occasions, since often repeated, becomes integrated and is normally not a source of intolerable disturbance. In other words, the primal scene, in being a long running play, is not the momentous event it appears in the analyses of Western middle-class patients with their very different living conditions, notions of privacy, and mystification around the 'parental bedroom'"[18] (Kakar 1985, 442). While I agree with Kakar's point that cultural norms regarding privacy and organization of domestic space, as well as social, living conditions are key factors in assessing the relevance of a construct such as the Oedipal complex; 'Abd as-Sabur presents this factor as quite important in the psychological and emotional disturbances experienced by his Egyptian protagonist.

In 'Abd as-Sabur's drama, the role of the stepfather could be analogous to the role of the paternal uncle (who also is Layla's father) in the classical rendition of the *Majnun Layla* love story, just as the treacherous Husam's role could be somewhat comparable to that of the "outsider" husband in the tenth-century version. In the latter, Majnun is unable to marry his beloved because first, her father bars him from having contact with her, and second, a man from a distant and remote tribe ends up marrying her. This "intruder figure" (represented by paternal surrogate figures such as the stepfather, paternal uncle, or Husam as the rival-traitor, etc.) stands for the Oedipal father in the boy-child's fantasy—stands for the father who interferes in the merger relation that the boy really desires with ultimately his mother.[19]

Sa'id's relation with Layla (or more precisely, his inability to have a relation with Layla) is mediated through and by his past relations with his mother, father, and/or stepfather. Psychoanalytic thought holds that an adult's relations with current love objects are always mediated by and through his/her past relations with the primary objects of love. Sa'id's unresolved Oedipal conflict flares up, for example, when he discovers Layla in the bedroom with Husam, his rival. This discovery is experienced by him as a reenactment of the primal scene with all of its Oedipal intensity: hence, not only does Sa'id tries to kill the Oedipal rival, Husam, but upon hearing that Layla and this rival have just made love, he blacks out, with his last words being: "*Layla Layla ummi*" (Layla, Layla, my mother). Precisely these words are uttered by the young boy Sa'id, as he witnesses the coercive parental bedroom drama depicted at the close of the penultimate segment in scene I, act II.

CONCLUDING REMARKS

Much ink has been spilled over the question of whether or not the Oedipal complex is universal. This question, of course, engages the issue that is raised in this essay's beginning, namely the one of the nexus between psychoanalysis and culture. A number of non-Western analysts and critics have, on various grounds, challenged the notion of a universal Oedipal complex. A. K. Ramanujan has written about the "negative Oedipus-type" in the Indian setting, wherein "a father wants to do away with his son" rather than the other way around (1999). A. Bouhdiba has questioned, whether in the context of Muslim Arab familial relationships, one can reasonably speak of a universal Oedipal complex: "In other words, the Oedipus complex cannot be a cultural abstraction, and in place of a monistic notion of a univocal and universal relation between the child and its mother, we have to substitute a multiplicity of possible modes of relation. We must also be more attentive to what makes these modes of relation diverge than converge" (1977, 127).

While I concur with Bouhdiba, what is striking about the Oedipal content in 'Abd as-Sabur's play is how it *does* lend support to the universality of the intrapsychic relational configurations delineated by Freud and his followers. I certainly cannot offer any answers to the weighty question of whether or not there exists a universal Oedipal complex, but I maintain that 'Abd as-Sabur's contemporary Egyptian drama is suggestive of an Oedipal complex that stems from, in Kakar's words, "a shared, universal experience of infancy and childhood within the structure of the family" (Kakar 1985, 444). This "psychological universalism" (in Kakar's words) or "developmental infrastructure" (in Peter Homans' words) is "composed of the unconscious, dream-based childhood world of experience that all people share and that persists in social and cultural systems" (Homans 1984, 148–49).

As acknowledged in this chapter's beginning, there are drawbacks to the application of psychoanalytic constructs (such as the Oedipal complex) to religiocultural contexts (and their literary products) that are very different from those in which psychoanalysis originated. These drawbacks stem from the perception that psychoanalysis is reductionist, Euro-centric, anti-religious, and ahistorical. My main contention regarding these perceived and actual drawbacks of applied psychoanalysis is that I do not think they override the significant gains that can accrue from the judicious and meaningful integration of Freudian and, especially, post-Freudian psychodynamic concepts in the contiguous fields of Islamic Studies and Arabic literary/cultural studies.[20] Lastly, such an application and integration contributes to the crucially important project of what Kakar terms the "relativizing" of psychoanalytic configurations:

> Perhaps it is clear from my examples that in arguing for a relativizing of psychoanalysis through an inquiry into non-Western experience, I do not question the great developmental constants psychoanalysis has uncovered. These are, of course, based on a shared, universal experience of infancy and childhood within the structure of the family. My notions of relativity have more to do with establishing the boundary conditions for various analytic concepts, determining their relative importance within the edifice of psychoanalytic thought, and separating what is Western-cultural in psychoanalytic formulations from what is truly universal. (1985, 444)

16

Cultural Nationalism in Indo-Muslim Art

Manail Anis Ahmed

When one fig tree looks at another, both bear fruit.

—Medieval Arabic Proverb

The story of cultural nationalism as illustrated through Indo-Muslim art is an interesting one. The Indian subcontinent, arguably the most populous landmass on the face of the earth, has produced and inspired generations of artists, both natives and visitors. As home to one of the world's oldest civilizations, the Indus Valley and its environs have also witnessed sumptuous imperial patronage. Centuries of stability, wealth, and strategic advantage enabled the nurturing and production of great art and architecture that still stands as a testament to the ages. Successive waves of invasion, immigration, and resettlement have given rise to a hybridity of styles and diversity of values, syncretized in artistic production to always produce to a new style of art: ever absorbent, multiply influenced, and essentially Indian.[1]

The rise of Indo-Muslim consciousness in the years immediately preceding India's independence from British colonial rule and its continued development forms the focus of this chapter. I will begin with a brief discussion of how Islam and India impacted each other to cause an Indianization of Islam in the subcontinent. Then I will talk about art produced under Muslim rule in India as a preface to the rise of a specific Indo-Muslim cultural nationalism. Following this, I will make a brief foray into the artwork of two Muslim artists of the subcontinent, Abdur Rehman Chughtai and Maqbool Fida Hussain. I conclude with some synthesizing remarks on the role of art and nationalism in the establishment of historical identity and modern nationhood.

THE INDIANIZATION OF ISLAM

Historical India happens to be home to some of the world's oldest religions: the Vedic religion is an important part of Indian history that is a legitimate conceptual predecessor to the attainment of enlightenment by the rebel prince Gautama, known and beloved as the Buddha (563–483 B.C.), and the subsequent transmission of a code that eventually came to be known as Buddhism. Much later, from the eighth century onward, successive waves of Muslim invasions left in their wake a religion transplanted from Arabia, one that very soon became indigenized and developed its own peculiarly Indian character. Though later Western missionary zeal succeeded in producing small patches of Christianity in the subcontinent, in a manner of speaking, no religion was able to match Islam in its adoption of Indian color and texture. It molded itself to the land and its peoples, infusing local Hindu populations with Turkic vocabulary, Persianate fashion, and Arabic flair, and soon gave rise to a colorful medley of Indian traditions. Guru Nanak (1469–1539) founded Sikhism in the fifteenth century as a unique byproduct of the melding of Hindu and Muslim traditions. Meanwhile Islam, starting from its status as the religion of the rulers and a faith to be acquired via politically motivated marriages, became favored over time for conversion by lower caste Hindus. After the coming of British colonialism and the rise of religious nationalism, the question of governance of the largest religious minority in India, the Muslims, caused great political upheaval, ultimately resulting in the creation of Pakistan in 1947, and the largest human migration the world has ever witnessed. Large numbers of Muslims, however, remained in India, but for the purposes of this chapter, we will consider historical India as a whole.

Being Muslim in historical India[2] was an interesting, challenging, and significant thing. According to Islam (2002),

> Religion was unquestionably a vital factor in the life of medieval South Asia. This was all the more so among the followers of Islam, for Islam encompasses a doctrine, as well as a way of life. Islam is a well-defined faith and has always demanded a clear and exclusive commitment from its followers. Islam also succeeded in fostering among its followers a relatively greater uniformity of organization and conduct than could be found among the followers of other faiths . . . in South Asia, Islam demanded *and received*, relatively speaking, more adherence and conformity than did the other faiths in the same region. Being a Muslim powerfully influenced one's dress, food, daily routine, and, indeed, entire way of living." (p. 68)

However, it is interesting to cast a glance at just how such "adherence" to the religion was both demanded and received by the Muslims of historical India.

Out of the melding of Arab religion and Persian traditions on Indian soil, there arose a colorful syncretism. The hybrid culture of Indian Islam is distinct from any other Islamic culture, be it Middle Eastern, Levantine, Persian/ Turkic, Hispano-Muslim, or North African. This "Indianization" of Islam manifests itself in many ways—the great mystical traditions of Islam that arose from South Asia are still very much alive in the form of Sufism. Sufi philosophy, theology, monism, and poetry thrived in an environment of musicality, lyricality, and tolerance (Shafii 1985). The echoes of Vedic and Buddhist voices were evident in these perspectives. They combined with pre-Islamic Arabic ideals of valor and Persian literary tropes of unrequited love to produce a corpus of Sufi literature and culture that continues to grow, in an uninterrupted continuous historical tradition, to this day. Music was another realm in which Hindu and Muslim traditions melded in a harmonious gestalt (Manuel 1996). South Asian Muslim rites of passage, such as weddings and funerals, also took on a strongly Indian flavor. Religious rituals in both traditions starting emulating each other. North Indian Hindu nobility started to observe the *Muharram*[3] rituals of Shi'i Muslims. The shrines and tombs of Muslim saints and sages across the subcontinent developed a devotional following that Hindus and Sikhs. Muslims likewise started investing spiritual and religious significance in local deities and homegrown lore, celebrating Hindu festivals like *Holi* with gusto (Akhtar 2005).

ART UNDER MUSLIM RULE IN INDIA

Whereas Islam first arrived on the southwestern coast of India by sea, giving rise to a proud community of Moplah Muslims in Kerala in the seventh century, it was only in A.D. 712 that it became formally established on Indian soil. However, the main thrust of its intellectual and cultural force only came to be felt almost three centuries later, when the Central Asians started crossing the mountain passes in India's Northwestern frontier, until the twelfth century when Afghans, Turks, and Persians set down more permanent roots in India. Although cultural and artistic activities under Muslim leadership, or even those having Muslim influence, were continuously taking place, the high noon of Muslim rule under which artistic brilliance was achieved in India (the legacy of which is still alive in our minds and hearts) was to take place in the sixteenth century, during the apex of Mughal rule. This manifested itself in the realms of architecture, poetry, music, and painting.

Qutb *minar*, the tower commemorating the numerous invasions of Afghan armies into the heartland of India, was raised in Delhi in 1193. This decade marked the advent of the "Slave Dynasty," of whose architectural and artistic ambitions brought to fruition, dazzled India. The *Quwwat-ul-Islam* (Might of Islam) mosque (A.D. 1199) in the old city of Delhi incorporated stylistic elements of Hindu temples. This is a wonderful example of the incorporation of Indian motifs into Islamic architecture to give birth to a uniquely Indian artistic style. Beginning with this project, Muslim rulers employed local Hindu craftsmen to produce masterpieces of Indian Muslim art and architecture. Traditional Hindu corbelling techniques, for instance, were used in the construction of Islamic arches, embellished with Qur'anic inscriptions in *Naskh* (literally, "copying" in Arabic) and *Nastaliq* (elegantly blended Arabic and Persian) styles of calligraphy, interspersed with floral designs of Indian origin. The result of such collaboration was an "Indo-Muslim" art, which saw its zenith during the reign of Jalaluddin Mohammad Akbar (1556–1605), the magnificent Mughal ruler of the sixteenth century.

It was Emperor Akbar's grandson, Shah Jahan (ruled 1628–1658) who brought Indo-Muslim architecture to its zenith. The Taj Mahal, which took from 1632 to 1654 to complete, was built as a mausoleum for his beloved queen, Mumtaz Mahal. It replicates the basic plan of Akbari period buildings in Delhi, but has pure white marble facades contrasted with tracery in black stone, inlaid in geometric patterns and Arabic inscriptions. Its high central dome, towering minarets, and shimmering whiteness defy its mammoth size, lending it a visual lightness and delicacy. All this has placed it among the finest examples of Indo-Muslim art extant.

Arts of the book, within which the position of figural painting in the Muslim milieu has always been ambiguous, nevertheless had been flourishing for many centuries in Iran, Turkey, Central Asia, and other parts of the Muslim world by Akbar's time. The rulers of the Islamic world allowed themselves a great deal of latitude in this regard, gaining moral support from the prophetic tradition: "Allah is beautiful, and loves beauty" (in Arabic, *Allahu jameelun yuhibbul jamal*). The phenomenon of miniature painting thus grew around a tradition of poetry and literature—book-size paintings were produced as manuscript illustrations accompanying Persian verse, Arabic scientific texts and travelogues, and Central Asian court chronicles. When the Mughals rose to power and achieved unrivalled dominance and wealth in the subcontinent, they made it a point to step up patronage of this art form, and indigenized otherwise Islamic motifs into very recognizably Indo-Muslim ones. When, by the eighteenth century, Mughal hegemony receded to an eventual overthrow and the advent of colonial rule, their patronage had already recast the character of Indian miniature painting in a definitive manner.

It was at this point of departure that Indian artists and art in general came under close scrutiny of the imperial gaze. The Indian arts served foremost as a tool for understanding and assessment during the earliest imperial encounters, and later as a political device whereby the inclinations, tastes, and skills of the "natives" could be subsumed by the paternalistic ambitions of the British. Indian art underwent a concerted campaign at Westernization at the hands of the British: an exercise that altered subcontinental art forever, both by its introduction of Western artistic techniques, such as academic naturalism, as well as by its preparation of subcontinental artists to receive global influences. Thus, in that sense, the colonial encounter with Indian art in general and Indo-Muslim art in particular can be said, at the very least, to have helped along the agenda of cultural nationalism in art, to some small degree.

ART AND MODERN INDIAN NATIONALISM

The Aesthetic Influence of Colonialism

The story of Indo-Muslim art and the role of such art in the making a new Indian nationalism, both before and after the partition of the subcontinent, makes for interesting reading. The British East India Company established itself in Bengal, with full military force and as an unabashed governing power, in the year 1757. Just as in all other spheres, India was meant to be colonized in the realms of art, architecture, and connoisseurship. This was achieved in various ways and to various interesting ends.

After 1757, European art institutions and practices were gradually introduced on the subcontinent. As early as the end of the eighteenth century, Indian artistic patronage had begun to be influenced by British ideals of taste. For all their hostility toward the British and their suspicion of Western motives, the Indian upper classes, and eventually society in general, came to be deeply influenced by British conceptions of beauty and skill. This can partly be explained by the appeal of early adaptation to "fashion": meaning, the sooner Indian natives were able to overcome their fear and hostility toward the colonizers and the sooner they were able to reconcile themselves to the shift in patterns of power and patronage, the "trendier" they could become by appropriating (or pretending to) British artistic conventions and standards of taste.

Therefore, nawabs, maharajas, and merchant princes, encouraged in their newly acquired and carefully nurtured taste for Western art by the new British rulers themselves, began to generously patronize traveling European artists. The works of such artists as William Hodges (1744–1797), Tilly Kettle (1734–1786), Thomas Daniell (1749–1840), and his nephew William Daniell (1769–1837) became popular not only back home in London, where they became critically acclaimed commercial successes, but also in India itself. A glance at the Daniell's melded portrait of Indian architectural styles, frozen in time and displayed with an exaggerated amount of romantic nostalgia for an "exotic, untouched Orient" drives this point home quite powerfully.

This is not to say, however, that India had hitherto been ignorant of Western artistic activities. As early as Emperor Jalaluddin Mohammad Akbar's reign in the sixteenth century, artists and their patrons in the Mughal courts had shown a serious interest in Western styles and techniques. This possibly helped in the later willingness of Indian artists to incorporate these techniques into their own works. The advent of technology facilitated this development. The sudden ease with which reproductions could be made by virtue of the proliferation of lithography and printing presses made Western models of art far more accessible to Indian artists—comparable in today's world, for instance, to the ease with which images and ideas circulate globally through the Internet.

European schools of art were set up by the British in major metropolitan centers, such as Bombay, Madras, Lahore, and Lucknow, to name a few. However, it was not until the 1850s, the apex of colonial power in British India, that Western art schools set about on a systematic, stated transformation of Indian taste. Mitter (2002) argues that it was not just accessibility that led to the "occidental orientations" of Western artists. The growing influence of Western art on Indian taste was included in a deliberate plan on the part of the British to introduce the cultural values of the West in India. "One of the first tasks the East India Company officials set themselves was to 'improve' the skills of the Indian artists by teaching them scientific drawing. The general British opinion of Indian painting was typified by the Victorian painter, Valentine Prinsep, who lamented that the Delhi painters never worked from nature. They were remarkable solely for their mechanical capacity and 'admirable patience'" (Mitter 2002, 238).

To support this argument, Mitter quotes Lord Macaulay's "Minute" of 1835 and Wood's "Education Despatch" of 1854. During a debate on education for Indians, Macaulay spoke of creating "a class of persons, Indian in blood and colour, but English in taste, in opinions, in morals and in intellect (quoted in Mitter 2002, 234). In 1854, Wood stated that it was "the purpose of the British to share with India the useful knowledge with which Providence had blessed them, including, as a kind of by-product, art schools that would teach naturalist art" (quoted in Mitter 2002, 234). This epitomized the high tide of Westernization, a tide that was suddenly overturned after the "mutiny" of 1857. After this, exclusion rather than assimilation became the keynote; a cautious and contained intervention became the administrative policy. However, Mitter points out with many telling examples and pictorial representations, a most unpleasant feature of imperial rule. This was the scorn with which many British treated Indians who tried to adopt Western ways, especially those who spoke English.[4] Their resentment against the Westernized, educated Indian elite was indeed deep-seated. The paternalistic ambitions of the Raj were seemingly more compatible with concerns for the poor and illiterate peasantry than with the threatening competitiveness of the disaffected intelligentsia. On the other hand, the rising resentment of the general Indian populace against the *bhadralok* (Bengali for Westernized Indians) led to the creation of a genre of painting with them as the targets of a coarse, publicly distributed satire that parodied their nouveau riche pretensions. This type of painting, popularly distributed through the medium of print technology, was produced by the traditional Bengali *pat* (scroll) painters in the Kalighat style. Around the same time, print technology enabled the widespread diffusion of images in colonial Calcutta, as Kalighat, on its outskirts, emerged as a major center of pilgrimage.

Thus, for all its earnestness in the desire for intellectual compatibility, equality, and integration with Western ideals through the adoption of academic naturalism, the Bengal school's nationalist aspirations failed, arguably, in the face of a preconceived idea of nationalism in the minds of Indians, and a prejudiced narrow-mindedness of aesthetic taste on the part of the British.

Hindu and Muslim Cultural Nationalism

In this environment of mutual resentment and mistrust between the Indians and the British, the emergence of *swadeshi* ideology (cultural nationalism based on Indian heritage and invoking a sense of pride in the Indian past) proved to be most useful, at least for some. Artists, writers, and leaders of elite cultural taste, such as Rabindranath Tagore (1861–1941), his nephew Abanindranath Tagore (1871–1951), the radical Englishwoman Annie Besant (1847–1933), and Abanindranath's young student-artists, such as Kshitindranath Mazumdar (1891–1975), Nandalal Bose (1882–1966), and Jamini Roy (1887–1972) stressed to Indian youths the value of harking back to a glorious Hindu past. The myths and folk tales in Hinduism, and India's otherwise rich and colorful history were revived, retold, illustrated, and disseminated.[5] The movement flourished under the Englishman E. B. Havell's leadership at the Calcutta Art School, where Abanindranath Tagore proudly declared, "I have mastered drawing Buddha, Nanda (Nandalal Bose) is drawing Shiva, and Kshitin (Kshitindranath Mazumdar) in drawing Chaitanya" (www.chitralekha.org/abanindranath.htm, 2001). Art in the older Indian traditions was encouraged. *Swadeshi* nationalism, arguably, helped restore Hindu self-respect. The British Empire, a self-confident nation with an obviously strong sense of identity, rested on its laurels of cultural superiority. In holding India up as culturally superior to the West, Indians were simply turning the aesthetic knife around upon their rulers.

However, *swadeshi* nationalism as it manifested itself in art neglected to include one major group of disaffected Indians: the Muslims. It is true that Abanindranath Tagore did a series of paintings depicting Mughal rulers and even earlier Muslim figures, among others. His works—*The Last Moments of Shah Jahan* (1900), *Omar Khayyam* (1909), and *Aurangzeb Examining the Head of Dara* (1911)—are wonderfully detailed, superbly crafted, enormously self-conscious documents of Indian history. It could even be argued that his intensely psychological treatment of the subject matter sensitively and presciently highlighted Muslim issues of cultural identity in India. But, paintings along such lines were few and far between. For all its well-meaning inclusiveness, *swadeshi* nationalism was an overwhelmingly Hindu nationalism. Within it, Indian Muslims could find little solace.

Simultaneously, a "pan-Islamic" movement was gathering momentum in Asia. Prominent Muslim leaders of cultural and political opinion were beginning to more accurately voice the grievances of a once-glorious Muslim empire whose end was in sight. In India, Bahadur Shah Zafar II (1775–1858), the last ruler of the Mughal dynasty, was exiled to Rangoon by the British—where he spent his last days in poignant poetic lamentation: "How unfortunate Zafar is! For his grave, he got not even two yards, in his beloved land."[6]

Elsewhere, the Ottoman Empire was on its last legs, facing annihilation by Christian Europe. Muslims in British India at this point launched the Khilafat movement (1919–1924) to ensure that the British, victors of World War I, kept a promise made at Versailles. The promise was that the Islamic Caliphate, then claimed by the Ottoman emperor, would not be abolished. The brothers Maulana Mohammad Ali (1874–1951) and Shaukat Ali (1873–1938), together with Maulana Abul Kalam Azad (1888–1958) and Hasrat Mohani (1875–1951), spearheaded this movement.

Cultural nationalism among Muslims took many other forms, not always directly political. Earlier educationists, such as Sayed Ahmed Khan (1817–1898), knighted by the British in 1888 for his services to the Empire, had stressed the importance of Western scientific education and the learning of English to ensure the inclusion of Muslims in the eventual British vision of Indian governance.[7] In 1875, Sir Sayed founded the Mohammedan Anglo-Oriental College in Aligarh and produced a series of translations of English scientific texts in Urdu to make this information available to Muslim students. Renamed Aligarh Muslim University in 1920, the institution became a hotbed of nationalist Muslim politics and produced proponents of diverse ideologies. Some of them advocated the acquiring of Western scientific education in order to keep up with the advances made by the imperializing West. Others subscribed to the separatist tendencies of right-leaning Islamic scholars.

Muhammad Iqbal (1877–1938), poet, thinker, and much-touted visionary of the hotly debated Muslim dream that would later take shape as Pakistan, was also an important figure in this process of Muslim "renaissance" in British India. Later termed the "poet-philosopher of Islam," Iqbal was very active in Indo-Muslim politics, heading the All-India Muslim League in the early 1930s. Born in Sialkot, Punjab, and educated in law at Cambridge, Iqbal received his doctorate at the University of Munich with a dissertation on "The Development of Metaphysics in Persia" in 1928. Returning to Lahore and beginning simultaneous careers in law, politics, and poetry, Iqbal deeply impressed and widely influenced a whole generation of Muslim Indians. Among his contemporaries was a Muslim painter named Abdur Rehman Chughtai.

CHUGHTAI: AN ISLAMIC ARTIST PAR EXCELLENCE

Abdur Rehman Chughtai (1897–1975) is one of the most important artists in the telling of the subcontinental story. An outstanding painter from Lahore, Chughtai "represents the awakening of Muslim political and cultural identity in India partly in response to Hindu cultural nationalism" (Nesom 1984, 10). Chughtai was trained in basic Islamic ornamental design by an artisan attached to a local mosque. In 1911, he enrolled in the Mayo School of Art in Lahore, a British art institution now known as the National College of Art, but the death of his father and his family's ensuing circumstances forced him to leave school to make a living. Later hired as a drawing teacher by the art school, he eventually became the head instructor in chromo-lithography there.

Chughtai was arguably the finest artist in the subcontinent to personalize Muslim classics. He drew his inspiration from such Islamic sources as the twelfth century *Rubai'yat* of Omar Khayyam (1048–1122), the mythic tales of the Arabian Thousand and One Nights (*Alf Layla wa Layla*), the poetry of classical Persian poets from Shiraz such as Mosleh al-Din Sa'adi (1210–1290) and the Sufi Shamsuddin Mohammed Hafiz (1324–1393), and the inspirational, revivalist writings of Muhammad Iqbal. In order to understand Chughtai's politics, one must first look carefully at the politics of his time. At the high noon of British Empire, Indian nationalism manifested itself in a myriad of ways. General resentment and rising indignation against the colonizers had, by 1857, led to the infamous Sepoy rebellion ("mutiny") against the British. Both Hindu and Muslim civilians and soldiers were aggrieved—their closely held religious and personal beliefs appeared to be ridiculed and their loyalty to the Crown seemed futile, unrewarded, and too servile. National pride of the natives of the Indian subcontinent was damaged beyond repair.

Chughtai traced his family's roots to Persian architects at the Mughal court and drew great solace and inspiration from this lineage. Growing up in Lahore, he was familiar both by virtue of his religious education at the local mosque and his training with the artisan attached to that mosque, with principles of Islamic design and architecture. He lived his life among the *bazaars, masajid* (mosques), and *maqabir* (tombs) that were a legacy of the Sultanate and Mughal eras, and this un-self-conscious seepage is evident in his works. In 1916, he visited Delhi to view Mughal architecture, and the painstaking attention to architectural detail in his subsequent productions attests to the faithfulness with which he portrayed Islamic design and ornamentation.

Chughtai's role in the development of an Indo-Muslim nationalist art during colonial occupation cannot be denied. His identification with the Mughals was obviously related to Muslim reaction in the face of Hindu nationalism, and the worldwide pan-Islamic movement that was under way at the time. Muslim fears of a Hindu-majority India were recognized when they were granted the right to separate representation by the Minto-Morley Act of 1909. It must be kept in mind that by the end of the nineteenth century, now that British Empire in India was clearly viewed by the Indians as occupier and enemy, the rules of engagement had become more complicated. It was no longer only "us" (Indians) against "them" (the British). The subcontinent was now coming to a point where the promise of the British leaving India was actually in sight. The stakes were now higher for Indians—how would they govern themselves? Who would rule whom? Among the religious minorities (i.e., all who were not Hindu), how would the largest group assert themselves on the political and cultural map of a newly independent India?

But in order to place Chughtai's painting in its proper context, the story of nationalism in Indian art as a whole must first be understood. *Swadeshi* nationalism had manifested itself in Indian art to a great extent as a reaction to Western painterly principles of academic naturalism. Earlier, such as in the paintings of Raja Ravi Varma (1848–1906), the *swadeshi* agenda co-opted academic naturalism, so to speak, and made it a tool in the hands of local artists with which they produced a uniquely Indian colonial art. Such art, like that of Shaykh Muhammad Amir of Karaya (company artist of the eighteenth century), hired by the British for his renderings of Indian subjects in the techniques of Western academic naturalism, and the uncle and nephew team Raja Ravi Varma (1848–1906) and Raja Raj Varma (1863–1918), closely resembled the aquatints of British painters like yet another uncle and nephew team, Thomas Daniell (1749–1840) and William Daniell (1769–1837). Yet, Indian nationalist art posited itself less as resistance and the production of propaganda than as assertion of identity and the creation of an indigenous style. By these standards, Raja Ravi Varma's art was considered inadequately nationalistic. Abanindranath Tagore (1871–1951), on the other hand, dabbled in naturalist art in his youth but slowly turned first to oil paintings along Mughal themes, and then to watercolors in the Japanese traditional style. His atmospheric nationalist works reveal a combination of Japanese wash-technique with a very Mughal arrangement of planes.

In 1905, Lord Curzon, Viceroy of India, partitioned Bengal, causing political unrest, the boycott of British goods by Indian nationalists, and an upsurge in *swadeshi* ideology. E. B. Havell, then head of the Calcutta art school, invited Abanindranath Tagore to join him, thus forming the major art movement later known as the Bengal School. Artists, such as Nandalal Bose (1882–1966), Kshitindranath Mazumdar (1891–1975), Jamini Roy (1887–1972), Asit Haldar (1890–1964), and Mukul Dey (1895–1989), were trained with the intent of rediscovering "the lost language of Indian art." In this environment, the Muslim minority, anxiously observing the rise of militant Hinduism and its claim to represent all Indians, sought to construct its own identity based on a wider pan-Islamic basis. It is at this juncture that we must place Abdur Rehman Chughtai — an artist whose paintings attempted to express, according to Mitter (2001), "nostalgia for the decline of Mughal grandeur in his sensuous, erotic pictures of decadence."

At the same time, Abanindranath Tagore was also an influence on Chughtai, who had visited Calcutta along with Delhi in 1916, and acknowledged the importance of Tagore's contribution to modern art. Tagore hoped to promote a new style of revivalist oriental art in the Northwest through Chughtai, whose remarkably fine drawing received critical acclaim from other artists practicing in the Orientalist style. In 1920, Chughtai gained a position in the Punjab Fine Art Society of Lahore. By then, his work had become renowned.

While Chughtai worked along the lines of Abanindranath Tagore initially, he later realized the quantitative difference between the paintings of the two. Chughtai's early work, *Jahanara and the Taj*, shows the clear influence of Abanindranath's *The Last Moments of Shah Jahan*. But in retrospect, Chughtai discounted Tagore's works as lacking the authenticity of true Muslim experience. "I painted from the Rubai'yat [of Omar Khayyam]," he complained, "but Bengal had already put its stamp on it" (Chughtai, quoted in Nesom 1984). He obviously felt his vision of the Muslim past was more authentic, thus more legitimate. "My paintings not only paint Omar Khayyam's thoughts but embody the Islamic values which were part of me. . . . On account of their background, the emphasis [of the Bengal School] was different" (Chughtai, quoted in Nesom 1984).

Of course, such claims to artistic authenticity all but invite contradiction, being so ambiguous. It has been argued that Abanindranath Tagore drew upon Muslim classics for inspiration throughout his life. But it should not be forgotten that if Tagore was inclusive of Muslim literature, Chughtai also did not disregard Hindu mythology in his paintings. His early watercolor *Radha and Krishna* is a case in point—a moving portrait of the divine couple that proves his lack of hesitation in treating Hindu themes with the same lyricality and nostalgia that imbued all his other works.

Chughtai's importance as a revivalist Muslim artist in these tumultuous times cannot be disregarded. The poet Muhammad Iqbal, on his return to India from Germany, had begun writing poetry in Persian, conceiving of it as a pan-Islamic lingua franca. In the same spirit, Chughtai turned to what he considered his heritage—Persian art. Arabesque, calligraphy, and intensely meticulous rendering of architectural details characterized his works. Recurrent tropes in Urdu and Persian poetry are to be witnessed yet again in Chughtai's paintings—his lines flow like the black tresses of the beloved, the sweet conflations in form of his female subjects are reminders of the domed rooftops dotting Muslim cityscapes of the time. In this sense, the sensuality and erotic value of Chughtai's works cannot be denied—whether figural or architectural, representational or symbolic. He claimed as his artistic forebear the Persian master Riza-I-Abbasi (1565–1635), from the Isfahan court of Shah Abbas, whose elegant single-page compositions, bound in manuscript albums, are now to be found throughout the world's major serious collections of Islamic art.

Yet, this self-consciousness did not extend to the artist's realization of himself as essentially a revivalist living and working in, and influenced by, a thoroughly and uniquely South Asian, modern ethos. To a Westerner, for instance, what would be most strikingly noticeable on first glance is the sheer Orientalism of Chughtai's works—languorous, dream-like, and expressly nostalgic as they are. But, it must be remembered that Chughtai did not always paint a certain way—the perfection of the assertion of his Muslim identity and sense of self, his *"khudi"* (authentic self, in Urdu) in Iqbal's terms, was an evolutionary process. Trained by a humble mosque artisan, at first Chughtai painted romantic genre scenes of Punjabi women in pastoral settings. It was only over time, with self-education in the classics of Muslim literature and his maturing as a political, as well as sensual artist, that Chughtai was able to express a breathtaking reinterpretation of a very eastern *art nouveau*.

I have created Scheherazade, Badr'ul Badr, Aladin, Sindbad, Harun al-Rashid . . . and have given form to Sa'di, Omar Khayyam and Hafiz, all those who upheld the past grandeur of Islam. . . . If the artist or poet does not take active part in politics, he should at least be active in national life. Art is our national heritage, but convincing art cannot come from imitating European forms, nor is the belief in Western progress conducive to national well-being. Bihzad and Riza, who did not depend on Leonardo or Raphael for their achievements, would have approved of my work. An artist can only be universal by being rooted in his own culture. (Chughtai, quoted in Nesom 1984)

The creative interaction that took place between Chughtai and the poet Muhammad Iqbal also makes for interesting reading. Serving as the artist's inspiration, the poet wrote in his preface to the *Muraqqa-e-Chughtai* (Album of Chughtai): "With the exception of architecture, the art of Islam (music, painting, and poetry) is yet to be born—the art that aims at the human assimilation of divine attributes" (Cousins and Iqbal 1928, 3). Hoping for an artistic collaboration comparable to that of Dante and Goethe, Chughtai was engaged by Iqbal to illustrate the English translations of his poems. The sudden death of the poet forced this ambitious project to be cancelled in its infancy, but the *Muraqqa* was published in Lahore in 1928. It illustrates about fifty plates by Chughtai, comprising gouaches, colored drawings, and pencil sketches, preceded by an introduction by the British art scholar James Cousins. The second part of the book comprises the poetry of Mirza Asadullah Khan Ghalib (1796–1869), undisputedly the finest poet of the Urdu language and the voice of a dying generation that lived among the last vestiges of Muslim greatness, fading along with the fading glory of the Mughal Empire.

Chughtai was an artist who painted a world long gone: decaying, voluptuous, degenerative cosmos of languid women, beautiful starlit skies, opulent interiors, and delusions of grandeur. Perhaps, it can also be claimed that Chughtai's most important contribution to South Asian art was not in the realm of Muslim cultural nationalism, but in that of personal vision and imaginative flights of fancy. His artistic license transcended the confines of a temporal, politically imbued point. In either case, his contribution was an important one.

Chughtai's works of art are important in that they represent a small part of the story of Muslim revivalist thought and cultural nationalism in colonial India, at a time when it was beset with all manner of sociopolitical issues of identity. In a land like historical India, it had never been easy being Muslim. Perhaps a few moments spent looking at one of Chughtai's beautiful, eroticized, languorous paintings made, for those few moments, some part of being a Muslim in India easier.

With the partition of the subcontinent in 1947, and the creation of the modern nation-states of India and Pakistan, artists in both countries worked hard to develop distinctive voices. Of these, many were voices of lament at the cruel and illogical division of the landmass that was historical India. In Pakistan, Muslim artists sought to establish a clear connection with the Islamic heritage of the subcontinent. Political circumstances and state patronage further ensured that state-sponsored activities, such as portraiture, calligraphy, and to a lesser extent architecture, gained prominence within the artistic realm. As a result, Ismail Gulgee (b. 1926) and S. H. Askari (b. 1915) gained prominence as state portraitists. Sadequain (1930–1987), widely regarded as "the Holy Sinner," infused Arabic calligraphy with a personality, depth, and pathos mirrored only by the cacti of the Sindh desert he so lovingly represented. In the 1950s, Shakir Ali (1916–1975), fresh from Europe, taught and later became principal of the National College of Arts in Lahore. Anna Molka Ahmed (1917–1994), coming from London to Lahore with her husband, and Zubeida Agha (1922–1977), also trained in Europe, were remarkable female painters credited with bringing modernism home to Pakistan. A different scenario was contemporaneously unfolding in India.

HUSSAIN: MUSLIM, BUT NOT ISLAMIC

A living post-partition Muslim artist who has captured and kept the attention of the Indian art world for many decades now is Maqbool Fida Hussain. He is referred to as a modernist, even though his artistic range varies from Bollywood hoardings and portraits in oil on canvas to computer-generated multimedia presentations, installations, and 35mm film. Born into a poor family in Pandharpur, Northern India, Hussain's mother died before his second birthday. His father remarried and moved the family to Indore, where Hussain set out with his painter's tools, beginning his artistic journey without any formal training. In 1935, he finally moved to Bombay and enrolled at the J. J. School of Art (founded, incidentally, in 1857—the year of the sepoy rebellion against the British—and named after Sir Jamsetjee Jeejebhoy, its benefactor). Starting off as a painter of cinema billboards and hoardings, Hussain was a struggling artist until his work suddenly came to be noticed, placing him in the august company of other successful artists such as Francis Newton Souza (1924–2002). Very quickly, the artist shot to fame and began to be exhibited widely, winning high honors beginning with an exhibition at the Bombay Art Society in 1947—the year of India's independence from British rule. Today, Hussain's international stature as an artist is indisputably established and his works fetch exorbitant prices at global auctions.

Whereas the artist has courted controversy on many counts through his long, illustrious career, what often becomes eclipsed in all the media frenzy is his strong commitment to Indian nationhood. Given that no artist, even by trying, is ever able to distance himself from his context, Hussain is notable in that even within his seemingly innocuous paintings of movie stars and celebrities, questions lurk about self, nationhood, values, and ideals that only the brave have the heart to raise. As he once said,

> India was never a nation. . . . This is the first time it is struggling to become a nation. It might collapse . . . the very fact that it is struggling is dangerous and exciting . . . this is perhaps the most exciting period in history. I don't think it is just going to drown in the sea. It has an inner sense of centuries; it would take centuries to destroy it . . . for me India's humanity is what is important, not its borders. (Hussain, quoted in Herwitz 1988, 17)

Hussain was of age at the time of the subcontinent's division into India and Pakistan. It was in 1947, in fact, that his work *The Potters* won an award at a Bombay Art Society exhibition. In the post-independence period in India, opting to stay instead of emigrating to the newly formed state of Pakistan, despite being a Muslim, made a staunchly nationalist political statement of another kind. "When I look back, I realize that the nationalist movement also meant Hindu-Muslim unity. We were brought up on those ideals. That is why, when our country was partitioned into India and Pakistan, our family never thought of emigration. We felt we belonged to the place where we had lived for generations" (Hussain, quoted in Herwitz 1988, 17).

At this point, being a nationalist in India meant joining the march toward modernity, and the artist's contribution toward this ideology was his panoramic work *Zameen* (Earth 1955), connoting an India that was at once real, mythical, and symbolic. Prior to this, as a declaration of his commitment to modernity, Hussain had already joined the Progressives, a group of young artists, including Francis Newton Souza and Syed Haider Raza, (1922–) committed to describing the new Indian reality immediately after the subcontinent's independence from colonial rule.

In 1984, Hussain visited the British Museum library in London. There he came across books on the Indian "mutiny" and other material that triggered his memories of the British Raj, as he had experienced it as a child in Indore. The result was a critically acclaimed series of watercolors that cast a harsh light both on the conduct of the British in India, as well as on the natives who tried to emulate them, to the extent of humiliation. He highlighted the slavish mentality of the natives, in a controversial move clearly indicative of a rise in nationalist sentiment, Indian indignation against colonialism, and a very self-conscious pride in one's own cultural heritage.

As opposed to Chughtai's constant assertion of Muslim identity, Hussain's nationalist modus operandi involved a return to the stories and lore that emerged indigenously from the motherland, India. Interestingly enough, it was a socialist (Ram Manohar Lohia), and not a cultural nationalist, who influenced this return to roots. In the 1960s, Hussain embarked on a grand project, painting the *Ramayana* and the *Mahabharata*, those great Indian epics, and transported them by bullock cart to various villages. "I painted the epic not from the religious angle, but for the people," he claimed about them, boasting of how villagers sat enthralled for hours staring at the paintings, while folk singers sang the illustrated epics. Just as Abanindranath Tagore had done before him with his treatment of Muslim subjects, Hussain examined the psychosocial dimensions of the Hindu epics with his paintings.

However, for all his well-meaning nationalist sentiment, Hussain was unable to avoid the wrath of religious fundamentalists, both at home and abroad. In a recent development, right-wing Hindu extremists have accused Hussain of portraying Hindu deities in a manner that was hurtful to the sentiments of their devotees—going so far as leveling charges against him of obscenity, indecency, and having an anti-Hindu bias. The fact that he is a Muslim has also been used as a weapon against him. Ironically, in the recent worldwide backlash against depictions of the Prophet Mohammad in caricatured cartoons, M. F. Hussain's representations of Hindu deities have been cited by Indian Muslims as the other side of the same coin. In February 2006, the artist was arrested and charged under the Prevention of Insults to National Honor Act (295A of the Indian Penal Code), which states: "Whoever, with deliberate and malicious intention of outraging the religious feelings of any class of citizens of India, by words, either spoken or written, or by signs or by visible representations or otherwise, insults or attempts to insult the religion or the religious beliefs of that class, shall be punished with imprisonment of either description for a term which may extend to three years, or with fine, or with both."

On being questioned about these developments, Hussain's stance was: "My work has not been understood. But a time will come when people will appreciate my art." He thinks the outrage is a natural reaction from some sections of society. "People tend to resent any new form of art. After the Renaissance, the works of the Impressionists created a hue and cry in society. People felt that those strikingly colorful paintings were an insult to art. Today, however, the paintings are regarded as classics. My work is modern art, a symbolic and poetic interpretation of reality. This art is only fifty years old and the masses have yet to accept it."

It is notable that the artist thinks of himself as a link in the chain of historical and artistic continuity, and places himself in a position comparable to the heralding of a newer renaissance in another place and at another time. The world shall just have to wait and see whether this belief withstands the test of time.

CONCLUDING REMARKS

Cultural nationalism in Indo-Muslim art takes us back many centuries. Yet, it is also being repainted, recast, and retold today to explain new geopolitical realities. Partition of the Indian subcontinent into India and Pakistan in 1947, for instance, has had a significant impact on the direction of "Indo-Islamic" art in the region. In India, Muslim artists increasingly leaned toward modern abstract movements while immersing themselves in themes and forms derived from Hindu mythology. A prominent example of this is the impressive body of work by Maqbool Fida Hussein. Muslim artists of the subsequent generation (e.g., Farhan Mujeeb, Zeba) tend to strike a balance between Hindu and Islamic aesthetic legacies. In contrast, Pakistan has spawned a whole generation of artists that has vigorously revived the Islamic miniature painting tradition. Their documentation of hitherto unseen times in a well-known and much-loved format has generated great interest both in academic circles, as well as in the world's sophisticated and globalized art market. Shahzia Sikander (1969–), a New York-based Pakistani artist currently featured at the Museum of Modern Art, combines Mughal miniature and Japanese wash-techniques with a lively, impudent critique of the Hindu/Muslim divide and contemporary South Asian identity. The traveling *Karkhana* (workshop in Urdu) project, bringing together six Pakistani miniaturists to form a painters' assembly line, imprints individual ideas, in successive layers, upon the same piece to radical, breathtaking effect. Within the country also, Western art movements have infiltrated and sometimes taken over the artistic imagination to produce widely differing yet for the most part commercially successful results.

Islam's encounter with India has left behind a rich legacy of cultural traditions. Both the region and the religion continue to evolve rapidly in today's *realpolitik*. The manifestation of Indo-Muslim nationalism through art, especially in the years immediately preceding the division of the subcontinent, is an instructive phenomenon. It not only affirms the role of the arts in the raising of national consciousness, but also shows us some surprising ways in which a similar kind of sentiment can be expressed in artistic media, to widely differing ends. But perhaps most importantly, it makes us aware of the challenges artists must face in their quest for identity, nationality, and a place to feel truly at home with their imagination.

VI

EPILOGUE

17

Muslims in the Psychoanalytic World

Salman Akhtar

The time has come to utilize the tools of contemporary social sciences and critical theory to interrogate some of the fundamental notions of identity and belonging which has shaped and colored Muslim politics for so long. The Muslim world needs to recognize, accept, and even celebrate the internal differences and plurality within itself.

—Noor 2003, 325

Sigmund Freud, the founder of psychoanalysis, was a Jew. While skeptical about religion in general and hardly observant of the rituals of his own faith, Freud was intensely proud of his Jewish identity. This homoethnic comfort was, at least in part, responsible for the fact that, in the course of his discovery of psychoanalysis and of its early evolution, most of his associates and pupils were Jewish. The Wednesday Psychological Society he founded in 1902 had an exclusively Jewish membership that consisted of, beside himself, Alfred Adler, Hugo Heller, Max Graf, Paul Federn, and Wilhelm Stekel. And by 1908, when this select group expanded to become the Vienna Psychoanalytic Society, most members or frequent visitors (e.g., Karl Abraham, Max Eitingon, Sandor Ferenczi, and Otto Rank) were Jewish. At one level, this was congenial to Freud. At another level, it worried him. He feared that such a homoethnic cloister might be harmful to the future of psychoanalysis and the discipline might be reduced to "a Jewish national concern" (letter to Karl Abraham, Freud May 1908). This clashed with his robustly broad vision and his yearning to disseminate psychoanalytic ideas to the world at large.

NON-JEWISH ANALYSTS

Christians

Thus motivated, Freud welcomed the thoroughly Welsh and Christian Ernest Jones to the psychoanalytic circle. He especially courted the unmistakably Nordic Carl Gustav Jung and, for a long while, regarded him as his professional heir. Though Freud's effort to anoint Jung as his successor floundered, the synagogue of the unconscious became open to Christian individuals. While the majority of psychoanalysts in Europe and, later, the Americas still remained Jewish, the number of Christians joining the field gradually grew and so did the contribution of these non-Jewish analysts to the theoretical and technical conceptualizations of psychoanalysis. Prominent early analysts who were Christians include Wilfred Bion, W. R. D. Fairbairn, Harry Guntrip, Karl Menninger, Richard and Edith Sterba, James Strachey, Harry Stack Sullivan, and Donald Winnicott. Prominent contemporary analysts who are Christians include Homer Curtis, Peter Fonagy, Glen Gabbard, Dorothy Holmes, James McLaughlin, William Meissner, Bernard Pacella, Warren Procci, Nadia Ramzy, Ana-Marie Rizutto, Harry Smith, Charles Socarides, Neville Symington, and Stuart Twemlow. Together these distinguished individuals, and many others, who remain unnamed here owing to space limitations, have certainly laid Freud's early concern to rest.

Hindus

In a later and less-recognized development, the foundation of Indian Psychoanalytic Society in 1922 (and its rapid affiliation with the International Psychoanalytic Association, with the help of Ernest Jones) made it possible for Hindus to enter the psychoanalytic field.[1] Akhtar and Tummala-Narra (2005) have reviewed the subsequent development of psychoanalysis in India and amplified the various aspects of the Hindu involvement in psychoanalysis. The predominantly Hindu contributors to Akhtar's (2005) edited volume *Freud Along the Ganges* also demonstrate that Hindu thought and psychoanalysis have much to offer each other. The preeminent Indian psychoanalyst Sudhir Kakar's (1990a; 1990b; 1991a; 1991b; 1996; see also Kumar 2005) wide-ranging oeuvre has made this amply evident through a highly sophisticated synthesis of psychoanalytic depth psychology and the mythic and cultural idiom of India.

Sikhs and Parsis

A corollary of the Hindu passport for psychoanalysis was the entry of Indian Sikhs and Parsis (Zoroastrians of Persian origin) in the profession. The most prominent member of this group was Harwant Singh Gill, a Sikh man from India who trained in England and wrote thoughtful papers on Oedipal triumph (1987) and the importance of an absent father (1988). Others from Sikh community who have made significant contributions to psychoanalysis are Baljeet Mehra, a senior training analyst at the British Psychoanalytic Society, and Jaswant Guzder, who is both an outstanding artist and psychoanalyst based in Montreal.

Having "assimilated" Christians, Hindus, Sikhs, and Parsis (e.g., Sarosh Forbes and Eileen Bharucha) in its originally exclusive Jewish fold, psychoanalysis has now come to encounter the Muslim world. And it immediately faces a question. Why is it that the followers of Islam, the world's second largest religion, are so underrepresented in the field of psychoanalysis?

Muslims

Seeking answers to this question compels one to consider the demographic lay of the land where psychoanalysis has taken root. In doing so, one is forced to acknowledge that the discipline is a cultural phenomenon of the Western Europe and the Americas. Therefore, it has drawn adherents from the largely Christian and Jewish population of these regions. Areas of Europe with a sizable population of Muslims (e.g., Bosnia, Kosovo, Albania) were not reached by psychoanalysis; factors such as economic hardship, socialist forms of government, nonavailability of psychoanalytic literature in Serbian, and the absence of homoethnic psychoanalytic role models, rather than features of Islam per se, seem responsible for this nonpenetration of psychoanalytic thought in the Balkans. With some variation, the same might hold true for other regions of the world with large Muslim populations.[2] As a result, the entry of Muslims in the psychoanalytic profession has been largely via the immigrant population in countries where psychoanalysis was already well established. Approximately forty Muslims have thus obtained psychoanalytic training from the institutes recognized by the International Psychoanalytic Association. This group is comprised by individuals who have migrated from Algeria, Cyprus, Egypt, India, Iran, Morocco, Pakistan, and Turkey, though all analysts of such nationalities are not Muslim by religion. Currently, to the best of my knowledge, about twenty Muslim psychoanalysts are practicing in the United States and Canada, with the remaining being in various countries of Europe (especially France), Latin America, and Australia. Although little factual data is available, it seems safe to assume that these individuals differ in the degree of their religiosity and ability to conduct treatment in their native languages (e.g., Arabic, Pashto, Persian, Punjabi, Sindhi, Turkish, and Urdu).

Whether, as a cohort, these individuals have made (or will make) any unique contributions to the theory and practice of psychoanalysis and to what

extent such work might be traceable to their religious identities (as opposed
to their regional, personal, and training backgrounds) remain open questions
at this point in time.

THE CASE OF MASUD KHAN

The most well known individual belonging to this group is the *enfant-terrible*
of psychoanalysis, namely Masud Khan (1924–1989). He arrived in England
from India in 1943 (i.e., when India was under British rule). Trained in England during the late 1940s and early 1950s, Khan rose to international prominence in psychoanalysis. He was analyzed by Ella Freeman Sharpe, John
Rickman, Donald Winnicott, and, later, briefly by Jacques Lacan.[3] He also had
several "informal therapeutic encounters" (Cooper 1993, 14) with Anna Freud,
who had been one of his supervisors during the analytic training. Khan quali-
fied in child analysis after he had begun to work as an adult analyst.

Over the course of his professional development, Khan became a highly
sought out teacher and was appointed a training analyst at the Institute of
Psychoanalysis in London. He was editor of the International Psychoanalyti-
cal Library for over twenty years, associate editor of the *International Journal of Psychoanalysis* for over a decade, the foreign editor of the *Nouvelle Re-
vue de Psychoanalyse*, and a codirector of Sigmund Freud Copyrights.

Khan was a prolific author and made "imaginative contributions to
psychoanalytic theory" (Sandler 2004, 33) especially as it pertains to "cumulative trauma" (Khan 1963), phobic and counterphobic mechanisms in the
schizoid personality, lying fallow, "idolization" of the self, alienating impact
of sexual perversions, and role of silence as well as playfulness in the consolidation of human mind and in the psychoanalytic situation (Khan 1974;
1980; 1983). "Most members of the British Society considered him a distinguished, if controversial, member and were proud of his contributions" (Sandler 2004, 33). The following excerpts from his large body of work support
their stance.

- On schizoid character: "These patients suffered separation from their mother
  in early childhood to which they had reacted, not with a sense of loss and
  mourning, but an excessive internalization both of the idealized maternal object and the idealized self . . . an interplay between seeking objects of a special character and in a special way and their compulsive jettisoning . . . constituted their truly dynamic private existence" (Khan 1966, 70–72).

- On psychoanalytic setting: "We create a void and absence from our presence
  to create that space of illusion where the patient can use symbolic discourse,

and which we receive symbolically and interpret in similar idiom" (Khan 1971, 266).

- On sexual perversion: "The capacity to create the emotional climate in which another person volunteers to participate is one of the few real talents of the perverts. . . . A make-believe situation is offered in which two individuals temporarily renounce their separate identities and boundaries and attempt to create a heightened maximal body-intimacy of orgastic nature. There is always, however, one proviso. The pervert himself cannot surrender to the experience and retains a split off, dissociated manipulative ego control of the situation. This is both his achievement and failure in the intimate situation" (Khan 1964, 22).

- On pornography: "I believe that pornography alienates its accomplices both from their self and the other. What masquerades as mutual and ecstatic intimacy through somatic events is in fact a sterile and alienated mental concoction. It is this characteristic that made me once remark that pornography is the stealer of dreams" (Khan 1979, 222).

- On dreams: "Certain intrapsychic functions and ego capacities are necessary for a person to be able to put together a 'good dream' from his sleep experience. Prominent among these are the ego's capacity to sustain the sleep wish, controlling excessive influx of the primary process, and appropriate dosage of 'day residues' to structuralize the latent 'dream wish' into a contained dream text" (Khan 1983, 42).

- On lying fallow: "Lying fallow is a transitional state of experience, a mode of being that is alerted quietude and receptive wakeful lambent consciousness. . . . Although this mood is essentially and inherently private and personal, it needs an ambiance of companionship in order to be held and sustained. In isolation or deprivation, one can neither arrive at this mood nor sustain it. Someone—a friend, a wife, a neighbor—sitting around unobtrusively, guarantees that the psychic process does not get out of hand, that is, become morbid introspective or sullenly doleful" (Khan 1983, 185).

Khan's conceptualizations were poetic, his clinical work was intriguing, and his prose was disarmingly elegant. However, with passage of time, all this began to deteriorate. What was once radiantly innovative became disturbingly outrageous. Khan succumbed to the physical and emotional ailments he had long struggled with, and this led him to behave in grossly unethical ways and make draconian errors of moral judgment. His tragic professional downfall has by now become a part of psychoanalytic legend (Limentani 1992; Cooper 1993; Hopkins 1998; Godley 2001; 2004). The emphasis in these writings has been on Khan's character pathology that did become increasingly transparent over time. In brave exception to such "one person psychology" view, Hopkins

(1998) and Sandler (2004) include the potential contributions of the British psychoanalytic milieu of that time and especially Khan's analyst, Donald Winnicott's, technical failures in containing his analysand's destructiveness. According to Sandler: "Winnicott was unable to hold the frame in his analysis of Khan. . . . Khan was taught by Winnicott and attended clinical seminars led by him: after qualification, he was supervised by Winnicott during 1951 on his first child training case. When Khan's second analyst died early in that same year, he chose to go into analysis with Winnicott—then in his first term as President of the British Society. The analysis began toward the end of 1951 and, within the first two years, Khan, the analysand, was collaborating with Winnicott, his analyst, on a book review written by them both and published in the *International Journal* in 1953 (Winnicott and Khan 1953). Khan (1975) himself says that it was four years later, in 1957, when Winnicott invited him to put together his first collection of papers, for which Khan wrote the introduction. . . . Winnicott's active public support for Khan's advancement within the British Society represents another important boundary violation" (2004, 35).

Sandler (2004) acknowledges that "the British Society had neither the will nor the strength to discipline" Khan and displayed an "all pervasive collusion towards Winnicott's personal use of a candidate" (p. 36, 40). Laudable though Sandler's contribution is, it does not go deep enough into the issues involved. Declaring the origins of the dyadic conundrum as "matters of speculation" (p. 35), Sandler's paper manages to overlook that serious erotic limitations in Winnicott's (Rodman 2003)—and, for that matter, in Anna Freud's (Young-Bruehl 1988)—life could have compromised their ability to help the hopelessly promiscuous Khan. Another factor not taken into account is the potential influence of India's struggle for independence and its achieving freedom from the British close to the time the three "Anglo-Indian" analyses of Khan (with Sharpe, Rickman and Winnicott) took place. The potential role of "colonial transference" and, more importantly, "colonial countertransference" in these failed analyses is thus omitted.

It is also interesting to note that Sandler refers to Khan as a "Pakistani-Indian" (2004, 33). Since no such nationality exists or has ever existed, one is forced to wonder about this label. Is it a clumsy compromise to accommodate the fact that the region of India where Khan hailed from was included in 1947 in the newly formed Pakistan? Since not once in her article does Sandler identify Khan as a Muslim, one also wonders if the designation "Pakistani-Indian" is her way of avoiding the word "Muslim."

All this becomes more intriguing in the light of the fact that Khan, in his last book (1988) that acted as the proverbial last straw and led to his downfall, declared himself to be "a devout Muslim" (p. 53). To my mind, this melodramatic announcement was an affectation in consonance with Khan's belligerent anti-Semitism (evident in that very book) and the title of "Prince" that he had merrily given himself toward the last years of his life. Each of these measures was based on shaky grounds in reality. Khan was hardly a practicing Muslim. His anti-Semitism was "peculiarly unconvincing" (Paterson 1991, 110)[4] and his "prince-hood" was self-invented. All three measures (i.e., pseudo-religiosity, pseudo-animosity, and pseudo-royalty) attempted to keep a crumbling self intact with the band-aid of paranoid grandiosity. The result, as might be expected, was the opposite. Khan became more disorganized and was finally removed from the membership of the British Psychoanalytic Society. Some of his analysands (e.g., Godley 2001) felt harmed by him, others (e.g., Cooper 1993) came to his defense while recognizing his weaknesses. Still others (e.g., Christopher Bollas, Adam Phillips) became shining stars of British psychoanalysis. Khan himself was ostracized and died a lonely man. Nonetheless, a group of individuals did remain supportive of him until the very end.

Ambivalences of such sort and an outright loathing of Khan on the part of many analysts,[5] have led some to invalidate his contributions. The line of argument asks: If he was so disturbed, how can his works be taken seriously? Such stance overlooks that psychopathology and creativity frequently coexist, and in the field of psychoanalysis, a large number of major contributors have been informed from within. Freud's (1900a) interpretation of dreams and discovery of Oedipus complex, Anna Freud's (1922) elucidation of beating fantasies, and Kohut's (1979) paper on the two analyses of Mr. Z. are but a few examples of this sort. Khan's psychopathology might have similarly informed his theorizing. Suppression of object hunger by selfless devotion to others, use of sexual excitement to enliven a dead self, oscillation between hollowness and megalomania, and the potentially vitalizing role of authenticity gained via withdrawal and silence are themes present both in Khan's lived life and psychoanalytic writings. The dots are not difficult to connect. That said, it is clear that Khan continues to occupy a significant, if disturbing, place in the psychoanalytic universe. He is mentioned here in some detail because of his prominent and pioneering status in the relatively small cadre of analysts who happen to be Muslims.

At the same time, it would be erroneous to attribute Khan's transgressions to his religion. They were the end-product of complex biopsychosocial factors that included narcissistic character pathology, metastatic cancer, multiple surgical operations, alcoholism, and the loneliness consequent upon being a highly gifted, wealthy, brown-skinned, Muslim immigrant in an exclusively white, Judeo-Christian fraternity that dished out equal amounts of admiration and mistrust to him. To assign the source of Khan's difficulties to Islam would be tantamount to suggesting that Wilhelm Reich's claim that he could make rain happen (Spurgeon English, personal communication, April 1982) and Ernest Jones' sexual indiscretions (Brome 1983) were caused by their being Jewish and Christian, respectively. It will also be unjust to restrict the tale of Muslims in the psychoanalytic world to the painful episode of Masud Khan. There are many other Muslims who have made prominent contributions to our field. However, before proceeding with a discussion of their works, it might not be out of place to raise a more basic question.

DOES THE ANALYST'S RELIGION MATTER?

The possibility that the analyst's personal characteristics might have a signif-icant impact upon the conduct of analysis has only recently become a serious consideration. While a patient entering psychoanalysis was required to have a "fairly reliable character" (Freud 1905, 263), the analyst was assumed to possess such stability or to have acquired it after undergoing an analysis him-self. This attitude was most strikingly evident in the studies of "analyzability" (e.g., Bachrach and Leaff 1978; Erle and Goldberg 1984; Rothstein 1982) that listed factor after factor that made a patient suitable for analysis, but said lit-tle about the contributions of the analyst. Clearly, Freud's early reminder that "each analyst's achievement is limited by what his or own complexes and re-sistances permit" (1910, 145) did not find a conceptual foothold in these stud-ies of analyzability. Their implication was that the analyst's personality hardly figures in the conduct of analysis; only the technique matters. Yet an-other illustration of this tendency is the fact that the Jewish refugee analysts in the Americas of the 1940s and 1950s made no reference to the impact of the cultural difference between them and their patients (Akhtar 1999). One was left to believe that analysis was analysis, regardless of who was doing it and where and under what circumstances it was taking place. To think other-wise was scary since it could be misconstrued as derogation of the validity of objective methods in psychoanalysis.

To be sure, there were exceptions to such cautious thinking. Winnicott (1947), for instance, noted that "the idiosyncratic tendencies of the analyst, determined by his personal history can make his work different in style and quality from that of his colleagues" (p. 199). Despite this reminder, the im-pact of the psychoanalyst's personality upon his technique remained insuffi-ciently studied, leading Klauber (1968) to emphasize that a theory of tech-nique "which ignores the immense influence on the psychoanalytic transaction of the value systems of the patient and analyst alike ignores a ba-sic psychic reality behind any psychoanalytic relationship. What has to be taken into account is what the Greeks might have called the *ethos* of patient and analyst—a word meaning originally an accustomed seat—in addition to the *pathos* of more labile reactions" (p. 128, italics in the original).

Far from being matters of expressive idiom and unobjectionable aspects of lifestyle, the value system of the dyad affects the clinical exchange in significant, if subtle, ways. Patient's value system and "ideals may take forms compatible or incompatible with the ideals of individual analysts: propensities toward austerity or luxury, toward the acceptance or nonacceptance of commonly held standards of choice of work, or even of dress, which may be treated by one psychoanalyst as symptoms and by another with toleration" (Klauber 1968, 131).

At this point, the analyst's religious beliefs and his overall attitude toward religion enter the clinical picture. To be sure, values of the sort we are concerned with here are also the product of the socioeconomic status, parental dictates and lifestyles, era and nation in which one has been raised and is practicing, educational institutions attended, and superego modification via extrafamilial identifications during late adolescence and early adulthood. However, religion also plays a role here. If, for instance, the analyst is indifferent or hostile to religion, he is likely to be highly skeptical toward his analysand's spiritual yearnings. He may side step such issues, subtly devalue them, or quickly reduce them to their alleged instinctual origins. On the other hand, if the analyst is religious, his attitude toward such associations is likely to be more tolerant and permissive.

The analyst's religiosity, or lack thereof, might also affect his attention when his patients bring up certain specific issues. Matters involving abortion, homosexuality, impending death, and life after death especially tend to evoke countertransference reactions that are, at least in part, governed by the analyst's religious beliefs. The specific religion to which the analyst belongs can also come to play an important, even if subtle role, in the clinical exchange involving these issues. Consider the following examples as well.

- A Hindu surgeon reports that he bows his head to the elephant-headed deity, *Ganesha*, that sits on his office desk before walking toward the operating room.
- A Jewish lawyer declares that Muslims are basically primitive and praises Israel for the assassination of the Hamas leaders.
- A Lutheran college student struggles with difficulty in finding boyfriends and potential marital partners owing to her religiously-based refusal to have premarital sex.
- A Muslim analysand expresses his outrage at the recent newspaper cartoons ridiculing the Prophet Mohammed; he says that the murder of Theo van Gogh, the Dutch documentary maker, was a legitimate retribution for his mockery of Muslim customs.

Now ask yourself whether religious and nonreligious Jewish, Christian, Hindu, and Muslim analysts would listen to these associations in exactly the same manner? As much as we would like to believe that they would, the doubt that this might not be the case nags at our theoretical conscience. We would like to believe that the religious backgrounds of these analysts would not preclude their receiving this material with equanimity and that they will all attend similarly to the surface as well as the in-depth and symbolic aspects of these communications, especially as they pertain to transference-countertransference developments. However, this view may be idealistic. It overlooks the fact that countertransference experience in such situations becomes quite vulnerable to the tricks of "shared ethnic scotoma" (Shapiro and Pinsker 1973), "acculturation gaps" (Prathikanti 1997), "excessive culturalization of the analytic ego" (Akhtar 1999), and "nostalgic collusions" (Akhtar 2006). To be sure, this does not have to happen, but the fact is that it *can* happen. And, that is the point, namely, that the religious background of the analyst (and the sociopolitical stances consequent upon it) *can* come into play under certain circumstances and alter the pathways of empathy and interpretation.

TALKING SPECIFICALLY OF ISLAM

Linguistic Enrichment

As the numbers of Muslim psychoanalysts and analysands grow, so does the probability of analytic treatment being conducted in new languages (e.g., Arabic, Persian, Turkish, Urdu, and so on). This could, in turn, open up unfamiliar associative networks (Amati-Mehler et al. 1999) to otherwise commonplace fantasy and relational themes and enrich psychoanalytic imagery and metaphor. Affect theory might also be advanced, since analysands speaking in languages hitherto unfamiliar to clinical psychoanalysis might bring forth emotions that have not been well-recognized in the exclusive reliance on European languages.

Developmental Enrichment

Analyzing Muslim patients would provide access to their childhood backgrounds and, thus, help psychoanalysts to encounter patterns of child-rearing that (despite variations with patients' regional culture) are influenced by Islam. This could force a redrawing of the boundaries of what psychoanalysis considers to be modal and normative in the realm of personality development. Bonovitz's (1998) provocative statement that "if Margaret Mahler had emigrated to India rather than the United States, what theory of separation-individuation would she have woven from her observations of Indian mothers and their babies?" (p. 178) is apt in this context. Regarding Muslim child-rearing practices per se, one aspect of clinical importance might be the psychological impact of circumcision that, among Muslims of South East Asia, is typically performed at the ages of four or five. Occurring at this age, circumcision can cause body image disturbances and increase castration anxiety as opposed to its relative "harmlessness" when it is done soon after birth (as is customary among Jews).[6] Other such developmental influencing factors might also surface as one begins to be familiar with this terrain.

Technical Enrichment

Muslim analysands who are in treatment with non-Muslim analysts might develop specific transferences that differ from those of non-Muslim ananlysands (Gorkin 1996). And, Muslim analysts might be targets of unique transferences from their non-Muslim patients (Abbasi 1997). Their religious background, often identifiable by their characteristically Arabic, Persian, and Turkish-derived names, can pull forth a rich variety of prejudices and stereotypes. Holmes (1982) notes that such "points of access to a patient's transferences" (p. 8) give rise to rich associations that need to be carefully deciphered. Attention to such overtly ethnic clues to deeper transferences should not make the analyst overlook the fact that not every utterance the patient makes about people of the analyst's ethnicity and religion is transferentially significant. A robust tension between skepticism and credulousness must be maintained. At times, however, a firm limit-setting to the patient's inquisitiveness about the analyst's religion is needed in order for the unconscious associations to become available for interpretation (Akhtar 2006).

Conceptual Enrichment

The work of Muslim psychoanalysts might also open up new areas of confluence between psychoanalysis and history, literature, anthropology, and existentialism. The interface between Sufi meditative techniques and painstaking analytic deconstruction of psychic surface (Shafii 1985) is an illustration of such novel overlaps. The evocative use of the great Urdu poet Mirza Asadullah Khan Ghalib's poetry in the discussion of mental pain (Akhtar 2001) and countertransference dilemmas emanating from analyst's bilingualism (Akhtar 1999; 2006) is another example of new areas of confluence that have the potential of enriching the literary and aesthetic dimensions of psychoanalysis.[7]

Psychopolitical Enrichment

Representing various non-Western regions of the world, Muslim analysts are also prone to extend psychoanalytically-informed studies of ethnic tensions and conflict resolution to new territorial contexts. Tensions between Turks and Greeks on the vivisected island of Cyprus (Volkan 1979) and between Hindus and Muslims in India (Akhtar 2005b) thus become foci of psychoanalytic attention. Such studies familiarize Western analysts with a vocabulary of prejudice that is specific to these less known realms and inform the locally concerned individuals that tensions that seem highly specific ultimately represent ubiquitous human tendencies. In this context, the finding of a striking similarity between the Jew-hating Christians in California and Muslim-hating Hindus in the Indian region of Punjab (Adorno and Frenkel-Brunswick 1950; Varma et al. 1973) is especially informative and heartening.

ENTER VAMIK VOLKAN

Born in a Muslim-Turkish family on the island of Cyprus and medically trained in Ankara, Turkey, Vamik Volkan arrived in the United States in 1957. He obtained his psychiatric training at the University of North Carolina in Chapel Hill. After a few years of employment at Cherry Hospital, Goldsboro, North Carolina and Dorothea Dix Hospital in Raleigh, North Carolina, Volkan moved to University of Virginia School of Medicine in Charlottesville, and made it his permanent home. He did his psychoanalytic training at the Washington Psychoanalytic Institute, where he had an analysis with Stanley Olinick. Over the years that have followed, Volkan has evolved a professional career that has brought him great accolades and renown, while extending the purview of psychoanalytic inquiry into novel realms.

Volkan's early long-term work with severely regressed patients, including some who were schizophrenics, is an impressive testimony to what a humane devotion to understanding the disturbed mind can achieve. Many such patients got better organized psychically and better adapted socially under his psychotherapeutic care. His work greatly enriched the understanding of their primitive internalized object relations and the magical use of inanimate objects by them. This body of work culminated in the publication of three books, *Primitive Internalized Object Relations* (Volkan 1976), *Infantile Psychotic Self and Its Fates* (Volkan 1995), and *The Seed of Madness* (Volkan and Akhtar 1997).

Volkan extended his clinical work to borderline and narcissistic patients and described many hitherto unrecognized concepts in this realm. These include the "glass bubble" (Volkan 1979a) and "transitional fantasies" (Volkan 1973) of narcissistic patients and the affect storms, primitive splitting (Volkan 1976), and satellite states (Volkan and Corney 1968) of the borderline individuals. For the treatment of the latter, Volkan devised a step-by-step approach, describing it in detail with the help of ample clinical illustrations (Volkan 1987).

Another clinical domain that drew Volkan's attention was that of unresolved grief reaction. Designating the condition as "established pathological mourning," Volkan (1981) outlined its phenomenology, metapsychology, and psychodynamics. He introduced the concept of "linking objects" in this context. This denoted a physical object that is "actually present in the environment that is psychologically contaminates with various aspects of the dead and the self . . . the significance of this object does not fade as it does in uncomplicated mourning. Rather, it increasingly commands attention with its aura of mystery, fascination, and terror" (1981, 101). A noticeable feature of linking objects is that they can neither be rationally used nor discarded. They are usually hidden away in the house and might remain so for years. Looking at them stirs up pain, as well as a vague sense of fear. Pain is caused by the physical object's reminding one of the original loss. Fear results from the mechanism of projective identification that endows the physical object with menacing and accusatory qualities.

Volkan also delineated a specific type of short-term psychotherapy directed at resolving frozen grief reactions (Volkan et al. 1975). He also extended his work on grief reactions to the imperative role of mourning in general. Echoing Klein's (1940) emphasis upon the significance of the capacity to mourn for healthy development, Volkan wrote his first book (Volkan and Zintl 1993) for readership beyond that of mental health professionals. This turn to normative phenomena also became evident in his work on sibling relationships (Volkan and Ast 1997), where, once again, he introduced many new concepts including "womb fantasies," "deposited representations," "living linking objects," and so on.

Volkan's increasing devotion to the understanding of identity disturbances, unresolved mourning, and sibling relationships had a counterpart in what has come to be called "applied psychoanalysis." He extended his psychoanalytic understanding of these matters to the Turkish-Greek conflict that had plagued his island nation of Cyprus and led to its division in two sections (Volkan 1979b). And, he authored a book called *The Need for Enemies and Allies* (1988), which showed his increasingly involvement in matters beyond those of individual psychopathology. The book's subtitle, *From Clinical Practice to International Relations*, aptly heralded this shift in Volkan's career path.

In 1987, Volkan founded and directed Center for The Study of Mind and Human Interaction at the University of Virginia School of Medicine. This center became an interdisciplinary clearing house and meeting point for diplomats, historians, scholars of religion and political science, and psychoanalysts. It brought out the journal *Mind and Human Interaction*, which became a significant forum for the left-leaning, secular, applied psychoanalytic voice. Besides sponsoring conferences and deepening international dialogue at the Center itself, Volkan has stepped out in the field and has done an enormous amount of work on the grassroots level. He has participated in the study and attempted resolution of national and international conflicts under the auspices of the Carter Center and the FBI. The trouble spots he has dealt with include Turkey and Greece; Israel, Egypt, and Palestine; Bosnia, Serbia, and the former Yugoslavia; South Ossetia and the Republic of Georgia; Latvia, Estonia, and Russia; Albania; and Waco, Texas.

Based upon these field experiences, Volkan authored a series of books including *Turks and Greeks* (Volkan and Itzkowitz 1994), *Blood Lines* (1997), *The Third Reich in the Unconscious* (Volkan, Ast, and Greer 2002), and *Blind Trust* (Volkan 2004). Levine (2006) has recently reviewed Volkan's "enormous contributions to psychoanalysis and political science" (p. 280) and noted that they "argue persuasively for including a psychological, particularly an unconscious psychological, dimension into any understanding of ethnic, national, and international conflict. Taken together, they provide readers the beginnings of a sophisticated, psychoanalytically informed theory of large-group dynamics, the concepts needed to understand the relationship and interplay between individual and large-group identity, and numerous vivid and compelling illustrations drawn from contemporary events" (p. 274).

Clearly, the psychoanalytic study of the psychology of large groups can illuminate the area of ethnic conflicts and strategies of their resolution. Levine (2006) concludes that "it is our good fortune—and Vamik Volkan's enormous contribution to psychoanalysis and political science—that he has begun to help us address this task" (p. 280).

In sum, Volkan's contributions can be categorized into: (1) clinical texts outlining phenomemology, dynamics, and treatment strategies, (2) psychopolitical writings that advance the understanding of ethnic conflicts and offer strategies for their amelioration, and (3) actual fieldwork where such strategies are put into action via the efforts of "track II diplomacy." Volkan has also contributed to psychoanalysis by being the teacher and mentor of a large number of young mental health professionals. His over three-decade-long faculty tenure at the University of Virginia School of Medicine and his careful encouragement and grooming of aspiring psychoanalysts in Izmir and Istanbul, Turkey, give ample testimony of this dimension of his career.

Paul Fink, a former president of the American Psychiatric Association (1988–1989) and a distinguished psychiatric and psychoanalytic educator in his own right, has described Volkan, the man, in the following succinct passage:

> Volkan is a remarkable man. In his own quiet way, he has been able to have huge effects in bringing nations together, which is much more difficult than bringing individual people together. He is an excellent diplomat and uses all of his psychiatric and psychoanalytic skills to be a real force, nonintrusive but truly and exceptionally able to think through issues and problems and work with warring factions to bring about peaceful solutions. It is clear to many of Volkan's colleagues that he is a true peacemaker, someone who has risen above his birth, education, and his profession to take on tasks that are hardly imagined by most people. (personal communication, April 22, 2005)

It is, therefore, not surprising that Volkan was nominated for Nobel Prize for Peace in 2005, and although he did not get the award, his nomination still remains active. Regardless of the outcome of these efforts, it can be safely said that Volkan has already brought great respect to the field of psychoanalysis, to himself, and to those close to him, and, in the context of this chapter, to psychoanalysts who are Muslims.

OTHER MUSLIM ANALYSTS

In the emphasis upon recounting the highly public careers of Masud Khan and Vamik Volkan, it should not be overlooked that other Muslims have also made significant contributions to the psychoanalytic field. Some of these contributions have been on the administrative and social interface of psychoanalysis. Others pertain to its clinical enterprise. Foremost in the first category is leadership of IPA-UN (International Psychoanalytic Association–United Nations) Liason Committee by Afaf Mahfouz. Under friendly and unfriendly and just and unjust conditions,[8] Mahfouz has persevered in carrying on the task of establishing, sustaining, and advancing a dialogue between the psychoanalytic and diplomatic worlds. Her efforts have led to many opportunities for psychoanalysts to present their views on social topics (e.g., prejudice, women's rights) to various component groups of United Nations. This is a profound contribution to the field indeed.

Also to be noted are the educational contributions of Talaat Mohammed and Roknedin Safavi to the activities of the New Orleans and Cleveland Psychoanalytic Societies, respectively. Shahid Najeeb's contributions to the Australian Psychoanalytic Society are also notable. Still other Muslim psychoanalysts have held administrative positions and taught in psycho-analytic institutes and contributed to psychoanalytic literature.[9] Aisha Abbasi, a training and supervising analyst at the Michigan Psychoanalytic Institute, has written poignantly (1997) on interethnic transferences and countertransferences. Siassi's (2000; 2004) essays on cross-gender transfer-ences and on forgiveness, Mann's work (2004, 2006) on ethnic identity for-mation, and Sholevar's numerous contributions (e.g., 1985; 1989; 1995; 1997) in the realm of psychoanalytically informed family therapy are other outstanding examples of such contributions.

I too have written on important topics in psychoanalysis. Prominent among these are articles on optimal distance (1992a), pathological optimism and in-ordinate nostalgia (1996), psychodynamics of terrorism (1999a), distinction between needs and wishes (1999), mental pain (2000), forgiveness (2002), and dehumanization (2003). These articles, along with my earlier work on severe personality disorders, have been gathered in four books (Akhtar, 1992b; 1995; 1999b; 2003). However, it is my perspective on immigration, beginning with a *JAPA* (*Journal of the American Psychoanalytic Association*) award-winning paper (Akhtar 1995a) and culminating in a book (Akhtar 1999) and other subsequent contributions on the subject (Akhtar 2007; Akhtar and Choi 2002; Huang and Akhtar 2005), that is in many ways a centerpiece of my work. This work not only discusses the psychosocial variables that affect the outcome of migration and vicissitudes of subsequent identity trans-formation, but also the technical guidelines for treating immigrant patients, as well as the specific dilemmas of practicing as an immigrant analyst; my having edited books on the cross-currents between psychoanalysis and Indian thought (Akhtar 2005) and between psychoanalysis and Islam (this book) also demonstrates my drive to synthesize my psychoanalytic life with my Indian-Muslim origins. This last mentioned topic brings up an important question pertaining to the matters at hand, namely, are we discussing *Muslim* analysts or *immigrant Muslim* analysts or simply *immigrant* analysts here? What is the impact of immigration upon the life and work of the analysts that we are talking about?

THE ROLE OF IMMIGRATION

All the analysts mentioned here are immigrants. All have migrated as adults. All have had to undergo the bittersweet process of postmigration transforma-tion of identity (Akhtar 1995a; 1999) to a greater or lesser extent. How these well-intentioned, talented, and ambitious individuals have mastered this "trauma of dislocation" (Akhtar 2007) and how this geocultural laceration has impacted upon their clinical work, applied psychoanalytic endeavors, and theoretical outlooks are matters worthy of careful scrutiny. While a step-by-step correlation of the evolving professional careers of these analysts with meticulously gathered biographical details is needed for making definitive comments upon this issue, three broad trends are already discernable. These are exemplified by the works of Khan, Volkan, and me.

Khan, born in 1929, spent the first twenty-two years of his life under the British rule in India. He arrived in England in October, 1946 (i.e., merely ten months before India gained independence from the British and the region Khan hailed from "went" to the newly formed Pakistan). Not only was the timing of his migration tumultuous, but the fact that he was relocating to the very country that had colonized his motherland could hardly be devoid of psychological impact. Two other factors complicated his situation. Being the sole Indian in the British Psychoanalytic Society—indeed in the entire psychoanalytic world—Khan lacked homoethnic role models or mentors; ethnically, linguistically, and culturally he was utterly alone. Moreover, his being wealthy—not to say, his narcissistic flare of displaying that wealth—also contributed to the class-conscious British developing ambivalence toward him. Being analyzed and supervised by his white colonizers could hardly be easy for Khan, and for that matter, for the latter as well. One result of all this was that he did not—could not—assimilate his cultural background in his psychoanalytic work. "Had his background been more integrated and conceptualized, he might not have needed to enact it" (Cooper 1993, 113). Ilahi feels that acknowledging cultural differences was difficult for Khan since "it might have meant acknowledging his feelings of shame and opening up a whole area which he had closed off" (quoted in Cooper 1993, 99).

The split between home culture and adopted culture (Akhtar 1999) became professionally clandestine, though not without occasionally breaking through "Islamic pronouncements on his analysand's weakness" (Bollas 1989, 39). The latter tendency acquired a grotesque and caricatured shape toward the last years of Khan's life when he was physically ill and ostracized by his peers. The cultural wound at the core of his heart never healed. It bled profusely and became infected.

The impact of migration upon Vamik Volkan's career trajectory seems to be remarkably different. Volkan migrated not to England, but to the United States with which his Turkish background had little common history. The cultural shift was palpable but not acrimonious; Turkey of the 1960s after all, was an open and secular society with little Islamist fervor that is beginning to appear at its demographic corners today. Developing a rapid interest in the phenomena associated with ego-splitting and resultant disturbances of identity permitted Volkan to carry on the mourning work of migration in displaced fashion. An early article empathizing with African-American patients' poetry (Volkan 1963) and the inability of some borderline patients to negotiate over optimal distance with their love objects (Volkan and Corney 1968) also indicated of this preconscious leaning. More important was his early monograph about the political situation of Cyprus, from when he had hailed.

Interestingly, Volkan's clinical writings did not bring his immigrant status to bear upon his listening attitude and technical interventions. His work remained "All-American," but a dramatic shift to an exclusively psycho-political realm allowed this inner cultural dissonance a sublimated forum. Frequent international travel, repeated encounters with ethnically different groups, participation in track II diplomacy, founding of an interdisciplinary center for political psychology, and the authorship of a large body of psychopolitical texts became measures to creatively express the inner disjunction between the two cultures of his lived life. Braque's dictum that "art is a wound turned to light" thus found a vivid illustration.

In contrast to Khan's explosive cultural split and Volkan's self-healing through bringing warring ethnic factions together, I have taken a third route.[10] A long phase of study and investigation of ego-splitting (Akhtar and Byrne, 1983), identity diffusion (Akhtar 1984), and overt and covert divide in the manifestations of character pathology (Akhtar 1992) prepared me to undertake a direct study of the multifaceted impact of immigration upon identity (Akhtar 1995a; 1999a) and vulnerability to nostalgia (Akhtar 1999d). More significantly for the purpose of psychoanalytic theory and technique, I delineated the clinical strategies needed in the treatment of immigrant patients (Akhtar 1999) and also the technical challenges found by immigrant analysts (Akhtar 2006) in their daily work with both "native" and homoethnic patients. Unlike Khan's pseudo-cultural proclamations and Volkan's painstaking psychopolitcal efforts, I have attempted to synthesize my linguistically and culturally Indian Muslim self with my clinical conceptualizations in a direct manner. The difference between immigrant analyst, Muslim analyst, and simply an analyst has thus become heightened and diminished at the same time. The fine line between the accepted and the "other" has become more pronounced and thinner at the same time. Winnicott (1953), who championed the paradoxical nature of life in general and creativity in particular, would be happy.

CONCLUDING REMARKS

After commenting briefly upon the entry of Christians, Hindus, Sikhs, and Parsis in the profession of psychoanalysis, I have focused upon the role of

Muslims in the field. Taking the potential impact of the analyst's religion upon his empathic receptivity and technical interventions as a starting point, I have elucidated five areas (linguistic, developmental, technical, conceptual, and psychopolitical) of possible enrichment of psychoanalysis by Muslim analysts. In addition, I have devoted close attention to the lives and works of two renowned Muslim analysts, namely Masud Khan and Vamik Volkan. I have attempted to highlight Khan's important contributions to psychoanalysis and to locate his downfall in the sexually befuddled relational matrix and postcolonial ambience of British psychoanalysis. I have sought to delineate the progression of Volkan's rich and impressive career from a dedicated clinician of despair to a psychoanalytically informed healer of worldwide ethnic conflicts. I have also commented upon the impact of these and other such analysts being immigrants living in societies that differ remarkably from those of their origin.

My aim in this discourse has been to create awareness of the contributions of Muslim analysts to psychoanalysis and to make it possible for them to stand shoulder-to-shoulder with their Jewish, Christian, Hindu, Sikh, and Parsi colleagues without a cloak of ethnic invisibility. To be known in one's authenticity is, after all, one of the most significant gratifications of the ego. It is only with such personal integrity and social acceptance that one can enhance one's own efficacy and enter into genuine mutuality with others.

18

Whose Side Are You On?

Muslim Psychoanalysts Treating Non-Muslim Patients

Aisha Abbasi

Truth never changes, though over time we come to appreciate more and more of it, and this greater awareness is commensurate with the growth and development of the person who discovers and uses it.

—Shahid Najeeb, 2007, p. 235

In his book, *The Color of Water: A Black Man's Tribute to His White Mother*, James McBride (1996) writes,

As a boy, I always thought my mother was strange. She never cared to socialize with our neighbors. Her past was a mystery she refused to discuss. She drank tea out of a glass. She could speak Yiddish—she was the commander in chief of my house—The nuts and bolts of raising us was left to Mommy, who acted as chief surgeon for bruises ("Put iodine on it"), war secretary ("If somebody hits you, take your fist and crack'em"), religious consultant ("Put God first"), chief psychologist ("Don't think about it"), and financial advisor ("What's money if your mind is empty?"). Matters involving race and identity she ignored. (9)

Fortunately and unfortunately, that is something we as psychoanalysts cannot and should not do. Our patients bring in their emotional conflicts into treatment in a variety of ways. At times, patients are clearly aware of what they are struggling with and are able to speak about it directly. At other times, conflicts are highlighted indirectly in associations that have to do with patients' descriptions of their relationships, their appearance, their professional identities, the homes they live in, and their families. And at yet other moments, intrapsychic conflict manifests itself in treatment as patients talk about their religious, ethnic, and cultural identities. It is the psychoanalysts' task, with regard to all of these associations, to listen to these thoughts as rooted both in the patients' external and internal reality. For example, a patient, struggling in her analysis with issues relating to gender identity and her conflicts about being female versus being male, talked in a session about looking for a home in a neighborhood that felt "transitional" to her and wondered what she would have to give up to get the kind of home she wanted. I heard these associations as, being connected to her search in reality for a new home, her ongoing search for a place she felt she belonged to (rather than an old feeling of being unwanted, even by her mother), as well as a metaphor that described her current state of being in flux emotionally, with regard to her sense of herself as female versus male. I believe it is most helpful if an analyst can listen in the same way to patients' associations about their own and the analysts' ethnic, religious, and cultural identity. However, this is easier said than done.

We see over and over again in our day-to-day lives and in our work as analysts, the difficulty often encountered by the speaker and the listener when the topic turns to issues of religion, ethnicity, and culture; in particular, when the speaker and listener have to converse about differences between the two of them and deal with prejudices residing in the minds of both. This chapter intends to address particular clinical issues that come up in psychoanalytic treatment when the analyst and patient come from very different backgrounds. In particular, I will be talking about matters of religious and ethnic identity as they have come up in my work (as a psychoanalyst from a Muslim background) with patients in America, before and after September 11, 2001.

BEFORE AND AFTER SEPTEMBER 11

In an earlier article (Abbasi 1997), I described my work with a young Jewish man who had very negative feelings about Muslims. In that article I wrote,

> All patients, and all analysts, are different from each other. But in all analyses, the way in which the patient experiences and uses the difference between himself and the analyst is determined by the patients' needs and conflicts. There are some analyses in which the differences may not come up in bright shades and colors. There are others, as with my patient, where the differences present in an array of blinding, dizzying colors because it serves a certain, defensive, purpose. (5)

In my work with that particular patient, I noted that there was a fine and fluctuating tension between the world of external reality and the world of internal perceptions and meanings in the patient's mind. I was impressed by the way in which the external differences were first emphasized by the patient, creating in his mind major obstacles in the path of the psychoanalytic work. However, as I acknowledged the external realities he was talking about (the conflict between Muslims and Jews in the Mideast, his immersion in Orthodox Judaism at a certain point in his life, the teachings of his Rabbi who referred to Muslims as "dogs") and attempted to understand what these external realities might represent for him, analytic exploration could then deepen. We gradually learned that there were many reasons he needed to emphasize the external differences between us. We also understood over time that these reasons had to do with his internal struggles and his childhood history with his mother, father, and siblings. It is significant that as I worked with that young man, many years before the September 2001 attacks on the World Trade Center, I experienced very little inner tension within myself, with regard to the religious differences between us. It was not difficult for me to listen to my patient's associations when he referred to Muslims as dogs and when he told me about other very negative thoughts he had toward Muslims, as well as the derogatory remarks made by one of his Rabbis about Muslims.

At that time, I found my own feelings to be in sharp contrast with comments made by a Jewish analytic colleague whom I discussed the case with. He remarked that if he had a patient in analysis with him who made such derogatory remarks about Jews, he could not analyze the patient. In a similar vein, Knafo (1999) has written about a man she began work with when she was a doctoral candidate. The patient was a Jew whose parents were concentration camp survivors. In his second session with the analyst, the patient described sadomasochistic masturbation fantasies in which he imagined naked women about to die in Nazi gas chambers, describing that at the point of their imagined deaths, he would achieve orgasm. The analyst became aware, as the patient looked at her while talking about this, that he had included the analyst in his violent, sadistic fantasy. She experienced a sense of horror and felt she could not work with him. Knafo (1999) writes that she wondered later what made it impossible for her to treat this man and felt that she was "unable to process this man's hostility in a therapeutic manner because it was made manifest in the most abhorrent imagery from the Holocaust."

I believe that it was not a strain for me to be quite optimally analytic in the treatment of the patient I described in my 1999a article, because his attacks upon Muslims felt rather safely distant from my life experiences. Even though I was a Muslim, I was born and raised in Pakistan, a country where I had no actual contact with Jewish people. The Mideast conflict between Jews and Muslims was something I had grown up hearing about and, from time to time, the Pakistani government certainly voiced sympathy for the Muslims in the Mideast. However, these events had not touched me (or so I thought) in a meaningful way during my childhood, teenage, and early adult life. I came to America in 1987. Other than a few interactions with Jewish people during earlier travels to Europe, it was only after I came to America that I became more involved with Jews. It therefore seemed to me when I was treating the patient I wrote about earlier, that his denigration of Muslims did not touch me in a very personal way, did not feel like a narcissistic attack on my sense of my ethnic and religious identity, and was quite comfortable for me to deal with as simply another analytic issue. In retrospect, I believe that in addition to his feelings about the Jewish-Muslim conflict not being "experience-near" for me, another reason I may have seemingly felt optimally able to explore his feelings and fantasies, was that I was warding off a clearer and deeper awareness in my own mind, of his intense hostility and sadism, my anxiety about similar feelings in myself and my fear of his destructive wishes toward me (Abbasi 1997). Such understanding is often available to us only in retrospect.

I clearly noticed a difference in my ability to listen and to explore my patients' feelings and fantasies about the differences between us after the events of September 11, 2001. The Mideast conflict between Muslims and Jews no longer remained a "distant" issue in my analytic work with patients in America. Muslim terrorists had bombed the World Trade Center in New York. The differences between Muslims and non-Muslims were very real and close to home now, both for my patients and for me. Let me quote here from Leary's (2006) article, "How Race is Lived in the Consulting Room" in which she beautifully sums up the change that occurred in America after September 11. She writes,

> In the intervening years since September 11, the face of race in America has almost literally been transformed. Racial reasoning continues to include the familiar declension into 'us versus them' even as those accepted as 'us' reflect new alliances—a growing number of New Yorkers say that they're witnessing a change in race relations since the terrorist attacks. The shift in racial attitudes, noticed in the days and weeks following September 11 but enduring since then, has been manifest in an increased rapprochement between blacks and whites and a lessened tendency to 'overreact' [sic] to perceived injustices. By contrast, the dynamics of prejudice and defensive exclusion now extend most openly to South Asians, to people from Middle Eastern backgrounds, to those who are Muslim. This, sadly, has become the psychology of the new "normal." (75)

My patients reacted to the disastrous, violent tragedy of September 11 in a variety of ways. All were obviously deeply shaken by the sudden, catastrophic event. For each one, it brought up personal tragedies and fears. They were very concerned that I might be experiencing problems of being harassed in my day-to-day life. In terms of this event highlighting our religious differences, most of my patients initially responded by reassuring me that they knew I was not like the terrorists. They also expressed relief that they were not like the terrorists.

Sitting with my patients in the weeks following September 11, I found myself recognizing, dimly, the defensive nature of these remarks, but also feeling relieved by them. I felt limited in my ability to fully process the material in a meaningful way. I could not clearly understand why this was happening. A woman who had been in analysis with me four times a week for about three years suddenly announced she had to cut back to three times weekly. She cited financial difficulties. The announcement felt abrupt and I tried to work with her around the idea that some anxieties lay behind this decision. She seemed quite ready to consider this, but nonetheless felt her decision was a reasonable extension of financial concerns she had been describing in the analysis over the last several months. I had a vague feeling I was missing something, but did not know what that was. Over the next few months, I became more and more aware that my sense of analytic dislocation after September 11 had to be better understood. My private associations unfolded into a growing realization that I was affected by this event, not just because it brought the Jewish-Muslim conflict near to me in the present, but also because it evoked memories I had suppressed—memories from my younger years, memories I knew about but had minimized. These had to with anti-Semitic comments made in my home by my parents during my childhood and adolescent years, as they talked about the daily news or discussed the situation in the Middle East with their friends. I struggled with a clearer awareness of the problem; here I was, in America, most of my practice consisting of Jewish patients, some of my best friends being Jewish and having worked with a Jewish analyst who had worked very hard to help me address these issues in my analysis. And I believed I had dealt with my feelings about the differences between us. I was humbled by the realization that I had more work to do, with regard to my own prejudices; work I had not felt emotionally ready to undertake in earlier years. As I felt somewhat more in touch with my own prejudices and their link to my earlier history and my parents, I became aware (in a newer way) of my fear of my own feelings of rage toward my early caretakers—a rage dealt with through faulty identifications with them, and displaced onto various others, including Jews, these "others," seemingly safer targets than my parents. A fairly standard understanding of prejudice! In the midst of these painful, slowly growing self-realizations, I went back to talking with my patient about why she had cut back her sessions so soon after September 11. I wondered whether the bombing of the World Trade Center had scared her for many different reasons. Haltingly, she now revealed that her husband's retirement portfolio, which they depended on for their living expenses, had been unstable before the events of September 11, but had capsized after the attacks. Her husband had said it was all because of "fucking Muslims." He'd like to take all of them out to sea and drown them. They had ruined everything good. I felt we were finally able to speak about what had felt unspeakable to both of us. As we analyzed her rage, her fear of it, her sense of split loyalties. and her distrust of me, the patient became freer and bolder in her exploration of these feelings and about seven months later, increased her analytic frequency back up to four times a week.

CONDUCTING PSYCHOANALYSIS ACROSS THE BOUNDARIES OF "DIFFERENCE"

A review of the psychoanalytic literature beginning from the early 1950s and until very recent years, demonstrates a certain diversity of opinion among analysts in terms of how patients' thoughts about differences of ethnicity, religion, and cultural background between them and their analysts can be understood and worked with. In 1954, Oberndorf wrote, "Nevertheless, from a therapeutic standpoint, transference in its positive form is most likely to be easily established and examined (analyzed) between patient and hospital and patient and physician if their psychological biases do not differ too widely. The fear of the stranger, originating in the young child's feeling of security in the accustomed, and need for protection in the face of the unfamiliar person or place are almost instinctive (p. 757)."

In his article, Oberndorf clearly seemed to be suggesting that patients could best be treated by analysts who were of a similar background. He cited some specific situations in which a patient might prefer an analyst of a different background, but for the most part felt that if analyst and patients came from a similar background, the patient could be more easily helped in terms of understanding his psychological issues. Almost fifty years later, Leary (2006) wrote: "Race and ethnicity are an important area for analytic inquiry. The analyst's working subjectivity regarding his or her racial assumptions must be subject to honest and compassionate scrutiny. This requires a willingness to bear a measure of discomfort in order to make it possible to learn with and from patients. If Winnicott was correct in suggesting that there's no such thing as a baby, then perhaps there is no such thing as a black or a white (without the other). Whenever patients talk about the Other, they're inevitably talking about themselves, and so are we" (87).

In fifty years, psychoanalytic theory has obviously come a long way in looking at issues of differences between patients and analysts as matters that need to be fully and clearly explicated and investigated in treatment, rather than being obstacles or hurdles to psychoanalytic work.

Some very significant contributions have been made by various analysts in the area of addressing special issues of theory and technique while working with people across cultures, religions, and race. These include Devereux (1953),

Bernard (1953), Grier (1967), Schachter and Butts (1968), Calnek (1970), and Ticho (1971). Further important contributions were made by Fisher (1971), Garza-Guerrero (1973), Myers (1977), and by Goldberg, Myers, and Zeifman (1974). Further articles on this topic were published in the 1980s by Zaphiropoulos (1982), Basch-Kahre (1984), and Kakar (1985). In the 1990s, psychoanalytic literature moved beyond the initial issues of transference and countertransference in such treatments. More sophisticated problems were grappled with in some very important articles written by Holmes (1992), Amati-Mehler (1993), and Roland (1994). Akhtar's seminal article, "A Third Individuation: Immigration, Identity, and the Psychoanalytic Process," (1995a) was published in the *Journal of the American Psychoanalytic Association* and it captured a wealth of ideas regarding the effect of immigration on one's identity and the impact of immigration on the psychoanalytic process. Moncayo (1998), Apprey (1999), Tang and Gardner (1999), and Knafo (1999) further enhanced our understanding of these issues with their articles. In addition, Leary (1995; 1997; 2000; 2003) presented her evolving ideas about the impact of race and racial differences on the psychoanalytic process in a series of articles. Psychoanalysts obviously no longer had doubts about the viability and success of analytic treatment conducted when the analyst and patient had major differences of class, culture, race, or religion. Their explorations were more focused on understanding specific issues that might arise in such treatments.

In a book chapter titled "The End of Analyzability," Moskowitz (1996) concludes,

> Freud wrote that psychoanalysis is a cure through love. We are limited in our ability to work psychoanalytically with people only by or in our inability to love and be loved by them. People have loved and been loved across all boundaries of culture and class. The question of analyzability then becomes a question of the analysts' capacity to understand the other, to be able to enter into the patient's psychic world. To the extent that a life can be understood, it can be analyzed. Each analyst can learn not who is analyzable, but, to paraphrase Green "who is analyzable by me?" (191)

My own particular view with regard to specific issues of theory and technique in cross-cultural analyses is as follows:

- Patients can be effectively and usefully analyzed by analysts whose backgrounds (culture/race/ethnicity/religion) are very different from those of the patient.
- In my 1999a article, I suggested that "particular differences between analysts and patients may cause a kind of 'cloudiness' on the analytic horizon which makes it difficult for the analyst to see things which would be

fairly simple to see in other analyses where the gross and obvious differences within the analytic dyad, and its various meanings for patient and analyst, are not such an issue" (7). In a similar vein, Basch-Kahre (1984) also felt that the analyst's lack of knowledge with regard to the specifics of development, child rearing, and values and conventions of the analysand's background, make the analyst blind to the usual features that might indicate to us that the analysand is approaching conflict territory. She believed that these difficulties cause analysis to proceed at a slower pace, but did not thwart it. I am not even sure that these difficulties cause analysis to proceed at a slower pace. It seems to me that these difficulties are something that the analyst needs to be aware of, but the more the analyst is able to talk about them with the patient, the less likely it is that they will cause insurmountable problems.

- My stance is that differences between patient and analyst are a reality that must be acknowledged in the analysis by both, and then a way must be found to understand the differences, first at the level of manifest reality and then as they relate to the patient's inner conflicts. This is very much in-line with technique proposed by many other analysts, including, for example, Holmes (1992).
- Working across differences becomes difficult for the analyst when the analyst's narcissistic equilibrium is disrupted by the patient's comments about "differences."

Leary (2006) captures this last mentioned point very well when she writes, "racial enactments are occasions, at least, potentially, of clinical productivity to the extent that the analytical couple is able to tolerate and learn from their engaging in each other's psychology. At the same time, they are also moments of clinical exposure for both the analyst, as well as for the patient. Racial enactments typically involve the very issues—idealization, envy, jealousy, and devaluation, likely to upset one's narcissistic equilibrium" (85).

She goes on to say, "I believe that in the consulting room, racial enactments involve instances of stereotype activation. Patient, analyst, or both are confronted with a self-image that threatens self-condemnation from the other. In addition to interfering with narcissistic equilibrium, the very effort to overcome the stereotype can disrupt the capacity for what Holmes (1999) elegantly describes as a therapist's ability to be resourceful" (86). An example of this from my own clinical work is that of a young Jewish woman who had occasion to enter my home office through my foyer rather than the usual separate entry because of remodeling going on in my home. She turned to me at the beginning of her session and said that as she had walked through the foyer today she smelled what seemed to her to be Pakistani or Indian food cooking in the kitchen. It was an unpleasant smell for her and reminded her of the slums in London, a city she had recently spent several months in. I found myself feeling shocked at her remarks, surprised that the smell of my native foods, so beloved and comforting to me, would be so repulsive to her. She registered the look on my face before she lay down on the couch. As we talked about what it evoked for her, I began to wonder why I had felt so shocked. I then realized that her remarks had evoked old feelings of shame in me that had very little to do with food and more to do with early caretakers in my life. In other words, my narcissistic equilibrium had been disturbed, and it made it difficult for me to work effectively and optimally as an analyst until I could find my bearings again.

I will now present detailed clinical material from my work with a patient who had been seeing me for a few years before September 11, 2001. I believe this material highlights the very points that I have just written about.

CLINICAL MATERIAL

Mrs. A was about twenty-seven years old when she started seeing me. She had recently moved from Florida, where she had been born and raised. The only daughter of a father who had migrated to America from Spain in his late twenties and an American-born mother of Polish descent, Mrs. A had gone to college in Florida and then to graduate school on the East coast, then started working at a well-known financial institution in New York. She met her husband at a national conference. They worked for the same company, but he was living and working in Michigan. After they became involved with each other and realized they wanted to get married, she decided she would move to Michigan, feeling that the lifestyle would be less busy and, financially, things would be easier when they had children, if she wanted to work part-time.

Mrs. A came to see me after she had her first child, a son. She was concerned that her childhood history might affect her ability to be a good mother and was aware of certain problems in her relationship with her husband. Mrs. A's father was a successful physician who had come to America for his residency training. Her mother met her father at the hospital where he was in training and she was a nurse. After a romantic, whirlwind courtship, the two married and her mother sponsored her father for a green card, thus making it easier for him to stay on in the country and become an American citizen. Mrs. A's father became very successful professionally and quite wealthy. The mother did not work after the first few years of her marriage.

Mrs. A was born four years after her parents got married. Her childhood memory of her parents was that they were essentially loving, but physically often absent, very much involved in the social scene. She was left in the care of competent, kind nannies, who were often changed because one or both of her parents found some flaw in them. Her parents did not seem to be aware of the impact of all of this on her. She was a very pretty, engaging child and charmed all who met her, with her bright smile and intellectual precocity. It was only after a few years of analysis that Mrs. A could even begin to be more in touch with how lonely and isolated she felt in those early years of her life and recalled thinking of herself as a princess in a lavish prison.

When Mrs. A was about five, her mother became pregnant. Her understanding over the years was that this had not been a planned pregnancy. Apparently, her father had wanted a second child soon after Mrs. A was born, but her mother felt "one was enough." Now, in her second pregnancy, her mother became depressed and felt physically sick most of the time. Mrs. A's relationship with her mother, already limited to begin with, became even more painful as her mother stayed in bed more and more and withdrew from everyone. Years later, her mother admitted she had wanted to have an abortion, but the father would not agree. In a further tragic twist of fate, the baby, a boy, was stillborn at term; the result, doctors said, of a cord around the neck that cut off the baby's air supply during the last phase of labor. Life for Mrs. A became even more stifling. Her mother became severely depressed after the stillbirth and had to be treated with antidepressant medications. Mrs. A had vague memories of nurses attending to her mother at home, while mother spent more and more time in her room. She recalled her mother sobbing one day, saying to her father, "He was so blue . . . the poor baby was so blue."

Slowly, life got back to "normal" in their household. The parents resumed their rather frenzied social activities; Mrs. A was enrolled in a private school and started taking lessons in music, tennis, swimming, and horseback riding. She developed into an externally very sophisticated, talented young girl, hiding tremendous anxiety and depressive feelings behind a veneer of great charm. When she was about fourteen, there was another storm in her life. She heard loud arguments between her parents and threats of divorce. Neither of them brought up the issue with her directly and she felt terrified that if she asked, whatever she was told would be too painful to bear. Finally, her mother told her that her father was having an affair with a divorced nurse at his hospital. They had been seen around town, with the nurse's nine-year-old son in tow. Neither parent seemed to have viewed this as being in any way linked to the death of their baby boy, over eight years ago.

Mrs. A had vivid memories of those months, during which her mother would yell and scream at her father and her father would respond nonchalantly, saying she was making a big deal out of nothing. He claimed he and this woman were just friends and it would all "blow over." At times, her mother would break dishes and throw the television remote at the father, shouting that if it hadn't been for her, he wouldn't even be in America—she had helped him get a green card and become a citizen here. The father would threaten to take the mother to a psychiatrist, insisting that she was "losing it." Mrs. A would at times intervene, insisting he tell them the truth and pointing out that her mother was not crazy, only reasonably angry and frustrated. The father would smile and say that she was a good girl and she should not worry herself. By the end of that year, the affair seemed to have ended. Again, her life resumed its usual routine, her parents somehow managing, at least superficially, to put the betrayal and rancor behind them. She could not understand how really terrible things could happen and then never be talked about again.

Mrs. A described her husband as a warm, loving, good-looking Jewish man. She did not convert to Judaism before her marriage, but gradually became more involved with his synagogue after they got married. Over the years of her analysis, she became seriously interested in converting formally to Judaism. This desire became more marked after she had her son. The main problems she was aware of when she started treatment were her anger at men when she felt disdained and put down, either at work or in personal relationships. She was afraid she would say something so angry in response that she would be inappropriate. In addition, she felt very quickly suspicious of her husband and was afraid he would have an affair. This was causing great tension between them; she also recognized, hazily, that she was very quick to feel neglected by her friends and her husband if they were slightly distracted when she wanted their attention. She was a very loving, dedicated mother, but was aware of an inner strain she experienced, a sense of impatience with her son, when he was "clingy and needy." We could see the links between these issues and her relationships with her parents, as well as the cumulative effects of the quiet emotional neglect she had suffered as a child and the more dramatically traumatic effect of the events when she was about six and fourteen.

During the course of Mrs. A's analysis, much work was done on helping her understand the impact that her childhood events had on her. Issues related to her father's immigration to America, the fact that he had not been born and raised here, and the connection between this and me being an immigrant analyst whose ethnicity was different from hers were also quite visible in the analysis.

However, these issues came into very sharp focus after the terrorists' bombing of the World Trade Center in September 2001. Soon after the bombing, Mrs. A reported at the beginning of a session that she was having thoughts that felt "paranoid" to her. She said that she had seen my husband outside my home (where I had my office) recently, and it made her think about Al Qaeda. She was having "strange" thoughts that perhaps my husband and I were connected to Al Qaeda and that I might turn her in to them if they were able to take over America. Her thought was that I would turn her over to them because she was a non-Jewish woman, married to a Jewish man and, as such, would be seen as an enemy of the Muslims and of Al Qaeda. Over the next few weeks, she had several thoughts about whose side I was on. I said she obviously had no way of knowing whose side I was on, but it was important for us to understand how this tragic reality of the World Trade Center bombing was affecting her perceptions of me and her feelings about our analytic relationship. I will now present three sessions that took place a few months after the attacks of September 11, 2001.

Session 1: Monday

The patient said she realized she was late with the payment of her analytic bill from last month. She was waiting to confirm the amount of money available in their checking account with her husband. He had been very busy the last few days and was away in the evenings for meetings. After a pause, she went on to say that she was having thoughts about her husband's colleague, Z. A few months ago, Z had asked for donations to a certain organization. Z is an Arab American who was born and raised in America. Recently, her husband laughingly said that maybe Z was funding Al Qaeda with their donated money. The patient added, "I don't really believe that." Then she went on to say that driving to her analytic session today, she saw that the Star of David in the window of a new synagogue close to my home had been broken. It was so sad, this enmity between people. Apparently, the window had been broken by an anti-Semitic group. She felt more Jewish, more and more identified with Jews like her husband. I said perhaps she was having more concerns about my being non-Jewish, a Muslim. She said "No, I don't think of the conflict in the Middle East as being a Jewish-Muslim conflict. I think of it only as being a Jewish-Arab conflict." I said this was quite remarkable, the way she was delineating the Mideast conflict. She must be quite aware that the Arabs who were in conflict with the Jews in the Mideast were Muslims. Maybe she was afraid of looking into all of this with me. I reminded her that soon after the terrorist attacks, she had been afraid I might hand her over to Al Qaeda. I said, "You've been wondering who is on whose side. I wonder if in addition to the religious, ethnic, and cultural reality that we are both currently dealing with, in terms of the differences between us, could some of these feelings you're describing also have to do with the split loyalty you experienced in yourself with regards to your parents? Like the Jews and the

Muslims, and you being able to see the issues on both sides. As a child, you at times you felt your mother was right, and other times your father was. At certain moments, you felt badly for one of them or the other. At yet, other moments, you didn't know who to trust. Perhaps, what you're feeling with me now mirrors the struggles you experienced as a child about who was on whose side?"

Session 2: Tuesday

The patient walked in, asking rather insistently whether we were starting a minute or so late. I checked and said that by my clock we were starting on time. She said she was almost sure we were starting a little late. I then said maybe we would understand more about this later. In the meantime, I would make sure we had the usual forty-five minute session.

The patient lay down on the couch and began to talk about her son B. He was still sick. His chest was congested and he had a slight fever. She and her husband, D., were further upset yesterday because his mother, L., called from the emergency room of a local hospital. She said she thought she was having a heart attack. It turned out she was having palpitations. L. tended to make up things; at times she lied outright.

Mrs. A. then talked more about her mother-in-law, whom she disliked because of her condescending, intrusive behavior. D. was worried about Mrs. A's decision to not go to his mother's summer home in Northern Michigan that year. Mrs. A said she had decided she would stay in town with her son during the week in August that she generally took Ben to be with his grandmother; because she was fed up with the mean, unsympathetic way in which L. treated everyone. However, D. was worried this would really upset his mother. He wanted to make an excuse, telling his mother that his wife had a friend's wedding to participate in that week in August.

I said, "So, you're saying L. lies and so does D." Mrs. A responded, "Yes, I guess sometimes people are afraid to tell each other the truth. For some reason, I'm thinking about my parents now. I know I haven't resolved all my issues about them. You were saying recently that I often view my mother as all-good and my father as all-bad. That is true. I seem to see my mother more as a victim—but I am beginning to feel freer with her in terms of disagreeing with her. I'm not as worried about being mad at her, so I don't feel I have to overcompensate by being nicey-nice. I wish it didn't feel so painful though; sometimes she really gaslights me. We talk about things that were bad in my childhood and she behaves as if I'm distorting things."

I wondered, in light of these associations, whether Mrs. A felt I had been gaslighting her with regard to the time at the beginning of the session. She said, "I thought you didn't want to acknowledge your clock could be slow." I asked what she thought would make me not want to acknowledge something like that. She said she wasn't sure. I then asked if she thought this distrust of me and the idea that I might try to gaslight her could have to do with issues we were speaking about yesterday. Mrs. A responded, "I think that is your issue. I don't know how you got to the Jewish-Muslim issue yesterday." I said it was meaningful that she couldn't remember. After all, she had come in yesterday talking about her conversation with her husband and his laughing comment that his friend was funding Al-Qaeda with money donated by them. She had had these thoughts right after she talked about not having paid me yet.

In an angry, uncomfortable tone, Mrs. A said, "I still think it's your issue. I've never had thoughts like that about you." I asked, "Never?" With an embarrassed laugh, she said, "No, that's not true. I did feel after 9/11 that you might turn me in to Al Qaeda for being married to a Jewish man. It's really scary talking about these things here." I asked what made it so scary. She answered, "Hate gets stirred up. Windows might get broken, like that star of David window, other ones. . . . " "Ah," I said. "Which other windows come to mind?" In a startled tone, she replied, "So strange, but I thought of your waiting room window. Then I had a sudden urge to break everything there . . . now I'm thinking about the lovely blue flowers you have there today [painted daisies] and I feel as thought I want to cut off the heads of all the blue flowers."

Session 3: Wednesday

Mrs. A came in five minutes late. She said B.'s doctors thought he might need breathing treatments. "They suspect he has an allergic asthma—gets this way when he has a viral infection. He will grow out of it. It's difficult, having to see different doctors in the practice." I asked how many there were, in all. She said about six or seven. Whom she sees depends on who is available on a given day, at a given time. I said, "Sounds somewhat like the multiple nannies going through your home when you were little."

She said, yes, she wasn't too happy with this practice. In fact, she wasn't happy with her internist either. He was quite rude. She wondered why she stayed on with him; it was as though she had to choose between people who were good at what they did but were mean, or people who were inefficient and inept but comforting. "I think that's what I was feeling with you yesterday, that if I get mad at you, I will no longer be able to get your good help. You'd think, 'who do you think you are?'" I asked what she imagined would make me think that. Mrs. A replied, "That's like my mother. My anger is always unacceptable to her. It feels crazy to me that I would be sitting in your waiting room, thinking what it would be like to break everything. I think that's why I went to the thought of just cutting off the heads of the flowers—as though that's less crazy." I said, "Can it be that when you are so angry, you begin to feel afraid you are like your mother used to be with your father at times? And maybe he was right that she was crazy—and so are you. Not just angry, but crazy."

"I do feel crazy about the whole Jewish-Muslim issue. I still feel you are finding meanings in my words that have to do with your thoughts." I asked if she was worried that I was an anti-Semite. She said, "Well, no, not that, but I feel I didn't even realize that Palestinians and Yasser Arafat are all Muslims." I said I was sure that was correct. In an astonishing mental process designed to protect her from unacceptable feelings, she seemed to have successfully compartmentalized various pieces of knowledge she had. I asked if she had ever watched the television coverage after 9/11, in which there was constant information about the terrorists being Muslim, the Palestinians being Muslim, and so forth. She laughed, anxiously, and said that of course she had. She really must have blocked this all out. "Why do you suppose you need to do that?" I asked. "What could be so frightening about these thoughts and feelings?"

Mrs. A responded, "I am thinking about the terrorists flying into the WTC windows. I wonder what you think of those people and of others like them. It's similar to my thoughts about smashing your waiting room window. I didn't tell you before, but I had also thought I wanted to smash everything you have on display on that long table in the waiting room. I imagined these are things your other patients gave you, perhaps those who finished treatment. I wondered about the candle I gave you last Christmas. It wasn't there. It feels as though everyone else is more important to you, even the patients who've left. I am still here and you seem to have forgotten me." I said, "I think this is how you felt with your parents throughout your childhood, especially with your mother and most specially, when she became so depressed, self-absorbed, and unavailable to you after your brother was born dead." Mrs. A started crying and was quiet for a long time. Then she said through her tears, "Blue was the color my mother said he was, when he was born—like the flowers in your waiting room that I wanted to chop off. I am so angry. I just want to be your most special patient, your most special little girl." And then sobbing, she added, "I just wanted to be my mom's special little girl."

CONCLUDING REMARKS

I will leave a detailed exploration of this clinical material to my reader. I believe the material speaks for itself, in terms of elucidating ideas I have brought up earlier in this chapter. I would like only to say that I see myself primarily as a psychoanalyst, attempting to understand my patients' material. I am not a sociologist, nor a religious leader, member of a particular advocacy group, or a political activist. If I find myself tempted in an analytic session to behave as one of the above, I realize that something the patient has said is getting to me in a very personal way and try to think about it. At times, I do get pulled into enactments around such material and can then understand what happened, only after it has happened. For the most part though, I find over and over again that the seemingly most external events being described by a patient are ultimately deeply connected to internal feelings and personal issues. It is a helpful beacon of light in the darkness that threatens to engulf an analysis, when "transferences of alienation" (Lieberman 1997) are activated and cause the patient to feel that she cannot possibly be understood or continue treatment with an analyst because of their external differences.

Notes

CHAPTER 1. BASIC HISTORY AND
TENETS OF ISLAM: A BRIEF INTRODUCTION

1. This historical review is drawn largely from Hodgson (1974) and Esposito (1999).

2. This debt began before the creation of earth, when human souls collectively recognized God's authority (*Quran*, 7:172). Each soul enters its human body within the first 120 days of gestation. Each individual is born innocent, without sin, and with an innate inclination toward God. Once individuals mature, around adolescence, they become morally accountable for their actions.

3. There are several interesting distinctions between the Quranic and Biblical narrative of Adam and Eve. First, Satan, not Eve tempted Adam according to the *Quran* (20:120). Furthermore, God forgave Adam and Eve because they repented; therefore, there is no tradition of "original sin." The primary lesson of the Quranic story is that humans will inevitably sin, mankind has a tendency to forget their responsibility to follow God's command, and God will forgive those who repent.

4. In a famous tradition of the Prophet, Allah lists ninety-nine names for "himself" to capture the multifaceted nature of the divine essence, with ninety-nine representing an essence that can never be completely captured. Allah has no gender; however, there is not a gender neutral pronoun in Arabic, therefore, God is often referred to as "He" without the connotation of masculinity. Among God's names are The Most Forgiving (Al-Raheem), The Most Generous (Al-Kareem), and The Most Knowledgeable (Al-Raouf). Many Muslim names are prefixed by "Abd," which literally means servant, such that Abdul-Raheen is the servant of the Most Forgiving. These ninety-nine names are discussed throughout Muslim literature and poetry and expressed in artwork throughout different cultures.

5. See Rahman (1994) for a more comprehensive and nuanced reference to the contents of the *Quran*.

6. Throughout Muslim cultures, whether Arab, African, Indian, Indonesian, and so forth, "Salam-u-'alaikum" is a universal Muslim greeting that means "Peace be onto you."

7. Among the most famous traditions of the Prophet is: "Verily, actions are judged by intentions." The Prophet urged Muslims to consider why an action is performed, and he cautioned his followers that without the proper intention, ritual acts of worship would lose their moral charge and be rendered meaningless, empty movements of the body.

8. Ibid., 48–49.

9. *Quran* 94:5–8, "(5) And, behold, with every hardship comes ease: (6) Verily, with every hardship comes ease! (7) Hence, when thou art freed [from distress], remain steadfast, (8) and unto thy Sustainer turn with love."

10. *Quran* 2:155–156, "(155) An most certainly shall We try you by means of danger, and hunger, and loss of worldly goods, of lives and [labor's] fruits. But give glad tidings unto those who are patient in adversity (156) who, when calamity befalls them, say, 'Verily, unto God do we belong and, verily, unto Him we shall return.'" This last verse is commonly expressed to a Muslim whose loved one has passed away, emphasizing the cycle of life and the transitory quality of worldly life.

11. See *Quran* 96:1–5, "Read by in the name of thy Sustainer, who has created, (2) created man out of a germ-cell. (3) Read—for your Lord is the Most Bountiful One, (4) Who taught (man) by the use of the pen [verse] (5) Taught man what he did not know." There are many translations of the *Quran*, and Asad's (1980) is used in this manuscript.

12. Worshipping anything aside from God is considered the most grievous sin in Islam because it undermines God's unique and ultimate authority.

13. The issue of gender relationships in Islam is complicated by interpretation of sacred text, regional cultural practices, and historical factors (Ahmed 1992).

14. In Shiite theology. the ummah's religious authority after the Prophet's death is passed down to the Prophet's cousin (the Prophet has no surviving son) Ali and are called "Imams." Imam is an Arabic word that connotes the religious leader and is also used to name the leader of a mosque in both Sunni and Shiite traditions. By the eighth century, Ali's great-great grandson Ja'far Al-Siddique, an eminent Islamic legal scholar, became recognized by Shiites as the Imam of the Muslim community. The genealogy of Shiite Imams split after Imam Ja'far into the two dominant Shiite sects known as the Twelvers and the Seveners, who differ with regards to the continuation of the lineage after the seventh Imam. These two sects continue to be important today; the modern Islamic Republic of Iran is ruled by Twelver Shiism doctrine. The Ismailis, a dominant group within the Seveners, played an important role in the global proselytizing of Islam and the development of many Muslim institutions, such as Al-Azhar University of Cairo, Egypt, and Agha Khan University in Karachi, Pakistan.

15. The Safavid dynasty beginning in the fifteenth century, in which Twelver Shiism was the state religion, peaked its expansion in the seventeenth century, and was limited to modern day Iran and parts of eastern Iraq.

16. Since the Iranian edict on Salman Rushdie's book, *Satanic Verses* (1989), the term *fatwa* has been misused to mean a death threat. A *fatwa* is decreed when a new legal question that is not addressed in the *Quran*, Sunna, or by case precedent.

17. Many Muslims philosophers would cite Quranic verses (45:3–5) such as, "(3) Behold, in the heavens as well as on earth there are indeed messages for all who [are willing to] believe, (4) And in your own nature, an in [that of] all the animals which He scatters [over the earth] there are messages for people who are endowed with inner certainty, (5) And in the succession of night and day, and the means of subsistence which God sends down from the skies, giving life thereby to the earth after it had been lifeless, and in the change of winds: [in all this] there are messages for people who use their reason."

18. Contemporary Arab psychiatrists argue this is among the earliest writings in psychotherapy.

19. See Leonard (2003) for an overview of the patterns of development of Muslim American communities.

20. Jackson (2005) provides a detailed account of the relationship of African American theology and the evolution of African-American Sunni Islam.

21. For worldview and cultural assessments, see Josephson and Peteet's (2004) *Handbook of Spirituality and Worldview in Clinical Practice*, as well as the Committee on Cultural Psychiatry Group for the Advancement of Psychiatry's (2002) *Cultural Assessment in Clinical Psychiatry*.

CHAPTER 2. THE PROPHET MUHAMMAD: MAN, FOUNTAINHEAD, AND LEADER

1. I will spell important words such as Muhammad, the *Qur'an*, Makkah, and Madinah in the closest way they sound in Arabic. I will keep the way others spell them in my reference to them.

2. I am using the word Orientalist to describe those who used knowledge as power in the service of political programs. I realize that there were many "Orientlists" who were not part of these systems. I prefer to call them Westerners, who wrote sensitively and fairly about the East.

3. The depth of Orientalism is illustrated by Gibbs. Despite a thoughtful introduction and warnings about bias, Gibbs states that the Muslims think of themselves as Muslims and not Mohammadans. They consider that name derisive because they do not worship Mohammad. And yet he called his Book "Mohammedanism."

4. As I said, "Orientalist" is not synonymous with "Western." Of the several books that I read about the life of the Prophet, the best were written by Westerners: Rodinson, (1971), and Watt (1974).

5. In reviewing the life of Mohammad, I relied on the following sources: six books (Gibbs 1970; Haykal 1968; Indamdar 2001; Jaffer 2003; Rodinson 1971; Watt 1974), one book chapter (Hammidullah 1969), and a translation of the *Qur'an* (Pickthal 2002). I will refer to any of these references specifically when the information is important or unique.

6. Muhammad's father died before he was born. In such a situation, the absence of a father is considered a loss.

7. This information comes from the index of another translation of the *Qur'an* (al-Hilali and Khan; 1417 hegira, *Translation of the Noble Qur'an in the English*

Language, Madina, K.S.A.: King Fahd Complex for the Printing of the Holy *Qur'an*). While the index is excellent, I did not use the translation because I found some of the words translated from Arabic to English to be politically motivated to explain Islam according to religious order in Saudi Arabia. There is no such thing as an objective translation. The others were just less so.

8. The first Surah, The Fatihah (the Opening), is only seven verses. Caring for the orphans appear as early as the ninety-fourth verse of the *Qur'an*, which consist of thousands of verses.

9. These claims were made in the biographies of Muhammad that were written more than a century after his death.

10. The Arabic words used to describe what Watt calls "dreams or visions" are interesting. In Arabic, three words were used to describe three such experiences. The first word was *wahi*, which can be translated to inspiration or revelation. The second word was *Ra'aho*, which in simpler Arabic means "to see him." In a third "vision" (to be described later), the Arabic word was *roiyah*, which is accurately translated as vision. Thus, all three words imply that something from outside was perceived by the Prophet, to support the idea that this was the angel Gabriel. It can be suggested from reading the descriptions of these experiences that the psychological explanations are that they were hallucinatory religious experiences or dreams.

11. "Unusual," to us as clinicians. We do not see the manifestations of the unconscious this way in our clinical practices.

12. The term *umma* has changed its meaning. During that time it clearly referred to community. Today, it refers to "nation," which is not what Muslims refer to.

13. Like me, many others have seen this said on television by people like Pat Robertson, Jerry Falwell, and other less known evangelists.

14. I use quotation marks, because while the translation to English is "adoptive," the Arabic words were not what we use today to denote adoption. However, adoption, as we understand it in the West, is still not allowed in Islam.

15. The continuous importance of that period in the current Islamic consciousness is that the military wing of the largest Shiite group in Iraq is called the Badr brigade.

16. The books report that the Jews went to a city called Khybar, north of Madinah, but eventually, they went to Syria.

17. As I am writing this, the issue of the Danish cartoons illustrating the Prophet has exploded.

18. We can have an empirical study now. If I survive after the publication of this book, then I was right. If I do not, then I was "dead" wrong.

19. According to Ali (1993), Muhammad's domestic life may be divided into four periods: "Up to twenty-five, he led a celibate life, from twenty-five to fifty-four years, he lived in a married state with one wife; from fifty-four to sixty, he contracted several marriages, and lastly from sixty till his death, he did not contract any new marriage" (p. 187). Ali lists the women Muhammad married during middle age (Aishah, Saudah, Hafsah, Zainab, Umm Salamah, Zainab, Juwairiyah, Umm Habibah, Safiyyah, Mary, and Maimunah) and traces their tribal and familial backgrounds in an attempt to place these liaisons in their sociocultural and political context of the era.

20. Such discouragement/nonacceptance of a deepening of the ties between children and their adoptive parents stands in sharp contrast to the Prophet's and Islam's benevolent attitude toward orphans that I mentioned earlier in this chapter.

CHAPTER 3. RAPTURE AND POETRY: RUMI

1. The *nay* (rhymes with may) is an ancient Persian musical instrument cut out of bamboo stalks. The sound of the *nay* is ethereal, sweet and gentle, capable of producing nearly all the musical potentialities of the human voice. One of Rumi's most poignant lamentations centers around his invitation to hear the *nay*'s narrative of loss and separation expressed in unrequited longing to return to the place where his existence once began and to reunite with those he once formed a collective whole.

CHAPTER 5. DESTINY AND NATIONALISM: MOHAMMAD ALI JINNAH

1. The disastrously erroneous theorizing about mother-child interaction in India by Kurtz (1996) constitutes a recent example of such naïve theoretical colonialism.

2. This was the name of a horse presented by Prophet Mohammad to his grandson Imam Hussain. Actually, the horse was originally named *Murtajiz*, but when it was riddled with arrows on both his flanks, Imam Hussain poetically named him *Zuljinnah* (which meant an animal with with two wings). The figure of this animal remains a major inspiration for Shia mourners, recalling Iman Hussain's martyrdom during the war of Karbala (circa A.D. 680).

3. At the age of twelve, Jinnah spent nearly six months with his beloved paternal aunt, Manbai, in Bombay. There, according to his sister Fatima Jinnah (1893–1967), who was his confidante and identified with his late-life Muslim ethnocentrism, Jinnah received schooling at the Muslim Anjuman-e-Islam. According to his secretary, M. H. Syed, however, the school he attended was the secular Gokul Das Tej Primary School (Wolpert 1984, 6). Such contradictions are found all though the public narrative of Jinnah's life.

4. This literal deletion of "bhai-hood" would be followed decades later by a more malignant erasure of the fraternal sentiments Jinnah, an Indian Muslim, had with his fellow Hindu citizens.

5. Gandhi and Nehru, who had also gone to England for studies, reacted differently to their encounter with the colonizing country. Gandhi flirted briefly with the British cultural scene and then "discovered" that a Hindu idiom was more suited for his personal and public life. Nehru, standing equidistant from Jinnah's "anglicization" and Gandhi's "Hinduization," seamlessly assimilated the democratic and literary traditions of the West into his elite Indian lifestyle.

6. In order to grasp the magnitude of such income, one has to convert yesterday's rupees into today's rupees, and then convert the latter into today's dollars. This is a

tricky business. Changes in the purchasing power of money, the varying conversion rates between rupees and dollars over the decades that have since passed, and the factor of ever-growing inflation make any effort at such calculation hard, if not impossible. A crude estimate of $10,000 a month (in 1910 American dollars) does however comes to mind. In today's terms, this amounts to nearly $80,000 per month!

7. From his name, Kanji Dwarkadas would seem to be Hindu. Perhaps Wolpert (1984) refers to him as a Parsi in an effort to minimize Jinnah's Hindu connections. This tendency is also evident in Ahmed's (1997) finding esoteric Muslim origins of the Hindu names in Jinnah family and in Fatima Jinnah's factually incorrect statement (cited in Wolpert 1984, 6) that Jinnah went to an Islamic school during his brief stint as a child in Bombay. Such delinkages from the Hindu surrounding and a concomitant "over-Islamization" is evident in many of Jinnah's biographers, as well as in Jinnah himself.

8. Her desperate letters to him, often describing her dreams in detail, are quite literary and make for fascinating reading (Dwarkadas 1963).

9. Dina never joined her father in Pakistan. She married Neville Wadia (a Parsi who had converted to Christianity) and continued to live in Bombay. Vehemently opposed to this union, Jinnah broke off all relations with her and referred to her as "Mrs. Wadia" in his subsequent correspondence.

10. To be sure, Indians were constantly exploring all sorts of avenues, besides parliamentary reform, to gain independence from the British. Gandhi's "noncooperation movement" and Subhash Chandra Bose's (1987–1945) armed resistance were the most prominent of these "alternate" strategies.

11. Future events, especially the draconian laws which led to the British massacre of Indians at the Jallianwalla Bagh in 1919, made Gandhi regret his decision to support the British.

12. Born in Bhagpur near Nasik in the western Indian state of Maharashtra in 1883, Savarkar became politically active at a young age. While still an undergraduate, he founded *Abhinav Bharat*, an organization dedicated to wresting freedom from the British, if necessary with the help of arms. For his courage, he came to be known as "Veer" (bold) Savarkar. Arriving in England in 1906 to study law, he set up the Free India Society as a recruiting front for his group in Bombay. A member of the latter group shot and killed Sir Cuzon Wyllie in 1909, and Savarkar, living in London, became embroiled in the political fallout of this murder. He was arrested in 1910 and extradited to India. When he was being taken by ship to India, Savarkar jumped into the sea and swam to the French coast, braving gunfire from the ship. He was arrested at Marseille by the British police. The French Government protested against this arrest on French soil to the Hague International Court. This brought Veer Savarkar to prominence. After being tried for sedition in 1910 at Bombay, he was sentenced to fifty years of rigorous imprisonment at the Cellular Jail in the Andaman Islands. He spent twelve long years of hard labor there and, upon his return to Bombay, founded the *Rashtriya Sevak Sangh* in 1925. He is assumed to be the instigator of Gandhi's assassination in 1948 (Collins and Lapierre 1985; http://en.wikipedia.org.wiki.savarkar).

13. Of course, in feeling this way, he was conveniently ignoring the fact that a large number of Indian Muslims adored Gandhi and followed him without question. Gandhi's endorsement of the *Khilafat* movement, which supported the Turkish Caliph

against the victorious British Empire, was partly responsible for this. A second, equally important, reason was that a large number of Indian Muslims felt a great sense of loyalty to their country, took active part in the freedom struggle, and were opposed to the idea of country's partition.

14. The fear of Japanese invasion of India was no idle fantasy. Japan had captured India's Andaman and Nicobar Islands by 1942, and in early 1944, had crossed Indian borders and took control of Kohima in the far eastern region of Nagaland.

15. Fascinatingly, Chowdhry Rahmat Ali, the man who had originated the idea of a separate Muslim nation carved out of India and coined the name "Pakistan," was far from delighted at this point. Regarding the newly formed country to be smaller than what he had envisioned, Ali launched a movement to secure the repeal of the June 3, 1947 Plan which had ensured the formation of Pakistan. Consequently, he was denied Pakistani citizenship and was told to leave the country. He died in 1951 and was buried in Cambridge, England.

16. Transgenerational deposits of unmetabolized representations are seen most clearly in replacement children (i.e., those who are conceived during a period when the mother is mourning the loss of someone very close to her) (Cain and Cain 1964; Poznanski 1972; Volkan 1981). Under such circumstances, the child develops a divided self; one part of him represents his authentic strivings, and the other part, an identification with what the deceased person stood for or might have accomplished.

17. His first wife's death seems less emotionally significant; it was an arranged marriage of very short duration after all.

18. Gandhi was taking away "Mother India's" adoration. Nehru was taking away Gandhi's affection. Kanji was taking away Ruttie's love. Caught at the far corner of these triangles, Jinnah might have painfully reexperienced the repeated diminution of maternal attention when she gave birth to his seven younger siblings. His current anguish was compounded.

19. The "union" of West and East Pakistan lasted only twenty-four years. The Punjabi oppression of Bengalis (on both administrative and cultural fronts) ultimately led the latter to revolt and created the separate nation of Bangladesh (from what had been East Pakistan) in 1971.

20. Prominent among this group were Khan Abdul Ghaffar Khan ("Frontier Gandhi"), Mukhtar Ahmad Ansari, Hakim Ajmal Khan, Maulana Abul-Kalam Azad, Rafi Ahmad Kidwai, and Ansar Harvani. While each was distinguished in his own way, the status of Maulana Azad remains heads and shoulders above all. His story is especially instructive when compared to that of Jinnah. Born in Mecca (of an Indian father and Arabian mother) in 1888, Azad grew up in Calcutta from age ten onward. His father was a scholar of Islam and was deeply revered by the local Muslim community. Being the son of a *Pir* (wise man and guide), Azad himself was the recipient of honor and homage throughout the years of his growing up. Steeped in the readings of Islamic theology, history, and jurisprudence, Azad nonetheless grew up to be a highly secular Indian nationalist. Disdainful of Muslim League's demand for Pakistan, Azad fought for India's independence and was the president of the Indian National Congress from 1940 to 1946. Of note here is the fact that Azad's deep and authentic Muslim roots did not preclude his secular leanings, whereas Jinnah's

questionable Muslim ancestry and total lack of religious faith led him to become the great "savior" of Muslims. The difference between healthy and pathological narcissism (Kernberg 1975) accounts for this. Azad, possessing a solid identity, could move beyond his early beginnings without the fear of becoming internally unmoored. Jinnah, on the other hand, lacked a sense of inner security and had evolved a grandiose self-image, which could barely accommodate compromises; this is especially true of the last part of his life when he was suffering from many narcissistic injuries.

CHAPTER 7. ISLAM AND FAMILY STRUCTURE

1. For a consideration of the sociocultural context of Prophet Mohammad's multiple marriages, see Ali (1993). George Awad (chapter 2 of this book) also touches upon this issue.

2. Even this portrayal of a traditional Indian Muslim wedding does not exhaust all the subcontinental variations of rituals and ceremonies. The relative influence of Hindu customs is most marked among Bangladeshi Muslims and least among Pakistanis, with the Indians standing somewhere in between.

3. Female circumcision, often erroneously associated by the West with Islam, is actually an African tribal ritual.

CHAPTER 8. ISLAM, SEX, AND WOMEN

1. These more moderate attitudes toward sexuality are rarely acknowledged in the Western media, where sensationalistic stories about the plight of Muslim women tend to take center stage. "Yet, despite the spread of ultraconservative version of Islam over the past few decades, these societies are not the norm in the Muslim world. In Egypt, female cops patrol the streets. In Jordan, women account for the majority of students in medical school. And, in Syria, courtrooms are filled with female lawyers" (Ali 2005, 33).

2. Interestingly, the vast Muslim empires of the Middle Ages and early modern period had little need and few means to impose orthodoxy on the people of the region; indeed, wide divergences from the rules set out in the Shari'a were tolerated or even justified in the past. It was only more recently, with the rise of European imperialism and most strongly in the aftermath of World War II and decolonization, that socioreligious movements and trends to enforce Islamic law gained political and cultural currency (Said Amir Arjomand, personal communication, October 2005).

3. The Shari'a constitutes the basis of a religious law, which insofar as it was revealed by God to Muhammad, is believed to transcend "both humanity and temporality" (Mernissi 1987, 21). While in theory, the Shari'a is meant to dictate to all followers how Islam should be practiced, Islamic history has seen as widely varying interpretations of the text, as there are political and cultural differences among the diverse groups that comprise the Muslim world. Hence, we see the fundamental break

between the Sunni and Shi'a sects of Islam, as well as numerous divisions among Sunni schools, such as the Hanafi, Hanbali, Maliki, and Shafi, whose hermeneutical divergences put to question the absoluteness of these laws on the basis of their divine order (Imam 2005, 52). At present, partially in reaction to perceived Western excesses, a politically motivated, selective reinterpretation of these laws has gained currency in a number of Islamic countries. This reactionary turn to religion has almost universally advocated a rigid control of women, who are perceived to be the most imminent threat to the patriarchal structure of Islamic society.

4. Ahmed (1992) details the pervasiveness of misogynistic practices among various groups in Mesopotamia and the Mediterranean Middle East, whose culture and institutions form a large part of Islam's inheritance. She contends that hierarchical class structures and legal systems of the urban societies to the east gave rise to proprietary attitudes toward women and that a "fierce misogyny was a distinct ingredient of Mediterranean and eventually Christian thought in the centuries immediately preceding the rise of Islam" (p. 35).

5. This point is made most strongly by Mernissi (1987) and Sabbah (1984), who both draw on al-Ghazali's writings to insist that orthodox Islamic discourse presents sexual desire as a mere expedient to obtaining progeny and, as such, denies the particularity of the object (woman) toward which that desire is directed.

6. The lewd, vulgar humor and derogatory representation of women characterizing such popular stories is by no means exclusive to Islamic popular culture. We find similar preoccupations with the illicit or scandalous sexual behavior of women in medieval European texts and in particular in the French "fabliau" genre. Such ribaldry abounds even in canonical texts like Chaucer's *Canterbury Tales* and Boccaccio's *Decameron*.

7. These stories were orally circulated for centuries before they were finally written down and compiled under this title in the thirteenth century (Haddawy 1990, xi–xii). We recall that in the overarching frame tale (Haddawy 1990, 3–16), King Shahrayar and his brother Shahzaman are both betrayed by their wives, who are caught fornicating with servants and slaves of the palace. For a long time, Shahrayar takes his vengeance on all of womankind, each night taking to bed and then putting to death a virgin from his kingdom, until the wise Shahrazad, by captivating him with her bedtime stories, distracts him from his wrath and ultimately wins his love. For more on sources and manuscripts, see Haddawy's *The Arabian Nights* (New York: Norton).

8. It must be noted that it is precisely such hyperbolic rhetoric that underwrites not just legal institutions in Islamic countries, but also other forms of social regulation. For instance, even in societies where veiling has not been mandated by the state, women who do not abide by the accepted codes of modesty are subject to disapproval and shame-inducing denunciations. It is not surprising, then, that it is often women themselves who, having internalized these regulatory discourses, become the greatest champions of the patriarchal status quo of Muslim society, as well as the injustices they endure in Islam's name.

9. It would seem from the stories depicting the woman's "seduction" by large beasts, that Oedipal defeat is presupposed: how could a man possibly compete

sexually against a rival of such mammoth proportions? We may speculate that if man is resigned to the impossibility of ever outdoing the gargantuan father and winning back the wife/mother, he would rather bypass the triadic scenario altogether. Indeed, this insistence on containing conflict within a dyadic paradigm—where the man seeks only to evade castration/emasculation by keeping the woman under a tight leash rather than to wage a losing battle against another man—becomes particularly evident when we consider the practice of honor killing, which will be discussed at length below.

10. Of course, we do not mean to suggest that Hafez is representative of all Sufi or free-thinking Muslim thinkers or that the three *ghazals* we have chosen, in the interest of brevity, for our demonstration here speak to all the "positive" attitudes toward sexuality and desire in the Muslim world. Other poets in the Iranian tradition with which we are most familiar—such as Sa'adi, Jami, Nezami, Attar, and Sana'i, to name but a few—could also be seen to reflect the liberal strain of Islamic thought in their works. For a broader sampling of writings related to gender relations drawn from Sufi poems and philosophical prose from across the Islamic world and also directly from the *Koran*, we refer the reader to Murata's (1992) important study.

11. The original Persian text of all poems is drawn from the Enjavi edition of Hafez's *Divan*. All translations are the authors'. An attempt has been made to offer as literal a reproduction of the poet's meaning as possible. Needless to say, this approach falls far short of recreating the musical cadence, meter, and rhyme of the original verse. The reader is thus asked to bear in mind that a powerful sensuality of the lyrical form, which is lost in translation, reinforces and highlights the sensual content of the poems that are to be discussed here.

CHAPTER 9. SUFI PERSPECTIVE ON HUMAN SUFFERING AND ITS RELIEF

1. In Sufi literature, many words are used synonymously with *pir: kamil*—perfect, complete, full. In Sufism, this refers to the one who is complete with all qualities of humanity; *murad*—wishes, willed, desired. In Sufism, this refers to the one who leads the seekers on the path of truth toward freedom from the self *(fana)*; *murshid*—a guide to the right way, a spiritual advisor, and a guide on the path of integration; *shaykh*— a venerable old man, a chief, a superior of the dervishes; *tabib ruhani*—physician of the soul; *qutb*—pole, axis, or pivot. In Sufism, this refers to the one who is the head of the Sufi order (Nurbakhsh, 1953, pp. 3–4).

2. Through the Sufi meditative experience, the inhibitory grip of the brain cortex is temporarily released, and the hypothalamus and sympathetic and parasympathetic systems are allowed to function automatically—free from the interference of the cortex. When the hypothalamus and vagus nerve are free, the affective states *(halat)* of hope, fear, love, and so forth are experienced without cognitive interference. Tears come without any reason, joy without explanation. The proprioceptic sensation of vibration and hair-raising goose bumps are experienced with or without cognitive awareness.

CHAPTER 11. CHRISTIANITY AND ISLAM: THE AXIS OF BALKANS AND THE WEST

1. Asymmetry is a central and hotly debated analytic concept under headings like mutuality versus asymmetry, therapist's authority (Mitchell 1998). It is a useful concept in thinking about the analytic relationship or the parent/child relationship in which there is a developmental, maturational task at hand. Here it is used in the sense of asymmetry of large groups. The powerful, dominant large group, when it is perceived as such, is under the scrutiny of the weaker one and is the recipient of intense idealizing/devaluing projections. One the one hand, the dominant one has a propensity to treat the nondominant one as a "thing" or "object"; it may initiate projective identificatory processes that will lead to the construction of the "other" that is in the line with the images of that the "self," the dominant one, has about the weaker one. In the analytic literature on narcissistic disorders, this is described as the "glass bubble" phenomenon (Volkan 1979, 405-31). On a more ordinary level, the relationship from the perspective of the dominant one is reminiscent of the experience we have at the zoo where we watch wildlife documentaries on television. Once the nemesis of humans, beasts like wolves or bears are now objects of human curiosity. And behind the protection of a thick glass barrier or a television screen, we see in them what we can identify in ourselves—sexuality, aggression, and fights for dominance.

2. The Balkans, where a substantial number of Turk/Muslim communities were created during Ottoman expansion, is still considered as the land of "Our Ancestors" by many Turks. On the other hand, many nations that arose from former Ottoman lands in Southeastern Europe attribute their relative backwardness—as compared to Western Europe—to Ottoman domination of many centuries; "If Ottomans had not subjugated us, we would be in much better shape" is a common rhetoric. "Turk" is clearly an insult for the current nationalities of the Balkans. It is also noteworthy that in the mind of Turks, these nationalities—Greek, Bulgarian, Serbian—still carry a valence. In Turkey, if you want to insult someone, calling him "Greek" or "Gavur" (infidel) is very effective. "Bulgarian" doesn't have the same impact, but "may do the job" and one can hardly invoke any sentiments in Turks by calling them German, British, French, or Italian.

CHAPTER 12. JEWISH-MUSLIM RELATIONS: MIDDLE EAST

1. This section draws on W. Montgomery Watt (1960), *Muhammad: Prophet and Statesman* (Oxford: Oxford University Press); Norman A. Stillman (1979), *The Jews of Arab Lands: A History and Source Book,* (Philadelphia: Jewish Publication Society of America); and Reza Aslan (2005), *No god But God: The Origins, Evolution, and Future of Islam* (New York: Random House).

2. The traditional Muslim biography of Muhammad is the editorial revision by Ibn Hisham of Ibn Ishaq's *al-Sira al-Nabawiyya*, 2 vols. (Cairo, 1955); *The Life of Muhammad,* abridged English translation, Alfred Guillaume (Karachi, 1955).

3. See her *Studies in Arabic Literary Papyri* (Chicago, 1957–1972).

4. Montville, Joseph V., (1993), "The Healing Function in Political Conflict Resolution," in Dennis J.D. Sandole and Hugo van der Merwe, eds., *Conflict Resolution Theory and Practice: Integration and Application,* (Manchester: Manchester University Press) pp. 112–28; and Montville, Joseph V. (2001), "Justice and the Burdens of History," in Mohammed Abu-Nimer, ed., *Reconciliation, Justice, and Coexistence: Theory and Practice* (Lanham, MD: Lexington Books), pp. 129–44.

5. See his *Under Crescent and Cross: The Jews in the Middle Ages* (Princeton: Princeton University Press), 1994.

CHAPTER 13. HINDU–MUSLIM RELATIONS: INDIA

1. A recent example of such outlandishness is the *fatwa* issued by Mufti Abdul Quddus Rumi, a Muslim cleric in Agra, which excommunicated fifty-four Muslims and nullified their marriages because they declared that singing the nationalist song, *Vande Matram*, was not un-Islamic (*India Abroad*, p. A-18, March 19, 2004).

2. The *Somnath* temple was finally rebuilt after India's independence from the British in 1947. The impetus for its reconstruction was provided by Sardar Patel, the first Home Minister of postcolonial India, during his visit to Junagadh in November, 1947. The ruins of the old temple were pulled down in October 1950, and Rajendra Prasad, the first President of Republic of India, performed the idol installation ceremony in May 1951 (Jafferlot 1996, 84).

3. On surface, the distinction between Islamic monotheism and Hindu polytheism is obvious. However, a closer look reveals that the matter is much more complex. While not declaring Mohammad or his son-in-law Ali to be "gods," the reverence Muslims have toward them, as well as many other subsequent seers and sages tends to distribute their worshipping attitude a bit more widely. Conversely, while having a vast array of deities, Hinduism ultimately proposes one supreme God. The related matter of idol worship is similarly complex. On the surface, Muslims do not worship idols and Hindus do. However, the Muslim turning toward Mecca during prayers, rituals Muslims perform during *Hajj* (pilgrimage to Mecca), and the Muslim regard for various *mazaars* (graves) and *dargahs* (shrines) in India look suspiciously like idol worship to me. Conversely, all thoughtful Hindus know that the idols they worship are merely iconic way stations to a supreme God that is boundless and beyond reification.

4. A fourth member, the great singer Tansen (A.D. 1535–1592) is reported to be a born Muslim by some and a Hindu convert to Islam by other historians. What remains certain is that he died a Muslim and is buried in Gwalior, Madhya Pradesh.

5. Aurangzeb was an exception in this regard, but he treated Muslim musicians with equal degree of contempt. In realms other than music, too, his harshness was directed at both Hindus and Muslims. He saddled Hindus with all sorts of religious, social, and legal hardships *and* he instituted severe punishments for Muslims over their omission of five daily prayers and fasting during the month of Ramazan.

6. The Indian liquor baron, Vijay Mallya, a Hindu, recently bought the fabled sword of the Muslim king Tipu Sultan (A.D. 1749–1799) at a London auction for over $3 million. Calling the sword a unique piece of Indian history, Mallya said that he had bought it to restore the "rightful legacy" (quoted in *India Abroad*, p. A-18, April 16, 2004) to Karnataka, the South Indian state to which Tipu Sultan belonged. Mallya's grand gesture underscored the essentially secular and multicultural spirit of India.

7. These Hindus frequently had Dutt and Mohiyal as their last names. Their recent generations have, by and large, abandoned the mixed religious heritage of the group, finding it as embarrassingly deviant.

8. Such "Hinduization" of Islam in Bengal, especially the local Muslims' love of the Bengali language, would later play a role in the 1971 birth of Bangladesh as a separate nation.

9. Fascinatingly, the claim that Hindus and Muslims of India are two irreconcilable "nations" is made by both the Hindu and Muslim extremists. The thinking of the Muslim League's Mohammad Ali Jinnah and Shiv Sena's Bala Saheb Thackeray seems to be in complete agreement on this matter.

10. Their agony has been poignantly captured in the 1973 movie *Garam Hawa*. The fact that the movie is produced and directed by M. S. Sathyu, a South Indian Hindu, is a powerful testimony to the essentially secular spirit of India.

11. He was assassinated on January 30, 1948 (i.e., less than six months after India's independence and partition). His murderer Nathu Ram Godse had strong ideological ties to the right-wing Hindu nationalist leader Veer Savarkar. The "crime" for which Gandhi allegedly "deserved" to be killed was his kindness and "indulgence" toward Muslims!

12. I have elsewhere (Akhtar 1999b) elaborated on the differences between immigrants and exiles when it comes to the matters of nostalgia, future orientation, and overall social adjustment.

13. Muslims frequently adopted Hindu names while entering the film industry and Hindus often took on Muslim *nom de plumes* while contributing to Urdu literature. The complex societal factors underlying such choices certainly deserve further attention.

14. The works of these poets and their predecessors directly pertaining to India's topography and culture has been collected in a four-volume set called *Hindustan Hamara* (Akhtar 1975). Beside such overt reference, Urdu poetry has drawn more subtle and profoundly significant themes from ancient Hindu thought. The impact of Advaitic Vedantism is especially evident in poems of Mirza Ghalib and the more recent poet Ali Sardar Jafri.

15. A Shia Muslim from Ghaziabad, Uttar Pradesh, Rahi Masoom Raza , wrote the screenplay and dialogues of the fifty-two-hour-long television series based upon the great Hindu epic *Mahabharata* shown to rapt audiences across India during the early 1990s.

16. The husband-wife duo of Javed Akhtar and Shabana Azmi defies categorization. They are film personalities, stage and television performers, political presences, and social activists of immense virtuosity and international stature.

17. Whereas there might be inadvertent omissions in this account given my modest knowledge of history, there are some matters that I have deliberately bypassed in the service of narrative economy. Prominent among these are the massacres by Nadir Shah, Ahmed Shah Abdali, and Taimur Lung (the infamous "Tamerlane" of the West); Muslim-Muslim battles over the Delhi throne; Faizi's and Firdausi's literary and historical works; the gardens made by Mughal emperors; the fine arts of calligraphy and miniature painting under the sponsorship of Muslim rulers; the North-South difference in Hindu-Muslim relations; the complex saga of Sikh–Muslim relations; the Muslim *Nawab*—Hindu money lender tension created by the British strangulation of finances in Oudh; the impact of *Khilafat* movement in the Indian–Muslim politics; the role played by the Deoband *ullema* (Muslim scholars) and academics of Aligarh Muslim University in the social concerns of Indian Muslims; the patriotic and exhortative songs written by Muslim poets (e.g., Jan Nisar Akhtar's "*Awaaz do hum ek hain*") during the Indo-Chinese and Indo-Pakistani wars; the details of both the *Babri Masjid* destruction and Gujrat riot; and, finally the fiction (e.g., Tharoor 2001) and poetry (e.g., Alexander 2004), that has evolved about various communal riots.

18. Pakistan, formed with the heady notion of Muslim fraternity, also began to develop a similar "villain hunger" once it no longer had Hindus to demonize. The most striking result of such need for "enemies," was the Punjabi-Bengali tension that ultimately led to the formation of Bangladesh. The subsequent anti-Hindu activities in Bangladesh and the Shia-Sunni strife in Pakistan (not to mention the anti-Ahmadi violence) testify to the ever unquenched nature of man's need for enemies.

19. Such quotas were arrived to reflect the proportion of this group's population in the country. The total of reserved jobs was restricted to 49 percent in accordance with a ceiling set by the Supreme Court to maintain the credibility of the equal opportunity clause of the constitution.

20. Hitherto marginalized in national level politics the Hindu nationalist party BJP, which had a mere 2 seats in a 534-member national parliament in 1984, garnered 86 seats by 1989, 118 seats by 1991, and a whopping 328 seats by 1993. BJP Leadership "told India's electorate that if the countries of Western Europe and the United States can call themselves Christians, India should be free to call itself Hindu" (Rudolph and Rudolph 1993, 28). That this was against the country's constitution apparently did not matter!

21. This hypernationalism of the diaspora Hindus has striking parallels with the Muslim immigrants of London coming up with the idea of Pakistan during the 1940s (Collins and Lapierre 1975) and the Sikh immigrant community of the United Kingdom and Canada aiding and abetting the *Khalistan* (a separate nation for the Indian Sikhs) movement of the 1980s.

22. Advani's *rathyatra* had an uncanny similarity with the Serbian leader Milosevic's tour of Yugoslavia to stir up Serbian nationalism. At each stop of his rambling sojourn, Milosevic reminded the Serbs of their defeat by the Ottoman Turks nearly seven hundred years ago. At each stop, the remains of the defeated Serbian King Salazar were buried and exhumed in order to inflame Serbian passions against the Bosnian and Kosovar Muslims, who were declared to be the descendants of Turks. A genocide of the latter group followed.

23. To be sure, the British did many harmful things to the Indian society during their nearly 100-year reign. However, this should not make one overlook their positive contributions that include the construction of railroads and "hill stations" (mountain resorts), propagation of the English language, various judicial and administrative measures, Western attire, and the all-important game of Cricket. India's capital, New Delhi, with its majestic and sweeping boulevards and roundabouts, is almost exclusively built by the British. The nation's parliament meets in buildings constructed by the British and its President, Prime Minister, and all other cabinet officers live in houses planned and built by the British.

24. The Indian government's family planning campaign during the 1960s and 1970s certainly gained momentum from the "Hum do, Humare do" ("Two of us, two of ours") billboards scattered throughout India.

25. Actually, such movies are being made less and less often these days. The reasons for this remain unclear. Could it be that the amount of societal aggression against Muslims is now so close to surface that it can no longer be defended by such cinematographic fawning?

26. These ideas were mentioned to me by Joseph Montville during an informal conversation circa 2000. For his important contributions in the realm of conflict resolution, see Montville 1987; 1991.

27. The importance of such civic bridges was also demonstrated in a study (Varshney 2002) comparing the positive Hindu-Muslim relations in Calicut with the frequently tense ones in Aligarh. About 90 percent of Hindu and Muslim families in Calicut reported that their children play together against a mere 42 percent in Aligarh!

28. Note in this connection the relief experienced by Jews when Nazi concentration camp officers are traced and brought to trial. Akin is the reaction of the African immigrant community in Germany to the harsh sentence against three skinheads handed down by a Berlin judge in connection with the murder of a worker from Mozambique (*Philadelphia Inquirer* 2000).

29. An almost literal translation of the two lines would be: "What the politicians and social engineers would do in the end, only they know/My message is one of love; let us see how far its reach turns out to be."

CHAPTER 15. OEDIPUS IN EGYPT: A TWENTIETH-CENTURY RENDITION OF *MAJNUN LAYLA*

1. Very few psychoanalytic studies have been undertaken of Islamic rituals, the *Qur'an*, representations of Allah, biographical material concerning the prophet Muhammad, the family dynamics underlying the Sunni-Shi'ite split, Arabo-Islamic literature, modern diasporic Islam—to list just a few areas in which a psychological dimension may be enlightening.

2. As a poet, his biographical name is Qays ibn al-Mulawwah and he was born in the Hijaz, a region of the Arabian peninsula, during the latter half of the seventh century. (Khan 2005, 288).

3. Unless otherwise indicated, nearly all translations from *Majnun Layla* are mine.

4. Cf. Madjnun Layla in *Encylopaedia of Islam*, 2nd ed., V, 1986, pp. 1102–07.

5. In the latter half of the twentieth century, *Majnun Layla* arrived in the west as well; in Germany, it was made into a symphony. The British musician, Eric Clapton, drew upon Nizami's Persian rendition to fashion his musical composition called "Layla."

6. Ahmad Shawqi, regarded as the supreme poet throughout the Arab world during the early part of the twentieth century, turned to writing drama during the last four years of his life, and M. Badawi credits him with "helping to render drama as acceptable form of literature" at that time (Badawi book on Modern Arabic poetry). At the end of the nineteenth century, historical plays, melodramas, tragedies, comedies and political plays were already being written in Arabic (a number of these were translations, adaptations, or imitations of European models). With the turn of the century, there appeared a more seasoned type of writer who was familiar not only with the traditional Arabic heritage, but also with the classical/modern masterpieces of Europe; foremost among these was Ahmad Shawqi.

7. The Egyptian film entitled *Qays Layla* came out in 1960 and was directed by Ahmad Diya al-Din.

8. A. Shawqi's drama, consisting of five acts, relies on a certain repertoire of episodes and scenes from the classical version that by the twentieth century had become signature marks of the romance.

9. Drama as a Western genre was imported by modern Arabic literature, and the experimentation with it was a distinct phase in modern Arabic literary history. The plays of Shakespeare, Moliere, Racine, and Eliot had been translated and read by modern Arab writers, and their impact was keenly felt.

10. Cf. Allen 2000 for the significance of the Nahdah.

11. Egyptian playwrights, despite their intense nationalism, were open to foreign influences from European dramatists—even experimental ones such as Samuel Beckett and Bertolt Brecht. Both Beckett and Brecht had an impact upon 'Abd as-Sabur. (Khairallah 1995, 175) Indeed, with the revolution of 1952 in Egypt, Marxism also exerted a great influence on young, leftist Egyptian intellectuals and writers.

12. It may be asked was Freud known to Salah 'Abd as-Sabur? Were Freud's works translated and read by Egyptian literateurs? Though it is difficult to answer this question with regard to 'Abd as-Sabur specifically, the Egyptian writer and critic Gamal al-Ghitani (born about fifteen years after as-Sabur) has discussed how he read Freud in translation by the time he was a teenager. At the time, Freud's *The Interpretation of Dreams* had been translated by one Mustafa Safouan through the printing press, Dar al-Kutub, and al-Gitani states that he "almost memorized entire pages of it" because he could not afford to buy it (Ghazoul 1994). He apparently read other works by Freud as well. It would seem, therefore, that some of Freud's oeuvre was translated into Arabic and read by the Arab world during the 1950s and 1960s.

13. Throughout this synopsis, I paraphrase and borrow from the summary presented by A. Khairallah (1995, 168–69).

14. In Nizami's Persian thirteenth-century rendition entitled *Layli Majnun* as translated by Gelpke (1966), too, psychoanalytic dimensions are present—as examined by

Sudhir Kakar and John Munder Ross. Sudhir Kakar and John Munder Ross, "Love in the Middle Eastern World," in *Tales of Love, Sex and Danger*, eds. Sudhir Kakar and John Munder Ross (NY: Basil Blackwell, 1986). Kakar and Ross delve into the merger and separation aspects of the love that Majnun has for Layla: "The preservation of Layla, to the extent that he denies himself erotic access to her, is paramount. He senses that in having her he will destroy illusion" (p. 66).

15. The 'Udhri romances ostensibly foreground a monagamous bond between a pair of lovers, but a close scrutiny of these tales reveals that a third party is always present and that the configuration of erotic bonds is actually triangular and scarcely chaste. Certainly, the existence of the erotic triangle in romance and lyric is a well-documented fact. Freud's essays "A Special Type of Object Choice Made by Men" and "The Taboo of Virginity" help to illuminate some aspects of this triangle. Sigmund Freud, *Sexuality and the Psychology of Love*, ed. Philip Rieff (New York: Macmillan Publishing Co., 1963).

16. Afsaneh Najmabadi, "The Erotic Vatan [Homeland] as Beloved and Mother: To Love, To Possess, and to Protect." *Comparative Studies in Society and History*, 1997, 39 (3):442–67. Najmabadi's article also makes references to the *Layla Majnun* story in the context of (Iranian) nationalism.

17. I tend toward an idiomatically correct translation rather than a literal one.

18. A number of other non-Western critics have addressed the issue of whether there exists a universality of the Oedipal complex, including A. K. Ramanujam (1999) and G. Obeyesekere. Cf. Obeyesekere's *The Work of Culture* including especially the chapters entitled "Oedipus: the Paradigm and its Hindu Rebirth" as well as "The Parricide in Buddhist History."

19. Kakar has pointed out that Majnun's own father in the premodern versions of the love story is not the Oedipal father, but rather "he is a figure who strives to push the boy away from [the mother], to draw the once androgynous and indulged creature into the 'real' world of his adult male culture" (Kakar and Ross 1988, 68).

20. Part of the problem is that most scholars and critics in the North American academy are not informed of what has happened in the field of psychoanalysis since the prevalence of the drive psychology of Freud. There has been a proliferation of various relational models within psychoanalysis, and these models (with names such as Mahler, Winnicott, Kernberg, Kohut, Erikson associated with them) embrace different conceptions of human development, different ideas about the unconscious and conscious realms and departures in psychoanalytic technique. All of this renders these relational models, as Kakar has pointed out, generally more amenable to cross-cultural applications (1985, 446–47). The rise of these relational models has meant, among other things, a shift in focus from the Oedipal to pre-Oedipal period in infancy and childhood—a shift that has boded well for both feminism and multiculturalism. North American academe has been flirting for some time with the French psychoanalytic theoreticians, such as Jacques Lacan and Julia Kristeva, but it is relatively unaware of how relational models of psychoanalysis as evinced in the scholarship of the object relations school or self psychology insightfully can be drawn upon to examine diverse religious and cultural phenomena.

CHAPTER 16. CULTURAL NATIONALISM IN INDO-MUSLIM ART

1. India is, throughout this chapter, meant to represent the historical entity, not the current sovereign state. Any discussion of Indo-Muslim art would be incomplete without the other major political entity in the subcontinent of Pakistan.

2. The historian Barbara Metcalf, in her presidential address to the 47th Annual Meeting of the Association for Asian Studies in Washington, DC in 1995, explained the various facets of this phenomenon, including the convenient construction of "grand" narrative—colonial, nationalist, supremacist and separatist, to make sense of the presence of Muslims, and Islam, in India.

3. The first month of the Islamic lunar or *hijri* calendar, during which the martyrdom of the Prophet Mohammad's grandson Husain took place in Karbala in A.D. 680. Shi'i Muslims commemorate this event with forty days of mourning. The rituals of Indian Muslims on such occasions are obviously influenced greatly by Hindu religious traditions.

4. Separately, Lady Curzon (the wife of the Viceroy of India) collected examples of Indian English with which to amuse her friends. Punch, the London-based satirical newsmagazine, created a caricature of an English-educated Bengali "baboo"—a buffoon shown condescendingly affectionately with touching cultural pretensions. F. Anstey's creation of 1895, Baboo Jabberjee B.A., was "head over heels in love with Art, and the possessor of two magnificent colored lithographs" (quoted in Mitter 2002, 150) *Baboo-speak*, with all its malapropisms, its confusion of English and Bengali syntaxes, and its bombastic phrases, was played up to comical effect.

5. The illustrated comic book series *Amar Chitra Katha* is today's equivalent— a modern and widely read tool for the popular dissemination of Hindu folklore.

6. *Kitna hai badnaseeb Zafar, dafn ke liye*
Do guz zameen bhi mil na saki, ku-e-yaar mein
The translation of Bahadur Shah Zafar's original Urdu verse is my own.

7. The paternalistic ambitions of the British merit a separate, lengthier discussion, but suffice it to say that some forms of cultural nationalism, in art as well as in education, were infinitely more preferable to the British than direct political involvement by Indians.

CHAPTER 17. MUSLIMS IN THE PSYCHOANALYTIC WORLD

1. Correspondence between Freud and Girindrashekhar Bose (1887–1953), the "father of Indian psychoanalysis," had begun a year earlier and lasted till 1937 (see Ramana 1964).

2. The largely Westernized and secular Muslim nation of Turkey is an exception in this regard. Enthusiasm about psychoanalysis is great there, and psychoanalytic study groups in Istanbul and Izmir are quite active. At least six British- or French-trained Muslim psychoanalysts are currently practicing in Turkey. Many younger individuals are traveling to Greece for their training analyses while receiving supervision within

their country. All in all, there is a strong movement to establish a formal Turkish Psychoanalytic Society and Institute.

3. Khan personally told me this in a memorable, even though rambling and occasionally disturbing, "conversation" that lasted over three hours. I have put quotes around the word conversation because by the time of our meeting in May 1988, Khan was almost totally unable to speak and communicated by writing (I intend to write about my encounter with Khan someday in detail).

4. Two other prominent British analysts, namely Baljeet Mehra and Charles Rycroft, have expressed similar reservations about Khan's "antisemitism" (quoted in Cooper 1993).

5. Alan Stone, a past president of the American Psychiatric Association (1979–1980) told me that Joseph Sandler once referred to Masud Khan as "a moral leper" (personal communication, April 1988).

6. de Klerk (2003; 2004), however, asserts to the contrary. Deftly synthesizing biographical details of Freud's life (including his circumcision), Freud's various references to circumcision, medical aspects of such an intervention in neonatal life, and psychoanalytic observational data of children, de Klerk concludes that circumcision even at a very early stage of life is traumatic and, even though unrecognized, might form the "prehistoric" substrate on which the later castration anxiety develops.

7. Talking of aesthetics brings a hitherto unmentalized "contribution" of Muslims to the psychoanalytic world. This refers to the nearly ubiquitous presence of "oriental" rugs weaved by Muslim artisans in Iran, Pakistan, India, Turkey, and Afghanistan in analytic offices all over the world.

8. Her presence at the United Nations Conference on Xenophobia and Racism held in Durban, South Africa (August 2001) was a source of great controversy. While not even present at a particular session where certain groups spoke strongly against Israel and Zionism, Mahfouz was vilified by a faction of North American psychoanalysts as being anti-Semitic; one analyst implied that she was in cahoots with Osama bin Laden (Afaf Mahfouz, personal communication, May 2006). While many analysts (both Jewish and non-Jewish) did come to her defense, the emotional and social toll of the former's attack was far from negligible. Such emotional poignancy aside, the intrigue surrounding the matter and the fascinating dramtis personae involved in it beg for a book length treatment from an author like Janet Malcolm!

9. Three such individuals belonging to the American Psychoanalytic Association did not wish to be identified by name. To what extent this refusal was based upon personal feelings about their Muslim origins and what role did the anxiety of being identified publicly as a Muslim in the psychoanalytic profession or, more importantly, the current day United States play in it remains unclear. The following observation by Mamdani (2004) is clearly pertinent in this context.

"After an unguarded reference to pursuing a 'crusade,' President Bush moved to distinguish between 'good Muslims' and 'bad Muslims.' From this point of view, 'bad Muslims' were clearly responsible for terrorism. At the same time, the president seemed to assure Americans that 'good Muslims' were anxious to clear their names and consciences of this horrible crime and would undoubtedly support 'us' in a war against 'them.' But this could not hide the central message of such discourse: unless proved to be 'good,' every Muslim was presumed to be 'bad.' All Muslims were now under obligation to move their credentials by joining in a war against 'bad Muslims.'"

10. Factors other than that of personal character also seem responsible for the different outcomes of immigration in the case of Khan, Volkan, and me. Khan had grown up in a colonized nation and had migrated to the colonizing one. Volkan and I had no such historical baggage to carry. Khan and Volkan lacked homoethnic role models. I, on the other hand, had a long-term mental relationship with Khan during the years I was under training, and had the benefit of being directly taught and supervised by Volkan. Ethnoculturally, I was less alone. Two other differences exist. The era in which Khan's and Volkan's migrations took place were preglobalization and before the advent of fast electronic communications across countries. This might have rendered the schism between their cultures of origin and adoption harder to manage. Finally, by the time I entered psychoanalysis, and especially these days, the profession was beginning to undergo a cultural rejuvenation (Akhtar 1998). There was evidence of theoretical pluralism and also a greater demographic inclusiveness in the profession. "Mentalization" (Fonagy and Target 1997) of immigration-related conflicts and their assimilation into psychoanalytic theory and technique thus became possible for me.

References

Abbasi, A. 1997. When Worlds Collide in the Analytic Space: Aspects of a "Cross-Cultural" Analysis. Paper presented at the winter meetings of the American Psychoanalytic Association, December 1999.

Abd al Ati, H. 1977. *The Family Structure in Islam*. Plainfield, IN: American Trust Publications.

Abdul-Rauf, M. 1989. *Marriage in Islam*. Alexandria, VA: Al-Saadawi Publications.

Abdullah, A. and Al-Suhrawardy, A. 1990. *The Sayings of Muhammad*. New York: Citadel Press.

Aberbach, D. 1989. Creativity and survivor: The struggle for mastery. *The International Review of Psycho-analysis* 16:273–86.

Abraham, K. 1911. On the determining power of names. In *Clinical Papers and Essays on Psychoanalysis*, pp. 31–32. New York: Brunner/Mazel, 1967.

———. 1924. A short study of the development of libido. In *Selected Papers of Karl Abraham, M.D.*, pp. 235–44. London: Hogarth, 1927.

Abu-Rabi', I. 2004. *Contemporary Arab Thought: Studies in Post-1967 Arab Intellectual History*. London and Sterling, VA: Pluto Press.

Adams, L., Al Rubaiy, A., and Lamonte, R. 1984. Implications for education and child-rearing: The role of women in the Middle East. *School Psychology International* 5:167–74.

Adorno, J., and Frenkel-Brunswick, E. 1950. *The Authoritarian Personality*. New York: W.W. Norton.

Afetinan, A. 1971. *M. Kemal Ataturk'ten Yazdiklarim (What I Wrote Down from M. Kemal Atatürk)*. Istanbul: Milli Egitim Basimevi.

Ahmed, A. S. 1997. *Jinnah, Pakistan, and the Islamic Identity*. London: Rutledge.

Ahmed, L. 1992. *Women and Gender in Islam: Historical Roots of a Modern Debate*. New Haven, CT: Yale University Press.

Akhtar, J. N., ed. 1975. *Hindustan Hamara, Vols. I–IV*. New Delhi: Hindustani Book Trust.

Akhtar, S. 1992a. *Broken Structures: Severe Personality Disorders and Their Treatments*. Northvale, NJ: Jason Aronson.

———. 1992b. Tethers, orbits and invisible fences: Clinical, developmental, sociocultural, and technical aspects of optimal distance. In *When the Body Speaks: Psychological Meanings in Kinetic Clues*, eds. S. Kramer and S. Akhtar, 21–57. Northvale, NJ: Jason Aronson.

———. 1995a. A third individuation: Immigration, identity, and the psychoanalytic process. *Journal of the American Psychoanalytic Association* 43:1051–84.

———. 1995b. *Quest for Answers: A Primer for Understanding and Treating Severe Personality Disorders*. Northvale, NJ: Jason Aronson.

———. 1996. "Someday . . ." and "if only . . ." fantasies: Pathological optimism and inordinate nostalgia as related forms of idealization. *Journal of the American Psychoanalytic Association* 44:723–53.

———. 1999. *Immigration and Identity: Turmoil, Treatment, and Transformation*. Northvale, NJ: Jason Aronson.

———. 1999a. The psychodynamic dimension of of terrorism. *Psychiatric Annals* 29:350–55.

———. 1999b. *Inner Torment: Living Between Conflict and Fragmentation*. Northvale, NJ: Jason Aronson.

———. 1999c. The distinction between needs and wishes: implications for psychoanalytic theory and technique. *Journal of the American Psychoanalytic Association* 47:113–51.

———. 1999d. The immigrant, the exile, and the experience of nostalgia. *Journal of Applied Psychoanalytic Studies* 1:123–30.

———. 2000. Mental pain and the cultural ointment of poetry. *International Journal of Psychoanalysis* 81:220–44.

———. 2001. A note on the ontongenetic origins of prejudice. *Journal of The Indian Psychoanalytic Society* 55:7–13.

———. 2002. Forgiveness: Origins, dynamics, psychopathology, and technical relevance. *Psychoanalytic Quarterly* 71:175–211.

———. 2003. Dehumanization: Origins, manifestations, and remedies. In *Violence or Dialogue? Psychoanalytic Reflections or Terror and Terrorism*, ed. S. Varvin and V. D. Volkan, 131–45. London: International Psychoanalytic Association.

———. 2005. *Freud along the Ganges: Psychoanalytic Reflections on the People and Culture of India*. New York: The Other Press.

———. 2007a. The trauma of dislocation: Laceration of the non-human aspects of the waking screen and its emotional consequences. In *Space and Intuition: Realities, Metaphors, and Psychoanalysis*, ed. M. T. Hooke and S. Akhtar. London: International Psychoanalytic Association.

Akhtar, S., and Byrne, J. P. 1983. The concept of splitting and its clinical relevance. *American Journal of Psychiatry* 140:1013–16.

Akhtar, S., and Choi, L. 2003. When evening falls: The immigrant's encounter with middle and late age. *American Journal of Psychoanalysis* 64:183–91.

Akhtar, S., and Tummala-Narra, P. 2005. Psychoanalysis in India. In *Freud along the Ganges: Psychoanalytic Reflections on the People and Culture of India*, ed. S. Akhtar, 1–25. New York: The Other Press.

Al-Amily, H. M. 2005. *The Book of Arabic Wisdom: Proverbs and Anecdotes*. Northampton, MA: Interlink Books.

Alexander, M. 2004. *Raw Silk*. Evanston, IL: Triquarterly Books.

Al-Hilali, M. T., and Khan, M. M. 1417 hegira. *Translation of the Noble Qur'an on the English Language*. Madina, KSA: King Fahd Complex for the Printing of the Holy *Qur'an*.

Ali, L. 2005. Not ignorant, not helpless. *Newsweek*, December 12, p. 33.

Ali, M. M. 1993. *Muhammad The Prophet*. Dublin, OH: Ahmadiyya Anjuman Isha.

Alkan, M. O. 2003. *Tarihin sesli taniklari: plaklar* (Vocal witnesses of history: LPs). *Toplumsal Tarih* 117:12–19. Istanbul, Turkey.

Allen, R. 2000. *An Introduction to Arabic Literature*. Cambridge: Cambridge University Press.

Amati-Mehler, J., Argentieri, S., and Canestri, J. 1993. *The Babel of the Unconscious: Mother Tongue and Foreign Languages in the Psychoanalytic Dimension*, trans. J. Whitelaw-Cucco. Madison, CT: International Universities Press.

Ambali, M. A. 1987. The Nigerian adolescent: A consideration of aspects of the role of religion in counseling. *Nigerian Journal of Guidance and Counseling* 3:24–31.

Apprey, M. 1999. Reinventing the self in the face of received transgenerational hatred in the African American community. *Journal of Applied Psychoanalytic Studies* 22:131–43.

Arasteh, A. R. 1965. *Rumi the Persian: Rebirth in Creativity and Love*. Lahore, Pakistan: S. Ashraf Publishers.

Armstrong, K. 2000. *Islam: A Short History*. New York: Modern Library.

Asad, M. 1980. *The Message of The Quran*. Gibraltar: Dar Al-Amadulus.

Aslan, R. 2005. *No god but God: The Origins, Evolution, and Future of Islam*. New York: Random House.

Atatürk, M. K. 1925. *Ataturk un Soylev ve Demecleri* (Speeches and Statemens by Ataturk), 2 vols., ed. E. Z. Karal. Ankara: Turk Tarih Kurumu, 1952, 1959.

———. 1930. *Hurriyet* (Freedom). In *M. Kemal Ataturk'ten Yazdiklarim* by A. Afetinan, pp. 77–97. Istanbul: Milli Egittim Basimevi, 1971.

Attar, F. 1966. *Muslim Saints and Mystics: Episodes from the Tadhkirat al-Auliya*, transl. A. J. Arberry. Chicago, IL: University of Chicago Press.

Austin, A. 1997. *African Muslims in Antebellum America: Transatlantic Stories and Spiritual Struggles*. New York: Garland Press.

Avalon Project. 1988. *Hamas Covenant*, p. 5. New Haven, CT: Yale Law School.

Aydemir, S. S. 1969. *Tek Adam* (The Singular Man), 3 vols. Istanbul: Remzi Kitabevi.

Babayan, K. 1994. The Safavid synthesis: From Qizilbash Islam to Imamite Shi'ism. *Iranian Studies* 27:135–61.

Bachrach, H., and Leaff, L. 1978. "Analyzability": A systematic review of the clinical and quantitative literature. *Journal of the American Psychoanalytic Association* 26:881–920.

Badawi, M. 1975. *A Critical Introduction to Modern Arabic Poetry*. Cambridge: Cambridge University Press.

———. 1987. *Modern Arabic Drama in Egypt*. Cambridge: Cambridge University Press.

———. 1992. Arabic drama since the Thirties. In *Modern Arabic Literature: The Cambridge History of Arabic Literature*, ed., M. M. Badawi. Cambridge: Cambridge University Press.

Badran, M. M. C. and Cooke, M. 1990. *Opening the Gates: A Century of Arab Feminist Writing*. Bloomington: University of Indiana Press.

Bali, R. 2004. *Celal Bayar'in Amerika Ziyareti* (Celal Bayar's visit to America). *Toplumsal Tarih* 122:14–21.

Barkay, G. T. 2003. *Amerikan iliskileri: Iki adim ileri bir adim geri* (Turkish-American relations: Two steps forward, one step backward) *Toplumsal Tarih* 120:70–74.

Barks, C. 1995. *The Essential Rumi*. New York: Harper Collins.

Basch–Kahre, E. 1984. On difficulties arising in transference and countertransference when analyst and analysand have different socio-cultural backgrounds. *International Review of Psycho-Analysis* 11:61–67.

BBC News. 2005. President urges Turkey debate. June 22.

Becker, E. 1973. *The Denial of Death*. New York: Free Press.

Beg, A. 1977. Ed, *Quaid-e-Azam Centenery Bouquet*. Islamabad: Babur and Amer Publications.

Benedek, T. 1938. Adaptation to reality in early infancy. *Psychoanalytic Quarterly* 7:200–14.

Beres, D. 1951. Communication in psychoanalysis and in the creative process: A parallel. *Journal of the American Psychoanalytic Association* 5:408–23.

Bergen, P. 2002. *Holy War, Inc*. New York: Simon and Schuster.

Bergmann, M. S. 1980. On the intrapyschic function of falling in love. *Psychoanalytic Quarterly* 49:56–77.

Berkeley-Hill, O. 1921. A short study of the life and character of Mohammed. *International Journal of Psycho-Analysis* 2:31–53.

Berman, P. 2003. *The New York Times*, March 23, 2003, p. 4.

Bernard, V. 1953. Psychoanalysis in members of minority groups. *Journal of the American Psychoanalytic Association* 1:256–57.

Bernfeld, S. 1923. Uber eine typische Form de männlichen Pubertät, *Imago*, IX.

Birand, M. A. 2004. *Turkiye isteklerinin buyuk bolummunu Kabul ettirdi* (Turkey got the majority of her wishes). *Milliyet* (Turkish daily newspaper), December 18.

Bird, B. 1956. A consideration of the etiology of prejudice. *Journal of the American Psychoanalytic Association* 4:490–513.

Blum, H. P. 1995. Sanctified aggression, hate, and the alteration of standards and values. In *The Birth of Hatred: Developmental, Clinical, and Technical Aspects of Intense Aggression*, ed. S. Akhtar, S. Kramer, and H. Parens, 15–38. Northvale, NJ: Jason Aronson.

———. 1996. Perspectives on internalization, consolidation, and change. In *The Internal Mother*, ed. S. Akhtar, S. Kramer, and H. Parens, 173–201. Northvale, NJ: Jason Aronson.

Bocock, R. 1993. Religion, hatred and children: A Freudian sociological analysis. In *How and Why Children Hate*, ed. V. Varma, 124–35. Philadelphia, PA: Jessica Kingsley Publishers.

Bodansky, Y. 1999. *Bin Laden: The Man Who Declared War on America*. New York: Crown Publishing/Random House.

Bolitho, H. 1954. *Jinnah: The Creator of Pakistan*. London: John Murray.

Bollas, C. 1989. Obituary: Masud Khan—portrait of an extraordinary psychoanalytic personality. *The Guardian*, June 26, p. 39.

Bonovitz, J. 1998. Reflections of the self in the cultural looking glass. In *The Colors of Childhood: Separation-individuation Across Cultural, Racial, and Ethnic Differences*, ed. S. Akhtar and S. Kramer, pp. 169–98. Northvale, NJ: Jason Aronson.

Bouhdiba, A. 1977. The child and the mother in Arab-Muslim society. In *Psychological Dimensions of Near Eastern Studies*, ed. L. Carl Brown. Princeton, NJ: Princeton University Press.

Bowlby, J. 1958. The nature of the child's tie to his mother. *International Journal of Psychoanalysis* 39:350–73.

Bowlby, J. 1969. *Attachment and Loss: Vol. I, Attachment*. New York: Basic Books.

Brome, V. 1983. *Ernest Jones: Freud's Alter Ego*. New York: W.W. Norton.

Brown, L. C., and Itzkowitz, N. 1977. *Psychological Dimensions of Near Eastern Studies*. Princeton, NJ: Darwin Press.

Cain, A. C., and Cain, B. S. 1964. On replacing a child. *Journal of the American Academy of Child Psychiatry* 3:443–56.

Calnek, M. 1970. Racial factors in the countertransference: The Black therapist and the Black client. *American Journal of Orthopsychiatry* 40:39–46.

Candor, C. 2004. *Tarihimizin buyuk gunu* (The grand day of our history). *Dunden Bugune Tercuman* (Turkish daily newspaper), December 18.

Carolan, M., Bagherinia, G., Juhari, R., Himelright, J., and Mouton-Sanders, M. 2000. Contemporary Muslim families: Research and practice. *Contemporary Family Therapy* 22:67–79.

Carroll, J. 2001. *Constantine's Sword: The Church and the Jews: A History*. Boston: Houghton Mifflin.

Celenza, A. *Sexual Boundary Violations: Therapeutic, Supervisory, and Academic Contexts*. Lanham, MD: Jason Aronson.

Cohen, M. R. 2005. *Letter from Doha*, foreword, July 22, p. 2.

Collins, L. and Lapierre, D. 1975. *Freedom at Midnight*. London: Collins.

Cooper, J. 1993. *Speak of Me as I Am: The Life and Work of Masud Khan*. London: Karnac Books.

Cousins, J. and Iqbal, M. 1928. *Muraqqa-e-Chughtai: Paintings of M. A. Rahman Chughtai*. Lahore: Jahangir.

Craven, R. C. 1997. *Indian Art: A Concise Introduction*. London: Thames & Hudson.

Darques, R. 2000. *Salonique au XXe siecle: De la cite Ottomane a la metropole Grecque*. Paris: CNRS Editions.

de Klerk, E. 2003. Het trauma van Freuds besnijdenis. *Tijidschrift voor Psychoanalyse* 9:136–52.

———. 2004. Kastrationangst und beschneidung. *Psyche* 58:464–70.

Deikman, A. 1977. Sufism and psychiatry. *Journal of Nervous and Mental Diseases* 165:318–29.

Dennis, A. 2002. *Osama bin Laden: A Psychological and Political Portrait.* Lima, OH: Wyndam Hall Press.

Deren, S. 2002. From Pan Islamism to Turkish nationalism: Modernization and German influence in the late Ottoman period. In *Disrupting and Reshaping: Early Stages of Nation Building in the Balkans, Europe and the Balkans International Network*, ed. M. Dogo and G. Franzinetti, 117–39. Ravenna: Longo Editore.

Deutsch, H. 1933. Motherhood and sexuality. *Psychoanalytic Quarterly* 2:476–88.

Deutsche Welle News Bulletin. 2004. What Brussels really thinks about Turkey. December 15.

Devereux, G. 1953. Cultural factors in psychoanalytic therapy. *Journal of the American Psychoanalytic Association* 1:629–55.

Dimen, M. 1991. Deconstructing difference: Gender, splitting, and transitional space. *Psychoanalytic Dialogues* 1:335–52.

Djebar, A. 1985. *Fantasia: An Algerian Cavalcade*, trans. D. S. Blair. London: Quartet Books.

Dyer, G. 2004. Sonia Gandhi's big mistake. *The Philadelphia Inquirer*, May 21, p. A-19.

Earl of Cromer. 1908. *Modern Egypt.* New York: McMillan.

Eidelberg, S. 1977. The chronicle of Solomon Bar Simson. In *The Jews and the Crusaders.* Madison: University of Wisconsin Press.

Eigen, M. 1983. Dual union: Milner's view of psychic creativeness. *International Review of Psychoanalysis* 10:415–28.

El-Sadat, A. 1979. *In Search of Identity: An Autobiography.* New York: Harper Colophon Books.

Emin, A. 1922. *Buyuk Milet Meclisi reisi Baskumandan Mustafa Kemal ile mulakat* (An Interview with Mustafa Kemal Pasha, President of the Grand National Assembly and Commander-in-Chief). Reported in the newspaper *Vaki*, 10 January.

Encyclopedia of Asian History and Asian Society. 1988. New York: Asia Society.

Encyclopedia Britannica Yearbook. 1997. Islam. Chicago: Encyclopedia Britannica.

Encylopaedia of Islam. 1986. Madjnun Layla. In 2nd ed., V: 1102–7.

Erensu, S., and Adanali, Y. A. 2004. Turkey in the eye of the beholder: Tracking perceptions on Turkey through political cartoons. *KONTUR nr* 10:58–72.

Erikson, E. H. 1950. *Childhood and Society.* New York: W.W. Norton.

Erle, J., and Goldberg, D. A. 1984. Observations on the assessment of analyzability by experienced analysts. *Journal of the American Psychoanalytic Association* 32: 715–37.

Esposito, J. L. 1999. *The Oxford History of Islam.* New York: Oxford University Press.

———. 2005. *Islam: The Straight Path.* Oxford: Oxford University Press.

Etezady, M. H. 1995. Narcissism: Primary-secondary, fundamental, or obsolete? In *The Vulnerable Child*, vol. 2, ed. T. Cohen, M. H. Etezady, and B. Pacella, 3–9. New York: International Universities Press.

Fairbairn, W. R. D. 1952. *An Object Relations Theory of Personality*. New York: Basic Books.

Fanon, F. 1986. *Black Skin, White Masks*. London: Pluto Press.

Faqir, F. 2005. Intrafamily femicide in defence of honour: The case of Jordan. In *Women and Islam*, vol. 2, ed. H. Moghissi, pp. 104–24. New York: Routlege.

Farah, C. E. (2003). *Islam*. Hauppauge, NY: Barron's Educational Series.

Fisher, N. 1971. An interracial analysis: Transference and countertransference significance. *Journal of the American Psychoanalytic Association* 19:736–45.

Foley, T. 2003. Extending comity to foreign decrees in international custody disputes between parents in the United States and Islamic nations. *Family Court Review* 41:257–75.

Fonagy, P. 2001. *Attachment Theory and Psychoanalysis*. New York: Other Press.

Fonagy, P., and Target, M. 1997. Attachment and reflective function: Their role in self-organization. *Development and Psychopathology* 9:679–700.

Freud, A. 1922. Beating fantasies and daydreams. *International Journal of Psychoanalysis* 4:89–93.

———. 1936. *The Ego and the Mechanisms of Defense*. New York: International Universities Press.

Freud, S. 1900. The preface to The Interpretation of Dreams. *Standard Edition* 4:26.

———. 1900a. Interpretation of dreams. *Standard Edition* 4/5:1–626.

———. 1905. Three essays on the theory of sexuality. *Standard Edition* 7:135–243.

———. 1908. Letter dated 1908. In *The Complete Correspondence of Sigmund Freud and Karl Abraham 1907–1925*, ed. E. Falzedar and A. Haynal, 2002.

———. 1910. The future prospects of psychoanalytic therapy. *Standard Edition* 11:141–51.

———. 1916. Some character types met with in psychoanalytic work. *Standard Edition* 14:311–31.

———. 1917. A childhood recollection from Dichtung und Wahrheit. *Standard Edition* 17:145–57.

———. 1918. The taboo of virginity. *Standard Edition* 11:191–208.

———. 1919. The uncanny. *Standard Edition* 17:217–56.

———. 1921. Group psychology and the analysis of the ego. *Standard Edition* 18:145–72.

———. 1926. Inhibitions, symptoms, and anxiety. *Standard Edition* 20:87–156.

———. 1927. The future of an illusion. *Standard Edition* 21:5–56.

———. 1930. *Civilization and Its Discontents*. *Standard Edition* 21:59–145.

———. 1933. New introductory lectures to psychoanalysis. *Standard Edition* 22:5–182.

———. 1963. *Sexuality and the Psychology of Love*, ed. Philip Rieff. New York: Macmillan Publishing.

Friedman, T. 2002. *Longitudes and Attitudes*. New York: Farrar Straus Giroux.

Fromkin, D. 2001. *A Peace to End All Peaces*, 96–105. New York: Henry Holt and Co.

Fromm, E. 1956. *The Art of Loving*. New York: Harper and Row.

Gabbard, G., and Lester, E. 1995. *Boundaries and Boundary Violations in Psychoanalysis*. New York: Basic Books.

Galwash, A. A. 1963. *The Religion of Islam*. Cairo, Egypt: Imprimerie Misr S.A.E.

Gamard, I. 2004. *Rumi and Islam. Selections From His Stories, Poems and Discourses, Annotated and Explained*. Woodstock, VT: Skylight Paths Publishing.

Garza-Guerrero, A. 1973. Culture shock: Its mourning and the vicissitudes of identity. *Journal of the American Psychoanalytic Association* 22:408–29.

Gatade, S. 2003. Hating Romila Thapar. pp. 1–6. Available at www.Crosscurrents.org.

Gay, P. 1988. *Freud: A Life for Our Times*. New York: W.W. Norton.

Gelpke, R., trans. 1966. *The Story of Layla and Majnun*. London: Bruno Cassirer.

Ghazoul, F., and Harlow, B. 1994. *The View from Within: Writers and Critics on Contemporary Arabic Literature*. Cairo: American University in Cairo Press.

Ghazvini, M. and Ghani, J., eds. [1389] 1941. Diwan-I-Khwajeh Shamsuddin Mohammad Hafiz. Tehran: Zawawar.

Ghent, E. 1990. Masochism, submission, surrender. *Journal of Contemporary Psychoanalysis* 26:109–57.

Gibbs, H. A. R. 1970. *Mohammedanism*. London: Oxford New York: Oxford University Press.

Gill, H. S. 1987. Effects of oedipal triumph: Collapse or death of rival parent. *International Journal of Psychoanalysis* 68:251–57.

———. 1988. Working through resistances of intrapsychic, environmental origin. *International Journal of Psychoanalysis* 69:535–40.

Godley, W. 2001. Saving Masud Khan. *London Review of Books* 23:3–7.

———. 2004. Commentary. *International Journal of Psychoanalysis* 85:42–43.

Goldberg, E., Myers, W., and Zeifman, I. 1974. Some observations on three interracial analyses. *International Journal of Psychoanalysis* 55:495–500.

Goldstein, J., Freud, A., and Solnit, A. 1973. *Beyond the Best Interest of the Child*. New York: The Free Press.

Gole, N. June 2001. *PBS Frontline Interview: Women and Islam*, 2005, from http://www.pbs.org/wgbh/pages/frontline/shows/muslims/themes/women.html

Gopal, S. 1991. *Anatomy of a Confrontation: The Babri Masjid–Ram Janmabhumi Issue*. New Delhi: Penguin Books.

Gorkin, M. 1996. Countertransference in cross-cultural psychotherapy. In *Reaching Across Boundaries of Culture and Class*, ed. R. Perez-Foster, M. Moskowitz, and R. A. Javier, 47–70. Northvale, NJ: Jason Aronson.

Graham-Brown, S. 1988. *Images of Women: The Portrayal of Women in Photography of the Middle East, 1860–1950*. New York: Columbia University Press.

Grier, W. 1967. When the therapist is Negro: Some effects on the treatment process. *American Journal of Psychiatry* 123:1587–92.

Grinberg, L., and Grinberg, R. 1989. *Psychoanalytic Perspectives on Migration and Exile*. New Haven, CT: Yale University Press.

Grotstein, J. S. 2004. Spirituality, religion, politics, history, apocalypse and transcendence: An essay on a psychoanalytically and religiously forbidden subject. *International Journal of Applied Psychoanalytic Syudies* 1:82–95.

Group for the Advancement of Psychiatry. 2002. *Cultural Assessment in Clinical Psychiatry*. Washington, DC: American Psychiatric Publishing.

Gunaratna, R. 2002. *Inside Al Qaeda: Global Network of Terror*. New York: Berkley Books.

Gurel, D. 1985. The first encounter of Crusaders and Turks. In *Tarih ve Toplum*, 18:28–30, transl. from *Historie anonyme de la permier croisade*, eds. L. Brehmier and P. Champion, 1924.

Haddad, Y. Y., and A. T. Lummis. 1987. *Islamic Values in the United States*. Oxford: Oxford University Press.

Haddawy, H., and Mahdi, M. 1990. Introduction. In *The Arabian Nights* (1st ed., pp. ix–xxx). New York: Norton.

———. 1990. Prologue: [The Story of King Shahrayar and Shahrazad, his Vizier's Daughter]. In *The Arabian nights* (1st ed., pp. 3–16). New York: Norton.

Hafez, S. [1345] 1966. *Divan-e Khwaja Hafez Shirazi*, ed. S. A. Enjavi. Tehran: Haydari.

Hamilton, J. W. 1969. Object loss, dreaming, and creativity: The poetry of John Keats. *Psychoanalytic Study of the Child* 24:488–531.

Hammidullah, M. 1969. Introduction to Islam. In *Compendium of Muslim Texts*. Paris: Centre Culturel Islamique.

Hartmann, H. 1939. *Ego Psychology and the Problem of Adaptation*. Trans. D. Rapaport. New York: International Universities Press.

Hart, M. H. 1996. *100: A Ranking of the Most Influential Persons in History*. New York: Citadel Press.

Harvani, A. 1996. *Gandhi to Gandhi: Private Faces of Public Figures*. New Delhi: Gyan Publishing House.

Hasan, M. 1991. Competing symbols and shared codes: intercommunity relations in modern India. In *Anatomy of a Confrontation: The Babri Masjid–Ram Janmabhumi Issue*, ed. S. Gopal, 99–121. New Delhi: Penguin Books.

Hassan, M., and Khalique, A. 1987. Impact of parents on children's religious prejudice. *Indian Journal of Current Psychological Research* 2:47–55.

Haykal, M. H. 1968. *The Life of Mohammad* (Hayat Muhammad). Cairo: Maktabat Al-Nahda Almisrya.

Herwitz, D. 1988. *Husain*. Bombay: Tata.

Hitler, A. 1925. *Mein Kempf, Band 1 und 2*. Munchen: F. Eher Nachf. Verlag.

Hodgson, M. 1974. *The Venture of Islam: Conscience and History in a World Civilization*. Chicago: The University of Chicago Press.

Holmes, D. 1992. Race and transference in psychoanalysis and psychotherapy. *International Journal of Psychoanalysis* 73:1–11.

Holy Koran, translation and commentary by A. Y. Ali. Beirut, Lebanon: Dar al Arabia Publishing.

Hopkins, L. 1998. D. W. Winnicott's analysis of Masud Khan: A preliminary study of failures in object usage. *Contemporary Psychoanalysis* 34:5–47.

Homans, P. 1984. Once again, psychoanalysis, East and West: A psychoanalytic essay on religion, mourning, and healing. *History of Religions* 24:1.

Hourani, G. 1985. *Reason and Tradition in Islamic Ethics*. Cambridge, England: Cambridge University Press.

Huang, F., and Akhtar, S. (2005). Immigrant sex: The transport of affection and sensuality across cultures. *American Journal of Psychoanalysis* 65:179–88.

Hujwiri, A. U. J. 1967. *Kashf al-Mahjub: The Oldest Persian Treaties on Sufism*, trans. R. A. Nicholson. London: Luzac and Company.

Huntington, S. 1993. The clash of civilization. *Foreign Affairs*, June, 72:22–49

———. 2004. The Hispanic challenge. *Foreign Policy*, March/April, 30–45

Hussaini, M. M. 1996. *Marriage and Family in Islam*. Bolingbrook, IL: Al-Meezan International.

Ian, M. 2000. The unholy family: From satanism to the chronos complex. *Journal for the Psychoanalysis of Culture and Society* 5:285–89.

Ibn 'Arabi, M. 1971. *Sufis of Andalusia: The Ruh al-quds and al-Durrat al-fakhira*, trans. R. W. J. Austin. London: George Allen and Unwin Ltd.

Imam, A. 2005. The Muslim religious right ("fundamentalists") and sexuality. In *Women and Islam: Critical Concepts in Sociology*, vol. 2, ed. H. Moghissi, pp. 51–69. New York: Routledge.

Inalcik, H. 1987. Faith devri uzerinde tetkikler ve vesikalar (Documents and Investigations on the Era of the Conqueror). *Turk Tarih Kurmu*.

———. 2004. *Osmanli Imparatorlugu Klasik Cag* (Ottoman Empire–Classical Period) Istanbul: YKY.

Inamdar, S. 2001. *Muhammad and the Rise of Islam: The Creation of Group Identity*. Madison, CT: Psychological Press.

India Abroad. 2004. March 19, p. A-18.

India Abroad. 2004. April 16, p. A-18.

al-Isfahani, al-Faraj A. 1992. *Majnun Layla*. In: *Kitab al-Aghani* 2:1–97. Cairo: Al-Hay'ah al-Misriyah al-'Ammah lil-Kitab.

Islam, R. 2003. *Sufism in South Asia: Impact on 14th Century Muslim Society*. Karachi: Oxford University Press.

Itzkowitz, N. 1972. *Ottoman Empire and Islamic Tradition*. Chicago, IL: University of Chicago Press.

Jackson, S. 2005. *Islam and the Black American: Looking Toward the Third Resurrection*. New York: Oxford University Press.

Jaffer, A., and Jackson, A., eds. 2004. *Encounters: The Meeting of Asia and Europe, 1500–1800*. London: V&A.

Jaffer, M. 2003. *The Book of Muhammad*. New York: Viking Press.

Jafferlot, C. 1996. *The Hindu Nationalist Movement in India*. New York: Columbia University Press.

Jagruthi, M. 2004. *Women and Communalism*. Bangalore: Jagruthi Publications.

James, W. 2002. *The Varieties of Religious Experience: A Study in Human Experience*. New York: The Modern Library.

Jayyusi, S., and Allen, R. 1995. *Modern Arabic Drama: An Anthology*. Bloomington: Indiana University Press.

Josephson, A., and Peteet, J. 2004. *Handbook of Spirituality and Worldview in Clinical Practice*. Washington, DC: American Psychiatric Publishing.

Kakar, S. 1985. Psychoanalysis and non-Western cultures. *International Review of Psycho-Analysis* 12:441–48.

———. 1990a. *The Inner World: A Psycho-Analytic Study of Child and Society in India*. London: Oxford University Press.

———. 1990b. *Intimate Relations: Exploring Indian Sexuality*. Chicago: University of Chicago Press.

———. 1991a. *Shamus, Mystics, and Doctors: A Psychological Inquiry into India and Its Healing Traditions*. Chicago: University of Chicago Press.

———. 1991b. *The Analyst and the Mystic: Psychoanalytic Reflections on Religion and Mysticism*. Chicago: University of Chicago Press.

———. 1996. *The Colors of Violence: Cultural Identities, Religion, and Conflict*. Chicago: University of Chicago Press.

Kakar, S., and Ross, J. M. 1988. Love in the Middle Eastern world. In *Tales of Love, Sex and Danger*, eds. Sudhir Kakar and John Munder Ross. New York: Basil Blackwell.

Karsh, E., and Karsh, I. 1999. *Empires of the Sand: The Struggle for Mastery in the Middle East*, 326–341. Cambridge, MA: Harvard University Press.

Kernberg, O. F. 1974. Mature love: Pre-requisites and characteristics. In *Object Relations Theory and Clinical Psychoanalysis*, pp. 215–39. New York: Jason Aronson.

———. 1975. *Borderline Conditions and Pathological Narcissism*. New York: Jason Aronson.

———. 1976. *Object Relations Theory and Clinical Psychoanalysis*. New York: Jason Aronson.

Khairallah, As'ad. 1980. *Love, Madness, and Poetry: An Interpretation of the Majnun Legend*. Beirut: Orient-Institut der Deutschen Morgenlandischen Gesellschaft.

———. 1995. The Individual and Society: Salah 'Abd as-Sabbur's *Layla al-Majnun*. In *Gesellschaftlicher Umbruch und Histories im zeitgeneossischen Drama der islamischen Welt*, eds. Johann Christoph Burgel and Stephan Guth, 161–77. Stuttgart: F. Steiner.

Khan, H. I. 1964. *The Sufi Message of Hazrat Inayat Khan*, vol. 10. London: Barrie and Jenkins.

Khan, M. 1995. *The Meanings of Sahih Al-Bukani* (Arabic-English translation). Medina, Saudi Arabia: Islamic University Press.

Khan, M. M. R. 1964. Intimacy, complicity, and mutuality in perversions. In *Alienation in Perversions*, 18–30. New York: International Universities Press, 1979.

———. 1966. Role of phobic and counterphobic mechanisms and separation anxiety in schizoid character formation. In *The Privacy of the Self*, 69–81. New York: International Universities Press, 1974.

———. 1971. The role of illusion in the analytic space and process. In *The Privacy of the Self*, 251–69. New York: International Universities Press, 1974.

———. 1974. *The Privacy of the Self*. London: Hogarth Press.

———. 1975. Introduction. In *Collected Papers: Through Paediatrics to Psychoanalysis*, ed. D. W. Winnicott. London: Hogarth Press.

———. 1979. *Alienation in Perversions*. London: Hogarth Press.

———. 1983. *Hidden Selves*. London: Hogarth Press.

———. 1988. *When Spring Comes*. London: Chatto and Windus.

Khan, R. 2005. Qays ibn al-Mulawwah (circa 680–710). In *Dictionary of Literary Biography, vol. 311: Arabic Literary Culture, 500–925*, eds. M. Cooperson and S. M. Toorawa, 288–91. Detroit, MI: Thomson Gale.

Khan, S. A. 1884. Lecture at Gurdaspur, January 27, 1884. In *Lectures by Sir Syed Ahmad Khan*, 176. Aligarh: Aligarh Muslim University Press.

Khatami, M. 1998. Speech at the United Nations General Assembly. Available at www.dialoguecentre.org/PDF/proposal.pdf

Kilicbay, M. A. 1985. Istanbul'un latinler tarafindan zabti (The Latin Conquest of Istanbul). *Tarih ve Toplum* 18:31–36. Iletisim Yayincilik Istanbul.

Killingmo, B. 1995. Affirmation in psychoanalysis. *International Journal of Psycho-Analysis* 76:503–18.

Klauber, J. 1968. The psychoanalyst as a person. In *Difficulties in the Analytic Encounter*, 123–39. New York: Jason Aronson.

Klein, M. 1935. A contribution to the psychogenesis of manic-depressive states. In *Love, Guilt, and Reparation and Other Works, 1921–1945*, pp. 262–89. New York: Free Press, 1992.

———. 1940. Mourning and its relation to manic-depressive states. In *Love, Guilt, and Reparation and Other Works, 1946–1963*, 1–24. New York: The Free Press.

———. 1946. Notes on some schizoid mechanisms. *International Journal of Psychoanalysis* 27:99–110.

———. 1975. *Love, Guilt and Reparation and Other Works: 1921–1945*. New York: A Delta Book.

Knafo, D. 1999. Anti-Semitism in the clinical setting: Transference and countertransference dimensions. *Journal of the American Psychoanalysis Association* 47:35–63.

Kohut, H. 1971. *The Analysis of Self: A Systematic Approach to the Psychoanalytic Treatment of Narcissistic Personality Disorder*. New York: International Universities Press.

———. 1972. Thoughts on narcissism and narcissistic rage. *Psychoanalytic Study of the Child* 27:360–400.

———. 1975. Originality and repetition in science. In *The Search for the Self*, vol. 3, ed. by P. Ornstein. Madison, CT: International Universities Press.

———. 1977. *The Restoration of the Self*. New York: International Universities Press.

———. 1979. The two analyses of Mr. Z. *International Journal of Psychoanalysis* 60:3–10.

Kologlu, O. 1990. Dunya Siyaseti ve Islam Birligi (World Politics and Unity of Islam). *Tarih ve Toplum* 83:12–17 Istanbul.

Koran. Ed. and trans. A. Yusaf Ali. Lahore, Pakistan: Ashraf Publications.

Kumar, M. 2005. In a bid to restate the culture-psyche problematic: Revisiting "The Essential Writing of Sudhir Kakar." *Psychoanalytic Quarterly* 2.

Kurtz, S. 1996. *All the Mothers are One: Hindu India and the Cultural Reshaping of Psychoanalysis*. New York: Columbia University Press.

bin Laden, Osama. 2002. *The Travail of a Child Who Has Left the Land of the Holy Shrines*, trans. Abd-ar-Rahman al-Ashmawi. *The New York Times*, April 2, p. 16.

Leary, K. 1995. Interpreting in the dark: Race and ethnicity in psychoanalytic psychotherapy. *Psychoanalytic Psychology* 12:127–40.

———. 1997. Race, self-disclosure and "forbidden talk": Race and ethnicity in contemporary clinical practice. *Psychoanalytic Quarterly* 163–89.

———. 2000. Racial enactments in dynamic treatment. *Psychoanalytic Dial* 10: 639–53.

———. 2006. How race is lived in the consulting room. In *Unmasking Race, Culture, and Attachment in the Psychoanalytic Space*, ed. K. White, pp. 75–89. London: Karnac Books.

Leonard, K. 2003. *Muslims in the United States: The State of Research*. New York: Russell Sage Foundation.

Lévi-Strauss, C. 1953. *Discussion of an Appraisal of Anthropology Today*, ed. S. Tax. Chicago, IL: University of Chicago Press.

———. 1958. *Structural Anthropology*. New York: Anchor.

Levine, H. 2006. Large group dynamics and world conflict: The contributions of Vamik Volkan. *Journal of the American Psychoanalytic Association* 54:273–80.

Lewis, B. 1984. *The Jews of Islam*. Princeton: Princeton University Press.

Lieberman, J. 1997. Discussion of Aisha Abbasi's paper, "When Worlds Collide in the Analytic Space," presented at the winter meetings of the American Psychoanalytic Association, New York, NY.

Lichentenberg, J. D. 1989. *Psychoanalysis and Motivation*. Hillsdale, NJ: The Analytic Press.

Limentani, A. 1992. Obituary of M. Masud R. Khan. *International Journal of Psychoanalysis* 73:155–159.

Lings, M. 1971. *A Sufi Saint of the Twentieth Century, Shaikh Admad al-Alawi: His Spiritual Heritage and Legacy*. Berkeley: University of California Press.

Lockman, Z. 2004. *Contending Visions of the Middle East: The History and Politics of Orientalism*. Cambridge: University Press.

Loewenberg, P. 1995. *Fantasy and Reality in History*, pp. 93–107. Oxford: Oxford University Press.

Ludden, D. 1996. *Contesting the Nation: Religion, Community, and the Politics of Democracy of India*. Philadelphia: University of Pennsylvania Press.

Madhok, B. 1970. *Indianisation?* New Delhi: S. Chand and Company.

———. 1983. Persecuted or pampered? *Illustrated Weekly of India*, January 9.

Mahler, M. S., Pine, F., and Bergman, A. 1975. *The Psychological Birth of the Human Infant*. New York: Basic Books.

Mamdani, M. 2004. *Good Muslim, Bad Muslim: America, the Cold War, and the Roots of Terror*. New York: Pantheon Books.

Mani, V. 1975. *Puranic Encyclopaedia*. Delhi: Motilal Banarsidass Publishers.

Manji, I. 2003. *The Trouble with Islam Today: A Muslim's Call for Reform in Her Faith*. New York: St. Martin's Griffin.

Mann, M. 2004. Immigrant parents and their emigrant adolescents: The tension of inner and outer worlds. *American Journal of Psychoanalysis* 64:143–53.

———. 2006. The formation and development of individual and ethnic identity. *American Journal of Psychoanalysis* 66:211–24.

Manuel, P. 1996. Music, the media, and communal relations in North India, past and present. In *Contesting the Nation: Religion, Community, and the Politics of Democracy of India*, ed. D. Ludden, 119–28. Philadelphia: University of Pennsylvania Press.

Marks, L. 2004. Sacred practices in highly religious families: Christian, Jewish, Mormon, and Muslim perspectives. *Family Process* 43:217–31.

McBride, J. 1996. *The Color of Water: A Black Man's Tribute To His White Mother*. New York: Riverhead Books.

McCoud, A. 1993. *African American Islam*. New York: Rutledge.

Mernissi, F. 1987. *Beyond the Veil: Male-Female Dynamics in Modern Muslim Society*, rev. ed., Bloomington: Indiana University Press.

Miliora, M. 2004. The psychology and ideology of an Islamic terrorist leader: Usama bin Laden. *International Journal of Applied Psychoanalytic Studies* 2:121–39.

Milli Gazette (Turkish daily newspaper), December 18, 2004.

Mitchell, S. 1988. *Relational Concepts in Psychoanalysis: An Integration*. Cambridge, MA: Harvard University Press.

Mitchell, S. A. 1988. The analyst's knowledge and authority. *Psychoanalytic Quarterly* 67:1–31.

Mitter, P. 1994. *Art and Nationalism in Colonial India, 1850–1922*. Cambridge: Cambridge University Press.

———. 2001. The Raj, Indian artists and Western art. In ed. J. K. Bautze, *The Ehrenfeld Collection—Indian and Western Painting 1780–1890*. London: Art Services International.

Modell, A. (1976). The holding environment and the therapeutic action of psychoanalysis. *Journal of the American Psychoanalysis Association* 24:255–307.

Modell, A. H. 1970. The transitional object and the creative act. *Psychoanalytic Quarterly* 39:240–50.

Mohammad-Arif, A. 2002. *Salaam America: South Asian Muslims in New York*. London: Anthem Press.

Mohan, S. 1997. *Awadh Under the Nawabs*. New Delhi: Manohar Publications.

Moncayo, R. 1998. Cultural diversity and the cultural and epistemological structure of psychoanalysis: Implications for psychotherapy with Latinos and other minorities. *Psychoanalytic Psychology* 15:262–86.

Montville, J. V. 1987. The arrow and the olive branch: a case for track II diplomacy. In *Conflict Resolution: Track II Diplomacy*, eds. J. W. McDonald Jr., and D. B. Bendahmane, 5–20. Washington, DC: U.S. Government Printing Office.

———. 1991. Psychoanalytic enlightenment and the greening of diplomacy. In *The Psychodynamics of International Relationships*, vol. 2, ed. V. D. Volkan, J. V. Montville, and D. A. Julius, 177–92. Lexington, MA: Lexington Books.

Moore, R. J. 1983. Jinnah and the Pakistan demand. *Modern Asian Studies* 17:529–61.

Moses-Hrushowsky, R. 1994. *Deployment: Hiding Behind Power Struggles as a Character Defense*. Northvale, NJ: Jason Aronson.

Moskowitz, M. 1996. The end of analyzability. In *Reaching Across Boundaries of Culture and Class: Widening The Scope of Psychotherapy*, ed. R. Perez Foster, M. Moskowitz, and R. Javier. Northvale, NJ: Jason Aronson.

Mukherjee, A. 1991. Colonialism and communalism. In *Anatomy of a Confrontation: The Babri Masjid–Ram Janmabhumi Issue*, ed. S. Gopal, 164–78. New Delhi: Penguin Books.

Murata, S. 1992. *The Tao of Islam: A Sourcebook on Gender Relationships in Islamic Thought*. Albany: State University of New York Press.

Myers, W. 1977. The significance of the colors Black and White in the dreams of Black and White patients. *Journal of the American Psychoanalytic Association* 25:163–81.

Naidu, S. 1918. *Mohammad Ali Jinnah: The Ambassador of Hindu-Muslim Unity*. Madras: Genesh and Company.

Najeeb, S. 2007. The religion of psychoanalysis, or ode to a nightingale. In *Explorations in Psychanalytic Ethnography*, ed. J. Mimica, p. 235. Oxford: Berghahn Books.

Nasafi, A. 1962. *Kitab al-Insan al-Kamil*, ed. M. Mole. Tehran, Iran: Department D'Iranologie, de l'Institute Franco-Iraninan.

Nasr, S. H. 1991. *Islamic Spirituality I: Foundations*. New York: Crossroad.

———. 2003. *Islam: Religion, History, and Civilization*. San Francisco: Harper-Collins.

Nayar, K. 2004. Defeat is a jigsaw puzzle—piece it together and you have an old story: Arrogance. *The Indian Express*, May 18.

Neher, A. 1980. *The Psychology of Transcendence*. Englewood, NJ: Prentice Hall.

Nesom, M. 1984. *Abdur Rehman Chughtai: A Modern South Asian Artist*. Ann Arbor: University of Michigan.

Nicholson, R. A. 1926. *The Mathnavi of Jalau'ddin Rumi*. London: Cambridge University Press.

Niederland, W. G. 1976. Psychoanalytic approaches to artistic creativity. *Psychoanalytic Quarterly* 45:185–212.

Noor, F. 2003. What is the victory of Islam? In *Progressive Muslims: On Justice, Gender, and Pluralism*, ed. O. Safi, 310–33. Oxford, UK: Oneworld Publications.

Nurbakhsh, D. J. 1953. *Mureed va Murad*. Tehran: Khaneqah-i-N'imutullahi.

———. 1978. Sufism and psychoanlysis I: What is Sufism. *International Journal of Social Psychiatry* 24:204–12.

Oberndorf, C. P. 1954. Selectivity and option for psychiatry. *American Journal of Psychiatry* 100:754–58.

Obeyesekere, G. 1990. *The Work of Culture: A Symbolic Transformation in Psychoanalysis and Anthropology*. Chicago: University of Chicago Press.

———. 1999. Further steps in relativization: The Indian Oedipus revisited. In *Vishnu on Freud's Desk: A Reader in Psychoanalysis and Hinduism*, ed. T. G. Vaidyanathan and J. J. Kripal, 147–62. Delhi: Oxford University Press.

Oldenburg, V. T. 2001. *The Making of Colonial Lucknow: 1856–1877* (The Lucknow Omnibus Edition). New Delhi: Oxford University Press.

Olsson, P. 2005. *Malignant Pied Pipers of Our Time: A Psychological Study of Destructive Cult Leaders From the Reverend Jim Jones to Osama bin Laden*. Baltimore, MD: Publish America.

Ortayli, I. 1985. Imparatorlugun En Uzun Yuzyili (The Longest Century of the Empire). *Iletisim Yayinlari Istanbul*.

Parens, H. 1999. Toward the prevention of prejudice. In *At the Threshold of the Millennium: A Selection of the Proceedings of the Conference*, vol. 2, 131–41. Lima, Peru: Prom Peru.

Paris, E. 1995. *The End of Days: The Story of Tolerance, Tyranny, and the Expulsion of the Jews from Spain*. Amherst, NY: Prometheus Books.

Paterson, M. 1991. Obituary: Masud Khan. *Free Associations* 21:109–11.

Pickthal, M. M. 2002. *The Meaning of the Glorious Qur'an*. Beltsville, MD: Amana Publications.

Pine, F. 2006. Theories of motivation in psychoanalysis. In *Textbook of Psychoanalysis*, ed. E. Person, A. Cooper, and G. Gabbard, 3–9. Washington, DC: American Psychiatric Press.

Post, J. M. 1983. Woodrow Wilson re-examined. *Political Psychology* 4:289–306.

———. 1991. Saddam Hussein of Iraq. *Political Psychology* 12:279–89.

Post, J. M., and Robins, R. S. 1993. *When Illness Strikes the Leader*. New Haven, CT: Yale University Press.

Poznanski, E. O. 1972. The "replacement child": A saga of unresolved parental grief. *Behavioral Pediatrics* 81:1190–93.

Prasad, K., Chenoy, K. A. M., Singh, K., Mohan, D., Chhabra, S., and Shukla, S. C. 1993. *Report of the Inquiry Commission submitted to the Citizen's Tribunal on Ayodhya*. New Delhi: Secretariat, Citizen's Tribunal on Ayodhya.

Prathikanti, S. 1997. East Indian American families. In *Working with Asian Americans: A Guide for Clinicians*, ed. E. Lee, 79–100. New York: Guilford.

Quataert, D. 2003. *The Ottoman Empire 1700–1922*. Cambridge: Cambridge University Press.

Radhakrishnan, S. 1975. *The Present Crisis of Faith*. New Delhi: Orient Paperbacks.

Rahman, F. 1994. *Major Themes of The Quran*. Minneapolis, MN: Bibliotheca Islamica.

al-Rai 'i, Ali. 1992. The prose stylists. In *Modern Arabic Literature: The Cambridge History of Arabic Literature*, ed. M. M. Badawi. Cambridge: Cambridge University Press.

Ramana, C. V. 1964. On the early history and development of psychoanalysis in India. *Journal of the American Psychoanalytic Association* 12:110–34.

Ramanujam, A. K. 1999. The Indian Oedipus. In *Vishnu on Freud's Desk: A Reader in Psychoanalysis and Hinduism*, ed. T. G. Vaidyanathan and J. J. Kripal, 109–36. Delhi: Oxford University Press.

Rehman, T., and Dziegielewski, S. 2003. Women who choose Islam: Issues, changes, and challenges in providing ethnic-diverse practice. *International Journal of Mental Health* 32:31–49.

Rejwan, N. 1980. Jews under Muslim rule: Creative symbiosis. *The Jerusalem Post*, February 6, p. 4.

———. 1997. Jews and Arabs: The cultural heritage. *Israel Review of Arts and Letters* 105:1.

Rice, C. 1964. *The Persian Sufis*. London: Allen and Unwin.

Richard, A. Jr. 1991. The economic uses and impact of international remittances in rural Egypt. *Economic Development and Cultural Change* 39:695–722.

Robins, R. S. 1986. Paranoid ideation and charismatic leadership. *Psychohistory Review* 5:15–55

Robinson, A. 2001. *Bin Laden: Behind The Mask of the Terrorist*. New York: Arcade Publishing.

Rodinson, M. 1976. *Mohammed*. New York: Penguin Books.

Rodman, F. R. 2003. *Winnicott: Life and Work*. Cambridge, MA: Perseus Books Group.

Roland, A. 1988. *In Search of Self in India and Japan: Toward a Cross-Cultural Psychology*. Princeton, NJ: Princeton University Press.

——. 1994. Identity, self, and individualism in a multicultural perspective. In *Race, Ethnicity, and Self*, ed. E. Salett and D. Kolsow, 143–69. Washington, DC: National Multicultural Institute.

——. 1996. *Cultural Pluralism and Psychoanalysis: The Asian and North American Experience*. New York: Routledge.

Rose, G. J. 1964. Creative imagination in terms of ego "core" and boundaries. *International Journal of Psychoanalysis* 45:75–84.

Rothstein, A. 1982. Analyzability. *International Journal of Psychoanalysis* 67:177–88.

Roushdy-Hammady, I. 2006. Sheer and opaque screens: The medical ethnography of Arabic television, a phenomenological quandary of communal memory, suffering, and resistance. In *Leading to the 2003 Iraq War: The Global Media Debate*, ed. A. Nikolaev and E. Hakanen. Hampshire, UK: Macmillan Ltd.

Roy, O. 2004. *Globalized Islam*, 290–325. New York: Columbia University Press.

Royle, R., Barrett, M., and Takriti, Y. 1999. Religious identity in Egyptian Muslim and Christian children aged 6–13 years. *Arab Journal of Psychiatry* 10:120–27.

Royster, J. E. 1979. Sufi as psychotherapist. *Psychologia* 22:225–235.

Rudolph, S., and Rudolph, L. I. 1993. Modern hate. *The New Republic*, March 22, 24–29.

Ruether, R. 1974. *Faith and Fratricide: The Theological Roots of Anti-Semitism*. New York: Seabury Press.

Rumi, M. J. M. 1925. *The Mathmawi of Jalal-uddin Rumi*, vol. 1, ed. R. A. Nicholson. Leiden, Holland: E. J. Brill.

Rushdie, S. 1989. *Satanic Verses*. New York: Viking.

Sabbah, F. A. 1984. *Woman in the Muslim Unconscious*. New York: Pergamon Press.

as-Sabur, Salah 'Abd. 1970. *Layla wal-Majnun*. Cairo: General Egyptian Society for Writing and Publishing.

Sandler, A. M. 2004. Institutional responses to boundary violations: The case of Masud Khan. *International Journal of Psychoanalysis* 85:27–42.

Sandler, J. 1960. The background of safety. *International Journal of Psychoanalysis* 41:352–56.

Sandler, J., and Rosenblatt, B. 1962. The concept of the representational world. *Psychoanalytic Study of the Child* 17:128–55.

Sarraj, A. N. 1914. *Kitab al-luma fit't-tasawwuf*, ed. R. A. Nicholson. Leiden, Holland: E. J. Brill.

Schachter, J., and Butts, H. 1968. Transference and countertransference in interracial analyses. *Journal of the American Psychoanalytic Association* 16:792–808.

Schimmel, A. 1975. *Mystical Dimension of Islam*. Chapel Hill: University of North Carolina.

Scholem, G. 1965. *On the Kabbalah and Its Symbolism*, transl. R. Manhein. New York: Schocken Books.

Scholem, G. 1973. *Sabbatai Sevi: They Mystical Messiah 1626–1676*. Princeton, NJ: Princeton University Press.

Scott, J. W. 1988. Deconstructing equality-versus-difference: Or, the uses of post-structuralist theory for feminism. *Feminist Studies* 14:33–50.

Settlage, C. 1992. Psychoanalytic observations on adult development in life and in the therapeutic relationship. *Psychoanalysis and Contemporary Thought* 15:349–75.

Shafii, M. 1985. *Freedom from the Self: Sufism, Meditation, and Psychotherapy*. New York: Human Sciences Press.

Shafii, M. and Shafii, S. L. 1982. *Pathways of Human Development: Normal Growth and Emotional Disorders in Infancy, Childhood, and Adolescence*. New York: Thieme-Stratton.

Shah, I. 1964. *The Sufis*. Garden City, NY: Doubleday.

Shakespeare, W. 1593. *King Richard III*. In *The Complete Works of William Shakespeare*, vol. 1, ed. W. G. Clark and W. A. Wright, pp. 209–46. New York: Nelson Doubleday, 1972.

Shapiro, E. R., and Carr, A. W. 1991. *Lost in Familiar Places*, 23–26. New Haven, CT: Yale University Press.

Shapiro, E., and Pinsker, H. 1973. Shared ethnic scotoma. *American Journal of Psychiatry* 130:1338–41.

Sharar, A. H. 1921. *Lucknow: The Last Phase of an Oriental Culture* (The Lucknow Omnibus Edition), trans. E. S. Harcourt and F. Hussain. New Delhi: Oxford University Press, 2001.

Shavit, Y., and Pierce, J. 1991. Sibship size and educational attainment in nuclear and extended families: Arabs and Jews in Israel. *American Sociological Review* 56:321–30.

Shawqi, A. 1933. *Majnun Layla*. trans. A. J. Arberry. London: Luzac & Co.

Sholevar, G. P. 1985. Marital assessment. In *Contemporary Marriage*, ed. D Goldberg, 290–311. Homewood, IL: Dorsey.

———. 1989. Resocialization of family therapy into psychiatry. *Contemporary Psychiatry* 8:242–45.

———. 1995. Family development and life cycle. In *Psychiatry*, vol. 2, ed. R. Michels, pp. 1–9. Philadelphia, PA: J. B. Lippincott.

———. 1997. Initial and diagnostic interviews. In *Textbook of Child and Adolescent Psychiatry*, ed. J. M. Weiner, 103–15. Washington, DC: American Psychiatric Press.

Siassi, S. 2000. Male patient—female analyst: Elucidation of a controversy. *Journal of Clinical Psychoanalysis* 9:93–112.

———. 2004. Transcending bitterness and early paternal loss through mourning and forgiveness. *Psychoanalytic Quarterly* 73:915–37.

Sikand, Y. 2004. Hindu followers of a Muslim imam. *American Federation of Muslims of Indian Origin: News Brief* 14:6.

Smith, K. 1996. The shadow of God. *The Hungarian Quarterly* 144:14–24.

Sokullu Mehmet Pasa. 2005. *Turk Tarihi* (Turkish History). www.dallog.com.

Spitz, R. A. 1965. *The First Year of Life*. New York: International Universities Press.

Steinberg, B. 1996. *Shame and Humiliation: Presidential Decision Making on Vietnam.* Montreal: McGill-Queen's University Press.

Sterba, R. 1947. Some psychological factors in Negro race hatred and in anti-Negro riots. *Psychoanalysis and the Social Sciences* 1:411–27.

Stern, D. N. 1985. *The Interpersonal World of the Infant.* New York: Basic Books.

Stern, J. 2003. *Terror in the Name of God: Why Religious Militants Kill.* New York: Harper Collins.

Stillman, N. A. 1979. *The Jews of Arab Lands: A History and Source Book.* Philadelphia: The Jewish Publication Society of America.

Strath, B. 2001. *Europe and the Other and Europe as the Other.* Brussels: Peter Lang P. I. E.

Sun Tzu. 500 B.C. *The Art of War.* Minneola, NY: Dover Publications.

Symington, N. 2004. The spirituality of natural religion. *International Journal of Applied Psychoanalytic Studies* 1:61–72.

Tang, N., and Gardner, J. 1999. Race, culture, and psychotherapy: Transference to minority therapists. *Psychoanalytic Quarterly* 68:1–20.

Teja, J. S., and Akhtar, S. 1981. The psychosocial problems of FMG's with special reference to those in psychiatry. In *Foreign Medical Graduates in Psychiatry: Issues and Problems*, ed. R. S. Chen, pp. 321–38. New York: Human Sciences Press.

Thapar, R. 2004. The future of the Indian past. *The Economist*, May 22 to 28, 2004, 9–10.

Tharoor, S. 2001. *Riot.* New Delhi: Penguin Books.

Thomson, J. A., Harris, M., and Volkan, V. D. 1993. *The Psychology of Western European Neo-Racism.* Charlottesville, VA: Center for the Study of Mind and Human Interaction.

Ticho, G. 1971. Cultural aspects of transference and countertransference. *Bulletin of the Menninger Clinic* 35:313–34.

Timur, T. 1993. Oriyentalist Resim Tarihi ile ilgili notlar (Notes on the History of Orientalist Painting). *Tarih ve Toplum* 112:34–39. Istanbul.

Turkman, E. 1962. *The Essence of Rumi's MAS NEVY.* Konya, Turkey: ERIS Bookseller.

Twain, M. 1966. *The Innocents Abroad.* New York: Signet Classics.

Uyar, H. 2004. Avrupa Uolunda kacirlan firsatlar (Chances missed on the road to Europe). *Toplumsal Tarih* 132:52–59. Istanbul.

Valiuddin, M. 1972. *Love of God.* London: Camelot Press.

van der Veer, P. 1994. *Religious Nationalism: Hindus and Muslims in India.* Berkeley: University of California Press.

Varshney, A. 2002. *Ethnic Conflict and Civic Life: Hindus and Muslims in India.* New Haven, CT: Yale University Press.

Varma, V. K., Akhtar, S., Kulhara, P. N., Vasudeva, P., and Kaushal, P. 1973. Measurement of authoritarian traits in India. *Indian Journal of Psychiatry* 15:156–75.

Volkan, V. D. 1963. Five poems by Negro youngsters who faced a sudden desegregation. *Psychiatric Quarterly* 37:607–16.

———. 1973. Transitional fantasies in analysis of narcissistic personality. *Journal of the American Psychoanalytic Association* 21:351–56.

———. 1976. *Primitive Internalized Object Relations*. New York: International Universities Press.

———. 1979. The "glass bubble of a narcissistic patient." In *Advances in Psychotherapy of the Borderline Patient*, ed. J. LeBoit and A. Cappori. New York: Jason Aronson.

———. 1979a. *Cyprus: War and Adaptation*. Charlottesville: The University Press of Virginia.

———. 1979b. The "glass bubble" of a narcissistic patient. In *Advances in Psychotherapy of the Borderline Patient*, ed. J. LeBoit and A. Capponi, 405–31. New York: Jason Aronson.

———. 1981. *Linking Objects and Linking Phenomena: A Study of Forms, Symptoms, Metapsychology, and Therapy of Complicated Mourning*. New York: International Universities Press.

———. 1987. *Six Steps in the Treatment of Borderline Personality Organization*. Northvale, NJ: Jason Aronson.

———. 1988. *The Need to Have Enemies and Allies: From Clinical Practice to International Relationships*. Northvale, NJ: Jason Aronson.

———. 1995. *The Infantile Psychotic Self and Its Fates*. Northvale, NJ: Jason Aronson.

———. 1997. *Blood Ties: From Ethnic Conflict to Ethnic Terrorism*. New York: Farrar, Strauss, and Giroux.

———. 2004. *Blind Trust: Large Groups and Their Leaders in Times of Crises and Terror*. Charlottesville, VA: Pitchstone Publishing.

Volkan, V. D., and Akhtar, S. (1998). *The Seed of Madness*. Madison, CT: International Universities Press.

———. 1997. *Bloodlines: From Ethnic Pride to Ethnic Terrorism*. New York: Farrar, Straus, and Giroux.

———. 2004. *Blind Trust*. Charlottesville, VA: Pitchstone Publishing.

Volkan, V. D., Akhtar, S., Dorn, R. M., Kafka, J. S., Kernberg, O. F., Olsson, P. A., Rogers, R., and Shanfield, S. B. 1998. The psychodynamics of leaders and decision making. *Mind and Human Interaction* 9:129–81.

Volkan, V. D., and Ast, G. 1997. *Siblings in the Unconscious and Psychopathology*. Madison, CT: International Universities Press.

Volkan, V. D., Ast, G., and Greer, W. 2002. *The Third Reich in the Unconscious*. New York: Brunner and Routledge.

Volkan, V. D., Cilluffo, A. F., and Sarvay, T. L. 1975. Re-grief therapy and the function of the linking object as a key to stimulate emotionality. In *Emotional Flooding*, ed. P. T. Olsen, 179–224. New York: Human Sciences Press.

Volkan, V. D., and Corney, R. T. 1968. Some considerations of satellite states and satellite dreams. *British Journal of Medical Psychology* 41:283–90.

Volkan, V. D., and Itzkowitz, N. 1984. *The Immortal Ataturk: A Psychohiography*. Chicago: University of Chicago Press.

———. 1994. *Turks and Greeks: Neighbors in Conflict*. Cambridgeshire: Eothen Press.

Volkan, V. D., Julius, D. A., and Montville, J. V., eds. 1990. *The Psychodynamics of International Relationships*, vol. 1. Lexington, MA: Lexington Books.

Volkan, V. D., and Zintl, E. 1993. *Life After Loss: The Lessons of Grief*. New York: Charles Scribner's Sons.

Watt, W. M. 1974. *Muhammad: Prophet and Statesman*. London: Oxford University Press.

Waelder, R. 1936. The principle of multiple function. *Psychoanalytic Quarterly* 5:45–62.

Weich, M. H. 1978. Transitional language. In *Between Reality and Fantasy*, ed. S. Grolnick, L. Bashin, and W. Meunsterberger, 411–23. New York: Jason Aronson.

Weil, A. 1970. The basic core. *Psychoanalytic Study of the Child* 25:442–60.

Wells, L. B. 2005. *Jinnah's Early Politics: The Ambassador of Hindu-Muslim Unity*. New Delhi: Permanent Black.

Wheatcroft, A. 2004. *Infidels*. New York: Random House Publishing.

Whinfield, E. H. 1973. *Teachings of Rumi*. London: Octagon Press.

Winnicott, D. W. 1947. Hate in the countertransference. In *Collected Papers: Through Paediatrics to Psychoanalysis*, 194–203. London: Hogarth Press, 1958.

———. 1953. Transitional objects and transitional phenomena. *International Journal of Psychoanalysis* 34:89–97.

———. 1960. Ego distortion in terms of true and false self. In *The Maturational Processes and the Facilitating Environment*, pp. 140–52. New York: International Universities Press, 1965.

———. 1971. *Playing and Reality*. London: Tavistock Publishing.

Winnicott, D. W., and Khan, M. M. R. 1953. Book review of *Psychoanalytic Studies of the Personality* by W. R. D. Fairbairn. *International Journal of Psychoanalysis* 34:329–33.

Wolf, E. 1988. *Treating the Self: Elements of Clinical Self Psychology*. New York: The Guilford Press.

Wolpert, S. 1984. *Jinnah of Pakistan*. Karachi: Oxford University Press.

Yilmaz, S. 2003. Iki Dunya Savasi arasinda Turk–Amerikan Illiskileri (Turkish American relations in the inter-war period). *Toplumsal Tarih* 120:86–91. Istanbul.

Young-Bruehl, E. 1988. *Anna Freud: A Biography*. New York: Summit Books.

Zaphiropoulos, M. 1982. Transcultural parameters in the transference and countertransference. *Journal of the American Academy of Psychoanalysis* 10:571–84.

Zepp, I. G. 1992. *A Muslim Primer*. Fayettville: University of Arkansas Press.

Index

Adam and Eve: in *Quran,* 128; *Quran* compared to the *Bible* for story of, 351

adoption: Islamic views on, 36–37; *Quran* on, 35–36

Advani, L. K., 253, 377

Afghanistan: bin Laden, Osama's, appeal to, 115–16; bin Laden, Osama's, leadership and Soviet Union war with, 109, 111; USA's mistakes made with, 115

Aisha: infidelity concerns with, 33–34; Muhammad and controversial marriage to, 35

Akbar, Jalaluddin Mohammad, 237

Ali, Chowdrhy Rahmat: Jinnah on views of, 89; Pakistan and citizenship of, 361

Ali, M. M., 355

Ali, Noble Drew, 17

Allah: history of term of, 5; Islam and singularity of, 7, 25; Jihad in name of, 199; Jinnah and prayer to, 88; Muhammad as intermediary for, 31; names of, 351

Amar Chitra Katha, 386

A'mr Husn, 8

ANZAC. *See* Australian and New Zealand Army Corps

aqiqa, 138

Arab(s): Egyptian *Asrar al-Banat* and challenges to audience of, 278–79; Egyptian movies and representation of, 268–70; Egyptian movies impacted by Israel's conflict with, 270–71; Egypt's *Al-Mumya* and representation of, 274–75; Muslims and intellectual growth through people who are not, 12–13; Muslims differentiated from, xiv–xv; sexuality and Sabbah's research on erotic literature of, 147–48; USA and *The Mummy*'s representation of, 274; USA and *Munich*'s representation of, 279–81; USA and *Syriana*'s representation of, 279–80; USA movies and representation of, 268–70, 275

Arabic Radio and Television (ART), 279

ART. *See* Arabic Radio and Television

art: Chughtai and influence of Persians and, 306; India and impact of *swadeshi* nationalism on, 304–5; India and introduction of European

practices and institutes of, 299–300; Islam and, xvi; Pakistan's Muslims and their, 307–8. *See also* Indo-Muslim art
Asharites, 134
al-Ashmawi, Abd-ar-Rahman, Dr., 112
Aslan, Reza, 222–25
Asrar al-Banat (The Girls' Secrets), 278–79
asymmetry, 205, 371–72
Atatürk, Mustafa Kemal: ANZAC eulogy of, 215; birth of, 66; childhood in Salonika of, 66–67; Christianity and Islam unification attempts of, 216; creativity developed in, 70; creativity of language created by, 75; death of, 70; death of siblings of, 71; dinner gatherings hosted by, 73–74; education in military of, 67; Efendi and, 73; essays of, 70–72; government exile of, 67–68; history and importance of, 63–64; Muslim leaders and inspiration from, 65; religion of mourning mother impacting, 72; Republic of Turkey and presidency of, 68–70; Turkey and Westernization of, 69–70; Turkey's religious beliefs and changes from, 72, 75; World War I success of, 68, 215–16
al Ati, Abd, 128
Aurangzeb, Alamgir: Hindus and suppression from, 236, 375; Muslims and suppression from, 375
Australian and New Zealand Army Corps (ANZAC), 216
Azad, Maulan Abul-Kalam, 80, 90, 302, 361
Azzam, Sheik Yussuf Abdallah: bin Laden, Osama, and differences with, 111; bin Laden, Osama, influenced by, 107–8, 116

Baboo-speak, 386
Babri Masjid, 252–54
Badawi, M., 287
Badr, 31–32
Bakr, Abu, 10
the Balkans: Gladstone on conflict in, 205–6; Ottoman Empire invading, 201; Turkey and views on, 372
Bergen, Peter, 107
Berman, Paul: on Al Qaeda, 104; on Qtub, Sayyid, 108
Bernfeld, Siegried, 114
Bible: Adam and Eve's story in *Quran* compared to, 351; Muhammad influenced by *New Testament* and, 221
bin Laden, Mohammad: bin Laden, Osama, and limited time with, 105–6; death of, 105; success of, 104–5
bin Laden, Osama: Afghanistan and appeal of, 115–16; Afghanistan's war with Soviet Union and leadership of, 109, 111; Azzam and differences with, 111; Azzam's influences on, 107–8, 116; Bergen on father figure search of, 107; bin Laden, Mohammad, and limited time with, 105–6; birth of, 104; creativity's absence in group-self led by Hitler and, 117–18; cult leaders compared to, 103–4, 113; education of, 107; Fahd and friendship with, 106–7; followers of, 114; Hitler compared to, 117; Islam's liberation from Western world and teachers of, 109; legacy in question of, 103; media covering terrorism and, 116–17; mother and shame of, 105–6; mother and stepmother relationships with, 105; poetry of, 111–13; psychoanalysis of anti-Western attitude of, 110, 118; Qtub, Sayyid, and influences on Al Qaeda and,

108–9; Saudi Arabian leadership and differences on USA with, 109–10, 115, 118; sibling's teasing of, 106; suicide bombers recruited by, 116; terrorism and possible reasons of, 103; al Turabi's influence on, 109; al-Zawahiri's influence on, 111

Bose, Girindrashekhar, 387

Bowlby, John, 164, 192

Buddhism, 296

Bush, George W., president: on Muslims as good or bad, 388; Turkey angered by requests of, 64–65

Carroll, James, 226

Casablanca, 270

case study. *See* Hasan; Mehran; Mrs. A

childhood: Atatürk in Salonika and, 66–67; Islam rituals in, 137–38; Jinnah and confusion with religion during, 95–96; of Jinnah and views of Freud, Sigmund, 96; Jinnah's health during, 96; of Mrs. A, 344–45; of Mrs. A and impact on psychoanalysis, 349; Muhammad impacted by separation and loss in, 24–25, 354; Winnicott on creativity in, 74

children: creativity and, 53–54, 60; Freud on religion and, 181; of Khadija, 26; of Muhammad, 26; Muslim immigrant family problems with latency and, 191–94. *See also* childhood

Christian(s): Europe and Jews compared to, 219; history of Jews and treatment in Europe by, 227; Jews and anti-Semitism from, 220; Muhammad's views on, 224–25; psychoanalysis and, 316

Christianity: Atatürk's attempts at unifying Islam and, 216; Islam and deteriorating relations with, 200; Islam compared to, 63–64; Islam's

history with, 201–2; Jinnah and, 98; Judaism and reconciliation with, 228–29; Judaism demonized in early, 226–27; sexuality in Islam compared to, 142

Chrysostom, John, St., 227

Chughtai, Abdur Rehman: colonialism influencing, 303–4; education of, 303; Hussain compared to, 309; Indo-Muslim art development and role of, 304, 306–7; Iqbal collaborating with, 307; Islamic lineage of, 304; Persian art influencing, 306; Riza-I-Abbasi influencing work of, 306; Tagore compared to, 305–6; Tagore influencing work of, 305; on Western influence on his work, 306–7

cinema. *See* movies

circumcision: de Klerk on Freud and, 387; of Jews compared to Muslims, 138

A Citizen, a Detective, a Thief. See Muwatin wa-Mukhbir wa-Harami

colonialism: Chughtai influenced by, 303–4; Indian relations between Muslims and Hindus affected by England and, 238–39; Indo-Muslim art aesthetically influenced by England and, 299–301; Islamic world history influenced through, 15–16; Muslims and villain hunger of Hindus after, 249–50

The Color of Water: A Black Man's Tribute to His White Mother (McBride), 335

Conker, Nuri, 74

Constantine's Sword (Carroll), 226–27

Constantinople, and Ottoman Empire conquest, 202–3

creativity: Atatürk developing, 70; Atatürk's creations in language and, 75; bin Laden, Osama, and Hitler, and absence of, 117–18; children and,

53–54, 60; development of, 54–55; intuition and, 55–56; origins of, 53, 60; process of, 55, 60; universality of, 54; Winnicott on childhood and, 74. *See also* art; poetry
Cripps, Stafford, Sir, 93
Croft, Frederick Leigh, Sir, 83
the Crusades, and racism, 200

Daniell, Thomas, 299–300
death: of Atatürk, 70; of Atatürk's siblings, 71; of bin Laden, Mohammad, 105; of Emibai, 83; Freud, Sigmund on father and, 106; of Jinnah, 88; of Jinnah's mother, 83; of Khadija, 7–8, 26; of Khan, Masud, 321; of Petit, 86; Rumi's views on, 50–51
de Klerk, E., 387
depressive position, 59–60
divorce: Islam and, 130–31; *Quran* on, 131
Djebar, Assia, 152
Dönmes, 73
dreams, 319
Ducas, 202
Dwarkadas, Kanji, 86, 359–60
Dyer, Gwynne, 256

East India Company, 299–300
education: of Atatürk in military, 67; of bin Laden, Osama, 107; of Chughtai, 303; Hindu right wingers changing Indian history in curriculum in, 255–56; of Hussain, 308; of Jinnah, 83, 359; of Mrs. A, 343–44; Muhammad on women and, 141; Muslim and Hindu conflict in India and solutions in, 257–58; of Volkan, 326
Efendi, Shemsi: Atatürk's identification with, 73; Dönme background of, 73; rituals of, 69
Egypt: 9/11's impact on movies from, 281–82; Arab audiences challenged by *Asrar al-Banat* from, 278–79; Arabs represented in movies from, 268–70; Arabs represented in *Al-Mumya* from, 274–75; Badawi on theater revival in, 287; European influence on playwrights in, 383; Israel's conflict with Arabs impacting movies from, 270–71; *Layla Wal-Majnun* and background of Revolution in, 289–90; *Majnun and Layla* by Shawqi in, 286–87; marriage tradition for Muslims in, 136; movies and feminism in, 276–77; movies from, 267; movies with belly dancers from, 272–73; women represented in movies from, 268–69, 271–73
Einstein, Albert, 48
El Fadl, Khaled Abou, 63
Emibai, 83
England: India and demise of reign of, 93–94; India and positive contributions from, 377–78; Indian citizens patronizing artists from, 299–300; Indian relations between Muslims and Hindus effected by colonialism of, 238–39; Indians and racism from, 300–301; Indo-Muslim art aesthetically influenced by colonialism of, 299–301; Indo-Muslim art and Westernization attempts of, 298–99; Jinnah and changes upon move to, 83–84, 97; Jinnah's activism and India v., 98; Muslims joining uprising with India against, 239; Ottoman Empire's negative image from, 208
erfan (gnosis): Persian poetry and, 56–57; Rumi's view of existence grounded by, 51–52, 60; science compared to, 51
EU. *See* European Union
Europe: Egyptian playwrights influenced by, 383; history of Jews and treatment of Christians in, 227;

immigration causing identity confusion in, 214–15; India and introduction of art institutes and practices of, 299–300; Jews compared to Christians in, 219; *Majnun and Layla* in, 382; Muslim countries and modernization attempts of USA and, 64–65; Ottoman Empire and defeat at Lepanto against, 204; Ottoman Empire and racism in views of, 203–4; Ottoman Empire diminished by, 201–2, 205–6; Ottoman Empire's fashion spreading to, 204–5; as-Sabur and influence of, 383; Turkey insulted by cartoons from, 211–12, 355; women and sexism in, 366–67

European Union (EU): Turkey and history of negotiations with, 211–13; Turkey and membership challenges for joining, 77

experimental knowledge, 47

Fahd, Abdul Aziz, 106–7

faith: culturing, 43–44; defining, 43; Khan, Masud's, anti-Semitism and Islamic, 320–21; personal and varying relationships with, 58–59; Rumi and, 45, 62; Rumi's poetry and, 58, 62

family: Hasan and problems with, 183–84; Mehran and struggles with, 190–91; of Mrs. A, 343–45; Muslim immigration challenges of, 185–86, 188, 191; Muslims and latency child problems with immigrant, 191–94; 9/11 creating problems for Muslim immigrants and, 194; USA life and challenges of Muslims and, 181–83, 188. *See also* family structure

family structure: *Asharites* compared to *Mutazilites* in, 134; Islam and regional variations of, 125; Islam and relationship to, 123–24; *Quran* and parental duties in, 131–33; Sufism and, 134–35

Fana (freedom from the self), 168

Fantasia: An Algerian Cavalcade (Djebar), 152

Fatima, 87

fatwa (legal opinion), 12, 34, 353

feminism: Egyptian movies and, 276–77; of *Layla Wal-Majnun,* 290; Shafiq and movements for, 276–77

Fink, Paul, 329

Freud, Anna, 114, 149

Freud, Sigmund, 31; Bose corresponding with, 387; on death of father, 106; de Klerk on circumcision and, 387; Islam and studies of psychoanalysis and, 283–84; Jinnah's and childhood views of, 96; Judaism and concerns of, 315; *Layla Wal-Majnun* and psychoanalysis of, 292; on religion and children, 181; on *Richard III,* 100

Fromm, Erich, 164–65

Gallipoli, 215–16

Gandhi, Mohandas Karamchand, 79; assassination of, 376; Indian Muslims and views on, 360; Jinnah and friction with, 92–94, 98–99; Jinnah compared to, 90–91; Nehru and favor of, 98; Nehru compared to, 359

Garam Hawa, 376

al-Ghazali, Imam Hamed, 14, 79, 147

Ghaznavi, Mahmud, 235

Gill, Harwant Singh, 317

The Girls' Secrets. See Asrar al-Banat

Gladstone, William Ewart, 205–6

God: Islam and belief in oneness of, 125; Islam and worship of, 352; Sufism's view of human separation from, 161–63. *See also* Allah; religion

Goitein, Shlomo Dov, 219

Gole, Nilufer, 150

Hafez, 267; on love, 161; poetry of, 155–58; sexuality of women as

viewed by, 157–58; Sufism ideals expressed by, 154
Hajj (pilgrimage to Mecca), 123
halat (mystical states), 172
Hamas (Islamic Resistance Movement), 217; on Jews and World War I, 226
Hanafi, 134
Hanbali, 134
haqq. See God
Hasan (case study child): family problems of, 183–84; Islamic conversion of Westerners and interest of, 184–85; Mecca trip and classmate ridicule of, 184; Muslim special schooling of, 184–85; religion and fear of, 185; USA traditions avoided by, 186–87
al Haythem, Ibn, 13
Hijrah (immigration, exile), 30–34
Hindu(s): Aurangzeb and suppression of, 236, 375; *Babri Masjid* attack and orchestration of Advani and, 253; England's colonialism effecting India's relations between Muslims and, 238–39; Hussain's work and opposition from right-wing of, 310; India and constitutional solutions for Muslim conflict with, 262–63; India and cultural solutions for Muslim conflict with, 258–59; India and economic solutions for Muslim conflict with, 260–61; India and education for solution of Muslims and conflict with, 257–58; India and experiential measures as solutions for Muslim conflict with, 259–60; India and issues of Muslims and, 231–32, 243–44, 246–47; India and judicial solutions for Muslim conflict with, 261–62; India and political solutions for Muslim conflict with, 261; India history in education curriculum changed by right wing of, 255–56; Indian government and Muslims incorporating, 236–37; Indian

Muslims and banning of *The Satanic Verses* alienating, 246; India's division into Pakistan and unresolved mourning of, 248–49; Jinnah and Muslims divided from, 240–41; Jinnah and view of, 95; Jinnah's ancestry of, 83; Jinnah unifying Muslims and, 90; movies and Muslims adopting names of, 376; Muslim *Babri Masjid* mosque destroyed by, 252–54; Muslim history of Indian domination causing trauma for, 248; Muslim reaction to recent attacks in India of, 254–55; Muslim religion compared to, 375; Muslim representation in movies of, 258–59; Muslims and cultural exchange between, 234, 237–40; Muslim's and postcolonial villain hunger of, 249–50; Muslims and varying views of nationalists and general public of, 233; Muslim's constitutional privileges in India alienating to, 246; Muslims destroying *Somnath* temple of, 235; Muslims in India and economic threat posed to, 250; Muslim's lack of Indian progressive secular leadership alienating to, 245–46; Muslim's pathological nostalgia alienating to, 244–45; Muslim's prejudicial attitudes toward, 245; Muslim's religious practices alienating to, 244; NRIs and confusion with India culture and, 251–52; Pakistan's division from India causing fighting amongst Muslims and, 241–42; psychoanalysis and, 316; *swadeshi* nationalism in India impacting, 301–2; Urdu language and contributions of, 238; USA media used against Muslims by NRI's and, 253
history: of Allah as term, 5; Atatürk's importance in, 63–64; of cultural stereotypes, 213–14; Hindu right

wingers changing Indian education curriculum and, 255–56; Hindus caused trauma from Muslims dominating India in, 248; of Indo-Muslim art, 297–99; of Islam and relationship to Christianity, 201–2; of Islamic world influenced through colonialism, 15–16; of Islam's expansion and political authority, 9–11; of Jews and early relationship with Muslims, 217–20; of Jews and treatment from European Christians, 227; of Mecca, 7, 24; of Muhammad, 6–9; of Muslims and societal improvements in India, 235–36; of *pir* and corruption, 171–72; of *Quran,* 5; of science books in Arabic, 13–14; of sexuality and gender inequality in Islam, 145–46; shariah's interpretations throughout Islam and, 366; of Sufism, 146; of Sunna, 5; of Turkey's negotiations with EU, 211–13; of USA and African-American Muslims, 17–18

Hitler, Adolf: bin Laden, Osama, compared to, 117; creativity's absence in group-self led by bin Laden, Osama, and, 117–18; Savarkar praising, 240

the Holocaust, 228

Holy Spirit, 47–48

Holy War, Inc. (Bergen), 107

honor killing, 152–53

Hujwiri, A. U. J., 163

Huntington, Samuel, 215

Hussain, Maqbool Fida: Chughtai compared to, 309; education of, 308; Hindu right wingers and opposition to work of, 310; Indian nationalism in work of, 308–9; on Pakistan and immigration, 309

ibn Abdullah, Muhammad. *See* Muhammad

ibn Abi-Taleb, Ali, 10

ibn Affan, Uthman, 10

iman (faith), 5

imitational knowledge, 47

immigrant(s): 9/11 causing problems for Muslim family of, 194; Muslim psychoanalysts who are, 330–32; Muslims and latency child problems with family of, 191–94; Muslims who are politically exiled compared to choosing to be an, 193

immigration: European identity confusion due to, 214–15; Hussain on Pakistan and, 309; Khan's psychoanalyst career impacted by, 331; Muslim family and challenges with, 185–86, 188, 191; Muslims in USA and, 16–17; USA and identity confusion due to, 214–15; Volkan's psychoanalyst career impacted by, 331–32. *See also Hijrah;* immigrant(s)

Inch' Allah Dimanche, 151–52

Incoherence of the Philosophers (Al-Ghazali), 14

Indamdar, 23–24

India: Buddhism in, 296; Daniell's success in, 299–300; England and Muslims joining uprising with, 239; England and racism toward people of, 300–301; England's artists patronized by citizens of, 299–300; England's positive contributions to, 377–78; England's reign ending for, 93–94; European art institutions and practices introduced to, 299–300; Gandhi and views of Muslims in, 360; Hindu conflict with Muslims and constitutional solutions for, 262–63; Hindu conflict with Muslims and economic solutions for, 260–61; Hindu conflict with Muslims and experiential measures as solutions for, 259–60; Hindu conflict with Muslims and judicial solutions for, 261–62; Hindu conflict

with Muslims and political solutions
for, 261; Hindu conflict with
Muslims and solutions in education
for, 257–58; Hindu conflict with
Muslims and solutions of cultural
measures for, 258–59; Hindus caused
trauma from Muslim history of
domination of, 248; Hindus
economically threatened by Muslims
in, 250; Hindu's unresolved
mourning of Pakistan's division
from, 248–49; history in education
curriculum changed by right wing
Hindus in, 255–56; Hussain's work
and nationalism of, 308–9; Indo-
Muslim art impacted by Pakistan
separating from, 310–11; Islam and
hybridization of culture in, 296–97,
386; Jinnah's activism and England
v., 98; Jinnah's disregard for
Muslim's from, 100; Jinnah's early
association with politics in, 84–85;
marriage tradition for Muslims in,
135–36; Muslim and Hindu relations
effected by English colonialism of,
238–39; Muslim architecture
influenced by, 297–98; Muslim
cultural nationalism in, 302–3;
Muslim reaction to recent attacks of
Hindus in, 254–55; Muslims and
Hindus fighting over Pakistan's
division from, 241–42; Muslims and
history of societal improvements
made in, 235–36; Muslims and
issues with Hindus in, 231–32,
243–44, 246–47; Muslim's
constitutional privileges alienating to
Hindus in, 246; Muslim's growing
secularism in politics of, 256;
Muslims incorporating Hindus in
government of, 236–37; Muslim's
lack of progressive secular leadership
alienating to Hindus in, 245–46;
Muslims plundering, 234–35;
Muslim's recent cultural

contributions to, 242–43; Nehru on
separation of Pakistan from, 94;
NRIs and confusion with Hindu
culture and, 251–52; psychoanalysis
and Sikhs and Parsis from, 316–17;
Radcliffe separating Pakistan from,
94; *The Satanic Verses* banned by
Muslims alienating Hindus in, 246;
Saudi Arabia ties of Muslims in, 244;
Savarkar on Muslims in, 241;
swadeshi nationalism ignoring
Muslims in, 302; *swadeshi*
nationalism impacting art in, 304–5;
swadeshi nationalism impacting
Hindus in, 301–2; Vedic tradition in,
296. *See also* Indo-Muslim art
Indo-Muslim art: architecture in, 298;
Chughtai's role in development of,
304, 306–7; cultural nationalism in,
295; England and Westernization
attempts on, 298–99; England's
colonialism and aesthetic influence
on, 299–301; history of, 297–99;
miniature painting in, 298; Pakistan
separating from India impacting,
310–11
intuition: creativity drawing on, 55–56;
science and, 56. *See also* intuitive
knowledge
intuitive knowledge, 47
Iqbal, Mohammad, Sir, 87, 303, 306;
Chughtai collaborating with, 307
iradah, 176
Iran: Mehran and teasing for being from,
189; 9/11 and racism toward, 189;
poetry in, 56, 367; Shi'ism in, 146
al-Isfahani, Faraj, 284–85
ishq (intense love), 166; origins of, 167;
psychoanalysis' transference
compared to Sufism and *pir* and,
175–76; Rumi on loss of self and,
167; as-Sadiq on, 175; Sufism and
experience of, 167–68
Islam: adoption and views of, 36–37;
Allah's singularity in, 7, 25; *aqiqa*

and cultural variations in, 138;
architecture of, xv; art of, xvi;
Atatürk's attempts at unifying
Christianity with, 216; bin Laden,
Osama, and teachers on liberation
from Western world for, 109;
childhood rituals in, 137–38;
Christianity and deteriorating
relations with, 200; Christianity
compared to, 63–64; Christianity's
history with, 201–2; Chughtai's
lineage in, 304; colonialism
impacting world of, 15–16;
compassion and mercy in, 159–60;
definition of, 4–6, 123; divorce and,
130–31; family structure and
relationship to, 123–24; family
structure regional variations with,
125; Freud, Sigmund, and
psychoanalysis studies on, 283–84;
God and worship in, 352; God's
oneness and importance to, 125; *Hajj*
in, 123; Hasan's interest on
Westerner's converting to, 184–85;
history of expansion and political
authority in, 9–11; history of gender
inequality in sexuality in, 145–46;
India and hybridization of culture of,
296–97, 386; Jinnah and non-
practice of, 88–89; Judaism and
reconciliation with, 229–30;
Judaism's respect in early, 225–26;
Khan, Masud's, anti-Semitism and
faith in, 320–21; Khan, Masud's,
professional downfall and blame
placed on, 321–22; *Majnun and
Layla*'s popularity throughout, 286;
marriage and importance to, 126–27;
marriage ceremony in, 135; marriage
contract importance to, 137;
misconceptions of, 3–4;
Muhammad's warning for, 103;
Ottoman Empire's identity and
importance of, 207–8;
psychoanalysis and, xvii–xviii;
psychoanalysis' conceptual
enrichment from, 325;
psychoanalysis' developmental
enrichment from, 324–25;
psychoanalysis linguistic enrichment
from, 324; psychoanalysis'
psychopolitical enrichment from,
326; psychoanalysis' technical
enrichment from, 325; religion
distinguished between cultural norms
for, 131–32, 144–45; religions of
various origin and shared teachings
to, 126; Satan and, 4–5; seminal
contributions of, xv; sexuality
effected by wife *v.* mother-in-law in,
151–52; sexuality in Christianity
compared to, 142; sexuality in
Judaism compared to, 142; sexuality
of women in, 143, 150–51, 153;
shariah and interpretations
throughout history of, 366; shariah
and justification of practices in, 143;
submission and, 141; submission
differentiating from surrender in,
158–59; tawakkul principle of, 6;
tenets essential to, 125, 182;
universality of, 38; Western world's
search for leader of, 64; women and
submission in, 143–44; *Zakat* in,
123. *See also* Pan Islam; shariah;
Shiite(s); Sufism; Sunni(s)
Islamic Resistance Movement. *See*
Hamas
Israel: creation of, 220; Egyptian
movies impacted by Arabs and
conflict with, 270–71

jaan, 50
James, William, 28
Jew(s): Christians and anti-Semitism
toward, 220; circumcision for
Muslims compared to, 138; Europe
and Christians compared to, 219;
Hamas on World War I and, 226;
history of Europe and Christians

treatment of, 227; Muhammad and Medina clans of, 221–23; Muhammad's views on, 224–25; Muhammad *v.,* 35; Muslims and early history with, 217–20; Muslims and hostility for Meccan support of, 223–24; Muslims and psychoanalysis of, 336–39; Muslims and war with, 32–33; Ottoman Empire and, 218–19; Quraysh tribe and loyalties of, 222–23; Spain expelling Muslims and, 218. *See also* Dönmes

Jihad, 199

Jinnah, Mohammad Ali: on Ali, Chowdrhy Rahmat's, views, 89; Allah and prayer of, 88; ancestral roots of, 82–83; birth of, 81; birth of daughter of, 85; childhood and health of, 96; Christianity and, 98; controversy of, 80; Croft helping, 83; death of, 88; death of mother of, 83; education of, 83, 359; Emibai marriage to, 83; England and changes of, 83–84, 97; England *v.* India and activism of, 98; Fatima supporting, 87; Freud, Sigmund, and views on childhood and, 96; Gandhi and friction with, 92–93, 98–99; Gandhi compared to, 90–91; Hindu ancestry of, 83; Hindu's view of, 95; ideological changes in life of, 95; Indian Muslims disregarded by, 100; Indian politics and early association of, 84–85; Islam and non-practice of, 88–89; legacy of, 79–80; Mountbatten and demands of, 93–94; Muslim foundations of, 82; Muslim League and, 89; Muslims and Hindus divided by, 240–41; Muslims and Hindus united by, 90; Muslim separatists joined by, 87; Muslims represented in Congress Party by, 89–90; Muslim's view of, 95; Naidu on, 85, 89; name change of, 84; Nehru and friction with, 92, 99;

Pakistan and reinvention of, 99–100; Pakistan created and, 87–89, 92–93; Petit marriage to, 85; religion and confusion in childhood of, 95–96; RSS's rise in power and, 91; self-invention of, 94; sexuality of, 97; Wolpert on, 79

Jonaid of Baghdad, 173

Jones, Ernest, 316

Judaism: Christianity and reconciliation with, 228–29; Christianity in early stages and demonizing of, 226–27; Chrysostom on, 227; Freud, Sigmund, and concerns with, 315; the Holocaust and, 228; Islam and early respect for, 225–26; Islam and reconciliation with, 229–30; Mrs. A and, 345–47; psychoanalysis and, 315; *Quran* and passages on, 224; sexuality in Islam compared to, 142. *See also* Jew(s)

Jung, Carl Gustav, 316

Kakar, Sudhir: on Oedipal complex, 292, 294; on Oedipal complex in *Majnun and Layla,* 383–84; psychoanalysis and, 316

Kemal, Namik, 67

Kernberg, O. F., 173

Khadija: children of, 26; death of, 7–8, 26; Muhammad's marriage to, 7, 25; Muhammad supported by, 27

Khairallah, As'ad, 286–87

Khalli Balak min Zuzu (Watch Out for Zuzu), 272

Khan, Hazrat Inayat, 171

Khan, Masud: death of, 321; on dreams, 319; Islam and blame for professional downfall of, 321–22; Islamic faith and anti-Semitism of, 320–21; on lying fallow, 319; on pornography, 319; psychoanalysis and legacy of, 318–19; psychoanalysis and professional downfall of, 319–21; psychoanalyst career impacted by immigration for, 331; on psychoanalytic setting, 318–19; Sandler on, 319–20; on schizoid character, 318; on sexual perversion, 319; Winnicott and controversial collaboration with, 320

Khan, Syed Ahmad, Sir, 231, 302

Khojas, 82

Al-Khwarizimi, 13

al-Kindi, 3

Kitab, 135

Kitab al-Aghani (Book of Songs) (al-Aghani), 284–85

Kitab al-Jabr wa-l-Muqabala (Al-Khwarizimi), 13

Knafo, D., 337

Kohut, H., 173

Layla. See Majnun and Layla

Layla Wal-Majnun (Layla Majnun), 284; Egyptian Revolution as backdrop for, 289–90; feminism of, 290; *Majnun and Layla* referenced in, 289, 292–93; psychoanalysis of Freud, Sigmund, and, 292; al-Rai'i on, 290; as-Sabur adding Oedipal complex subtext to, 288–92; summary of, 288

Leary, K.: on 9/11 and racism in USA, 338; on psychoanalysis and differences in background, 340, 342

Lepanto, 204

Levine, H., 328

Lewis, Bernard, 219

Literary Criticism: Its Principles and Methodology (Qtub), 108

Madinah. *See* Medina

Mahabbat (affection), 166

Mahfouz, Afaf: anti-Semitism and accusations toward, 387; psychoanalysis contributions of, 329

Mahfuz, Nagib, 277

Majnun and Layla: Egyptian production of Shawqi's version of, 286–87; European versions of, 282; Islam and popularity of, 286; Kakar on Oedipal complex subtext in, 383–84; Khairallah on adaptations of, 286–87; *Layla Wal-Majnun* referencing, 289, 292–93; Oedipal complex subtext in, 289; story of, 284–85. *See also Kitab al-Aghani*

Makkah. *See* Mecca

Malcom X, 17–18

Maliki, 134

Marks, L., 181–82

marriage: Egyptian Muslim tradition of, 136; Indian Muslim tradition of, 135–36; Islam and ceremonial, 135; Islam and contract of, 137; Islam and importance of, 126–27; of Jinnah to Emibai, 83; of Jinnah to Petit, 85; Muhammad and Aisha and controversy of, 35; of Muhammad and Khadija, 7, 25; Muhammad and political advantages in, 35; Muhammad and Zaynab and controversy of, 35–37; *Quran* and mate selection for, 127–29; *Quran* on polygamy and, 129–30; sexism in views on, 127; Syrian Muslim tradition of, 136–37. *See also* divorce; *Kitab*; *Nikah*

Mawdudi, Mawlana, 16

McBride, James, 335

Mecca: Hasan and ridicule from classmates for trip to, 184; history of, 7, 24; Muhammad and opposition from, 29–30, 222; Muhammad conquering, 37–38; Muslim persecution in, 7–8; Muslims and *Truce of Hudaybah* with, 37; Muslims and war at Badr with, 31–32; Muslims and war at Uhud with, 32–33; Muslims hostility toward Jews for supporting, 223–24; Surrahs of, 30. *See also Hajj*

media: bin Laden, Osama, and terrorism in, 116–17; Hindu NRIs in USA against Muslims through, 253; Muslim women in Western, 365

Medina: Muhammad and *Hijrah* period in, 30–34; Muhammad and Jewish clans in, 221–23; Muhammad creating constitution of, 223; Muhammad relocation to, 8, 30

meditative process, 171, 176, 179, 369

Mehran (case study child): family struggles of, 190–91; Iranian nationality causing teasing of, 189; problems of, 187–88

men: Muslims and women's emasculation of, 148–49; *Quran* and dress code of women and, 126–27

Metcalf, Barbara, 386

mihr, 167

Mir, Muntasir, 199

Mitter, P., 300

Modell, Arnold, 71

Mohammad-Arif, Aminah, 181

The Moorish Scenic Temple, 17

Moses, 225

Moskowitz, M., 341

Moslem. *See* Muslim

Mountbatten, Earl Louis, 93–94

movies: Egypt and, 267; Egypt and 9/11's impact on, 281–82; Egypt and belly dancers in, 272–73; Egypt and feminism in, 276–77; Egypt and representation of Arabs in, 268–70; Egypt and representation of women in, 268–69, 271–73; imagery and power in, 267–68; Israel's conflict with Arabs impacting Egypt and, 270–71; Muslim representation from Hindus in, 258–59; Muslims adopting Hindu names for work in, 376; USA and 9/11's impact on, 279–82; USA and representation of Arabs in, 268–70, 275

Mrs. A (case study): 9/11 impacting psychoanalysis of, 345–46, 348–49; childhood impacting psychoanalysis of, 349; childhood of, 344–45; education of, 343–44; family of, 343–45; Judaism and, 345–47; Al Qaeda and paranoia of, 346–48; trust issues of, 347–48

Muhammad: action and intention according to, 352; adolescence of, 25; adult life of, 25–26; Aisha and controversial marriage to, 35; Ali, M. M., on domestic life of, 355; Allah and intermediary of, 31; angel Gabriel speaking to, 27–28; birth of, 24; books written on, 21–24; childhood loss and separation impacting, 24–25, 354; children of, 26; Christians and views of, 224–25; farewell pilgrimage of, 38; history of, 6–9; Islam and warning of, 103; James on visions of, 28; Jewish clans in Medina an, 221–23; Jews and views of, 224–25; Jews *v.*, 35; Khadija's marriage to, 7, 25; Khadija's supporting, 27; marriages for political advantage of, 35; Mecca conquered by, 37–38; Mecca's opposition toward, 29–30, 222; Medina and *Hijrah* period of, 30–34; Medina and relocation of, 8, 30; Medina constitution created by, 223; message of, 5; *New Testament* and the *Bible* influencing, 221; Orientalist views in studies on, 23, 27–28; *Quran* and relationship to, 6–7, 22–23; revelations in early teachings of, 29; Rushdie and ridicule of, 34; Satanic verses of, 34; *ummah* formed by, 30–31; visions of, 26–27; on women and education, 141; Zaynab and controversial marriage to, 35–37

Muhammad and the Rise of Islam: The Creation of Group Identity (Indamdar), 23–24

Muhammad, Elijah, 17–18

Muhammad, Warith Deen, 17–18

The Mummy (USA), 274

Al-Mumya (The Mummy) (Egypt), 274–75

Munich, 279–81

Muslim(s): achievements in recent memory of, xvi–xvii; Arabs differentiated from, xiv–xv; Atatürk providing inspiration to leaders of, 65; Bush on good or bad kinds of, 388; circumcision for Jews compared to, 138; definition of, 4; England and uprising of India joined by, 239; England's colonialism effecting India's relations between Hindus and, 238–39; family and immigration challenges of, 185–86, 188, 191; family problems with latency child and immigrating, 191–94; Gandhi as viewed by India and, 360; greeting of all, 352; Hasan and special school for, 184–85; Hindu movies and representation of, 258–59; Hindu religion compared to, 375; Hindus alienated by Indian constitutional privileges of, 246; Hindus alienated by lack of Indian progressive secular leadership of, 245–46; Hindus alienated by pathological nostalgia of, 244–45; Hindus alienated by religious practices of, 244; Hindus and cultural exchange between, 234, 237–40; Hindus and prejudicial attitudes of, 245; Hindus and varying views of radicals and general public of, 233; Hindus caused trauma from history of India and domination of, 248; Hindus destroying *Babri Masjid* mosque of, 252–54; Hindus in India and economic threat of, 250; Hindu's postcolonial villain hunger of, 249–50; Hindu's recent attacks in India and reaction of, 254–55; Hindu's *Somnath* temple destroyed by, 235; history of India society and improvements from, 235–36; history

of USA and African-Americans who are, 17–18; honor killing and, 152–53; immigrant by choice compared to politically exiled, 193; India and constitutional solutions for Hindu conflict with, 262–63; India and cultural nationalism of, 302–3; India and cultural solutions for Hindu conflict with, 258–59; India and economic solutions for Hindu conflict with, 260–61; India and education for solution of Hindu and conflict with, 257–58; India and experiential measures as solutions for Hindu conflict with, 259–60; India and growing political secularism of, 256; India and issues of Hindus and, 231–32, 243–44, 246–427; India and judicial solutions for Hindu conflict with, 261–62; India and political solutions for Hindu conflict with, 261; Indian culture and recent contributions of, 242–43; Indian government and incorporation of Hindus by, 236–37; Indian Hindus and alienation from banning of *The Satanic Verses* by, 246; Indian influence in architecture of, 297–98; India plundered by, 234–35; intellectual growth through non-Arabs and, 12–13; Jews and early history with, 217–20; Jews and psychoanalysis of, 336–39; Jews and war with, 32–33; Jews supporting Mecca and hostility of, 223–24; Jinnah and foundation as, 82; Jinnah and Hindus divided from, 240–41; Jinnah and view of, 95; Jinnah in Congress Party and representing, 89–90; Jinnah joining separatists and, 87; Jinnah's disregard for India and, 100; Jinnah unifying Hindus and, 90; literature of, xvi; marriage tradition in Egypt for, 136; marriage tradition in India for,

135–36; marriage tradition in Syria for, 136–37; Mecca and *Truce of Hudaybah* with, 37; Mecca and war at Badr with, 31–32; Mecca and war at Uhud with, 32–33; Mecca's persecution of, 7–8; media in West on women who are, 365; men's fear of emasculation by women and, 148–49; movies and Hindu names adopted by, 376; 9/11 and immigrant family problems of, 194; 9/11 and USA's relations with, xiii–xv, 181, 199–200; Pakistan and art of, 307–8; Pakistan's division from India causing fighting amongst Hindus and, 241–42; populations around world of, xiv–xv, 133; psychoanalysis and, 317–18, 329–30, 387; psychoanalysts who are immigrants and, 330–32; Al Qaeda's appeal to USA and, 113; Al Qaeda's recruiting technique for, 114; Quraysh tribe defeating, 223; religion and relationship with, 3–4; religion *v.* science in, 13; Saudi Arabia ties of India and, 244; Savarkar on India and, 241; sexuality of elderly women who are, 152; Spain expelling Jews and, 218; statistics on, 3; *swadeshi* nationalism in India ignoring, 302; USA and challenges facing, 18; USA and Europe and modernization attempts for countries of, 64–65; USA and immigration of, 16–17; USA and media used by Hindu NRIs against, 253; USA life and family challenges of, 181–83, 188; Western values impacting, 16; women and value of virginity for, 279. *See also* Indo-Muslim art; Khojas; Muslim League; Shiite(s); Sunni(s)
Muslim League: Jinnah and, 89; RSS and friction with, 240
Mutazilites, 134

Muwatin wa-Mukhbir wa-Harami (A Citizen, a Detective, a Thief), 281

Naidu, Sarojini, 85, 89
Najeeb, Shahid, 335
Nasafi, A., 165
Al-Naser Salah al-Din (The Victor Saladdin), 281
Nasr, S. H., 123
Nation of Islam (NOI), 17
NATO. *See* North Atlantic Treaty Organization
nay, 60, 356
Nayar, Kuldip, 256
Nehru, Jawaharlal, 80; Gandhi compared to, 359; Gandhi's favoring of, 98; India's separation with Pakistan and views of, 94; Jinnah and friction with, 92, 99
New Testament: Muhammad influenced by the *Bible* and, 221; *Quran* compared to, 22
Nikah, 135
9/11. *See* September 11, 2001
Nobel Prize for Peace, 329
NOI. *See* Nation of Islam
nonresident Indians (NRIs): Hindu and Indian culture confused in, 251–52; USA and success of, 250–51; USA media used against Muslims by Hindus and, 253
Noor, F., 315
North Atlantic Treaty Organization (NATO), 210
NRIs. *See* nonresident Indians

Oberndorf, C. P., 340
Oedipal complex: Kakar on, 292, 294; Kakar on *Majnun and Layla* and subtext of, 383–84; *Layla Wal-Majnun* and as-Sabur adding subtext of, 288–92; *Majnun and Layla* and subtext of, 289; universality of, 293–94, 383
Omar, Mullah Huhammad, 110

Orientalists, 27–28, 354

Ottoman Empire: architectural achievements of, 204; the Balkans invaded by, 201; Constantinople and conquest of, 202–3; England's negative image of, 208; Europe and diminishing of, 201–2, 205–6; Europe and fashion of, 204–5; European victory at Lepanto against, 204; Europe's racism and views of, 203–4; Islam's importance to identity of, 207–8; Jews in, 218–19; Pan Islam and Western view of, 207; Suleiman the First and image of, 203; Twain on, 209; Westernization and modernization attempts of, 69–70, 206; Western views of inferiority toward, 208–9

Ozal, Turgut, 76

Pakistan: Ali, Chowdrhy Rahmat and citizenship in, 361; Hindu's unresolved mourning of India's division into, 248–49; Hussain on immigration and, 309; Indo-Muslim art impacted by India and separation of, 310–11; Jinnah and creation of, 87–89, 92–94; Jinnah's reinvention with, 99–100; Muslim art in, 307–8; Muslims and Hindus fighting over India's division into, 241–42; Nehru on separation from India of, 94; Radcliffe separating India from, 94; villain hunger of, 377

Pan Islam, 207, 302

Paris, Erna, 218

Parsis, 316–17

patient(s): psychoanalysis and external reality *v.* internal reality of, 336–37; psychoanalysis theories on differences between psychoanalysts and, 340–43; psychoanalyst and impact of value system of, 323, 336; psychoanalyst's duty and impact of cultural identity and religion of,

335–36. *See also* Hasan; Mehran; Mrs. A

Persian(s): Chughtai's work influenced by art of, 306; *erfan* and poetry of, 56–57; poetry and challenges of Western translation from language of, 57; poetry's high regard by, 56; Rumi and contribution to longevity of language of, 45–46; *yaar* and poetry of, 57–58

Petit, Ruttenbai: death of, 86; Jinnah marriage to, 85

pir (spiritual physician): attributes of, 167–69; corruption in history of, 171–72; psychoanalysis compared to Sufism and advice from, 175; psychoanalysis' transference compared to Sufism's *ishq* for, 175–76; religions of other cultures and guides similar to, 171; seeker's self-devotion to, 169–70; Sufism and necessity of, 170; Sufism and search for, 170–71; Sufism and seeker assessment of, 173–744; Sufism initiation with, 171–72; *zikr* breathing practice taught by, 171

poetry: of bin Laden, Osama, 111–13; of Hafez, 155–58; in Iran, 56, 367; Persians and challenges in Western translation of, 57; Persians and *erfan* in, 56–57; Persians and *yaar* in, 57–58; Persians high regard for, 56; of Rumi on human dilemma of separation from nature, 161–63; Rumi's faith and, 58, 62; Rumi's universality in, 46; of Sufism and sexuality of women, 146, 153–58

polygamy, and marriage in *Quran*, 129–30

Poonja, Jinnahbhai, 82

pornography, 319

Prinsep, Valentine, 300

the Prophet. *See* Muhammad

psychoanalysis: of bin Laden's anti-Western attitude, 110, 118; Christians and, 316; Gill and, 317; Hindus and, 316; Indian Sikhs and Parsis and, 316–17; Islam and, xvii–xviii; Islam and conceptual enrichment of, 325; Islam and developmental enrichment of, 324–25; Islam and linguistic enrichment of, 324; Islam and psychopolitical enrichment of, 326; Islam and studies of Freud, Sigmund, and, 283–84; Islam and technical enrichment of, 325; Jews and Muslims in, 336–39; Judaism and, 315; Kakar and, 316; Khan, Masud on setting of, 318–19; Khan, Masud's legacy in, 318–19; Khan, Masud's professional downfall in, 319–21; *Layla Wal-Majnun* and Freud, Sigmund, and, 292; Leary on differences in background impacting, 340, 342; Levine on Volkan's contributions to, 328; Mahfouz's contributions to, 329; Mrs. A and 9/11 impacting, 345–46, 348–49; Mrs. A and childhood impacting, 349; Muslims and, 317–18, 329–30, 387; patient's internal reality *v.* external reality in, 336–37; psychoanalyst and patient differences and theories for, 340–43; psychoanalyst prejudice impacting, 339, 343; religion and differences after 9/11 impacting, 338–39; Sufism and avoidance compared to resistance in, 176–78; Sufism and focus on self compared to psychic trauma in, 178; Sufism and *ishq* for *pir* compared to transference in, 176; Sufism's advice from *pir* compared to, 175; Sufism's forgetfulness and ignorance compared to repression and denial in, 165–66; Sufism's views on origin of suffering and anxiety compared to, 172–73; Sufism's views on separation anxiety compared to, 164–65; in Turkey,

387; Volkan and applied, 327–28; Volkan's legacy in, 326, 328–29
psychoanalyst(s): Khan's immigration impacting career as, 331; Muslim immigrants who are, 330–32; patient's value system impacting, 323, 336; personality impacting success of, 322–23; psychoanalysis impacted by prejudice of, 339, 343; psychoanalysis theories on differences between patients and, 340–43; religion and cultural identity of patient and duty of, 335–36; religion's impact on, 323–24; Volkan's immigration impacting career as, 331–32
Pukhta (maturity), 168

Al Qaeda: Berman on, 104; Mrs. A and paranoia with, 346–48; Muslims and recruiting techniques of, 114; Qtub, Sayyid's, influence on bin Laden, Osama, and, 108–9; USA and Muslims and appeal of, 113
Qtub, Muhammed, 108
Qtub, Sayyid: Berman on, 108; bin Laden, Osama, and Al Qaeda influenced by, 108–9; philosophy of, 108–9
Quran: Adam and Eve's story in, 128; Adam and Eve's story in the *Bible* compared to, 351; adoption and attitude of, 35–36; divorce in, 131; family structure and parental duties in, 131–33; history of, 5; Judaism in, 224; marriage and mate selection according to, 127–29; marriage and polygamy in, 129–30; Moses in, 225; Muhammad's relationship to, 6–7, 22–23; *New Testament* compared to, 22; orphans mentioned in, 25; Rahman, Fazlur, on, 5–6; suicide bombers and misinterpretations of, 113; terms key to, 5–6; women's and men's

dress code according to, 126–27.
See also Surrah(s)
Quraysh tribe: Jews aligning with,
222–23; Muslims defeated by, 223
Qutb, Sayyed, 16

racism: the Crusades and accounts of,
200; of England citizens toward
Indians, 300–1; of Europe toward
Ottoman Empire, 203–4; Gladstone's
views on Turkey and, 205–6;
Iranian's after 9/11 and, 189; Leary
on USA after 9/11 and, 338; religion
and, 232
Radcliffe, Cyril, Sir, 94
Rahman, Fazlur, 5–6
Rahman, Sheik Omar Abdel, 108, 111
al-Rai'i, Ali, 290
rapture, 52–53
Rashid, Harun, Caliph, 14
Rashtriya Sevak Sangh (RSS): Jinnah
and rise in power of, 91; Muslim
League and friction with, 240;
Savarkar founding, 91
Raza, Rahi Masoom, 376
Al-Razi, 13–14
Rejwan, Nissim, 219
religion: Atatürk changes for Turkey
and, 72, 75; Atatürk impacted by his
mourning mother and her, 72; Freud,
Anna, on sexuality and adolescents
compared to fanatics of, 149; Freud,
Sigmund, on children and, 181;
Hasan and fear from, 185; Hindu's
alienated by Muslim's practices of,
244; of Hindus compared to
Muslims, 375; identity formation
and, 182–83, 193; Islam and
distinguishing between cultural
norms and, 131–32, 144–45; Islam
and shared teachings with other
forms of, 126; Jinnah's childhood
and confusion with, 95–96; Muslims
and science *v.*, 13; Muslims
relationship with their, 3–4; Ozal's

changes in Turkey with, 76; *pir* and
similar guides in other forms of, 171;
psychoanalysis after 9/11 and
differences in, 338–39;
psychoanalyst and impact of,
323–24; psychoanalyst's duty on
impact of patient's cultural identity
and, 335–36; racism from, 232;
science compared to, 29. *See also*
Buddhism; Christianity; Hindu(s);
Islam; Judaism; Vedic tradition
revelations, in Muhammad's early
teachings, 29
Richard III (Shakespeare), 100
Riza-I-Abbasi, 306
Rosenthal, Erwin, 219–20
RSS. *See* Rashtriya Sevak Sangh
Rumi, Jalal-uddin Mohammad: birth of,
43; death and views of, 50–51;
depressive position of, 59–60; *erfan*
grounding view of existence of,
51–52, 60; evolution according to,
50; faith and, 45, 62; Holy Spirit and
beliefs of, 47–48; human existence
and views of, 46–47; intuitive
knowledge, experimental knowledge,
imitational knowledge, and, 47; on
ishq and loss of self, 166; legacy of,
44; on moral conflicts, 166; nay
performance and view of, 60, 356;
Persian language longevity and
impact of, 45–46; poetry and faith of,
58, 62; poetry and universality of,
46; poetry on human dilemma of
separation from nature written by,
161–63; science compared to world
view of, 48, 60; Sufism and, 49; on
Sufism and avoidance of seeker,
176–77
Rushdie, Salman, 34

Sabbah, Fatna, 147–48
Sabr (patience), 168
as-Sabur, Salah Abd, 284; European
influence on work of, 383; *Layla*

Wal-Majnun and Oedipal complex subtext added by, 288–92; Shawqi compared to, 287–88
as-Sadiq, Imam Ja'far, 175
salam (peace), 5–6
Salonika, 66–67
Sandler, A. M., 319–20
Sarraj, A. N., 172
Satan: Islam and, 4–5; Muhammed and verses of, 34
The Satanic Verses: fatwa misused and edict on, 34, 353; Indian Muslims alienating Hindus over banning of, 246
Saudi Arabia: bin Laden, Osama, and differences on USA with leadership of, 109–10, 115, 118; Indian Muslims and ties to, 244. *See also* Mecca; Medina
Savarkar, Vinayak Damodar: biography of, 360; Hitler praised by, 240; on Muslims in India, 241; RSS founded by, 91
schizoid position, 59
science: *erfan* compared to, 51; history of Arabic books on, 13–14; intuition and, 56; Muslims and religion *v.* 13; religion compared to, 29; Rumi's world view compared to, 48, 60
September 11, 2001 (9/11): Egypt and movies after, 281–82; Iranian's receiving racism after, 189; Leary on racism in USA after, 338; Mrs. A's psychoanalysis impacted by events of, 345–46, 348–49; Muslim immigrant family problems after, 194; psychoanalysis and differences in religion after, 338–39; USA and movies after, 279–82; USA and Muslim relations after, xiii–xv, 181, 199–200
sexuality: Arabic erotic literature and Sabbah's research on, 147–48; Freud, Anna, on religious fanatics compared to adolescents in terms of, 149; al-

Ghazali and views toward, 147; Hafez's views on women and, 157–58; history of Islam and gender inequality of, 145–46; Islam and wife *v.* mother-in-law effecting, 151–52; of Islam compared to Christianity, 142; of Islam compared to Judaism, 142; of Jinnah, 97; Khan, Masud, on perversion in, 319; of Muslims and elderly women, 152; shariah on, 144; Sufism and poetry on women and, 146, 153–58; women and beasts and implications of, 147, 367; of women in Islam, 143, 150–51, 153
Sezer, Ahmet, 64
Shafi, 134
Shafiq, Durriyah, 276–77
Shakespeare, William, 100
shariah (Islamic law): development of, 11–12; history of Islam and interpretations of, 366; Islamic practices justified through, 143; on sexuality, 144
Shawqi, Ahmad: Egyptian production of *Majnun and Layla* by, 286–87; legacy of, 382; as-Sabur compared to, 287–88
Shi'ism: Iran and, 146; sects of, 352; Sufism compared to, 146
Shiite(s): emergence of, 10; Sunnis compared to, 11, 134
Sikhs, 316–17
Sina, Ibn, 13–14
Sokullu, Grand Vizier, 204–5
Somnath temple, 235
Soviet Union: bin Laden, Osama's, leadership in Afghanistan war with, 109, 111; USA's friendship with Turkey and political motives with, 209–10
Spain, 218
Stillman, Norman, 218
Sufism: aim of, 48–49; emergence of, 14–15; family structure according to,

134–35; forgetfulness and ignorance of humans as viewed in, 163–64; God and separation from human in, 161–63; Hafez expressing ideals of, 154; *halat* and, 172; history of, 146; *ishq* experience in, 166; meditative process in, 134, 176,179, 369; *pir* and assessment of seeker in, 173–74; *pir* and initiation into, 172–73; *pir* as necessity to, 170; *pir* searching in, 171–72; psychoanalysis and psychic trauma compared to focus on self in, 178–79; psychoanalysis and resistance compared to avoidance in, 176–78; psychoanalysis and transference compared to *ishq* with *pir* in, 175–76; psychoanalysis compared to *pir*'s advice in, 175; psychoanalysis's repression and denial compared to forgetfulness and ignorance in, 165–66; psychoanalysis's views on origin of suffering and anxiety compared to, 172–73; psychoanalysis's views on separation anxiety compared to, 164–65; Rumi and, 49; Rumi on avoidance of seeker in, 176–77; seven stages of devotion for, 49–50; sexuality of women in poetry of, 146, 153–58; Shi'ism compared to, 146; therapeutic methods in, 178–79. *See also* Shi'ism

suicide bomber(s): bin Laden, Osama, recruiting, 116; *Quran* and misinterpretations from, 113

Suleiman the First, 203

Sunna, 5

Sunni(s): legal schools of, 11–12; schools of law for, 134; Shiites compared to, 11, 134. *See also* *Asharite(s)*; *Mutazilite(s)*

Surah(s) (chapters): of Mecca, 30; of women, 33

swadeshi nationalism: Hindus in India impacted by, 301–2; Indian art impacted by, 304–5; Muslims in India ignored by, 302

Syria, 136–37

Syriana, 279–80

Tagore, Abanindranath: Chughtai compared to, 305–6; Chughtai's work influenced by, 305

Taj Mahal, xvi, 298

taqwa, 6

tawakkul, 6

terrorism: bin Laden and possible reasons for, 103; media covering bin Laden, Osama, and, 116–17. *See also* suicide bomber(s)

Thackeray, Bala Saheb, 262

The Thousand and One Nights, 148

Truce of Hudaybiyah, 37

al Turabi, Hassan Abdullah, 109

Turkey: Atatürk and Westernization of, 69–70; Atatürk becoming president of Republic of, 68–70; Atatürk's changes for religious beliefs of, 72, 75; the Balkans and views on, 372; Bush and requests angering, 64–65; EU history of negotiations with, 211–13; EU membership challenges facing, 77; European cartoons insulting, 211–12, 355; NATO acceptance of, 210; Ozal and religion in, 76; psychoanalysis in, 387; racism in Gladstone's views on, 205–6; USA and souring relations with, 210–11; USA's political motives with Soviet Union and friendship with, 209–10

Twain, Mark, 209

Uhud, 32–33

umma (community): meaning changing for, 355; Muhammed forming, 30–31

The Uncovering of the Veils (*Kashf Al-Mahjub*) (Hujwiri), 163

United States of America (USA): 9/11's impact on movies from, 279–82;

Afghanistan and mistakes made by, 115; Arabs represented in movies of, 268–70, 275; Arabs represented in *The Mummy* from, 274; Arabs represented in *Munich* from, 279–81; Arabs represented in *Syriana* from, 279–80; bin Laden, Osama, and Saudi Arabian leadership differing on, 109–10, 115, 118; Hasan avoiding traditions of, 186–87; Hindu NRIs using media against Muslims in, 253; history of African-American Muslims in, 17–18; identity confusion with immigration in, 214–15; Leary on racism after 9/11 in, 338; Muslim countries and modernization attempts of Europe and, 64–65; Muslim family challenges for life in, 181–83, 188; Muslim immigration to, 16–17; Muslims and challenges of living in, 18; 9/11 and Muslim relations in, xiii–xv, 181, 199–200; NRIs success in, 250–51; Al Qaeda's appeal to Muslims and, 113; Turkey and souring relations with, 210–11; Turkey befriended for political motives with Soviet Union of, 209–10
Urdu language, 238
USA. *See* United States of America

The Varieties of Religious Experience (James), 28
Varma, Raja Ravi, 304–5
Vedic tradition, 296
The Victor Saladdin. See Al-Naser Salah al-Din
Volkan, Vamik: applied psychoanalysis of, 327–28; education of, 326; Fink on, 329; Levine on contributions to psychoanalysis of, 328; Nobel Prize for Peace and, 329; psychoanalysis and legacy of, 326, 328–29; psychoanalyst career impacted by immigration for, 331–32; on unresolved grief reaction, 327

Wadia, Neville, 360
war: bin Laden, Osama's leadership with Afghanistan against Soviet Union in, 109, 111; of Jews and Muslims, 32–33; of Mecca and Muslims at Badr, 31–32; of Mecca and Muslims at Uhud, 32–33. *See also* World War I
Watch Out for Zuzu. See Khalli Balak min Zuzu
Winnicott, Donald W.: on creativity in childhood, 74; Khan, Masud, and controversial collaboration with, 320
Wolpert, Stanley, 79
women: Egyptian movies and representation of, 268–69, 271–73; Europe and sexism toward, 366; Hafez's views on sexuality of, 157–58; Islam and sexuality of, 143, 150–51, 153; Islam and submission of, 143–44; media in West on Muslims and, 365; Muhammad on education and, 141; Muslims and men fearing emasculation from, 148–49; Muslims and value of virginity for, 279; *Quran* and dress code of men and, 126–27; sexuality of beasts and, 147, 367; sexuality of elderly Muslim, 152; Sufism and poetry on sexuality of, 146, 153–58; Surrahs of, 33. *See also* feminism
World War I: Atatürk's success in, 68, 215–16; Hamas on Jews and, 226

yaar, 57–58

Zakat (giving alms to the poor), 123
al-Zawahiri, Ayman: background of, 110–11; bin Laden, Osama, and influence of, 111
Zayd, 35–36
Zaynab, 35–37
zikr, 172
Zuljinnah, 82, 359
Zvi, Shabbatai, 73

About the Editor and Contributors

Aisha Abbasi, M.D., training and supervising analyst, Michigan Psychoanalytic Institute, Farmington Hills, Michigan.

Manail Anis Ahmed, M.A., research assistant, Section on Indian Art, Philadelphia Museum of Art, Philadelphia, Pennsylvania.

Salman Akhtar, M.D., professor of psychiatry and human behavior, Jefferson Medical College; training and supervising analyst, Psychoanalytic Center of Philadelphia, Philadelphia, Pennsylvania.

George Awad, M.D., training and supervising analyst, Toronto Psychoanalytic Institute, Toronto, Ontario, Canada. (Deceased.)

M. Hossein Etezady, M.D., faculty member, Psychoanalytic Center of Philadelphia, Philadelphia, Pennsylvania.

Hamada Hamid, D.O., resident, Departments of Neurology and Psychiatry, New York University School of Medicine, New York City.

Norman Itzkowitz, Ph.D., professor emeritus of Near Eastern studies, Princeton University, Princeton, New Jersey.

Samar A. Jasser, M.D., resident, Department of Psychiatry, University of Pennsylvania Health System, Philadelphia, Pennsylvania.

M. Sagman Kayatekin, M.D., staff psychiatrist and psychoanalytic psychotherapy supervisor, Austen Riggs Center, Stockbridge, Massachusetts.

Ruqayya Yasmine Khan, Ph.D., assistant professor, Department of Religion, Trinity University, San Antonio, Texas.

Manasi Kumar, doctoral candidate, Department of Psychology, University College London, U.K.

Mali A. Mann, faculty member, San Francisco Psychoanalytic Institute, San Francisco; clinical assistant professor of psychiatry, Stanford University Medical School, California.

Joseph V. Montville, Ph.D., director of preventive diplomacy, Center for Strategic and International Studies, Washington, D.C.

Peter A. Olsson, M.D., adjunct clinical professor of psychiatry, Baylor College of Medicine; assistant professor of Psychiatry, Dartmouth Medical School, Lebanon, New Hampshire.

Iman Roushdy-Hammady, Ph.D., auxiliary professor of medical anthropology, Drexel University, Philadelphia, Pennsylvania.

Mohammad Shafii, M.D., professor of psychiatry and director of the Division of Child Psychiatry, University of Louisville School of Medicine, Louisville, Kentucky.

Guillan Siassi, M.A., doctoral candidate in comparative literature, University of California at Los Angeles.

Shahrzad Siassi, Ph.D., senior faculty, New Center for Psychoanalysis, Los Angeles California.

Vamik D. Volkan, M.D., training and supervising analyst, Washington Psychoanalytic Institute; professor emeritus of psychiatry, University of Virginia School of Medicine, Charlottesville, Virginia.